International Law and Society

The International Library of Essays in Law and Society
Series Editor: Austin Sarat

Titles in the Series:

International Law and Society

Empirical Approaches to Human Rights

Edited by

Laura A. Dickinson

University of Connecticut, USA

ASHGATE

Published by
Ashgate Publishing Limited
Gower House
Croft Road
Aldershot
Hampshire GU11 3HR
England

Ashgate Publishing Company
Suite 420
101 Cherry Street
Burlington, VT 05401-4405
USA

Ashgate website: http://www.ashgate.com

British Library Cataloguing in Publication Data
International law and society: empirical approaches to
human rights. – (The international library of essays in law
and society)
1. Human rights 2. International Law 3. International
relations 4. Sociological jurisprudence
I. Dickinson, Laura A.
341.4'8

Library of Congress Control Number: 2007921468

ISBN: 978–0–7546–2611–4

Printed in Great Britain by TJ International Ltd, Padstow, Cornwall

Contents

PART III HUMAN RIGHTS DISCOURSE AND SOCIAL MOVEMENTS

Acknowledgements

The editor and publishers wish to thank the following for permission to use copyright material.

Blackwell Publishing Limited for the essay: Lisa Hajjar (1997), 'Cause Lawyering in Transnational Perspective: National Conflict and Human Rights in Israel/Palestine', *Law and Society Review*, **31**, pp. 473–504. Copyright © 1997 Law and Society Association.

Cambridge University Press for the essay: William W. Burke-White (2005), 'Complementarity in Practice: The International Criminal Court as Part of a System of Multi-level Global Governance in the Democratic Republic of Congo', *Leiden Journal of International Law*, **18**, pp. 557–90. Copyright © 2005 Foundation of the Leiden Journal of International Law.

Chicago Journal of International Law for the essay: Ellen Lutz and Kathryn Sikkink (2001), 'The Justice Cascade: The Evolution and Impact of Foreign Human Rights Trials in Latin America', *Chicago Journal of International Law*, **2**, pp. 1–33.

Columbia Journal of Transnational Law for the essay: Janet Koven Levit (1999), 'The Constitutionalization of Human Rights in Argentina: Problem or Promise?', *Columbia Journal of Transnational Law*, **37**, pp. 281–355.

Copyright Clearance Center for the essays: Laurence R. Helfer (2002), 'Overlegalizing Human Rights: International Relations Theory and the Commonwealth Caribbean Backlash Against Human Rights Regimes', *Columbia Law Review*, **102**, pp. 1832–911; Balakrishnan Rajagopal (2003), 'International Law and Social Movements: Challenges of Theorizing Resistance', *Columbia Journal of Transnational Law*, **41**, pp. 397–433.

Oxford University Press for the essay: Ryan Goodman and Derek Jinks (2003), 'Measuring the Effects of Human Rights Treaties', *European Journal of International Law*, **14**, pp. 171–83. Copyright © 2003 EJIL.

University of Chicago Press for the essays: Richard A. Wilson (2000), 'Reconciliation and Revenge in Post-Apartheid South Africa: Rethinking Legal Pluralism and Human Rights', *Current Anthropology*, **41**, pp. 75–87, 87a–87b. Copyright © 2000 Wenner-Gren Foundation for Anthropological Research; Sally Engle Merry and Rachel E. Stern (2005), 'The Female Inheritance Movement in Hong Kong: Theorizing the Local/Global Interface', *Current Anthropology*, **46**, pp. 387–409. Copyright © 2005 Wenner-Gren Foundation for Anthropological Research.

Yale Law Journal for the essay: Oona A. Hathaway (2002), 'Do Human Rights Treaties Make a Difference?', *Yale Law Journal*, **111**, pp. 1935–2042. Reprinted by permission of The Yale Law Journal Company and William S. Hein Company.

Series Preface

The International Library of Essays in Law and Society is designed to provide a broad overview of this important field of interdisciplinary inquiry. Titles in the series will provide access to the best existing scholarship on a wide variety of subjects integral to the understanding of how legal institutions work in and through social arrangements. They collect and synthesize research published in the leading journals of the law and society field. Taken together, these volumes show the richness and complexity of inquiry into law's social life.

Each volume is edited by a recognized expert who has selected a range of scholarship designed to illustrate the most important questions, theoretical approaches, and methods in her/his area of expertise. Each has written an introductory essay which both outlines those questions, approaches, and methods and provides a distinctive analysis of the scholarship presented in the book. Each was asked to identify approximately 20 pieces of work for inclusion in their volume. This has necessitated hard choices since law and society inquiry is vibrant and flourishing.

The International Library of Essays in Law and Society brings together scholars representing different disciplinary traditions and working in different cultural contexts. Since law and society is itself an international field of inquiry it is appropriate that the editors of the volumes in this series come from many different nations and academic contexts. The work of the editors both charts a tradition and opens up new questions. It is my hope that this work will provide a valuable resource for longtime practitioners of law and society scholarship and newcomers to the field.

AUSTIN SARAT
William Nelson Cromwell Professor of Jurisprudence and Political Science
Amherst College

Introduction

In one of the most quoted statements in the international law literature, Louis Henkin suggested 35 years ago that 'almost all nations observe almost all principles of international law and almost all of their obligations almost all of the time' (Henkin, 1979, p. 47). The truth of this observation, however, has not been subjected to sufficient empirical scrutiny. On the one hand, obedience to international legal norms has too often been taken simply as an article of faith among those most committed to international law and legal institutions. Thus, liberal internationalists (for example, Doyle, 1983; Burley, 1992) have traditionally assumed that liberal democratic states comply with international law because their norms and values resonate with those contained in international agreements. Other scholars (see, for example, Franck, 1995; Trimble, 1990) have suggested that if international rules are deemed procedurally and substantively 'fair', they compel compliance. And those studying 'transnational legal process' have argued that states obey international law because they come to internalize international norms and values over time (see for example, Koh, 1997; O'Connell, 1999). Yet, for years there were only fitful efforts to test these hypotheses with comprehensive data on international law compliance.

On the other hand, international relations sceptics of international law have long used rational choice, game theoretic and so-called 'realist' models to argue that international law does *not* have any independent valence and that a nation-state obeys international law only when doing so is in that state's own self-interest (see for example, Morgenthau, 1978 [1948]; Goldsmith and Posner, 2004). But these arguments too have tended not to be empirically grounded, relying far more on logical models and hidden (or not so hidden) assumptions concerning state behaviour. And while constructivist scholars (for example, Finnemore, 1996; Ruggie, 1998) have challenged realist assumptions and argued that international law *itself* shapes what comes to be thought of as the state's interest, this proposition, like the others, has not been sufficiently tested on the ground.

Recently, this lack of emphasis on empirical studies in international law has begun to change. Perhaps spurred on by the general trend towards empiricism in the legal academy, legal scholars are beginning to test the impact and efficacy of international law. However, this work is still in its infancy and tends to be informed primarily by the methodologies of quantitative political science research. Accordingly, the empirical study of international law has not sufficiently embraced the broad range of empirical approaches to legal questions that is emblematic of the law and society movement. Meanwhile, law and society scholars – with some notable exceptions – have historically focused on domestic legal regimes and have therefore not sufficiently analysed international law.

The purposes of this volume, therefore, are twofold. First, the book seeks to acquaint international law and international relations scholars with the variety of law and society approaches to studying legal questions. Second, it aims to focus more attention within the law and society movement on international law.

As to the first purpose, it seems to me that international law generally – and international human rights law in particular – *needs* law and society insights, because these are insights about how laws on paper translate themselves into the behaviour, assumptions and practices of officials, social movements and people on the ground. As with all rights, there is a social dimension to their internalization and efficacy. Law and society scholars have been studying and analysing this process for years, but primarily in the domestic context. And although international law and international relations scholars are increasingly interested in testing whether (and how) states comply with international law, these nascent studies are almost solely quantitative and have not generally been harnessed to broader law and society insights about law's operation in daily life. Accordingly, international law would greatly benefit from the kind of rich, multifaceted studies that characterize sociolegal scholarship. Such studies would help us develop a more complete understanding of the complex and multivariate processes through which states and the various actors within states – governmental and inter-governmental bureaucrats, as well as members of non-governmental organizations (NGOs), corporations, social movements, and individuals – internalize, ignore or resist the norms and values encoded in international law.

At the same time that international law scholars need law and society insights, law and society scholars can learn something from going international. Because of their focus on law on the ground, law and society scholars are perhaps unduly dismissive of international law in all forms because they do not perceive a state sanction. Indeed, sociologically-oriented legal scholars tend to be realists in international law terms because of their scepticism about paper rules. 'Where is the sanction?' they ask. 'Where is the power? Where is the bureaucracy of enforcement – the police and other such institutional actors?'

This approach, however, ignores the fact that populations may internalize norms, even if those norms are not articulated through instruments of coercive power. As research on legal consciousness in the domestic context has shown, law's power may manifest itself in categories of thought and everyday attitudes, and these social beliefs may derive, at least in part, from legal norms that are *not* associated with a coercive sanction (Ewick and Silbey, 1998). Similarly, international human rights treaties and treaty processes – even without strong sanctioning power – can operate to name categories of offences, create transnational networks of governmental and non-governmental actors concerned with these categories, empower local actors to take action on certain issues, and shape and shift local understandings and practices (see for example, Merry, 2003). Thus, international human rights are an important terrain for study and understanding of broad law and society issues.

Finally, a third goal of this book is to rekindle long-running law and society debates about the merits of quantitative versus qualitative analysis, yet play it out on the terrain of international human rights law. For example, to what extent do arguments in favour of either quantitative or qualitative work change when addressing international, as opposed to domestic, law? What forms of statistical analysis are appropriate in this area, given the practical difficulties in measuring both human rights violations and compliance? Are the concerns about using statistics different in the international realm?

Indeed, international human rights law in some ways resembles the contractual forms familiar from commercial practice. As in commercial law, there is a standardized model or template, which migrates and gets adopted from nation to nation and from legal culture to legal culture. Yet, the very same forms may have very different cultural meanings or interpretations in different contexts, and in each context we encounter a different set of state actors, NGOs and local social movements – different people with different things to gain and lose from adopting or rejecting the template. Thus, with regard to an international human rights provision, we may see in some cultures a strong effect; the ratification of a treaty leads to a reduction in human rights abuses and the establishment of human rights monitoring organizations. But in other settings there may be absolutely no effect; the categories contained in the human rights treaties may be received officially, but then are promptly buried. Or, the interpretation of a treaty and its tools of legal enforcement may become more robust over time, so much so that they may generate a backlash. Accordingly, a simple statistical model that tallies formal ratification may not capture the wide variety of implementation practices that are occurring.

On the other hand, with respect to more qualitative studies, such as interpretive ethnographies, are there different limitations and possibilities for this work in the international sphere? Is it harder to draw generalizable conclusions from such studies given the breadth and scope of international law and the diversity of actors in the international system? And finally, to the extent that one wants to do empirical work – qualitative or quantitative – what are the relevant sources of law, and who are the relevant actors to be studied?

In an attempt to stimulate dialogue and debate about all of these questions, this volume brings together a small sampling of recent empirical work in international human rights law. The volume is divided into three main categories, corresponding to those areas of human rights law that have so far inspired the most attention from empirically-oriented scholars: (1) the extent of nation-state compliance with international human rights norms; (2) the degree to which nation-states internalize international human rights norms; and (3) the interaction between international human rights norms and local and transnational social movements. In each of these areas, we see scholars engaging with both the theoretical and methodological questions raised above, and these essays therefore offer both a useful glimpse of the emerging empirical discourse on international human rights and a fertile source of ideas for future development in this area.

Human Rights Discourse and National Compliance

Part I, which addresses the compliance question, begins with Oona Hathaway's important, though controversial, statistical analysis of states' compliance with human rights treaties, a project that has yielded some surprising and counterintuitive results. Using data from the US State Department Country Reports on Human Rights Practices, she argues that ratification of major human rights treaties is, paradoxically, often associated with a decline in human rights conditions. She attempts to explain these results by suggesting that treaty ratification may lead international actors to reduce political pressure on states to protect human rights, thereby allowing such states to get by without actually making real improvements in their human rights practices. She therefore contends that the requirements for treaty ratification should be increased and that human rights advocates should perhaps rethink their strategy of pressing for universal ratification of human rights treaties.

Chapter 2, by Ryan Goodman and Derek Jinks, emphasizes the importance of Hathaway's broad-ranging study, but also critiques her approach on a number of grounds. To begin with, the authors identify defects in Hathaway's research design. For example, they fault her for focusing on the moment of treaty ratification, when other events such as treaty signature or the enactment of implementing legislation may be more significant. They also point out measurement errors, most notably Hathaway's failure to account for the likelihood that increased reporting of abuses may actually indicate an *improved* human rights climate. Next, the authors raise concerns about the conclusions Hathaway draws from her data. Although Hathaway suggests that international actors tend to reduce pressure on states once those states have ratified human rights treaties, she does not present any quantitative data to support this claim. Indeed, the opposite may be the case, because ratification may lead to the formation of an internal domestic human rights constituency to monitor compliance and lobby for reform. At the same time, if ratification is really costless, as Hathaway postulates, the model cannot explain the non-participation of many states in treaty regimes or why ratification would 'signal' anything to other states. Nor does her theoretical model account for how states might incorporate international norms or the incentives that form or guide state choices. Finally, Goodman and Jinks worry about the policy prescriptions that Hathaway makes, arguing that broad ratification of human rights treaties may play an important role in the process of building both national and transnational human rights cultures. They suggest that a 'softer kind of empiricism, something more sociological than economic', may be a better approach to address these issues (Goodman and Jinks, 2003, p. 183).[1]

Like Hathaway, Laurence Helfer (Chapter 3) seeks to use the insights of work in international relations, and in particular a quantitative approach, to test assumptions about compliance that often appear in the international literature. Rather than a global study of human rights practices, however, Helfer focuses on a case study of three Caribbean countries and their history with ratification of human rights treaties. In the 1990s, the governments of Jamaica, Trinidad and Tobago, and Guyana, all of which had previously signed and ratified the International Covenant on Civil Political Rights and its Optional Protocol, along with the American Convention on Human Rights (with the exception of Guyana, which only signed the treaty), changed course by denouncing the treaties and withdrawing from the jurisdiction of the tribunals established to oversee the treaties. While the denunciation was at least partly caused by a backlash against regional human rights courts associated with imperialist domination in the Caribbean, Helfer draws a lesson with a possible broader application. He argues that the withdrawals can also be understood as a response to the 'overlegalization' of the government's human rights commitments. Overlegalization, he contends, arises primarily when the terms of an initial treaty bargain change. For example, a supranational tribunal may expand a treaty's mandatory substantive reach (thereby increasing obligations on the signing country), narrowly interpret state derogations from the treaty, or require states to implement the tribunal's own technically non-binding recommendations. In each of these circumstances, a state may end up rebelling against a treaty whose scope has been enlarged beyond the parameters that were understood at the time of signing. Alternatively, overlegalization can arise when a treaty's obligations are underenforced at the time a state ratifies the treaty, but then increase over time. Helfer contends that overlegalization of human rights treaties helps explain the Caribbean backlash, and suggests that the idea of overlegalization can provide depth and nuance to prevailing theories of international human rights compliance.

---

[1]   Goodman and Jinks have begun to develop such an approach by studying what they term 'acculturation', the social processes through which states change their behaviour because they are embedded in an international system (Goodman and Jinks, 2004).

In Chapter 4, the political scientist Andrew Moravcsik also uses empirical evidence to make a significant contribution to the study of states' compliance with human rights norms. In a nuanced elaboration of liberal internationalism, Moravcsik contends that states ratify human rights treaties in order to protect domestic liberal democratic values. Using data from Europe, he shows that the strongest supporters of human rights treaties have been newly democratizing states, while more established democracies have resisted ratification. Thus, he claims that support for the treaties reflects the desire of new democracies to bind themselves in order to protect still fragile rights.

Human Rights Discourse and Domestic Norms

Part II focuses on a question closely tied to compliance: are norms contained in international law *internalized* by domestic and transnational communities, and, if so, how? As noted previously, this idea of international norm internalization is most closely identified with the idea of 'transnational legal process' championed by Harold Hongju Koh. Instead of asking 'Why do nations *comply* with international law?', Koh pursued the perhaps more fundamental question 'Why do nations *obey* international law?'. The difference is more than mere semantics. As Janet Koven Levit has observed, 'compliance is norm-conforming behavior conditioned by exogenous forces . . . while obedience is endogenous, the voluntary accession to a norm incorporated into internal value systems' (Levit, 1999, p. 285).

Koh defines 'transnational legal process' as the mechanisms by which: first, interaction among transnational actors generates international norms; second, further interaction in national and supranational fora leads to interpretation of norms; and, third, concomitant internalization of international norms into domestic legal systems results in compliance and, if the internalization strategy is effective, ultimate obedience (Koh, 1997). Moreover, Koh emphasizes that understanding this process requires looking beyond the state to other transnational actors, including individuals, corporations, NGOs, public interest organizations, subgovernmental organizations, regional organizations and international organizations. Thus, this framework has the advantage of taking seriously the idea that norms may seep into a legal system in ways more complicated than simply formal rules or policies. 'Yet, more is needed to fully flesh out the idea of transnational legal process, to see how the process of norm internalization actually takes place outside of the official organs of government' (Berman, 2005, p. 545). Thus, while it may be true, for example, that '[i]nternational articulation of rights norms has reshaped domestic dialogues in law, politics, academia, public consciousness, civil society, and the press' (Cassel, 2001, p. 122), it is another matter entirely to try to study this 'reshaping' process in concrete settings.

It is significant, therefore, that a growing number of scholars have begun to look at the internalization question. In a sense, these scholars pick up where Hathaway and the majority of others who study compliance leave off. Although Helfer's work is an exception, most of these scholars focus primarily on the state, rather than looking to groups or individuals within or outside the state. Moreover, as important as Hathaway's work is, it does not consider the possibility that international human rights norms may be internalized over time, *regardless* of the degree of initial compliance in the first few years after ratification. Yet, any comprehensive story about long-term compliance with international law must ultimately take account of the processes by which norms are transmitted, internalized, changed or rejected.

Janet Koven Levit's essay (Chapter 5) uses Argentina as a case study to explore these questions. According to Levit, Argentina has the strongest formal commitment to human rights in the Americas because it directly incorporates the core human rights treaties into its 1994 constitution. At the same time, it accords those treaties a status above federal law and perhaps even gives them a constitutional character. Yet, strikingly, Levit shows that these norms have not been internalized into Argentine legal culture. Surveying Supreme Court and lower court decisions issued since the adoption of the new constitution, Levit shows that judges and lawyers have not implemented these human rights norms substantively or accorded them the high status that the constitution seems to provide. She suggests, drawing on the debates over the adoption of the constitutional provisions, that the lack of internalization stems from the fact that broader social groups, such as NGOs, did not participate in the adoption of the constitutional provisions, which were mainly incorporated to signal to regional and international lending organizations that Argentina was committed to human rights. As a result, at least at the time of Levit's essay, the norms had not yet penetrated particularly far into Argentine society. However, she noted that further norm internalization was still possible.

Indeed, Levit has subsequently written that her criticisms and concerns 'were perhaps premature', noting that Argentina's constitutionalization of human rights has, since she wrote her essay, proven to be a 'catalyst' for changes in legal consciousness in that country (Levit, 2005). Such changes may be reflected in the recent Argentine Supreme Court decision invalidating the country's amnesty laws protecting those who committed human rights violations in the 'Dirty War' of the 1970s. In 1987, the Supreme Court had upheld the constitutionality of these laws. But when confronted again with the issue 15 years later, the court concluded, first, that the amnesty laws were unconstitutional because they were inconsistent with the provisions of the American Convention on Human Rights, and, second, that forced disappearances were crimes against humanity and could not be shielded by a domestic statute of limitations. Both rulings would have been unthinkable in an earlier era. Thus, Levit's essay illustrates that formal compliance with, or codification of, international norms may have little impact (particularly in the first few years afterwards) unless such formal compliance is accompanied by popular (or at least elite) norm internalization. But her subsequent follow-up indicates that the formal compliance may function as the first step towards deeper norm internalization and may even be a catalyst for broader changes in legal consciousness.

While Ellen Lutz and Kathryn Sikkink (Chapter 6) do not describe themselves as belonging to the transnational legal process school, their 'ideational' approach resonates with both Koh's and Levit's idea of norm internalization. The authors, scholars of diplomacy and political science respectively, argue that neither the self-interested actions of powerful state hegemons, as the realists contend, nor the desire of liberal democratic states to entrench their democratic values, as the liberal internationalists maintain, can fully account for the way international human rights norms are transmitted across borders and internalized. Rather, they suggest that the inherent pull of the ideas contained within international law, combined with events that foster the legitimacy of those ideas, result in shifts in beliefs and behaviour. Like the transnational legal process scholars, they stress the importance of considering a range of institutional actors, including government bureaucrats, NGOs and judges. And, like Levit, they rely on public statements and actions of these various groups to make their assessments. In contrast at least to Levit's initial Argentina assessment, however, Lutz and Sikkink conclude that the norm of criminal accountability for gross human rights violations has in fact gained broad acceptance in Latin America. They suggest that this development has taken place through a 'boomerang' process in which advocacy groups within Latin American countries have sought justice transnationally in European and American courts and, in turn, this transnational litigation has spurred on domestic and regional efforts to promote democracy and the rule of law. In addition, they maintain that this process fits into a larger 'norm cascade', a kind of snowball effect of increasing support for human rights and democracy throughout the region. They contend that this result provides support for their 'ideational' approach because it cannot be fully explained by realism (since United States policies and court decisions had a much less significant effect than those of non-hegemonic European countries) or liberal internationalism (since the shift can only partly be explained by new democracies' desire to entrench the rule of law).

The next case study (Chapter 7), a collaborative effort of the Human Rights Center and the International Human Rights Law Clinic at the University of California, Berkeley, along with the Centre for Human Rights at the University of Sarajevo, again looks at how international law diffuses (or fails to diffuse) into local legal consciousness. The authors analyse perceptions of the International Criminal Tribunal for the Former Yugoslavia (ICTY) among Bosnian lawyers and judges of all ethnic types. Based on extensive interviews, the essay presents legal actors' reactions that extend beyond the formal articulations of law in judicial decisions or legislative debates. Strikingly, this study also suggests a transmission gap between international norms and institutions and their reception on the ground. Even among Bosnian Muslims, whom one might expect to be the most sympathetic to the work of the ICTY, there has been tremendous mistrust of, and scepticism about, the tribunal and the norms it is enforcing. Indeed, according to the study, lawyers and judges from all ethnic groups generally perceive the trials to be highly politicized and do not view the prosecutors and judges as applying legal rules neutrally and impartially. In addition, many of those throughout the legal community were surprisingly uninformed about the work of the ICTY. The authors of the study posit that the scepticism and lack of awareness may stem in part from the civil law framework of Bosnian legal culture, a framework that is somewhat at odds with the more common-law influenced tribunal. In addition, the authors suggest that the remoteness of the tribunal, situated far from Bosnia in the Hague, lacking any Bosnian representation on its bench and plagued by a poor public outreach programme, may have contributed to this disconnect. Finally, Bosnians may also have seen inherently distrustful of any legal institution, given their previous experience with the highly politicized justice system of communist Yugoslavia. This sort of qualitative study offers a sobering reminder that formal articulations of international legal norms may have little to do with acceptance or adoption of such norms among domestic populations.

On the other hand, William Burke-White's essay (Chapter 8) suggests a more robust relationship between the new international criminal court (ICC) and conceptions of the role of international law categories and institutions on the ground in the Democratic Republic of Congo, where successive repressive dictatorships and ongoing civil war have resulted in widespread atrocities. Like the Bosnia project, Burke-White's study is based on interviews with a variety of domestic actors about their perceptions of the ICC and the international crimes to be tried before the court. However, unlike the Bosnian study, Burke-White found that actors across the spectrum – from potential defendants before the ICC to judges and lawyers – were acutely aware of, and perhaps even shaping their behaviour in response to, the potential work of the court. His results are particularly striking because he conducted his interviews even before the ICC took up the case of the Congo as its first investigation. The actors on the ground were thus already responding to the mere *possibility* that the ICC would begin investigations into atrocities in the Congo.

Finally, in Chapter 9 anthropologist Richard Wilson analyses the translation, incorporation, rejection and reshaping of international human rights norms in South Africa. Wilson conducted interviews with victims who testified before South Africa's Truth and Reconciliation Commission (TRC), which adopted a distinctive approach to post-conflict justice. Rather than providing for criminal trials of those who committed atrocities during South Africa's apartheid regime, the TRC granted amnesty from criminal prosecution to those involved in political crimes who came forward to tell their stories in public, so long as the TRC determined that the alleged perpetrators had given a full and fair accounting of those crimes. The TRC thus reflected an appropriation and reshaping of international human rights discourse. In its reports and the statements of its individual members, the TRC articulated a goal of promoting human rights culture through 'reconciliation' rather than 'revenge'. Wilson argues, however, that the TRC pushed this internationalist agenda only by squelching a discourse of revenge and criminal accountability articulated by many victims. Relying on his interview data, Wilson shows that a large number of victims did not get to testify, and those who did found that the TRC staff organized and managed their testimony in such a way that it was reduced to the empirical data that the TRC required. In addition, in its reports on victim testimony, the TRC selectively constructed a narrative of redemption, reconciliation and forgiveness, excluding other views. Although Wilson acknowledges that the TRC process was born out of a political compromise that offered the possibility of amnesty to the old military guard in exchange for a peaceful transition to democracy, he suggests that the TRC sacrificed the language of criminal accountability – as well as vengeance – too readily. Indeed, he goes so far as to contend that criminal accountability is the foundation of creating a culture of human rights. And while scholars have criticized Wilson both for his arguable conflation of vengeance and criminal accountability and for his suggestion that the TRC could have gone further beyond the political compromise that required amnesty, the richness of his empirical account adds undisputable depth to the analysis of the TRC's proceedings. Moreover, his work demonstrates the complex ways in which human rights categories shift and change as they are transmitted from the international to the domestic context (and back again). Moreover, even within the domestic setting, such categories are the continuing sites of contest over meaning and application.

Human Rights Discourse and Social Movements

Such contests over international law categories are the subject of the essays in Part III, which considers the role social movements play in both deploying and shaping human rights discourse. Although the question of social movements is often overlooked by international law scholars (who tend to gravitate towards more formal legal actors), sociologists, anthropologists and even some political scientists have begun to look at ways in which social groups use and resist categories of international human rights law and, at the same time, interact with the institutions, both domestic and international, that apply those categories. Thus, the relationship between domestic and transnational social movements and the international human rights system provides another important site for empirical research.

Sociologist Balakrishnan Rajagopal (Chapter 10) argues that international law scholars must do a better job of understanding the ways in which social movements in the developing world have shaped and changed international law categories and the institutions that apply them. Indeed, too often international human rights dialogue on both the left and the right operates under the assumption that Western human rights norms are being imposed on 'local' culture. 'Such claims reflect a familiar story about the production and reception of legal consciousness, in which the West is the primary site of legal production – exporting such goodies as secularism and the "rule of law" – and the Third World is the happy receptor of such knowledge and structures' (Sunder, 2003, p. 1459). Rajagopal resists these sorts of assumptions, using an approach that is both theoretical and empirical. Thus, even as he draws on Foucault, Fanon, Gramsci and Chatterjee to explain the significance of social movements in the international sphere, he provides rich real-life examples of how social movements engage international legal discourse and institutions. For example, he shows how the Mexican Zapatistas appropriated the language of human rights and to some extent changed that language to engage in a broader political struggle. He also argues that the agitation of those in the anti-globalization movement has provoked significant reforms at the World Bank, including a broader respect for rights and social safety nets in the provision of development assistance and the establishment of institutional complaint mechanisms for those negatively affected by aid projects. Moreover, Rajagopal criticizes human rights discourse for itself truncating important categories of resistance, particularly claims concerning economic justice.

Like Rajagopal, sociologist Lisa Hajjar (Chapter 11) is interested in the relationship between international human rights discourse and social movements, but she examines the relationship through the lens of a particular group of mediating actors: cause lawyers. In particular, Hajjar examines the ways in which the Israeli–Palestinian struggle has affected the use of international human rights discourse by lawyers representing Palestinian defendants in the military court system in the West Bank and Gaza. Relying on extensive interviews with Jewish-Israeli, Arab-Israeli, and Palestinian lawyers, Hajjar argues that these defence lawyers, while all left-leaning and generally sceptical of the Israeli occupation, have very different strategies for deploying international human rights arguments. Moreover, the difference in strategy seems to depend quite a bit on the lawyer's own understanding of his or her role as part of a broader social movement. For example, Jewish-Israeli lawyers were most likely to use international human rights law arguments to criticize specific government policies connected with the Israeli occupation. Seeing themselves as reformers, they have sought to avoid plea deals so that they could challenge such policies in court. Meanwhile, Arab-Israeli lawyers have been more likely to use human rights discourse to critique the occupation altogether, both in and out of court. And Palestinian lawyers, who are more likely to view *both* the occupation *and* the military court system as illegal, were actually the least likely to use the legal categories of human rights and humanitarian law in court, because they viewed any in-court arguments as a capitulation and therefore a watering-down of the claims of the broader Palestinian movement. Consequently, they tended to engage in plea bargaining and invoke human rights discourse in extralegal ways through the media, rather than in court. Hajjar's rich study therefore reminds us that international human rights discourse can be deployed in many different ways, both in formal legal arguments and in popular fora, and that the strategies employed may depend more on one's perceived social movement agenda than on any technical legal category.

Finally, in Chapter 12 anthropologists Sally Merry and Rachel Stern show how human rights discourse can actually help provide an effective vehicle for social movements to access and leverage political power. They argue that the language of international human rights provided a new impetus and discursive framework in the long struggle of Hong Kong women to make inheritance laws more egalitarian. Based on extensive interviews with participants, Merry and Stern suggest that the entry into force of the Convention on the Elimination of all forms of Discrimination Against Women (CEDAW) in 1981 provided legal categories that Hong Kong women (along with international women's rights NGOs) used to reshape an old debate about traditional inheritance. Previously waged as a struggle about family and kinship structure, the debate changed to one about women's equality. Moreover, the human rights discourse helped women mobilize domestically by renaming their grievances and bringing them together as a social group. At the same time, the newer terms of the debate resonated with the international media, providing a greater catalyst for change.

The Hong Kong study provides a fitting end to this volume because it suggests myriad ways in which international human rights may change on the ground conditions. But such effects are only likely to turn up in very fine-grained qualitative studies. Thus, large quantitative analyses of formal effects may miss important changes wrought by a treaty such as CEDAW. On the other hand, such qualitative studies run the risk of using anecdotal examples that obscure a large picture that may not fit the researcher's intuitive beliefs (or ideological predispositions).

Obviously, the answer is that both types of studies are necessary because they each provide important checks on the data gathered by the other. Yet, too often, the different research methods are associated with different disciplinary backgrounds, and the level of dialogue among those performing this important empirical research is far too infrequent. Indeed, if there is one thing that the essays in this volume − taken as a whole − demonstrate, it is that empiricists of international human rights law need each other, and international law, international relations, and law and society scholars must engage in constant interdisciplinary dialogue if they are collectively to provide a richer, more empirically grounded picture of how the international human rights system functions both in the halls of government and the streets of towns throughout the world.

References

Berman, Paul Schiff (2005), 'From International Law to Law and Globalization', *Columbia Journal of Transnational Law*, **43**, pp. 485–556.

Burley, Anne-Marie (1992), 'Law Among Liberal States: Liberal Internationalism and the Act of State Doctrine', *Columbia Law Review*, **92**, pp. 1907–996.

Cassel, Douglass (2001), 'Does International Human Rights Law Make a Difference?', *Chicago Journal of International Law*, **2**, pp. 121–35.

Doyle, Michael W. (1983), 'Kant, Liberal Legacies, and Foreign Affairs', *Philosophy and Public Affairs*, **12**, pp. 205–35.

Ewick, Patricia and Silbey, Susan S. (1998), *The Common Place of Law: Stories from Everyday Life*, Chicago: University of Chicago Press.

Finnemore, Martha (1996), *National Interests in International Society*, Ithaca, NY: Cornell University Press.

Franck, Thomas M. (1995), *Fairness in International Law and Institutions*, Oxford: Oxford University Press/Clarendon Press.

Goldsmith, Jack L. and Posner, Eric A. (2004), *The Limits of International Law*, New York: Oxford University Press.

Goodman, Ryan and Jinks, Derek (2003), ' Measuring the Effects of Human Rights Treaties', *European Journal of International Law*, **14**, pp. 171–83.

Goodman, Ryan and Jinks, Derek (2004), 'How to Influence States: Socialization and International Human Rights Law', *Duke Law Journal*, **54**, pp. 621–703.

Henkin, Louis (1979), *How Nations Behave, Law and Foreign Policy*, New York, NY: Columbia University Press, 2nd edn.

Koh, Harold Hongju (1997), 'Why Do Nations Obey International Law?', *Yale Law Journal*, **106**, pp. 2599–659.

Levit, Janet Koven (1999), 'The Constitutionalization of Human Rights in Argentina: Problem or Promise?', *Columbia Journal of Transnational Law*, **37**, pp. 281–355.

Levit, Janet Koven (2005), 'The Constitutionalization of Human Rights in Argentina', talk delivered at University of Saskatchewan, 22 September 2005 (manuscript on file with author).

Merry, Sally Engle (2003), 'Constructing a Global Law – Violence Against Women and the Human Rights System', *Law and Social Inquiry*, **28**, pp. 941–74.

Morgenthau, Hans J. (1978 [1948]), *Politics Among Nations* (5th edn), New York: Alfred A. Knopf.

O'Connell, Mary Ellen (1999), 'New International Legal Process', *American Journal of International Law*, **93**, pp. 334–51.

Ruggie, John Gerard (1998), 'What Makes the World Hang Together: Neo-Utilitarianism and the Social Constructivist Challenge', *International Organization*, **52**, pp. 855–85.

Sunder, Madhavi (2003), 'Piercing the Veil', *Yale Law Journal*, **112**, pp. 1399–72.

Trimble, Phillip R. (1990), 'International Law, World Order, and Critical Legal Studies', *Stanford Law Review*, **42**, pp. 811–45.

Part I
Human Rights Discourse and National Compliance

[1]

Do Human Rights Treaties Make a Difference?

Oona A. Hathaway[†]

CONTENTS

† Associate Professor, Boston University School of Law. Associate Professor Designate, Yale Law School. J.D., Yale Law School. I thank the Carr Center for Human Rights Policy and the Center for Ethics and the Professions, both of Harvard University, for their support of this project and participants in workshops at both centers for their comments on an early draft of this Article. I thank Casey Caldwell, Teomara Hahn, Neil Austin, Seyoon Oh, Atif Khawaja, Steve Morrison, Matthew Eckert, and Jaehong Choi for their research assistance and Katherine Tragos for her data entry and research assistance. I owe a debt to Victor Aguirregabiria for consulting with me on the statistical portions of this Article, and Yulia Radionova, Martino De Stephano, and especially Firat Inceoglu for their research assistance with the statistical portions of this Article. I am also indebted to the library staff at Boston University School of Law for providing extraordinary support for and assistance with this project. Finally, I am grateful to participants in the Boston University Faculty Workshop, Karen J. Alter, Ian Ayres, Lawrence Broz, Douglass W. Cassel, Jr., Daniel Farber, Ward Farnsworth, Andrew Guzman, Philip Hamburger, Jim Hathaway, Robert Howse, Robert Keohane, Alvin Klevorick, Harold Hongju Koh, Kristin Madison, Christopher McCrudden, Andrew Moravcsik, Benjamin I. Page, A.W. Brian Simpson, Mark West, and especially Jacob S. Hacker for their thoughtful comments on earlier drafts of this Article.

International lawyers for the most part assume that, as Louis Henkin memorably put it, "almost all nations observe almost all principles of international law and almost all of their obligations almost all of the time."[1] This assumption undergirds the work of many legal scholars and practitioners, who endeavor to explicate and form the law presumably because they believe that it has real impact. Indeed, the claim that international law matters was until recently so widely accepted among international lawyers that there have been relatively few efforts to examine its accuracy.[2] Yet this view long coexisted with a much more skeptical conception of international law among international relations scholars—a conception that holds that, in the immortal words of Thucydides, "[t]he

---

1. LOUIS HENKIN, HOW NATIONS BEHAVE 47 (2d ed. 1979) (emphasis omitted); see ABRAM CHAYES & ANTONIA HANDLER CHAYES, THE NEW SOVEREIGNTY: COMPLIANCE WITH INTERNATIONAL REGULATORY AGREEMENTS 3 (1995) ("[F]oreign policy practitioners operate on the assumption of a general propensity of states to comply with international obligations."); ANDREW T. GUZMAN, INTERNATIONAL LAW: A COMPLIANCE BASED THEORY (Univ. of Cal. at Berkeley Sch. of Law, Public Law and Legal Theory Working Paper No. 47, 2001); Abram Chayes & Antonia Handler Chayes, On Compliance, 47 INT'L ORG. 175, 176 (1993); Harold Hongju Koh, Why Do Nations Obey International Law?, 106 YALE L.J. 2599, 2599 (1997) (book review). But see Francis A. Boyle, The Irrelevance of International Law: The Schism Between International Law and International Politics, 10 CAL. W. INT'L L.J. 193 (1980) (arguing against the importance of international law); Robert H. Bork, The Limits of "International Law," NAT'L INT., Winter 1989-1990, at 3 (same).

2. See Benedict Kingsbury, The Concept of Compliance as a Function of Competing Conceptions of International Law, 19 MICH. J. INT'L L. 345, 346 (1998) ("[T]he first empirical task is to determine whether, as is often asserted by international lawyers, most States and other subjects of international law conform to most legal rules most of the time. We have impressions which may rise to the level of "anecdata," but in many areas we simply do not have systematic studies to show whether or not most States conform to most international law rules most of the time . . . ." (citations omitted)); Koh, supra note 1, at 2599-600 ("[S]cholars have generally avoided the causal question: If transnational actors do generally obey international law, why do they obey it, and why do they sometimes disobey it?"); S.M. Schwebel, Commentary, in COMPLIANCE WITH JUDGMENTS OF INTERNATIONAL COURTS 39, 39 (M.K. Bulterman & M. Kuijer eds., 1996) ("Compliance is a problem which lawyers tend to avoid rather than confront."). There are some notable exceptions. E.g., Douglass Cassel, Does International Human Rights Law Make a Difference?, 2 CHI. J. INT'L L. 121 (2001) [hereinafter Cassel, Does International Human Rights Law Make a Difference?]; Douglass Cassel, Inter-American Human Rights Law, Soft and Hard, in COMMITMENT AND COMPLIANCE: THE ROLE OF NON-BINDING NORMS IN THE INTERNATIONAL LAW SYSTEM 393 (Dinah Shelton ed., 2000); Linda Camp Keith, The United Nations International Covenant on Civil and Political Rights: Does It Make a Difference in Human Rights Behavior?, 36 J. PEACE RES. 95 (1999); Beth A. Simmons, International Law and State Behavior: Commitment and Compliance in International Monetary Affairs, 94 AM. POL. SCI. REV. 819 (2000); Edith Brown Weiss & Harold K. Jacobson, A Framework for Analysis, in ENGAGING COUNTRIES: STRENGTHENING COMPLIANCE WITH INTERNATIONAL ENVIRONMENTAL ACCORDS 1 (Edith Brown Weiss & Harold K. Jacobson eds., 1998) [hereinafter ENGAGING COUNTRIES]. In recent years, legal scholars have paid more attention to the question of compliance. Indeed, the 91st Annual Meeting of the American Society of International Law was entitled, "Implementation, Compliance and Effectiveness." AM. SOC'Y OF INT'L LAW, PROCEEDINGS OF THE 91ST ANNUAL MEETING: IMPLEMENTATION, COMPLIANCE AND EFFECTIVENESS (1997).

1938   The Yale Law Journal   [Vol. 111: 1935

strong do what they can and the weak suffer what they must,"[3] with little regard for international law.[4]

The disinclination of international lawyers to confront the efficacy of international law is nowhere more evident—or more problematic—than in the field of human rights law. After all, the major engines of compliance that exist in other areas of international law are for the most part absent in the area of human rights. Unlike the public international law of money, there are no "competitive market forces" that press for compliance.[5] And, unlike in the case of trade agreements, the costs of retaliatory noncompliance are low to nonexistent, because a nation's actions against its own citizens do not directly threaten or harm other states. Human rights law thus stands out as an area of international law in which countries have little incentive to police noncompliance with treaties or norms. As Henkin remarked, "The forces that induce compliance with other law . . . do not pertain equally to the law of human rights."[6]

Are human rights treaties complied with? Are they effective in changing states' behavior for the better? These are critical questions not only for our assessment of human rights treaties, but also for our understanding of the effects of international law more generally. If states act primarily in pursuit of their self-interest, as dominant theories of international relations generally assume, a finding that human rights law frequently alters state behavior would be deeply puzzling, for human rights treaties impinge on core areas of national sovereignty without promising obvious material or strategic benefits. Indeed, a finding that human rights treaties play an important constraining role would provide powerful evidence for the view, embraced by many scholars and practitioners of international law, that state action is critically shaped by the persuasive power of legitimate legal obligations. Examining the effects of human

---

3. THUCYDIDES, HISTORY OF THE PELOPONNESIAN WAR 394 (R. Crowley trans., 1920).

4. *See, e.g.*, MICHAEL BYERS, CUSTOM, POWER, AND THE POWER OF RULES: INTERNATIONAL RELATIONS AND CUSTOMARY INTERNATIONAL LAW 8 (1999) ("International Relations scholars have traditionally had little time for [questions of international law]. Instead, they have regarded international law as something of an epiphenomenon, with rules of international law being dependent on power, subject to short-term alteration by power-applying states, and therefore of little relevance to how states actually behave."); George W. Downs et al., *Is the Good News About Compliance Good News About Cooperation?*, 50 INT'L ORG. 379 (1996); Beth A. Simmons, *Money and the Law: Why Comply with the Public International Law of Money?*, 25 YALE J. INT'L L. 323, 323-24 (2000) ("[M]ost legal scholars and practitioners believe that the rules at the center of their analysis do indeed matter . . . . Scholars of international relations, . . . however, have been far more skeptical.").

5. *See* Simmons, *supra* note 4, at 326 (arguing that "competitive market forces" in the form of "[t]he risk of deterring international business [are] what give[] international monetary law its constraining influence").

6. HENKIN, *supra* note 1, at 235.

rights treaties thus offers a rare opportunity to put dominant views of international law to the test.[7]

This Article undertakes that test with a large-scale quantitative analysis of the relationship between human rights treaties and countries' human rights practices. The analysis relies on a database encompassing the experiences of 166 nations over a nearly forty-year period in five areas of human rights law: genocide, torture, fair and public trials, civil liberties, and political representation of women. This data set is the empirical window through which I examine two separate but intimately related questions. First, do countries comply with or adhere to the requirements of the human rights treaties they have joined? Second, do these human rights treaties appear to be effective in improving countries' human rights practices—that is, are countries *more* likely to comply with a treaty's requirements if they have joined the treaty than would otherwise be expected?[8]

A quantitative approach to these questions makes it possible to trace relationships between treaty ratification and country practices that would be difficult, if not impossible, to detect in qualitative case-by-case analyses.[9] In an analysis of individual cases, there is virtually no way to know whether better or worse human rights practices are due to treaty ratification or instead to any number of other changes in country conditions, such as a change in regime, involvement in civil war, or a change in economic context. Designed correctly, therefore, comprehensive statistical analysis can isolate more effectively the particular effects of treaty ratification on country practices. And such an analysis can achieve a breadth of coverage that would be infeasible in a qualitative case-by-case analysis.

To be sure, the quantitative approach is not without drawbacks. Although a quantitative analysis can have a scope that is impractical in a qualitative analysis, it necessarily brushes over the nuances of historical context that can only be garnered from a case-study approach. This is, of course, an argument not for abandoning quantitative analysis but instead for supplementing it with qualitative evidence.[10] A second obvious drawback of

---

7. One other article undertakes a similar quantitative test of the relationship between human rights practices and treaty ratification and finds results similar to those reported in this Article. Keith, *supra* note 2.

8. Edith Brown Weiss and Harold K. Jacobson provide a framework of analysis for what has traditionally been referred to simply as "compliance" that separates out notions of "implementation," "compliance," and "effectiveness." *See* Weiss & Jacobson, *supra* note 2, at 4-6.

9. For some excellent case studies of these relationships, see, for example, ENGAGING COUNTRIES, *supra* note 2; THE POWER OF HUMAN RIGHTS (Thomas Risse et al. eds., 1999); and A.W. BRIAN SIMPSON, HUMAN RIGHTS AND THE END OF EMPIRE (2001).

10. Indeed, this Article is the first step in a broader project that will include a series of case studies that will test the findings of the statistical analyses and verify, strengthen, and deepen the arguments made in this Article. My earlier study of the impact of free trade agreements in the United States takes just such a case-study approach. *See* Oona A. Hathaway, *Positive Feedback:*

1940   The Yale Law Journal   [Vol. 111: 1935

statistical inquiry is that the accuracy of the analysis necessarily depends on the accuracy of the data on which it rests. To address this problem, I draw on several different data sources and cross-check all my results against more than one source. Nonetheless, to the extent that the data on which my study rests are imperfect, there remains a risk that the conclusions I draw are similarly imperfect. The questions that this Article addresses are worth considering even if the answers fall short of certainty and even if much room remains for additional quantitative and qualitative research.

From the standpoint of leading perspectives on international law, the results of my research are counterintuitive. Although the ratings of human rights practices of countries that have ratified international human rights treaties are generally better than those of countries that have not, noncompliance with treaty obligations appears to be common. More paradoxically, when I take into account the influence of a range of other factors that affect countries' practices, I find that treaty ratification is not infrequently associated with worse human rights ratings than otherwise expected. I do, however, find evidence suggesting that ratification of human rights treaties by fully democratic nations is associated with better human rights practices. These findings are not fully consistent with either the classic interest-based or the norm-based views of international law. If treaties are simply window-dressing for the self-interested pursuit of national goals, then there should be no consistent relationship between ratification and state behavior, positive or negative. If, by contrast, they have a powerful normative hold, then ratification of human rights treaties should be associated with better practices—not only by fully democratic nations—and should never be associated with worse practices.

My findings do not necessarily tell us that treaties lead to worse human rights practices. Countries with worse practices may be more inclined to ratify treaties, or we may simply know more about violations committed by countries that sign human rights treaties, making countries that ratify look worse than they are. Yet given that I find not a single treaty for which ratification seems to be reliably associated with better human rights practices and several for which it appears to be associated with worse practices, it would be premature to dismiss the possibility that human rights treaties may sometimes lead to poorer human rights practices within the countries that ratify them.

This suggestion is not as outrageous as it might at first appear. The counterintuitive results may be explained at least in part, I argue, by a conception of international treaties that takes account of their dual nature as both instrumental and expressive instruments. Treaties are instrumental in

---

The Impact of Trade Liberalization on Industry Demands for Protection, 52 INT'L ORG. 575 (1998).

that they create law that binds ratifying countries, with the goal of modifying nations' practices in particular ways. But treaties also declare or express to the international community the position of countries that have ratified. The position taken by countries in such instances can be sincere, but it need not be. When countries are rewarded for positions rather than effects—as they are when monitoring and enforcement of treaties are minimal and external pressure to conform to treaty norms is high— governments can take positions that they do not honor, and benefit from doing so.[11] In this respect, human rights treaties lie in contrast to Article VIII of the IMF's Articles of Agreement, for which compliance information is readily available and which Beth Simmons has found to have a significant positive influence on state behavior.[12]

This perspective helps explain why treaty ratification might sometimes be associated with worse human rights practices than otherwise expected. Countries that take the relatively costless step of treaty ratification may thereby offset pressure for costly changes in policies. Because monitoring and enforcement are usually minimal, the expression by a country of commitment to the treaty's goals need not be consistent with the country's actual course of action.

Although ratification of human rights treaties appears to have little favorable impact on individual countries' practices, this finding does not preclude the possibility that treaties have favorable effects on human rights across the board. And human rights treaties may have positive effects on ratifying countries over the long term, creating public commitments to which human rights activists can point as they push nations to make gradual, if grudging, improvements down the road. Indeed, these dynamics are not mutually exclusive. Treaty ratification may set in play both positive and negative forces, which together often lead to little or no net effect on state practices.

This Article proceeds in four stages. Part I discusses the existing international relations and legal literature on compliance with international law, dividing contending schools into two broad camps: rational actor

---

11. In this Article, I use the terms "nation," "country," and "government" interchangeably to refer to various domestic-level governing institutions through which a series of individuals take actions and make decisions. The process of national decisionmaking and the interaction between domestic and international players is of course important to a complete understanding of treaty compliance. This Article explores the role of domestic politics to a limited extent by examining the impact of the level of democratization of a country on its human rights practices and on its propensity to ratify human rights treaties, and by discussing possible explanations for countries' compliance practices. *See, e.g., infra* text accompanying note 246. The role of domestic politics in treaty compliance is the subject of my ongoing research and will be addressed more fully in future work.

12. Simmons, *supra* note 2, at 832 (finding that "[o]nce we control for most of the obvious reasons a government may choose to restrict its current account, Article VIII status still emerges as a truly significant influence on the probability of choosing to restrict [the current account]").

models and normative theory. By developing an inclusive framework for understanding the international-relations and international-law literature on compliance, I aim to clarify the basic fault lines in the debate and further existing efforts to conceive of these two previously divided disciplines as a unified whole. Part II discusses the design of the empirical analysis and reviews the results. The analysis uses a wide range of evidence to evaluate a central question of international law: Do human rights treaties make a difference in state behavior? I begin by comparing the practices of treaty ratifiers with those of nonratifiers to show that the extent of compliance is not only lower than might be expected, but also varies within the universe of nations in revealing ways. I then turn to the crucial quantitative tests, examining the relationship between treaty ratification and country practices in the context of a range of other factors expected to influence country practices, including economic development, civil and external wars, and levels of democratization.

Part III returns to the theory in light of the evidence, pitting contending explanations against the empirical findings and developing my own argument for the paradoxical results that I find. Drawing upon and amending existing theories of international law, I argue that treaties must be understood as dual instruments, in which both expressive functions and instrumental ends sometimes uneasily coexist. The results of the empirical analyses indicate that state expressions of commitment to human rights through treaty ratification may sometimes relieve pressure on states to pursue real changes in their policies and thereby undermine the instrumental aims of those very same treaties. The concluding Part IV discusses possible favorable effects of human rights treaties that may be overlooked by the quantitative analysis and considers the ways in which the expressive and instrumental roles of treaties might be better aligned to ensure that international human rights laws will more effectively lead to improvements in the lives of those they are meant to help.

I. EXISTING LITERATURE ON TREATY COMPLIANCE AND EFFECTIVENESS

Until fairly recently, the question of international law compliance fell by the wayside of both international law and international relations scholarship. Legal scholars examined and explicated the rules of state international behavior, generally taking as a given that the rules would have impact. International relations scholars, for their part, had little interest in international law. The centrality in international relations of realist thinking, which accepted the view that nation-states operated "in a tenuous net of breakable obligations," discouraged careful examination of the role of transnational institutions and hence of international law.[13]

At the same time, the few advances that each discipline made in examining international compliance were largely ignored by the other. Writings on international law were largely concerned with the formation, promulgation, and codification of international laws. Although scholars of international law obviously understood that these rules are not self-executing and that nations vary in the degree to which they adhere to them, relatively little attention was given to the broader economic and political environment that conditions the making of international law and nations' responses to it. This environment was, by contrast, the very focus of much of the international relations literature, yet international relations scholars did not explore whether and how international law fits into it. Perhaps most indicative of the mutual isolation of the two disciplines was the general failure of international law scholars to use quantitative techniques and rational choice theory, which had emerged as important tools of analysis in political economy but had generally taken a back seat to more traditional modes of legal argumentation and analysis in writing on international law. In turn, international relations scholars often ignored international law scholarship altogether.

In recent years, the chasm between the disciplines has narrowed as international law and international relations theorists have begun to share insights.[14] Yet compliance with and effectiveness of international human rights law remains a dark corner into which few have bothered to peer. Here, I sketch out the primary existing theories of international law compliance and effectiveness in both international law and international relations scholarship, taking special note of the few instances where human rights law is specifically considered. In light of the growing harmony and discourse between international law and international relations scholarship,

---

13. Stanley Hoffmann, *The Role of International Organization: Limits and Possibilities*, 10 INT'L ORG. 357, 364 (1956).

14. In law, much of the attention to international relations theory began with Kenneth W. Abbott, *Modern International Relations Theory: A Prospectus for International Lawyers*, 14 YALE J. INT'L L. 335 (1989) [hereinafter Abbot, *Modern International Relations Theory*]. Progress since then has been slow but steady on both sides. Witness the Summer 2000 issue of *International Organization*, the flagship of international relations scholarship, which was devoted to international relations approaches to international law, and the *American Journal of International Law*, which has devoted several articles to charting the burgeoning interdisciplinary scholarship. *See, e.g.*, Kenneth W. Abbott, *International Relations Theory, International Law, and the Regime Governing Atrocities in Internal Conflicts*, 93 AM. J. INT'L L. 361 (1999); Anne-Marie Slaughter Burley, *International Law and International Relations Theory: A Dual Agenda*, 87 AM. J. INT'L L. 205 (1993); Anne-Marie Slaughter et al., *International Law and International Relations Theory: A New Generation of Interdisciplinary Scholarship*, 92 AM. J. INT'L L. 367 (1998). For further commentary, see THE ROLE OF LAW IN INTERNATIONAL POLITICS (Michael Byers ed., 2000); and the American Society of International Law's planned conference in 2002, "The Legalization of International Relations/The Internationalization of Legal Relations."

1944   The Yale Law Journal   [Vol. 111: 1935

I opt to blend the two scholarships in defining two broad approaches, which I group under the labels "rational actor models" and "normative theory."[15]

Before I begin a review of the literature in more detail, two caveats are in order. First, as any brief review of a rich literature must, the following discussion skims only the surface of deeply complex theories in order to draw out their implications for human rights treaty compliance. Second, by delineating the distinctions among the theories, I do not intend to suggest that they are mutually exclusive. Each approach provides useful and often complementary insights into the puzzle of treaty compliance. Indeed, the goal of this Article is not to supplant, but to supplement, these theories so that they are individually and collectively better equipped to explain treaty compliance.

A. *Rational Actor Models*

The theories I term "rational actor models" have at their heart a shared belief that states and the individuals that guide them are rational self-interested actors that calculate the costs and benefits of alternative courses of action in the international realm and act accordingly. In this view, international law does not hold a privileged position. It is one of a series of tools available to the relevant actors in their ongoing battle to achieve their self-interested ends. Compliance does not occur unless it furthers the self-interest of the parties by, for example, improving their reputation, enhancing their geopolitical power, furthering their ideological ends, avoiding conflict, or avoiding sanction by a more powerful state. The three variants of this model outlined below differ primarily in the types and sources of interests that they claim motivate country decisions.

1. *Realism: Compliance as Coincidence*

In what was once the most widely accepted theory of state action among international relations scholars (and is now of growing influence in international law), international treaties and institutions exist only because powerful states benefit from their presence. The most traditional version of this approach, labeled "classical realism," was dominant in academic and policy circles in the years following World War II. In this view, states are

---

15. My framing mirrors that of Robert O. Keohane. Robert O. Keohane, *International Relations and International Law: Two Optics*, 38 HARV. INT'L L.J. 487 (1997). For good summaries of the relationship between international relations theory and international legal scholarship, see Slaughter Burley, *supra* note 14; and Slaughter et al., *supra* note 14. *See also* Abbott, *Modern International Relations Theory*, *supra* note 14, at 337-38; John K. Setear, *An Iterative Perspective on Treaties: A Synthesis of International Relations Theory and International Law*, 37 HARV. INT'L L.J. 139 (1996); Beth A. Simmons, *Compliance with International Agreements*, 1 ANN. REV. POL. SCI. 75 (1998).

motivated exclusively by their geopolitical interests.[16] International law exists and is complied with only when it is in the interests of a hegemon or a few powerful states, which coerce less powerful states into accepting the regime and complying with it. International law is therefore in this view largely epiphenomenal.[17]

The strong version of this view no longer holds sway,[18] in large part because its dismissal of international regimes ran into difficulty in the 1970s and 1980s when its predictions rapidly diverged from empirical reality.[19] Instead, classical realism has given way in the last two decades to a more nuanced approach, termed by its proponents "neorealism" or "structural realism," that shares with classical realism a conception of states as unitary actors and a focus on the international system as the relevant level of analysis. Neorealists abandoned classical realism's exclusive focus on international power arrangements and instead use concepts drawn from game theory and economics—known under the broad rubric of rational choice theory—to understand and explain international cooperation and discord. Like classical realism, however, neorealism, as conceived of in Kenneth Waltz's foundational *Theory of International Politics*[20] and its progeny, leaves little room for international institutions. Rather, international politics take place in an international environment defined by anarchy and filled with states that are "unitary actors who, at a minimum, seek their own preservation and, at a maximum, drive for universal domination."[21] In this view, therefore, if compliance with international law occurs, it is not because the law is effective, but merely

---

16. *See* EDWARD HALLETT CARR, THE TWENTY YEARS' CRISIS 1919-1939 (Harper & Row 1946) (1939); HANS J. MORGENTHAU, POLITICS AMONG NATIONS (3d ed. 1966); Keohane, *supra* note 15, at 489 ("The 'instrumentalist optic' focuses on interests and argues that rules and norms will matter only if they affect the calculations of interests by agents."); Hans J. Morgenthau, *Positivism, Functionalism, and International Law*, 34 AM. J. INT'L L. 260 (1940).

17. *See* HENKIN, *supra* note 1, at 49 (labeling as "[t]he cynic's formula" the realist view that "since there is no body to enforce the law, nations will comply with international law only if it is in their interest to do so; they will disregard law or obligation if the advantages of violation outweigh the advantages of observance").

18. For critiques of classical realism, see, for example, ROBERT O. KEOHANE, AFTER HEGEMONY (1984); and Duncan Snidal, *The Limits of Hegemonic Stability Theory*, 39 INT'L ORG. 579 (1985).

19. *See, e.g.*, Jeff Frieden, *Sectoral Conflict and Foreign Economic Policy, 1914-1940*, 42 INT'L ORG. 59 (1988) (seeking to understand why the United States was so slow to assume a position of leadership in the interwar years despite its power position in the world); Judith Goldstein, *Ideas, Institutions, and American Trade Policy*, 42 INT'L ORG. 179 (1988) (finding that American trade policy remained liberal in the 1970s and 1980s despite the country's relative decline within the international economy); Michael Mastanduno, *Trade as a Strategic Weapon: American and Alliance Export Control Policy in the Early Postwar Period*, 42 INT'L ORG. 121 (1988) (finding that the United States was unable to maintain the trade regime it preferred in the 1950s, even though it was at the zenith of its hegemonic power).

20. KENNETH N. WALTZ, THEORY OF INTERNATIONAL POLITICS (1979).

21. *Id.* at 118.

because compliance is coincident with the path dictated by self-interest in a world governed by anarchy and relative state power.

Both strands of realist theory face a difficult task when called upon to explain the existence of and compliance with human rights regimes. The observation by a state of the human rights of its citizens provides little or no direct benefits to other states. It is therefore difficult for realists to explain why states would be willing to incur the costs of setting up a regime to protect human rights, surrender to that regime the power to control and monitor some aspects of their interactions with their own citizens, commit to bring themselves into line with treaty requirements, and agree to engage where necessary in sanctioning activity to bring others into compliance.

Perhaps the most widely shared view of such laws among realist scholars is that efforts to secure human rights are, in essence, "cheap talk"—an example of governments using liberal ideological arguments to justify actions that they take in pursuit of wealth and power.[22] In this view, state behavior that is consistent with the requirements of human rights treaties can only be explained as mere coincidence because no state would actually change its behavior in response to a human rights treaty absent some independent motivation.

Some neorealist scholars, by contrast, accept that a state's commitment to human rights can be genuine and can indeed be no less important in explaining the motivations of countries than material interests.[23] Kenneth Waltz, for instance, accepts the possibility that some countries are genuinely committed to human rights and explains human rights regimes as simply a result of powerful nations seeking to impose their commitment to human rights on other nations.[24] In this view, states comply with human rights norms because they are coerced into doing so by more powerful nations. This neorealist explanation, however, is not entirely consistent with observed reality. In practice, the most powerful nations are often not among

---

22. *See* CARR, *supra* note 16; MORGENTHAU, *supra* note 16. Of course, there remains a gaping hole in the logic of this argument: If nations are really just motivated by self-interest and international relations are simply guided by the interests of the most powerful states, why do countries bother with cheap talk about human rights? Part III of this Article attempts to provide an answer.

23. Jack Donnelly, *International Human Rights: A Regime Analysis*, 40 INT'L ORG. 599, 616 (1986).

24. WALTZ, *supra* note 20, at 200. Waltz states:
Like some earlier great powers, we [the United States] can identify the presumed duty of the rich and powerful to help others with our own beliefs about what a better world would look like. England claimed to bear the white man's burden; France spoke of her *mission civilisatrice.* . . . For countries at the top, this is predictable behavior.
Id. Curiously, Waltz does not explain where the powerful nations' commitment to human rights comes from or why nations would be willing to sacrifice more tangible interests and benefits in pursuit of human rights.

those pressing for human rights treaties.[25] Indeed, the United States, which has been indisputably the strongest world power since World War II, has shown some antipathy toward human rights law, having ratified as of 1999 only seven of nineteen non-International Labour Organization universal human rights treaties with binding legal effect, compared with a median of ten for the 165 other countries included in my database.[26] Thus realist and neorealist approaches suggest that if state action is consistent with the requirements of international human rights law, it is most likely the result of coincidence rather than the force of the law. Consequently, they would likely predict no significant relationship between human rights treaty ratification and government behavior.

2. *Institutionalism: Compliance as Strategy*

In contrast with realist models, institutionalism takes system-wide institutions seriously. Institutionalists, including most notably Robert Keohane,[27] seek to explain why international institutions exist and how they influence state action.[28] Like neorealism, institutionalism for the most part

---

25. *See, e.g.*, Andrew Moravcsik, *The Origins of Human Rights Regimes: Democratic Delegation in Postwar Europe*, 54 INT'L ORG. 217, 219-20 (2000) (arguing that "[a]lthough established democracies [in Europe] supported certain human rights declarations, they allied with dictatorships and transitional regimes in opposition to reciprocally binding human rights enforcement" (emphasis omitted)).

26. Author's calculations, based on ratification information on treaties filed with the Secretary General of the United Nations. *See* United Nations Treaty Collection, *at* http://untreaty.un.org/English/access.asp (last visited Apr. 2, 2002). I label as "universal human rights treaties" those treaties included in U.N. CTR. FOR HUMAN RIGHTS, HUMAN RIGHTS: A COMPILATION OF INTERNATIONAL INSTRUMENTS 419, U.N. Doc. ST/HR/1/Rev.5, U.N. Sales No. E.94.XIV.1 (1994), that are open to signature by any member of the United Nations without geographical or other restriction and that have binding legal power. *See id.* at xii. Several scholars have discussed the apparent aversion of the United States to human rights law. *See, e.g.*, Cormac T. Connor, *Human Rights Violations in the Information Age*, 16 GEO. IMMIGR. L.J. 207, 230 (2001) ("In 1953, Secretary of State John Foster Dulles asserted that the United States did not intend to ratify any international human rights treaties. Official antipathy to international human rights instruments has been entrenched ever since courts have found the provisions of the Universal Declaration to be non-binding." (footnotes omitted)); M. Christian Green, *The "Matrioshka" Strategy: U.S. Evasion of the Spirit of the International Convention on Civil and Political Rights*, 10 S. AFR. J. HUM. RTS. 357, 370-71 (1994) ("The United States has been the target of international criticism not so much for its own violations as for its unwillingness to use its position in the world to set a good example for others. The United States has a role to play as a member of the vanguard of nations trying to advocate human rights not only in theory, but in practice. It should assume this role and work for the improvement of rights in the world community rather than grudgingly ratifying treaties, while at the same time concealing their goals within layer upon layer of qualifications."); Kenneth Roth, *The Charade of US Ratification of International Human Rights Treaties*, 1 CHI. J. INT'L L. 347, 352-53 (2000) ("Washington's cynical attitude toward international human rights law has begun to weaken the US government's voice as an advocate for human rights around the world.").

27. *See* KEOHANE, *supra* note 18.

28. Other works in this vein include LISA L. MARTIN, COERCIVE COOPERATION (1992), LISA L. MARTIN, DEMOCRATIC COMMITMENTS (2000), Robert Jervis, *Security Regimes*, 36 INT'L ORG. 357 (1982), Lisa L. Martin, *Institutions and Cooperation: Sanctions During the Falkland*

1948 The Yale Law Journal [Vol. 111: 1935

views states as unified principal actors that behave on the basis of self-interest.[29] It also shares neorealist assumptions that anarchy and the distribution of power among states are the underlying principles of world politics.[30] Indeed, an early variant of this approach—dubbed "modified structural realism"[31]—differs from realism primarily in that it takes institutions, often referred to as "regimes,"[32] seriously.[33] In this view—which has been variously recast as "intergovernmental institutionalism,"[34] "neoliberal institutionalism,"[35] and "new institutionalism,"[36]—regimes exist in order to facilitate agreements and are complied with largely because of the rational utility-maximizing activity of states pursuing their self-interest. Regimes thus allow countries to engage in cooperative activity that might not otherwise be possible by restraining short-term power maximization in pursuit of long-term goals.[37] When it occurs, therefore,

---

Islands Conflict, INT'L SECURITY, Spring 1992, at 143, and Arthur A. Stein, *Coordination and Collaboration: Regimes in an Anarchic World,* 36 INT'L ORG. 299 (1982).

29. Robert O. Keohane, *Institutional Theory and the Realist Challenge After the Cold War, in* NEOREALISM AND NEOLIBERALISM 269, 271 (David A. Baldwin ed., 1993) ("[I]nstitutionalist theory assumes that states are the principal actors in world politics and that they behave on the basis of their conceptions of their own self-interests.").

30. For a thoughtful essay exploring the relationship between neoliberal institutionalism and neorealism, see ROBERT O. KEOHANE, *Neoliberal Institutionalism: A Perspective on World Politics, in* INTERNATIONAL INSTITUTIONS AND STATE POWER 1 (1989).

31. *See* Slaughter Burley, *supra* note 14, at 221 ("Keohane recast modified Structural Realism as 'Neoliberal Institutionalism.'"). Some significant works on compliance in this vein include KEOHANE, *supra* note 18, at 61-64, ROBERT O. KEOHANE & JOSEPH S. NYE, POWER AND INTERDEPENDENCE (1977), Robert O. Keohane, *The Demand for International Regimes,* 36 INT'L ORG. 325 (1982), and Robert O. Keohane, *Theory of World Politics: Structural Realism and Beyond, in* NEOREALISM AND ITS CRITICS 158, 192-95 (Robert O. Keohane ed., 1986). Other works on this topic include ORAN R. YOUNG, INTERNATIONAL COOPERATION: BUILDING REGIMES FOR NATURAL RESOURCES AND THE ENVIRONMENT (1989), ORAN R. YOUNG, INTERNATIONAL GOVERNANCE: PROTECTING THE ENVIRONMENT IN A STATELESS SOCIETY (1994), Duncan Snidal, *Coordination Versus Prisoners' Dilemma: Implications for International Cooperation and Regimes,* 79 AM. POL. SCI. REV. 923 (1985), Duncan Snidal, *The Game Theory of International Politics,* 38 WORLD POL. 25 (1985), and Oran R. Young, *The Effectiveness of International Institutions: Hard Cases and Critical Variables, in* GOVERNANCE WITHOUT GOVERNMENT 160 (James N. Rosenau & Ernst-Otto Czempiel eds., 1992).

32. Stephen D. Krasner, *Structural Causes and Regime Consequences: Regimes as Intervening Variables, in* INTERNATIONAL REGIMES 1, 2 (Stephen D. Krasner ed., 1983) (defining "regimes" broadly as "principles, norms, rules and decision-making procedures around which actors' expectations converge in a given area"). Relatedly, Keohane and Nye define "regimes" as "sets of governing arrangements" that include "networks of rules, norms, and procedures that regularize behavior and control its effects." KEOHANE & NYE, *supra* note 31, at 19.

33. For more on the evolution of modified structural realism, see Friedrich Kratochwil & John G. Ruggie, *International Organization: A State of the Art on an Art of the State,* 40 INT'L ORG. 753 (1986).

34. *See, e.g.,* Andrew Moravcsik, *Negotiating the Single European Act: National Interests and Conventional Statecraft in the European Community,* 45 INT'L ORG. 19, 27 (1991).

35. KEOHANE, *supra* note 30, at 7.

36. Duncan Snidal, *Political Economy and International Institutions,* 16 INT'L REV. L. & ECON. 121, 121 (1996).

37. *See* Robert O. Keohane, *The Demand for International Regimes, in* INTERNATIONAL REGIMES, *supra* note 32, at 141; Krasner, *supra* note 32.

compliance with international legal rules can be explained as a winning long-term strategy to obtain self-interested ends.

As Duncan Snidal has pointed out, the increased attention to international regimes by international relations scholars did not, at least initially, signal a new focus on international law. The definition of "regimes" adopted early on by most theorists required neither formal institutions nor enforcement powers, and much of the ensuing literature on regimes focused on informal cooperation and largely ignored traditional international organizations and international law.[38] Yet the most recent work in this vein has adopted a broader view of institutions[39] that encompasses law as well as international legal institutions.[40] In this view, legal institutions, like other institutions, are seen as "rational, negotiated responses to the problems international actors face."[41]

This reconceptualization of institutionalism among international relations scholars to include international law is one of many signs of the increasing convergence of international law and international relations. Until recently, however, it was left largely to international legal scholars to bring international law into the institutionalist framework. In part in response to the challenge that realism has posed to international law, legal scholars began to reconceptualize the role of law and politics in the international realm.[42] In the last decade, a few legal scholars adopted the interests-based approach of institutionalism, but, unlike most international relations scholars, they placed law at the center of the analysis.[43] Yet despite institutionalism's increasing acceptance, it has been applied only recently in any comprehensive way to international legal compliance. Jack Goldsmith and Eric Posner use an institutionalist approach that views compliance with international law as the result of interactions between

---

38. Snidal, *supra* note 36, at 124.
39. Modern work in this vein generally uses the terms "regime" and "institution" interchangeably. *See, e.g.*, Ronald B. Mitchell & Patricia M. Keilbach, *Situation Structure and Institutional Design: Reciprocity, Coercion, and Exchange*, 54 INT'L ORG. 891, 893 (2001) ("We also use the term regime interchangeably with institution.").
40. *See, e.g.*, Barbara Koremenos et al., *The Rational Design of International Institutions*, 55 INT'L ORG. 761, 762-63 (2001) ("We define international institutions as explicit arrangements, negotiated among international actors, that prescribe, proscribe, and/or authorize behavior. . . . The 1961 Vienna Law on Treaties is a good example."). For a collection of recent institutionalist work from the political science perspective, see the issue of *International Organization* in which the Koremenos article appears.
41. Koremenos et al., *supra* note 40, at 768 (emphasis omitted).
42. *See* Slaughter Burley, *supra* note 14, at 209-14.
43. John K. Setear, for instance, uses an institutionalist approach informed by rational choice theory to analyze the rules of release and remediation in the law of treaties and the law of state responsibility. *See* John K. Setear, *Responses to Breach of a Treaty and Rationalist International Relations Theory: The Rules of Release and Remediation in the Law of Treaties and the Law of State Responsibility*, 83 VA. L. REV. 1 (1997); *see also* Setear, *supra* note 15 (taking an institutionalist approach to the law of treaties).

1950 The Yale Law Journal [Vol. 111: 1935

rational, self-interested states to critique customary international law.[44] And in a recent paper, Andrew T. Guzman puts forward a comprehensive institutionalist view of state action in the international realm as a function of interests and power rather than legitimacy or ideology.[45] In Guzman's framework, countries take into account both direct sanctions and more indirect sanctions in the form of reputational costs, which he operationalizes through a game-theoretic model of repeated interaction, in deciding whether to comply with international legal rules.[46] They weigh these costs against the benefits they will obtain from compliance, and, based on this calculus, decide how to act.

This institutionalist view of international law can be seen as a necessary and overdue counterpart to the longstanding consent-based approach to international law. International lawyers have long pointed to state consent as the central basis for the binding nature of international law.[47] The consent-based approach is centered, as its name suggests, on the notion that states can bear no obligation to which they have not consented.[48] Proponents of this view of international law see international treaties as simply a means for states to consent to abide by certain well-specified obligations. Once a state has accepted such an obligation, the argument continues, the obligation becomes binding and a nation must comply with it.[49] The institutionalist approach outlined above helps fill a gap in consent theory by offering a possible explanation for why, if international law binds only countries that consent to it, international law exists and has any force at all. International law exists and has force, the institutionalist would say, because it provides a means of achieving outcomes possible only through coordinated behavior. States consent to commit themselves because doing so is the only way to achieve certain goals. They then comply with

---

44. *See* Jack L. Goldsmith & Eric A. Posner, *A Theory of Customary International Law*, 66 U. CHI. L. REV. 1113 (1999) (using the game-theoretic concepts that form the central focus of much international relations scholarship to provide an account of how customary international law arises, why nations comply with it, and how it changes over time).

45. GUZMAN, *supra* note 1.

46. Interestingly, Guzman's framework is in many ways entirely consistent with the managerial model discussed *infra* text accompanying notes 72-84, despite efforts by both sets of authors to emphasize the differences between the two approaches. Indeed, Guzman's work could be seen as providing a formal model of the amorphous threat of alienation from the "complex web of international arrangements" that is emphasized by Chayes and Chayes. *See infra* text accompanying note 82.

47. Setear, *supra* note 15, at 156 ("Most international lawyers would probably summarize the underlying structure of the law of treaties in a single phrase: the consent of sovereign nations.").

48. This view is reflected in the famous *S.S. Lotus* case, in which the Court of International Justice stated: "The rules of law binding upon States therefore emanate from their own free will . . . ." S.S. Lotus (Fr. v. Turk.), 1927 P.C.I.J. (ser. A) No. 10, at 18 (Sept. 7); *see also* Louis Henkin, *International Law: Politics, Values and Functions*, 216 RECUEIL DES COURS D'ACADEMIE DE DROIT INTERNATIONAL 27 (1989) ("[A] State is not subject to any external authority unless it has voluntarily consented to such authority.").

49. *See* CHAYES & CHAYES, *supra* note 1, at 185 ("It is often said that the fundamental norm of international law is *pacta sunt servanda* (treaties are to be obeyed).").

obligations already made as long as the reputational costs and direct sanctions that would result from noncompliance outweigh the costs of continued compliance.[50] In this view, then, law provides a real constraint, but only insofar as violating it entails real costs. Law carries no weight divorced from the quantifiable sanctions and costs imposed in the case of its violation.

Explaining compliance with human rights law is almost as daunting a task for institutionalist theory as it is for realist theory. In the institutionalist view, compliance with international human rights treaties must be explained as the result of rational self-interested behavior on the part of states, the result of a reasoned weighing of the costs and benefits of alternative modes of action. But on the whole, the benefits of human rights treaty compliance appear minimal while the costs often are not. In cases where the treaty requires actions that are consistent with a country's practices at the time the treaty is adopted, the costs of compliance are obviously negligible. Treaties can, however, require fairly extensive changes in domestic institutions and practices. One of the treaties examined here, for example, requires a ratifying country to put in place "legislative, administrative, judicial or other measures to prevent acts of torture in any territory under its jurisdiction."[51] Countries that are parties may thus be required to make potentially costly system-wide changes in order to bring themselves into compliance. Why might countries be willing to do this? In the institutional model, they do so because of the threat of direct sanctions or harm to reputation.[52] Direct sanctions in the form of economic or military reprisal for human rights treaty violations are so rare, however, that states are unlikely to conform their actions to a treaty solely on that basis.[53] And the threat of retaliatory noncompliance with the treaty does not have the power that it does in other contexts, such as trade or arms agreements, as a threat that a treaty party will violate the treaty in retaliation for violations by another party is untenable. The institutional model is left, then, with reputation as the primary anchor of compliance for all but those countries for which compliance is costless: States comply with human rights treaties

---

50. For the only comprehensive work on compliance from the rationalist view, see GUZMAN, *supra* note 1.

51. Convention Against Torture and Other Cruel, Inhuman or Degrading Treatment or Punishment, *adopted* Dec. 10, 1984, art. 2, § 1, S. TREATY DOC. NO. 100-20, at 20 (1988), 1465 U.N.T.S. 85, 114 (entered into force June 26, 1987) [hereinafter Torture Convention].

52. Relatedly, states may be willing to make such changes to create and maintain a regime that satisfies their long-term interests. But such motivations depend on the existence of strong monitoring and enforcement to cause members to restrict their short-term interest-seeking to obtain long-term goals. Where direct sanctions are minimal, however, such motivations disappear.

53. *See* ECONOMIC SANCTIONS RECONSIDERED 16-32 (Gary Clyde Hufbauer et al. eds., 2d ed. 1990) (listing all of the uses of economic sanctions for foreign policy purposes between 1914 and 1990 and finding that out of 119 cases of sanctions, 63 of which involved sanctions imposed only by the United States, fewer than 25 were motivated in significant part by human rights concerns).

to obtain or maintain a reputation for compliance and hence good international citizenship. In the institutional model, therefore, if countries change their behavior in response to human rights treaties, it is largely because of concern for their reputation.

3. *Liberalism: Compliance as By-Product of Domestic Politics*

A third rational actor model of international law compliance discards the assumption, which undergirds realism and institutionalism, that states are properly viewed as unitary rational agents. Termed "institutional liberalism" (or sometimes "liberal institutionalism"), this approach disaggregates the state and places the focus on domestic political processes. The approach finds its intellectual antecedents in the work of Immanuel Kant, in particular his essay *Perpetual Peace*.[54] In the essay, Kant argues that the first condition of perpetual peace is that "the civil construction of every nation should be republican,"[55] because republican governments (i.e., representative democracies) rely on the consent of the citizens to engage in war and must therefore "consider all its calamities before committing themselves to so risky a game."[56] Kant's claim was later taken up by international relations scholars who claimed that although "liberal" states engage in war, they do not engage in war with *one another*.[57] In its modern iteration, liberal international relations theory has come to stand for the straightforward proposition that domestic politics matter.[58]

The liberal approach holds that interstate politics are much more complex than realists and institutionalists acknowledge. States are not unitary, but rather are the sum of many different parts. Understanding those parts—the political institutions, interest groups, and state actors—is essential to fully understanding state action on the world stage. As Andrew Moravcsik puts it: "Societal ideas, interests, and institutions influence state behavior by shaping state preferences, that is, the fundamental social purposes underlying the strategic calculations of governments."[59] In other

---

54. IMMANUEL KANT, *Perpetual Peace*, *in* PERPETUAL PEACE AND OTHER ESSAYS ON POLITICS, HISTORY, AND MORALS 107 (Ted Humphrey trans., Hackett Publ'g Co. 1983) (1795).

55. *Id.* at 112.

56. *Id.* at 113.

57. The central work on this topic is Michael W. Doyle, *Kant, Liberal Legacies, and Foreign Affairs*, 12 PHIL. & PUB. AFF. 205 (1983). Doyle's findings were confirmed by a series of empirical studies, including most notably Zeev Maoz & Nasrin Abdolali, *Regime Types and International Conflict, 1816-1976*, 33 J. CONFLICT RESOL. 3 (1989).

58. GRAHAM ALLISON & PHILIP ZELIKOW, ESSENCE OF DECISION 39 (2d ed. 1999).

59. Andrew Moravcsik, *Taking Preferences Seriously: A Liberal Theory of International Politics*, 51 INT'L ORG. 513, 513 (1997).

words, one cannot fully understand state decisions in the international realm without understanding the domestic politics that underlie them.[60]

Anne-Marie Slaughter has taken the lead in bringing the liberalist view to the attention of legal scholars. She argues in an early piece in this vein that just as liberal states act differently toward one another in waging war, they act differently toward one another in the legal realm.[61] From this insight, she constructs what she terms a "liberal internationalist model" of transnational legal relations that seeks to explain why and how relations among liberal states differ from those between liberal and nonliberal states. In short, she argues that because of their political structure, liberal states are more likely to resolve disputes with one another peacefully in the "zone of law" than they are when the disputes are with nonliberal states.[62] In a more recent article, Slaughter and her coauthor Laurence Helfer make a similar argument with regard to the effectiveness of international or "supranational" adjudication, which, although distinct from treaty law, bears some important similarities.[63] They argue that liberal democratic governments will be more likely to comply with supranational legal judgments than are other states because international legal obligations mobilize domestic interest groups that in turn pressure the government to comply.[64] More specifically, they claim that "government institutions committed to both the rule of law and separation of powers . . . in systems where the individuals themselves are ultimately sovereign[] are primed to be the most receptive to the tools that a supranational tribunal has at its disposal."[65] Thus compliance with international law comes, in the liberalist view, from the favorable effect of international law and legal institutions on domestic interests—a phenomenon not limited to, but more likely to be found in, liberal states.

Liberal theory is susceptible to the charge that although it can provide explanations for government actions after the fact, it has difficulty generating predictions ex ante. Indeed, at an extreme, the theory can be reduced to the unenlightening truism that if a country acts in a particular

---

60. *See* Stephan Haggard & Beth A. Simmons, *Theories of International Regimes*, 41 INT'L ORG. 491, 499 (1987) (arguing that realist and institutionalist theories "downplay the central insight of interdependence theorists: foreign policy is integrally related to domestic structures and processes").

61. Anne-Marie Burley, *Law Among Liberal States: Liberal Internationalism and the Act of State Doctrine*, 92 COLUM. L. REV. 1907, 1920-21 (1992); *see* Anne-Marie Slaughter, *International Law in a World of Liberal States*, 6 EUR. J. INT'L L. 503 (1995); Anne-Marie Slaughter, *The Liberal Agenda for Peace: International Relations Theory and the Future of the United Nations*, 4 TRANSNAT'L L. & CONTEMP. PROBS. 377 (1995); Slaughter Burley, *supra* note 14.

62. Burley, *supra* note 61, at 1916-22.

63. Laurence R. Helfer & Anne-Marie Slaughter, *Toward a Theory of Effective Supranational Adjudication*, 107 YALE L.J. 273, 278 (1997).

64. *Id.* at 331-35.

65. *Id.* at 334.

way, it must be because domestic politics made it do so. Yet it is arguably better suited to explaining compliance with human rights treaties than are either of the other two rational actor models. In the liberalist view, human rights treaties, like other sources of international law, must affect state action by affecting domestic interests. A state's ratification of a human rights treaty creates an international legal obligation that domestic interest groups can use to mobilize pressure on domestic political institutions to take action in conformance with that obligation. This process is particularly strong in liberal states, which are structured to translate domestic interests into state action. Moreover, according to this view, such states are more likely to abide by human rights treaties because they are more likely to be receptive to the claim that once a treaty is consented to, it creates an obligation that must be obeyed.[66] Liberalism thus generates a testable hypothesis: Liberal nations are more likely to comply than others, and treaties are more likely to lead to favorable changes in the practices of liberal nations than in the practices of others.

Andrew Moravcsik's recent work on human rights treaty ratification from the perspective of a variant of the liberal approach—termed "republican liberalism"—gives reason to suspect that the story regarding human rights treaty compliance may be more complicated than the above analysis suggests. Examining the formation of the European Convention on Human Rights,[67] Moravcsik argues that newly established and potentially unstable democracies are more likely to be supporters of binding human rights regimes than are either established democracies or nondemocracies.[68] They do so, he explains, in order to "lock in" democratic rule through the enforcement of human rights.[69] If Moravcsik is correct and if, as one might reasonably hypothesize, new democracies tend to have worse human rights practices than do more established democracies,[70] then it is possible that

---

66. *Cf.* Helfer & Slaughter, *supra* note 63 (making a similar argument with regard to supranational adjudication).

67. Convention for the Protection of Human Rights and Fundamental Freedoms, *opened for signature* Nov. 4, 1950, 213 U.N.T.S. 221 (entered into force Sept. 3, 1953) [hereinafter European Convention on Human Rights].

68. *See* Moravcsik, *supra* note 25. This thesis will be much more fully tested in a work in progress, Oona A. Hathaway, The Puzzle of Human Rights Treaty Formation: When and Why Do Nations Join Human Rights Regimes? (Jan. 2002) (unpublished manuscript, on file with author).

69. Moravcsik, *supra* note 25, at 228.

70. I find support for the supposition that newly established democracies, defined as countries with an 8 to 10 point democracy rating on a scale of 1 to 10 that have been in place fewer than thirty years, *see infra* Appendix B, Section G; *see also* Moravcsik, *supra* note 25, at 231-32 (defining newly established democracies—in a study of negotiations that took place in 1950—as those established between 1920 and 1950), have worse practices than established democracies. In my data (in which higher ratings reflect worse practices), established democracies have Torture ratings of 1.71, compared to 2.50 for newly established democracies; Fair Trial ratings of 1.23, compared to 1.96 for newly established democracies; Civil Liberty ratings of 1.35, compared to 2.54 for newly established democracies; Genocide ratings of 0, compared to 0.035 for newly established democracies; and 89% Men in Parliament, compared to 95% for newly established

there is an unexpected selection effect that would lead to lower apparent rates of compliance with human rights treaties. Of course, Moravcsik's argument regarding countries' reasons for joining treaties does not suggest that human rights treaties worsen the practices of newly established democracies. Indeed, the argument appears to rest on the assumption, shared by others in the liberal camp, that democracies will be likely to exhibit better human rights practices if they have signed a treaty than if they have not. If this were not the case, it is not clear why domestic actors would see treaty ratification as a means of "locking in" democratic rule.[71] Thus, while Moravcsik's republican liberal theory suggests a more nuanced story regarding expected patterns of compliance, it too appears to predict that human rights treaties will be more effective in changing behavior in liberal nations than in others.

B. *Normative Models*

The theories of international law compliance that I group under the label "normative models" share the conviction that the interest-based rationalist models miss something fundamental about the international legal framework: the persuasive power of legitimate legal obligations. Scholars adopting this approach argue that state decisions cannot be explained simply by calculations of geopolitical or economic interests or even the relative power of domestic political groups. A complete description of state action in the international realm, they argue, requires an understanding of the influence and importance of ideas. How and why ideas matter, however, remains a source of disagreement. I describe below three separate models that seek to explain the influence of ideas on international law compliance: the managerial model, the fairness model, and the transnational legal process model.

1.   *The Managerial Model: Compliance Is Due to a Norm of Compliance and Fostered by Persuasive Discourse*

Perhaps the most prominent normative approach, called the "managerial model" by its progenitors Abram and Antonia Chayes, places the spotlight on the process of international discourse. This view, which is informed by and draws together Chayes and Chayes's extensive practical international law experience, teaching, and writing, adopts a "cooperative, problem-solving approach" to international law compliance, as against

---

democracies. *See infra* Section II.A (describing human rights measures). I do not find any evidence, however, that newly established democracies ratify human rights treaties more readily than do established democracies. *See infra* note 184.

71. Moravcsik, *supra* note 25, at 228.

what they term the "enforcement model" of compliance.[72] The common belief that it is necessary for a treaty to incorporate coercive enforcement measures in order to achieve a high rate of compliance reflects, they claim, "an easy but incorrect analogy to domestic legal systems."[73] Coercive economic or military sanctions for treaty violations cannot be the primary mechanism of obtaining compliance with treaties. Such sanctions are too politically and economically costly and often ineffective at changing behavior.[74] Moreover, because they are so costly, they are rarely administered and tend to be intermittent and ad hoc, and hence unlikely to serve as legitimate, effective deterrents.[75]

Instead of assuming that international legal obligations must be backed up with threats in order to be effective, Chayes and Chayes begin with the expectation that states have a propensity to comply with their international treaty obligations. This propensity to comply comes about in large part, they claim, because treaties generate legal norms, which necessarily carry a widely accepted obligation of obedience.[76] Norms are obeyed not simply because of the penalties a violation carries; rather, the obligation to obey legal norms exists even in the absence of a threat of reprisal.[77] Although it is difficult to explain why countries respond to this sense of obligation, Chayes and Chayes argue that it is no more difficult than explaining why they would respond to self-interest.[78] In short, then, states obey treaties largely because their prior agreement to do so has created a normative obligation they cannot ignore—states accept and abide by the notion of *pacta sunt servanda.*[79]

When noncompliance occurs, in this view, it is usually not because of a calculated weighing of costs and benefits of treaty adherence but instead because of insufficient information or capacity on the part of the state.[80] To

---

72. CHAYES & CHAYES, *supra* note 1, at 3. For a strong critique of this approach and a defense of the enforcement model, see Downs et al., *supra* note 4.

73. CHAYES & CHAYES, *supra* note 1, at 2.

74. *Id.* at 2-3.

75. For more on Chayes and Chayes's views of military and economic sanctions, see *id.* at 34-67.

76. The assumption that countries tend to comply with international law is, they argue, supported by three types of considerations: efficiency, interests, and norms. Compliance with established treaty norms is efficient; treaties supply a standard operating procedure by which government actors can operate. Because a treaty is a consensual instrument, it must also serve the parties' interests, as they otherwise would not have agreed to it. They therefore must have some interest in maintaining its viability. And, finally, treaties are accepted to be legally binding instruments, which are obeyed because of shared norms of law abidance. *Id.* at 3-9.

77. *Id.* at 116.

78. *Id.* at 118.

79. "The rule that agreements and stipulations, esp. those contained in treaties, must be observed." BLACK'S LAW DICTIONARY 1109 (7th ed. 1999).

80. Specifically, noncompliance occurs because of "ambiguity and indeterminacy of treaty language," "limitations on the capacity of parties to carry out their undertakings," and time lags or failure of the treaty to adapt to changing conditions. CHAYES & CHAYES, *supra* note 1, at 9-17.

combat noncompliance, Chayes and Chayes therefore advocate a strategy based not on coercion but on "managing" compliance. This multifaceted approach focuses on ensuring transparency regarding the requirements of the regime and the parties' performance under it, creating a dispute settlement mechanism, and building capacity for compliance. These elements merge into a broader effort to *persuade* noncomplying countries to act in accordance with the law. It is this persuasion, they argue, that is central to treaty compliance. As they put it, "[T]he fundamental instrument for maintaining compliance with treaties at an acceptable level is an iterative process of discourse among the parties, the treaty organization, and the wider public."[81] This process is effective not because of the threat of direct penal sanctions but rather because of the threat of alienation from the "complex web of international arrangements" that have become central to most nations' security and economic well-being.[82] In this view, therefore, persuasive discourse in a system where there is a norm of treaty compliance is the key to obtaining and maintaining international law compliance.

All of the normative theories—and the managerial model is no exception—share the fundamental claim that it is the transformative power of normative discourse and repeated interactions between transnational actors, rather than the calculation of political, military, or financial advantage, that is responsible for the formation and continuation of human rights regimes. Norms, in other words, have a causal influence on human rights regimes. International cooperation regarding human rights occurs, it is claimed, because of the persuasive power of normative beliefs regarding human rights. This process of norm proliferation and socialization is aided by the human rights activism of nongovernmental organizations, which motivate international discourse on human rights, establish international networks of people and institutions to monitor human rights violations, and rally public opinion in support of efforts to convince governments to create human rights regimes and press other states to join them.[83] Normative theorists thus reject the notion that governments abide by human rights treaties for instrumental reasons. The fundamental motive behind these

---

81. *Id.* at 25.
82. *Id.* at 27.
83. *See* MARTHA FINNEMORE, NATIONAL INTERESTS IN INTERNATIONAL SOCIETY (1996); DAVID HALLORAN LUMSDAINE, MORAL VISION IN INTERNATIONAL POLITICS (1993); ROBERT W. MCELROY, MORALITY AND AMERICAN FOREIGN POLICY (1992); Thomas Risse-Kappen, *Ideas Do Not Float Freely: Transnational Coalitions, Domestic Structures, and the End of the Cold War*, 48 INT'L ORG. 185 (1994); Kathryn Sikkink, *The Power of Principled Ideas: Human Rights Policies in the United States and Western Europe, in* IDEAS AND FOREIGN POLICY 139 (Judith Goldstein & Robert O. Keohane eds., 1993).

1958   The Yale Law Journal   [Vol. 111: 1935

treaties is not rational adaptation, they claim, but transnational socialization.[84]

The managerial model provides some specific arguments regarding compliance that can be used to deduce predictions regarding state compliance with human rights regimes. In particular, it predicts that countries have a propensity to comply with treaties and that noncompliance will be limited to situations in which there are ambiguities, limitations on capacity, or temporal issues. The sources of noncompliance identified by Chayes and Chayes are indisputably correct—countries cannot immediately comply with legal obligations they do not understand, with which they do not have the capacity to comply, or that take time to implement. What is more debatable—and hence tested in this Article—is the assertion that compliance with human rights treaties will generally exist where these sources of noncompliance are absent.

2. *The Fairness Model: Compliance Occurs when Rules Are Legitimate and Just*

A prominent strand of the normative explanatory framework finds the source of support for international regimes in the legitimacy of the norms and rules that compose them.[85] Phillip Trimble, for example, argues that international law is a form of "rhetoric" whose persuasiveness depends on its legitimacy, which in turn depends on the process whereby it arises, its consistency with accepted norms, and its perceived fairness and transparency.[86]

In the most recent comprehensive statement of this approach, Thomas Franck claims that the key element explaining treaty adherence and compliance is fairness.[87] The question Franck poses is not, "Do nations comply?," but rather "[I]s international law fair?"[88] This is the central question, he claims, because rules that are not fair exert little "compliance pull."[89] In order to be legitimate or fair, rules must be both substantively and procedurally fair—their ends must lead to distributive justice and they "must be arrived at discursively in accordance with what is accepted by the parties as *right process*."[90]

---

84. Jack Donnelly, *International Human Rights: A Regime Analysis,* 40 INT'L ORG. 599 (1986); Martha Finnemore & Kathryn Sikkink, *International Norm Dynamics and Political Change,* 52 INT'L ORG. 887 (1998).

85. *See, e.g.,* BRUCE RUSSETT, GRASPING THE DEMOCRATIC PEACE (1993).

86. Phillip R. Trimble, *International Law, World Order, and Critical Legal Studies,* 42 STAN. L. REV. 811, 833 (1990) (book review).

87. THOMAS M. FRANCK, FAIRNESS IN INTERNATIONAL LAW AND INSTITUTIONS (1995).

88. *Id.* at 7.

89. Thomas M. Franck, *Legitimacy in the International System,* 82 AM. J. INT'L L. 705, 712 (1988).

90. FRANCK, *supra* note 87, at 7.

The fairness model, like the managerial model, thus points not to state calculations of self-interest as the source of state decisions to act consistently with international legal obligations, but instead to the perceived fairness of the legal obligations. Compliance with international law, in this view, is traced to the widespread normative acceptance of international rules, which in turn reflects the consistency of the rules with widely held values and the legitimacy of the rulemaking process.[91] Specifically, Franck claims that four primary factors determine the legitimacy of a rule and thus state compliance with it.[92] First, there must be "determinacy" so that the rule's requirements are transparent and its fairness thereby "made manifest" (this is an obvious counterpart to Chayes and Chayes's claim that "ambiguity" is a major source of noncompliance).[93] Second, the rule must have attributes that signal that it is an important part of a system of social order, a characteristic Franck labels "symbolic validation."[94] Third, the rule must exhibit "coherence"—it must treat like cases alike and "relate[] in a principled fashion to other rules of the same system."[95] Finally, the rule must be closely connected to (i.e., "adhere to") the secondary rules of process used to interpret and apply rules of international obligation.[96]

In this framework, the greatest strength of human rights regimes is arguably their symbolic validation. As Franck notes, the violation of any aspect of human rights has assumed the "greater gravity of a trespass against a major public policy of the community."[97] Human rights rules also appear to be supported by the procedural and institutional framework of the international community (thereby meeting Franck's "adherence" condition). Human rights treaties vary, however, in their determinacy and coherence. Franck argues that the process put into place by the International Covenant on Civil and Political Rights[98] has caused "[a] perception of fairness" to begin to displace the "opprobrium of expedient politics in human rights discourse"[99] because its provision for case-by-case review of alleged violations by the quasi-judicial Human Rights Committee of independent experts means that the rules are more impartially applied. This impartial application, in turn, creates greater coherence and determinacy in

91. Franck, *supra* note 89.

92. FRANCK, *supra* note 87, at 30.

93. *Id.* at 99 ("The determinacy of a rule directly affects its legitimacy because in increasing the rule's transparency, its fairness is made manifest, and thus its compliance pull on members of the international community is increased."); *see id.* at 30-34.

94. *Id.* at 34-38.

95. *Id.* at 38.

96. *Id.* at 41-46.

97. *Id.* at 124.

98. International Covenant on Civil and Political Rights, *adopted* Dec. 19, 1966, S. EXEC. DOC. E, 95-2, at 23 (1978), 999 U.N.T.S. 171 (entered into force Mar. 23, 1976) [hereinafter Covenant on Civil and Political Rights].

99. FRANCK, *supra* note 87, at 103.

1960   The Yale Law Journal   [Vol. 111: 1935

the requirements of the treaty.[100] But Franck's analysis may be too sanguine regarding the effectiveness of the provisions of the Covenant on Civil and Political Rights and other similar human rights treaties.[101] While the human rights system may be legitimate in form, it appears less so in practice, and hence its compliance pull must be less strong under the fairness framework than Franck estimates. Nonetheless, the fairness theory appears to argue, as does Franck himself, that human rights treaties are largely fair and therefore likely to foster compliance.

3. *The Transnational Legal Process Model: Compliance Occurs Because Norms Are Internalized*

The most recent addition to the normative theoretical framework is Harold Koh's theory of transnational legal process.[102] Koh shares with Franck and Chayes and Chayes a conviction that the secret to better enforcement of international law is not coerced compliance, but voluntary obedience. He fills a logical gap left by these theorists by providing an explanatory framework for understanding how and why the process of norm-internalization that he considers the key to compliance, or obedience, occurs. Koh claims that the process of norm-internalization has three phases. It begins when one or more transnational actors provoke an interaction with another, thereby requiring enunciation of the norm applicable to the interaction. The interaction generates a legal rule that can be used to guide future transnational interactions. Over time, a series of such interactions causes the norms to become internalized, and eventually, this iterative process leads to the reconstitution of the interests and identities of the participants.[103]

---

100. *Id.* at 104-05.

101. There are 1203 overdue reports in the human rights treaty system, while only 1613 reports have ever been considered. Seventy-one percent of all state parties to human rights treaties have overdue reports, and 110 states have five or more overdue reports. ANNE F. BAYEFSKY, THE UN HUMAN RIGHTS TREATY SYSTEM: UNIVERSALITY AT THE CROSSROADS 8 (2000), http://www.yorku.ca/hrights/Report/finalreport.pdf; *see* Philip Alston, *Final Report on Enhancing the Long-Term Effectiveness of the United Nations Human Rights Treaty System*, U.N. ESCOR, 53d Sess., Agenda Item 15, ¶ 37, U.N. Doc. E/CN.4/1997/74 (1996). In its 1999 Annual Report, the Human Rights Committee reported that since 1977, it had received 873 communications (despite the fact that the Optional Protocol that governs the individual complaint system under the treaty covers over one billion people around the world). Of those, the Committee had concluded 328 by issuing its views, declared 267 inadmissible, discontinued 129, and not yet concluded 149. *See* INTERNATIONAL HUMAN RIGHTS IN CONTEXT 740 (Henry J. Steiner & Philip Alston eds., 2d ed. 2000).

102. Koh, *supra* note 1; *see* Harold Hongju Koh, *The 1998 Frankel Lecture: Bringing International Law Home*, 35 HOUS. L. REV. 623 (1998) [hereinafter Koh, *Bringing International Law Home*]; Harold Hongju Koh, *How Is International Human Rights Law Enforced?*, 74 IND. L.J. 1397 (1998) [hereinafter Koh, *How Is International Human Rights Law Enforced?*].

103. Koh, *supra* note 1, at 2646.

Transnational legal process, in contrast with the two other models of normative theory discussed above, opens the black box of the state. The process of norm-internalization on which the theory rests occurs via transnational actors—usually foreign policy personnel of the governments involved, private norm entrepreneurs, and nongovernmental organizations, which form an "epistemic community" to address a legal issue.[104] As transnational actors interact, Koh argues, they generate patterns of activity that lead to norms of conduct, which are in turn internalized into domestic structures through executive, legislative, and judicial action. Domestic institutions thereby enmesh international legal norms, generating self-reinforcing patterns of compliance. In this way, repeated participation in the transnational legal process leads nations to obey international law. Obedience to international law thus comes about not simply because of external enforcement of legal rules, but because repeated interaction leads nations gradually to internalize legal rules. Indeed, in Koh's view, "True compliance is not so much the result of externally imposed sanctions . . . as internally felt norms."[105]

The transnational legal process framework presents a coherent explanation for compliance with human rights regimes. Noting that in the area of human rights, national governments are often unwilling to enforce treaties against one another, Koh argues that the transnational legal process approach offers a means of combating this apathy. To encourage interaction, more actors, including intergovernmental and nongovernmental organizations and private parties, ought to be encouraged to participate in the process.[106] And to produce interpretations of human rights norms, fora dedicated to this purpose should be created or adapted from existing institutions.[107] Finally, domestic internalization of the norms can occur through a variety of means, including incorporation into the legal system through judicial interpretation, acceptance by political elites, and the like.[108] Indeed, Koh exhorts those seeking to encourage countries to abide by international human rights law to use all the tools at their disposal—not simply external power and coercion, not simply self-interest of states, not simply encouragement of liberal legal identity, not simply promotion of shared values, and not simply facilitation of legal process, but all of these at once.[109]

The approach of transnational legal process helps explain why human rights norms are obeyed even in the face of contrary self-interest on the part

---

104. *Id.* at 2648.
105. Koh, *How Is International Human Rights Law Enforced?*, *supra* note 102, at 1407.
106. Koh, *supra* note 1, at 2656.
107. *Id.*
108. *Id.* at 2656-57.
109. Koh, *How Is International Human Rights Law Enforced?*, *supra* note 102, at 1407-08.

1962   The Yale Law Journal   [Vol. 111: 1935

of participating states. It fosters better understanding of the process by which international legal norms can be generated and internalized into domestic legal systems and thereby provides a guide for those seeking to bring about changes in country practices on an international scale.[110] However, in providing a very detailed explanation for compliance, the transnational legal process model loses some predictive power. Once a norm has been internalized and obeyed, the transnational legal process model provides a means of tracing the players and process that led the country to obey. Yet it is difficult to predict in advance which norms will become internalized through the three-step process of interaction, interpretation, and internalization. In its current form, which awaits book-length treatment, the theory does not tell us what characteristics of a norm or country lead to compliance. Nor does it explain why norms in favor of compliance, rather than against it, are internalized. While this tradeoff of predictive value for explanatory value is undoubtedly intentional, it does cabin the uses to which the theory can be put.[111]

The rationalist and normative strands of international law and international relations scholarship recounted here provide coherent contrasting accounts of international legal compliance. The next Part tests the claims of the two approaches and their variants in the area of human rights using a comprehensive analysis of countries' human rights practices and their relationship to human rights treaty ratification. The results, while necessarily limited to the area of human rights treaties, carry implications for theories of treaty compliance more generally.

II. TESTING COMPLIANCE

The analysis presented in this Part confronts the question: Do human rights treaties make a difference in countries' human rights practices? Normative theory suggests that they should unless specified sources of noncompliance, such as insufficient information or incapacity on the part of the state, are present.[112] Rationalist theory is more equivocal, with each variant making slightly different predictions regarding the expected relationship between treaty ratification and human rights practices. Realist

---

110. Indeed, Koh has put forward a guide for United States human rights policy for the twenty-first century that draws on and builds upon his transnational legal process framework. *See* Harold Hongju Koh, *A United States Human Rights Policy for the 21st Century*, 46 ST. LOUIS U. L.J. 293 (2002). More so than any of the theories outlined in this Article, Koh's theory of transnational legal process speaks directly to those who seek, as he puts it, to "bring international law home"—the lawyers, activists, politicians, and others who carry out the process of norm-internalization. Koh, *Bringing International Law Home, supra* note 102, at 680-81.

111. *See* Jacob S. Hacker, *Learning from Defeat?: Political Analysis and the Failure of Health Care Reform in the United States*, 31 BRIT. J. POL. SCI. 61, 91-92 (2001) (discussing the difference between predictability and explainability).

112. *See, e.g., supra* text accompanying notes 76, 86-92.

theory, which views such treaties largely as cheap talk, would predict little or no relationship between ratification and practice. Institutionalists, on the other hand, would expect treaty ratification to be associated with better human rights practices. If the reputational benefits of treaty compliance are the primary source of country compliance, as Andrew Guzman's model suggests, one would expect countries that ratify human rights treaties to comply with their requirements but not if doing so requires changes in practices. Indeed, in this view, it appears likely that only countries for whom compliance is costless or nearly costless will ratify. Finally, liberalists would predict that for democracies at least, treaty ratification will be associated with better human rights practices. The question this Part examines thus provides a good starting point for testing the relative strengths of the theories against the empirical evidence.

The analysis in this Part explores two related issues—compliance and effectiveness. I begin by discussing the challenges inherent in a project that seeks to address these two issues and the ways in which I have attempted to meet these challenges. I then turn to the quantitative analyses. I first examine whether countries comply with or adhere to the requirements of the human rights treaties they have joined.[113] I then address the more difficult question of whether treaties are *effective* in improving countries' human rights practices.

A. *The Challenges of Measuring Compliance and Effectiveness*

Any study seeking to evaluate compliance with and effectiveness of human rights treaties faces a serious measurement problem. This problem has two aspects. First, compliance and effectiveness are imprecise terms that can be open to multiple interpretations. It is therefore important to be clear about what it is that the study seeks to measure. Second, measuring state human rights practices is complicated by the relative dearth of comprehensive information. Indeed, a central difficulty that all quantitative studies of human rights practices face—and the present one is unfortunately no exception—is the relative scarcity of accurate information on state practices.[114]

---

113. The data sources for treaty ratification are described in Appendix B. In this Article, I look only at whether a country has ratified a treaty. I do not take into account any reservations the country may have made to the treaty. I do this both because quantifying reservations in a consistent way would be extremely difficult and because a reservation to a treaty is only valid if it does not defeat the object and purpose of the treaty. Vienna Convention on the Law of Treaties, *opened for signature* May 23, 1969, art. 19, S. EXEC. DOC. L, 92-1, at 16 (1971), 1155 U.N.T.S. 331, 336-37. A reservation that falls within this limitation ought not significantly affect the reserving country's human rights practices covered by the treaty.

114. *See, e.g.*, Robert E. Robertson, *Measuring State Compliance with the Obligation To Devote the "Maximum Available Resources" to Realizing Economic, Social, and Cultural Rights*, 16 HUM. RTS. Q. 693, 703-13 (1994) (discussing the difficulties of measuring compliance with

1964   The Yale Law Journal   [Vol. 111: 1935

I begin with the more tractable challenge of specifying the relationship between treaties and state behavior. I explore two facets of what traditionally has been referred to collectively as "compliance"— compliance and effectiveness.[115] The notion of compliance also has several different dimensions: compliance with procedural obligations, such as the requirement to report; compliance with substantive obligations outlined in the treaty; and compliance with the spirit of the treaty.[116] This study focuses attention on the last two of these forms of compliance. Because I aim to measure compliance with a treaty's letter and spirit, I focus on countries' actual treatment of their inhabitants, rather than their cooperation with procedural requirements or with the legislative implementation requirements of the treaty.[117] In principle, therefore, determining whether a country complies with a treaty merely requires comparing the relevant activity with the treaty's requirements. Yet this is not as simple as it at first seems. To begin with, compliance is not an on-off switch; it is an elastic concept that allows for different gradations.[118] Laws often incorporate a

---

certain provisions of the International Covenant on Economic, Social and Cultural Rights); *see also* Jack Donnelly & Rhoda E. Howard, *Assessing National Human Rights Performance: A Theoretical Framework*, 10 HUM. RTS. Q. 214 (1988) (seeking to establish a framework for assessing states' human rights performance); James M. McCormick & Neil J. Mitchell, *Human Rights Violations, Umbrella Concepts, and Empirical Analysis*, 49 WORLD POL. 510 (1997) (arguing for the use of a disaggregated, multidimensional measure of human rights violations); Herbert F. Spirer, *Violations of Human Rights—How Many?: The Statistical Problems of Measuring Such Infractions Are Tough, but Statistical Science Is Equal to It*, 49 AM. J. ECON. & SOC. 199 (1990) (reviewing statistical problems encountered in measuring and analyzing human rights violations). The four most prominent sources of comprehensive cross-national time series information on a broad spectrum of human rights practices are the United States Department of State *Country Reports on Human Rights*, Human Rights Watch's reports, Amnesty International's *Country Reports*, and Freedom House's *Freedom in the World* reports. (There are, of course, many other sources of data on human rights practices, but most do not cover all or nearly all countries in the world over a substantial period of time, as is necessary for the instant analysis.) Each of these data sources has advantages and drawbacks. The State Department reports, for instance, have been charged with political bias. *E.g.*, David Carleton & Michael Stohl, *The Role of Human Rights in U.S. Foreign Assistance Policy: A Critique and Reappraisal*, 31 AM. J. POL. SCI. 1002, 1007 (1987) (citing and briefly discussing reports of Americas Watch, Helsinki Watch, and the Lawyers Committee for International Human Rights and critiquing the State Department reports for political bias). The Freedom House reports, which are the only ones of the four to provide a quantifiable measure of human rights practices, have been criticized for lack of replicability and reliability. Christopher Mitchell et al., *State Terrorism: Issues of Concept and Measurement*, in GOVERNMENT VIOLENCE AND REPRESSION 1, 20 (Michael Stohl & George A. Lopez eds., 1986). The Amnesty International and Human Rights Watch reports are relatively short and do not cover every country every year, making them a poor source for social scientific inquiry.

115. Weiss & Jacobson, *supra* note 2, at 4-6 (disaggregating the notions of implementation, compliance, and effectiveness).

116. *Id.* at 4 (identifying various dimensions of compliance).

117. This focus on state practice permits a comparison of the practices of ratifying and nonratifying countries. A broader focus would make a comparison difficult, as nonratifying countries cannot necessarily be expected to comply with the procedural or legislative requirements of a treaty. This narrower focus also centers attention on what ought to be the central concern—whether treaties make a difference in people's lives.

118. *See* CHAYES & CHAYES, *supra* note 1, at 17.

zone within which behavior is considered to "conform" even if it is not consistent with the letter of the legal obligation. And there are different levels of nonconformance: Just as traveling at forty miles per hour over the speed limit is different in kind from traveling ten miles per hour over the speed limit, so too is rampant corruption in a court system different in kind from occasional failure to bring accused persons to trial quickly. Compliance with human rights treaties must therefore be defined on a continuum based on the degree to which behavior deviates from the legal requirements of the treaties.

Effectiveness is directly related to, but distinct from, compliance. A country may comply with a treaty—its actions comport with the requirements of a treaty—but the treaty may nonetheless be ineffective in changing its practices. In evaluating effectiveness, I therefore seek to determine whether there is any evidence indicating that countries' practices are different when they have ratified a given treaty than they would have been expected to be absent ratification.

The second and more difficult challenge encountered in a study of compliance and effectiveness of human rights treaties is posed by the task of measuring countries' practices. I choose in this study to examine five subject areas—genocide, torture, civil liberty, fair and public trials, and political representation of women—that cover a broad spectrum of human rights and draw their measures from a variety of sources. Genocide and torture are the most widely prohibited human rights violations. Both are the subject of international treaty instruments and are among the few human rights that are virtually universally acknowledged to be a violation of customary international law.[119] Indeed, the norms against torture and genocide are widely regarded as *jus cogens* and therefore nonderogable.[120] The norms against torture and genocide are also relatively clear and precisely specified.[121] Next on the spectrum are civil liberty (encompassing freedom of expression, freedom of association, the independence of the judiciary, rule of law, and personal autonomy) and the right to a fair and

---

119. *See* RESTATEMENT (THIRD) OF FOREIGN RELATIONS LAW OF THE UNITED STATES § 702 (1986).

120. Filartiga v. Pena-Irala, 630 F.2d 876, 890 (2d Cir. 1980) ("[T]he torturer has become—like the pirate and slave trader before him—*hostis humani generis*, an enemy of all mankind."); Regina v. Bartle, *ex parte* Pinochet, [2000] 1 A.C. 147 (H.L. 1999) (recognizing the inviolability of the international prohibition against torture and therefore allowing extradition proceedings against General Augusto Pinochet to go forward); Ellen L. Lutz & Kathryn Sikkink, *International Human Rights Law and Practice in Latin America*, 54 INT'L ORG. 633, 634 (2000); Eduardo Moisés Peñalver, *Redistributing Property: Natural Law, International Norms, and the Property Reforms of the Cuban Revolution*, 52 FLA. L. REV. 107, 138 (2000) ("[C]ommon examples of [j]us cogens include the duty to respect human rights and the prohibition of genocide.").

121. Torture Convention, *supra* note 51, art. 1, S. TREATY DOC. NO. 100-20, at 19, 1465 U.N.T.S. at 113-14 (defining torture); Convention on the Prevention and Punishment of the Crime of Genocide, *adopted* Dec. 9, 1948, art. 2, S. EXEC. DOC. O, 81-1, at 7 (1949), 78 U.N.T.S. 277, 280 (entered into force Jan. 12, 1951) [hereinafter Genocide Convention] (defining genocide).

public trial, both of which are covered by decades-old international treaty instruments, but neither of which is regarded as a norm of customary law.[122] Finally, I examine the influence of treaties on one of the least entrenched international human rights—women's political equality.[123]

I choose to examine these five areas of human rights in part because they permit me to minimize two of the three factors contributing to noncompliance outlined by Chayes and Chayes—ambiguity and lack of capacity. I seek to address ambiguity by focusing my analysis on treaties for which the interpretation of the broad requirements of the treaty is widely shared (though particular applications of those requirements may be contested), and I resolve any significant differences of legal opinion on the requirements of the treaty in favor of the countries under study.[124] With the exception of women's political equality, the areas on which I focus are ones in which the treaty governs only activity by the state or its agents, thus enhancing state capacity to effect the required changes.[125] Of course, simply because an activity is carried out by state actors does not necessarily mean that it is within the capacity of the state to change it, but it does suggest that the state's capacity will be greater than where the state must affect the activity of private actors in order to comply. I address the third source of noncompliance—the time lag between undertaking and performance—by tracking countries over a nearly forty-year period. I likewise seek to eliminate the related sources of noncompliance identified by Franck by selecting cases in part because they largely satisfy the determinacy condition (the obligations of the treaty are clearly specified) and the

---

122. *See infra* text accompanying notes 141-157 (describing the data on fair trials and civil liberty).

123. *See infra* text accompanying notes 158-161 (describing the data on women's political equality).

124. For example, the dispute over whether punishment inflicted pursuant to the Sharia constitutes "torture" in violation of the Torture Convention was resolved in this study in favor of the countries arguing that it does not constitute torture.

125. In coding the torture practices of countries, I considered only torture committed by agents of the state. Genocide is defined by the authors of the State Failure Problem Set from which I drew my data in part as "the promotion, execution, and/or implied consent of sustained policies *by governing elites or their agents*—or in the case of civil war, either of the contending authorities—that result in the deaths of a substantial portion of a communal group or politicized non-communal group." Ted Robert Gurr et al., Codebook: Internal Wars and Failures of Governance, 1954-1996, at 11 (May 19, 1997) (unpublished manuscript, on file with author) (emphasis added). The Civil Liberty index also measures freedoms largely in the control of the state, such as free and independent media, free religious institutions, free public and private religious expression, freedom of assembly, freedom of political organization, free trade unions, and peasant organizations or the equivalent. *Cf.* FREEDOM HOUSE, FREEDOM IN THE WORLD: THE ANNUAL SURVEY OF POLITICAL RIGHTS AND CIVIL LIBERTIES 1999-2000, at 584 (Adrian Karatnycky ed., 2000) (providing a civil liberties checklist). Finally, whether or not a state provides a fair and public trial is a matter largely within the hands of the state. These areas all contrast markedly with the examples of areas where the state "lacks capacity" cited by Chayes and Chayes, such as agreements to reduce environmental pollutants, which require the state to influence private behavior. *See* CHAYES & CHAYES, *supra* note 1, at 13-15.

coherence condition (like cases are treated alike) for legitimacy. By minimizing these obvious and widely accepted sources of noncompliance in the study, I can better focus attention on the central area of disagreement between normativists and rationalists, namely, whether and why nations comply (or do not comply) with clear, determinant, and coherent treaties to which they have some capacity to conform their actions.

I draw the measures of state practices in the five areas examined from four different sources: the Center for International Development and Conflict Management at the University of Maryland, College Park, the United States Department of State *Country Reports on Human Rights*, Freedom House's *Annual Survey of Political Rights and Civil Liberties*, and the Inter-Parliamentary Union. The database consists of 166 countries from 1960 to 1999, for a total of 6474 separate observations.[126] Because the database covers multiple countries over multiple years, I sometimes refer to a single observation as a "country-year," though for ease of reference I usually employ the less precise term "country."

None of the sources I use provides a perfect measure of countries' compliance with the requirements of a given treaty. Some of the measures are better than others, but each has its flaws. Indeed, an examination of the four sources demonstrates a tradeoff between the objectivity of the data sources and the level of tailoring of the sources to the relevant treaties. For example, I draw the data on torture and fair trials from the State Department reports.[127] The strength of these data is the close tailoring of the data to the requirements of the treaties, which was possible because I coded the data in the State Department's narrative accounts with direct reference to the requirements of the relevant treaties. The primary weakness is the susceptibility of the State Department reports to charges of political bias.[128] The data on genocide are drawn from an independent organization not known for particular biases.[129] Yet the fit between the definition of genocide used in constructing the data and the very narrow definition of genocide in the Genocide Convention is imperfect. Similarly, the data on the percentage of men in parliament have the advantage of being entirely objective, yet again the fit between the data and the requirements of the treaty is imperfect.

While the problems of objectivity and fit ought not be ignored, they also ought not be overstated. Studies of the State Department *Country*

---

126. A list of the 166 states included in the database (one of which is the United States) appears in Appendix C. Notably, none of the analyses takes advantage of the full database, as there are significant gaps in the data for many of the variables, and an entire observation is dropped whenever any portion of the data is missing. Nonetheless, with the exception of the analyses of the regional treaties, most of the analyses are based on well over 1000 observations.

127. *See infra* notes 137-151 and accompanying text.

128. *See supra* note 114.

129. *See infra* note 132 and accompanying text.

1968   The Yale Law Journal   [Vol. 111: 1935

Reports on Human Rights have shown that their assessments of the human rights practices of countries differ only marginally from the assessments of Amnesty International, particularly after 1985, the period for which I use the State Department data.[130] And where the fit between measures of country practices and treaty requirements is imperfect, the measures chosen are nonetheless strongly indicative of the success of countries in putting in place practices and institutions designed to achieve the requirements of the treaties. Moreover, it is imperative to note that I base each broad analytical conclusion on data drawn from at least two different data sources and do not rely on any empirical result that cannot be cross-validated. This approach mirrors that of the only other extant quantitative study of the relationship between human rights treaty ratification and country human rights practices.[131]

To give a more precise picture of the sources and definitions of the five areas under study, I discuss each in turn below.

1. *Genocide*

I obtained the data on genocide from the Center for International Development and Conflict Management at the University of Maryland, College Park.[132] The Center defines "geno/politicide" as

> the promotion, execution, and/or implied consent of sustained policies by governing elites or their agents—or in the case of civil war, either of the contending authorities—that result in the deaths of a substantial portion of a communal group or politicized

---

130. *E.g.*, Steven C. Poe & C. Neal Tate, *Repression of Human Rights to Personal Integrity in the 1980s: A Global Analysis*, 88 AM. POL. SCI. REV. 853, 855 (1994) ("Because of the rather high correlation between the two measures in our sample [i.e., the Amnesty International reports and the State Department reports] (zero-order correlation = 0.83), we instead chose to substitute the value coded for the State Department scale when profile information was unavailable on a country in the Amnesty International reports and vice versa (in the few cases where it was necessary) as the best available approximation of those scores."); *id.* at 862 (displaying a graph that shows increasing convergence between the data derived from the State Department reports and the data from the Amnesty International reports over time, with no more than an approximate 0.1-point difference in mean index on a scale of 1 to 5 between the two measures after 1985).

131. Keith, *supra* note 2. Keith states:
> For this study, the perfect measure of human rights behavior might include an indicator of *each* right that is protected in this treaty. . . . It would be extremely difficult to gather data that could adequately measure *each* of these rights. However, political scientists have developed two standards-based indices that are believed to be an acceptable measure for this study: the Freedom House Political and Civil Rights indices and Stohl et al.'s Personal Integrity measure [referred to here as the "Purdue Political Terror Scale," *see infra* note 170]. Using both of these sets of measures to test my hypothesis will allow for cross-validation.

Id. at 101 (citations omitted).

132. Ted Robert Gurr et al., Internal Wars and Failures of Governance, 1954-1996 (May 19, 1997) (unpublished data, on file with author).

noncommunal group. In genocides the victimized groups are defined primarily in terms of their communal (ethnolinguistic, religious) characteristics. In politicides, by contrast, groups are defined primarily in terms of their political opposition to the regime and dominant groups. . . . In the case of geno/politicide authorities physically exterminate enough (not necessarily all) members of a target group so that it can no longer pose any conceivable threat to their rule or interests.[133]

In operationalizing the criteria, the Center provides: "(1) Authorities' complicity in mass murder must be established. . . . (2) The physical destruction of a people requires time to accomplish: it implies a persistent, coherent pattern of action. . . . (3) The victims to be counted are unarmed civilians, not combatants."[134] The Center records the magnitude of each genocidal episode based on the annual number of deaths, placed on a scale that ranges from 0 to 5.[135] With the exception of its inclusion of politicides (admittedly a substantial difference), the definition reasonably closely matches the definition of genocide offered in the Genocide Convention:

[G]enocide means any of the following acts committed with intent to destroy, in whole or in part, a national, ethnical, racial or religious group, as such: (a) Killing members of the group; (b) Causing serious bodily harm or mental harm to members of the group; (c) Deliberately inflicting on the group conditions of life calculated to bring about its physical destruction in whole or in part; (d) Imposing measures intended to prevent births within the group; (e) Forcibly transferring children of the group to another group.[136]

2. Torture

I generated the data on torture by coding the sections on torture in the United States Department of State *Country Reports on Human Rights*. The Torture index, which I constructed by referring directly to the requirements of the relevant treaties,[137] ranges from 1 to 5. In arraying countries'

---

133. Gurr et al., *supra* note 125, at 11.
134. *Id.*
135. The scale is as follows: 0 = less than 300 annual deaths; 0.5 = 300-1000; 1.0 = 1000-2000; 1.5 = 2000-4000; 2.0 = 4000-8000; 2.5 = 8000-16,000; 3.0 = 16,000-32,000; 3.5 = 32,000-64,000; 4.0 = 64,000-128,000; 4.5 = 128,000-256,000; 5.0 = 256,000 or more. *See id.* at 12.
136. Genocide Convention, *supra* note 121, art. 2, S. EXEC. DOC. O, 81-1, at 7, 78 U.N.T.S. at 280.
137. The Torture Convention defines torture as
any act by which severe pain or suffering, whether physical or mental, is intentionally inflicted on a person for such purposes as obtaining from him or a third person information or a confession, punishing him for an act he or a third person has committed or is suspected of having committed, or intimidating or coercing him or a

1970   The Yale Law Journal   [Vol. 111: 1935

practices on this scale, I considered "beatings," which were frequently mentioned separately from "torture," to be a subcategory of torture when they constituted affirmative acts of physical or mental abuse in prison or by police or other governmental officials. In this subcategory, I included maltreatment used to extract confessions or in initial interrogations. I disregarded punishments carried out pursuant to a country's legal system, even if that system may be considered by some to sanction torture. Hence, I did not consider punishment carried out pursuant to the Sharia to constitute torture. When possible, I coded a country's practices using key words identified in the reports to indicate the frequency of the use of torture. I did not code widespread poor prison conditions (e.g., overcrowding, inadequate food, lengthy detentions prior to trial) as torture unless the conditions of detention were so severe as to constitute mistreatment or abuse aimed at intimidating, penalizing, or obtaining a confession from detainees. I gave weight to all information reported unless it was specifically noted to be likely untrue. In assigning a rating to a country, I gave the highest category to which it corresponded. Hence, if there were reports of "widespread torture" but no "beatings," the country-year would nonetheless be assigned a 5. I rated country practices as described below:

1: There are no allegations or instances of torture in this year. There are no allegations or instances of beatings in this year; or there are only isolated reports of beatings by individual police officers or guards all of whom were disciplined when caught.

---

third person, or for any reason based on discrimination of any kind, when such pain or suffering is inflicted by or at the instigation of or with the acquiescence of a public official or other person acting in an official capacity. It does not include pain or suffering arising from, or inherent in or incidental to, lawful sanctions.

Torture Convention, *supra* note 51, art. 1, S. TREATY DOC. No. 100-20, at 19, 1465 U.N.T.S. at 113-14. The American Torture Convention defines torture as

any act intentionally performed whereby physical or mental pain or suffering is inflicted on a person for purposes of criminal investigation, as a means of intimidation, as personal punishment, as a preventive measure, as a penalty, or for any other purpose. Torture shall also be understood to be the use of methods upon a person intended to obliterate the personality of the victim or to diminish his physical or mental capacities, even if they do not cause physical pain or mental anguish.

The concept of torture shall not include physical or mental pain or suffering that is inherent in or solely the consequence of lawful measures, provided that they do not include the performance of the acts or use of the methods referred to in this article.

Inter-American Convention To Prevent and Punish Torture, *adopted* Dec. 9, 1985, art. 2, 25 I.L.M. 519, 521 (entered into force Feb. 28, 1987) [hereinafter American Torture Convention]; *see also* European Convention for the Prevention of Torture and Inhuman or Degrading Treatment or Punishment, *opened for signature* Nov. 26, 1987, pmbl., Europ. T.S. No. 126, at 2, 27 I.L.M. 1152, 1154 (entered into force Jan. 2, 1989) [hereinafter European Torture Convention] (prohibiting, but not defining, torture); African Charter on Human and Peoples' Rights, *adopted* June 27, 1981, art. 5, 21 I.L.M. 58, 60 (entered into force Oct. 21, 1986) [hereinafter African Charter on Human Rights] (same).

2: At least one of the following is true: There are only unsubstantiated and likely untrue allegations of torture; there are "isolated" instances of torture for which the government has provided redress; there are allegations or indications of beatings, mistreatment or harsh/rough treatment; there are some incidents of abuse of prisoners or detainees; or abuse or rough treatment occurs "sometimes" or "occasionally." Any reported beatings put a country into at least this category regardless of government systems in place to provide redress (except in the limited circumstances noted above).

3: At least one of the following is true: There are "some" or "occasional" allegations or incidents of torture (even "isolated" incidents unless they have been redressed or are unsubstantiated (see above)); there are "reports," "allegations," or "cases" of torture without reference to frequency; beatings are "common" (or "not uncommon"); there are "isolated" incidents of beatings to death or summary executions (this includes unexplained deaths suspected to be attributed to brutality) or there are beatings to death or summary executions without reference to frequency; there is severe maltreatment of prisoners; there are "numerous" reports of beatings; persons are "often" subjected to beatings; there is "regular" brutality; or psychological punishment is used.

4: At least one of the following is true: Torture is "common"; there are "several" reports of torture; there are "many" or "numerous" allegations of torture; torture is "practiced" (without reference to frequency); there is government apathy or ineffective prevention of torture; psychological punishment is "frequently" or "often" used; there are "frequent" beatings or rough handling; mistreatment or beating is "routine"; there are "some" or "occasional" incidents of beatings to death; or there are "several" reports of beatings to death.

5: At least one of the following is true: Torture is "prevalent" or "widespread"; there is "repeated" and "methodical" torture; there are "many" incidents of torture; torture is "routine" or standard practice; torture is "frequent"; there are "common," "frequent," or "many" beatings to death or summary executions; or there are "widespread" beatings to death.

A researcher working under my guidance performed the initial coding. A second researcher then coded a random sample of 20% of the data to test reproducibility reliability.[138] Intercoder reliability, which I assessed using

---

138. "Reproducibility reliability is the extent to which coding decisions can be replicated by different researchers." Stephen Lacy & Daniel Riffe, *Sampling Error and Selecting Intercoder*

1972 The Yale Law Journal [Vol. 111: 1935

Cohen's Kappa statistic,[139] was 80%. Because the information in the reports is scarce prior to 1985, I deemed it insufficiently reliable and therefore included only data obtained from the reports from 1985 to 1998 in the data set, even though earlier reports are available. As with all of the human rights measures, where the data source does not cover a country or provides insufficient information on a country in a particular year to allow for coding, that entry is left blank in the database. As the United States is never covered by the State Department *Country Reports on Human Rights*, all the entries for the United States's torture practices are blank in the database. Because the United States is only one of 166 countries in the database, this omission ought not have a significant impact on the results. A complete copy of the data appears in Table 6.[140]

3. *Fair Trial*

I created the Fair Trial index by coding, with the help of two research assistants, the sections in the State Department *Country Reports on Human Rights* that addressed issues relating to fair trials. To code these sections, I identified ten elements of a paradigmatic fair trial by reference to the Covenant on Civil and Political Rights, the American Convention on Human Rights, the European Convention on Human Rights, and the African Charter on Human Rights. The identified elements of a fair trial include the following: an independent and impartial judiciary,[141] the right to counsel,[142] the right to present a defense,[143] a presumption of innocence,[144]

Reliability Samples for Nominal Content Categories, 73 JOURNALISM & MASS COMM. Q. 963, 963 (1996).

139. Jean Carletta, *Assessing Agreement on Classification Tasks: The Kappa Statistic*, 22 COMPUTATIONAL LINGUISTICS 249, 252-53 (1996).

140. *See infra* Appendix C.

141. *See* African Charter on Human Rights, *supra* note 137, art. 26, 21 I.L.M. at 63 ("States parties to the present Charter shall have the duty to guarantee the independence of the Courts . . . ."); American Convention on Human Rights, *opened for signature* Nov. 22, 1969, art. 8, § 1, 1144 U.N.T.S. 123, 147 (entered into force July 18, 1978) ("Every person has the right to a hearing, with due guarantees and within a reasonable time, by a competent, independent, and impartial tribunal, previously established by law . . . ."); Covenant on Civil and Political Rights, *supra* note 98, art. 14, S. EXEC. DOC. E, 95-2, at 25-26, 999 U.N.T.S. at 176-77 ("[E]veryone shall be entitled to a fair and public hearing by a competent, independent and impartial tribunal established by law."); European Convention on Human Rights, *supra* note 67, art. 6, § 1, 213 U.N.T.S. at 228 ("In the determination of his civil rights and obligations or of any criminal charge against him, everyone is entitled to a fair and public hearing within a reasonable time by an independent and impartial tribunal . . . .").

142. *See* African Charter on Human Rights, *supra* note 137, art. 7, 21 I.L.M. at 60 ("Every individual shall have the right to . . . defence, including the right to be defended by counsel of his choice . . . ."); American Convention on Human Rights, *supra* note 141, art. 8, § 2, 1144 U.N.T.S. at 147 ("[E]very person is entitled, with full equality, to the following minimum guarantees: . . . the right of the accused to . . . be assisted by legal counsel of his own choosing, and to communicate freely and privately with his counsel; . . . the inalienable right to be assisted by counsel provided by the State, paid or not as the domestic law provides, if the accused does not defend himself personally or engage his own counsel within the time period established by

the right to appeal,[145] the right to an interpreter,[146] protection from ex post facto laws,[147] a public trial,[148] the right to have charges presented,[149] and

law . . . ."); Covenant on Civil and Political Rights, *supra* note 98, art. 14, § 3, S. EXEC. DOC. E, 95-2, at 26, 999 U.N.T.S. at 177 ("[E]veryone shall be entitled to . . . defend himself in person or through legal assistance of his own choosing . . . ."); European Convention on Human Rights, *supra* note 67, art. 6, § 3, 213 U.N.T.S. at 228 ("Everyone charged with a criminal offence has the following minimum rights: . . . to defend himself in person or through legal assistance of his own choosing or, if he has not sufficient means to pay for legal assistance, to be given it free when the interests of justice so require.").

143. *See* African Charter on Human Rights, *supra* note 137, art. 7, 21 I.L.M. at 60 ("Every individual shall have the right to . . . defence . . . ."); American Convention on Human Rights, *supra* note 141, art. 8, § 2, 1144 U.N.T.S. at 147 ("[E]very person is entitled, with full equality, to the following minimum guarantees: . . . [t]he right of the accused to defend himself personally or to be assisted by legal counsel of his own choosing . . . ."); Covenant on Civil and Political Rights, *supra* note 98, art. 14, § 3, S. EXEC. DOC. E, 95-2, at 26, 999 U.N.T.S. at 177 ("[E]veryone shall be entitled to . . . defend himself in person or through legal assistance of his own choosing . . . ."); European Convention on Human Rights, *supra* note 67, art. 6, § 3, 213 U.N.T.S. at 228 ("Everyone charged with a criminal offence has the following minimum rights: . . . to defend himself in person or through legal assistance of his own choosing . . . .").

144. *See* African Charter on Human Rights, *supra* note 137, art. 7, 21 I.L.M. at 60 ("Every individual shall have the right to . . . be presumed innocent until proved guilty . . . ."); American Convention on Human Rights, *supra* note 141, art. 8, § 2, 1144 U.N.T.S. at 147 ("Every person accused of a criminal offense has the right to be presumed innocent so long as his guilt has not been proven according to law."); Covenant on Civil and Political Rights, *supra* note 98, art. 14, § 2, S. EXEC. DOC. E, 95-2, at 26, 999 U.N.T.S. at 176 ("Everyone charged with a criminal offence shall have the right to be presumed innocent until proved guilty according to law."); European Convention on Human Rights, *supra* note 67, art. 6, § 3, 213 U.N.T.S. at 228 ("Everyone charged with a criminal offence shall be presumed innocent until proved guilty according to law.").

145. *See* African Charter on Human Rights, *supra* note 137, art. 7, 21 I.L.M. at 60 ("Every individual shall have the right to . . . an appeal to competent national organs . . . ."); American Convention on Human Rights, *supra* note 141, art. 8, § 2, 1144 U.N.T.S. at 147 ("[E]very person is entitled, with full equality, to the following minimum guarantees: . . . the right to appeal the judgment to a higher court . . . ."); Covenant on Civil and Political Rights, *supra* note 98, art. 14, § 2, S. EXEC. DOC. E, 95-2, at 26, 999 U.N.T.S. at 176 ("Everyone charged with a criminal offence shall have the right to be presumed innocent until proved guilty according to law.").

146. *See* American Convention on Human Rights, *supra* note 141, art. 8, § 2, 1144 U.N.T.S. at 147 ("[E]very person is entitled, with full equality, to the following minimum guarantees: . . . the right of the accused to be assisted without charge by a translator or interpreter, if he does not understand or does not speak the language of the tribunal or court . . . ."); Covenant on Civil and Political Rights, *supra* note 98, art. 14, § 3, S. EXEC. DOC. E, 95-2, at 26, 999 U.N.T.S. at 177 ("[E]veryone shall be entitled to . . . have the free assistance of an interpreter if he cannot understand or speak the language used in court."); European Convention on Human Rights, *supra* note 67, art. 6, § 3, 213 U.N.T.S. at 228 ("Everyone charged with a criminal offence has the following minimum rights: . . . to have the free assistance of an interpreter if he cannot understand or speak the language used in court.").

147. *See* African Charter on Human Rights, *supra* note 137, art. 7, 21 I.L.M. at 60 ("No one may be condemned for an act or omission which did not constitute a legally punishable offence at the time it was committed. No penalty may be inflicted for an offence for which no provision was made at the time it was committed."); American Convention on Human Rights, *supra* note 141, art. 9, 1144 U.N.T.S. at 148 ("No one shall be convicted of any act or omission that did not constitute a criminal offense, under the applicable law, at the time it was committed."); Covenant on Civil and Political Rights, *supra* note 98, art. 15, S. EXEC. DOC. E, 95-2, at 27, 999 U.N.T.S. at 177 ("No one shall be held guilty of any criminal offence on account of any act or omission which did not constitute a criminal offence, under national or international law, at the time when it was committed."); European Convention on Human Rights, *supra* note 67, art. 7, 213 U.N.T.S. at 228 ("No one shall be held guilty of any criminal offence on account of any act or omission

timeliness.[150] We then coded each element by country and year for compliance, partial compliance, or noncompliance. After coding each element, we aggregated the individual results to obtain a final code on a four-point scale, with a lower index indicating better practices. Due to the volume of work and time involved in coding trial practices in this manner, I limited the scope of inquiry to every third year, beginning in 1985 and ending in 1997. While State Department reports covering fair trial practices are available in years prior to 1985, they are of insufficient detail to compare reliably to reports in later years. Intercoder reliability across the entire Fair Trial index was 82%. The data used to measure fair trials appear in Table 7.[151]

---

which did not constitute a criminal offence under national or international law at the time when it was committed.").

148. *See* American Convention on Human Rights, *supra* note 141, art. 8, § 5, 1144 U.N.T.S. at 147 ("Criminal proceedings shall be public, except insofar as may be necessary to protect the interests of justice."); Covenant on Civil and Political Rights, *supra* note 98, art. 14, § 1, S. EXEC. DOC. E, 95-2, at 25, 999 U.N.T.S. at 176 ("[E]veryone shall be entitled to a fair and public hearing by a competent, independent and impartial tribunal established by law."); European Convention on Human Rights, *supra* note 67, art. 6, 213 U.N.T.S. at 228 ("In the determination of his civil rights and obligations or of any criminal charge against him, everyone is entitled to a fair and public hearing within a reasonable time . . . . Judgment shall be pronounced publicly but the press and public may be excluded from all or part of the trial in the interests of morals, public order or national security in a democratic society, where the interests of juveniles or the protection of the private life of the parties so require, or to the extent strictly necessary in the opinion of the court in special circumstances where publicity would prejudice the interests of justice.").

149. *See* African Charter on Human Rights, *supra* note 137, art. 6, 21 I.L.M. at 60 ("No one may be deprived of his freedom except for reasons and conditions previously laid down by law. In particular, no one may be arbitrarily arrested or detained."); American Convention on Human Rights, *supra* note 141, art. 8, § 2, 1144 U.N.T.S. at 147 ("[E]very person is entitled, with full equality, to the following minimum guarantees: . . . prior notification in detail to the accused of the charges against him . . . ."); Covenant on Civil and Political Rights, *supra* note 98, art. 14, § 3, S. EXEC. DOC. E, 95-2, at 26, 999 U.N.T.S. at 177 ("[E]veryone shall be entitled to . . . be informed promptly and in detail in a language which he understands of the nature and cause of the charge against him . . . ."); European Convention on Human Rights, *supra* note 67, art. 6, § 3, 213 U.N.T.S. at 228 ("Everyone charged with a criminal offence has the following minimum rights: . . . to be informed promptly, in a language which he understands and in detail, of the nature and cause of the accusation against him.").

150. *See* African Charter on Human Rights, *supra* note 137, art. 7, 21 I.L.M. at 60 ("Every individual shall have the right . . . to be tried within a reasonable time by an impartial court or tribunal . . . ."); American Convention on Human Rights, *supra* note 141, art. 8, § 2, 1144 U.N.T.S. at 147 ("[E]very person is entitled, with full equality, to . . . adequate time and means for the preparation of his defense . . . ."); Covenant on Civil and Political Rights, *supra* note 98, art. 14, § 3, S. EXEC. DOC. E, 95-2, at 26, 999 U.N.T.S. at 177 ("[E]veryone shall be entitled . . . to be tried without undue delay . . . ."); European Convention on Human Rights, *supra* note 67, art. 6, 213 U.N.T.S. at 228 ("[E]veryone is entitled to a fair and public hearing within a reasonable time . . . .").

151. *See infra* Appendix C.

4. *Civil Liberty*

I draw the Civil Liberty variable from Freedom House's *Comparative Survey of Freedom.*[152] It is reported on a 1 to 7 scale, with 1 being the best and 7 the worst. The scale is constructed from answers to a "Civil Liberties Checklist" that includes freedom of expression and belief, association and organizational rights, rule of law and human rights, and personal autonomy and economic rights.[153] As broad as the civil liberties checklist is, it overlaps quite well with the equally broad treaties for which I use it as a measure of compliance. The Covenant on Civil and Political Rights protects freedom of expression and belief in Articles 18, 19, and 27; association and organizational rights in Articles 1, 18, 21, and 22; rule of law and human rights in Articles 6, 7, 9, 14, 15, 16, 17, 25, and 26; and personal autonomy and economic rights in Articles 1, 3, 8, 12, 22, 23, and 25.[154] The African Charter protects freedom of expression and belief in Articles 8 and 9; association and organizational rights in Articles 10, 11, and 20; rule of law and human rights in Articles 3, 5, 6, 7, 23, and 26; and personal autonomy and economic rights in Articles 12, 14, 18, 19, and 21.[155] The American Convention on Human Rights protects freedom of expression and belief in Articles 12 and 13; association and organizational rights in Articles 15 and 16; rule of law and human rights in Articles 3, 5, 7, 8, 24, and 25; and personal autonomy and economic rights in Articles 1, 17, 21, and 22.[156] Finally, the European Convention on Human Rights protects freedom of expression and belief in Articles 9 and 10; association and organizational rights in Article 11; rule of law and human rights in Articles 3, 5, and 6; and personal autonomy and economic rights in Articles 8, 12, and 14.[157]

5. *Women's Political Equality*

I measured women's political equality using the percentage of men in each country's legislature.[158] The data are derived from data published by the Inter-Parliamentary Union.[159] Although the Convention on the Political

---

152. For the set of ratings for the entire history of the *Freedom in the World* reports, see Freedom House, Country Ratings, *at* http://www.freedomhouse.org/ratings/index.htm (last modified May 8, 2001). Freedom House graciously provided the ratings to me in a database format.

153. *See* FREEDOM HOUSE, *supra* note 125, at 584-85.

154. Covenant on Civil and Political Rights, *supra* note 98.

155. African Charter on Human Rights, *supra* note 137.

156. American Convention on Human Rights, *supra* note 141.

157. European Convention on Human Rights, *supra* note 67.

158. Where a country's legislature is divided into two houses, I added the two houses together before calculating the percentage of men in the legislature.

159. INTER-PARLIAMENTARY UNION, WOMEN IN PARLIAMENTS 1945-1995: A WORLD STATISTICAL SURVEY (1995).

1976   The Yale Law Journal   [Vol. 111: 1935

Rights of Women of course does not require equal numbers of women and men to serve in a country's legislature, the preamble does provide:

> The Contracting Parties . . . [r]ecogniz[e] that everyone has the right to take part in the government of his country, directly or indirectly through freely chosen representatives, and has the right to equal access to public service in his country, and desir[e] to equalize the status of men and women in the enjoyment and exercise of political rights, in accordance with the provisions of the Charter of the United Nations and the Universal Declaration of Human Rights . . . . [160]

Moreover, two of the three substantive articles in the treaty directly address women's participation in government. Articles II and III provide that "[w]omen shall be eligible for election to all publicly elected bodies, established by national law, on equal terms with men, without any discrimination," and that "[w]omen shall be entitled to hold public office and to exercise all public functions, established by national law, on equal terms with men, without any discrimination." [161] Consequently, a measure of women's direct political participation—which of course depends on women's access to direct participation in government—appears likely to be strongly correlated with country compliance with the treaty's goals.

B. *Do Countries Comply?*

This first portion of the quantitative analysis examines whether countries that ratify human rights treaties tend to conform their activity to the requirements of the treaties. I do not aim here to demonstrate any causal relationship between treaty ratification and country practices. Rather, my purpose in this portion of the analysis is simply to determine whether countries that have ratified human rights treaties are more likely to conform their conduct to the treaties than are countries that have not ratified the same treaties, regardless of the reasons for conformance. In short, I seek here only insight into whether countries that ratify these treaties have better human rights practices than those that do not.

An initial analysis of the relationship between treaty ratification and country ratings (as shown in Tables 1 and 2) indicates that, for the most part, countries that have ratified human rights treaties have better human rights ratings than those that have not. On this first test, therefore, the

---

160. Convention on the Political Rights of Women, *opened for signature* Mar. 31, 1953, pmbl., 27 U.S.T. 1909, 1911, 193 U.N.T.S. 135, 136 (entered into force July 7, 1954).
    161. *Id.* arts. II-III, 27 U.S.T. at 1911, 193 U.N.T.S. at 138.

TABLE 1. HUMAN RIGHTS RATINGS: RATIFYING COUNTRY-YEARS
VERSUS NONRATIFYING COUNTRY-YEARS
(BETTER AVERAGES IN BOLD)

Treaty	Human Rights Metric	Average Ratifying	Average Non-ratifying	Number of Observations
Genocide Convention	Genocide[a]	**0.074** (0.008)	0.093 (0.009)	6640
Torture Convention	Torture[b]	**2.70** (0.042)	2.76 (0.030)	2228
Article 21	Torture	**2.06** (0.058)	2.85 (0.025)	2223
Covenant on Civil and Political Rights	Fair Trial[c]	**2.15** (0.045)	2.42 (0.056)	740
Optional Protocol	Fair Trial	**1.98** (0.062)	2.39 (0.041)	740
Covenant on Civil and Political Rights	Civil Liberty[d]	**3.77** (0.045)	4.66 (0.038)	4076
Optional Protocol	Civil Liberty	**2.94** (0.054)	4.65 (0.033)	3996
Conv. on the Political Rights of Women	Men in Parliament[e]	**0.91** (0.002)	0.93 (0.002)	3990
American Torture Convention	Torture	3.26 (0.093)	**2.96** (0.068)	332
African Charter on Human Rights	Torture	2.99 (0.042)	**2.65** (0.071)	703
European Torture Convention	Torture	1.86 (0.060)	**1.67** (0.079)	379
American Convention on Human Rights	Fair Trial	2.66 (0.088)	**2.33** (0.237)	110
African Charter on Human Rights	Fair Trial	2.45 (0.066)	**2.24** (0.114)	234
European Convention on Human Rights	Fair Trial	**1.23** (0.056)	1.36 (0.091)	126
American Convention on Human Rights	Civil Liberty	**3.22** (0.061)	3.80 (0.115)	633
African Charter on Human Rights	Civil Liberty	**4.95** (0.058)	5.36 (0.049)	1271
European Convention on Human Rights	Civil Liberty	**1.63** (0.041)	3.34 (0.252)	630

[a] Genocide is measured from 0 (no genocide) to 5 (rampant genocide).
[b] Torture is measured from 1 (little or no torture) to 5 (rampant torture).
[c] Fair Trial is measured from 1 (fair) to 4 (not fair).
[d] Civil Liberty is rated from 1(high liberty) to 8 (low liberty).
[e] Men in Parliament is the fraction of the country's legislature that are men.

Note: For all of the human rights measures a lower index indicates better practices.
Standard deviations in the data appear in parentheses.

record appears to validate the contention of normative theory that countries are likely to comply with their international legal commitments. Probing slightly deeper, however, I find reason to question these optimistic results. Although countries that have ratified treaties have better human rights ratings on average, I find that not only does noncompliance seem to be rampant—a finding that would be consistent with some of the rational actor models identified above—but countries with poor human rights ratings are sometimes *more* likely to have ratified the relevant treaties than are countries with better ratings, a finding that is largely unexplained by either the normative or the rationalist theories.

As Table 1 shows, a comparison of the human rights ratings for country-years (referred to below for ease of reference as "countries") in which human rights treaties have been ratified with those in which they have not reveals that ratifiers generally have better average human rights ratings than nonratifiers (the better averages are in bold). This is true for all the universal human rights treaties examined. Countries that have ratified the Covenant on Civil and Political Rights[162] appear to have better average civil liberties and fairer trials, with average ratings of roughly a full point and a third of a point lower than for nonratifiers, respectively. The same is true of those that have ratified the Optional Protocol to that Covenant;[163] indeed the difference between ratings of ratifiers and nonratifiers is greater. Countries that have ratified the Convention on the Political Rights of Women[164] have an average of 91% of their legislature made up of men, compared to an average of 93% for nonratifying countries.

For the Torture Convention, the differences in average level of human rights ratings for ratifiers versus nonratifiers are small. Countries that have ratified the Convention have an average Torture index of 2.70, compared to 2.76 for nonratifiers; countries that have ratified Article 21[165] to that Convention (which provides for state-to-state complaints) have an average Torture index of 2.06 compared to 2.85 for nonratifiers. (The results for this analysis and all others of Article 21 described in this Article are nearly identical to those for Article 22[166] to that Convention, which provides for individual complaints, because forty-two of the forty-five countries that have accepted Article 21 accepted Article 22 in the same year.) The Genocide Convention likewise exhibits a small difference between means: 0.074 for ratifying countries, which is marginally better than the 0.093 for nonratifying countries.

---

162. Covenant on Civil and Political Rights, *supra* note 98.
163. Optional Protocol to the International Covenant on Civil and Political Rights, *adopted* Dec. 19, 1966, 999 U.N.T.S. 302 [hereinafter Optional Protocol].
164. Convention on the Political Rights of Women, *supra* note 160.
165. Torture Convention, *supra* note 51, art. 21, S. TREATY DOC. NO. 100-20, at 26-27, 1465 U.N.T.S. at 118-20.
166. *Id.* art. 22, S. TREATY DOC. NO. 100-20, at 27-28, 1465 U.N.T.S. at 120.

The finding that countries that ratify human rights treaties have better ratings than those that do not is not universal. Indeed, the regional treaties that outlaw torture[167] show the opposite result: The countries that have ratified the treaties appear to have *worse* torture practices than the countries that are members of the sponsoring regional organization but have not ratified the treaties,[168] and the differences are particularly striking for the American Torture Convention and for the African Charter. The same is true of the American and African regional treaties requiring fair and public trials: Countries that have ratified the treaties have worse ratings on average than countries that are members of the sponsoring regional organization but have not ratified the treaties.[169] I arrive at similar results using an independent measure of repression.[170] Moreover, even where the ratings of ratifiers are better than those of nonratifiers, the differences are not as large as one might expect.

Table 2 shows the results of a similar analysis performed on fully democratic countries (defined as those with democracy ratings of 10 on a scale of 1 to 10).[171] The data indicate that fully democratic countries exhibit similar patterns of compliance to the group of nations as a whole, perhaps calling into question some liberals' predictions that democratic countries will be more likely to comply with their international legal commitments than nondemocracies.[172] Although the human rights ratings of full

---

167. For the regional torture conventions, I use the European Torture Convention and the American Torture Convention rather than the European Convention on Human Rights and American Convention on Human Rights (both of which also prohibit torture) because the more particularized treaties give specific content to the torture prohibition and put in place mechanisms to make the prohibition on torture more effective.

168. Although today all the members of the Council of Europe have ratified the European Convention on Human Rights, this has not always been true. Until ratification of the Convention was made an effective condition of membership, most countries took several years or more to ratify the Convention after joining the Council. Because the data set is a time series, this is the basis for the comparison of ratifying country-years (again, referred to here with the shorthand "countries") versus nonratifying country-years in the European context.

169. The treaties specifically require the elements of fair and public trials measured by the Fair Trial index. For more on the index, see *supra* notes 141-151 and accompanying text.

170. I obtain nearly identical results using the Purdue Political Terror Scale (PTS), a measure of political repression put together by researchers at Purdue University based on the United States Department of State reports and the Amnesty International annual reports on country human rights practices. *See* Michael Stohl, Purdue University Political Terror Scale, *at* http://www.ippu.purdue.edu/info/gsp/govern.htm (last visited Jan. 29, 2002). Using this measure, I find that countries that ratify the African Charter on Human Rights have an average PTS (State) index of 2.89 versus 2.50 for nonratifiers (on a scale of 1 to 5, where lower is better), and an average PTS (Amnesty) index of 2.96 versus 2.73 for nonratifiers. Similarly, I find that countries that have ratified the European Torture Convention have an average PTS (State) index of 1.67 versus 1.47 for nonratifiers, and an average PTS (Amnesty) index of 2.32 versus 1.61 for nonratifiers.

171. Countries with a democracy rating of 10 make up roughly 18% of the entire sample. For more on the democracy scale, see *infra* Appendix B, Section G.

172. *See supra* text accompanying notes 61-65.

TABLE 2. HUMAN RIGHTS RATINGS OF FULL DEMOCRACIES:
RATIFYING COUNTRY-YEARS VERSUS NONRATIFYING COUNTRY-YEARS
(BETTER AVERAGES IN BOLD)

Treaty	Human Rights Metric	Average Ratifying	Average Non-ratifying	Number of Observations
Genocide Convention	Genocide	—	—	0
Torture Convention	Torture	1.66 (0.044)	**1.58** (0.062)	429
Article 21	Torture	**1.59** (0.048)	1.67 (0.056)	424
Covenant on Civil and Political Rights	Fair Trial	**1.12** (0.032)	1.35 (0.143)	141
Optional Protocol	Fair Trial	1.16 (0.041)	**1.14** (0.064)	139
Covenant on Civil and Political Rights	Civil Liberty	1.42 (0.027)	1.42 (0.048)	749
Optional Protocol	Civil Liberty	**1.41** (0.029)	1.43 (0.040)	731
Conv. on the Political Rights of Women	Men in Parliament	**0.89** (0.004)	0.94 (0.002)	865
American Torture Convention	Torture	2.33 (0.194)	**1.97** (0.151)	42
African Charter on Human Rights	Torture	2.14 (0.137)	**1.38** (0.177)	15
European Torture Convention	Torture	1.59 (0.049)	**1.42** (0.066)	289
American Convention on Human Rights	Fair Trial	1.45 (0.205)	**1.00** (0)	14
African Charter on Human Rights	Fair Trial	**1.00** (0)	1.33 (0.304)	5
European Convention on Human Rights	Fair Trial	1.15 (0.041)	**1.00** (0)	96
American Convention on Human Rights	Civil Liberty	1.75 (0.098)	**1.23** (0.085)	96
African Charter on Human Rights	Civil Liberty	2.00 (0)	2.00 (0)	18
European Convention on Human Rights	Civil Liberty	**1.32** (0.027)	1.63 (0.107)	475

Note: For all of the human rights measures a lower index indicates better practices.
Standard deviations in the data appear in parentheses.

democracies are usually better, the relationship between treaty ratification
and human rights ratings is very similar. Fully democratic countries that
have ratified the universal human rights treaties usually have better human
rights ratings, on average, than those that have not. As with the group of
nations as a whole, however, this pattern does not hold for regional treaties.
In six out of nine cases, ratification of regional treaties is associated with

worse, rather than better, ratings.[173] Similarly and somewhat more surprisingly, expanding the group of democratic countries examined to include those with democracy ratings of 6 or above suggests that democratic countries that ratify the Genocide Convention and the Optional Protocol (with regard to Civil Liberty) have worse practices than those that do not.[174] Thus, democratic countries appear to be no more likely to have better human rights practices when they have ratified treaties than the group of countries as a whole.

When we look at human rights treaty compliance from a slightly different perspective, however, a somewhat more pessimistic picture emerges. Figures 1 through 5 map treaty ratification rates for each human rights measure. For each treaty, I calculated and plotted the mean level of ratification of the group of countries at each level of the relevant human rights measure.[175] The graphical picture that emerges indicates that the countries with the worst human rights ratings are sometimes as likely as those with the best ratings to have joined the relevant human rights treaties. Many countries that ratify human rights treaties, it appears, regularly and predictably violate their voluntarily assumed human rights treaty obligations.

Although the figures show a consistently high level of noncompliance, their patterns vary. Figure 1 shows that approximately 50% of countries where no acts of genocide are recorded have ratified the Genocide

---

173. Unlike the group of nations as a whole, fully democratic countries that ratify the American Convention on Human Rights have worse Civil Liberty ratings on average than those that do not. And, unlike the group of nations as a whole, fully democratic nations that ratify the African Charter on Human Rights have better average Fair Trial ratings than those that do not ratify. This mean is based, however, on a population size of only five. Moreover, when the group of democratic countries is enlarged to include countries with a democracy rating of 6 or above, the mean Fair Trial rating of ratifying countries for the African Charter is worse than that of nonratifying countries. (There are thirty-seven observations involving countries in the OAU with a democracy rating of 6 or above.) The mean level of the Fair Trial measure for countries ratifying the African Charter on Human Rights is 2, versus a level of 1.5 for nonratifying countries.

174. Thirty-six percent of the entire data set has a democracy rating of 6 or greater. In the case of the Genocide Convention, the average level of Genocide if the treaty is ratified is 0.016, compared to 0.014 if it is not, for the 3077 observations in the database. In the case of the Optional Protocol, the average Civil Liberty rating if the treaty is ratified is 2.52, compared to 2.10 if it is not, for the 1576 observations in the database.

175. For instance, for genocide, which is measured on a scale from 0 to 5, I determined the mean level of ratification of the Genocide Convention for countries with a level 0 Genocide, a level 0.5 Genocide, a level 1 Genocide, and so on, and plotted them on the graph in Figure 1. Because the data cover nearly forty years (all of which post-date the entry into force of the Genocide Convention), each country is included multiple times in the data from which I generated the graph. Hence, the figures are not a point-in-time record of the relationship between human rights practices and ratification of the relevant treaty; rather, they reflect the relationship over the thirty-nine years covered by the data. I calculated ratification rates for the regional treaties using a subset of the database that included only countries that are eligible to join the relevant treaty. Hence, I limited the database to members of the Organization of American States for the American treaties, members of the Organization of African Unity for the African treaties, and members of the Council of Europe for the European treaties.

Convention, rising to 85% of countries reported to have committed an average of 1000 to 2000 acts of genocide (a 1 on the Internal Wars and Failures of Governance scale), falling to a low of less than 10% of countries reported to have committed 16,000 to 32,000 acts of genocide (a 3 on the scale), and rising again to a high of 47% of countries reported to have committed an average of 64,000 to 128,000 acts of genocide (a 4 on the scale).[176] In other words, countries with the worst Genocide ratings are just about as likely as those with the best to have ratified the Genocide Convention. For this Convention, it is impossible to test the liberalist prediction that full democracies are more likely to comply with human rights treaty requirements than others, as no country classified as a full democracy was found to have committed any genocide.[177]

FIGURE 1. GENOCIDE

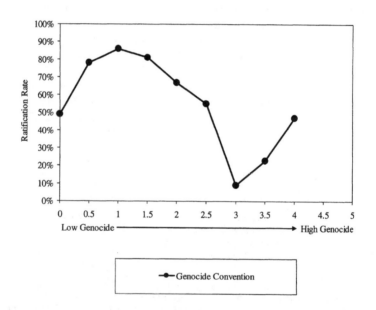

The relationship between country Torture ratings and ratification of the various treaties outlawing torture exhibits a similar pattern to that found

176. I omitted data points that relied on fewer than fifteen observations. For instance, fewer than fifteen country-years registered as a 4.5 or 5 on the Genocide scale.

177. Such countries ratified the Genocide Convention at an average rate of 40%. Countries with democracy ratings of 6 to 10 and with a Genocide rating of 0 ratified the Genocide Convention at an average rate of 49%. Although some of these countries received slightly higher Genocide ratings, not enough of these met the fifteen-observation minimum, and I therefore omitted these data from the graph. *See supra* note 176.

between treaty ratification and human rights ratings in the area of genocide. Figure 2 shows that the level of ratification of the universal Torture Convention has a relatively flat relationship to recorded levels of torture, with a gradual decline in the ratification rate as recorded torture levels rise and a small rise in the ratification rate as recorded torture levels reach their highest point. The results for the regional treaties are more interesting. As a whole, they exhibit a pattern that is inconsistent with normative and institutional theories, with ratification rates rising or remaining almost flat as Torture ratings worsen. On the other hand, Article 21 of the Torture Convention, which authorizes state parties to file complaints against states that have opted into the provision, exhibits a gradual and consistent downward trend—that is, countries with worse ratings are less likely to ratify.[178]

Plotting the relationship between human rights ratings and ratification of the Torture Convention by full democracies, I again find an upward slope at the start of the curve. Countries that appear the least likely to torture have a ratification rate of 51%. This rises initially to 73% for countries that register as a 2 on the 5-point Torture scale, and then falls back to 51% for countries with a Torture rating of 3. No full democracy warranted a Torture rating of 4 or 5.[179] I find a similar pattern for Article 21.

---

178. Again, I reach similar results using the Purdue Political Terror Scales. *See supra* note 170.

179. Although I do not include these results in the figure below, it is interesting to note that for this figure, as for all those that follow, when the group of democratic countries examined is expanded to include countries with democracy ratings of 6 or above, the results are very similar to those for the entire data set, though the ratification rates at each level of Torture tend to be slightly higher over most of the graph. For the Torture Convention, the ratification rates for countries with democracy ratings of 6 to 10 is 49% for those with Torture ratings of 1, 60% for those with ratings of 2, 47% for those with ratings of 3, 40% for those with ratings of 4, and 51% for those with ratings of 5. For Article 21, the ratification rates are 42% for those with ratings of 1, 33% for those with ratings of 2, 18% for those with ratings of 3, 8% for those with ratings of 4, and 2% for those with ratings of 5. For the ratification rates for the other conventions for countries with democracy ratings of 6 to 10, see *infra* notes 180-182.

1984   The Yale Law Journal   [Vol. 111: 1935

FIGURE 2. TORTURE

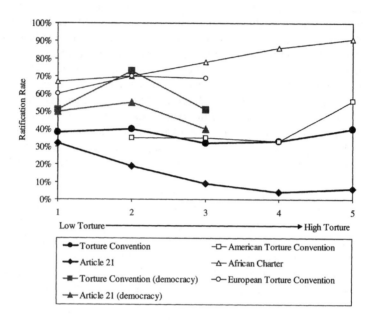

In some contrast with the results summarized in the figures above, ratification rates for treaties requiring fair and public trials are largely flat across the spectrum of fair trial levels, as Figure 3 shows. In some cases— the Covenant on Civil and Political Rights, the Optional Protocol, and the European Convention on Human Rights—ratification rates fall very gradually, varying by less than thirty percentage points across the full spectrum of Fair Trial ratings. The ratification rates for the American Convention on Human Rights and the African Charter on Human Rights rise by an equally small amount, again varying less than twenty-five percentage points across the entire graph. The ratification rates for the fully democratic countries fall somewhat more steeply than the others between the Fair Trial codes of 1 and 2, the only two data points for which there were sufficient observations to warrant inclusion on the graph. Ratification rates of full democracies are usually higher than, or nearly the same as, those of the group of nations as a whole.[180]

---

180. When the group of democratic countries is expanded to include all countries with democracy ratings of 6 or above, the curves exhibit a shape nearly identical to that of the full set of countries. For the Covenant on Civil and Political Rights, the ratification rates for countries with democracy ratings of 6 to 10 are 81% of those with a Fair Trial rating of 1, 69% of those with a rating of 2, 78% of those with a rating of 3, and 60% of those with a rating of 4. For the Optional Protocol, the ratification rates for countries with democracy ratings of 6 to 10 are 63% of

FIGURE 3. FAIR TRIALS

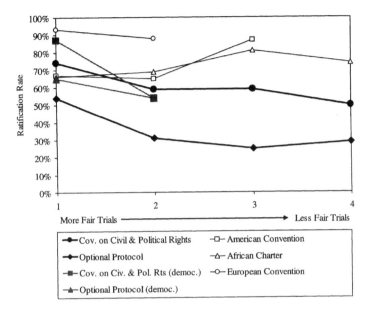

Figure 4, which shows the relationship between Civil Liberty ratings and treaty ratification, displays two sets of patterns. On the one hand, the Covenant on Civil and Political Rights, the Optional Protocol, and the European Convention on Human Rights all have downward sloping curves, with ratification rates falling as Civil Liberty ratings worsen. On the other hand, the American Convention on Human Rights, the African Charter on Human Rights, the Covenant on Civil and Political Rights (limited to full democracies), and the Optional Protocol (limited to full democracies) exhibit a parabolic shape: In each case, the ratification rates for countries with Civil Liberty ratings of 2 or 3 are notably higher than for countries with both better and worse ratings.[181]

---

those with a rating of 1, 48% of those with a rating of 2, 51% of those with a rating of 3, and 53% of those with a rating of 4.

181. When the group of democratic countries is expanded to include all countries with a democracy rating of 6 or above, the parabolic shape disappears, and the curve reverts to a shape much more similar to that for the set of countries as a whole. For the Covenant on Civil and Political Rights, the ratification rates for countries with democracy ratings of 6 to 10 are 70% for those with Civil Liberty codes of 1, 66% for those with codes of 2, 62% for those with codes of 3, 76% for those with codes of 4, 40% for those with codes of 5, and 29% for those with codes of 6. For the Optional Protocol, the ratification rates for countries with democracy ratings of 6 to 10 are 53% for those with codes of 1, 52% for those with codes of 2, 47% for those with codes of 3, 39% for those with codes of 4, 11% for those with codes of 5, and 6% for those with codes of 6. There are an insufficient number of observations of democratic countries with codes of 7 to warrant inclusion in the graph.

FIGURE 4. CIVIL LIBERTY

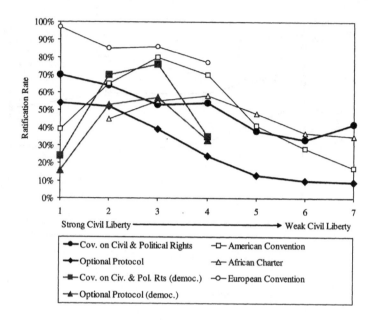

Finally, Figure 5 shows the relationship between the percent of legislators that are male and ratification of the Convention on the Political Rights of Women. To produce the graph, I broke the data into quartiles based on the percent of the legislature made up by men. The result is a gradual downward sloping curve, falling from a high of a 60% ratification rate for the quarter of countries with the lowest percentage of men in parliament to a low of 37% for the quarter of countries with the highest percentage of men in parliament. For democracies, the pattern is similar, though the ratification rates are higher across the board and fall off somewhat more quickly between the first and the second quartiles.[182]

---

182. This observation holds for both the narrower and broader categories of democracy. For countries with democracy ratings of 6 to 10, the ratification rates are 76% for the first quartile, 68% for the second, 57% for the third, and 45% for the fourth.

FIGURE 5. PERCENTAGE OF MEN IN PARLIAMENT

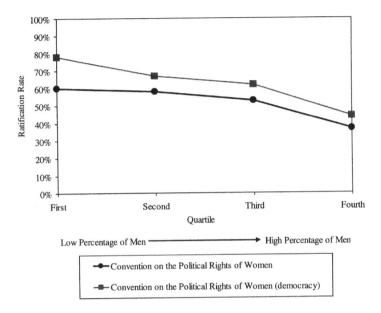

The evidence shown in these figures gives reason to question both the normative and the rationalist accounts. Normative theory suggests that the curves will be downward sloping, with higher rates of ratification associated with better human rights practices. Yet as the above figures show, this pattern is only sometimes observed. Moreover, even where the shape of the curve is downward sloping, the ratification levels of the worst human rights offenders remain consistently over 30%, contradicting the suggestion of normative theory that compliance with treaty requirements is the norm. The evidence indicates that noncompliance not only occurs, but is quite common.

Most of the rationalist theories do not fare much better. If treaty ratification is simply cheap talk, as realists would have it, why do we witness patterns in state ratings that show consistent relationships to treaty ratification? If, however, only countries for which compliance is easy—so-called least-cost compliers—sign treaties, as institutionalist theory suggests, then why do we see countries with the worst ratings ratifying treaties at high rates, sometimes even higher than those of the countries with the best ratings? And why are countries with poor ratings much less likely to have ratified the Optional Protocol and Article 21? Liberals seem to have part of the story correct—democracies with worse ratings do have lower rates of ratification. Moreover, full democracies that exhibit the worst human rights

1988   The Yale Law Journal   [Vol. 111: 1935

ratings generally have not ratified treaties at high rates. Nonetheless, liberal theory is unable to explain why full democracies with the best ratings not infrequently have lower ratification rates than those with slightly worse ratings.[183]

Finally, although each theory can account for some of the results, none either individually or collectively can explain why the Torture and Genocide Conventions appear to have the smallest impact on human rights practices of all the universal treaties or why regional treaties seem more likely than universal treaties to exhibit a frequent association between increasing rates of ratification and worsening human rights ratings. And with the possible exception of republican liberal theory, they would be hard-pressed to explain why we often find countries with worse human rights ratings ratifying at higher rates than those with better ratings.[184] As the discussion below demonstrates, the puzzle only deepens when we examine whether treaty ratification is associated with better or worse human rights ratings than would otherwise be expected.

---

183. As Figures 2 and 4 show, full democracies (countries with a democracy rating 10 on a scale of 1 to 10) that have the best ratings are less likely to ratify the relevant human rights treaties than are full democracies with slightly worse ratings.

184. For the republican liberal explanation, see Moravcsik, *supra* note 25, at 225-30. If newly established, unstable democracies have worse practices than established, stable democracies, as my data seem to suggest, then the supposition that newly established and potentially unstable democracies are more likely to be supporters of binding human rights regimes than are either established democracies or nondemocracies might help explain a positive association between ratification and worse human rights practices. *See supra* text accompanying notes 67-71. It is worth noting, however, that a comparison of the mean ratification rates of newly established democracies (defined here as those with democracy ratings of 8 to 10 on a 1 to 10 scale that were fewer than thirty years old at the time the treaty under examination came into force) with established democracies (defined here as those with democracy ratings of 8 to 10 on a 1 to 10 scale that were thirty years old or more at the time the treaty under examination came into force) across all the country-years following enactment of the treaty under consideration does not show a higher propensity to ratify among newly established democracies. Established democracies are more likely to ratify than newly established democracies in five out of eleven treaties—the Convention on the Political Rights of Women (73% versus 72%), Article 21 (19% versus 14%), the Optional Protocol (39% versus 38%), the Genocide Convention (73% versus 69%), and the European Convention on Human Rights (92% versus 90%)—and newly established democracies are more likely to ratify than more established democracies in four out of eleven treaties—the Covenant on Civil and Political Rights (53% versus 51%), the Torture Convention (30% versus 23%), the American Convention on Human Rights (77% versus 46%), and the European Torture Convention (44% versus 27%). For the remaining two treaties, there were no countries that met the established democracy criteria and hence a comparison was impossible. When the definition of "democracy" is expanded to include countries that are rated 6 to 10 on a 1 to 10 scale, I find that in eight out of eleven treaties, established democracies are more likely to ratify than are newly established democracies, and in one out of eleven treaties—the American Convention on Human Rights—newly established democracies are more likely to ratify than established democracies. Again, for the remaining two treaties, there were no countries that met the "established democracy" criteria. These findings do not preclude the possibility that newly established democracies are more likely to ratify than are established democracies, controlling for other characteristics. This hypothesis will be much more fully tested in a work in progress. *See* Hathaway, *supra* note 68.

C. Are Treaties Effective?

Although the preceding examination of the relationship between treaty ratification and human rights ratings yields interesting insights into country compliance behavior, it has one notable shortcoming: It cannot tell us whether the patterns that we observe are due to the impact of treaties or instead to factors that are associated both with ratification and with countries' human rights ratings. The observation that countries that ratify treaties generally have better human rights ratings on the whole than those that do not does not mean that ratifying countries have better ratings *as a result of* ratifying the treaties. Rather, it is possible that this observation arises because the same factors that lead to good human rights ratings also lead countries to ratify human rights treaties. For this reason, a demonstration that countries' conduct usually conforms to their voluntarily accepted treaty obligations does not provide an answer to those who are skeptical of international law, as law that has no effect on behavior cannot really be said to be law at all.

In the analyses summarized below, I examine whether countries that have ratified treaties are more likely than they otherwise would be to conform their actions to the requirements of the treaty. In other words, do the treaty requirements appear to be effective in changing countries' practices? The results suggest that not only is treaty ratification not associated with better human rights practices than otherwise expected, but it is often associated with worse practices. Countries that ratify human rights treaties often appear less likely, rather than more likely, to conform to the requirements of the treaties than countries that do not ratify these treaties.

Determining whether countries that have ratified human rights treaties are more likely than we would otherwise expect to act in ways consistent with the requirements of the treaties is not a simple matter. It requires, to begin with, a theory of what factors, other than treaties, affect countries' human rights practices. Fortunately, there is a fairly extensive strain of political science literature that seeks to explain cross-national variation in respect for human rights.[185] This Article draws on and builds upon these

---

185. *See, e.g.,* DOUGLAS A. HIBBS, JR., MASS POLITICAL VIOLENCE: A CROSS-NATIONAL CAUSAL ANALYSIS 182 (1973) (finding a positive relationship between "internal war" and "negative sanctions" by government); Conway W. Henderson, *Conditions Affecting the Use of Political Repression,* 35 J. CONFLICT RESOL. 120, 132 (1991) (conducting a cross-national study for 1986 and finding that democracy and energy consumption per capita (a measure of economic wealth) are negatively correlated with political repression and that inequality is positively correlated with political repression); Conway W. Henderson, *Population Pressures and Political Repression,* 74 SOC. SCI. Q. 322 (1993) (hypothesizing a link between population density and repression, but finding no statistically significant relationship and finding that population growth has a statistically significant positive relationship to the level of repression); Neil J. Mitchell & James M. McCormick, *Economic and Political Explanations of Human Rights Violations,* 40 WORLD POL. 476 (1988) (finding weak support for the contention that wealthier nations have

earlier studies, using them as a guide to selection of the control variables. Based in part on these studies, the control variables that I expect to be associated with poorer human rights records include international war, civil war, population size, population growth, and whether the regime in power is relatively new. The variables that I expect to be associated with better human rights records include democracy,[186] gross national product per capita, global economic interdependence, and dependence on foreign aid. I expect economic growth to have both positive and negative effects on human rights practices.[187] Descriptions of the data sources for these control variables are set out in Appendix B.

Unless otherwise indicated, I also include in the analyses a control variable to capture otherwise unaccounted-for country-to-country variation in the data (a "country dummy" variable), as well as a time-trend variable intended to capture otherwise unaccounted-for variation in the data across time.[188] The final control variable that I use in the analyses is the prior year's measure of the human rights practice (a "lagged dependent variable"), which I expect to be a strong predictor of a given country's human rights record in any given year. The use of this variable addresses a significant statistical problem that is encountered in analyzing pooled cross-sectional data.[189] With all these controls in place, the crucial variable of interest is whether a nation has signed the relevant human rights treaty. To account for the fact that the effect of treaties may be cumulative and long-term, I measure this variable as a sum of the number of years since the treaty was ratified.[190]

---

better human rights records than poorer nations); Poe & Tate, *supra* note 130, at 861, 866-67 (finding that population size has a positive and statistically significant impact on political repression and that democracy and economic standing have a negative and statistically significant impact); Steven C. Poe et al., *Repression of the Human Right to Personal Integrity Revisited: A Global Cross-National Study Covering the Years 1976-1993*, 43 INT'L STUD. Q. 291, 306 (1999) (finding that population size, population growth, and civil war have a positive and statistically significant impact on political repression and that democracy, per capita GNP, and economic growth have a negative and statistically significant impact).

186. It is possible that democracies are not only more likely to have better practices but that they are more likely to have cumbersome ratification processes that lead them to ratify treaties at a lower rate than otherwise expected. Because I control for the level of democracy in the analysis, this dynamic ought not have a substantial effect on the results.

187. *Compare* Mancur Olson, *Rapid Growth as a Destabilizing Force*, 23 J. ECON. HIST. 529 (1963) (arguing that economic growth will increase repression because it increases instability), *and* Conway W. Henderson, *Conditions Affecting the Use of Political Repression*, 35 J. CONFLICT RESOL. 120, 126 (1991) (hypothesizing that "the greater the rate of growth in the economy, the more likely the government will be to use repression"), *with* Poe et al., *supra* note 185, at 294 (suggesting that increasing prosperity has the opposite effect, satisfying those who would otherwise rebel and thereby promoting stability and reducing the need for repression).

188. For more on these variables, see *infra* Appendix B.

189. *See infra* notes 326-327 and accompanying text (discussing autocorrelation).

190. I expect that human rights treaties, if they have effects on country practices, do so relatively slowly. *See* CHAYES & CHAYES, *supra* note 1, at 16 ("The effort to protect human rights by international agreement may be seen as an extreme case of the time lag between undertaking and performance."). Operationalizing the treaty variable this way has the effect of

I obtained the results for all the analyses except that involving the Convention on the Political Rights of Women using ordered probit analysis with robust standard errors.[191] For the Convention on the Political Rights of Women, I used an ordinary least squares analysis with robust standard errors, because I measure compliance using the percentage of men in the legislature—a continuous variable, as opposed to the ordinal indices I use to measure compliance with the other treaties.[192] Tables 3 through 5 summarize the direction of the relationship these analyses suggest between the ratification of each identified human rights treaty and relevant country practices. More details regarding the variables and the design of the analyses, as well as the complete results of the analyses, can be found in Appendices B and C.

This approach aims to determine whether country-years in which the analyzed treaty is ratified exhibit better or worse human rights ratings than would otherwise be expected.[193] Because the analyses use both time series and cross-national data, the results capture both across-country and across-time variation in country ratings. In other words, the analyses show whether, controlling for other factors, there are either systematic differences between the measures of human rights practices of countries that have

---

magnifying changes in country practices over time, whether positive or negative. See *infra* note 298.

191. I use ordered probit analysis here because the dependent variable data are ordinal. See TIM FUTING LIAO, INTERPRETING PROBABILITY MODELS: LOGIT, PROBIT, AND OTHER GENERALIZED LINEAL MODELS 37 (1994). The drawback of using this model, however, is that the coefficients are not as easily interpreted. See *id.* at 37-47; *see also* WILLIAM H. GREENE, ECONOMETRIC ANALYSIS (4th ed. 2000). Although the coefficients from an ordered probit analysis are indicative of the relationship between the independent variables and the dependent variable, the coefficients cannot be interpreted as the marginal effects of the independent variables on the dependent variable (as they can, for instance, with the ordinary least squares model). To discern the marginal effects of the independent variables on the dependent variable, additional calculations are required. Greene explains:

> In the general case, relative to the signs of the coefficients, only the signs of the changes in $Prob(y = 0)$ and $Prob(y = J)$ are unambiguous! The upshot is that we must be very careful in interpreting the coefficients in th[e] [ordered probit] model. . . . Indeed, without a fair amount of extra calculation, it is quite unclear how the coefficients in the ordered probit model should be interpreted.

GREENE, *supra*, at 877-78.

192. Because Men in Parliament is a percentage bounded between 0 and 1, a tobit model is arguably more appropriate here. J. SCOTT LONG, REGRESSION MODELS FOR CATEGORICAL AND LIMITED DEPENDENT VARIABLES 212-13 (1997). However, the tobit model yields the same results for the purposes of this Article as the ordinary least squares (OLS) model, which yields coefficients that are more easily interpreted. The coefficient for ratification of the Convention on the Political Rights of Women using either a two-limit or a right-censored tobit model is −0.00005, with a standard error of 0.00006. The coefficient is not statistically significant. The coefficient for ratification of the Convention on the Political Rights of Women by fully democratic countries using either tobit model is −0.0004, with a standard error of 0.0001. It is statistically significant at the 99% level.

193. Linda Camp Keith takes a similar approach to an analysis of the relationship between ratification of the Covenant on Civil and Political Rights and countries' human rights practices. Although Keith uses a somewhat different model (she employs ordinary least squares), her results for this treaty are quite similar to mine. Keith, *supra* note 2, at 110-12.

1992   The Yale Law Journal   [Vol. 111: 1935

ratified treaties and those that have not, or systematic differences between the period before they have ratified treaties and the period after they have done so. If treaty ratification is associated with better ratings (fewer detected violations) than otherwise expected, that should be indicated by a statistically significant and negative coefficient for the treaty variable. If treaty ratification is associated with worse ratings (more violations) than otherwise expected, that should be indicated by a statistically significant and positive coefficient for the treaty variable. Hence, in the following tables, a positive sign indicates that a country's human rights ratings tend to be *worse* if a country has ratified, whereas a negative sign indicates that they tend to be *better*.

Before reviewing the results produced by this approach, it is worth once again noting that multivariate quantitative analysis, no matter how carefully done, is a useful but imperfect tool for examining complex questions of human action.[194] The results of the analyses below therefore do not provide a definitive answer to the question posed by this Article. The findings do, however, provide some important insights into the effect of treaties on country practices and, in turn, suggest promising avenues for future research.

Table 3 summarizes the results for five universal human rights treaties and the optional provisions of the Torture Convention and the Covenant on Civil and Political Rights, provisions that must be separately ratified in order to be binding. This summary shows that, when the treaty ratification variable is statistically significant, it is associated with *worse* human rights ratings than would otherwise be expected (as noted earlier, a positive sign indicates more observed violations). Consider, for example, the Genocide Convention. The positive and statistically significant coefficient for the treaty variable in the analysis indicates that countries that have ratified the Genocide Convention have more violations, on average, than those that do not, controlling for a range of country characteristics, otherwise unaccounted-for change over time, and country-to-country variation. The

---

194. There are several potential concerns regarding the statistical analysis below, including most notably selection bias, measurement error, and lack of mutual independence of the units. I discuss selection bias and systematic measurement error, both of which can bias results, in more depth *infra* notes 213-214 and accompanying text. The assumption of mutual independence of the units can also be a problem with analyses of pooled cross-sectional data (here, the data set includes multiple years for single countries). Scholars have proposed various correctives, but each has its weaknesses. *See* Morris P. Fiorina, *Divided Government in the American States: A Byproduct of Legislative Professionalism*, 88 AM. POL. SCI. REV. 304, 309 (1994); James Stimson, *Regression in Space and Time: A Statistical Essay*, 29 AM. J. POL. SCI. 914, 945 (1985). My use of a dummy variable for each country and a lagged dependent variable should partially address the mutual independence problem, *see* Fiorina, *supra*, at 309, though it is impossible to rule out the possibility that there is some remaining effect on the statistical significance of the coefficients.

TABLE 3. RELATIONSHIP BETWEEN TREATY RATIFICATION
AND HUMAN RIGHTS RATINGS (UNIVERSAL TREATIES)

Treaty	Human Rights Measure	Direction of Relationship	R-Squared or Pseudo R-Squared
Genocide Convention	Genocide	+	0.42
Genocide Convention	Genocide (no country dummies)	(+)	0.51
Torture Convention	Torture	(+)	0.39
Torture Convention	Torture (no country dummies)	+	0.31
Article 21	Torture	(+)	0.39
Covenant on Civil and Political Rights	Fair Trial	(+)	0.31
Optional Protocol	Fair Trial	(−)	0.30
Covenant on Civil and Political Rights	Civil Liberty	(−)	0.61
Optional Protocol	Civil Liberty	(+)	0.61
Conv. on the Political Rights of Women	Percentage of Men in Parliament	(−)	0.87

Note: Except where otherwise indicated, these results control for country characteristics through the use of country dummy variables. All results appearing in parentheses are not statistically significant at the 95% level.[195]

statistical significance does not hold, however, when I omit controls for country-specific effects. In both the analysis in which country dummies are used and in the analysis in which they are omitted, all the other substantive variables that are statistically significant are significant in the expected direction, with a single exception.[196] Together, the variables account for 42% of the variation in the measure of genocide when country dummies are included and 51% of the variation when they are not (indicated by a pseudo R-squared of 0.42 and 0.51, respectively).

---

195. Tests of statistical significance are intended to show whether "a difference is real, or just due to a chance variation." DAVID FREEDMAN ET AL., STATISTICS 487 (1980). A test of significance only matters, therefore, when there is a possibility of chance variation. It is common accepted practice to regard a time series such as that in use here "as being an observation made on a family of random variables." Emanuel Parzen, *An Approach to Time Series Analysis*, 32 ANNALS MATHEMATICAL STAT. 951, 952 (1961); *see also* Keith, *supra* note 2, at 102 (presenting the results of multivariate analyses using a database including 178 countries over an eighteen-year period); Simmons, *supra* note 2, at 829-30 (presenting the results of multivariate analyses using a database including 133 countries over periods averaging twenty years).

196. The sign for the aid dependency variable in the analysis that includes country dummies has the opposite sign from what I would have expected. *See* Table 8, *infra* Appendix C.

1994   The Yale Law Journal   [Vol. 111: 1935

The results for the Torture Convention are similar. Although the treaty variable is not statistically significant when dummy variables for each country are included, it is statistically significant and positive without them. In both cases, the results for the other substantive variables that are statistically significant have the expected signs. The analyses account for 39% of the difference in Torture ratings when dummy variables for countries are included in the analysis and 31% of the difference in Torture ratings when dummy variables for countries are not included.

The results for the remaining treaties consistently show no statistically significant relationship between treaty ratification and human rights ratings. Countries that ratify Article 21 of the Torture Convention do not show a statistically significant difference in measured torture levels from what would otherwise be expected; those that ratify the Covenant on Civil and Political Rights or the Optional Protocol do not show a statistically significant difference in the measures of fair trial practices and civil liberties; and those that ratify the Convention on the Political Rights of Women do not show a statistically significant difference in the percentage of men in parliament. In every case, virtually all the other substantive variables that are significant have the expected sign.[197] The null result for the treaties appears to be relatively robust: Except where otherwise indicated, the treaty variables remain statistically insignificant when I drop country dummies from the analyses and when I rerun the analyses using only the statistically significant variables and the treaty variables (the results of these analyses are not included in the table unless their results differ importantly). Taken together, the results for the group of universal treaties indicate that treaty ratification is usually not associated with statistically significantly different human rights ratings from what would otherwise be expected. More surprisingly, however, when ratification is associated with statistically significantly different human rights ratings, it is associated with worse, rather than better, human rights ratings than would otherwise be expected.

The results for similar analyses of regional human rights treaties lend credence to these findings. Table 4 summarizes the results for the five regional treaties, the impact of some of which is assessed using two or three

---

197. The most unexpected result is the finding that state failure has a statistically significant negative relationship to the measure of fair trials when ratification of the Covenant on Civil and Political Rights is used as the treaty variable. *See id.* There are a couple of possible explanations for this unexpected result. One is that the source of information for the index of fair trials, the State Department, might have had difficulty collecting information regarding government trial practices during times of state government collapse, thus leading to lower (hence better) Fair Trial ratings during these periods. The other unexpected result is the positive relationship between democracy and the percentage of men in parliament, which runs contrary to the presumption that democracy should be associated with better human rights records. *See id.* This result is not entirely surprising, however, given that quotas requiring minimum levels of female representation in parliament are more common in nondemocratic states than in democratic ones.

different measures of human rights practices addressed by the treaties. As with the assessment of compliance, I test the effectiveness of regional treaties for ratifying countries only against nonratifying countries that are members of the regional organization sponsoring the relevant treaty (which therefore could have joined the treaty at issue).[198]

TABLE 4. RELATIONSHIP BETWEEN TREATY RATIFICATION
AND HUMAN RIGHTS RATINGS (REGIONAL TREATIES)

Treaty	Human Rights Measure	Direction of Relationship	R-Squared or Pseudo R-Squared
American Torture Convention	Torture	+	0.35
African Charter on Human Rights	Torture	(−)	0.28
African Charter on Human Rights	Torture (no country dummies)	+	0.23
European Torture Convention	Torture	(+)	0.44
American Convention on Human Rights	Fair Trial	−[a]	0.46
African Charter on Human Rights	Fair Trial	(+)	0.25
European Convention on Human Rights	Fair Trial	+	0.36
European Convention on Human Rights	Fair Trial (no country dummies)	+	0.57
American Convention on Human Rights	Civil Liberty	+	0.57
African Charter on Human Rights	Civil Liberty	−[a]	0.54
European Convention on Human Rights	Civil Liberty (no country dummies)	(+)	0.70

[a] The results for the treaty variable for the American Convention on Human Rights (with Fair Trial as the dependent variable) and the African Charter on Human Rights (with Civil Liberty as the dependent variable) are not stable across alternative specifications.

The results of these analyses suggest that ratification of regional human rights treaties is not infrequently associated with worse than expected human rights practices. Of the three regional treaties on torture, one (the European Torture Convention) shows no statistically significant relationship between treaty ratification and torture; one (the African Charter on Human Rights) shows a statistically significant positive relationship

198. Hence, I limited the database to members of the OAS for the analyses involving American treaties, to members of the OAU for analyses involving African treaties, and to members of the COE for analyses involving European treaties.

1996   The Yale Law Journal   [Vol. 111: 1935

between ratification and Torture ratings (meaning that ratification is associated with more recorded torture), but only when country dummies are omitted from the analysis;[199] and one (the American Torture Convention) shows a statistically significant positive relationship between ratification and Torture ratings both when country dummies are included and when they are not (only the results for the former analysis are presented). Except where otherwise indicated, the results for the treaty variables are the same when I omit country dummies and when I drop nonsignificant variables.

I obtain similar results in my analyses of the relationship between countries' Fair Trial ratings and ratification of regional human rights treaties requiring fair trial practices. Of the three relevant regional treaties, two have statistically significant relationships to countries' reported fair trial practices. I find a statistically significant and negative relationship between ratification of the American Convention on Human Rights and the Fair Trial measure. If accurate, this result would be the first instance thus far in which ratification of a human rights treaty is associated with better ratings. Unfortunately, there is reason to doubt the results: Unlike the others, they are not stable across alternative specifications. In contrast to the American Convention, the African Charter on Human Rights appears to have no statistically significant relationship to the Fair Trial measure. And I find a positive and statistically significant relationship between ratification of the European Convention on Human Rights and the Fair Trial measure, suggesting that ratification of the European Convention on Human Rights is associated with more unfair trials. Because of the small number of observations for this analysis, it is impossible to include both country dummies and all of the substantive control variables. When I run the analysis with country dummies but omit all other control variables except the lag variable, I find a statistically significant and positive relationship. I find similar results when I run the analysis with all of the control variables but without country dummies. The analyses explain between 25% and 57% of the variation in the Fair Trial index, but the results for a few of the variables are not as expected.[200]

---

199. *See infra* Appendix B, Section M (explaining the reasons for including country dummies in the analyses).

200. In the analysis of the European Convention on Human Rights, the coefficient for "new regime" is significant and negative, suggesting that new regimes provide fairer trials than would otherwise be expected given other country characteristics. Similarly, in the analysis for the African Charter on Human Rights, the coefficients for "international war" and "state failure" are significant and negative, suggesting that countries engaging in war and experiencing state failure provide fairer trials than would otherwise be expected. These results may be due to the difficulties presented to the State Department, which constructs the *Country Reports on Human Rights* from which I drew the index, in obtaining information on the fair trial practices of countries during times of upheaval (such as war and regime transition), and its practice of giving the benefit of the doubt to newer regimes in compiling the reports.

The relationship between ratification of regional human rights treaties and civil liberties is also mixed. On the one hand, ratification of the American Convention on Human Rights is associated with worse Civil Liberty ratings than expected. On the other hand, ratification of the African Charter on Human Rights is associated with better Civil Liberty ratings than expected. Once again, however, this encouraging finding for the efficacy of international human rights law does not hold: The latter result is not stable across alternative specifications. The European Convention on Human Rights splits the difference, showing no statistically significant relationship between treaty ratification and Civil Liberty ratings. (I was unable to obtain any results using country dummies, probably because of insufficient variation in the dependent variable in many European countries.) The analyses predict a large percentage of the variation in the Civil Liberty ratings—between 54% and 70%—but the results for some of the control variables are not as expected.[201]

In order to test the prediction of liberal theory that democratic countries will be more likely to change their behavior in response to their international legal commitments, I reran the analyses of the universal treaties including an additional variable that tests the impact of treaty ratification on measures of human rights for countries with democracy ratings of 10.[202] As summarized in Table 5, the results suggest that fully democratic countries may sometimes be more likely to have better human rights practices if they ratify a human rights treaty than would otherwise be expected. Most notably, when the data set is limited to countries with some variation in their Genocide levels, fully democratic countries that ratify the Genocide Convention have statistically significantly better Genocide ratings than expected. This lies in direct contrast to the results for the group of nations as a whole, as summarized in Table 3. And whereas ratification of the Optional Protocol and Convention on the Political Rights of Women bears no apparent relationship to the practices of the group of nations as a whole, fully democratic countries that ratify the Optional Protocol have statistically significantly better Civil Liberty ratings and those that ratify the Convention on the Political Rights of Women have a statistically

201. In the analysis of the European Convention on Human Rights, the coefficient for international war is significant and negative (indicating that it is associated with better Civil Liberty ratings) and the coefficient for aid dependency is significant and positive (indicating that it is associated with worse Civil Liberty ratings).

202. This variable is created by interacting the treaty variable with a new dummy variable that indicates 1 only where the country's democracy rating is 10 and 0 elsewhere. In addition, I added the new dummy variable labeled "full democracy" in Table 10 as a separate independent variable to ensure that the results for the interacted variable would accurately reflect only the impact of treaty ratification for fully democratic countries.

International Law and Society

1998   The Yale Law Journal   [Vol. 111: 1935

TABLE 5. RELATIONSHIP BETWEEN TREATY RATIFICATION
AND HUMAN RIGHTS RATINGS (FULLY DEMOCRATIC NATIONS)

Treaty	Human Rights Measure	Direction of Relationship	R-Squared or Pseudo R-Squared
Genocide Convention[a]	Genocide	–	0.12
Torture Convention	Torture	+	0.38
Article 21	Torture	+	0.38
Covenant on Civil and Political Rights	Fair Trial	(+)	0.31
Optional Protocol	Fair Trial	(+)	0.31
Covenant on Civil and Political Rights	Civil Liberty	(–)	0.61
Optional Protocol	Civil Liberty	–	0.61
Conv. on the Political Rights of Women	Percentage of Men in Parliament	–	0.87

[a] Genocide Convention results include countries with democracy ratings from 8 to 10.

significantly lower percentage of men in parliament. The Torture Convention, however, appears to have the same effect on full democracies that it does on the group of countries as a whole: The results for this treaty variable are statistically significant and positive, indicating that fully democratic nations that ratify the treaty appear to engage in more violations than would otherwise be expected (this contrasts with positive but insignificant results for the group of nations as a whole that ratify the treaty, except when the impact of the Torture Convention is measured without country dummies).[203] Article 21 has a similar effect on full democracies (this contrasts with positive but insignificant results for the group of nations as a whole). Finally, ratification of the Optional Protocol has no statistically significant relationship to Fair Trial ratings of full democracies, and ratification of the Covenant on Civil and Political Rights has no statistically significant relationship to either the Fair Trial or the Civil Liberty ratings of

---

203. These results may initially appear to contradict the findings summarized in Figure 2, which show ratification rates of the Torture Convention for full democracies initially rising and then falling off precipitously as Torture ratings rise, suggesting that for full democracies, worse practices are associated with lower, not higher, ratification rates. But what Figure 2 does not show is that the number of countries in each category is lower as Torture ratings rise, with 226 observations for a 1, 142 for a 2, and 55 for a 3. The analysis summarized in Table 5 treats each observation equally, thus the higher ratification rate for countries with a rating of 2 than for those with a 1 has a large impact on the results, as does controlling for a variety of other factors that influence human rights practices.

full democracies (the results are the same for the group of nations as a whole). For the most part, these largely encouraging results do not hold when the universe of democratic nations is expanded to include countries with democracy ratings of 6 to 10.[204]

Taken as a whole, the empirical evidence regarding the patterns of human rights treaty compliance appears largely inconsistent with existing theories. First and foremost, although countries that ratify treaties usually have better ratings than those that do not,[205] noncompliance appears common.[206] Indeed, those with the worst ratings sometimes have higher rates of treaty ratification than those with substantially better ratings. Second and relatedly, treaty ratification is not infrequently associated with worse, rather than better, human rights ratings than would otherwise be expected.[207] Unexpectedly, treaty ratification is more often associated with worse human rights ratings in areas where rights are deeply entrenched in international law than in areas that are of more recent provenance.[208] Third, noncompliance appears less common and less pronounced among countries that have ratified the Optional Protocol to the Covenant on Civil and Political Rights and Article 21 of the Torture Convention, and countries that have ratified these provisions generally have substantially better human rights ratings than those that have not.[209] However, it is possible that this is due largely to a greater proclivity among those with better practices to sign

---

204. Only the Genocide Convention shows significant and negative results for the larger group of democratic nations (suggesting that practices of ratifying countries are better than otherwise predicted). In every other case, the results are either not significant or are significant and positive (suggesting worse practices for democratic ratifying countries). For the Genocide Convention, the coefficient for the interacted variable is −0.034 (significant at the 95% level), and the standard error is 0.013. For the Torture Convention, the coefficient for the interacted variable is −0.030 (not significant), and the standard error is 0.036. For Article 21, the coefficient for the interacted treaty variable is 0.017 (not significant), and the standard error is 0.061. For the Covenant on Civil and Political Rights (with Fair Trial as the dependent variable), the coefficient is 0.052 (not significant), and the standard error is 0.031. For the Optional Protocol (with Fair Trial as the dependent variable), the coefficient for the interacted variable is 0.075 (significant at the 95% level), and the standard error is 0.036. For the Covenant on Civil and Political Rights (with Civil Liberty as the dependent variable), the coefficient for the interacted variable is −0.010 (not significant), and the standard error is 0.010. For the Optional Protocol (with Civil Liberty as the dependent variable), the coefficient for the interacted variable is 0.029 (significant at the 95% level), and the standard error is 0.013. For the Convention on the Political Rights of Women, the coefficient for the interacted variable is 0.0001 (not significant), and the standard error is 0.0002.

205. See Table 1, *supra* Section II.B (comparing the mean rating for countries that have ratified treaties to the mean rating of those that have not).

206. This is revealed most strikingly by Figures 1-5, *supra* Section II.B, which show that countries with the worst human rights ratings often have very high rates of treaty ratification.

207. See Tables 3-4, *supra*.

208. Most notably, as Table 3, *supra*, shows, ratification of the Genocide and Torture Conventions is associated with statistically significantly worse Genocide and Torture ratings. Ratification of the other universal treaties, on the other hand, has no statistically significant relationship to human rights ratings.

209. See Table 1 and Figures 2-4, *supra* Section II.B.

the provisions rather than to the effect of the provisions on state behavior.[210] Fourth, ratification of regional treaties appears to be more likely than ratification of universal treaties to be associated with high rates of noncompliance and with worse human rights practices than would otherwise be expected.[211] Finally, full democracies appear to be more likely to comply with their human rights treaty obligations than the group of nations as a whole and more likely when they ratify treaties to have better practices than otherwise expected.[212]

There are two possible nonsubstantive explanations for these results. First, it is possible, though not likely, that the results are due in part or whole to systematic measurement error. Such measurement error may account in part for the correlation between ratification of treaties and worse human rights ratings than otherwise expected if it is, for instance, more difficult to get information about the human rights practices of countries that have not ratified treaties than it is to get information about those that have. There are good reasons to believe that such measurement error does not account for the results of the analyses,[213] but the possibility cannot be entirely ruled out.

---

210. The analyses summarized in Tables 3-5, *supra*, suggest that countries that have ratified the Optional Protocol and Article 21 have no better practices than would otherwise be expected, and indeed ratification of Article 21 by fully democratic countries is associated with worse Torture ratings.

211. The comparison of means in Table 1, *supra* Section II.B, for example, indicates that countries that ratify the regional treaties that address torture and fair trial practices generally have worse average ratings than those that do not. Figures 2-4, *supra* Section II.B, show that, in the torture, fair trial, and civil liberty areas, poor human rights ratings are associated with high rates of ratification of regional human rights treaties. And the statistical analyses summarized in Table 4, *supra*, indicate that many of the regional treaties analyzed are associated with worse, rather than better, human rights ratings than otherwise expected.

212. Although the mean human rights ratings of full democracies that have ratified are not substantially different from the ratings of those that have not, *see* Table 2, *supra* Section II.B, the means are better across the board for full democracies. In part because full democracies do not tend to engage in the worst human rights violations, they do not tend to have high rates of ratification associated with poor ratings. *See* Figures 2-4, *supra* Section II.B. Most strikingly, full democracies appear to be more likely to improve their practices when they ratify universal treaties than is the group of nations as a whole, as the results summarized in Table 5, *supra*, suggest.

213. First, the uniformity of the results across different subject areas evaluated with different sources of data suggests that a reporting effect is unlikely to be the source of the counterintuitive finding. Second, and more important, in the instances in which I can directly evaluate the impact of ratification on the evaluation of human rights practices—in my coding of the State Department *Country Reports on Human Rights*—I find that when treaty ratification is noted, the reports almost universally appear to give countries lighter, rather than heavier, scrutiny for the year of ratification and for a short period thereafter. In essence, the reports appear to give newly ratifying countries the benefit of the doubt in the immediate wake of treaty ratification. If this observation is correct, this would suggest that the results *understate*, rather than overstate, the association of treaty ratification with worse human rights practices. And finally, if the results were due to greater reporting of violations in the wake of treaty ratification, we would expect to find that ratification would always or nearly always be associated with higher violation ratings. But instead the results suggest that the association between ratification and practices is strongest in the most entrenched areas of human rights and for regional treaties—variations that are difficult to explain by sole reference to a reporting effect.

Second, the results might be affected by reciprocal causation. It could be, after all, that the relationship between treaties and practices runs the other direction. We have already seen that countries with poorer human rights ratings are sometimes more likely to sign human rights treaties than those with somewhat better ratings. It might be supposed, as a result, that the finding of an apparent negative association between treaties and practices is due to this tendency (practices causing ratification) rather than to any actual effects that treaties have on practices. Recall, however, that the analysis controls for a wide array of factors expected to shape the human rights practices of countries. Reciprocal causation would bias the results only to the extent that countries with worse practices are more likely to ratify than those with better practices, controlling for the influence of these factors.[214] Yet I cannot at this point rule out the possibility that counterintuitive results of the analysis are due to a perverse selection effect.

Bearing these reasons for caution in mind, it is nonetheless the case that much of the evidence regarding the apparent relationship between human rights treaty ratification and human rights practices is perplexing for advocates of idealism and rationalism alike. Contrary to the predictions of normative theory, treaty ratification appears to be frequently associated with worse, rather than better, human rights practices. Even more confoundingly, this adverse relationship between treaty ratification and country human rights ratings appears more pronounced in the most established areas of human rights—torture and genocide—and for regional treaties. Rationalist theories also face anomalies. Contrary to realists' expectations, ratification is not simply (or at least not always) epiphenomenal. Rather, ratification appears sometimes to have an effect on practices, simply not the effect one would anticipate. Institutionalists, like normative scholars, expect treaty ratification to be associated with better human rights practices, at a minimum because they expect the least-cost compliers to be more likely to ratify the treaties than countries for which compliance would be more costly. Of the existing theories, liberal theory appears the most promising, as it correctly predicts that democracies will be more likely than others to have better human rights ratings when they ratify treaties. But liberals are for the most part unable to explain why ratification of treaties on the whole, and of regional treaties in particular, often appears to be associated with worse human rights practices than would otherwise be expected.[215] Nor can they explain why fully democratic nations have worse

214. There are statistical methods for addressing selection bias, but using them would require identifying an instrumental variable for the human rights practice that is uncorrelated with the probability of ratification—something I have thus far been unable to do. *See* Joshua D. Angrist et al., *Identification of Causal Effects Using Instrumental Variables*, 91 J. AM. STAT. ASS'N 444 (1996).

215. Even if newer democracies have worse practices than established democracies and are more likely to join human rights treaties more readily than are established democracies, this

2002   The Yale Law Journal   [Vol. 111: 1935

Torture ratings when they ratify the Torture Convention than would otherwise be expected. In the next Part, I consider a possible explanation for the empirical findings and seek to place the insights of liberal theory into a broader context.

III. THE DUAL ROLES OF HUMAN RIGHTS TREATIES

Previous analyses of treaty compliance have focused primarily on the direct effect of the binding commitment of ratification on country practices. Rationalists for the most part claim that countries will comply with treaties only when doing so enhances their interests, whether those interests are defined in terms of geopolitical power, reputation, or domestic impact. Normative scholars, on the other hand, claim that strict self-interest is less important to understanding international law compliance than is the persuasive power of legitimate legal obligations. Neither considers the possibility that countries comply (or fail to comply) with treaties not only because they are committed to or benefit from the treaties, but also because they benefit from what ratification says to others. In contrast to these approaches, my argument is that we cannot fully understand the relationship between human rights treaty ratification and human rights practices unless we understand that treaties operate on more than one level simultaneously. They create binding law that is intended to have particular effects, and they express the position of those countries that join them. Like other political instruments, in short, treaties play both instrumental and expressive roles.[216] This theory of the dual roles of human rights treaties draws upon and throws new light on both the normative and rationalist models of international law compliance—and, I argue, may provide a missing key to explaining the paradoxical patterns of interaction between human rights treaty ratification and human rights practices.

Before turning to this explanation, however, it is important to consider why human rights treaties so often appear to have no statistically significant effect on practices. Although treaty ratification does often appear to be associated with worse human rights treaty practices—a result that is counterintuitive and therefore demands explanation—there are more instances in which treaty ratification has no apparent impact. Although we should be wary of reading too much into a null result, we also cannot ignore

---

selection effect would likely not explain the results reported here. *Cf. supra* note 184. The analyses in this Section, unlike those in the previous Section, test for whether practices are better or worse than they otherwise would have been, given other country characteristics (including level of democracy and whether the regime is new or not).

216. *See* MURRAY EDELMAN, THE SYMBOLIC USES OF POLITICS 12 (1977) ("In Himmelstrand's terms, political acts are both instrumental and expressive.").

it. It is striking, after all, that treaties, even though they do not consistently make practices worse, seem so consistently not to make them better.

There are any number of possible explanations for these findings. Much of the strength of international human rights law comes from NGOs and Western liberal states' critical attention to nations with poor human rights practices. However, neither NGOs nor Western states tend to limit their focus to treaty ratifiers. Indeed, as discussed below, the opposite may be true. The increasingly pervasive culture of human rights and processes of norm internalization tend to affect states regardless of whether they have ratified particular treaties. Perhaps this is due in part to the fact that UN Charter-based mechanisms may act against ratifiers and nonratifiers alike. In the regional context, we might also expect few differences between ratifying and nonratifying states because regional bodies—particularly the Council of Europe (COE) and the Organization of American States (OAS)—place requirements on members that make ratification of an individual treaty either mandatory or superfluous—in either case, the treaty might reasonably be expected to have little independent effect on practices.[217]

It is also possible that these findings are due at least in part to the heavy resistance of nations' human rights practices to change.[218] With few exceptions, the lagged dependent variable in the model summarized in Tables 3-5 is statistically significant and positive, indicating that one of the best predictors of a country's rating in a given year is its rating the previous year.[219] This consistency in ratings over time is probably due at least in part to the central role that bureaucratic inertia plays in government abuses of human rights. Individuals and institutions become habituated to the use of repressive means of retaining control. As a result, repressive behavior lingers long after the initial impetus for it disappears. The more government employees use repressive tactics, the more accepted such tactics become. At the same time, governments build up institutions around the use of these practices, and the institutions and individuals needed to manage conflict using nonrepressive means disappear or perhaps are never part of government in the first place. In short, governments and the individuals who make decisions within them become habituated to engaging in human rights violations, and this behavior takes time and continued conscious effort to change. Major shocks to the system—such as a change in government—provide limited windows of opportunity for effecting large

---

217. I am grateful to Douglass Cassel for immensely thoughtful comments on this topic.

218. This resistance to change might even loosely be called "path-dependent." See, e.g., Oona A. Hathaway, *Path Dependence in the Law: The Course and Pattern of Legal Change in a Common Law System*, 86 IOWA L. REV. 601 (2001). Chayes and Chayes refer to this resistance to change in the human rights area as a "time lag." See CHAYES & CHAYES, *supra* note 1, at 16.

219. *See* Tables 8-10, *infra* Appendix C.

2004   The Yale Law Journal   [Vol. 111: 1935

changes in the system. Indeed, when major changes in human rights practices occur, it is often because of such an event.[220] But even then, change is not inevitable; to the extent that low-level government officials remain in place during shifts in the top levels of government, government oppressive practices often remain as well.[221] The same is of course true of countries that observe human rights. Once norms favoring human rights are entrenched, they can be difficult to dislodge.

But this does not tell the entire story, for human rights practices do change and are often responsive to human rights treaty ratification as well as other factors. The major task of this Part, then, is to suggest how we might begin to explain the unexpected patterns that emerge from the quantitative analysis—why, that is, countries with worse human rights practices sometimes appear to ratify treaties at higher rates than those with better practices, why treaty ratification often appears to be associated with worse human rights practices than otherwise expected, why noncompliance is apparently less pronounced among countries that have ratified the Optional Protocol and Article 21, why ratification of regional treaties appears more likely to worsen human rights practices than to improve them, and why, finally, full democracies appear more likely when they ratify treaties to have better practices than otherwise expected. The dual nature of treaties—as instrumental and expressive tools—provides a starting point for explaining these results.

The instrumental role of treaties is well understood. I therefore focus here primarily on outlining the expressive role of treaties. The notion that the law has an "expressive" function is not new, though earlier work on the expressive function of the law has focused almost exclusively on the domestic context.[222] Situated in opposition to the dominant focus on law's

---

220. For example, my examination of the years in which the Fair Trial coding changed by two points or more from the previous year reveals that the most common easily discernable reason for changes in ratings is a change in government, usually from democracy to nondemocracy or vice versa.

221. *See* ANN SEIDMAN & ROBERT B. SEIDMAN, STATE AND LAW IN THE DEVELOPMENT PROCESS 145-69 (1994) (describing the "rise of the bureaucratic bourgeoisie").

222. *See, e.g.*, Elizabeth S. Anderson & Richard H. Pildes, *Expressive Theories of Law: A General Restatement*, 148 U. PA. L. REV. 1503 (2000); Robert Cooter, *Do Good Laws Make Good Citizens? An Economic Analysis of Internalized Norms*, 86 VA. L. REV. 1577, 1593-94 (2000); Robert Cooter, *Expressive Law and Economics*, 27 J. LEGAL STUD. 585 (1998); Dan H. Kahan, *What Do Alternative Sanctions Mean?*, 63 U. CHI. L. REV. 591, 597 (1996); Lawrence Lessig, *The Regulation of Social Meaning*, 62 U. CHI. L. REV. 943 (1995); Jason Mazzone, *When Courts Speak: Social Capital and Law's Expressive Function*, 49 SYRACUSE L. REV. 1039 (1999); Richard H. McAdams, *A Focal Point Theory of Expressive Law*, 86 VA. L. REV. 1649 (2000); Richard H. Pildes, *Why Rights Are Not Trumps: Social Meanings, Expressive Harms, and Constitutionalism*, 27 J. LEGAL STUD. 725 (1998); Paul H. Robinson & John M. Darley, *The Utility of Desert*, 91 NW. U. L. REV. 453, 471-73 (1997); Cass R. Sunstein, *On the Expressive Function of Law*, 144 U. PA. L. REV. 2021, 2022 (1996); *see also* ELIZABETH ANDERSON, VALUE IN ETHICS AND ECONOMICS 33-37 (1993) (discussing expressive norms); H.L.A. HART, PUNISHMENT AND RESPONSIBILITY (1968) (arguing that one of the functions of criminal law is to express social judgments); ROBERT NOZICK, THE NATURE OF RATIONALITY 26-35 (1993)

sanctioning function, much of this work is aimed at demonstrating that law influences behavior not only by threatening to sanction undesirable actions, but also by what it says.[223] Broadly speaking, it argues that the social meanings of state action are little recognized but in some cases as important as the action's material impact.[224] The most widely discussed form of legal expressive theory thus tells actors (particularly state actors) to act in ways that "express appropriate attitudes toward various substantive values."[225]

Although the work of these scholars forms part of the backdrop for this Article, the conception here of the expressive function of the law is distinct, largely because this Article focuses on the international rather than domestic context. Unlike in the domestic context, in the international realm only the parties who voluntarily accede to the laws are bound to abide by them (with the notable exception, of course, of customary law, which is not the focus of this Article). As a consequence, the expressive role of the law takes on political dimensions not at issue in the domestic legal context.

The expressive role of treaties described in this Article has two aspects, the first arising from treaties' legal nature and the second from their political nature. Treaties, like domestic laws, work by expressing the position of the community of nations as to what conduct is and is not acceptable; they tell the international community what are the norms and code of conduct of civilized nations.[226] Yet treaties also have an expressive function that arises from what membership in a treaty regime *says about the parties to the treaties*. When a country joins a human rights treaty, it engages in what might be called "position taking," defined here as the public enunciation of a statement on anything likely to be of interest to domestic or international actors.[227] In this sense, the ratification of a treaty functions much as a roll-call vote in the U.S. Congress or a speech in favor of the temperance movement, as a pleasing statement not necessarily intended to have any real effect on outcomes.[228] It declares to the world that

---

(discussing the "symbolic utility" that arises out of symbolic meaning); Matthew D. Adler, *Expressive Theories of Law: A Skeptical Overview*, 148 U. PA. L. REV. 1363 (2000) (providing a critique of some variants of expressive theory); Jean Hampton, *An Expressive Theory of Retribution, in* RETRIBUTIVISM AND ITS CRITICS 1 (Wesley Cragg ed., 1992) (discussing an expressive theory of retribution).

223. McAdams, *supra* note 222, at 1650-51.

224. *See, e.g.*, Pildes, *supra* note 222, at 762.

225. Anderson & Pildes, *supra* note 222, at 1504.

226. This aspect of the expressive function is similar to the broad conception of the expressive function of law outlined by Cass Sunstein. *See* Sunstein, *supra* note 222, at 2024-25 ("In this Article I explore the expressive function of law—the function of law in 'making statements' as opposed to controlling behavior directly. I do so by focusing on the particular issue of how legal 'statements' might be designed to change social norms.").

227. This is a very slight twist on the definition of the term used by David Mayhew. *See* DAVID R. MAYHEW, CONGRESS: THE ELECTORAL CONNECTION 61 (1974).

228. *See* JOSEPH R. GUSFIELD, SYMBOLIC CRUSADE: STATUS POLITICS AND THE AMERICAN TEMPERANCE MOVEMENT (1963); MAYHEW, *supra* note 227, at 61-73 (discussing the phenomenon of "position taking" in the U.S. Congress).

2006 The Yale Law Journal [Vol. 111: 1935

the principles outlined in the treaty are consistent with the ratifying government's commitment to human rights.

I focus primarily in this Article on the second aspect of the expressive function because I believe it best helps to explain the empirical findings of my analyses. I do not mean in focusing on the second expressive aspect of treaties to suggest that the first is unimportant; indeed, as I discuss in more detail in the Conclusion, the first expressive function of treaties may change discourse about and expectations regarding country practices and thereby change practices of countries regardless of whether they ratify the treaties.

If the first step to explaining patterns of country treaty compliance is to recognize the expressive role of treaties, the second is to note that this expressive function can work either in unison with or in opposition to the instrumental role of the treaty. When a country is genuinely committed to the goals of the treaty and wishes to see them put into place, the country's expression in joining and remaining a party to a treaty is entirely consistent with its intended course of action: The country both signals support for the treaty's requirements and actually intends to act in ways consistent with those requirements. Treaties that include substantial monitoring or enforcement mechanisms embody some guarantees that the expressive and instrumental roles of the treaty will operate in tandem. For example, a country is unlikely to ratify a free trade agreement and then fail to abide by the terms of that agreement, because failure to abide by the terms of the agreement would likely be detected and lead to retaliatory action. For similar reasons, a country is unlikely to ratify a security pact or a treaty governing the use of airspace or the sea and then fail to abide by its terms. To the extent that monitoring and enforcement are effective, the expression of the commitment to the goals of such treaties is largely indivisible from the act of complying with the terms of the treaties.

But the expressive and instrumental roles of treaties do not always operate this seamlessly. When monitoring and enforcement of treaties is minimal, the expressive and instrumental roles may cease to cohere, and the expressive aspect of the treaty may become divorced from the instrumental aspect. Under such circumstances, a country may express a commitment to the goals of the treaty by joining it, yet fail to meet its requirements. Where there is little monitoring, noncompliance is not likely to be exposed. Therefore, the countries that join the treaty will enjoy the expressive benefits of joining the treaty, regardless of whether they actually comply with the treaty's requirements.[229] And where there is little enforcement, the costs of membership are also small, as countries with policies that do not adhere to the requirements of the treaty are unlikely to be penalized.

---

229. The threat, even if small, that a country's noncompliance may be exposed may be of greater significance to some countries than to others. *See infra* note 256 and accompanying text.

Where there is a disjuncture between expressive benefits and instrumental goals, it is possible that the expressive aspect of treaties will serve to relieve pressure for real change in performance in countries that ratify the treaty. Because such treaties offer rewards "for positions rather than for effects,"[230] countries can and will take positions to which they do not subsequently conform and benefit from doing so. This is particularly true of treaties enacted for the direct benefit neither of the joining parties nor of those pushing for enactment, but rather of uninvolved third parties. In this sense, human rights treaties can take on the character of "charitable" enactments that are "designed to benefit people other than the ones whose gratification is the payment for passage," and which, as a result, often suffer from indifferent enforcement and have little impact.[231]

There is arguably no area of international law in which the disjuncture between the expressive and instrumental aspects of a treaty is more evident than human rights. Monitoring and enforcement of human rights treaty obligations are often minimal, thereby making it difficult to give the lie to a country's expression of commitment to the goals of a treaty. The strongest means of treaty enforcement—military intervention and economic sanctions—are used relatively infrequently to enforce human rights norms,[232] in no small part because there is little incentive for individual states to take on the burden of engaging in such enforcement activity.[233] Because of the infrequency with which the international community resorts to such means of enforcement, the threat of their use does not contribute meaningfully to day-to-day compliance with the multitude of human rights treaties.[234] Moreover, as Louis Henkin puts it, "the principal element of horizontal deterrence is missing" in the area of human rights: "[T]he threat that 'if you violate the human rights of your inhabitants, we will violate the human rights of our inhabitants' hardly serves as a deterrent."[235]

---

230. MAYHEW, *supra* note 227, at 132. Again, David Mayhew is speaking here of the U.S. Congress, rather than the international treaty system, but the insight is nonetheless instructive.

231. *Id.* at 132-33. This, Mayhew claims, helps explain why the early Civil Rights Acts of 1957 and 1960, which benefited nonvoting Southern blacks but were passed to please Northern audiences, achieved little progress. *Id.* at 133. Mayhew notes that the same cannot be said for the Civil Rights Acts of 1964 and 1965. *See id.* at 133 n.106.

232. *See supra* note 53 and accompanying text.

233. *See* Henkin, *supra* note 48, at 253. Henkin states:

[T]he real beneficiaries [of human rights obligations] are not the State promisees but the inhabitants of the promisor State, and, in general, States—even if they have adhered to international agreements—do not have a strong interest in human rights generally, and are not yet politically acclimated and habituated to responding to violations of rights of persons abroad other than their own nationals.

Id. (citation omitted).

234. That is not to say that they play *no* role in improving human rights. *Cf.* Sarah H. Cleveland, *Norm Internalization and U.S. Economic Sanctions*, 26 YALE J. INT'L L. 1, 5 (2001) (arguing that "[e]conomic sanctions are an important weapon in transnational efforts to promote respect for fundamental rights and can have substantial behavior-modifying potential").

235. Henkin, *supra* note 48, at 253.

2008   The Yale Law Journal   [Vol. 111: 1935

Consequently, most human rights treaties rely not on sanctions to encourage compliance but instead on treaty-based and charter-based organs dedicated to monitoring compliance with particular treaties or particular sets of treaties, often through a system of self-reporting.[236] Were these monitoring systems effective, it is possible that the threat to reputation that they could pose to noncomplying countries would be sufficient to keep noncompliance at low levels. Yet most of these systems have proven woefully inadequate, with countries regularly and repeatedly failing to meet minimal procedural requirements with no repercussions.[237] Indeed, although treaties often require countries that join them to submit to semi-regular scrutiny by a treaty body, there is no real penalty for failure to participate in this process or for obeying the letter but not the spirit of the treaty requirements.[238] As a consequence, the failure of a country to comply with its treaty obligations is, in most cases, unlikely to be revealed and examined except by already overtaxed NGOs.[239]

At the same time, at least since World War II, there has been a great deal of pressure on countries to exhibit a commitment to human rights norms. Indeed, human rights treaties are a paradigmatic example of a charitable enactment in the international context. The audience of the decision to ratify human rights treaties is usually not the beneficiary of the agreement—the abused, oppressed, and suppressed of the world—but instead the political and economic actors located for the most part in wealthy liberal nations. Some of these actors, including various NGOs and

---

236. For clear descriptions and assessments of the intergovernmental human rights enforcement system, see INTERNATIONAL HUMAN RIGHTS IN CONTEXT, *supra* note 101, at 592-704; and THE UNITED NATIONS AND HUMAN RIGHTS (Philip Alston ed., 1992).

237. *See supra* note 101.

238. Comm. on Int'l Human Rights Law & Practice, *First Report of the Committee, in* INT'L LAW ASS'N, REPORT OF THE SIXTY-SEVENTH CONFERENCE HELD AT HELSINKI, FINLAND 336 (James Crawford & Michael Byers eds., 1996) (identifying the major deficiencies in the human rights treaty system and issuing recommendations for improving it); Rudolf Geiger, *The Violation of Reporting Obligations and the General Rules of State Responsibility, in* THE MONITORING SYSTEM OF HUMAN RIGHTS TREATY OBLIGATIONS 139, 139 (Eckart Klein ed., 1996) ("The rules of procedure of the treaty bodies provide for certain steps to be taken in order to induce a State to comply with its reporting duty. Such procedural steps may consist of a formal reminder by the treaty organ to the dilatory State or of a report to a superior organ (like the ECOSOC or the UN General Assembly). There are, however, no provisions covering the case should these measures fail."). For an excellent overview of many of the central debates regarding human rights treaty monitoring, see THE FUTURE OF UN HUMAN RIGHTS TREATY MONITORING (Philip Alston & James Crawford eds., 2000). *See also* PATRICK JAMES FLOOD, THE EFFECTIVENESS OF UN HUMAN RIGHTS INSTITUTIONS (1998) (describing and assessing the UN human rights system); HOWARD TOLLEY, JR., THE UN COMMISSION ON HUMAN RIGHTS (1987) (offering a history and assessment of the UN Commission on Human Rights).

239. Addressing this problem is a central mission of Amnesty International, Human Rights Watch, and the Lawyers Committee for Human Rights. Yet even together, they cannot monitor country compliance with each and every human rights treaty, nor do they attempt to do so. For more on fact-finding functions of international monitors, see INTERNATIONAL HUMAN RIGHTS IN CONTEXT, *supra* note 101, at 602-10; and THE UN HUMAN RIGHTS SYSTEM IN THE 21ST CENTURY 63-136 (Anne F. Bayefsky ed., 2000).

other domestic and international organizations, are genuinely committed to the ends of the treaties but have restricted access to information regarding the real impact of the treaties in individual countries. Others, including potential investors and perhaps nations wishing to provide aid assistance or to deepen economic or political ties, may be less genuinely committed to the ends of the treaties. They may instead be seeking evidence of commitment to the norms embedded in the human rights treaties that they can in turn use to placate more genuinely interested parties to which they must answer (including stockholders and customers of companies wishing to invest in the country and constituents of governments that wish to provide aid to or engage in deeper political or economic ties with the ratifying countries).[240] Countries that are parties to the treaties can therefore enjoy the benefits of ratification without actually supplying the human rights protections to which they have committed.[241] Consequently, treaty ratification may become a substitute for, rather than a spur to, real improvement in human rights practices.[242]

In arguing that the expressive and instrumental aspects of human rights treaties are divorced, I am not claiming that countries that ratify human rights treaties *necessarily* do not conform their actions to the requirements of the treaties. Although actions need not match expressions, this does not mean that they always do not. Moral norms are surely an important force for state and individual action, and human rights scholars are right to focus much of their attention on understanding the source of the ideological appeal of human rights.[243] Sincere commitment to a human rights treaty

---

240. Of course, the opposite may be true. It is possible that governments or members of governments that wish to resist deeper trade or political relationships with nations suspected of engaging in human rights violations may use a poor human rights record as an excuse for resisting deeper engagement.

241. This argument parallels that made by Mayhew regarding the U.S. Congress: "If the gratified receive muddled feedback on programmatic accomplishment, the actual supplying of the prescribed benefits becomes a distinctly secondary congressional concern." MAYHEW, *supra* note 227, at 132. Mayhew, in turn, was strongly influenced by GORDON TULLOCK, *Information Without Profit, in* PAPERS ON NON-MARKET DECISION-MAKING 141 (Gordon Tullock ed., 1967).

242. In this sense, human rights treaties might be viewed as an example of the claim by Giulio M. Gallarotti that international organization (IO) can lead to adverse substitution. He explains:

Nations are continually faced with difficult domestic and international problems whose resolution entails political, economic, or social costs. Although IO can alleviate short-run pressures and provide nations with an "out" from more costly solutions, doing so can be counterproductive in that it discourages nations from seeking more substantive and longer-term resolutions to their problems.

Giulio M. Gallarotti, *The Limits of International Organizations: Systemic Failure in the Management of International Relations*, 45 INT'L ORG. 198, 199 (1991). Gallarotti notes as support for this contention a statement by Secretary-General Pérez de Cuéllar that "[t]here is a tendency in the United Nations for governments to act as though passage of a resolution absolved them from further responsibility for the subject in question." *Id.* at 200 (quoting Pérez de Cuéllar).

243. Some scholars look to moral psychology, arguing that human rights ideals are intuitively attractive to human beings and recognized worldwide as valid. MARGARET E. KECK & KATHRYN SIKKINK, ACTIVISTS BEYOND BORDERS: ADVOCACY NETWORKS IN INTERNATIONAL POLITICS

2010   The Yale Law Journal   [Vol. 111: 1935]

may also arise out of somewhat less idealistic motives. Governments may see a treaty as a relatively costless means of spreading their ideals and principles to other nations. They may hope that the addition of another party to the treaty will build momentum for the formation of new customary law. They might even join the treaty with an eye to constraining their successors, who may or may not share their commitment to human rights, accepting constraints on their powers in the present in order to gain protection from oppressive behavior if they lose power in the future.[244] More generally, they may seek to use international commitments, including treaty ratifications, to gain political advantage at the domestic level in what may be termed a "reverse two-level game."[245]

Even when a country ratifies a treaty and subsequently fails to comply with its terms, it is not necessarily the case that the ratification was disingenuous. Countries may choose to ratify treaties with which they are not already in compliance because they genuinely aspire to improve their practices and they wish to invite international scrutiny of their progress. The practices of such countries may fail to improve for any number of reasons. Those at higher levels of government who are responsible for the ratification may find it difficult to effect change in the actions and decisions of those who actually engage in the violations, including police officers, members of the military, and other low-level state actors.[246] Indeed, this may help explain the often perverse results for my analyses of countries' torture practices—governments may simply find themselves unable to persuade police officers and members of the military to abandon the use of torture. It is also possible that the ratification may take place in the context of a divided government, with one arm of government joining the treaty

---

(1998); Sikkink, *supra* note 83. Others argue that cultural homogeneity is an important source of human rights agreements because states that share a common history, religion, cultural tradition, and values are more likely to agree upon human rights provisions. PAUL SIEGHART, THE INTERNATIONAL LAW OF HUMAN RIGHTS 26-27 (1983); Nisuke Ando, *The Future of Monitoring Bodies—Limitations and Possibilities of the Human Rights Committee, in* CANADIAN HUMAN RIGHTS YEARBOOK 1991-1992, at 169, 171-72 (1992); Jack Donnelly, *International Human Rights: A Regime Analysis,* 40 INT'L ORG. 599, 638 (1986). Yet others offer historical explanations for the appeal of human rights. ANDREW DRZEMCZEWSKI, EUROPEAN HUMAN RIGHTS CONVENTION IN DOMESTIC LAW 220 (1983); John H. Whitfield, *How the Working Organs of the European Convention Have Elevated the Individual to the Level of Subject of International Law,* 12 ILSA J. INT'L L. 27, 31 (1988). Regardless of the source to which they point, however, they all agree on one fundamental point: Human rights have an appeal that generates genuine commitment.

244. *See* Moravcsik, *supra* note 25.

245. This would entail something of a reversal of the relationship described by Robert D. Putnam in his seminal article, Robert D. Putnam, *Diplomacy and Domestic Politics: The Logic of Two-Level Games,* 42 INT'L ORG. 427 (1988). This reversal is further explored in my work in progress on human rights treaty formation. *See* Hathaway, *supra* note 68.

246. A.W. Brian Simpson points to this difficulty in the context of British compliance with the European Convention on Human Rights. *See* SIMPSON, *supra* note 9.

with a true desire to meet its terms but the other refusing to implement the changes required to follow through on the commitment.

The argument presented here therefore does not hinge on the assumption that countries will not comply, or do not intend to comply, with a treaty's requirements; rather, it relies on the fact that, for whatever reason, they may fail to do so and are not only unlikely to be sanctioned as a result but are likely to receive an expressive benefit regardless of their actual practices. Indeed, human rights treaties offer countries an expressive benefit precisely because at least some countries that ratify the treaties actually meet their terms. If every country that ratified a human rights treaty thereafter failed to comply with it, ratification of the treaty would likely cease to offer countries any expressive benefit. Because large numbers of countries do actually comply with the terms of the human rights treaties they ratify (as we have seen, countries that ratify human rights treaties do generally have better ratings on average than those that do not), and because it is difficult to determine which countries have met their treaty obligations and which have not, every country that ratifies receives an expressive benefit from the act of ratification, albeit one that is discounted to take into account the possibility that the country will fail to meet the treaty obligations it has accepted.[247]

This argument throws new light on institutional theories of treaty compliance. As noted in Subsection I.A.2, institutional theorists must rely on the indirect sanction of reputational effects of treaties as the primary anchor for human rights treaty compliance for all countries but those for which compliance is costless.[248] Yet, thus far, institutional scholars have not considered the indirect benefits of treaty ratification—the position-taking and signaling effects discussed above. If countries may obtain reputational benefits from ratifying some treaties while suffering little reputational cost from failing to observe the obligations assumed, countries may be substantially more likely to fail to comply with their treaty obligations. Indeed, it is possible that the expressive benefit of a treaty is at its greatest for precisely those countries not already in compliance with the treaty— those countries may have more to gain, and perhaps less to lose, than those with good practices and hence good reputations.[249] In assuming that

---

247. This situation is unlike the used car context analyzed in George A. Akerlof, *The Market for "Lemons": Qualitative Uncertainty and the Market Mechanism*, 84 Q.J. ECON. 488 (1970). Akerlof argued that due to quality uncertainty in the used car market, good used cars may no longer be sold. *Id.* In the treaty ratification context, however, the cost of the good to the "seller" has an inverse relationship to the quality of the "good." That is, the cost of ratification is likely lower for many of the countries that intend to comply with the requirements of the treaty. Thus, the discounting of the expressive benefit does not lead such countries to stop "selling" the good product (i.e. ratifying the treaties with the intention of actually complying with them).

248. *See supra* text accompanying notes 52-53.

249. *See infra* note 256.

2012   The Yale Law Journal   [Vol. 111: 1935

noncompliance will be detected, institutionalists have overestimated the indirect costs of noncompliance in treaties for which monitoring is minimal. As a result, institutional scholars' cost-benefit calculus for treaties that exhibit these characteristics overpredicts compliance. Where joining treaties might be expected to bring reputational benefits and where monitoring of the compliance with those treaties is minimal, institutional theorists ought to adjust their expectations regarding indirect sanctions and benefits accordingly.

Relatedly, the perspective on human rights treaties presented here provides an interesting twist on the claim by Daniel Farber that human rights protection acts as a "signal" that encourages investment in the country.[250] Farber argues that contrary to Richard Posner's claim that poor countries can ill afford to protect human rights because costly and ambitious legal reforms divert resources from projects more directly linked to economic growth, human rights protection can *encourage* economic growth.[251] Human rights protection, Farber explains, requires prioritizing long-term over short-term benefits.[252] A decision by a government to protect human rights thus indicates to investors that the government has a low discount rate and is therefore less likely to engage in expropriation.[253] Countries that make this signal of human rights protection encourage investment and thereby spur economic growth. But Farber's "rights as signals" argument assumes that the only way in which countries can signal to investors a commitment to human rights is actually to protect and enforce those rights. This does not take into account the problem of imperfect information about country practices, which is especially strong in the area of human rights. Because it is difficult to obtain information about human rights practices, investors are likely to look to obvious and readily discoverable indications of a country's human rights record in considering where to invest. One of these indicators is, as Farber points out, the existence of a constitution.[254] Another such indicator is membership in the major international and regional human rights treaty regimes, because the fact of ratification is highly public and easy to interpret. Actual protection or enforcement of rights—about which it can be difficult to obtain information—may therefore be less likely to be rewarded than the

---

250. Daniel A. Farber, Rights as Signals (Nov. 2, 2000) (unpublished manuscript, on file with author).

251. *Id.* at 1-8.

252. *Id.* at 15-18.

253. *Id.* at 23-26.

254. The adoption of a constitution no more guarantees that the rights defined therein will be enforced than does the adoption of a treaty. Many countries have good laws and constitutions that are not enforced. As Ann and Robert Seidman have spent decades demonstrating, this is not mere coincidence. ANN SEIDMAN ET AL., LEGISLATIVE DRAFTING FOR DEMOCRATIC SOCIAL CHANGE (2001) (providing a guide for legislative drafting that demonstrates how to write enforceable laws).

expression of a commitment to human rights, an expression that can be effectively made through the simple act of joining a treaty.[255]

The recognition of the dual roles of treaties helps explain the paradoxical findings of my analyses. If the expressive and instrumental roles of human rights treaties are divorced from one another (so that a country can express its willingness to be bound by a treaty by ratifying it and then fail to abide by its requirements) and if there is substantial external pressure on countries to conform to human rights norms, one would expect treaty ratification to be associated with regular noncompliance, which is of course what the evidence suggests. Indeed, because human rights treaties offer countries rewards for positions rather than effects, ratification of treaties can serve to offset pressure for real change in practices. This might help explain why we see evidence of a less linear relationship between human rights practices and treaty ratification than we would expect if the instrumental function of treaties held sway. Countries with worse human rights practices face greater potential costs of joining a treaty to the extent that they expect it to be monitored and enforced. But they also stand to gain more from the expression of adherence to the treaty, particularly where they are under external pressure to exhibit their commitment to human rights norms. At the same time, they may have less reputational capital to lose. If countries with worse human rights practices also have worse reputations for law-abidingness than those with better practices, they may be more willing to join treaties with which they are not certain they will be able to comply.[256] These cross-cutting pressures may well help account for the results of my analyses: Countries with worse human rights ratings often ratify treaties at higher rates than those with better ratings, and human

---

255. Signaling arguments generally assume that in order for an act to carry a signaling effect, it must entail real costs. *See, e.g.,* ERIC A. POSNER, LAW AND SOCIAL NORMS 19 (2000) ("Signals reveal type if only the good types, and not the bad types, can afford to send them, and everyone knows this."); Eric A. Posner, *The Strategic Basis of Principled Behavior: A Critique of the Incommensurability Thesis,* 146 U. PA. L. REV. 1185 (1998) (exploring the difference between actors' public representations and their actual behavior); *see also* Simmons, *supra* note 4, at 324 (arguing that states submit to International Monetary Fund obligations as a "signaling device . . . to convince private market actors as well as other governments of a serious intent to eschew the proscribed behavior," and thereby obtain "benefits of good standing in the international economic community"). Because I claim that countries that ratify treaties need not intend to carry out the requirements of the treaty, ratification would appear not to meet this condition. Assuming, however, that ratification does entail costs for some actors—those that actually do carry out a treaty's terms—and because it is difficult or impossible to distinguish these actors from those for whom ratification is virtually costless, ratification continues to issue a message, though perhaps not a signal as this literature would usually define it.

256. Conversely, countries with good practices and good reputations may be more reluctant to join treaties with which they are not certain they will be able to comply. Indeed, this may partially explain the United States's reluctance to join international human rights treaties. It may be highly risk-averse to being identified as failing to comply with human rights treaties to which it has committed. This dynamic will be explored further in a work in progress. *See* Hathaway, *supra* note 68.

2014   The Yale Law Journal   [Vol. 111: 1935

rights treaty ratification is often associated with worse ratings than otherwise expected.

In this light, it is also understandable that a perverse relationship between human rights treaties and countries' human rights ratings is sometimes found in more entrenched areas of human rights. The treaties prohibiting genocide and torture, which are nonderogable norms of international law,[257] impose little additional legal obligation on countries that are parties, because all countries are already bound under customary international law to respect the rights covered in the treaty. Joining these treaties thus entails only acceptance of relatively minimal additional reporting requirements. At the same time, the benefits of making a strong expression of adherence to the treaty norms can be substantial; the government of a country that is under pressure to adhere to international norms can use membership in the relevant treaty regime as evidence of its commitment to abide by the norms the treaty embodies. Because monitoring is imperfect and enforcement often minimal, any gap between expression and action is unlikely to be made public. For these reasons, we expect and indeed find evidence that in entrenched areas of human rights, treaty ratification by individual countries is more likely than in less entrenched areas of human rights to serve as a substitute for actual improvements in human rights practices.[258]

This same dynamic may provide at least a partial explanation for the empirical findings regarding the Optional Protocol to the Covenant of Civil and Political Rights and Article 21 to the Torture Convention. Both of these provisions provide for additional enforcement provisions that are binding only on treaty parties that opt in. The Optional Protocol provides that state parties that accept the Protocol must recognize the competence of the Human Rights Committee to receive and consider communications from other state parties alleging a violation by the state party of any rights set forth in the Convention.[259] Article 21 to the Torture Convention provides that an acceding state party must recognize the competence of the Committee Against Torture to receive and consider communications from other state parties indicating that it is not fulfilling its obligations under the

---

257. *See* sources cited *supra* note 120.

258. This argument provides an interesting twist on Thomas Franck's claim that "symbolic validation" is an important determinant of legitimacy and hence of whether a law will be met with compliance. *See* FRANCK, *supra* note 87, at 34-38. Although the characteristics that indicate symbolic validation—including ritual and pedigree—may lead countries to conform their practices to the principle that is validated, treaties possessing these characteristics are not necessarily more likely to enjoy high rates of compliance. Indeed, the argument of this Article is that the opposite may be true: Countries may be more likely to use such treaties to offset preexisting pressure for change in practices.

259. Optional Protocol, *supra* note 163, art. 1, 999 U.N.T.S. at 302.

Convention.[260] It exhibits nearly identical ratification patterns to Article 22 of the same Convention, which provides for an individual complaint mechanism similar in form to that put into effect in the Optional Protocol.[261] Although in principle these provisions establish much stronger enforcement mechanisms than the treaties as a whole, in practice they tend not to be particularly effective. Although the Protocol covers over one billion people, current estimates are that the Human Rights Committee can hear only about thirty complaints a year—clearly an insufficient number to establish a meaningful deterrent—and does not have the resources or mandate to follow up reliably and effectively on its recommendations.[262] Similarly, in the first thirteen years the Torture Convention was in force, the Committee Against Torture received 154 individual complaints, which resulted in thirty-three final views, of which sixteen found violations.[263] The state-to-state complaint procedure established under Article 21 has yet to be used.[264]

Because the Optional Protocol and Article 21 include somewhat stronger enforcement mechanisms, the expressive and instrumental roles of the provisions are less easily segregated. As a consequence, we would expect less frequent use of the expressive aspect of these provisions by countries that have little intention of complying with their requirements. The empirical evidence seems to bear out this expectation. Although the Optional Protocol and Article 21 are not associated with better ratings for the group of countries as a whole than otherwise expected (the results for these treaty variables are insignificant), they are also not associated with worse ratings.[265] This result is particularly noteworthy for Article 21, as ratification of the Torture Convention itself is associated with worse ratings.[266] Moreover, the comparison of ratification rates at various levels of human rights ratings demonstrates that noncompliance is lower for these

---

260. Torture Convention, *supra* note 51, art. 21, S. TREATY DOC. NO. 100-20, at 26, 1465 U.N.T.S. at 118-20.

261. *Id.* art. 22, S. TREATY DOC. NO. 100-20, at 27, 1465 U.N.T.S. at 120.

262. INTERNATIONAL HUMAN RIGHTS IN CONTEXT, *supra* note 101, at 740-41 (providing an overview of the current status of the individual complaint procedure under the Optional Protocol and noting that although the Committee had requested follow-up information with respect to the 253 cases in which it had found violations, it had received information with regard to only 152 of these cases); Henry J. Steiner, *Individual Claims in a World of Massive Violations: What Role for the Human Rights Committee?*, *in* THE FUTURE OF UN HUMAN RIGHTS TREATY MONITORING, *supra* note 238, at 15, 33 (noting that the current capacity of the Human Rights Committee offers "slender support for the rule of law").

263. INTERNATIONAL HUMAN RIGHTS IN CONTEXT, *supra* note 101, at 777.

264. *Id.* at 776 (noting that no interstate complaint has ever been brought under any of the UN treaty-body procedures).

265. *See* Table 3, *supra* Section II.C. Indeed, ratification of the Optional Protocol by full democracies is associated with *better* Civil Liberty ratings than expected. *See* Table 5, *supra* Section II.C.

266. *See* Table 3, *supra* Section II.C. The evidence is not unambiguously positive, however, as ratification of Article 21 by full democracies is associated with worse Torture ratings than expected. *See* Table 5, *supra* Section II.C.

provisions than for the treaties of which they are a part: Ratification rates among countries with the worst ratings are at or nearly at their lowest levels.[267]

The dual roles of treaties might also help explain what is perhaps the most puzzling of the empirical findings: Ratification of regional human rights treaties is relatively frequently associated with worse human rights ratings than would otherwise be expected. Ratification of regional human rights treaties may be more often and more markedly associated with worse human rights ratings than is ratification of universal human rights treaties because regional political and economic interdependence creates greater incentives for countries to express their commitment to community norms even when they are unable or unwilling to meet those commitments. In the regional context, the need to be an accepted member in what Chayes and Chayes term the "complex web of international arrangements" is particularly strong, as membership brings with it an array of economic and political benefits, and exclusion poses dangers.[268] For this reason, the sanction for violating regional international norms—the "'exclusion from the network of solidarity and cooperation'"—is particularly threatening.[269] Indeed, Beth Simmons's finding that governments' compliance with the IMF's Articles of Agreement is positively influenced by the compliance behavior of others in the region suggests that countries care a great deal about the practices and commitments of their neighbors.[270] Chayes and Chayes fail to note, however, that the threat of alienation may sometimes be soothed not only by actual compliance, but also by relatively toothless expressions of adherence to the relevant norm of international law. Where, as is often the case in the area of human rights, actual changes in practices are extremely costly and difficult to perceive, and treaty ratification is relatively costless and immediately apparent, ratification may be used to offset pressure for real change.

Of course, regional treaties do tend to include stronger enforcement and monitoring mechanisms than do universal treaties, and therefore the expressive and instrumental functions of the treaties should be more difficult to separate. The European Convention on Human Rights and the American Convention on Human Rights both put in place courts that can hold party states that accept the court's jurisdiction accountable for violations of rights established by the treaties,[271] and the treaties contain

---

267. *See* Figures 2-4, *supra* Section II.B.

268. CHAYES & CHAYES, *supra* note 1, at 27.

269. *Id.* (quoting ROBERT D. PUTNAM, MAKING DEMOCRACY WORK: CIVIC TRADITIONS IN MODERN ITALY 183 (1993)).

270. *See* Simmons, *supra* note 2, at 832.

271. *See* American Convention on Human Rights, *supra* note 141, ch. VIII, 1144 U.N.T.S. at 157-60 (establishing the Inter-American Court of Human Rights); *id.* art. 62, 1144 U.N.T.S. at 159 (providing that the Court has jurisdiction only if the state party whose conduct is at issue has

individual and state-to-state complaint mechanisms (parties to the American Convention must agree separately to the state-to-state complaint mechanisms in order to be subject to them).[272] Moreover, there are many examples of changes in law or practice by parties to the European Convention in response to decisions by the European Court of Human Rights.[273]

Yet although the regional treaty mechanisms are much stronger than those in the universal treaties, they nonetheless leave substantial room for noncompliance, in part because the strongest features are relatively infrequently used. Indeed, although the regional treaties vary to some degree in the stringency of their enforcement mechanisms, the better predictor of the impact of treaty ratification on practices is the emphasis the regional organization places on strong human rights records as a condition of membership. Although a clean human rights record was only recently made an explicit condition of membership by the European Union,[274] it has

---

entered into a special agreement or declared that it recognizes as binding, ipso facto, the jurisdiction of the Court on matters relating to interpretation of the Convention); European Convention on Human Rights, *supra* note 67, § 2, 213 U.N.T.S. at 234 (establishing the European Court of Human Rights).

272. American Convention on Human Rights, *supra* note 141, art. 45, 1144 U.N.T.S. at 155 (providing that states must make an additional declaration accepting the competence of the Commission to hear allegations by another state party against them); *id.* art. 44, 1144 U.N.T.S. at 155 (providing that any person or group of persons or any legally recognized nongovernmental entity may lodge a petition with the Commission containing denunciations or complaints of a violation by a state party); European Convention on Human Rights, *supra* note 67, art. 24, 213 U.N.T.S. at 236 (providing that any party to the Convention may refer to the Commission any alleged breach of the provisions of the Convention by any other party); *id.* art. 25, 213 U.N.T.S. at 236 (permitting individual applications to the Commission from any person, nongovernmental organization, or group of individuals claiming to be the victim of a violation by a state party).

273. *See* Robert Blackburn & Jorg Polakiewicz, *Preface* to FUNDAMENTAL RIGHTS IN EUROPE: THE EUROPEAN CONVENTION ON HUMAN RIGHTS AND ITS MEMBER STATES, 1950-2000, at ix, ix (Robert Blackburn & Jorg Polakiewicz eds., 2001) (providing a "detailed study of the practical effect of the [European] Convention [on Human Rights] upon and within the domestic legal and governmental systems of thirty-two of its member countries"). Perhaps the best-known example (at least in the United States) of a European Court of Human Rights case that precipitated a change in the domestic policy of a European Union member is *Lustig-Prean v. United Kingdom*, App. No. 31417/96, 29 Eur. H.R. Rep. 548, 572-87 (1999), which held that the discharge of two British nationals from the Royal Navy on the sole ground that they were homosexual violated Article 8 of the European Convention. Less than a year after the decision was rendered, the U.K. began permitting persons who are openly homosexual to serve in the British Armed Services. *See* T.R. Reid, *British Military Lifts Restrictions on Gays*, SUN-SENTINEL (Ft. Lauderdale), Jan. 13, 2000, at 14A.

274. Treaty of Amsterdam Amending the Treaty on European Union, the Treaties Establishing the European Communities and Certain Related Acts, Oct. 2, 1997, 1997 O.J. (C 340) 1 (entered into force May 1, 1999) [hereinafter Amsterdam Treaty]. The Amsterdam Treaty amended the Treaty on European Union Article 49 (formerly Article O) to require new member states to demonstrate respect for the principles of Article 6(1) of the Treaty on European Union in order to accede to the Union. *See* Treaty on European Union, Oct. 2, 1997, art. 49, 1997 O.J. (C 340) 145 [hereinafter Treaty on European Union]. The Amsterdam Treaty also amended the Treaty on European Union to establish a procedure whereby some membership rights in the EU can be suspended if a "serious and persistent breach" of human rights is found in a member state. Treaty on European Union, *supra*, art. 7, 1997 O.J. (C 340) at 154.

been an implicit membership issue for the EU at least since the 1970s.[275] It is also a condition of membership for the Council of Europe.[276] Membership in the OAS is open to all nation-states in the Americas,[277] but joining the organization requires signing the Charter of the OAS, which carries with it an ill-defined but nonetheless binding obligation not to violate the human rights of one's own nationals.[278] By contrast, the Charter of the Organization of African Unity makes virtually no mention of human rights, nor is the human rights record of a country relevant to membership.[279] Although the African Charter on Human Rights has much weaker enforcement mechanisms than its European and American counterparts,

---

275. *See* GEORGE A. BERMANN ET AL., EUROPEAN UNION LAW (2d ed. forthcoming 2002) (manuscript at 252, on file with author) (noting that in 1993, the European Council decided at Copenhagen that "membership requires that the candidate country has achieved stability of institutions guaranteeing democracy, the rule of law, human rights and respect for and protection of minorities"); Andrew Williams, *Enlargement of the Union and Human Rights Conditionality: A Policy of Distinction?*, 25 EUR. L. REV. 601, 602 (2000) ("Prior to . . . the 1980s, there was little evidence of an explicit human rights conditionality applied to potential members of the European Union. However, as entry was possible only through the unanimous approval of all the existing Member States, it was perhaps clear that any applicant for membership had to ascribe to the fundamental principles of the Union which since at least the early 1970s had included respect for human rights." (footnotes omitted)). For example, Turkey's bid to join the EU was rejected in 1997, in part because of its poor human rights record. *See* Stephen Kinzer, *Europeans Shut the Door on Turkey's Membership in Union*, N.Y. TIMES, Mar. 27, 1997, at A13 (quoting the German Foreign Minister as stating that Turkey did not qualify for membership because of its record on "human rights, the Kurdish question, relations with Greece and of course very clear economic questions"). Indeed, since 1998, the European Commission has begun producing reports on the progress of applicant nations toward accession in which they detail, among other things, the human rights records of the applicants. Tellingly, the section of the report that covers human rights always begins with an overview of the human rights treaties that the applicant country has ratified. It then details relevant changes in the country in the last year, focusing largely on legal changes and less on actual state practices. *See* Comm'n on Progress Towards Accession, Progress Reports (Oct. 13, 1999), *at* http://europa.eu.int/comm/enlargement/report_10_99/index.htm.

276. The Statute of the Council of Europe now effectively requires states to ratify the European Convention on Human Rights as a condition of membership in the Council. The Statute of the Council of Europe provides that "[e]very Member of the Council of Europe must accept the principles of the rule of law and the enjoyment by all persons within its jurisdiction of human rights and fundamental freedoms." Statute of the Council of Europe, May 5, 1949, art. 3, 87 U.N.T.S. 103, 106. Accession to the Council therefore may often require countries to enact legislative changes (for example, abolish the death penalty) and satisfy experts operating on behalf of the Council that the country meets minimum human rights standards.

277. *See* Charter of the Organization of American States, as Amended by the Protocols of Buenos Aires and Cartagena De Indias; the Protocol of Amendment of Washington; and the Protocol of Amendment of Managua, June 10, 1993, art. 4, S. TREATY DOC. NO. 103-22 (1994), 33 I.L.M. 981, 990 ("All American States that ratify the present Charter are Members of the Organization.").

278. *See id.* art. 3, § k, 33 I.L.M. at 990 ("The American States proclaim the fundamental rights of the individual without distinction as to race, nationality, creed, or sex."); *id.* art. 3, § i, 33 I.L.M. at 990 ("Social justice and social security are bases of lasting peace."); *id.* art. 44, 33 I.L.M. at 994 (enumerating various human rights that member states are expected to observe and respect); THOMAS BUERGENTHAL ET AL., PROTECTING HUMAN RIGHTS IN THE AMERICAS 26 (1982).

279. *See* Charter of the Organization of African Unity, May 25, 1963, 479 U.N.T.S. 39 (making virtually no mention of human rights); *id.* arts. I, IV, 479 U.N.T.S. at 72, 74 (stating that membership in the OAU is open to all "independent sovereign African State[s]").

ratification of the Charter is less often associated with worse human rights ratings than would otherwise be expected.[280] Thus, it is possible that the heightened external pressure to demonstrate adherence to human rights norms that is found in the regional context, especially in Europe and to a lesser extent in the Americas, leads nations to join regional human rights treaties at higher rates even when they do not intend, or are unable, to implement them fully, despite those treaties' stronger enforcement and monitoring provisions. Moreover, ratification of regional treaties may cause a significant lessening of external human rights-related pressure, thereby leading ratifying countries to make fewer real improvements in their practices than they might otherwise have made.

Finally, the theory helps us understand why democracies that have ratified human rights treaties may be more likely to have better practices than would otherwise be expected and less likely to engage in large numbers of human rights violations if they have ratified the relevant human rights treaty. The theory developed here portrays states as sometimes willing to view treaty ratification as an expressive tool that does not necessarily entail an intention to abide by a treaty's requirements. Such disingenuousness is, however, less likely in democracies, not only because democracies are arguably more likely to have a true normative commitment to the principles embedded in the treaties but also because democratic governments will likely find it difficult to engage in expressions that are inconsistent with their actions. This helps place the liberalist claims that democracies are more likely to abide by their treaty commitments in a broader context. As liberalists note,[281] liberal democracies contain powerful domestic interest groups that mobilize to pressure their governments to comply with their international legal obligations. In countries with an independent court system, the courts may also offer a forum for those seeking to obtain enforcement of treaty commitments. And the independent news organizations found in most such democracies can divine and expose failures of a government to meet its obligations, thus reducing any expressive benefits to be gained from insincere ratification of a treaty. Hence, democracies in general have a more difficult time divorcing the expressive function of treaties from the instrumental, and are therefore less likely to exhibit high rates of noncompliance when they have ratified a treaty.[282]

---

280. *See* Table 4, *supra* Section II.C.

281. *See supra* text accompanying notes 61-65.

282. One might hypothesize that democracies are less likely to ratify treaties and then fail to comply with them because democracies are simply less likely to ratify treaties in general, largely because democratic institutions create significant barriers to ratification. The assumption upon which this hypothesis rests, however, may not be entirely accurate: As Figures 1-5, *supra* Section II.B, demonstrate, democracies are often more, rather than less, likely to ratify human rights treaties than the group of countries as a whole.

2020   The Yale Law Journal   [Vol. 111: 1935

In sum, treaties shape behavior not simply by influencing tangible benefits and not simply because they create legitimate legal obligations, but also by providing nations with a powerful expressive tool. Where, as is usually the case in the area of human rights, there is little monitoring or enforcement, combined with strong pressure to comply with norms that are embodied in treaty instruments, treaty ratification can serve to offset, rather than enhance, pressure for real change in practices. Only by recognizing that treaties operate on an expressive as well as on an instrumental level can we fully understand observed compliance.

IV. LOOKING AHEAD: CAN TREATIES MAKE A DIFFERENCE?

Understanding the dual nature of human rights treaties can help us better understand the relationship between human rights treaty ratification and human rights practices. External pressure on countries to demonstrate a commitment to human rights norms creates strong incentives for countries to engage in favorable expressive behavior by ratifying human rights treaties. But because human rights treaties are generally only minimally monitored and enforced, there is little incentive for ratifying countries to make the costly changes in actual policy that would be necessary to meet their treaty commitments. Given this, it is perhaps not so surprising that we find the patterns we do in the empirical analysis. Ratifying a human rights treaty can relieve pressure for change imposed by international actors, who may rely more heavily on positions than effects in evaluating countries' records. This reduction in pressure may in turn lead a country that ratifies to improve its practices less than it otherwise might. This dynamic may be stronger in the regional context because regional political and economic interdependence generates greater external pressure on countries to exhibit a commitment to human rights norms. When countries ratify regional treaties, therefore, the falloff in external pressure for real improvement in practices may be greater and the reduction in the pace of real improvement may consequently also be greater. Finally, the strongest democracies may be more likely to adhere to their treaty obligations because the existence of internal monitors makes it more difficult for such countries to conceal a dissonance between their expressive and actual behavior or because liberal democracies have a true normative commitment to the aspirations embedded in the human rights treaties.

What does all this imply about the future of human rights treaties? We must not jump to conclusions about the worth of human rights treaties based solely on the quantitative analysis above. Even if accurate, the results do not preclude the possibility that human rights treaties have a favorable impact on human rights. Although countries that ratify human rights treaties on the whole appear not to have better human rights practices than would otherwise be expected, treaties may have broader positive effects not captured by the analysis. Treaties may lead to more aggressive enforcement by UN Charter-based bodies, which may take action against ratifiers and nonratifiers alike. And human rights treaties and the process that surrounds their creation and maintenance may have a widespread effect on the practices of *all* nations by changing the discourse about and expectations regarding those rights. The expressive function of treaties, after all, has two aspects: It expresses the position both of the individual nation-state and of the community of nations with regard to the subject of the treaty. Although the individual expression need not be consistent with the intentions of the country to put the requirements of the treaty into effect, the collective expression of a series of countries may have genuine effect. Indeed, when a treaty gains a sufficient following, it is generally viewed as expressing what conduct is and is not acceptable to the community of nations. The treaty can thus influence individual countries' perceptions of what constitutes acceptable behavior.[283]

What is important to note—and the reason that this effect would not be detected in the empirical analysis—is that this influence can be felt by countries regardless of whether they ratify the treaty or not. All countries, having received the message transmitted by the creation and widespread adoption of a treaty, are arguably more likely to improve their practices or at least less likely to worsen them than they would otherwise have been. Anecdotal evidence lends support to this view, as observance of the norms embodied in many human rights treaties has come to be seen as an important facet of good international citizenship in the post-World War II period. It is worth noting, however, that the empirical analysis does not offer support for this intuition.[284] Net of other factors that seem to have improved human rights practices over time, the general direction of change in countries' human rights ratings during the time period analyzed, as measured by the trend variable, does not show consistent upward movement across all the areas of human rights, much less consistent statistically significant upward movement. Whether treaties have generally favorable effects on practices therefore remains an important subject for further research and analysis.

In addition to this broader positive expressive effect, it is also possible that ratification of human rights treaties has an undetected long-term

---

283. Cassel posits a similar process. *See* Cassel, *Does International Human Rights Law Make a Difference?*, *supra* note 2, at 122 ("Over time, the extent to which international law serves as a useful tool for protection of human rights will depend mainly on its contribution to a broader set of transnational processes that affect the ways people think and institutions behave . . . .").

284. This may be true in part because the data on practices rarely predate the opening of the relevant treaties for signature. If the creation of human rights treaties has a positive impact on discourse, this impact is probably concentrated in the years immediately before and perhaps immediately after they open for signature, years that the data set may not cover.

2022   The Yale Law Journal   [Vol. 111: 1935

positive effect on individual ratifying countries as well. When a country ratifies a treaty, it may do so for purely disingenuous reasons (simply to gain the expressive benefit), for aspirational reasons (because the government or a part thereof is truly committed to the norms embodied in the treaty and wishes to commit the country thereto), or for self-interested reasons (perhaps because political or economic benefits are tied to ratification). Even where ratification of the treaty is not motivated by commitment to the norms embodied in the treaty, the act of ratification and the continued fact of membership in the treaty regime may also serve to slowly transform the country's practices as it gradually internalizes the norms expressed. Indeed, ratification creates an opportunity for those Harold Koh terms "norm entrepreneurs" to begin to provoke interactions aimed at gradual internalization of the norms embodied in the treaty.[285] Yet this process can take decades to lead to tangible change. Because most of my analyses rely on data that cover fewer than two decades, it is possible that I have simply not studied a long enough period to detect this type of long-term change. Or perhaps the reduction in external pressure for improvement that may result from a country's ratification of a treaty initially offsets any gains that may be made through the gradual process of internalization that ratification may set in motion. Or perhaps this positive influence of treaty ratification occurs alongside the negative expressive effect, thus leading to little or no net effect from treaty ratification—which is, indeed, the predominant finding of the quantitative analyses described in Part II. Again, this remains an important subject for future study.

Whatever the outcome of these inquiries, to the extent that noncompliance with many human rights treaties is commonplace, the current treaty system may create opportunities for countries to use treaty ratification to displace pressure for real change in practices. This is a problem that should be addressed. One obvious step toward improvement would be to enhance the monitoring of human rights treaty commitments, the current weakness of which may make it possible for the expressive and instrumental roles of the treaties to work at cross-purposes.[286] Although there is some public information on countries' human rights practices— indeed, that information forms the basis for this study—it is not specifically

---

285. *See* Koh, *Bringing International Law Home, supra* note 102, at 642-63, 646 (discussing the role of norm entrepreneurs in the process of internalization); *see also* Cassel, *Does International Human Rights Law Make a Difference?, supra* note 2, at 122 ("International human rights law also facilitates international and transnational processes that reinforce, stimulate, and monitor these domestic dialogues."); Thomas Risse & Kathryn Sikkink, *The Socialization of International Human Rights Norms into Domestic Practices: Introduction, in* THE POWER OF HUMAN RIGHTS, *supra* note 9, at 1, 5 (arguing that transnational advocacy networks "empower and legitimate the claims of domestic opposition groups against norm-violating governments").

286. For an interesting examination of monitoring of international treaties, see ADMINISTRATIVE AND EXPERT MONITORING OF INTERNATIONAL TREATIES (Paul C. Szasz ed., 1999).

aimed at evaluating compliance with human rights treaty obligations nor is it, as a general matter, well publicized. If failures to live up to treaty commitments were more regularly and widely exposed, it would be costly for countries to express a commitment to human rights norms without actually meeting their treaty obligations. Greater exposure of noncompliance could be achieved in part by further enhancing the roles of existing NGOs. But a comprehensive monitoring system cannot be supplied solely by private organizations, which can do little in the face of the refusal of states to assist or cooperate with their efforts. Revisions of the existing treaty system aimed at exposing and publicizing noncompliance are needed if the reputational costs of noncompliance are truly to be enhanced.

The main method of enforcement and monitoring under the major universal treaties is a largely voluntary system of self-reporting. The bodies cannot assess any real penalties when countries fail to comply with reporting requirements, and these bodies possess insufficient resources to give complete and critical consideration to the reports that are made.[287] At a minimum, therefore, revisions aimed at strengthening the self-reporting system should be considered.[288] Although the specific shape of the reforms can be debated, a few changes are clearly in order.

To begin with, bodies charged with implementing the treaties should be empowered to compel countries to participate in the reporting and monitoring systems to which they have subscribed. These bodies should include independent experts charged with scrutinizing state practices and empowered to engage in independent investigation and fact-gathering regarding relevant state activity. The bodies should provide NGOs with more regular opportunities to participate in the process of evaluating and assessing state practices. Moreover, they ought to make a greater effort to encourage publicity of their conclusions by improving press access and by making available to news organizations information that is readily understood by nonspecialists. Effective follow-up procedures should be in place to assess and assist countries' efforts to improve compliance. More fundamentally, future human rights treaties should be written with a closer eye to effective monitoring. Declarations of rights that are not easily defined and measured, or that are not accompanied by an effective plan for securing true remedies for violations of those rights, may actually be counterproductive.

---

287. *See supra* note 101.

288. *See, e.g.*, BAYEFSKY, *supra* note 101 (examining ways to improve the UN reporting system, in an exhaustive report on the UN human rights treaty system); THE FUTURE OF UN HUMAN RIGHTS TREATY MONITORING, *supra* note 238; Alston, *supra* note 101, ¶¶ 37-79; Dinah Po Kempner, *Making Treaty Bodies Work: An Activist Perspective, in* AM. SOC'Y OF INT'L LAW, *supra* note 2, at 475 (making similar proposals for reform to the UN human rights treaty system from an activist's perspective).

2024   The Yale Law Journal   [Vol. 111: 1935

The findings of this study may also give reason to reassess the current policy of the United Nations of promoting universal ratification of the major human rights treaties.[289] Although universal ratification of a treaty can make a strong statement to the international community that the activity covered by the treaty is unacceptable, pressure to ratify, if not followed by strong enforcement and monitoring of treaty commitments, may be counterproductive. Indeed, it may be worthwhile to develop, consider, and debate more radical approaches to improving human rights through the use of new types of treaty membership policies. If countries gain some expressive benefit from ratifying human rights treaties, perhaps this benefit ought to be less easily obtained. Countries might, for example, be required to demonstrate compliance with certain human rights standards before being allowed to join a human rights treaty.[290] This would ensure that only those countries that deserved an expressive benefit from treaty membership would obtain it. Or membership in a treaty regime could be tiered, with a probationary period during the early years of membership followed by a comprehensive assessment of country practices for promotion to full membership. Or treaties could include provisions for removing countries that are habitually found in violation of the terms of the treaty from membership in the treaty regime.

Reforms aimed at enhancing the effectiveness of treaties through stronger monitoring provisions or tighter membership policies must of course be made with great caution. To the extent that such changes would increase the costs associated with joining treaties, it is possible that states will respond by simply opting out of the international human rights treaty system altogether. It is clear that human rights treaties need not be entirely toothless in order for countries to join them: Although they all have relatively stringent enforcement provisions, well over 100 countries have ratified the Optional Protocol to the Covenant on Civil and Political Rights, nearly fifty have ratified Articles 21 and 22 to the Torture Convention, and all the members of the Council of Europe have ratified the European Convention on Human Rights. Indeed, it is possible that the greater expressive value of membership in a treaty with strict monitoring would offset some of the additional costs associated with membership.

---

289. The policy has been adopted by the United Nations and advocated most prominently by Philip Alston, acting as an independent expert appointed by the Secretary General. *See* Alston, *supra* note 101, ¶¶ 14-36 ("Universal ratification of the six core United Nations human rights treaties would establish the best possible foundation for international endeavors to promote respect for human rights.").

290. This would not be entirely unlike the procedure used by the World Trade Organization (WTO), which requires members to apply for membership and grants accession "on terms to be agreed" between the acceding government and the WTO. *See* Final Act Embodying the Results of the Uruguay Round of Multilateral Trade Negotiations, Apr. 15, 1994, art. XII, Legal Instruments—Results of the Uruguay Round vol. 1, 33 I.L.M. 1125, 1150 (1994).

Nonetheless, significant changes may provoke reactions that could harm, rather than enhance, the human rights treaty system, and hence reformers should proceed carefully.

Regardless of whether or not stronger monitoring and tighter membership policies are put in place, reforms aimed at enhancing countries' capability to comply with human rights treaties ought to be considered as well. The UN and regional organizations could play an important role in furthering treaty compliance and effectiveness if they not only better monitored treaties, but also provided countries with assistance in improving their human rights practices in order to meet treaty requirements. This assistance could include guidance in drafting effective legislation to protect rights and in crafting strategies for overcoming the institutional inertia that lies at the heart of intransigence in countries' human rights practices.[291] It could also include assistance to build internal capacity—to build the institutions required—to carry out the treaties' directives.[292] The United Nations and regional organizations are in a position to ease the transition costs for governments seeking to overcome inertia and implement true change. In making such assistance available while at the same time increasing monitoring, they can better ensure that countries will ratify treaties with the true intention of improving their practices.

In recent decades, faith in the power of international law to shape nations' actions has led to a focus on the creation of international law as a means to achieve human rights objectives. The treaties that have resulted may have played a role in changing discourse and expectations about rights, thereby improving the practices of all nations. Yet, based on the present analysis, ratification of the treaties by individual countries appears more likely to offset pressure for change in human rights practices than to augment it. The solution to this dilemma is not the abandonment of human rights treaties, but a renewed effort to enhance the monitoring and enforcement of treaty obligations to reduce opportunities for countries to use ratification as a symbolic substitute for real improvements in their citizens' lives.

---

291. Indeed, in many respects, the problem of international human rights treaty compliance can be seen as a specific instance of the broader challenge of translating law into social change. This insight is the foundation of decades of work by Ann and Robert Seidman, who have demonstrated that the mere passage of laws guaranteeing rights, without more, is not enough to make those rights reality. *See, e.g.*, SEIDMAN ET AL., *supra* note 254.

292. This is a function that Chayes and Chayes refer to as "capacity-building." CHAYES & CHAYES, *supra* note 1, at 25.

APPENDIX A: LIST OF TREATIES

Short Name of Treaty	Regional Org.[a]	Full Name and Citation of Treaty
Conv. on the Political Rights of Women		Convention on the Political Rights of Women, *opened for signature* Mar. 31, 1953, 27 U.S.T. 1909, 193 U.N.T.S. 135 (entered into force July 7, 1954).
Torture Convention		Convention Against Torture and Other Cruel, Inhuman or Degrading Treatment or Punishment, *opened for signature* Dec. 10, 1984, S. TREATY DOC. NO. 100-20 (1988), 1465 U.N.T.S. 85 (entered into force June 26, 1987).
Article 21		Convention Against Torture and Other Cruel, Inhuman or Degrading Treatment or Punishment, *opened for signature* Dec. 10, 1984, art. 21, S. TREATY DOC. NO. 100-20, at 26-27 (1988), 1465 U.N.T.S. 85, 118-20 (entered into force June 26, 1987).
Article 22		Convention Against Torture and Other Cruel, Inhuman or Degrading Treatment or Punishment, *opened for signature* Dec. 10, 1984, art. 22, S. TREATY DOC. NO. 100-20, at 27-28 (1988), 1465 U.N.T.S. 85, 120 (entered into force June 26, 1987).
Covenant on Civil and Political Rights		International Covenant on Civil and Political Rights, *adopted* Dec. 19, 1966, S. EXEC. DOC. E, 95-2, at 23 (1978), 999 U.N.T.S. 171 (entered into force Mar. 23, 1976).
Optional Protocol		Optional Protocol to the International Covenant on Civil and Political Rights, *adopted* Dec. 19, 1966, 999 U.N.T.S. 302.
Genocide Convention		Convention on the Prevention and Punishment of the Crime of Genocide, *adopted* Dec. 9, 1948, S. EXEC. DOC. O, 81-1 (1949), 78 U.N.T.S 277 (entered into force Jan. 12, 1951).
American Convention on Human Rights	OAS	American Convention on Human Rights, *opened for signature* Nov. 22, 1969, 1144 U.N.T.S. 123 (entered into force July 18, 1978).
American Torture Convention	OAS	Inter-American Convention To Prevent and Punish Torture, *adopted* Dec. 9, 1985, 25 I.L.M. 519 (entered into force Feb. 28, 1987).
European Convention on Human Rights	COE	Convention for the Protection of Human Rights and Fundamental Freedoms, *opened for signature* Nov. 4, 1950, 213 U.N.T.S. 221 (entered into force Sept. 3, 1953).
European Torture Convention	COE	European Convention for the Prevention of Torture and Inhuman or Degrading Treatment or Punishment, *opened for signature* Nov. 26, 1987, Europ. T.S. No. 126, 27 I.L.M. 1152 (entered into force Jan. 2, 1989).
African Charter on Human Rights	OAU	African Charter on Human and Peoples' Rights, *adopted* June 27, 1981, 21 I.L.M. 58 (entered into force Oct. 21, 1986).

[a] Regional treaties are designated by the respective organization: the Organization of American States (OAS), the Council of Europe (COE), or the Organization of African Unity (OAU). Treaties not identified with a region are universal.

APPENDIX B: DATA SOURCES, DEFINITIONS, AND EXPLANATIONS
FOR THE INDEPENDENT VARIABLES

Over the last two decades, a growing body of studies has used quantitative methods to explain human rights practices of countries.[293] The instant study draws upon and builds on these earlier studies by using them and the broader theoretical literature on human rights as the source for an inventory of hypotheses concerning human rights practices.[294] This inventory, in turn, forms the foundation for the control variables used in this work.[295] Below, I detail the definitions of and data sources for each of the control variables. I also discuss the rationale behind the inclusion of several nonsubstantive control variables.

A. *Treaty Variables*

To determine the correlation between treaty ratification and the human rights measures, I include a treaty variable as an independent variable in each of the analyses. I generated the treaty variables using data on treaties filed with the Secretary General of the United Nations from the United Nations Treaty Collection,[296] and on regional treaties from the regional treaty organizations.[297] The results for each treaty variable appear in bold in Tables 8-10 where they are statistically significant. The variable, measured as the sum of the number of years the treaty has been in effect (repeated for each country each year), gives greater weight to the ratification the longer it has been in effect. This makes it possible to take account of changes in behavior that take several years to accumulate.[298] This approach—the

---

293. *See* sources cited *supra* note 185.

294. This strategy of compiling hypotheses is outlined in HUBERT M. BLALOCK, JR., THEORY CONSTRUCTION: FROM VERBAL TO MATHEMATICAL FORMULATIONS (1969), and it is employed in Poe et al., *supra* note 185, at 292.

295. I discuss in greater detail the rationale behind the expectation that these variables will influence countries' human rights policies and the implications of empirical findings regarding their influence on countries' human rights practices in Oona A. Hathaway, Political and Economic Influences on Human Rights Practices: An Empirical Analysis (Jan. 2002) (unpublished manuscript, on file with author).

296. United Nations Treaty Collection, *at* http://untreaty.un.org/English/treaty.asp (last visited Apr. 2, 2002).

297. Org. of Afr. Unity, Status of Ratification, *at* http://www. up.ac.za/chr/ahrdb/ahrdb_statorat.html (last visited Apr. 2, 2002); Org. of Am. States, Inter-American Treaties Approved Within the Framework of the OAS, *at* http://www.oas.org/juridico/english/treaties.html (last visited Apr. 2, 2002); Council of Eur., *at* http://www.coe.int (last visited Apr. 2, 2002); Office of the High Comm'r for Human Rights, Convention Against Torture, Statistical Survey of Individual Complaints Dealt with by the Committee Against Torture (Feb. 20, 2002), *at* http://www.unhchr.ch/html/menu2/8/stat3.htm.

298. Constructing the variables this way has the effect of magnifying changes in country ratings over time, whether positive or negative—which, as I argue in Part II, is appropriate given

2028   The Yale Law Journal   [Vol. 111: 1935

inclusion of a series of control variables along with the treaty variable as independent variables—ensures that any result found for the treaty variable will be independent of the other included factors.

B. *International War*

The data for international war for this study are based upon data compiled by the Center for Systemic Peace (CSP).[299] Under international conflict, I include the events coded as "international event—interstate," which include conflicts between two polities as well as polities "resisting foreign domination (colonialism)."[300] The coding ranges from 0 (no war) to 10 ("extermination and annihilation").[301] Where there was more than one episode of war in a country during the same time period, I added the magnitudes for each to form a single rating number.[302]

C. *Civil or Ethnic War*

The data for civil or ethnic war, like the data for international war, are based upon data compiled by the CSP. Under internal conflict, I include both ethnic conflict—defined as "[c]ivil-intrastate [conflict] involving rival

---

the expectation that treaties will have gradual and cumulative effects on country practices. When I instead operationalize the treaty variables as 0-1 indicators, I find, as expected, many fewer statistically significant results, though all the results that remain significant are significant in the same direction. The coefficients for the Genocide Convention and Torture Convention reported in Table 8 are insignificant when the treaty variable is operationalized as a 0-1 indicator. Similarly, the coefficients for all the regional treaties except the African Charter on Human Rights (without country dummies, with Torture as the dependent variable) are insignificant when I use a 0-1 treaty indicator. (The African Charter shows a coefficient of 0.330, with a standard error of 0.125, which is significant at the 99% level.) For full democracies, the coefficients for Article 21 and the Convention on the Political Rights of Women are insignificant when I use a 0-1 treaty indicator. The coefficients for the Genocide Convention for full democracies (−1.096, with a standard error of 0.381) and for the Torture Convention for full democracies (0.650, with a standard error of 0.235) are significant at the 99% level in the same direction as with a summed treaty variable. I was unable to obtain convergence for ratification of the remaining treaties by full democracies. In only one instance do I find a statistically significant result with a 0-1 indicator that I do not find with a summed treaty variable. When I analyze the Covenant on Civil and Political Rights (for the group of countries as a whole) with the treaty variable as a 0-1 indicator, I find positive statistically significant results. (The coefficient is 0.331, the standard error is 0.096, and the level of statistical significance is 99%.) Thus operationalizing the treaty variable as a 0-1 indicator also suggests (albeit more weakly) that with the exception of fully democratic nations, ratification of human rights treaties by countries is often associated with worse ratings than would otherwise be expected.

299. *See* Monty G. Marshall, Major Episodes of Political Violence, 1946-1999 (Oct. 1, 2000), *at* http://members.aol.com/CSPmgm/warlist.htm.

300. *Id.*

301. *Id.*

302. For more on the coding scheme of the CSP database, see Center for Systemic Peace, Assessing the Societal and Systemic Impact of Warfare: Coding Guidelines, *at* http://members.aol.com/CSPmgm/warcode.htm (last visited Apr. 2, 2002).

political groups"[303]—and civil conflict—defined as "[e]thnic-intrastate [conflict] involving the state agent and a distinct ethnic group."[304] The coding methodology used for this variable is identical to that used for the international war variable.[305]

D. *Population Size*

The source of these data is the *World Development Indicators* CD-ROM.[306] It defines "Population, total" as follows: "Total Population is based on the de facto definition of population, which counts all residents regardless of legal status or citizenship. Refugees not permanently settled in the country of asylum are generally considered to be part of the population of their country of origin."[307]

E. *Population Growth*

This variable is calculated from the total population data in the *World Development Indicators* CD-ROM.[308] It is equal to the percent change in population from the previous year.

F. *New Regime*

This variable is dichotomous, with an indicator of 1 where a regime has been in place for five years or fewer and 0 in all other cases. The data on regime duration are drawn from the "durable" indicator in the Polity IV data set, a database that is widely used and well respected among social scientists.[309]

G. *Democracy*

There has been a rich debate on how best to define and measure democracy.[310] I use the best available comprehensive data on democracy,

---

303. Marshall, *supra* note 299.
304. *Id.*
305. *See supra* text accompanying note 302.
306. WORLD DEVELOPMENT INDICATORS (World Bank CD-ROM, 2000).
307. *Id.*
308. *Id.*
309. *See* Monty G. Marshall & Keith Jaggers, Polity IV Project: Political Regime Characteristics and Transitions, 1800-2000, *at* http://www.bsos.umd.edu/cidcm/inscr/polity/index.htm (last visited Mar. 12, 2002) (including a description of variables and a link to the data set).
310. *See, e.g.,* JOHN D. MAY, OF THE CONDITIONS AND MEASURES OF DEMOCRACY (1973) (cataloguing and critiquing several prior efforts at measuring democracy); ON MEASURING DEMOCRACY (Alex Inkeles ed., 1991) (providing a comprehensive analysis of the challenges

which are found in the Polity IV data set.[311] The Polity project defines democracy, which ranges from 0 (low) to 10 (high), as "general openness of political institutions."[312] The scale is constructed additively using coded data on six separate variables: competitiveness of executive recruitment, openness of executive recruitment, regulation of executive recruitment, constraints on the chief executive, regulation of political participation, and competitiveness of political participation.[313]

H. *Gross National Product per Capita*

The source of these data is the *World Development Indicators* CD-ROM.[314] It defines "GNP per capita (constant 1995 US$)" as follows:

> GNP per capita is gross national product divided by midyear population. GNP is the sum of gross value added by all resident producers plus any taxes (less subsidies) that are not included in the valuation of output plus net receipts of primary income (employee compensation and property income) from nonresident sources. Data are in constant 1995 U.S. dollars.[315]

I. *Global Economic Interdependence*

This indicator measures the percentage of gross domestic product made up by trade. The source of these data is the *World Development Indicators* CD-ROM.[316] It defines "Trade (% of GDP)" as follows: "Trade is the sum of exports and imports of goods and services measured as a share of gross domestic product."[317]

J. *Dependence on Foreign Aid*

This variable measures the percentage of the country's GDP made up by official development assistance, which includes disbursements of loans

---

inherent in measuring democracy); Kenneth A. Bollen, *Issues in the Comparative Measurement of Political Democracy*, 45 AM. SOC. REV. 370, 371-77 (1980) (discussing the controversial aspects and limitations of the then-commonly-used indices of democracy and proposing a revised index of democracy); Kenneth Bollen, *Liberal Democracy: Validity and Method Factors in Cross-National Measures*, 37 AM. J. POL. SCI. 1207, 1208-10 (1993) (examining the definition and measurement of liberal democracy).

311. Marshall & Jaggers, *supra* note 309.

312. Polity IV Dataset Variables List, *at* www.bsos.umd.edu/cidcm/inscr/polity/index.htm (last visited Mar. 12, 2002).

313. *Id.*

314. WORLD DEVELOPMENT INDICATORS, *supra* note 306.

315. *Id.*

316. *Id.*

317. *Id.*

and credits from the World Bank and International Monetary Fund, as well as official country-to-country assistance. The source of the data is the *World Development Indicators* CD-ROM.[318] It defines "Aid (% of GDP)" as follows:

> Official development assistance and net official aid record the actual international transfer by the donor of financial resources or of goods or services valued at the cost to the donor, less any repayments of loan principal during the same period. Aid dependency ratios are computed using values in U.S. dollars converted at official exchange rates.[319]

In the data set, I inserted 0 wherever the World Bank provided no data, on the assumption that the data would likely have been reported if official development aid had been provided, that countries for which there was no entry solely because GDP data were unavailable would be thrown out of the data set in the regression analysis, and that therefore this alteration would not skew the results. (It is apparent that the World Bank CD-ROM leaves the entry blank where no aid was provided, because most of the major industrialized countries have blank entries.)

K. *Economic Growth*

The source of these data is the *World Development Indicators* CD-ROM.[320] It defines "GDP growth (annual %)" as follows:

> Annual percentage growth rate of GDP at market prices based on constant local currency. Aggregates are based on constant 1995 U.S. dollars. GDP measures the total output of goods and services for final use occurring within the domestic territory of a given country, regardless of the allocation to domestic and foreign claims. Gross domestic product at purchaser prices is the sum of gross value added by all resident producers in the economy plus any taxes and minus any subsidies not included in the value of the products. It is calculated without making deductions for depreciation of fabricated assets or for depletion and degradation of natural resources. The residency of an institution is determined on the basis of economic interest in the territory for more than a year.[321]

---

318. *Id.*
319. *Id.*
320. *Id.*
321. *Id.*

2032   The Yale Law Journal   [Vol. 111: 1935

L. *State Failure*

This variable is dichotomous, with an indicator of 1 for any year in which there is a "complete collapse of central regime authority,"[322] and a 0 for any year in which there is not. The variable is drawn directly from the "state failure" indicator in the Polity IV data set.[323]

M. *Country Dummies*

I include in the analyses dummy variables for each country to control for otherwise unaccounted-for sources of variation in the data (omitted variable bias). (I do not include the coefficients in Tables 8-10.) I use the dummy variables because human rights practices may vary from country to country for cultural, historical, or other reasons not otherwise accounted for. The use of country dummies helps address this dimension of omitted variable bias. I run each analysis with and without country dummies, reporting the results without country dummies only if they vary importantly.

N. *Time Trend*

I seek to address a second dimension of omitted variable bias by including a time trend variable as an independent variable. Human rights practices may exhibit trends over time because of improving worldwide standards independent of the treaties, the proliferation of media and communications methods that make it more difficult to obscure human rights violations, the proliferation of nongovernmental organizations dedicated to monitoring countries' human rights practices, and other reasons independent of treaty ratification itself and not otherwise accounted for. A time trend variable is commonly used in time-series estimations to control for this type of variation and is known as the "secular trend" or the "long-term trend." It describes the long-term movements of the dependent variable, y_t. It does not imply that the series always moves in the same direction, but it does indicate an overall directional trend over the entire time period.[324] In economic applications, for example, the time trend is frequently used as a proxy for technical progress. In general, the time trend variable will pick up any time-related factors affecting the dependent variable.[325]

---

322. Polity IV Dataset Variables List, *supra* note 312 (internal quotation marks omitted).
323. Marshall & Jaggers, *supra* note 309.
324. PAUL NEWBOLD, STATISTICS FOR BUSINESS AND ECONOMICS 692 (4th ed. 1995).
325. CHRISTOPHER DOUGHERTY, INTRODUCTION TO ECONOMETRICS 183-84 (1992). An alternative approach would have been to include dummy variables for each year. I chose not to do

O. *Lagged Dependent Variable*

The lagged dependent variable—which is determined by the prior year's human rights rating—is aimed at addressing autocorrelation. When variables display some linear trends (as is of course true here), successive values tend to be fairly close together. One way of modeling such behavior is by means of an autoregression.[326] Here, the inclusion of a lagged dependent variable is effectively a first-order autoregressive scheme. The use of a lagged dependent variable to address autocorrelation in such circumstances is well-accepted practice.[327] Notably, the use of a lagged dependent variable generally does not have a substantial impact on the results for the treaty variable.[328]

---

so not only because this would have taken up 39 additional degrees of freedom, but also because the results would not have detected consistent change in the dependent variable over time. Moreover, worldwide events that are likely to affect human rights practices (such as widespread war, worldwide economic downturn, or the like) are addressed in substantial part by the inclusion of control variables that measure these events more directly.

326. JACK JOHNSTON & JOHN DiNARDO, ECONOMETRIC METHODS 52-53 (4th ed. 1997).

327. *See* Christian Davenport, *Multi-Dimensional Threat Perception and State Repression: An Inquiry into Why States Apply Negative Sanctions*, 39 AM. J. POL. SCI. 683, 698-99 (1995); Poe et al., *supra* note 185, at 306.

328. The results for the treaty variables are statistically significant in the same direction both with and without the lagged dependent variable with only a few exceptions. The coefficient for the Convention on the Political Rights of Women (for the group of countries as a whole) is negative and significant at the 99% level when I omit the lagged dependent variable. The coefficient is −0.001, with a standard error of 0.0004. The coefficient is insignificant, however, when standard errors are adjusted for clustering on country. The coefficient for the American Convention on Human Rights with the Fair Trial dependent variable is negative, but not significant, when I omit a lagged dependent variable (the coefficient is −0.266 and the standard error is 0.127). In the analyses of full democracies' practices, I find a newly significant coefficient for the Covenant on Civil and Political Rights with Civil Liberty as the dependent variable (the coefficient is −0.035, the standard error is 0.013, and the significance level is 99%) when I omit lagged dependent variables.

International Law and Society

2034   The Yale Law Journal   [Vol. 111: 1935

APPENDIX C: CODED DATA AND COMPLETE STATISTICAL RESULTS

TABLE 6. CODED DATA ON TORTURE

Country	85	86	87	88	89	90	91	92	93	94	95	96	97	98	99
Afghanistan	5	5	5	5	5	5	4		4	5	5	4	5	5	5
Albania	3	3	3	2	2	3	2	1	2	2	2	2	2	3	3
Algeria	1	3	3	4	2	3	3	3	5	5	5	5	5	5	5
Angola	3	3	3	3	3	3	3	4	2	2	2	2	4	4	5
Argentina	2	2	2	3	3	3	3	4	2	2	2	2	3	4	4
Armenia								2	2	1	2	2	4	4	4
Australia	1	1	1	1	1	3	3	3	2	3	1	2	3	2	2
Austria	1	1	2	1	1	2	2	2	2	2	2	2	2	2	2
Azerbaijan								3	2	2	4	4	4	4	4
Bahrain	2	3	3	3	3	3			3	3	5	4	3	4	4
Bangladesh	3	3	3	3	3	3	4	4	4	3	5	5	5	5	5
Belarus								2	2	3	4	3	3	2	2
Belgium	1	2	1	1	1	1	1	1	2	1	1	1	1	1	1
Benin	3	3	3	3	3	1	1	1	1	1	1	1	1	1	1
Bhutan	1	1	1	1	1	1	3	5	3	3		3	1	3	2
Bolivia	2	2	3	2	3	3	3	3	3	2	2	2	2	3	3
Bosnia and Herzegovina								4	4	4	5	3	3	3	4
Botswana	1	1	2	3	3	2	1	2	4	3	2	2	2	2	2
Brazil	5	5	5	5	5	5	5	5	4	4	4	4	4	4	5
Bulgaria	3	2	3	4	4	1	1	2	2	2	2	3	3	2	3
Burkina Faso	3	2	3	3	3	3	3	3	3	3	3	3	2	2	2
Burundi	2	2	2	3	3	2	2	4	3	3	3	3	2	3	3
Cambodia (Kampuchea)	5	4	4	4	3	3	2	3	3	3	3	3	4	3	5
Cameroon	2	3	1	2	3	2	4	4	5	4	5	4	3	3	3
Canada	1	1	1	1	1	1	1	2	1	2	2	1	1	1	1
Central African Republic	3	2	2	1	2	3	2	4	2	2	2	3	5	4	3
Chad	5	4	2	3	3	4	4	3	3	3	4	2	4	3	3
Chile	4	3	3	3	3	3	3	3	3	3	3	3	3	3	2
China	1	3	3	3	3	4	4	5	5	5	5	5	3	3	3
Colombia	3	3	3	2	5	5	5	3	5	3	3	4	5	4	3
Comoros	3	3	3	3	3	2	3	1	1	2	1	1	4	2	2
Congo, Republic of	3	3	3	4	3	4	4	2	3	3	3	5	4	3	2
Congo, Democratic Republic of	5	5	4	4	3	2	3	4	5	5	4	4	4	4	4
Costa Rica	1	1	1	1	2	2	1	2	2	2	2	2	2	2	2
Côte D'Ivoire	2	2	2	2	2	3	2	2	2	2	2	3	4	4	4
Croatia								2	3	4	3	1	2	2	2
Cuba	4	4	4	4	3	3	3	4	4	3	3	3	3	2	2
Cyprus	1	1	1	1	1	1	1	2	3	2	2	2	3	2	2
Czechoslovakia	3	3	2	2	2	1	1	1	1	1	2	2	2	2	4
Denmark	1	1	1	1	1	1	2	1	1	2	1	1	1	1	1
Djibouti	3	2	1	2	3	3	4	3	3	2	2	3	3	4	4
Dominican Republic	2	2	2	2	2	2	3	4	2	2	2	4	3	3	3
Ecuador	3	2	3	4	3	5	4	2	3	3	3	3	2	3	3
Egypt	3	3	3	4	4	4	4	4	4	4	5	4	4	4	4
El Salvador	4	3	3	3	4	4	4	3	3	3	3	2	2	2	2
Equatorial Guinea	3	3	4	3	3	5	5	5	5	5	4	4	3	4	3
Eritrea									1	2	2	1	2	2	2
Estonia	4	4	4	4	4	3		2	2	2	2	2	2	2	2
Ethiopia	4	4	4	3	4	4	5	2	2	3	2	2	3	3	2
Fiji	1	1	3	2	2	2	2	2	2	2	2	2	2	2	2
Finland	1	1	1	1	1	1	1	1	1	1	1	1	1	1	1
France	1	1	1	2	2	2	1	1	2	1	2	2	2	2	2
Gabon	2	2	1	3	3	2	3	3	4	4	3	3	3	3	2
Gambia	2	2	2	2	2	2	2	2	2	2	3	3	3	2	2
Georgia								4	5	4	3	4	4	5	4
Germany, United						1	1	1	2	2	2	2	2	2	2
Germany, East															
Germany, West	1	1	2	1	1										
Ghana	3	3	3	3	2	1	2	2	3	2	2	2	2	3	2
Greece	2	1	3	2	3	2	2	1	3	2	3	2	2	2	2
Guatemala	4	3	3	3	2	4	4	3	3	4	4	3	3	3	3
Guinea	2	2	2	3	2	3	3	2	3	3	3	3	4	4	4
Guinea-Bissau	4	3	2	3	3	2	2	3	4	3	3	2	2	4	3
Guyana	3	3	2	2	2	2	2	3	3	2	2	2	2	2	2
Haiti	3	2	3	3	3	4	3	4	4	5	2	4	4	4	4
Honduras	2	2	3	3	3	4	3	3	4	3	3	3	4	3	3
Hungary	1	2	1	1	1	1	1	2	2	2	2	2	2	2	2
Iceland	1	1	1	1	1	1	1	1	1	1	1	1	2	1	1
India	3	4	4	4	4	4	4	4	4	4	5	5	4	4	4

Indonesia	3	3	4	4	4	4	4	4	5	4	3	5	4	4	5
Iran	5	5	5	5	4	3	3	3	3	3	3	3	3	4	4
Iraq	5	5	5	5	5	5	5	5	5	5	5	5	5	5	5
Ireland	2	2	2	2	1	1	1	1	1	2	1	2	2	2	2
Israel	1	1	4	4	4	1	1	1	2	2	3	2	4	4	3
Italy	1	2	3	1	1	1	1	2	2	3	2	2	2	2	3
Jamaica	2	3	3	3	3	4	4	4	4	3	2	2	2	2	3
Japan	1	1	1	1	1	3	3	2	3	3	2	3	3	3	3
Jordan	2	2	3	3	3	1	3	3	3	3	3	3	3	3	3
Kazakhstan								3	1	2	3	3	3	3	3
Kenya	3	3	3	3	3	3	3	3	3	3	3	4	4	4	4
Korea, Republic of	3	3	3	2	3	4	3	3	2	3	3	3	2	3	3
Korea, DPR	4	4	4	4											
Kuwait	2	3	3	3	3	4	4	3	3	3	2	2	2	2	2
Kyrgyzstan								1	1	2	1	2	2	2	2
Laos	2	2	3	2	2	3	1	1	1	2	1	1	1	2	3
Latvia	4	4	4	4	3	3		1	2	2	2	2	2	2	2
Lebanon	3	2	3	4	3	3	2	3	3	3	3	3	3	4	4
Lesotho	2	2	2	3	2	2	2	2	2	3	2	1	2	2	2
Liberia	3	3	3	3	3	5	3	4	4	4	3	3	3	4	3
Libya	4	3	4	4		3	3	3	3	3	3	3	3	3	3
Lithuania	4	4	4	4	4	3		1	2	2	2	2	2	2	2
Luxembourg	1	1	1	1	1	1	1	1	1	1	1	1	1	1	1
Macedonia								2	2	2	2	2	2	2	2
Madagascar	3	3	3	3	3	2	2	1	3	3	3	3	3	3	3
Malawi	2	2	3	2	2	3	3	3	2	2	2	3	2	2	2
Malaysia	1	1	2	2	1	2	1	2	2	2	3	2	2	3	3
Mali	3	3	3	2	3	3	1	1	1	1	2	1	3	3	1
Mauritania	3	1	3	3	4	3	4	5	2	3	3	3	3	2	2
Mauritius	1	1	1	1	1	2	2	2	2	2	2	3	2	2	2
Mexico	3	3	3	3	3	3	5	5	4	3	3	5	5	5	5
Moldova								3	2	2	2	2	2	2	3
Mongolia							1	1	1	2	2	2	2	2	3
Morocco	3	4	3	3	4	3	3	3	3	3	3	3	3	3	3
Mozambique	4	3	3	4	4	3	3	3	3	4	4	4	4	4	3
Myanmar (Burma)	3	3	3	3	4	5	4	3	2	3	4	3	3	4	4
Namibia	3	3	2	3	3	3	3	3	3	2	2	2	2	2	3
Nepal	3	4	5	4	4	4	4	4	3	3	3	4	4	4	4
Netherlands	1	1	1	1	1	1	1	1	1	2	1	1	1	1	1
New Zealand	1	1	1	1	1	1	1	1	1	1	1	1	1	1	1
Nicaragua	4	3	4	4	4	3	3	3	3	3	4	3	3	3	3
Niger	3	2	2	3	2	3	3	2	2	2	1	2	2	1	2
Nigeria	3	1	2	3	3	4	4	5	5	5	5	5	5	5	3
Norway	1	1	1	1	1	1	1	1	1	2	1	1	1	1	1
Oman	1	1	1	2	2	1	2	1	2	2	2	2	2	2	2
Pakistan	5	3	3	4	4	4	4	4	5	5	5	4	5	5	5
Panama	2	2	4	3	4	2	3	3	2	2	2	2	2	2	2
Papua-New Guinea	1	1	1	1	3	3	4	3	3	3	2	3	2	3	3
Paraguay	4	4	3	3	3	4	3	4	3	3	3	3	3	4	4
Peru	4	4	5	4	5	5	4	5	5	5	4	5	5	5	5
Philippines	4	4	4	4	4	4	4	4	4	3	3	3	3	3	3
Poland	3	3	4	3	2	2	2	2	2	2		2	2	2	2
Portugal	1	2	2	1	1	3	2	2	3	2	2	2	1	2	3
Qatar	2	2	1	3	2	1	2	1	1	1	1	1	1	1	1
Romania	4	3	3	3	3	3	3	2	4	2	4	2	3	2	4
Russia (or former USSR)	4	4	4	4	4	4	3	4	3	3	5	4	4	5	5
Rwanda	3	1	1	1	1	2	4	3	4	5	2	2	3	3	3
Saudi Arabia	3	2	4	3	4	4	4	3	3	3	3	3	3	3	3
Senegal	3	2	2	2	3	4	3	3	3	3	3	3	3	3	3
Sierra Leone	3	3	3	3	3	2	2	2	3	3	2	4	4	5	2
Singapore	2	1	3	2	3	2	1	2	3	2	2	2	2	2	2
Slovak Republic								1	1	3	2	2	2	2	2
Slovenia							1	1	1	1	1	1	1	1	1
Somalia	3	3	4	4	3	3	3	4	3	3					
South Africa	3	4	4	4	4	3	3	3	4	4	3	3	3	3	3
Spain	3	3	3	2	1	1	1	2	2	3	4	3	3	3	3
Sri Lanka	3	3	3	4	4	3	4	4	4	5	3	3	3	3	3
Sudan	1	3	3	3	3	5	5	5	5	5	5	5	4	5	3
Swaziland	2	2	2	2	2	2	2	2	3	4	3	4	3	3	3
Sweden	1	1	1	1	2	1	1	1	1	1	2	2	2	2	1
Switzerland	1	1	1	1	1	1	1	1	1	2	1	1	3	4	2
Syria	5	5	4	5	5	5	5	5	5	5	5	5	5	5	5
Tajikistan								3	3	4	4	4	3	4	4
Tanzania	3	4	3	3	4	4	4	4	4	4	4	4	3	3	3
Thailand	2	3	3	3	3	3	3	3	3	3	3	4	2	2	3
Togo	4	5	4	3	4	3		3	4	4	3	3	3	3	3
Tonga							1	1	1	1	1	1	1	1	1
Tunisia	2	2	3	3	3	3	3	4	3	3	2	3	3	4	3
Turkey	5	5	5	3	5	4	4	4	4	4	4	5	5	5	5

Country															
Turkmenistan								2	1	4	4	4	4	4	4
Uganda	4	3	3	3	4	4	4	3	3	3	3	3	3	3	
Ukraine								2	2	3	4	3	3	4	3
United Arab Emirates	1	1	1	3	3	3	1	1	1	1	1	2	2	2	2
United Kingdom	3	2	1	2	1	1	2	3	3	2	2	2	2	2	2
United States															
Uruguay	1	2	1	1	1	2	3	2	3	2	2	2	2	3	2
Uzbekistan								2	3	3	3	4	4	4	4
Venezuela	2	2	3	3	3	4	4	3	5	5	3	3	3	3	4
Vietnam, North															
Vietnam, South															
Vietnam, United	4	4	3	3	2	4	2	2	1	2	2	2		2	2
Yemen, North															
Yemen, South															
Yemen, United	3	3	3	3	3	3	5	3	3	3	2	3	5	4	3
Yugoslavia	3	2	2	4	3	4	4	3	4	4		5	5	5	5
Zambia	3	3	3	3	3	3	2	4	4	4	4	3	3	3	3
Zimbabwe	4	4	3	3	4	4	4	3	2	2	2	2	3	3	3

TABLE 7. CODED DATA ON FAIR TRIALS

Country	85	88	91	94	97
Afghanistan	4	4	4		
Albania	3	3	2	2	2
Algeria	2	1	2	2	3
Angola	3	3	3	3	3
Argentina	2	1	2	3	2
Armenia				2	2
Australia	1	1	1	1	1
Austria	1	1	1	1	1
Azerbaijan				2	3
Bahrain	2	1	3	2	4
Bangladesh	2	4	3	2	3
Belarus				3	3
Belgium	1	1	1	1	1
Benin	3	4	1	2	2
Bhutan	2	2	2	1	3
Bolivia	2	3	4	3	3
Bosnia and Herzegovina					2
Botswana	1	1	1	3	1
Brazil	2	1	3	3	3
Bulgaria	3	3	1	2	2
Burkina Faso	1	3	4	1	2
Burundi	2	2	3	3	3
Cambodia (Kampuchea)	4	3	3	3	3
Cameroon	2	4	2	2	3
Canada	1	1	1	1	1
Central African Republic	1	2	3	2	2
Chad	3	4	2	2	2
Chile	2	2	2	2	1
China	4	4	3	4	3
Colombia	3	3	3	3	3
Comoros	1	1	1	3	1
Congo, Republic of	3	4	2	2	3
Congo, Democratic Republic of	4	4	4	3	3
Costa Rica	1	1	1	1	1
Côte D'Ivoire	1	2	2	3	3
Croatia				2	3
Cuba	3	3	4	3	3
Cyprus	1	1	1	1	1
Czechoslovakia	4	3	2	1	1
Denmark	1	1	1	1	1
Djibouti	2	2	2	2	3
Dominican Republic	2	3	3	3	4
Ecuador	3	3	4	3	4
Egypt	1	2	1	3	3
El Salvador	3	3	3	3	4
Equatorial Guinea	2	3	4	2	2
Eritrea				3	2
Estonia	2	2	2	1	1
Ethiopia	4	4	2	3	3
Fiji	1	1	1	2	1
Finland	1	1	1	1	1
France	1	1	1	1	1
Gabon	2	2	1	3	2
Gambia	1	1	1	3	1
Georgia				3	2
Germany, United			1	1	1
Germany, East	3	3			
Germany, West	1	1			
Ghana	2	3	4	1	3
Greece	1	2	1	2	3
Guatemala	2	2	2	2	2
Guinea	1	2	2	2	2
Guinea-Bissau	2	3	1	3	3
Guyana	1	1	1	2	3
Haiti	3	3	3	3	3
Honduras	2	3	3	2	4
Hungary	2	2	1	2	1
Iceland	1	1	1	1	1
India	1	2	3	4	3
Indonesia	3	3	3	3	3
Iran	4	3	3	3	3
Iraq	2	2	3	3	3
Ireland	1	1	1	1	1

Israel	1	2	2	2	3
Italy	1	2	2	2	2
Jamaica	2	2	2	2	2
Japan	1	1	1	1	1
Jordan	1	2	2	2	3
Kazakhstan				2	3
Kenya	3	3	3	2	3
Korea, Republic of	3	4	2	1	1
Korea, DPR	3	3	3	2	3
Kuwait	1	2	3	2	2
Kyrgyzstan				3	2
Laos	4	4	3	3	3
Latvia	2	2	1	1	2
Lebanon	3	3	3	3	2
Lesotho	1	2	2	2	3
Liberia	3	2		2	2
Libya	4	4	4	3	4
Lithuania	2	2	2	1	1
Luxembourg	1	1	1	1	1
Macedonia				3	1
Madagascar	1	1	3	3	3
Malawi	2	3	4	2	3
Malaysia	2	2	3	3	3
Mali	2	2	2	3	2
Mauritania	3	2	3	3	2
Mauritius	1	1	2	1	1
Mexico	4	3	2	3	3
Moldova				2	2
Mongolia			2	1	1
Morocco	2	3	3	2	2
Mozambique	2	2	4	3	3
Myanmar (Burma)	3	3	4	3	3
Namibia	2	2	3	2	2
Nepal	3	4	2	2	4
Netherlands	1	1	1	1	1
New Zealand	1	1	1	1	1
Nicaragua	4	3	2	3	3
Niger	3	3	2	3	3
Nigeria	2	3	4	3	4
Norway	1	1	1	1	1
Oman	2	3	3	2	3
Pakistan	3	3	4	4	4
Panama	3	4	3	4	4
Papua-New Guinea	1	1	2	1	1
Paraguay	3	4	3	3	2
Peru	2	3	3	3	3
Philippines	3	2	2	3	2
Poland	2	2	3	1	1
Portugal	2	1	1	2	2
Qatar	3	3	3	2	2
Romania	3	3	2	2	1
Russia (or former USSR)	3	3	3	3	4
Rwanda	1	3	3	3	2
Saudi Arabia	2	2	4	4	4
Senegal	1	2	2	3	3
Sierra Leone	3	3	3	3	
Singapore	2	3	4	4	4
Slovak Republic				2	1
Slovenia				1	1
Somalia	4	4		2	3
South Africa	3	4	3	3	1
Spain	1	1	2	2	1
Sri Lanka	2	2	2	2	2
Sudan	1	2	3	3	2
Swaziland	2	2	2	1	1
Sweden	1	1	1	1	1
Switzerland	1	1	1	1	1
Syria	3	4	4	4	4
Tajikistan				3	2
Tanzania	2	3	3	3	3
Thailand	3	3	3	3	2
Togo	3	3	2	2	2
Tonga	1	1	1	1	1
Tunisia	3	2	3	3	2
Turkey	2	2	2	2	2
Turkmenistan				3	3
Uganda	2	3	3	3	4
Ukraine				3	3
United Arab Emirates	2	1	1	1	3

United Kingdom	1	1	1	1	1
United States					
Uruguay	1	1	1	1	3
Uzbekistan				2	3
Venezuela	3	4	3	3	3
Vietnam, North					
Vietnam, South					
Vietnam, United	3	4	4	2	3
Yemen, North	2	2			
Yemen, South	2	2			
Yemen, United			2	2	3
Yugoslavia	2	3	3	3	3
Zambia	2	2	2	2	2
Zimbabwe	2	2	1	2	2

TABLE 8. RELATIONSHIP BETWEEN RATIFICATION OF UNIVERSAL
TREATIES AND HUMAN RIGHTS RATINGS, CONTROLLING
FOR VARIOUS COUNTRY CHARACTERISTICS

Short Treaty Name	Genocide Convention	Genocide Convention (no country dummies)	Torture Convention	Torture Convention (no country dummies)	Article 21	Covenant on Civil and Political Rights	Optional Protocol	Covenant on Civil and Political Rights	Optional Protocol	Convention on the Political Rights of Women
Human Rights Measure	Genocide	Genocide	Torture	Torture	Torture	Fair Trial	Fair Trial	Civil Liberty	Civil Liberty	Percentage of Men in Parliament
Treaty Variable	**0.047*** (0.021)	0.0094 (0.0059)	0.033 (0.020)	**0.021*** (0.010)	0.027 (0.025)	0.030 (0.047)	-0.002 (0.042)	-0.006 (0.008)	0.003 (0.008)	-0.0004 (0.0003)
International war	0.063 (0.086)	0.207** (0.047)	0.101 (0.068)	-0.002 (0.058)	0.097 (0.068)	0.072 (0.096)		-0.0059 (0.068)	-0.004 (0.068)	0.0010 (0.0006)
Civil or ethnic war	0.664** (0.082)	0.387** (0.029)	0.128** (0.033)	0.088** (0.018)	0.125** (0.033)	0.109 (0.070)	0.055 (0.068)	0.103** (0.024)	0.101** (0.024)	0.0005 (0.0005)
Population size	0.006** (0.002)	-0.0006 (0.0003)	-5.0e-6 (0.004)	0.0007** (0.0003)	0.0004 (0.0036)	0.005 (0.008)	0.005 (0.009)	0.0024 (0.002)	0.002 (0.002)	5.12e-6 (1.7e-5)
Population growth	9.08 (8.48)	-6.79 (5.05)	2.87 (5.48)	6.33 (3.31)	2.80 (5.49)	-4.53 (3.85)	-2.70 (4.13)	0.272 (2.96)	0.283 (2.95)	-0.052 (0.156)
New regime	0.096 (0.152)	0.291** (0.112)	-0.064 (0.084)	-0.024 (0.066)	-0.056 (0.082)	-0.275 (0.174)				0.001 (0.002)
Democracy	-0.031 (0.026)	-0.038* (0.018)	-0.049* (0.020)	-0.03** (0.009)	-0.048* (0.020)	-0.085* (0.041)	-0.096* (0.041)	-0.19** (0.019)	-0.19** (0.019)	0.0012** (0.0004)
GNP per capita	0.0003 (0.0003)	-4e-5 (2e-5)	-4.6e-7 (4e-5)	-3e-5** (5e-6)	-5.4e-6 (4e-5)	0.0002 (0.0001)	0.0002 (0.0001)	2e-7 (1e-5)	-1e-6 (1e-5)	-1e-6** (4.3e-7)
Global interdependence	-0.011* (0.006)	-0.005 (0.003)	-0.002 (0.002)	-0.001 (0.001)	-0.001 (0.002)	-0.002 (0.006)	-0.0005 (0.0056)			0.00011 (8e-5)
Aid dependency	0.050* (0.022)	-0.001 (0.008)	0.003 (0.006)	-0.006 (0.003)	0.003 (0.006)	0.003 (0.012)	-0.003 (0.011)	-0.004 (0.005)	-0.003 (0.005)	2e-5 (3e-5)
GDP growth	-0.04** (0.012)	-0.015 (0.009)	-0.002 (0.006)	-0.005 (0.006)	-0.002 (0.006)	-0.001 (0.012)	0.0003 (0.013)			0.0002 (0.0002)
State failure	-0.582 (0.537)	0.188 (0.414)	0.048 (0.359)	-0.178 (0.278)	0.066 (0.355)	-1.73** (0.614)				-0.011 (0.013)
Time	-0.11** (0.021)	-0.04** (0.008)	0.057** (0.014)	0.026** (0.009)	0.054** (0.011)	0.016 (0.046)	0.027 (0.032)	0.0033 (0.006)	-0.0005 (0.005)	-0.0003 (0.0003)
Lagged depend. var.	0.443** (0.086)	0.746** (0.081)	0.541** (0.051)	0.936** (0.044)	0.540** (0.051)	-0.133 (0.105)	-0.139 (0.105)	1.40** (0.069)	1.40** (0.069)	0.778** (0.091)
Constant										0.209 (0.023)
No. of obs.	628	3919	1639	1639	1639	373	373	2739	2739	3019
Log-likelihd.	-387.18	-480.52	-1492.8	-1681.6	-1492.3	-329.75	-334.64	-1996.4	-1996.7	
Chi-squared	6057.43	762.88	28840.12	893.57	24463.74			1980.40	1979.77	
Pseudo R-sq.	0.42	0.51	0.39	0.31	0.39	0.31	0.30	0.61	0.61	0.87

* Statistical significance at 95% level
** Statistical significance at 99% level

TABLE 9. RELATIONSHIP BETWEEN RATIFICATION OF REGIONAL HUMAN RIGHTS TREATIES AND HUMAN RIGHTS RATINGS, CONTROLLING FOR VARIOUS COUNTRY CHARACTERISTICS

Short Treaty Name	American Torture Convention	African Charter on Human Rights	African Charter on Human Rights (no country dummies)	European Torture Convention	American Convention on Human Rights	African Charter on Human Rights	European Convention on Human Rights	European Convention on Human Rights (no country dummies)	American Convention on Human Rights	African Charter on Human Rights	European Convention on Human Rights (no country dummies)
Human Rights Measure	Torture	Torture	Torture	Torture	Fair Trial	Fair Trial	Fair Trial	Fair Trial	Civil Liberty	Civil Liberty	Civil Liberty
Treaty Variable	0.313** (0.096)	-0.007 (0.041)	0.030* (0.014)	0.285 (0.154)	-1.2** (0.36)[a]	0.023 (0.114)	0.341* (0.151)	0.13** (0.04)	0.17** (0.03)	-0.05** (0.02)[a]	0.022 (0.012)
International war	-0.370 (0.727)	0.087 (0.107)	0.018 (0.084)			-2.44** (0.837)			0.776* (0.401)	-0.162 (0.127)	-6.9** (0.27)
Civil or ethnic war	0.233** (0.082)	0.146* (0.060)	0.070* (0.031)	-0.072 (0.307)	0.134 (0.235)	0.053 (0.123)		0.423 (0.356)	0.054 (0.054)	0.170** (0.046)	0.173 (0.109)
Population size	0.015 (0.033)	0.050 (0.036)	0.013** (0.004)	-0.187 (0.117)	0.006 (0.084)	0.037 (0.050)		-0.020 (0.011)	0.049** (0.013)	0.022 (0.016)	-0.001 (0.005)
Population growth	34.1 (33.4)	-1.14 (4.92)	-3.02 (3.79)	-1.28 (36.5)	123.81 (81.46)	-5.43 (4.06)		-380** (101.1)	-18.6 (21.6)	-5.46 (4.19)	8.16 (19.37)
New regime	0.108 (0.181)	-0.016 (0.138)	0.044 (0.116)	0.205 (0.382)	0.178 (0.579)	-0.006 (0.284)		-2.44* (1.10)	-0.167 (0.159)	0.051 (0.133)	0.387 (0.297)
Democracy	0.017 (0.052)	-0.044 (0.031)	-0.07* (0.02)	-0.216 (0.267)	-0.46** (0.15)	-0.019 (0.066)		-1.04** (0.27)	-0.28** (0.047)	-0.21** (0.037)	-0.33** (0.109)
GNP per capita	3e-4 (2e-4)	7e-5 (4e-4)	8e-5 (7e-5)	-3e-4 (1e-4)	8e-4 (7e-4)	-7e-5 (0.001)		-2e-4** (6e-5)	-8e-5 (2e-4)	1e-4 (1e-4)	-2e-5 (2e-5)
Global interdependence	0.003 (0.006)	-3e-4 (0.004)	0.002 (0.002)	0.011 (0.014)	0.030 (0.022)	-0.004 (0.008)		-0.08** (0.02)	-0.001 (0.005)	0.006 (0.004)	-0.009* (0.004)
Aid dependency	-0.003 (0.013)	9e-4 (0.008)	0.003 (0.005)	-0.319 (0.206)	-0.035* (0.017)	0.008 (0.016)		0.179 (0.264)	-3e-4 (0.010)	-0.007 (0.006)	0.317** (0.097)
GDP growth	-0.013 (0.020)	-0.008 (0.011)	-0.011 (0.010)	0.005 (0.026)	0.069 (0.040)	-0.009 (0.018)		-0.030 (0.067)	-0.011 (0.013)	-0.009 (0.006)	-0.061* (0.025)
State failure		0.046 (0.416)	-0.041 (0.324)			-1.88* (0.903)			0.093 (0.352)	0.084 (0.348)	
Time	-0.28** (0.098)	0.038 (0.040)	0.007 (0.019)	-3e-4 (0.128)	1.20** (0.365)	-0.023 (0.111)		0.121 (0.081)	-0.11** (0.036)	-0.010 (0.011)	0.027* (0.014)
Lagged depend. var.	0.420** (0.127)	0.607** (0.078)	0.806** (0.074)	0.156 (0.160)	-0.83** (0.30)	-0.209 (0.149)	-1.63* (0.82)	-0.172 (0.493)	1.09** (0.146)	1.37** (0.11)	2.38** (0.21)
No. of obs.	272	546	546	270	62	166	25	65	505	978	310
Log-likelihd.	-246.78	-544.68	-582.57	-176.20	-38.21	-152.99	-12.44	-24.41	-351.19	-727.65	-119.69
Chi-squared	303.45	431.95	227.52	233.05	110.58			24.18	416.24	670.91	2608.15
Pseudo R-sq.	0.35	0.28	0.23	0.44	0.46	0.25	0.36	0.57	0.57	0.54	0.70

* Statistical significance at 95% level
** Statistical significance at 99% level
[a] The results for the American Convention on Human Rights impact on Fair Trial and the African Charter on Human Rights impact on Civil Liberty become insignificant when the analysis is rerun with only significant variables.

TABLE 10. RELATIONSHIP BETWEEN RATIFICATION OF HUMAN RIGHTS TREATIES AMONG FULLY DEMOCRATIC NATIONS AND HUMAN RIGHTS RATINGS, CONTROLLING FOR VARIOUS COUNTRY CHARACTERISTICS

Short Treaty Name	Genocide Convention [a]	Torture Convention	Article 21	Covenant on Civil and Political Rights	Optional Protocol	Covenant on Civil and Political Rights	Optional Protocol	Conv. on the Political Rights of Women
Human Rights Measure	Genocide	Torture	Torture	Fair Trial	Fair Trial	Civil Liberty	Civil Liberty	Percentage of Men in Parliament
Ratification by Full Democracies	**−0.056****	**0.087****	**0.090***	0.065	0.084	−0.020	**−0.038***	**−0.0004***
	(0.011)	**(0.033)**	**(0.046)**	(0.056)	(0.061)	(0.013)	**(0.015)**	**(0.0002)**
Treaty variable	0.012	−0.025	−0.035	0.024	−0.023	−0.002	0.011	−0.0002
	(0.009)	(0.021)	(0.036)	(0.048)	(0.046)	(0.008)	(0.009)	(0.0003)
International war	0.143**	0.101	0.103	0.066	0.072	0.003	0.0005	0.001
	(0.041)	(0.068)	(0.068)	(0.095)	(0.097)	(0.068)	(0.068)	(0.0006)
Civil or ethnic war		0.130**	0.129**	0.113	0.124	0.103**	0.099**	0.0004
		(0.033)	0.033	(0.070)	(0.071)	(0.024)	(0.024)	(0.0005)
Population size		0.001	0.0005	0.005	0.004		0.002	−4e−8
		(0.004)	(0.0036)	(0.008)	(0.009)		(0.002)	(2e−5)
Population growth		2.34	2.58	−4.67	−4.73	0.233	0.221	−0.079
		(5.42)	(5.45)	(3.85)	(3.86)	(2.82)	(2.82)	(0.155)
New regime	0.277*	−0.039	−0.032	−0.287	−0.294	−0.162**	−0.153**	0.001
	(0.112)	(0.085)	(0.083)	(0.178)	(0.179)	(0.073)	(0.073)	(0.002)
Full democracy	0.534*	1.089**	1.182**	−1.95*	−1.68*	0.105	0.178	0.002
	(0.249)	(0.352)	(0.340)	(0.884)	(0.709)	(0.296)	(0.267)	(0.004)
Democracy		−0.058**	−0.061**	−0.076	−0.073	−0.183**	−0.185**	0.001**
		(0.021)	(0.021)	(0.042)	(0.044)	(0.020)	(0.020)	(0.0004)
GNP per capita		−2e−5	−1e−5	2e−4	1e−4	5e−6	3e−6	−7.8e−7*
		(4e−5)	(4e−5)	(9e−5)	(1e−4)	(1e−5)	(1e−5)	(3.8e−7)
Global inter-dependence		−0.001	−0.001	−0.003	−0.003			0.0001
		(0.002)	(0.002)	(0.006)	(0.006)			(8e−5)
Aid dependency		0.002	0.002	0.003	0.003			2e−5
		(0.006)	(0.006)	(0.012)	(0.012)			(3e−5)
GDP growth		−0.0018	−0.002	0.0003	0.002			−0.0002
		(0.006)	(0.006)	(0.012)	(0.013)			(0.0002)
State failure		0.022	0.032	−1.72**	−1.72**	0.088	0.088	−0.011
		(0.362)	(0.359)	(0.616)	(0.613)	(0.268)	(0.269)	(0.013)
Time	−0.007	0.061**	0.058**	0.019	0.043	0.004	−0.001	−0.0003
	(0.008)	(0.014)	(0.011)	(0.046)	(0.033)	(0.005)	(0.004)	(0.0003)
Lagged dependent variable		0.525**	0.529**	−0.146	−0.147	1.39**	1.39**	0.774**
		(0.051)	(0.051)	(0.106)	(0.106)	(0.069)	(0.069)	(0.092)
Constant								0.212
								(0.086)
No. of obs.	927	1597	1597	373	373	2739	2739	3019
Log-likelihood	−912.76	−1483.01	−1484.37	−328.76	−328.73	−1994.07	−1991.65	
Chi-squared	353.55	1800.23	1814.69			1990.71	1979.21	
Pseudo R-sq.	0.12	0.38	0.38	0.31	0.31	0.61	0.61	0.87

*   Statistical significance at 95% level
** Statistical significance at 99% level
[a]   Genocide Convention results include countries with democracy ratings from 8 to 10.

[2]

Measuring the Effects of Human Rights Treaties

Ryan Goodman* and Derek Jinks**

Abstract

Do human rights treaties improve human rights conditions on the ground? In the end, this critical question is empirical in character. The effectiveness of any regulatory strategy turns on whether its rules and institutions actually mitigate the problems they are designed to address. Although empirical questions require empirical study, bad data is worse than no data. In a recent study, Professor Oona Hathaway purports to quantify the effect of human rights treaty ratification on human rights violations. Her findings are striking. She contends that ratification is associated with worse human rights practices (when other important variables are held constant). Of course, it is unsurprising that some states continue to commit substantial human rights abuses even after ratifying human rights treaties. It is, however, startling to suggest that treaty membership — including the labelling, monitoring and reporting of abuses — actually increases violations. In our view, any study advancing such wildly counterintuitive claims carries a heavy burden. While we support the empirical study of these phenomena (and indeed we rely on many such studies in formulating our critique), we identify several problems with Hathaway's project. We suggest that these problems demonstrate serious deficiencies in her empirical findings, theoretical model and policy prescriptions.

Does international law constrain state behaviour? Fundamental to the project of international law is the assumption that legal commitments meaningfully condition the exercise of state power. That is, the normative appeal of international law is predicated upon the view that well-designed rules will — in general and on average — promote peace, stability and good governance. It is, in other words, a radical critique of international law to suggest that international legal regimes actually worsen the problems they were crafted to redress.

In an important, recent article, Professor Oona Hathaway purports to quantify the

* J. Sinclair Armstrong Assistant Professor of International, Foreign, and Comparative Law, Harvard Law School. J.D., Yale Law School; Ph.D., Yale University.

** Assistant Professor of Law, Saint Louis University School of Law. J.D., Yale Law School; M.Phil., Yale University. We are grateful for comments received from James Cavallaro, David Cope, Jack Goldsmith, Howell Jackson, William Landes, Catharine MacKinnon, Andrew Moravcsik, Jonathan Nash, Eric Posner, David Sloss, Henry Steiner, William Stuntz, and Cass Sunstein.

172   *EJIL* 14 (2003), 171–183

impact of treaty ratification on actual human rights violations.[1] Hathaway maintains that her analysis supports several important empirical claims, including: (1) countries with worse human rights records appear to ratify treaties at a higher rate than those with better records; (2) treaty ratification is associated with worse human rights practices than expected; (3) enforcement procedures reduce non-compliance; and (4) ratification is associated with better practices in full democracies.[2]

Hathaway asserts that these findings contradict empirical predictions of both rational actor and normative models of treaty compliance; and she offers a theoretical model that, in her view, more adequately explains the empirical evidence.[3] She states that treaties 'operate on more than one level simultaneously. They create binding law that is intended to have particular effects, and they express the position of those countries that join them.'[4] For Hathaway, this dual role of treaties helps explain the 'paradoxical patterns of interaction between human rights treaty ratification and human rights practices'.[5] She suggests that some states ratify treaties to signal to other important actors their commitment to human rights.[6] Because of the legal character of international human rights treaties, ratification is virtually costless in that unenforced treaty rules do not require any actual changes in state practice. More specifically, international actors (including states and non-governmental organizations) reward ratifying states by reducing political pressure to promote human rights standards, thereby actually increasing human rights violations.[7] In this way, the law and politics of international human rights treaties provide a structural incentive for some 'countries [to] take positions to which they do not subsequently conform'.[8]

Hathaway's project is, in our view, the most well-conceived empirical study of this question in the legal literature. Indeed, Hathaway's contribution to human rights scholarship will, we expect, influence empirical debates in the legal academy for some time to come. It is because we value this work that we seek to advance the debate with the following critical remarks. In this article, we argue that Hathaway's project is in important respects flawed. Specifically, we identify (1) defects in Hathaway's research design; (2) structural deficiencies in her theoretical model; and (3) troubling implications of her policy analysis.

Our position is that Hathaway's study does not adequately account for the ways in which, and the conditions under which, human rights norms are incorporated into national practice. Because the study seeks to understand more fully the relationship between international human rights law and domestic practices, we suggest that this

---

[1]   Hathaway, 'Do Human Rights Treaties Make a Difference?', 112 *Yale L.J.* (2002) 1935.
[2]   *Ibid.*, at 1999 (summarizing empirical findings).
[3]   *Ibid.*, at 1989–2002.
[4]   *Ibid.*, at 2002.
[5]   *Ibid.*
[6]   *Ibid.*, at 2005–2006 ('[Ratification] declares to the world that the principles outlined in the treaty are consistent with the ratifying government's commitment to human rights').
[7]   *Ibid.*, at 2007 (arguing that this expressive aspect of human rights treaties often 'serve[s] to relieve pressure for real change in performance in countries that ratify the treaty').
[8]   *Ibid.*, at 2007.

criticism is central. Indeed, both 'rational actor' and 'normative' theorists postulate that social processes structure the relationship between international law and state decision-making in that international law is part of the institutional environment within which states act. Of course, these theoretical approaches differ on other important matters, including the logic of social choice utilized by states and the nature of the social process guiding the incorporation of international norms. Because Hathaway does not account for these dynamics, her model is not designed to address the debates between 'rational actor' and 'normative' theorists. In our view, the incorporation of human rights norms is a process; treaty law plays an important role in this process; and Hathaway's study does not provide a reason to reject these views.

1 Empirical Analysis

Hathaway's independent variable (treaty ratification) and dependent variable (reported human rights violations) are subject to measurement errors that call into question her empirical findings. Treaty ratification is used as a proxy for the formal acceptance of international human rights law. And detected, reported human rights violations are used as a measure of actual human rights conditions. As we discuss below, both variables fail to account for the most important axes along which we would expect to see variation. The research design accordingly does not adequately encapsulate the nature of human rights abuses; and it does not account for various ways in which states are oriented to the international legal order.[9]

Hathaway's focus on ratification as the independent variable is questionable. Ratification is not the 'magic moment' of acceptance of human rights norms. Rather, ratification is a point in the broader process of incorporation; and the relative significance of this point will, we would expect, vary widely with diverse impacts on measures of compliance. As a matter of international law, core treaty obligations attach earlier in the incorporation process — that is, upon *signature* of the treaty.[10] As a matter of domestic law, many governments condition their acceptance of treaty obligations on the passage of implementing legislation.[11] Some human rights treaties

---

[9] As a separate matter, because of Hathaway's research design (particularly the use of pooled cross-sectional data), one of her major findings — that treaty ratification is associated with worse human rights ratings than otherwise expected — may be largely dictated by the fact that countries with worse practices tend to ratify human rights treaties earlier than others.

[10] Under the general law of treaties, 'a State is obliged to refrain from acts which would defeat the object and purpose of a treaty when . . . it has signed the treaty.' Vienna Convention on the Law of Treaties, opened for signature, 23 May 1969, Art. 18, 1155 UNTS 331. We should add two points here. First, the effect of this rule may obviously have systematic effects on compliance depending on whether the signatory has a Parliamentary or Presidential system of government. Second, in terms of the appeal of this type of formalistic argument, consider that Hathaway relies on a similar provision of the Vienna Convention in evaluating the obligation entailed by ratification with particular reservations. See Hathaway, *supra* note 1, at 1963 n.113.

[11] Jackson, 'Status of Treaties in Domestic Legal Systems: A Policy Analysis', 86 *AJIL* (1992) 310. The effect of this factor will likely vary according to whether a state's constitution is dualist or monist. Systematic effects may also vary according to the formal and informal political support required to pass such legislation.

174   *EJIL* 14 (2003), 171–183

(or particular treaty provisions) are considered self-executing; others are not. More fundamentally, ratification might represent the initiation, culmination or reconfiguration of a domestic political struggle.[12] A government's decision to ratify might be preceded by other actions of international legal significance (e.g., affirming the treaty's fundamental principles, pledging to join the treaty, signing the treaty) and followed by others (e.g., adopting implementing legislation, withdrawing crippling reservations). When these actions occur in the process of incorporation — and whether they do so simultaneously, clustered together, or over time — naturally varies. Moreover, the most important moment in the incorporation process for any given state might well be the decision of another country to ratify a significant human rights treaty. One could make a strong case, for example, that China's ratification of the International Covenant on Civil and Political Rights was one of the most significant recent developments for the human rights policies of Burma, Indonesia, North Korea and Singapore.[13] The central empirical task, we submit, is identifying the conditions under which the process moves forward — and the conditions under which it stalls.[14]

Hathaway's measure of the dependent variable is also problematic. It does not account for strategies governments often adopt in response to improved enforcement of a norm. The main problems here concern strategic behaviour and substitutability. In Latin America in the late 1970s and early 1980s, levels of torture, political imprisonment and unfair trials declined — but governments were replacing those tactics with 'disappearances'. Human rights groups and victims eventually succeeded in reducing the practice of disappearances as well, but the point for statisticians is clear. Measuring one area of human rights without concurrently measuring the others would have misconstrued the patterns and prevalence of human rights

---

[12]   Moravcsik, 'The Origins of Human Rights Regimes: Democratic Delegation in Postwar Europe', 54 *Int'l Org.* (2000) 217, at 219–220 (analysing use of treaties by newly established democracies to solidify liberal gains and to guard against future rollbacks); T. Risse, *et al.* (eds), *The Power of Human Rights: International Norms and Domestic Change* (1999), at 25–28 (modelling transitions from repressive to rights-respecting regimes and role of international treaties and norms at different phases in the process). In these dissimilar situations, the baseline of human rights protections and, more significantly, the purpose of ratifying the treaty (e.g., to improve human rights protections or to keep protections at a plateau) will vary.

[13]   It is also important to note that such interdependencies can be incorporated into a regression analysis. D. C. Montgomery *et al.*, *Introduction to Linear Regression Analysis* (3rd ed., 2001).

[14]   Additionally, Hathaway fails to account for reservations and official derogations, which permit a state to suspend particular rights under the terms of a treaty. For instance, her model records violations of fair trial rights as non-compliance with the ICCPR even in years in which a state has officially entered an official derogation legally suspending those obligations. Moreover, these are obviously periods in which we would expect such 'violations' to increase dramatically. Another study of the effect of the ICCPR suggests the importance of taking into account derogation years. See Keith, 'The United Nations International Covenant on Civil and Political Rights: Does It Make a Difference in Human Rights Behavior?', 36 *J. Peace Res.* (1999) 95, at 105 ('A separate analysis was conducted in which the states that derogated from the treaty were moved into the group of non-party states for the years in which they had officially notified the UN of their derogation. When this adjustment is made, the difference between states parties and non-party states personal integrity abuse increases substantially and become [sic] statistically significant . . .').

conditions on the ground. Some political scientists have tried to address this substitutability problem directly. They avoid measuring the effectiveness of a human rights treaty by its impact on only one right contained in the treaty.[15] Assume, for example, that a treaty prohibits both disappearances and unfair trials. The problem for models like Hathaway's is that greater compliance with one obligation (e.g., reduction in disappearances) can show up as lower compliance with another (e.g., increase in unfair trials). Therefore, a model studying only unfair trials would show human rights conditions worsening, even though the overall country conditions may be improving as the treaty's norms are gradually incorporated into domestic practice.

Another difficulty, as many human rights statisticians have explained, is that the standard variables in this field only measure *recorded and reported* human rights violations, not actual violations. The problem is that improving human rights conditions increases access to information on the extent of violations. As a leading political scientist in the field explained,

> [t]he availability and reliability of data for contemporary human rights studies deteriorates markedly when the focus shifts to the political, civil, and personal security issues. This is especially true for some of the worst human rights violations such as torture. . . . [I]t is virtually an axiom that the more repressive the regime, the more difficult it makes access to information about its human rights atrocities to researchers.[16]

Indeed, regimes that have not fully embraced human rights norms often censor local media, restrict the number and access of international reporters, and harass or threaten local individuals who might otherwise document violations. After describing these types of practices, sociologist Kenneth Bollen concluded, '[i]ronically, it is possible that a nation which is relatively open may appear lower in rights and liberties simply because violations are more likely to be reported to the outside world.'[17] This limitation in the data can produce perverse measurement results: the more rights-protective a state becomes the worse the state's record *may appear* in terms of *detected* human rights violations. In particular, Hathaway's model cannot, for example, adequately distinguish between (1) a state in which levels of torture increase post-ratification and (2) a state in which torture declines post-ratification but appears to increase because liberalization eases the process of documenting and reporting instances of torture.

The measurement errors created by using reported violations would not be a problem if the errors were random. These measurement errors in Hathaway's empirical model are, however, systematic (that is, non-random). The problem for

---

[15]   Keith, *supra* note 14, at 101 n. 8; cf. Lopez and Stohl, 'Problems of Concept and Measurement in the Study of Human Rights', in T. B. Jabine and R. P. Claude (eds), *Human Rights and Statistics: Getting the Record Straight* (1992) 226.

[16]   Goldstein, 'The Limitations of Using Quantitative Data in Studying Human Rights Abuses', in Jabine and Claude, *supra* note 15, at 44–45.

[17]   Bollen, 'Political Rights and Political Liberties in Nations: An Evaluation of Human Rights Measures, 1950 to 1984', in Jabine and Claude, *supra* note 15, at 200. Techniques are available for addressing some of these measurement problems. For example, the empirical model could control for (1) the relative freedom of the press; and (2) the relative level of NGO activity.

176   *EJIL* 14 (2003), 171–183

Hathaway's model is that treaty ratification triggers social and political processes that *exacerbate* this measurement error. First, the decision whether to ratify human rights treaties often turns on the effect that ratification would have on the documentation of human rights practices. Consider that a recent study commissioned by the United Nations concluded that '[t]he most common reason for non-ratification is that the treaties threaten the status quo. States resist ratification of treaties if they do not agree with the norms contained in the treaties, or do not wish their performance in these areas to be subjected to international scrutiny.'[18] Hence, for many governments, the decision to ratify suggests a willingness to increase access to information on, and dialogue about, domestic human rights practices.

Treaty ratification also accentuates the measurement problem by increasing the salience and legitimacy of human rights concepts. As recent case studies and much experience suggest, one beneficiary of such developments is non-governmental organizations (NGOs). Local human rights groups often acquire greater legitimacy and political prominence in their struggle against a repressive regime when the government makes formal, tactical concessions.[19] One such concession can be the signature or ratification of a human rights treaty.[20] The discourse of international human rights — facilitated by the educative campaign and media attention preceding and incident to ratification — should also spread the concept of rights guarantees to individuals who have not previously conceptualized abuses committed against them in these terms.[21] In many jurisdictions, treaty ratification makes possible the initiation of individual legal claims based on the treaty's substantive guarantees. As a consequence, it encourages lawyers and their clients to express injuries in terms of the newly established treaty obligations. To take an example from domestic law: more expansive sexual violence laws are likely to result in statistically higher levels of rape claims, irrespective of whether the actual rate of rape remains constant or declines. We should not expect treaties involving civil and political rights, nor their domestic implementing legislation, to operate differently.

Formal institutional arrangements accompanying ratification are also likely to increase awareness and documentation of human rights. Ratification of a universal human rights treaty creates a special array of relationships between a government and the UN treaty system. Under UN reporting requirements, states are encouraged to

---

[18] See generally Heyns and Viljoen, 'The Impact of the United Nations Human Rights Treaties on the Domestic Level', 23 *HRQ* (2001) 483, at 487–488 (article by authors of UN study reproducing their main findings and recommendations).

[19] Risse and Sikkink, 'The Socialization of International Human Rights Norms into Domestic Practices: Introduction', in Risse, *supra* note 12, at 25–28.

[20] Risse and Ropp, 'International Human Rights Norms and Domestic Change', in Risse, *supra* note 12, at 238.

[21] Heyns and Viljoen, *supra* note 18, at 488 ('[T]he treaties have had their greatest influence domestically in shaping the understanding of government officials and members of civil society as to what is to be considered basic human rights. Although a causal link cannot always be proven, it could hardly be considered coincidental that the very language of human rights in the parliaments and courts of the surveyed countries is largely that which the treaty system has been introducing and reinforcing since the middle 1960s').

monitor, track, and analyse human rights abuses. To this end, the UN Office of the High Commissioner for Human Rights has dedicated funds and services for helping states prepare periodic reports. Each reporting cycle, NGOs are also encouraged to produce 'shadow reports' for submission alongside the government's official reports. Donor agencies are especially inclined to fund this type of NGO activity. While many NGOs generally operate at the national level in their daily practices, such events provide opportunities for bringing their information to the attention of international actors.[22] These interactions lend national NGOs formal institutional legitimacy and a forum in which to address state practices.[23] As a result, the more a country engages with the treaty system, the more its actual human rights record on the ground will be exposed.[24] Indeed, an important goal of human rights treaty regimes is the capacity-building of international and national monitoring mechanisms. That is, improved human rights documentation and reporting are themselves part of the process of incorporation.

Although Hathaway addresses some of these measurement problems, her brief analysis is unsatisfying. She contends:

> if the results were due to greater reporting of violations in the wake of treaty ratification, we would expect to find that ratification would always or nearly always be associated with higher violation ratings. But instead the results suggest that the association between ratification and practices is strongest in the most entrenched areas of human rights and for regional treaties.[25]

However, variations would be expected to occur. For instance, reporting may be more highly associated with particular thematic issues or with regional systems because those treaties are more effective. The *more effective* the treaty regime is in combating governmental repression, the greater the consciousness and reporting of violations will be. Especially given language and resource barriers, regional treaty regimes may be more effective in encouraging the growth and activities of domestic NGOs.[26] And, the most entrenched areas of human rights (such as torture) involve practices that governments try hardest to conceal.[27] In addition, these are the areas that donors, NGOs and international actors prioritize when regulatory mechanisms are in place.

---

[22] For a rich discussion of these institutional relationships, see P. Alston and J. Crawford (eds), *The Future of UN Human Rights Treaty Monitoring* (2000).

[23] Risse and Sikkink, *supra* note 19, at 18.

[24] Heyns and Viljoen, *supra* note 18, at 487–488 ('Some countries are highly engaged with the system. They submit substantial reports, their NGOs bring individual complaints . The unfortunate result is that the countries that most often end up being singled out as human rights violators are those that are engaged').

[25] Hathaway, *supra* note 1, at 2000 n. 213.

[26] Heyns and Viljoen, *supra* note 18, at 520–521 ('[T]he UN is often seen as a remote, invisible, and anonymous body, one that speaks in foreign languages, with little knowledge of local conditions and customs. (This partly explains the greater popularity of regional systems, which are "closer to home")').

[27] Goldstein, *supra* note 16, at 44–45.

178   *EJIL* 14 (2003), 171–183

Given these problems with the independent and dependent variables,[28] we would expect that Hathaway's empirical model would not account for much of the variation in the data. Thus, we are unsurprised that Hathaway's study yields 'no statistically significant relationship between treaty ratification and human rights ratings' in most of its multivariate analyses.[29] This statistical point may require clarification: the lack of a *statistically significant* relationship between ratification and practices does not demonstrate that a treaty's impact is insignificant. Rather, statistically insignificant results suggest likely (and perhaps non-random) measurement errors in the independent and dependent variables.[30] That is, such findings are insufficiently robust to confirm or disconfirm any affirmative empirical proposition.

2 Theoretical Model

In addition to the empirical problems, the proffered theoretical model also raises several concerns. That is, even if we assume that Hathaway's quantitative analysis conclusively establishes her empirical propositions, the theoretical implications of these findings are unclear. Some of these theoretical concerns also indicate flaws in the empirical study.

First, the quantitative analysis does not test, nor is it designed to test, the validity of Hathaway's theoretical model. Although Hathaway's theoretical account suggests that the US government reduces pressure (e.g., by the State Department Human

---

[28]   Also, several of the human rights violations in Hathaway's model do not match the associated treaty obligations. One problem is over-inclusiveness. For, example, the Genocide Convention does not concern so-called 'politicide'; but Hathaway's reliance on the Maryland data set does. The Torture Convention does not cover extra-judicial killings, but Hathaway's variable for torture does. The Convention on Political Rights of Women (CPRW) does not require proportionate representation of women in legislatures, but Hathaway's variable for testing compliance measures proportionate legislative seats. In fact, state practice suggests that proportionate representation resulting from a governmental sex-based quota system arguably violates the CPRW. See, e.g., Declarations and Reservations to the Convention on the Political Rights of Women http://www.unhchr.ch/html/menu3/b/treaty1_asp.htm (Declaration of the Government of Bangladesh). Under-inclusiveness is also a concern. For example, the Genocide Convention prohibits practices beyond those that result in death, it does not require a specific proportion of the victim group to suffer the relevant injury, and it has no state action requirement. Hathaway's variable for genocide, however, concerns only policies by '[1] governing elites or their agents — or in the case of civil war, either of the contending authorities — that [2] result in the deaths of [3] a substantial portion of a communal group or politicized noncommunal group.' Hathaway, *supra* note 1, at 1968–1969 (internal quotation marks and citation omitted); see also *ibid.* at 1969 (describing a substantial portion as 'authorities physically exterminate enough members of a target group so that it can no longer pose any conceivable threat to their rule or interests') (internal quotation marks and citation omitted).

[29]   Hathaway, *supra* note 1, at 1994.

[30]   Hathaway suggests that tests of statistical significance are not as relevant to her research design. *Ibid.*, at 1993 n.195. The data set, however, does not approximate the total population. The data set does not contain countries; it contains 'country-years'. *Ibid.*, at 1978. The model only measures a subset of years out of the total population available. The data set also includes only some of the obligations under the treaties, and only some of the human rights treaties in the world. (The study also omits country years when reliable data sources are not available.) Importantly, Hathaway draws inferences from the data set to each of these populations.

Rights Reports under-reporting human rights violations) in the wake of treaty ratification, no documentation of this political pressure dynamic is offered.[31] The regression analysis does not purport to measure the relationship between (a) state human rights practices and (b) international human rights pressure and reporting. It is important to note that the theory is simply a post-hoc causal explanation (arguably) consistent with, but neither confirmed nor assessed by, the empirical findings. The problem is that important (untested) empirical assumptions are embedded in the theoretical model; and that these assumptions are not always consistent with the assumptions of her empirical model. For example, the empirical model relies on US State Department reports as an objective indicator of human rights practices. That methodological choice, in turn, produces a major flaw in the model. A factual predicate of Hathaway's theoretical model — State Department under-reporting post-ratification — suggests that the chief source of information for her dependent variable (official State Department reports) *is biased*. That is, if we accept that the State Department decreases pressure on a country by under-reporting human rights violations post-ratification, we must reject the State Department reports as a reliable measure of actual human rights conditions. Furthermore, because Hathaway's findings show increased reports of human rights violations post-ratification, the data run contrary to her theoretical prediction of politically motivated under-reporting post-ratification.

Second, the model does not adequately explain state treaty practice. Because Hathaway assumes that treaty ratification is virtually costless, her theoretical model does not account for various forms of non-participation in human rights treaties. For example, the model cannot adequately explain non-ratification or the various forms of qualified participation (such as ratification with reservations or formal notices of derogation). Conversely, the model does not convincingly explain why some problem states ratify treaties at all, given that joining the treaty would signal (as a formal legal matter) the state's acceptance of the human rights principles embodied in the treaty.

Third, Hathaway's conception of 'signalling' postulates a strained view of state treaty practice. The model assumes that international actors are so radically under-informed about human rights practices that treaty ratification alone is used as a proxy for improving conditions irrespective of the fact that ratification carries with it no hard sovereignty costs. That is, Hathaway's model is predicated on the tantalizing oxymoron of a 'costless signal'. However, international legal commitments constitute 'signals' if, and only if, they are in some sense meaningful commitments. In this sense, Hathaway's analysis is difficult to understand. On her view, signalling states often understand that ratification is virtually costless; and are, as a consequence, willing to ratify even if they have no intention of complying with its substantive provisions. On the other hand, the signalled states (and other important actors such as international NGOs) apparently do not understand that ratification is meaningless and, as a consequence, reward ratifying states for the very act of ratification. Moreover, on Hathaway's view, the signalled states do not learn over time that ratification is

[31]   *Ibid.*, at 2000 n. 213.

180   *EJIL* 14 (2003), 171–183

meaningless. In our view, Hathaway's model systematically underestimates the sovereignty costs of treaty ratification; and, as a consequence, fails to identify the ways in which universal treaty ratification promotes the 'globalization of freedom'.[32] Human rights treaty ratification (even if understood only as 'position taking') at a minimum sharply delimits the ways in which states may justify controversial practices. The resultant constraints on legitimation strategies are, we submit, sensibly understood as 'sovereignty costs' by states.[33] In addition, even modest legalization of human rights institutions magnifies this effect by promoting more precise, obligatory treaty rules.[34]

Fourth, Hathaway does not make explicit important theoretical presuppositions of her model. Hathaway assumes that international political pressure in the area of human rights, under some unspecified circumstances, *causes* states to introduce costly changes. In short, where persuasion fails, pressure often works. In addition, states, on her view, seek to conform their conduct to prevailing international standards while minimizing sovereignty costs. As a consequence, some states would ratify human rights treaties with no intention of altering domestic practices in order to stave off more intrusive (and effective) modes of promoting human rights norms. The model, however, neither identifies a causal mechanism by which international norms are incorporated into national practice, nor the deeper incentives that form or guide state choices. What social logic or process animates the international political order? How and under what conditions do norms travel? These questions have prompted the energetic debates in international relations/international law scholarship on compliance and the role of law in world politics. And, indeed, the 'rational actor' and 'normative' theories identified by Hathaway are defined in large part by their respective answers to these questions. Hathaway's theoretical model thus fails to fulfil the promise made at the beginning of her article to address or improve those debates.

That Hathaway fails to engage these issues is also problematic because her theory, as a result, may rest upon untested assumptions and potential internal inconsistencies. Consider, for instance, that Hathaway expressly questions several empirical predictions of rational actor and normative schools. The crucial point is that those empirical predictions are *derived from the theoretical commitments of the schools*. Because Hathaway does not make her own theoretical commitments clear, her model arguably employs theories of social action that imply the very empirical predictions she disputes.

Consider, for example, Hathaway's critique of realist empirical predictions, despite her own implicit reliance on realist theoretical assumptions. Hathaway suggests that realists (a specie of 'rational actor' theorists) would predict — contrary to her findings — that international human rights treaties would exert no regular causal influence

[32]   Koh, 'The Spirit of the Laws', 43 *Harv. Int'l L.J.* (2002) 23, at 26.
[33]   See generally S. Cohen, *States of Denial: Knowing about Atrocities and Human Suffering* (2001).
[34]   See generally J. Goldstein *et al.*, *The Legalization of World Politics* (2001).

on state practice.[35] This empirical prediction, however, is derived from realism's commitment to a rationalist theory of social choice that treats the interests and preferences of actors as essentially fixed during the process of strategic interaction. On this view, international human rights law is part of the institutional environment within which states rationally pursue given and fixed preferences. International law might, of course, exert influence on state practices by altering the costs or benefits of particular strategic options, but the central causal dynamic would be the state's rational pursuit of its prefigured preferences. As a consequence, international law, as a potential explanation of state choice, is epiphenomenal.[36] Because Hathaway's findings purportedly disconfirm the realist's causal prediction, does she also question the theoretical assumption from which this prediction is derived? This may be particularly problematic for Hathaway in that she seems to employ a rationalist theory of social action in her 'pressure' model. Of course, the fundamental point is that Hathaway's under-theorized explanation raises more questions than it answers.

3 Policy Analysis

Finally, Hathaway's brief policy analysis is unpersuasive and ultimately counterproductive. As previously discussed, Hathaway's theoretical model explains the effects reflected in her data in terms of the unique character of human rights treaties — ratification of these treaties is, on her view, 'costless'. Her policy recommendations, therefore, aim — first and foremost — to increase the costs of ratification (and thereby ensure that treaty ratification is meaningful). From this general prescription, she derives several specific suggestions that, in our view, subvert the process of norm internalization by discouraging universal ratification of human rights treaties.[37]

Because Hathaway's policy analysis is geared to solve one problem ('costless' ratification), she fails to account for the impact her proposals would have on other potentially positive effects of treaty ratification (effects not captured by her empirical or theoretical model). Hathaway explains that the empirical 'findings of this study may also give reason to reassess the current policy of the United Nations of promoting universal ratification of the major human rights treaties'.[38] Based on her theoretical analysis, Hathaway advocates making ratification more difficult: 'The solution . . . is . . . to enhance the monitoring and enforcement of treaty obligations to reduce opportunities for countries to use ratification as a symbolic substitute for real

---

[35] Hathaway. *supra* note 1. at 1944–1947. Hathaway arguably pushes this claim a bit too far. She is correct to point out that realists attribute no independent causal significance to legal rules. Realists do, however, acknowledge that states often comply with international rules. For realists, rules constrain and facilitate state behaviour without reconfiguring state interests and preferences. It is in this way that international rules have no autonomous and causal status. See, e.g., Simmons, 'Compliance with International Agreements', *Ann. Rev. Pol. Sci.* (1998) 75 (summarizing this approach).

[36] For an example of this type of analysis in international legal scholarship, see Goldsmith and Posner, 'A Theory of Customary International Law', 66 *U. Chi. L. Rev.* (1999) 1113.

[37] See, e.g., Alston, 'Beyond "Them" and "Us": Putting Treaty Body Reform into Perspective', in Alston and Crawford, *supra* note 22, at 501.

[38] Hathaway. *supra* note 1. at 2024.

182   *EJIL* 14 (2003), 171–183

improvements.'[39] But, by reducing the opportunities for 'shallow' ratification by problem countries, Hathaway's approach would undermine the considerable constitutive effects of these treaties.

In short, our principal policy contention is that broad ratification of human rights treaties plays an important role in the process of building national human rights cultures (and a transnational human rights culture). It is important to note that, even on Hathaway's view, states attempt to realize the signalling benefits of human rights treaty ratification precisely because the norms embodied in these treaties enjoy widespread (international) acceptance. As previously discussed, treaty regimes help foster this acceptance domestically by increasing the salience and legitimacy of human rights norms. In addition, universal (or broad-based) ratification furthers these objectives on the global plane by increasing the salience and legitimacy of these norms in the international community. In this sense, human rights treaties serve both a (global) expressive function and a (domestic) constitutive function. In terms of expressive significance, Hathaway acknowledges that 'treaties may have broader positive effects not captured by the analysis'.[40] That is, even if ratifications are directly associated with negligible or deleterious effects in particular states, on the whole such treaties can have 'a widespread effect on the practices of *all* nations by changing the discourse about and expectations regarding those rights'.[41] 'What is important to note — and the reason that this effect would *not be detected* in [Hathaway's] empirical analysis — is that this influence can be felt by countries regardless of whether they ratify the treaty or not.'[42] Hathaway even nods to legal process scholars by admitting her empirical analysis may not capture the long-term internalization effects within ratifying countries.[43] Despite these two types of effects — global and domestic — Hathaway asserts that we must remedy the short-term, negative effects on individual ratifying countries by raising the costs of ratification. Such a scheme, however, may well disrupt the gradual process of constructing a global normative order (a necessary step in the further legalization of international human rights regimes).

Conclusion

Public international law desperately needs work like Hathaway's — studies that connect the law to events on the ground. There is a real danger that, absent such efforts, international lawyers will act in ways that have negligible or perverse effects on the injustices they seek to combat. But because the stakes are so high, it is important that we make accurate connections between what the law does and what happens on the ground. Those connections cannot be ascertained through the

---

[39]   *Ibid.*, at 2025.

[40]   *Ibid.*, at 2021.

[41]   *Ibid.* (emphasis in original); see also *ibid.*, at 2006 ('[T]he first expressive function of treaties may change discourse about and expectations regarding country practices and thereby change practices of countries regardless of whether they ratify the treaties').

[42]   *Ibid.*, at 2021 (emphasis added).

[43]   *Ibid.*, at 2022.

research design that Hathaway employed. Perhaps the answer is to discard this type of statistical modelling and adopt a softer kind of empiricism, something more sociological than economic. Perhaps it's something else. We certainly have not given up hope for statistical approaches in this area, as there are many devices that can be employed to help conduct such studies. In any event, this much is clear: we still do not satisfactorily know the full effects of human rights treaties. Absent such knowledge, the best assumption remains the conventional one: human rights treaties advance the cause they seek to promote, not the other way around.

[3]

OVERLEGALIZING HUMAN RIGHTS: INTERNATIONAL RELATIONS THEORY AND THE COMMONWEALTH CARIBBEAN BACKLASH AGAINST HUMAN RIGHTS REGIMES

*Laurence R. Helfer**

As the ratification of human rights treaties increases and the use of supranational adjudication to challenge human rights violations becomes more widespread, international legal scholars and international relations theorists alike have started to examine the effects of the increasing legalization of human rights norms. This Article raises the claim that international human rights law can become overlegalized, and it draws upon international relations theory and new empirical evidence to explore a recent case study of overlegalization. The Article seeks to understand why, in the late 1990s, three Commonwealth Caribbean governments denounced human rights agreements and withdrew from the jurisdiction of international human rights tribunals. It concludes that, while the denunciations can be viewed as arising from certain features unique to the Caribbean—in particular a dispute over capital punishment or judicial imperialism by the region's highest appellate court—they can also be understood as a response to the overlegalization of the governments' human rights commitments. In addition, the Article reassesses realist, ideational, and liberal international relations theories of treaty formation and compliance in light of the Caribbean case study, concluding that the notion of overlegalization adds nuance to the predictive power of these three theories.

TABLE OF CONTENTS

* Professor of Law and Lloyd Tevis Fellow, Loyola Law School, Los Angeles. Thanks to Ellen Aprill, Jeff Atik, David Boyd, Allison Danner, Graeme Dinwoodie, Catherine Fisk, John Knox, Kal Raustiala, Ted Seto, Beth Simmons, Anne-Marie Slaughter, and Lawrence Solum, who commented on earlier drafts or discussed specific issues raised in those drafts, to Kristopher Diulio, Loyola Class of 2003, for excellent research assistance, and to Jennifer Laurin of the *Columbia Law Review* for her exceptionally thoughtful review of the manuscript. Earlier versions of this paper were presented at the 2002 American Society of International Law Annual Meeting, the Political Study of International Law Speaker Series at UCLA Law School, and at faculty workshops at Arizona, Loyola, Melbourne, and USC law schools.

INTRODUCTION

Questions of compliance dominate international human rights law. Although once the exclusive province of nonbinding norms with no clear avenues of enforcement, international human rights today is comprised of complex and constraining rules targeted at the heart of domestic legal systems. It contains precise and detailed requirements for governments, and it uses judicial or court-like dispute settlement mechanisms to which aggrieved private parties have direct access.[1] Strikingly, this progressive legalization[2] of human rights has thus far appeared to meet with state approval. States have adhered to human rights treaties in increasing numbers, such that near universal ratification of many treaties is now plausible.[3]

Yet does the legalization of international human rights norms necessarily increase state compliance with those norms? Can human rights be "overlegalized,"[4] making their substantive rules or review mechanisms too constraining of sovereignty and precipitating a backlash by governments? If so, when are such counter-reactions likely to arise and how can they be avoided?

International legal scholars and international relations theorists answer these questions very differently. Within the legal academy, it is an article of faith that law matters. The international legal literature is replete with assertions that governments, albeit to greater or lesser degrees in different contexts, value their treaty commitments and alter their conduct to meet them.[5] International legal scholars focus on success stories—well-publicized cases where compliance with treaty rules does occur and where domestic practices are altered as a result—and use those stories to extrapolate to conclusions about the overall efficacy of interna-

---

1. See Laurence R. Helfer, Forum Shopping for Human Rights, 148 U. Pa. L. Rev. 285, 288–89 (1999) (discussing history of international human rights petition system).

2. For a definition and discussion of "legalization," see infra Part I.A.

3. See United Nations, Economic and Social Council, Commission on Human Rights, Effective Functioning of Bodies Established Pursuant to United Nations Human Rights Instruments, Final Report on Enhancing the Long-term Effectiveness of the United Nations Human Rights Treaty System ¶¶ 14–36, U.N. Doc. E/CN.4/1997/74 (1997) (noting "significant improvement" in progress toward universal ratification of the "core" U.N. human rights treaties and setting forth recommendations to encourage achievement of goal). Too much weight should not be placed on the increase in treaty ratifications, however. It has been argued that the "widespread ratification of human rights treaties masks widely varying normative views" about compliance with human rights norms. Kenneth W. Abbott, International Relations Theory, International Law, and the Regime Governing Atrocities in Internal Conflicts, 93 Am. J. Int'l L. 361, 373 (1999); see also Stephen D. Krasner, Sovereignty: Organized Hypocrisy 32 (1999) ("At least until the 1990s . . . the correlation between the behavior of governments with regard to human rights and the number of United Nations accords they had signed was weak.").

4. For a definition and detailed discussion of overlegalization, see infra Part I.D.

5. The most famous of these assertions is Louis Henkin's, that "almost all nations observe almost all principles of international law and almost all of their obligations almost all of the time." Louis Henkin, How Nations Behave 47 (2d ed. 1979) (emphasis omitted).

tional law. These scholars also stress the evolutionary character of international law (and human rights law in particular), including its increasing number of regimes and institutions, its expansion to new settings and issue areas, and its penetration into national law. Only rarely do legal scholars seek to isolate the variables that contribute to compliance[6] or effectiveness,[7] or to support their conclusions with empirical evidence.[8]

By contrast, political scientists concerned with international legal regimes seek to develop empirically testable hypotheses about whether, and under what conditions, legal rules are effective in changing government behavior. These scholars also attempt to isolate the causal pathways by which compliance with those rules occurs. Most of the literature on these subjects is of a relatively recent vintage,[9] and the empirical challenges (particularly in the human rights context) of measuring compliance are considerable.[10] Yet international relations scholars have already generated a number of important theories about the relative importance of different explanatory variables (of which law is only one) in altering government conduct. Many of these hypotheses challenge, often fundamentally, the beliefs long held by international lawyers.

This Article lies at the intersection of international law and politics. It seeks to understand why, in the late 1990s, three Commonwealth Caribbean governments denounced human rights treaties, including treaties granting jurisdiction to two international human rights tribunals. The denunciations followed a series of rulings by the region's highest appellate court, the Judicial Committee of the Privy Council, restricting the

---

6. For rare exceptions, see Benedict Kingsbury, The Concept of Compliance as a Function of Competing Conceptions of International Law, 19 Mich. J. Int'l L. 345, 346 (1998) (linking different conceptions of compliance to different theories "of the relations of law, behavior, objectives, and justice"); Kal Raustiala, Compliance & Effectiveness in International Regulatory Cooperation, 32 Case W. Res. J. Int'l L. 387, 391–99 (2000) (defining distinct concepts of "compliance" and "effectiveness" and contrasting them with other concepts, such as "implementation").

7. One exception is Laurence R. Helfer & Anne-Marie Slaughter, Toward a Theory of Effective Supranational Adjudication, 107 Yale L.J. 273, 298–336 (1997) (identifying three sets of variables that co-vary with effective supranational adjudication in Europe).

8. For a recent and significant exception, see Oona A. Hathaway, Do Human Rights Treaties Make a Difference?, 111 Yale L.J. 1935, 1940, 1962–2002 (2002) (presenting extensive quantitative analysis of states' human rights practices and concluding that "noncompliance with treaty obligations appears to be common" and that "treaty ratification is not infrequently associated with worse human rights ratings than otherwise expected").

9. For a comprehensive survey of this literature, see Kal Raustiala & Anne-Marie Slaughter, International Law, International Relations, and Compliance, *in* Handbook of International Relations 538, 539–45 (Walter Carlsnaes et al. eds., 2002).

10. E.g., Douglass Cassel, Does International Human Rights Law Make a Difference?, 2 Chi. J. Int'l L. 121, 122, 131 (2001) (noting that numerous variables influencing government behavior problematize empirical proof of human rights law's effectiveness); Hathaway, supra note 8, at 1963–68 (discussing the challenges of measuring compliance with and effectiveness of human rights treaties through quantitative analysis).

execution of criminal defendants who had filed petitions with the international tribunals alleging violations of their rights. I refer to the governments' withdrawals from these treaties and from the jurisdiction of these tribunals as the "Commonwealth Caribbean backlash" against human rights regimes. My study of this backlash has two objectives. The first is to show how overlegalizing human rights can lead even liberal democracies[11] to reconsider their commitment to international institutions that protect those rights. The second objective is to use the Caribbean example as a case study[12] against which to test recent and competing international relations theories seeking to explain the conditions under which states comply with their treaty commitments.

The Commonwealth Caribbean backlash is intriguing on several levels. First, it runs counter to the largely progressive evolution of human rights law to date.[13] It tells the story of an unprecedented "exit"[14] by liberal democratic governments from international human rights regimes, a withdrawal that includes formal (and likely permanent) treaty denunciations.[15] Second, the case study describes a rich set of interactions between international jurists and their national counterparts. It thus adds to the growing literature that sees links between international tribunals and domestic courts as a key variable favoring treaty compliance.[16] Third, the case study is non-European. Much of the research

---

11. For a list of the major characteristics shared by liberal democratic states, see infra note 45.

12. For a discussion of the importance of case studies to international relations theories relevant to international lawyers, see Abbott, supra note 3, at 362–63.

13. See Cassel, supra note 10, at 126 (noting that "processes of rights protection—including human rights law—are . . . growing stronger"); Helfer, supra note 1, at 289 (noting that "rich and nuanced case law" has developed in human rights tribunals).

14. J.H.H. Weiler, The Transformation of Europe, 100 Yale L.J. 2403, 2411–12 (1991) (asserting that member states' relinquishment of option to "exit" from European Community correlated with exercising of "voice" in Community governance (citing Albert O. Hirschman, Exit, Voice and Loyalty: Responses to Decline in Firms, Organizations, and States (1970))).

15. Formal denunciations of human rights agreements or institutions are relatively rare (and often temporary) and generally have been carried out by nondemocratic governments. In 1999, for example, President Alberto Fujimori of Peru denounced the jurisdiction of the Inter-American Court of Human Rights. After Fujimori's exit from power and a return to democratic rule, Peru reacceded to the court's contentious jurisdiction in January 2001. Cassel, supra note 10, at 128. Greece followed a similar pattern in the early 1970s, withdrawing from the Council of Europe and its human rights system after a military coup and rejoining after a return to democracy. Kathryn Sikkink, The Power of Principled Ideas: Human Rights Policies in the United States and Western Europe, in Ideas and Foreign Policy: Beliefs, Institutions, and Political Change 130, 149–50 (Judith Goldstein & Robert O. Keohane eds., 1993). North Korea denounced the International Covenant on Civil and Political Rights (ICCPR) in 1997. Letter from Kim Yong Nam, Minister of Foreign Affairs, North Korea, to Kofi Annan, Secretary-General, United Nations (Aug. 23, 1997) (on file with the *Columbia Law Review*).

16. See, e.g., Karen Alter, The European Union's Legal System and Domestic Policy: Spillover or Backlash?, 54 Int'l Org. 489, 492 (2000) (asserting that "many if not most of the advances in European law have been the result of national courts referring preliminary

touting the efficacy of international law focuses on Europe, a region whose treaty regimes and international courts are among the most advanced and effective in existence.[17] Study of a non-European exemplar, particularly one rich in cross-court relationships, tests the robustness of theories developed in one region in other parts of the world. Fourth and finally, the case study is based on new empirical evidence. It incorporates detailed data on changing patterns in the filing and review of international human rights petitions against Commonwealth Caribbean governments during the 1990s, data that allow for a deeper assessment of the backlash's causes.

Before proceeding, however, a cautionary note is in order. The case study does not identify any single variable or set of variables that conclusively explains the actions of Commonwealth Caribbean governments. The complex series of events leading to the treaty denunciations does not so easily lend itself to such definitive causal conclusions. In addition, the study contains a number of specific features—such as the prominence of differing views over capital punishment, and appellate review by a national court located in a foreign jurisdiction—that are unlikely to recur in other contexts.

But if the details are unique to the Commonwealth Caribbean, the study has important implications for international law and international relations generally. It suggests that states precisely calibrate the legalized quality of treaty regimes to achieve particular objectives. Seen from this perspective, the legalization of international commitments is not unambiguously good, and overlegalized treaty regimes may pose particular dangers. Consider the World Trade Organization (WTO) as an example.[18] When it was launched in 1995, scholars praised the victory of trade "legalists," who trumpeted the WTO's sanctions-based dispute settlement system as an improvement over its more "diplomatic" predecessor (the

---

rulings to the [European Court of Justice (ECJ)]"); Helfer & Slaughter, supra note 7, at 309 (explaining that the ECJ and the European Court of Human Rights (ECHR) have increased their effectiveness in part by crafting their opinions to appeal to both the material interests and professional ideals of national courts and prospective litigants); Anne-Marie Slaughter, Judicial Globalization, 40 Va. J. Int'l L. 1103, 1104–12 (2000) [hereinafter Slaughter, Judicial Globalization] (describing process by which the ECJ and ECHR reviewed complaints arising from domestic legal settings and enhanced states' compliance with European Community treaties and the European Convention on Human Rights).

17. See John H. Barton & Barry E. Carter, The Uneven But Growing Role of International Law, *in* Rethinking America's Security: Beyond Cold War to New World Order 279, 287 (Graham Allison & Gregory F. Treverton eds., 1992) (describing judgments of the European Court of Human Rights as being "as effective as those of any domestic court"); see also Helfer & Slaughter, supra note 7, at 293–97 (describing the docket of the ECHR as "relatively teeming" and noting that "the rate of compliance by states with the ECHR's rulings is extremely high").

18. Final Act Embodying the Results of the Uruguay Round of Multilateral Trade Negotiations, Apr. 15, 1994, Legal Instruments—Results Of The Uruguay Round vol. 1 (1994), 33 I.L.M. 1140 (1994) [hereinafter Final Act].

General Agreement on Tariffs and Trade (GATT)).[19] Seven years on, the case for strongly legalized trade regimes is more uneasy. Governments do not habitually alter their domestic laws to comply with WTO rulings. And one of the remedies for noncompliance—retaliatory sanctions—causes the very trade distortions that the WTO was designed to avert.[20] The Caribbean backlash suggests that patterns of overlegalization can also develop for international human rights—an area that, paradoxically, is often viewed as underlegalized.[21]

The Caribbean backlash also generates important insights for international legal and international relations scholars. For political scientists, the case study provides an opportunity to test and refine competing arguments. Each of three major theoretical approaches—realist, ideational, and liberal—that seek to explain why states create and enforce legalized human rights regimes offers insights into why Caribbean states abrogated their treaty commitments. But no single theory offers a complete explanation, and the evidence presented here challenges hypotheses that each theory has advanced. For international legal scholars, the case study raises important issues of treaty structure, of international tribunals' appropriate functions, and of the role of state and nonstate actors in implementing treaty obligations.

The remainder of this Article proceeds as follows. Part I reviews the international relations literature on legalization and applies it in the context of human rights. It then describes three international relations theories—realist, ideational, and liberal—that offer competing hypotheses to explain why states enter into legalized commitments to protect human rights, the conditions under which states comply with those commitments, and the mechanisms by which human rights regimes evolve from their origins. Part I also introduces the contention that human rights agreements can become overlegalized, generating domestic opposition to a state's international obligations and pressure to exit from a treaty. It identifies two distinct types of overlegalization and undertakes a preliminary assessment of what causes human rights treaties to become more highly legalized.

---

19. See G. Richard Shell, Trade Legalism and International Relations Theory: An Analysis of the World Trade Organization, 44 Duke L.J. 829, 833–34 (1995).

20. See Judith Goldstein & Lisa L. Martin, Legalization, Trade Liberalization, and Domestic Politics: A Cautionary Note, 54 Int'l Org. 603, 620–21, 630 (2000) (arguing that the WTO's highly legalized rules may be suboptimal at achieving progressive liberalization of international trade); see also Steve Charnovitz, Rethinking WTO Trade Sanctions, 95 Am. J. Int'l L. 792, 792 & n.2 (2001) (asserting that trade sanctions "undermine[ ] the [WTO] trading system" and proposing "softer measures" as alternatives).

21. See Christine M. Chinkin, Book Review, 95 Am. J. Int'l L. 472, 473 (2001) (reviewing Human Rights in Global Politics (Tim Dunn & Nicholas Wheeler eds., 1999)) ("[H]uman rights activists and their organizations have invested significant resources in a strategy of legality—that is, a belief that claims are strengthened when encapsulated in law.").

Part II reviews the political, legal, and historical commonalities shared by Commonwealth Caribbean states, including their domestic regime types, their support of international human rights institutions, and their retention of the Judicial Committee of the Privy Council as their highest court of appeal. Part II then sets out a brief narrative of the events leading to the Caribbean backlash against human rights treaties, human rights tribunals, and the Privy Council. It identifies the relationships among domestic and international state and nonstate actors and provides data concerning the filing and review of petitions with human rights tribunals during the 1990s.

Part III views the Caribbean backlash through three different optics—one focused on capital punishment, the second addressing the judicial imperialism of the Privy Council, and the third emphasizing the overlegalization of human rights obligations—and explores the broader implications of analyzing the case study from these perspectives.

Part IV reviews the case study using the three international relations theories discussed in Part I. It identifies features of the Caribbean backlash that each theory helps to explain, as well as aspects where the case study questions existing hypotheses.

I. Legalization and the International Politics of Human Rights Treaties

A. *Identifying Legalization Variables in Human Rights Treaties*

International relations theories relating to human rights regimes are one component of a broader debate about the role of law in world politics. In a series of recent studies, a number of prominent scholars analyzed why international regimes and institutions in a number of issue areas are increasingly "legalized."[22] These scholars reject any suggestion that governments face a binary choice between legalized and nonlegalized norms, and instead measure legalization using three variables: obligation, precision, and delegation. "Obligation" refers to the binding nature of an institution's or a regime's rules; "precision" refers to the specificity of those rules; and "delegation" refers to the authority granted to neutral third parties to interpret and implement those rules, to resolve disputes relating to them, and (sometimes) to create new rules.[23]

These three components of legalization are not fixed; each may vary independently of the others, both within a single regime and across different regimes. Consider a few examples of these components in the

---

22. Judith Goldstein et al., Introduction: Legalization and World Politics, 54 Int'l Org. 385, 393–96 (2000).

23. Kenneth W. Abbott et al., The Concept of Legalization, 54 Int'l Org. 401, 401 (2000).

human rights context,[24] beginning with obligation. Human rights norms are found in instruments ranging from nonbinding documents, such as the Helsinki Accords,[25] to legally binding conventions and treaties, such as the American Convention on Human Rights (American Convention) or the International Covenant on Civil and Political Rights (ICCPR).[26] Within a single treaty system, some agreements are binding while others (both substantive and procedural) are optional or merely hortatory. States parties to the American Convention, for example, must comply with that treaty's substantive rules, but have the choice of whether to ratify the Protocol to Abolish the Death Penalty, or to recognize the jurisdiction of Inter-American Court of Human Rights.[27] Variations in obligation also exist among the decisions of international tribunals. Some decisions, such as those of the Inter-American Court, are legally binding;[28] others, such as those of the Inter-American Commission on Human Rights and the U.N. Human Rights Committee, are not.[29]

Precision differs widely across all human rights instruments, often varying inversely with levels of obligation. The soft law Helsinki Accords contain very clear and detailed rules, for example, while the hard law International Covenant on Economic, Social and Cultural Rights contains far more ambiguous prescriptions for government conduct.[30] Even

---

24. Non-human rights examples of these variations can be found in Kenneth W. Abbott & Duncan Snidal, Hard and Soft Law in International Governance, 54 Int'l Org. 421 (2000).

25. Conference on Security and Co-operation in Europe, Aug. 1, 1975, 14 I.L.M. 1292.

26. American Convention on Human Rights, Nov. 22, 1969, S. Exec. Doc. F, 95-2, at 41 (1978), 1144 U.N.T.S. 144 (entered into force July 18, 1978) [hereinafter American Convention]; International Covenant on Civil and Political Rights, adopted Dec. 19, 1966, S. Exec. Doc. E, 95-2, at 23 (1978), 999 U.N.T.S. 171 (entered into force Mar. 23, 1976) [hereinafter ICCPR].

27. American Convention, supra note 26, art. 62, S. Exec. Doc. E, 95-2, at 58, 1144 U.N.T.S. at 159; Protocol to the American Convention on Human Rights to Abolish the Death Penalty, June 8, 1990, 29 I.L.M. 1447.

28. American Convention, supra note 26, art. 68(1), S. Exec. Doc. E, 95-2, at 59, 1144 U.N.T.S. at 160 ("The States Parties to the Convention undertake to comply with the judgment of the Court in any case to which they are parties.").

29. See Optional Protocol to the International Covenant on Civil and Political Rights, adopted Dec. 19, 1996, art. 5(4), 999 U.N.T.S. 302, 303 (entered into force Mar. 23, 1976) [hereinafter Optional Protocol] (referring to decisions of the U.N. Human Rights Committee as "views"); Caballero Delgado & Santana Case, Inter-Am. Ct. H.R. 135, 154, OAS/Ser.L/V/III.33, doc. 4 (1995) (holding that a "recommendation" issued by the Inter-American Commission under articles 50 and 51 of the American Convention "does not have the character of an obligatory judicial decision for which the failure to comply would generate State responsibility"); see also Christina M. Cerna, International Law and the Protection of Human Rights in the Inter-American System, 19 Hous. J. Int'l L. 731, 752 (1997) (stating that the "[Inter-American Commission's] recommendations are not obligatory and the State may chose to comply or ignore them as it chooses"); Helfer & Slaughter, supra note 7, at 351 (discussing expressly nonbinding nature of Committee's decisions).

30. Compare, e.g., Conference on Security and Co-operation in Europe, supra note 25, pt. VII (stating that "[s]tates will recognize and respect the freedom of the individual to

within a single human rights treaty, some provisions are vague, such as the collective right to self-determination, while others are unequivocal and clear-cut, such as the bans on slavery and torture.[31]

Levels of delegation in human rights instruments are also extremely diverse. Most human rights treaties contain their own independent monitoring mechanisms to review states' compliance with their international commitments. These mechanisms take many forms, ranging from fully adversarial courts to nonadversarial managerial bodies, with many gradations in between. A large number of treaties contain some kind of judicial or court-like procedure for individuals and private parties to bring complaints alleging violations of their treaty rights against governments.[32]

The degree to which human rights treaties are legalized across each of these three elements is, at least initially, a function of state preferences. States consciously design human rights agreements in response to specific problems, choosing the degrees of obligation, precision, and delegation required to solve those problems.[33] But legalization is not costless. To the contrary, greater legalization necessarily requires a more far-reaching diminution of sovereignty, raising the important question of what motivates states to create legalized human rights agreements in the first place.

B. *International Relations Theories of Human Rights Treaty Formation*

As Andrew Moravcsik has noted, human rights law is different from most other forms of institutionalized international cooperation.[34] It is primarily intended not to regulate the external interactions of states but

---

profess and practise, alone or in community with others, religion or belief acting in accordance with the dictates of his own conscience"), with International Covenant on Economic, Social and Cultural Rights, adopted Dec. 16, 1966, art. 2(1), S. Exec. Doc. D, 95-2, at 13 (1978), 993 U.N.T.S. 3, 5 (entered into force Jan. 3, 1976) (obligating states parties "to take steps . . . to the maximum of its available resources, with a view to achieving progressively the full realization of the rights recognized in the present Covenant").

31. Compare, e.g., ICCPR, supra note 26, art. 1(1), S. Exec. Doc. E, 95-2, at 23, 999 U.N.T.S. at 173 ("All peoples have the right of self-determination."), with id. art. 8(1), S. Exec. Doc. E, 95-2, at 25, 999 U.N.T.S. at 175 ("No one shall be held in slavery; slavery and the slave-trade in all their forms shall be prohibited."). For other examples, see Ellen L. Lutz & Kathryn Sikkink, International Human Rights Law and Practice in Latin America, 54 Int'l Org. 633, 633–39 (2000) [hereinafter Lutz & Sikkink, International Human Rights Law] (discussing levels of obligation, precision, and delegation of torture, disappearances, and democracy in Latin America).

32. See Helfer, supra note 1, at 296–98 (discussing courts, tribunals, and treaty bodies that review human rights complaints under U.N.-based and regional human rights treaties).

33. Raustiala and Slaughter refer to these choices as a regime's "problem structure" and "solution structure." Raustiala & Slaughter, supra note 9, at 545.

34. Andrew Moravcsik, The Origins of Human Rights Regimes: Democratic Delegation in Postwar Europe, 54 Int'l Org. 217, 217 (2000) [hereinafter Moravcsik, Origins].

rather to hold governments accountable for conduct occurring within their own borders. Moreover, human rights law often empowers the objects of its protection—individuals, groups, and private parties—to enforce legal commitments through international courts and quasi-judicial bodies. These two features make human rights treaties a particularly deep form of international agreement.

Three different theories—realist, ideational, and liberal—provide different answers to the question of why states seek to create intrusive and legalized international commitments.[35] According to realist theorists, these commitments, including their review and enforcement institutions, are nothing more than a reflection of states' power and interests. Treaties and international organizations are thus of little concern to realists because they do not impose constraints on hegemonic states.[36] Realists' focus on power as the currency of international affairs does, however, offer an explanation for why nonhegemonic states ratify human rights treaties. Weaker governments "accept international obligations because they are compelled to do so by great powers."[37] The latter, seeking to export their ideological preferences and further their own political interests, coerce weaker states to join human rights agreements. Conversely, where powerful states oppose progressive human rights policies, realist theory holds that they can block the formation of human rights commitments by other nations.[38]

An ideational theory of human rights law stands on a very different footing. It posits that the source of human rights commitments "lie[s] not solely in preexisting state or societal interests but in strongly held principled ideas (ideas about right and wrong)."[39] These ideas exert their own persuasive power that shapes the interests and identity of both state and nonstate actors.[40] They also lead governments to create legalized commitments affirming the salience of the principles they embody and confirming collective legitimation on like-minded nations.

Liberal theory emphasizes states' rational pursuit of national interests, interests which reflect the preferences of their component constituencies and the "domestic and transnational social context in which they

---

35. For more extended discussions of these three theories, see id. at 220–29; Ellen Lutz & Kathryn Sikkink, The Justice Cascade: The Evolution and Impact of Foreign Human Rights Trials in Latin America, 2 Chi. J. Int'l L. 1, 5–7 (2001) [hereinafter Lutz & Sikkink, Justice Cascade].

36. See Kenneth W. Abbott & Duncan Snidal, Why States Act Through Formal International Organizations, 42 J. Conflict Resol. 3, 8 (1998) (noting this point, but stating that realist theorists underestimate the importance of international organizations, even to powerful states).

37. Moravcsik, Origins, supra note 34, at 221.

38. See Lutz & Sikkink, Justice Cascade, supra note 35, at 6.

39. Id. at 5; see also Sikkink, supra note 15, at 140 (arguing that "[o]ne cannot understand the emergence and adoption of human rights policies . . . without taking into account the unmediated role of ideas").

40. Lutz & Sikkink, Justice Cascade, supra note 35, at 5.

are embedded."[41] It asserts that governments bind themselves to human rights commitments to reduce the political uncertainty that is an inevitable byproduct of popular sovereignty. According to one leading liberal theorist, nascent democracies are acutely sensitive to this uncertainty and to the possibility of nondemocratic retrenchment. It is they, rather than established democracies, who press for international commitments and judicial review as a means of "'locking in' democratic rule through the enforcement of human rights."[42]

A key concept shared by both liberal and ideational scholars is a focus on the state as a transparent entity composed of disaggregated governmental and nongovernmental actors, each with its own distinct functions and interests.[43] The diverse and often divergent preferences of these actors allow for a rich series of domestic and transnational interactions. But the very fact that these parties act with at least nominal independence says much about the political structures in which they are embedded. For if a state is controlled by a totalitarian or other nondemocratic political authority, these actors (to the extent they exist at all) will have little or no ability to oppose the forces exercising political power. Thus, liberal theory, and to a lesser degree ideational theory, attach critical importance to domestic regime type as a predictor of a state's behavior and of its interactions with other states and international institutions.[44] States' status as liberal democracies[45] or rule of law socie-

41. Andrew Moravcsik, Taking Preferences Seriously: A Liberal Theory of International Politics, 51 Int'l Org. 513, 513 (1997); see also Jose E. Alvarez, Interliberal Law: Comment, 94 Am. Soc'y Int'l L. Proc. 249, 253 (2000) (describing liberal theory's "central insight" as "investigating the complex consequences of the disaggregated state"); Anne-Marie Slaughter, A Liberal Theory of International Law, 94 Am. Soc'y Int'l L. Proc. 240, 241 (2000) [hereinafter Slaughter, Liberal Theory] (stating that characteristics of liberal theory include its bottom-up view, its linking of the international and domestic spheres, its rendering of state-society relations as transparent, and its transformation of states into governments).

42. Moravcsik, Origins, supra note 34, at 228. Other commentators have questioned whether this hypothesis about a human rights treaty's supporters holds outside of Europe. See, e.g., Lutz & Sikkink, Justice Cascade, supra note 35, at 7 (questioning the hypothesis for Latin America).

43. This focus on disaggregation is not shared by realist theorists. But even for realists, the exporting of human rights policies by hegemonic states is undertaken by particular governmental subunits (i.e., the executive or legislative branch), whose actions, in turn, place pressure on other governmental subunits within weaker target states.

44. See Slaughter, Liberal Theory, supra note 41, at 249 ("Liberal international relations theory insists that differences in domestic regime type drive differences in positive behavior. Thus . . . [there is a] distinction between liberal and non-liberal states as a positive predictor of how states are likely to behave . . . within or toward international institutions.").

45. See, e.g., Michael W. Doyle, Kant, Liberal Legacies, and Foreign Affairs, 12 Phil. & Pub. Aff. 205, 207–09 (1983) (defining liberal democracies as having four major characteristics: (1) protection of private property; (2) a market economy; (3) equality under the law and respect for human rights; and (4) a representative government deriving its authority from the consent of individuals); Anne-Marie Slaughter, International Law in a World of Liberal States, 6 Eur. J. Int'l L. 503, 511 (1995) (defining a liberal democracy as

ties[46] has thus featured prominently in recent international relations scholarship relating to human rights and other legalized international commitments.[47]

C. *International Relations Theories of Human Rights Treaty Compliance*

Although each of the three international relations theories seeks to explain why states negotiate new human rights treaties, none of them alone conclusively predicts how states will act once a human rights regime has been established. States face a number of critical choices with respect to such extant regimes. These choices include whether to join a treaty already binding on other nations; whether to ratify optional or supplemental treaty provisions, such as those allowing for judicial or quasi-judicial review; whether to comply with agreed-to commitments; and whether to formally exit from a treaty.

International relations scholars recognize the inadequacy of existing theories fully to explain these issues. Thus, a recent study offering a liberal explanation for the creation of the European Convention on Human Rights (European Convention) acknowledges that "the determinants of the evolution of human rights regimes are unlikely to be identical to the determinants of their founding and are therefore unlikely to be explained entirely by republican liberal theory."[48] In a similar vein, in a study of human rights trials in Latin America, two ideational scholars state that they "do not know with certainty what motivated" newly democratic governments in that region rapidly to ratify existing human rights agreements, and they note that the historical evidence supports all three theoretical perspectives.[49]

---

a state that possesses "some form of representative government secured by the separation of powers, constitutional guarantees of civil and political rights, juridical equality, and a functioning judicial system dedicated to the rule of law").

46. See Beth A. Simmons, The Legalization of International Monetary Affairs, 54 Int'l Org. 573, 595 (2000) [hereinafter Simmons, Legalization] (arguing that states complying with the "rule of law" have strong court systems, stable political institutions, an established framework of property rights, and an orderly system of succession).

47. See Andrew Moravcsik, Explaining International Human Rights Regimes: Liberal Theory and Western Europe, 1 Eur. J. Int'l Rel. 157, 179–80 (1995) [hereinafter Moravcsik, Explaining] (arguing that certain features of liberal regime types were essential preconditions for success of European human rights system and comparing features of regime types found in Latin America); see also Robert O. Keohane et al., Legalized Dispute Resolution: Interstate and Transnational, 54 Int'l Org. 457, 478 (2000) (positing that liberal democracies will be most receptive to efforts to "embed international law in domestic legal systems"); Simmons, Legalization, supra note 46, at 597–98 (presenting results of empirical research supporting premise that compliance with international monetary obligations is more likely for rule of law states than for liberal states); Beth A. Simmons, Capacity, Commitment and Compliance: International Institutions and Territorial Disputes 17–18 (2002) (unpublished manuscript, on file with the *Columbia Law Review*) (examining hypothesis that domestic regime type is an indicator of the likelihood of Latin American states submitting territorial disputes to arbitration).

48. Moravcsik, Origins, supra note 34, at 246.

49. Lutz & Sikkink, Justice Cascade, supra note 35, at 7.

In seeking to discern how governments behave with regard to extant human rights agreements, recent international relations scholarship has reviewed the complex mechanisms by which state and nonstate actors interact within and across borders. Ideational and liberal scholars in particular have made significant contributions to identifying the causal pathways by which compliance occurs.[50]

1. *Ideational Theory: The Spiral Model of Human Rights Change.* — Leading ideational scholars have developed a five-step "'spiral model' of human rights change" that helps to explain compliance with human rights agreements.[51] In seeking to discern the forces that drive change at each stage of the spiral,[52] these scholars look both within the state and outside it. Internally, ideationalists focus on domestic nongovernmental organizations, which act as "compliance constituencies" to pressure government officials to adhere to international commitments.[53] Externally, these theorists highlight the importance of "transnational advocacy networks" or "principled issue-networks" comprised of concerned individuals, groups, and domestic and international government agencies and of-

---

50. Realist scholars have yet to respond to these ideational and liberal contributions. In part, this may result from a lack of interest in agreements that (realists assert) merely reflect rather than constrain state power. Because of such power, treaty compliance is merely a coincidence and can in fact be explained by a state acting in its self interest. See Hathaway, supra note 8, at 1944–46. Notwithstanding the absence of recent realist efforts to explain compliance with human rights agreements, this Article considers a realist explanation for the Caribbean backlash in infra Part IV.A.

51. See Thomas Risse & Kathryn Sikkink, The Socialization of International Human Rights Norms into Domestic Practices: Introduction, *in* The Power of Human Rights: International Norms and Domestic Change 1, 17–35 (Thomas Risse et al. eds., 1999) [hereinafter The Power of Human Rights].

52. In the first two stages of the spiral, states respond to domestic pressure for rights protections by repressing local advocacy groups, denying the validity of international jurisdiction, and asserting the counternorm of national sovereignty. Domestic nonstate actors also begin to forge links with transnational human rights networks during these early periods, allowing for increasing external pressure on state actors. Id. at 22–24. During the third stage of the spiral, governments begin to make minor "tactical concessions" in response to these internal and external pressures. Although governments often believe these concessions to be cosmetic or inconsequential, the discursive practices of advocacy groups entrap governments in their own rhetoric and initiate a dialogue that eventually changes both minds and interests. Id. at 25–28. The spiral's fourth stage occurs when human rights norms acquire "prescriptive status." States acknowledge the validity of human rights norms, internalize them into their domestic legal systems, and ratify international agreements protecting individual rights. Id. at 29, 31, 33. In the fifth and final stage of the spiral, governments engage in behavior that conforms to the international rules they have recognized and internalized, and pressure for change by nongovernmental organizations declines. Id. at 33. For additional discussion of the fourth and fifth stages of the spiral model as they relate to treaty ratification and treaty compliance, see infra notes 62–65 and accompanying text.

53. See Miles Kahler, Conclusion: The Causes and Consequences of Legalization, 54 Int'l Org. 661, 675 (2000) (reviewing conclusions of other studies); see also Goldstein & Martin, supra note 20, at 614–15 (discussing nonstate domestic actors favoring and opposing compliance with international trade agreements).

ficials, who work together to solve human rights problems.[54] Linking up with these transnational networks, domestic compliance constituencies create "boomerang" patterns of influence[55] on "vulnerable" states[56] by pressuring government officials "'from above' and 'from below.'"[57] Also central to ideationalist theory are "norm cascades," collections of norm-affirming events that lead states rapidly to conform their conduct to international standards and implement those standards in their domestic legal systems.[58] Once these norm cascades evolve beyond their tipping

---

54. See Margaret E. Keck & Kathryn Sikkink, Activists Beyond Borders: Advocacy Networks in International Politics 1 (1998); Kathryn Sikkink, Human Rights, Principled Issue-Networks, and Sovereignty in Latin America, 47 Int'l Org. 411, 415–16 (1993); see also Peter M. Haas, Introduction: Epistemic Communities and International Policy Coordination, 46 Int'l Org. 1, 3 (1992) (defining the related concept of "epistemic communities" as "network[s] of professionals with recognized expertise and competence in a particular domain and an authoritative claim to policy-relevant knowledge within that domain or issue-area").

55. According to Risse and Sikkink:

A "boomerang" pattern of influence exists when domestic groups in a repressive state bypass their state and directly search out international allies to try to bring pressure on their states from outside. National opposition groups, NGOs, and social movements link up with transnational networks and INGOs [international nongovernmental organizations] who then convince international human rights organizations, donor institutions, and/or great powers to pressure norm-violating states.

Risse & Sikkink, supra note 51, at 18; see also Keck & Sikkink, supra note 54, at 12–13 (describing operation of the boomerang pattern of influence).

56. Keck & Sikkink, supra note 54, at 29 ("Vulnerability arises both from the availability of leverage and the target's sensitivity to leverage; if either is missing, a campaign may fail.").

57. Risse & Sikkink, supra note 51, at 26 (citing Alison Brysk, From Above and Below: Social Movements, the International System, and Human Rights in Argentina, 26 Comp. Pol. Stud. 259, 261 (1993)).

58. See Lutz & Sikkink, International Human Rights Law, supra note 31, at 655 ("We suggest that norms cascades are collections of norm-affirming events. These events are discursive events—that is, they are verbal or written statements asserting the norm."). The concept of norm cascades is borrowed from a literature that focuses on domestic norms. See, e.g., Cass R. Sunstein, Free Markets and Social Justice 34–38 (1997) ("Norm cascades occur when societies are presented with rapid shifts toward new norms.").

International legal process scholars offer similar explanations for human rights changes, focusing on "the process whereby an international law rule is interpreted through the interaction of transnational actors in a variety of law-declaring fora, then internalized into a nation's domestic legal system." Harold Hongju Koh, Bringing International Law Home, 35 Hous. L. Rev. 623, 626 (1998); see also Harold Hongju Koh, Why Do Nations Obey International Law?, 106 Yale L.J. 2599, 2645–56 (1997) (book review) [hereinafter Koh, Why Do Nations Obey?] (identifying three phases in process by which nations comply with international norms: "interaction" with transnational actors, "interpretation" of international norm, and "internalization" of norm into domestic legal systems); Janet Koven Levit, The Constitutionalization of Human Rights in Argentina: Problem or Promise?, 37 Colum. J. Transnat'l L. 281, 285–87 (1999) (applying international legal process model to human rights issues in Argentina).

point,[59] states find it increasingly difficult to dispute the validity of international rules or engage in rights violations.[60]

What roles do treaty ratification and treaty compliance play in the ideational analysis? The ideationalists' spiral model understandably takes a long view of human rights change to include the practices of the most repressive governments that are the world's worst rights violators. Accordingly, treaty ratification generally does not occur until the spiral's fourth and penultimate stage, after a state has acknowledged the validity of human rights norms and international monitoring mechanisms and is engaging advocacy networks over compliance issues.[61]

The empirical evidence gathered by ideationalists suggests that although a few states may ratify international agreements as a tactical concession to opponents, most states are aware that treaty ratification has consequences. Thus, they will not accept international standards unless they are "prepared to live up to these standards domestically."[62] Although rights violations may occur during this period, states no longer question the validity of international norms but instead seek to justify or explain their conduct. Habitual rule-consistent behavior only occurs in the model's fifth and final stage, as human rights norms become fully institutionalized in domestic legal structures. As compliance improves, advocacy networks begin to demobilize.[63]

The spiral model does not, however, presume that human rights changes are either unidirectional or uniform across states. In the model's early stages, states can increase repression of domestic groups and cut off their contacts with transnational allies to stall advances in rights protection. Arresting change later in the process is far more difficult, however. Once a fully mobilized domestic opposition with transnational links has formed, "there is not much . . . oppressive rulers can do to fight off the pressure and to continue the violation of human rights."[64] In addition, not all states respond identically to international pressures. In a point that overlaps with liberal theory, ideational theorists claim that "[t]o the degree that a nation values its membership in an emerging com-

---

59. See Martha Finnemore & Kathryn Sikkink, International Norm Dynamics and Political Change, 52 Int'l Org. 887, 896, 901 (1998) ("After norm entrepreneurs [agents with strongly held notions of appropriate behavior within a relevant community of actors] have persuaded a critical mass of states to become norm leaders and adopt new norms, we can say the norm reaches a threshold or tipping point.").

60. Risse & Sikkink, supra note 51, at 21–22; Finnemore & Sikkink, supra note 59, at 904–05; see also Lutz & Sikkink, International Human Rights Law, supra note 31, at 638 (explicating the phenomenon of human rights "norm cascades" in Latin America in the 1980s).

61. Risse & Sikkink, supra note 51, at 29–30.

62. Thomas Risse & Stephen C. Ropp, International Human Rights Norms and Domestic Change: Conclusions, in The Power of Human Rights, supra note 51, at 234, 250. But see Hathaway, supra note 8, at 1999 (reporting results of statistical study concluding that noncompliance by states ratifying human rights treaties is common).

63. Risse & Sikkink, supra note 51, at 31–33.

64. Id. at 35.

munity of liberal states, it will be more vulnerable to pressures than a state that does not value such membership."[65]

In sum, ideationalists conclude that treaties do matter, and that their ratification is a necessary, although not a sufficient, condition for consistent observance of human rights standards.[66] Given the complexity of the spiral model and the divergent pathways to compliance that it generates, more studies and empirical data are needed to refine ideational hypotheses over when and why treaty compliance occurs.[67] These hypotheses are revisited in Part IV to assess the predictive power of ideational theory in light of the Caribbean backlash.

2. *Liberal Theory: The Role of Incorporation and Supranational Judicial Review in Securing Treaty Compliance.* — Scholars of liberal theory (working in human rights and other international fields) have focused on a different explanation for treaty compliance, derived from an analysis of the strategies states adopt to "implement" their international commitments.[68] These implementation strategies map across two distinct but interrelated variables: (1) the incorporation of international commitments into national law, and (2) the use of supranational judicial review to interpret those commitments and assess alleged violations.[69] As explained below, the presence of high values for each of these variables (that is, deeper

---

65. Id. at 24.

66. See, e.g., Risse & Ropp, supra note 62, at 276–77 (asserting that signing and ratifying international agreements is the first step toward institutionalizing human rights norms into domestic law, but that such "prescriptive status is inadequate in and of itself").

67. Other international relations scholars have questioned whether the norms-driven analysis of ideational and transnational legal process theorists adequately explains the evolution of a consensus favoring human rights protection. See Kahler, supra note 53, at 678 ("Although normative analysis identifies actors and processes, explanation too often appears to be post hoc."); Moravcsik, Origins, supra note 34, at 225 (questioning explanatory power of ideational theory); see also Raustiala & Slaughter, supra note 9, at 544 (noting that transnational legal process model conflates independent and dependent variables).

68. Raustiala, supra note 6, at 392 ("Implementation refers to the process of putting international commitments into practice: the passage of domestic legislation, promulgation of regulations, creation of institutions (both domestic and international), and enforcement of rules.").

69. See Raustiala & Slaughter, supra note 9, at 541–48 (describing these variables and others relating to compliance, including "problem structure; solution structure; solution process; norms; domestic linkages; and international structure"). The supranational judicial review variable is a particularized version of the "delegation" variable identified in the legalization literature, according to which the legalized attributes of an international regime are measured by whether states delegate interpretation, monitoring, and dispute settlement functions to a neutral third party. See supra Part I.A. Outside of the human rights context, however, such third parties often do not have (and from the perspective of optimal regime design, often should not have) any adjudicatory powers. See Raustiala, supra note 6, at 423–27 (discussing the success of nonbinding enforcement mechanisms in recent international environmental agreements). By contrast, the human rights landscape is rich in supranational courts, tribunals, and quasi-judicial review bodies. See Helfer, supra note 1, at 298–301 (describing the detailed procedures of three U.N. treaty bodies that monitor compliance with specific human rights treaties).

incorporation or a more powerful supranational tribunal) independently favors treaty compliance. Moreover, the two variables often interact synergistically in ways that enhance compliance opportunities.

Consider first the incorporation of international rules into domestic legal systems—what liberal and other scholars have variously described as "embeddedness,"[70] or "internalization."[71] In its legal incarnation, incorporation occurs when national judiciaries give a treaty direct effect (in American parlance, treat it as self-executing) or when national legislatures transpose a treaty into a constitution or statute. This penetration into the domestic sphere allows private parties to invoke the weight of national judicial authority to press for compliance with international rules.[72] Thus, holding other variables constant, liberal theory predicts that higher degrees of legal incorporation should be associated with higher levels of treaty compliance.[73]

Distinctly, states can create independent international institutions to review states' compliance with treaty commitments. Although human rights law contains the full spectrum of these bodies, liberal scholars devote particular attention to those courts and court-like institutions (often referred to as "supranational" or "transnational" tribunals) to which aggrieved individuals and groups have direct access.[74] As compared to judicial institutions before which only states may appear, such tribunals are more likely to receive a large number of cases challenging the treaty-compatibility of national government practices.[75] Whether this surge of individually initiated cases in itself enhances treaty compliance is unclear; at a minimum, it generates opportunities to impose domestic political pressure on governments to adhere to international rulings.[76]

---

70. Keohane et al., supra note 47, at 458.

71. Risse & Sikkink, supra note 51, at 5.

72. A prominent example of this in the human rights context is the incorporation of the European Convention on Human Rights into the domestic laws of the Convention's contracting parties. See generally Andrew Z. Drzemczewski, European Human Rights Convention in Domestic Law: A Comparative Study 260–303 (1983) (discussing signatories to the European Convention that have incorporated the treaty into domestic law, thereby allowing individuals to invoke the treaty or the ECHR's judgments in national judicial proceedings).

73. Keohane et al., supra note 47, at 478 ("Other things being equal, the more firmly embedded an international commitment is in domestic law, the more likely is compliance with judgments to enforce it.").

74. See Helfer & Slaughter, supra note 7, at 289; Keohane et al., supra note 47, at 458.

75. Keohane et al., supra note 47, at 474.

76. Alter, supra note 16, at 507–08; see also Kahler, supra note 53, at 675 (describing how, under regional human rights conventions, legalization and transnational dispute settlement "strengthened transnational networks that mobilized in support of domestic compliance constituencies"); Keohane et al., supra note 47, at 478 ("Individuals and groups can zero in on international court decisions as focal points around which to mobilize, creating a further intersection between transnational litigation and democratic politics.").

Thus, holding other variables constant,[77] the existence of supranational adjudication in a treaty regime should be associated with higher levels of treaty compliance.

Domestic incorporation of international commitments and supranational judicial review of those commitments each independently enhances prospects for treaty compliance. But neither alone is a sufficient guarantee of compliance. To the contrary, because these two attributes are endogenous choices available to states when designing treaty regimes, states may choose them only when they are predisposed to comply with international commitments.[78] Empirical evidence reviewed by liberal scholars, however, suggests that when both attributes coexist, compliance levels rise significantly. Most notably, the Treaty of Rome[79] and the European Convention[80]—treaties that require significant modifications to national laws—are characterized by deep incorporation, powerful supranational tribunals, and membership limited to liberal democracies. Both agreements exhibit high rates of compliance rivaling those found in domestic legal systems.[81]

How did incorporation and supranational judicial review function together to enhance treaty compliance in Europe? Studies of the Treaty of Rome and the European Convention, and of their supranational tribunals, the European Court of Justice (ECJ) and the European Court of Human Rights (ECHR), focus on two different time periods.[82] During an initial period after the treaties came into force, the two courts forged links with domestic state and nonstate actors interested in seeking compliance with their rulings. In particular, they sought to align the interests of private litigants (seeking to enforce treaty provisions that benefited them) with those of domestic court judges (seeking to augment their power of judicial review or, in the case of the European Community (EC), to bypass the authority of higher national courts by referring cases

---

77. Such variables include the "independence" of the international tribunal and the liberal or nonliberal regime type of states parties to the treaty creating it. See Keohane et al., supra note 47, at 459–62, 478–79.

78. Cf. Raustiala, supra note 6, at 392 (discussing treaty regimes in which compliance levels are high because states have adopted international standards that precisely match existing domestic practices).

79. Treaty Establishing the European Economic Community, Mar. 25, 1957, 298 U.N.T.S. 11.

80. Convention for the Protection of Human Rights and Fundamental Freedoms, Nov. 4, 1950, 213 U.N.T.S. 221 [hereinafter European Convention].

81. See supra note 17 and accompanying text.

82. See Alec Stone Sweet & Thomas L. Brunell, Constructing a Supranational Constitution: Dispute Resolution and Governance in the European Community, 92 Am. Pol. Sci. Rev. 63, 65 (1998); see also Anne-Marie Burley & Walter Mattli, Europe Before the Court: A Political Theory of Legal Integration, 47 Int'l Org. 41, 41 (1993) (describing different mechanisms by which ECJ promoted integration of European Community); Helfer & Slaughter, supra note 7, at 290–96 (recounting processes used by ECJ and ECHR to enhance their authority in relation to European governments).

directly to the ECJ).[83] Once such links were established, the tribunals adopted legal doctrines that enhanced their own authority and pressed for deeper incorporation, often in ways unanticipated by the treaties' drafters. In short, supranational jurists in Europe consciously sought to augment the two treaty regimes in ways that favored compliance.

D. *Human Rights Treaty Evolution and the Overlegalization of Human Rights*

As this brief overview of the two European courts illustrates, state compliance with legalized international commitments is often intimately related to the question of whether and how those commitments evolve over time.

Initially, the levels of obligation, precision, and delegation contained in a treaty, as well as the degrees (if any) of incorporation and supranational judicial review, are fixed by governments themselves as conscious acts of regime design.[84] Consider the choices governments face when

---

83. In the case of the ECJ, litigants filed cases in national courts, which in turn referred the cases to the ECJ for rulings on the treaty compatibility of national laws and policies. Enforcement of these rulings was left not to the vagaries of domestic politics, but instead entrusted to the same national jurists who had referred the cases, thereby enabling their enforcement as part of the domestic legal order. See Alter, supra note 16, at 492 (explaining how the ECJ encouraged national courts to use preliminary reference procedure and thereby "turned national courts into enforcers of European law in the national sphere"). In the case of both the ECJ and the ECHR, the court "craft[ed] opinions that encourage[d] national judges to view development of supranational law as a common project, while reassuring them that their own jurisdiction [would] be respected." Abbott, supra note 3, at 378; see also Helfer & Slaughter, supra note 7, at 297–98 (noting that the ECHR and ECJ "achieved substantial compliance with [their] judgments by forging relationships with domestic government institutions, both directly and indirectly through relationships with private parties").

84. See Raustiala & Slaughter, supra note 9, at 550 (reviewing literature on design of international regimes); see also Barbara Koremenos et al., The Rational Design of International Institutions, 55 Int'l Org. 761, 762 (2001) (arguing that "states use international institutions to further their own goals, and they design institutions accordingly" (emphasis omitted)).

Although the states that negotiate a human rights treaty have the most influence over setting its legalization and incorporation levels, individual ratifying states have some leeway to adjust those levels to suit their domestic particularities through the use of reservations. See Inter-American Commission on Human Rights, Signatures and Current Status of Ratifications: American Convention on Human Rights, available at http://www.cidh.oas.org/Basicos/basic4.htm (last visited Aug. 12, 2002) (on file with the *Columbia Law Review*) [hereinafter American Convention Ratification Chart] (listing reservations filed by states at time of ratification); United Nations, 1 Multilateral Treaties Deposited with the Secretary-General: Status as of 31 December 2001, at 181, 182–225, U.N. Doc. ST/LEG/SER.E/20, U.N. Sales No. E. 02.V.4 (2002); an updated version is available at http://untreaty.un.org/ENGLISH/bible/englishinternetbible/partI/chapterIV/treaty5.asp (on file with the *Columbia Law Review*) [hereinafter ICCPR Ratification Chart] (same). A reservation alters the receptivity of the reserving state's domestic legal system to international rules and institutions. A prominent (and controversial) example is the package of reservations, understandings, and declarations adopted by the United States when ratifying multilateral human rights treaties. Compare Kenneth Roth, The Charade of US Ratification of International Human Rights Treaties, 1 Chi. J. Int'l L. 347, 347 (2000) (lamenting that the

negotiating human rights agreements. Often the trade off is between a treaty's hard and soft law elements.[85] States may tolerate rather high levels of precision, but only if levels of obligation and delegation are more attenuated. This occurred in the European Convention, where governments approved a mandatory set of detailed substantive rules, but made the right of individual petition and recognition of the ECHR's jurisdiction wholly optional.[86] Other human rights regimes reflect similar efforts to mute full legalization, for example by making the right of individual petition mandatory but making the resulting decisions recommendatory rather than binding.[87]

Why are governments so concerned about a human rights treaty's legalization variables? The answer lies in the domestic political costs of protecting individual liberties. Altering domestic policies to conform to international human rights standards is not costless.[88] Such alterations impose external constraints on a government's ability to respond to legitimate social problems by regulating the behavior of individuals within its

---

United States, out of fear and arrogance, ratifies human rights treaties in such a way as to preclude any domestic effect), with Jack Goldsmith, Should International Human Rights Law Trump US Domestic Law?, 1 Chi. J. Int'l L. 327, 329 (2000) (defending the United States practice of limiting domestic effect of international human rights treaties because the domestic costs outweigh the domestic and international benefits). The validity of a reservation depends upon its compatibility with the object and purpose of the treaty. For a detailed discussion, see General Comment 24 (52) on Issues Relating to Reservations Made Upon Ratification or Accession to the Covenant or the Optional Protocols Thereto, or in Relation to Declarations Under Article 41 of the Covenant, U.N. GAOR, Hum. Rts. Comm., 50th Sess., Supp. No. 40, at 119, U.N. Doc. A/50/40 (1996), available at http://www.unhchr.ch/tbs/doc.nsf/symbol/69c55b086f72957ec12563ed004ecf7a?open document (on file with the *Columbia Law Review*) (identifying "the principles of international law that apply to the making of reservations and by reference to which their acceptability is to be tested and their purport to be interpreted").

85. See Abbott & Snidal, supra note 36, at 424–50 (discussing the advantages and disadvantages of hard and soft law and why states choose one form of international cooperation over the other); Raustiala, supra note 6, at 423–27 (exploring benefits of nonbinding instruments and the possibility that they may be more effective than legally binding treaties). See generally Commitment and Compliance: The Role of Non-Binding Norms in the International Legal System (Dina Shelton ed., 2000) (reviewing different subject areas of international law in which states have created nonbinding norms and standards).

86. Moravcsik, Origins, supra note 34, at 218.

87. Compare American Convention, supra note 26, art. 44, S. Exec. Doc. F, 95-2, at 53, 1144 U.N.T.S. at 155 (requiring states parties to grant individuals right of access to Inter-American Commission), with Caballero Delgado & Santana Case, Inter-Am. Ct. H.R. 135, 154, OAS/Ser.L/V/III.33, doc. 4 (1995) (confirming that a "recommendation" issued by the Inter-American Commission "does not have the character of an obligatory judicial decision"). Legalization under the ICCPR is even more attenuated, since states need not permit individuals to file complaints with the U.N. Human Rights Committee, and even if they do, the decisions of the Committee are not binding. See Helfer & Slaughter, supra note 7, at 341–43, 351.

88. See Hathaway, supra note 8, at 1951 ("Countries that are parties [to human rights treaties] may . . . be required to make potentially costly system-wide changes in order to bring themselves into compliance.").

borders or by allocating resources to other areas of social policy—both traditional aspects of state sovereignty. States have differential preferences for committing themselves to these external constraints, which may vary based on their regime type, level of socioeconomic development, responsiveness to domestic civil society, or desire to impose human rights obligations on other states.[89] As a result of these differing preferences, states intentionally design international agreements with varying levels of legalization to allow themselves a measure of flexibility to achieve societal objectives that rival the protection of individual rights.

This cost-benefit view of legalization may seem a more apt tool for analyzing treaties regulating international trade or international environmental law than agreements that protect individual liberties. But such balancing can also be a useful way to analyze human rights accords, given the pragmatic reality of the international system in which states determine a treaty's structure and retain the power to control if and when they will be bound by it through the acts of ratification and denunciation.[90] Moreover, the widespread prevalence of derogation and "clawback" clauses in human rights agreements[91] supports the argument that states

---

89. From a realist perspective, a powerful state might use weakly legalized treaties as part of a long-term strategy to pressure other states toward greater adherence to human rights standards. Since compelling other states to alter their human rights policies is not costless even for a hegemon, it might be rational for the powerful state to press for the ratification of a human rights treaty with low or moderate levels of legalization. Later, the state might add additional modes of financial or political pressure or seek to augment the treaty's legalization levels.

From an ideational perspective, a state might attempt to mollify domestic interest groups demanding human rights protections by negotiating and ratifying a human rights treaty with relatively weak legalization levels. According to the ideationalists' spiral model, however, ratification has consequences. It causes domestic and international advocacy groups to put increasing pressure on governments to improve their human rights performance.

From a liberal perspective, a partially legalized treaty might be the result of bargaining between newly democratic states (who seek high levels of obligation, precision, and delegation to lock in the requisites of democratic rule) and well-established democracies (who favor weaker human rights regimes or optional enforcement mechanisms to protect their sovereignty). See Moravcsik, Origins, supra note 34, at 228–29.

90. States may, of course, choose to make treaty ratification a one-way ratchet by precluding the possibility of exit. See Elizabeth Evatt, Democratic People's Republic of Korea and the ICCPR: Denunciation as an Exercise of the Right of Self-defence?, 5 Aust. J. Hum. Rts. 215, 219–20 (1998) (discussing Human Rights Committee's decision, in response to North Korea's attempt to denounce the ICCPR, that drafters intended to preclude states parties from denouncing the treaty).

91. Compare, e.g., American Convention, supra note 26, art. 27, S. Exec. Doc. F, 95-2, at 49, 1144 U.N.T.S. at 152 (identifying limited emergency situations in which states may derogate from treaty obligations but listing rights from which no derogation is permitted), with European Convention, supra note 26, art. 10(2) (listing "formalities, conditions, restrictions or penalties" states may impose on the right to freedom of expression where "prescribed by law" and "necessarily in a democratic society" in the interests of, inter alia, "national security, territorial integrity or public safety, for the prevention of disorder or crime, for the protection of health or morals").

consciously draft treaties that—with a few notable exceptions—are only partially legalized to strike a balance between the protection of individual liberties and other important societal objectives.[92]

A state's attempt to fix the attributes of a treaty's structure during the negotiation stage does not, however, guarantee that those attributes will remain fixed once the treaty enters into force.[93] Where a treaty's obligation, precision, or delegation levels increase over time, government discretion to achieve countervailing societal objectives in tension with human rights diminishes. For example, an agreement's substantive standards or its review procedures can progress from weak norms and procedures that only modestly constrain government conduct to more obligatory legal rules or review mechanisms that compel governments to act or refrain from acting. Indeed, this transformation can occur between any two points on a continuum that stretches from entirely nonbinding norms and review mechanisms at one end of the spectrum to entirely binding rules and review procedures at the other, with numerous intermediate points. "Overlegalization" exists where a treaty's augmented legalization levels require more extensive changes to national laws and practices than was the case when the state first ratified the treaty, generating domestic opposition to compliance or pressure to revise or exit from the treaty.[94]

This definition of overlegalization can be disaggregated into two distinct types, each of which makes different assumptions about the relationship between a state's desire and ability to comply with its human rights commitments and the compliance expectations reflected in the treaty. In addition, each type of overlegalization has different normative consequences that can be used to evaluate claims that a treaty regime has become overlegalized.

1. *Overlegalization that Changes Initial Treaty Bargains.* — In the first type of overlegalization, the obligation, precision, and delegation levels of a human rights treaty—in the form that it is ratified—optimally balance the ratifying state's desire to protect individual liberties against its desire to achieve other governmental objectives in tension with that protection. Overlegalization occurs when the treaty's legalization levels rise over time, constraining a state's ability to achieve this balance. This might occur, for example, where a supranational tribunal expands a treaty's

92. Such balancing is not permitted, of course, where states draft a treaty right in absolute terms. See, e.g., European Convention, supra note 80, art. 3 ("No one shall be subjected to torture or to inhuman or degrading treatment or punishment."); id. art. 4(1) ("No one shall be held in slavery or servitude."). Where states choose such language, they commit themselves to the proposition that no competing societal objective, however compelling, can justify the violation of that right.

93. For a discussion of what causes human rights treaties to evolve toward higher levels of legalization, see infra Part I.E.

94. The consequences of overlegalization may include an increase in noncompliance rates, proposals to amend a treaty to more accurately reflect state preferences, and denunciations of one or more instruments within a treaty regime.

mandatory substantive reach (thereby increasing obligation), narrowly interprets ambiguous derogation or "clawback" clauses (thereby increasing precision), or concludes that states are required to implement its non-binding recommendations (thereby increasing delegation).[95] Given the assumption of perfect correspondence between domestic preferences and the state's international commitments at the time of ratification, domestic opposition to compliance or pressure to exit from the treaty should increase if the state adheres to the treaty in its overlegalized form.

Challenges by a state objecting to the existence of this first type of overlegalization have some intuitive appeal. After all, the increase in legalization has "changed the rules of the game" for the ratifying state by adding new obligations, specifying existing obligations with greater particularity, or strengthening mechanisms for review and enforcement. These were not the commitments that the state agreed to undertake when it first joined the treaty regime.

This does not mean, of course, that optimal levels of legalization in a treaty cannot evolve over time to create more deeply legalized human rights commitments. Such a result might occur, for example, where states and their citizens develop preferences for stronger human rights protection in response to pressure from domestic and transnational advocacy groups (an ideational explanation) or from powerful states (a realist account), or where supranational tribunals successfully lock in the requisites of democracy (as liberal theory asserts).[96] But this type of overlegalization does illustrate how evolving treaty regimes can become too constraining, forcing governments to choose among noncompliance, revising the treaty, or denouncing it.

2. *Overlegalization that Improves Enforcement Opportunities.* — A second type of overlegalization is also plausible. This type relaxes the assumption of a perfect correlation between domestic preferences for human rights

---

95. See, e.g., Grigoriades v. Greece, 57 Eur. Ct. H.R. 2575, 2589 (1997) (holding that the ECHR's review of limitations on right to freedom of expression is not "limited to ascertaining whether the respondent State exercised its discretion reasonably, carefully and in good faith," but rather that the court must "look at the interference complained of in the light of the case as a whole and determine whether it was 'proportionate to the legitimate aim pursued' and whether the reasons adduced by the national authorities to justify it are 'relevant and sufficient'"); Marckx v. Belgium, 31 Eur. Ct. H.R. (ser. A) at 19 (1979) (explaining that ECHR interprets the European Convention "in light of present-day conditions" rather than adhering to human rights standards endorsed by the Convention's drafters); Bradshaw v. Barbados, Communication No. 489/1992, U.N. GAOR, Hum. Rts. Comm., 49th Sess., Supp. No. 40 vol. 2, at 305, 309, U.N. Doc. A/49/40 (1994) ("It is an obligation for the State party to adopt appropriate measures to give legal effect to the [nonbinding] views of the Committee as to the interpretation and application of the [ICCPR] in particular cases arising under the Optional Protocol.").

96. The striking success of the ECHR in expanding the obligations of the European Convention and its own review powers without creating diminished compliance with its judgments illustrates this possibility. See Helfer & Slaughter, supra note 7, at 311–12 (explaining ways in which ECHR augmented its authority and expanded reach of the European Convention).

protection within a state and the initial legalization levels in a human rights treaty. Instead, it assumes (perhaps more realistically) that such treaties are too onerous even at their inception to be fully adhered to without incurring significant costs or generating significant domestic opposition. Many states are unwilling or unable to incur these costs or to expose themselves to such opposition. Why, then, would they choose to ratify treaties containing commitments they are unlikely to meet?

Although ratification may signal a genuine desire to strive for compliance,[97] it may also reflect the political benefits states gain (for example, from their citizens or from powerful states with a human rights agenda) from the expressive act of ratification. In this view, ratification functions "as a pleasing statement not necessarily intended to have any real effect on outcomes. It declares to the world that the principles outlined in the treaty are consistent with the ratifying government's commitment to human rights."[98] But states also know that their failure to live up to this commitment may not be detected. Outside of Europe, treaty review procedures are generally weak and only limited opportunities exist to impose direct or indirect sanctions for noncompliance.[99] Because of this disjunction between a treaty's formal requirements and the practical opportunities for its enforcement, states can provide domestic levels of human rights protection that are lower than a treaty in fact requires. Under this set of assumptions, overlegalization occurs where opportunities to detect, expose, or remedy noncompliance increase over time, forcing states closer to the commitments formally enshrined in a treaty's text.[100]

Challenges to this second variant of overlegalization at first appear far from compelling. It hardly seems justifiable for a state to contest efforts to compel adherence to obligations that it willingly assumed. But if many states in fact fail to comply with the human rights treaties they ratify, as a recent comprehensive quantitative study concludes,[101] increases

---

97. According to one assessment, states intend to comply with their treaty commitments but are unable to do so, for example, because of unavoidable time lags associated with implementation or because they lack technical or administrative capacity or adequate resources. See Abram Chayes & Antonia Handler Chayes, The New Sovereignty: Compliance with International Regulatory Agreements 10 (1995) (describing "willful flouting" of treaties as infrequent). Proponents of this approach advocate "management" of compliance by nonconfrontational, nonbinding mechanisms that monitor behavior, build capacity, and resolve disputes informally, thereby persuading states to adhere to their treaty commitments. See id. at 22–28.

98. Hathaway, supra note 8, at 2005–06 (internal citation omitted).

99. See id. at 1938, 2008 (noting that "the major engines of compliance that exist in other areas of international law are for the most part absent in the area of human rights," and describing human rights monitoring systems as "woefully inadequate").

100. Given its focus on enforcement, this type of overlegalization should be associated with increases in delegation, either to supranational tribunals or to domestic courts.

101. See Hathaway, supra note 8, at 1999 (concluding that noncompliance with human rights treaties is common and that ratification is often associated with worse human rights ratings than would otherwise be expected). But see Koh, Why Do Nations Obey?,

in legalization could produce the same sorts of reactions by states that rely on weak enforcement mechanisms to obscure noncompliance as may be produced by overlegalization that changes initial treaty bargains. Increases in delegation that make it easier to detect noncompliance might thus be normatively unassailable, but still capable of producing a backlash in the form of treaty denunciations.

From a pragmatic perspective, these arguments raise critical questions of regime design. For example, should nonstate advocates for human rights or states with high compliance rates continue to accept treaties with strong substantive rules but weak enforcement mechanisms to maintain broad-based participation by states with poor human rights records? Or should they seek to "trap" noncomplying states in their formal commitments by encouraging supranational tribunals and domestic courts to undertake more stringent review of treaty obligations, even at the risk of exit by some states?[102] The normative implications are even more challenging. In the area of international trade, scholars have argued that there is an optimal level of imperfection in treaties that gives states leeway to address the uncertainties of the international marketplace.[103] According to these scholars, escape clauses and loopholes in a treaty's text[104] and weak or opaque review procedures are essential to ensure that agreements bend rather than break when negative economic shocks make noncompliance efficient.[105] Whether these concepts can be translated to the human rights context is uncertain given the deontological arguments that support such rights. But they, along with the prag-

---

supra note 58, at 2599 & n.2 (arguing that empirical studies "seem[ ] largely to have confirmed" Professor Henkin's "hedged but optimistic" assertion that "'almost all nations observe almost all principles of international law and almost all of their obligations almost all of the time'" (citing Henkin, supra note 5, at 47)).

102. Cf. George W. Downs et al., Managing the Evolution of Multilateralism, 52 Int'l Org. 397, 400–06 (1998) (discussing the relative merits of different types of multilateral structures relating to free trade and environmental protection, such as organizations with more or less inclusive memberships).

103. See George W. Downs & David M. Rocke, Optimal Imperfection? Domestic Uncertainty and Institutions in International Relations 76–77 (1995).

104. See B. Peter Rosendorff & Helen V. Milner, The Optimal Design of International Trade Institutions: Uncertainty and Escape, 55 Int'l Org. 829, 830 (2001) (defining "escape clauses" of international agreements as "any provision[s] of an international agreement that allow[ ] a country to suspend the concessions it previously negotiated without violating or abrogating the terms of the agreement"). The derogation clauses in human rights treaties discussed above function as escape clauses in times of national emergency. See supra note 91.

105. See Downs & Rocke, supra note 103, at 77; see also Catherine Powell, Dialogic Federalism: Constitutional Possibilities for Incorporation of Human Rights Law in the United States, 150 U. Pa. L. Rev. 245, 292 (2001) (stating that "[b]ecause international law is a low-viscosity system, noncompliance occurs 'without irreparably tearing the fabric of the governing legal orders'" (quoting Daniel Halberstam, Comparative Federalism and the Issue of Commandeering, in The Federal Vision: Legitimacy and Levels of Governance in the United States and the European Union 213, 225 (Kalypso Nicolaidis & Robert Howse eds., 2001))).

COLUMBIA LAW REVIEW   [Vol. 102:1832

matic issues discussed above, raise the unsettling possibility that the optimal level of compliance with a human rights treaty for a particular state might be less than perfect compliance, and that therefore increasing the treaty's legalization levels might be counterproductive.

E. *The Causes and Consequences of Overlegalization: A Preliminary Assessment*

The possibility that international human rights treaties can become overlegalized raises intriguing questions. First, what causes the agreements to evolve over time and become more heavily legalized? Second, which state and nonstate actors press for increased legalization? Finally, at what point does the move toward higher legalization levels result in overlegalization? Answers to these questions will depend upon variables such as the particular agreement at issue, its membership and subject matter, and the precise pathways by which legalization increases. This Section provides only a preliminary general assessment of these issues. A more detailed and contextualized analysis appears in Parts III and IV, which discuss the Commonwealth Caribbean backlash against human rights regimes and the ability of international relations theories to explain the backlash.

International relations scholars differ over what triggers human rights treaties to evolve from their origins. According to ideational and some liberal theorists, governments do not anticipate the domestic political consequences of treaty membership and as a result are vulnerable to pressures to expand the treaty.[106] Other liberal scholars, by contrast, assert that governments are fully aware that their initial decision to ratify a human rights agreement will create political pressure for further diminutions of sovereignty and that they design treaties accordingly.[107]

As this analysis makes clear, a diverse set of actors may press for treaty evolution. Executive or legislative officials may see advantages to revising a treaty's legalization levels after it enters into force. In such a case, overlegalization is less likely to occur since states themselves control the pace and extent of change. Nonstate actors—both domestic and transnational advocacy networks—can also seek to augment legalized commitments to achieve their objectives, often by enlisting the support of national courts or supranational tribunals. National courts augment legalization by giving a treaty direct effect or by construing domestic law in harmony with it—acts that increase the treaty's obligatory character by making its rules binding domestically as well as internationally.[108] Supra-

---

106. See, e.g., Kahler, supra note 53, at 681 (reviewing legalization studies supporting conclusion that sometimes "governments have not foreseen the consequences of links between their own domestic politics and legalized international institutions").

107. See, e.g., Moravcsik, Origins, supra note 34, at 243 (discussing formation of European Convention on Human Rights).

108. See Joel P. Trachtman, Bananas, Direct Effect and Compliance, 10 Eur. J. Int'l L. 655, 659 (1999) (arguing that when courts give international agreements direct effect, the

national jurists also pursue expansionist strategies, as the ECHR and ECJ illustrate. The greater independence of these tribunals, their access to private parties with the incentive to challenge treaty violations, and their links to national courts have allowed them to expand the substantive scope and legalization levels of the agreements they interpret "without triggering noncompliance, withdrawal, or reform by national governments."[109]

Where governments do not control a treaty's evolution, just how far can treaty commitments expand before states begin to resist them? Early liberal studies argued that once supranational tribunals had established relationships with national courts and private parties, supranational review would generate a "one-way ratchet" toward increasing levels of legalization and incorporation into domestic law.[110] Recent liberal scholarship has identified more complex interactions among supranational tribunals and state and nonstate actors which challenge this assumption. Contrary to prior findings, "[n]egative feedback loops may also emerge" in the relationships among these actors, diminishing the scope and importance of international commitments and lowering levels of treaty compliance.[111] Ideational scholars make similar claims regarding points in the spiral model of human rights change at which governments can return to repressive practices.[112]

Finally, for any pathway of treaty evolution, the pace of change must also be considered. The growth rate endorsed by a state's executive or legislative bodies may lag behind the rate of change that judicial and nonstate actors seek to impose. In Europe, for example, it took more than thirty years for all governments to ratify the European Convention's optional judicial review clauses, thus enabling a structural revision of the treaty to make such review mandatory.[113] Evolutionary strategies adopted

---

agreements can be automatically implemented and thus are more heavily legalized than treaties not given such effect); see also Keohane et al., supra note 47, at 466–67 (arguing that control of governments is at its apex where "autonomous national courts can enforce international judgments against their own governments").

109. Id. at 479–80; see also Alter, supra note 16, at 492 (noting how ECJ acted to increase obligation, precision, and delegation of European Union (EU) treaties).

110. Burley & Mattli, supra note 82, at 60 (discussing history of the ECJ).

111. Alter, supra note 16, at 512. As Karen Alter demonstrates in her study of the ECJ, the very success of the court in expanding the reach of European integration may have precipitated a backlash against it. Alter notes the limitations member states have placed on the ECJ's powers and the resistance some national courts have shown to implementing EU law. Id. at 512–15.

112. See Risse & Sikkink, supra note 51, at 18.

113. See Keohane et al., supra note 47, at 485 (noting that creation of Protocol 11, making jurisdiction of ECHR compulsory and permitting individuals direct access to the court, occurred after three-decade period during which all European governments voluntarily recognized ECHR's jurisdiction and granted individuals access to European Commission on Human Rights); see also Moravcsik, Explaining, supra note 47, at 181 (noting that human rights commitments "develop slowly, even among stable and advanced democracies").

by national courts or supranational tribunals may proceed more rapidly, as the histories of the ECJ and the Human Rights Committee reveal.[114]

The disjunctions between these differing rates of change highlight potential fault lines of overlegalization within evolving treaty systems. They also suggest that judicial actors pressing for increased legalization must exercise caution to avoid "provok[ing] a backlash that contribute[s] to disintegration" of a treaty.[115] In the case of the European Community, for example, such a backlash took the form of amendments to the EC treaties adopted by member states to "reverse or qualify" the effects of expansive ECJ rulings or to "constrain the ECJ's activism."[116] These governmental responses to overlegalization were largely incremental, however. Full-scale exit from the Community by a state dissatisfied with the ECJ's legalization efforts was not a viable option given the broad cross-section of issues contained in the EC treaties and the adverse effects of denunciation on domestic interest groups. As the next Part explains, however, no similar issue linkages deterred Commonwealth Caribbean states from denouncing their human rights obligations. As a result, when the region's highest court issued a highly unpopular decision that increased the treaties' legalization levels in the area of capital punishment, exiting the treaties became a viable political strategy for Caribbean governments.

II. THE HUMAN RIGHTS BACKLASH IN THE COMMONWEALTH CARIBBEAN

This Part describes the human rights backlash in the Caribbean. It begins by identifying the common political and legal structures shared by Commonwealth Caribbean nations as well as divergences among the three states who denounced human rights treaties—Jamaica, Trinidad & Tobago, and Guyana. It then turns to a roughly chronological narration of events beginning in the 1980s and leading up to the denunciations of human rights treaties and petition procedures by these three states between 1997 and 2000. The narrative focuses in particular on a watershed decision of the Privy Council, *Pratt v. Attorney-General for Jamaica*,[117] which generated a new set of interactions among supranational tribunals, national courts, private litigants, and transnational advocacy networks. The case, and the interactions it precipitated, illustrate one way in which a human rights agreement can become overlegalized. These events also provide a factual foundation for assessing how accurately the interna-

---

114. See Helfer & Slaughter, supra note 7, at 290–93, 338–66 (identifying strategies used by ECJ and Human Rights Committee to augment the legalized qualities of the respective treaties subject to their review).

115. Alter, supra note 16, at 490; see also Moravcsik, Explaining, supra note 47, at 182 ("Strongly pressuring countries to accept binding jurisdiction and the individual right of petition before they are ready to accept it voluntarily is to invite open non-compliance . . . .").

116. Alter, supra note 16, at 513.

117. [1994] 2 A.C. 1 (P.C. 1993) (appeal taken from Jam.).

tional relations theories described in Part I explain the Caribbean human rights backlash.

A. *Political and Legal Systems and Efforts to Protect Human Rights*

1. *Domestic Regime Types.* — Jamaica, Trinidad & Tobago, Guyana, and the nine other independent nations that comprise this region are all former colonies of the United Kingdom and present members of the British Commonwealth.[118] Upon achieving independence beginning in the early 1960s,[119] each nation retained key features of British law and politics, including Westminster-style parliaments[120] and common law legal systems.[121] Caribbean nations deviated from the British model, however, by adopting written constitutions that endorsed judicial review and a rule of constitutional supremacy over legislative and executive action.[122]

In terms of domestic regime type, all but one of the states in the Commonwealth Caribbean are liberal democracies.[123] Their govern-

---

118. See The Commonwealth, Who We Are, at http://www.thecommonwealth.org/dynamic/Country.asp (last visited Aug. 12, 2002) (on file with the *Columbia Law Review*) (listing members of the Commonwealth). The twelve nations are Antigua & Barbuda, The Bahamas, Barbados, Belize, Dominica, Grenada, Guyana, Jamaica, St. Kitts & Nevis, St. Lucia, St. Vincent & the Grenadines, and Trinidad & Tobago. Guyana and Belize, although not geographically part of the Caribbean, are generally included in the term "Commonwealth Caribbean" because of their historical and political links to Britain. See Rose-Marie Belle Antoine, Commonwealth Caribbean Law and Legal Systems 3 & n.1 (1999) (noting that Guyana and Belize are geographically part of South and Central America, respectively, but arguing that the "Commonwealth Caribbean" is a political region created from the British colonial experience).

119. Jamaica and Trinidad & Tobago became sovereign nations in 1962. Guyana followed in 1966. Laurel B. Francis, Caribbean Community States and State Succession, *in* Caribbean Perspectives on International Law and Organizations 84, 84 & nn.3–4, 85, 87 n.15 (B.G. Ramcharan & L.B. Francis eds., 1989).

120. See Arend Lijphart, Democracies: Patterns of Majoritarian and Consensus Government in Twenty-One Countries 1–20 (1984) (discussing the Westminster model of democracy); Anthony Payne, Westminster Adapted: The Political Order of the Commonwealth Caribbean, *in* Democracy in the Caribbean: Political, Economic, and Social Perspectives 57, 60–72 (Jorge I. Domínguez et al. eds., 1993) (evaluating Caribbean adaptation of Westminster model based on characteristics of "constitutionalism," "civilian supremacy," "bureaucratic and police neutrality," "competitive elections," and "pluralist representation").

121. Antoine, supra note 118, at 28–30. This is true even for Guyana, which retains only remnants of a Roman law system imposed by the Dutch. Id. at 51.

122. Id. at 41, 83; Sir Fred Phillips, Freedom in the Caribbean: A Study in Constitutional Change 124 (1977). For the three nations under study, these constitutions were drafted by local state and nonstate actors, albeit with strong support from the British Colonial Office. Id. at 79–80 (describing drafting of constitutions of Jamaica, Trinidad & Tobago, and Guyana and characterizing them as "autochthonous" or "home-grown" instruments (citing K.C. Wheare, The Constitutional Structure of the Commonwealth 93–95 (1960))); A.W. Brian Simpson, Human Rights and the End of Empire: Britain and the Genesis of the European Convention 870–73 (2001) (discussing support of Colonial Office for inclusion of bills of rights clauses in domestic constitutions of former British colonies).

123. See supra note 45 (defining liberal democracies).

ments are chosen by free and fair elections among competing political parties, their judiciaries are independent (if sometimes underfunded),[124] and state actors protect basic civil and political liberties as well as property rights while upholding the rule of law.[125] Indeed, the strength and resiliency of liberal democratic structures in the Commonwealth Caribbean are unique among developing nations and contrast sharply with the nearby nations of Central and South America, which have been governed by autocratic or unstable regimes until a democratizing trend took hold in the 1980s.[126]

Guyana is the only longstanding exception to these regional commonalities.[127] After the country's last free election under British rule in 1964, Guyana was governed for more than twenty years by Forbes Burnham, an autocratic socialist leader who declared his ruling party para-

---

124. See Albert Fiadjoe, Caribbean Public Law 151–53 (1996) (noting constitutional guarantee of judicial independence and discussing increasing development of lower court independence); Telford Georges, The Scope and Limitations of State Machinery, *in* Human Rights and Development: Report of a Seminar on Human Rights and Their Promotion in the Caribbean 40, 47 (Int'l Comm'n of Jurists & The Org. of Commonwealth Caribbean Bar Ass'ns eds., 1977) (arguing that judiciary is "adequate[ly]" independent with exception of lifetime tenure provisions). But see Antoine, supra note 118, at 223–26 (arguing that although judicial independence is embedded in Commonwealth Caribbean constitutions, problems of limited qualified personnel and financial resources may undermine achievement of true autonomy).

125. See Freedom House, Democracy's Century: A Survey of Global Political Change in the 20th Century 1, 4, at http://www.freedomhouse.org/reports/century.pdf (last visited Aug. 12, 2002) (on file with the *Columbia Law Review*) (identifying Commonwealth Caribbean states in the year 2000 as "democracies" in which "leaders are elected in competitive multi-party and multi-candidate processes in which opposition parties have a legitimate chance of attaining power or participating in power"); see also Ivelaw L. Griffith & Trevor Munroe, Drugs and Democratic Governance in the Caribbean, *in* Democracy and Human Rights in the Caribbean 74, 82 (Ivelaw L. Griffith & Betty N. Sedoc-Dahlberg eds., 1997) ("Relative to other states, Caribbean states have over the last fifty years been exceptional in the consistency of fair and free elections, the observation of political rights and civil liberties, competitive party systems, and the rule of law."); Merle McCormack, A Non-Governmental Organisation Perspective on Human Rights Action in the Caribbean, *in* International Human Rights Law in the Commonwealth Caribbean 348, 348 (Angela D. Byre & Beverley Y. Byfield eds., 1991) ("Commonwealth Caribbean countries have, by and large, retained a high level of Parliamentary democracy . . . .").

126. See Jorge I. Domínguez, The Caribbean Question: Why Has Liberal Democracy (Surprisingly) Flourished?, *in* Democracy and the Caribbean, supra note 120, at 1, 2–3; cf. Lutz & Sikkink, Justice Cascade, supra note 35, at 7 (noting "regional wave of redemocratization between 1978 and 1991" in Latin America).

127. Grenada is another limited exception to the region's strong liberal democratic history. The 1979 revolution in that country led to a four-year suspension of democratic political structures. See Clifford E. Griffin, Democracy and Political Economy in the Caribbean, *in* The Political Economy of Drugs in the Caribbean 113, 134 n.2 (Ivelaw L. Griffith ed., 2000); see also McCormack, supra note 125, at 350 (noting that the independence of the judiciary has been somewhat undermined in Grenada). Another minor exception is the nation of Antigua & Barbuda, where there have been claims of electoral fraud and corruption since 1976 with respect to the Antigua Labor Party. See Griffin, supra, at 136 n.2.

mount to the state, suppressed free elections, compromised the judiciary, and violated human rights. State socialism and one-party control began to erode after Burnham's death in 1985 and accelerated after free elections were held in 1992.[128] Additional free elections and changes of government followed, but as of 2001 Guyana was still making a slow and unsteady transition to democratic rule.[129]

  2. *Domestic and International Protection of Human Rights.* — Another point of regional commonality (again with only partial applicability to Guyana) is a moderately good record of protecting human rights in domestic legal systems.[130] According to annual surveys by Freedom House, the Commonwealth Caribbean ranks well above the global average in the enjoyment of political rights and civil liberties.[131] In addition, Commonwealth Caribbean constitutions contain detailed bills of rights closely modeled on the European Convention on Human Rights and the Universal Declaration on Human Rights.[132] Promotion of human rights also

---

  128. See Ivelaw L. Griffith, Democracy and Human Rights in Guyana, *in* Democracy and Human Rights in the Caribbean, supra note 125, at 156, 158–59; W. Marvin Will, NGOs and IGOs as Promoters of Liberal Democracy in the Caribbean: Cases from Nicaragua and Guyana, *in* Democracy and Human Rights in the Caribbean, supra note 125, at 51, 60–67.

  129. See Bureau of W. Hemisphere Affairs, U.S. Dep't of State, Background Note: Guyana (2001), available at http://www.state.gov/r/pa/ei/bgn/1984.htm (on file with the *Columbia Law Review*); U.S. Dep't of State, 1999 Country Reports on Human Rights Practices: Guyana (2000), available at http://www.state.gov/www/global/human_rights/ 1999_hrp_report/guyana.html (on file with the *Columbia Law Review*) [hereinafter 1999 Guyana Country Report].

  130. See Val T. McComie, Legal Contribution of the Caribbean to the Inter-American System, *in* Caribbean Perspectives on International Law and Organizations, supra note 119, at 432, 436 ("Respect for human rights is deeply rooted in the peoples of the Caribbean . . . ."); McCormack, supra note 125, at 349–50 (noting that in English-speaking Caribbean "human rights problems have tended to be isolated and incidental rather than systemic").

  For a discussion of problematic areas, including the criminal justice system, arbitrary detentions, and extra-judicial killings, see Florizelle O'Connor, The Jamaica Council for Human Rights: A Non-Governmental Organisation Case Study, *in* International Human Rights Law in the Commonwealth Caribbean, supra note 125, at 331, 333–45. A more detailed discussion of the human rights problems associated with Caribbean criminal justice systems appears infra Part III.C.

  131. The Freedom House ratings range from 1 to 7 for political rights and for civil liberties, respectively, with 1 being the most rights-protective rating. In the period between 1973 and 2000, the ratings for Jamaica ranged from 1,2 to 2,3; for Trinidad & Tobago from 1,1 to 2,3; and for Guyana from 2,2 to 5,5. Freedom House, Freedom in the World Country Ratings, 1972–1973 to 2000–2001, available at http://www.freedomhouse.org/ research/freeworld/FHSCORES.xls, (last visited Aug. 12, 2002) (on file with the *Columbia Law Review*). Guyana received the least rights-protective ratings (from 3,3 to 5,5) between 1974 and 1992 when democratic political structures were compromised and Freedom House designated the country as only "partly free." Guyana's rating has remained at 2,2 since 1993. Id.

  132. Antoine, supra note 118, at 157–58.

occurs through domestic NGOs and a system of ombudsmen who hear individual complaints of government abuses.[133]

The region's commitment to protecting human rights is not limited to the domestic sphere. Newly independent Commonwealth Caribbean governments also supported international institutions,[134] including those relating to human rights.[135] Jamaica and Guyana were early signatories to the ICCPR, in 1966 and 1968 respectively, and their ratifications followed nine years later in 1975 and 1977.[136] Trinidad & Tobago ratified the treaty in 1978 two years after revising its constitution.[137] Jamaica ratified the Optional Protocol to the ICCPR (Optional Protocol) in 1975, as did Trinidad & Tobago in 1980, both well before the rapid wave of ratifications in the 1990s; Guyana followed suit in 1993 (after its first free post-independence elections in 1992).[138] Adherence to Inter-American human rights rules and institutions was slower and more halting, largely because the Organization of American States (OAS) was created without Caribbean participation and because its basic instruments did "not reflect the reality and the interests of the Caribbean."[139] Jamaica did not ratify the American Convention until 1978, Trinidad until 1991 (at which time

133. Id. at 303–18; Rose D'Sa, National Institutions Concerned with the Promotion of Human Rights in Commonwealth Countries, in International Human Rights Law in the Commonwealth Caribbean, supra note 125, at 317, 324–27.

134. Prior to independence in the late 1950s, Caribbean governments formed a short-lived Federation of the West Indies. Phillips, supra note 122, at 21–77. Shortly thereafter, they formed a Caribbean Free Trade Association and later a Caribbean Common Market (CARICOM). G. Pope Atkins, Latin America and the Caribbean in the International System 185–87 (1999).

135. This accords with Andrew Moravcsik's study of the European human rights system, which argues that newly emergent liberal democracies look to international human rights regimes "to 'lock in' and consolidate democratic institutions." Moravcsik, Origins, supra note 34, at 220.

136. ICCPR Ratification Chart, supra note 84, at 181.

137. Id. at 182. See also Phillips, supra note 122, at 191–97 (discussing constitutional reforms in Trinidad & Tobago).

138. United Nations, 1 Multilateral Treaties Deposited With the Secretary-General: Status as of 31 December 2001, at 226–27, U.N. Doc. ST/LEG/SER.E/20, U.N. Sales No. E.02.V.4 (2002), available at http://untreaty.un.org/ENGLISH/bible/englishinternet bible/partI/chapterIV/treaty6.asp (on file with the Columbia Law Review) [hereinafter Optional Protocol Ratification Chart]; see Helfer & Slaughter, supra note 7, at 344 n.314 (noting increase in Optional Protocol ratifications between 1991 and 1995).

139. McComie, supra note 130, at 432; see also B.G. Ramcharan, Caribbean Community Perspectives on International Law and Organization, in Caribbean Perspectives on International Law and Organizations, supra note 119, at 1, 28 (noting that "Caribbean Community States have not been entirely at home in the OAS" and that "they have insisted on establishing and developing their own organizations"). Although Trinidad & Tobago and Jamaica joined the OAS in 1967 and 1969, respectively, Guyana was precluded from joining under a rule barring membership to any nation in a territorial dispute with an existing OAS member. That rule was revised in the 1980s, allowing Guyana to join in 1991. McComie, supra note 130, at 435–36; Organization of American States, Charter of the Organization of American States: General Information of the Treaty: A-41, available at http://www.oas.org/juridico/english/sigs/a-41.html (last visited Aug. 12, 2002) (on file with the Columbia Law Review) [hereinafter OAS Ratification Chart].

it also accepted the jurisdiction of the Inter-American Court of Human Rights[140]), and Guyana has yet to ratify the treaty.[141]

As a result of these ratifications, individuals who believed that the states had violated their rights under the ICCPR could file petitions with the U.N. Human Rights Committee, and those who asserted violations of the American Convention could file petitions with the Inter-American Commission on Human Rights. Each tribunal then reviewed the allegations in the petitions, sought responses from defending governments, and determined whether the countries had in fact violated their treaty obligations. The tribunals' findings were set out in nonbinding written decisions that often contained recommendations for the government concerned as to the measures necessary to remedy any violations.[142]

3. *Domestic Legal Systems: The Role of the Privy Council.* — Although Commonwealth Caribbean states gained political independence from the United Kingdom beginning in the 1960s, they did not sever their legal ties to that country. In addition to local trial and appellate courts, each state retained the London-based Judicial Committee of the Privy Council as its highest court of appeal. The Privy Council is comprised of a panel of British judges (all members of the House of Lords) which acted as the court of last resort for Britain's colonies, and which continues to serve that function for several Commonwealth states, including those in the Caribbean.[143]

Judicial review by the Privy Council is also an important component of human rights protection in the Commonwealth Caribbean. Beginning in the years immediately following independence, the court heard numerous appeals in which it interpreted the individual rights clauses in Caribbean constitutions. It began this task with circumspection, narrowly construing rights or relying on other constitutional provisions to limit their scope.[144] By the 1980s, however, the Privy Council's jurisprudence was divided between decisions that strictly interpreted individual rights

---

140. See American Convention, supra note 26, art. 62, S. Exec. Doc. F, 95-2, at 58, 1144 U.N.T.S. at 159 (setting out procedures for a state party to the American Convention to recognize the jurisdiction of the Inter-American Court of Human Rights).

141. American Convention Ratification Chart, supra note 84.

142. See Helfer, supra note 1, at 296–301 (describing procedures used by U.N. and regional human rights tribunals). In the case of Trinidad & Tobago, the Commission could refer disputes to the Inter-American Court of Human Rights for a legally binding ruling. See American Convention, supra note 26, arts. 61–62, S. Exec. Doc. E, 95-2, at 57–58, 1144 U.N.T.S. at 159 (setting forth procedures for referral of cases to Inter-American Court involving states that have recognized the court's jurisdiction).

143. Office of the Privy Council, Jurisdiction of Judicial Committee (2000), available at http://www.privy-council.org.uk/output/Page32.asp (on file with the *Columbia Law Review*).

144. See Phillips, supra note 122, at 124–27, 143–44, 159–60 (reviewing decisions narrowly construing freedom of expression, property protections, the reach of the judicial power, guarantees against unreasonable searches, and rights of redress).

clauses and others that endorsed a purposive and generous construction used by other common law courts and supranational tribunals.[145]

Throughout this period, the Privy Council's powers of judicial review remained controversial. As early as the 1970s, government officials and academics targeted the court as a vestige of colonialism.[146] Yet until the mid-1990s, Caribbean states (except Guyana[147]) made little effort to cast off the Privy Council as their highest court of review.[148] Although advocates of self-determination may find this puzzling, cogent pragmatic and political arguments explain the region's reluctance to sever its links to the London-based jurists.

From a practical perspective, the instances of Privy Council review were rather infrequent in fact, even when they were available in theory. Filing appeals in London was costly for litigants, and over the years the court developed doctrines to limit the exercise of its appellate jurisdiction, particularly in criminal cases.[149] These factors reduced the number of cases that the Privy Council decided on appeal from local Caribbean courts, and thus limited its ability to alter the Caribbean legal landscape.[150]

---

145. Compare Robinson v. The Queen, [1985] A.C. 956, 966–67 (P.C. 1985) (appeal taken from Jam.) (strictly construing constitutional provisions relating to right to legal representation), and Riley v. Attorney Gen. of Jam., [1983] 1 A.C. 719, 725–26 (P.C. 1982) (appeal taken from Jam.) (rejecting claim that extended stays on death row contravened constitutional prohibition on inhuman or degrading treatment), with Antoine, supra note 118, at 80–81 (mentioning Thornhill v. Attorney Gen., [1981] A.C. 61, 71 (P.C. 1979) (appeal taken from Trin. & Tobago), and discussing Minister of Home Affairs v. Fisher, [1980] A.C. 319, 328 (P.C. 1979) (appeal taken from Berm.) (both adopting rights-protective constructions of Caribbean constitutions)).

146. See Caribbean Task Force, Report of the Caribbean Task Force 102–03 (1974); see also Phillips, supra note 122, at 194, 625 (discussing criticism of appeals to the Privy Council and recommending creation of a regional appellate court to hear such appeals instead of Privy Council); cf. Sandra Fullerton Joireman, Inherited Legal Systems and Effective Rule of Law: Africa and the Colonial Legacy, 39 J. Mod. Afr. Stud. 571, 572 (2001) (labeling legal systems inherited by former European colonies in Africa as "the political detritus of colonisation").

147. Guyana severed its formal link to the Privy Council in 1970. See Antoine, supra note 118, at 89 n.6, 109 (citing Judicial Committee of Privy Council (Termination of Appeals) Act 1970, and discussing Guyanese case law after Guyana severed link to Privy Council).

148. See Hugh A. Rawlins, The Privy Council or a Caribbean Final Court of Appeal?, 6 Caribbean L. Rev. 235, 236 (1996) (stating that proposals to replace Privy Council with regional court of appeal have been treated "either as an intellectual debate for academic gratification or as a political or administrative exercise for the agenda of regional meetings").

149. See Antoine, supra note 118, at 230–34 (describing limitations on Privy Council jurisdiction, including in criminal cases, and concluding that "the Privy Council does not actually operate as a full appellate court"); Roget V. Bryan, Comment, Toward the Development of a Caribbean Jurisprudence: The Case for Establishing a Caribbean Court of Appeal, 7 J. Transnat'l L. & Pol'y 181, 207 (1997) (noting expense of Privy Council appeals).

150. From 1985 to 1994, there were 214 appeals from Commonwealth Caribbean courts to the Privy Council. The court decided 163 appeals after a hearing while it

For important questions of constitutional law, however, the political arguments for retaining appeals to the Privy Council were compelling.[151] First, Privy Council review, paid for by Britain, was cheap for the Caribbean governments; second, the court was "perceived to be incorruptible and aloof from local pressures"; and finally, it was staffed by "able common law judges."[152] The first rationale explains why Caribbean governments, overseeing new nations with many demands on the public fisc, supported the Privy Council. The second explains why the Caribbean public supported the court, and the third explains why Caribbean legal elites supported it.[153] As explained in the next section, however, this constellation of governmental, public, and elite backing shifted significantly in the 1990s.

B. *Criminal Justice Systems and the* Pratt *Case*

1. *The Rise of Death Rows in the Caribbean.* — Beginning in the 1980s, crime rates in the Commonwealth Caribbean, and homicide rates in particular, rose sharply. Government officials blamed South American drug cartels (which used the Caribbean as a transshipment point for drugs bound for the United States) and the general decline in the region's economic growth.[154] They responded by ending the unofficial moratoria on executions that had been in place since the 1970s.[155]

---

dismissed 68 appeals without a hearing. During the same period, litigants filed 292 petitions for special leave to appeal. Of these, the court granted only 87. M.A. De La Bastide, The Case for a Caribbean Court of Appeal, 5 Caribbean L. Rev. 401, 402–03 (1995).

   151. Although much of the Privy Council's appellate jurisdiction is discretionary and requires leave to appeal, Caribbean constitutions grant litigants a right of appeal in cases alleging violations of constitutional rights or freedoms. Antoine, supra note 118, at 230–31.

   152. Joseph O'Neill, The Ascent of Man, Granta, Winter 2000, at 187, 192; see also Jamaicans For Justice, Guide Sheet on the Privy Council and the Proposed Caribbean Court of Justice, at http://www.jamaicansforjustice.org/guide.htm (last visited Aug. 13, 2002) (on file with the *Columbia Law Review*) (noting that Privy Council was "free from any interference or pressure from politicians" in the Caribbean).

   153. See Antoine, supra note 118, at 237–38 (discussing arguments in favor of retaining Privy Council jurisdiction and noting that incorruptibility argument appealed "to a people fearful of political interference in a society which they view as politically partisan and sometimes corrupt").

   154. See Ivelaw Loyd Griffith, Drugs and Security in the Caribbean: Sovereignty Under Siege 53–92 (1997); Griffith & Munroe, supra note 125, at 78; O'Neill, supra note 152, at 191.

   155. See O'Neill, supra note 152, at 191 (reporting Trinidad & Tobago moratorium from 1979 to 1992); O'Connor, supra note 130, at 334–35 (Jamaican moratorium from 1976 to 1980); Guyana Rejects UN Protocol, South America Report, Jan. 1999, available at LEXIS, IAC (SM) Newsletter Database File (on file with the *Columbia Law Review*) (reporting that Guyana resumed executions in 1985).

Contrary to a trend in other parts of the world, Commonwealth Caribbean nations had never abolished the death penalty.[156] Some even made death a mandatory punishment for most, if not all, murder convictions.[157] Capital punishment was also highly popular with citizens, and it became even more so in the wake of rising homicide rates.[158] As a result of these combined pressures, an increasing number of criminal defendants received capital sentences and were placed on death row to await execution.

During the 1980s and early 1990s, complaints by these death row inmates began to reach the Privy Council, the Inter-American Commission, and the U.N. Human Rights Committee. One legal argument in particular began to appear with increasing frequency—the claim that a long period of detention on death row *in itself* was degrading or inhuman treatment or punishment proscribed by national constitutions and human rights treaties.[159] This argument, which challenged what came to

---

156. See Amnesty Int'l, State Killing in the English Speaking Caribbean: A Legacy of Colonial Times 2 (2002), at http://web.amnesty.org/aidoc/aidoc_pdf.nsf/index/AMR050032002ENGLISH/$File/AMR0500302.pdf (on file with the *Columbia Law Review*) [hereinafter State Killing] ("Against the international trend away from the use of the death penalty, executions have increased in the English speaking Caribbean . . . in recent years." (footnote omitted)); see also Bernard Babb, Fresh Move Towards Caribbean Court of Appeal, Caribbean Wk., Oct. 26–Nov. 8, 1996, at 2 (noting that "[n]early all Caribbean territories have retained the death penalty in their constitutions").

157. See, e.g., Offences Against the Person (Amendment) Act, No. 14-1992, 115 Jam. Gazette (Supplement) 1, 1–4 (Nov. 27, 1992) (on file with the *Columbia Law Review*) (amending section 2(1) of the Offences Against the Person Act to define "capital murder" and prescribe a penalty of death for murder committed, inter alia, against certain persons by virtue of their employment, position or status, as well as for murder committed in the course of certain other crimes, including "robbery," "burglary or housebreaking," "arson," or "any sexual offence"); Offences Against the Person Act, 3 The Laws of Trinidad and Tobago, ch. 11:08, § 4 (1990) ("Every person convicted of murder shall suffer death."); United Nations, Human Rights Committee, Second Periodic Report of States Parties Due in 1987: Guyana, U.N. Doc. CCPR/C/GUY/99/2 (1999), available at http://www.unhchr.ch/tbs/doc.nsf/(Symbol)/CCPR.C.GUY.99.2.En?Opendocument (on file with the *Columbia Law Review*) (discussing Guyana criminal laws imposing sentence of death upon conviction of murder). But see infra note 226 (discussing a recent Privy Council decision holding mandatory death sentences unconstitutional).

158. See Griffin, supra note 127, at 241–42 tbl.13.6 (reporting 1994 survey in which ninety-six percent of Trinidadians expressed support for capital punishment); Annabel Pilling, A Hanging Offence, The Times (London), Sept. 21, 1999, at D5 (noting results of February 1999 poll revealing that eighty-seven percent of adult Jamaicans favored capital punishment); Peter Richards, Rights-Caribbean: Region Stands Firm on Death Penalty, Inter Press Serv., June 9, 1999, available at LEXIS, Inter Press Service File (on file with the *Columbia Law Review*) (reporting surveys showing support for death penalty at eighty-eight percent in Barbados and seventy percent in Trinidad & Tobago).

159. See, e.g., Guy. Const. (Constitution of the Co-operative Republic of Guyana Act, 1980) pt. II, tit. 1, § 141(1) ("No person shall be subjected to . . . inhuman or degrading punishment or other treatment."); Jam. Const. ch. III, § 17(1) (same); Trin. & Tobago Const. ch. I, § 5(2)(b) ("Parliament may not . . . impose or authorise the imposition of cruel and unusual treatment or punishment."); American Convention, supra note 26, art. 5(2), S. Exec. Doc. F, 95-2, at 42, 999 U.N.T.S. at 174 ("No one shall be subjected to . . .

be known as the "death row phenomenon," did not contest the legality of capital punishment per se but rather the protracted delays associated with waiting for execution while appealing a conviction and sentence.[160]

2. *The* Pratt *Case.* — The Privy Council considered the death row phenomenon argument in a November 1993 decision known as *Pratt* v. *Attorney-General for Jamaica.*[161] The procedural history of *Pratt* is tortuous, with nearly a decade and a half of domestic appeals and international petitions. But the case merits detailed attention, both to illustrate the relationships between the Privy Council and the tribunals and to provide needed context for the legal and political responses to the Privy Council's decision reversing an earlier ruling and recognizing the death row phenomenon as a human rights violation.[162]

In January 1979, Earl Pratt and Ivan Morgan were convicted of murder and sentenced to death. The Jamaican Court of Appeal affirmed their convictions and death sentences in December 1980, but did not issue reasons for its decision until September 1984. The defendants could have petitioned the Privy Council for leave to appeal at any time after the Court of Appeal affirmed their convictions, although their practical ability to do so was severely hampered without a written decision. Instead, the defendants filed international petitions with the Inter-American Commission and the Human Rights Committee.[163]

In the first petition, brought to the Inter-American Commission in June 1981, Pratt complained about various unspecified procedural errors during his capital trial and appeal. The Commission rejected this claim in October 1984, although it asked Jamaica to commute his death sentence on humanitarian grounds.[164] Pratt then petitioned the Human Rights Committee in January 1986. His accomplice Morgan later filed a related petition and the two cases were joined. The petition alleged a number of violations of the ICCPR, including a claim based on the death row phenomenon.[165] In March 1986, while that petition was pending, the defendants sought leave to appeal to the Privy Council. In July of that year, the Privy Council refused to allow the appeal, although it expressed

---

cruel, inhuman or degrading treatment or punishment."); ICCPR, supra note 26, art. 7, S. Exec. Doc. E, 95-2, at 15, 999 U.N.T.S. at 175 (same).

160. See William A. Schabas, The Abolition of the Death Penalty in International Law 127–36, 236–38 (2d ed. 1997) (discussing application of death row phenomenon by different international human rights tribunals).

161. [1994] 2 A.C. 1 (P.C. 1993) (appeal taken from Jam.).

162. See Riley v. Attorney Gen. of Jam., [1983] 1 A.C. 719, 724–27 (P.C. 1982) (appeal taken from Jam.) (concluding that delays in carrying out executions did not violate the "inhuman or degrading punishment or other treatment" clause in Section 17 of Jamaican Constitution).

163. *Pratt*, [1994] 2 A.C. at 9–22.

164. Pratt v. Jamaica, Case 9054, Inter-Am. C.H.R. 111, 113, OEA/ser.L/V/II.66, doc. 10 rev. 1 (1985).

165. Pratt v. Jamaica, Communication Nos. 210/1986 & 225/1987, U.N. GAOR, Hum. Rts. Comm., 44th Sess., Supp. No. 40, at 222, U.N. Doc. A/44/40 (1989).

concern over the Court of Appeal's nearly four-year delay in issuing a written decision.[166]

The defendants' petition to the Human Rights Committee was more successful. In July 1986, the Committee issued an interim decision requesting that Jamaica stay the executions of Pratt and Morgan pending a review of their allegations. Jamaica refused to comply, however, and in February 1987 it issued a warrant of execution for both men. Later that month the Governor General did issue a stay, apparently because the defendants' petitions had been scheduled for hearings in March 1987 by both the Inter-American Commission and the Human Rights Committee.[167]

The Commission was the first of the two tribunals to act. In July 1987, it informed Jamaica that the nearly four-year detention on death row while defendants awaited the Jamaican Court of Appeal's decision "was tantamount to cruel, inhuman and degrading treatment" in violation of the American Convention.[168] In response to this decision, Jamaica once again vacillated on executing Pratt and Morgan, initially denying and then granting a stay while the defendants' parallel petition to the Human Rights Committee was pending. In March 1988, more than two years after the defendants first filed that petition, the Committee declared their claims to be admissible. A further thirteen months elapsed before the Committee issued its decision on the merits in April 1989. The Committee found a violation of the ICCPR based on the Court of Appeal's delay in giving reasons for affirming the defendants' convictions, and it recommended that Jamaica commute their death sentences.[169] But the Committee rejected the death row phenomenon claim, reasoning that "prolonged judicial proceedings do not per se constitute cruel, inhuman or degrading treatment even if they can be a source of mental strain for the convicted prisoners."[170]

---

166. *Pratt*, [1994] 2 A.C. at 22–23.

167. Id. at 23–24. The Commission's authority to reexamine Pratt and Morgan's cases three years after it dismissed their petition is unclear. The American Convention and the Commission's regulations preclude the Commission from considering a complaint that is pending before another human rights tribunal or that is "substantially the same as one previously studied by the Commission." American Convention, supra note 26, art. 47(d), S. Exec. Doc. F, 95-2, at 54, 1144 U.N.T.S. at 152; Reg. Inter-Am. C.H.R., art. 39(1)(b), reprinted in Inter-Am. Ct. H.R., Basic Documents Pertaining to Human Rights in the Inter-American System 75, 89, OEA/Ser.L.V/II.71, doc. 6 rev. 1 (1987). Although the defendants apparently provided the Commission with additional information after its 1984 ruling, that in itself does not explain the Commission's failure to follow its established rules of procedure. In addition, the Commission never published the 1987 decision in its official annual report and its existence became widely known only when the Privy Council issued its ruling in the case six years later. Schabas, supra note 160, at 287.

168. See Schabas, supra note 160, at 287 (discussing and quoting unpublished Commission decision).

169. *Pratt*, [1994] 2 A.C. at 24–26.

170. *Pratt*, U.N. Doc. A/44/40, at 222. The Committee cautioned, however, that in capital cases "an assessment of the circumstances of each case would be necessary." Id. For

Again Jamaica equivocated over whether to carry out the death sentences while it considered what legal weight to afford the tribunals' recommendations. The defendants then filed a motion for constitutional redress, which the Jamaican courts rejected.[171] When the Privy Council finally reviewed the defendants' constitutional claims, they had been incarcerated on death row for more than fourteen years.

In its November 1993 decision, the Privy Council canvassed the differing approaches to the death row phenomenon adopted by national courts and by the ECHR in the eleven years since its earlier judgment. Although these courts were divided over the issue, the Privy Council sided with those domestic and international jurists who had found prolonged detention on death row incompatible with constitutional or treaty-based bans on inhuman or degrading treatment or punishment.[172] The Privy Council acknowledged that much of the delay between sentence and execution could be attributed to capital defendants' efforts to invoke all available appellate procedures, and not necessarily to government error or flaws in the criminal justice system. Nevertheless, the court concluded that "[i]f the appellate procedure enables the prisoner to prolong the appellate hearings over a period of years, the fault is to be attributed to the appellate system that permits such delay and not to the prisoner who takes advantage of it."[173]

Turning to the question of remedies, the Privy Council considered how to balance the government's interest in speedy post-conviction review of capital cases against a defendant's interest in a full and fair hearing of his legal challenges. Facing a Jamaican judicial system that was slow and unresponsive, the court held that a delay in carrying out an execution exceeding five years would be presumptively unconstitutional and require a commutation of the death sentence to life imprisonment. Within this five-year window, the court allocated approximately two years to complete all domestic appeals and eighteen months to petition the Human Rights Committee.[174] Because Pratt and Morgan's death row de-

---

a discussion of the Committee's subsequent death row case law, see Helfer, supra note 1, at 327–31.

171. *Pratt*, [1994] 2 A.C. at 27. Section 25 of the Constitution of Jamaica allows any person alleging that any of his or her rights under the Constitution have been violated to "apply to the Supreme Court for redress." Jam. Const. ch. III, § 25(1).

172. *Pratt*, [1994] 2 A.C. at 30–33 (discussing decisions from Canada, ECHR, India, United States, and Zimbabwe).

173. Id. at 33.

174. Id. at 35. The court in *Pratt* appeared to hold that this eighteen-month period applied to petitions filed only with the Human Rights Committee. In a later ruling, however, the Privy Council suggested that the eighteen-month window was applicable even where a death row defendant petitioned both the Committee and the Inter-American Commission in succession. See Thomas v. Baptiste, [2000] 2 A.C. 1, 21 (P.C. 1999) (appeal taken from Trin. & Tobago) (stating that state could have prescribed for the tribunals a maximum of eighteen months for death row defendants to complete international petitions "whether the petitioner made only one application or applied successively to more than one international body or made successive applications to the same body").

tention substantially exceeded this five-year limit, the Privy Council held that "[t]o execute these men now after holding them in custody in an agony of suspense for so many years would be inhuman punishment within the meaning of" the Jamaican Constitution.[175]

3. *The Domestic Effects of Pratt.* — The *Pratt* case had an immediate and extreme impact on Caribbean criminal justice systems. Jamaica promptly commuted the death sentences of 105 prisoners already detained on death row for more than five years. Trinidad & Tobago commuted the sentences of fifty-three death row inmates and Barbados commuted nine death sentences.[176] Local appellate courts put other cases on hold to concentrate on capital appeals.[177] And ambiguities in the decision and its application to other Caribbean states compelled the Privy Council to devote a considerable portion of its docket to death row appeals from Caribbean courts between 1994 and 2000.[178]

The *Pratt* case also radically altered perceptions of the Privy Council among government officials, local judges, and some legal elites, who condemned its "revolutionary" break from past jurisprudence, its usurpation of Caribbean legislative powers, and the "great dislocation" it engendered in "the system of the administration of justice."[179] The court's stature also declined among the Caribbean public, who criticized the overturning of death sentences by "London judges who did not have to live with the consequences of their decisions."[180] Eventually, both expert and popular opinion came to view *Pratt* as an attempt to undermine use of the death penalty, which had become a popular tool for combating the region's escalating murder rates.[181]

4. *The International Effects of Pratt.* — *Pratt* also had a pronounced effect on the international human rights regimes to which Caribbean states were parties. To understand why, recall that the Privy Council's

---

175. *Pratt*, [1994] 2 A.C. at 33.

176. David Simmons, Judicial Legislation for the Commonwealth Caribbean: The Death Penalty, Delay and the Judicial Committee of the Privy Council, 3 Caribbean L. Bull. 1, 6 (1998) [hereinafter Simmons, Death Penalty].

177. De La Bastide, supra note 150, at 407; see also Ramesh Lawrence Maharaj, The Death Penalty: Legal and Constitutional Issues, 9 Caribbean L. Rev. 137, 152 (1999) (noting "legislative and administrative reforms" of the domestic appeals process).

178. See Bob Howard & Anne Westcott, Death Under the Sun, The Times (London), Jan. 18, 2000, at D16 (reporting statement by Privy Council judge that twenty-five percent of court's docket is devoted to death row appeals from the Commonwealth Caribbean).

179. Antoine, supra note 118, at 81, 109; see also De La Bastide, supra note 150, at 407–08 ("The question, however, is whether these are the sorts of decisions that should be taken in London by judges who have no contact at first hand with the societies to whom the decisions apply.").

180. O'Neill, supra note 152, at 192.

181. Id. at 193; Simmons, Death Penalty, supra note 176, at 2 (Attorney General of Barbados asserting that *Pratt* "frustrated the desires of Governments in this region to carry out the death penalty" and "infuriated populations who see their Governments rendered virtually powerless by decisions of legal policy set . . . by judges sitting in London and applying British and European notions").

choice of a five-year execution window was influenced by two factors. The first was the court's assessment of the functions and permissible delays of the domestic appellate process, a subject with which it was intimately familiar as the region's court of last resort. The second factor was the court's appraisal of the functions and abilities of human rights tribunals, a subject about which it was far less knowledgeable.[182] This lack of understanding had serious consequences for the region's human rights regimes.

Consider first the Privy Council's statements in *Pratt* regarding the Inter-American Commission and the Human Rights Committee. The court expressed a generally positive view of the tribunals' roles in reviewing death row petitions. Notwithstanding the fact that the tribunals' decisions were not legally binding, the court took pains not to "discourage Jamaica from continuing its membership of these bodies and from benefiting from the wisdom of their deliberations,"[183] and urged that their decisions "be afforded weight and respect" by the government.[184] But the Privy Council also stated that either tribunal should complete its review of a petition "with reasonable dispatch and at most within eighteen months," and that petitions were likely to be "infrequent" once Jamaica eliminated the delays for domestic appeals.[185]

Both of these predictions were based on a misperception of how human rights petition procedures function. As for the time required to review death row petitions, the court in *Pratt* failed to recognize the tribunals' institutional incapacity to review cases quickly.[186] The tribunals are part-time bodies which meet only a few times per year and manage an increasingly crowded docket with inadequate material and financial resources.[187] For these reasons, each tribunal generally takes up to two years—and often longer—to process each case from its initial filing to a

---

182. For example, in a decision applying the *Pratt* principle to the Bahamas, the Privy Council initially set the execution window at three years and six months based on its conclusion that the Bahamas had failed to ratify either the American Convention or the Optional Protocol and thus no international petition procedures were available to individuals. Henfield v. Attorney Gen. of Bah., [1997] 1 A.C. 413, 423–25 (P.C. 1996) (appeal taken from Bah.). The court later corrected this error, recognizing that individuals could still petition the Inter-American Commission concerning alleged violations of the American Declaration of the Rights and Duties of Man. Fisher v. Minister of Pub. Safety & Immigration, [1998] 1 A.C. 673, 684–85 (P.C. 1997) (appeal taken from Bah.).

183. Pratt v. Attorney Gen. for Jam., [1994] 2 A.C. 1, 35 (P.C. 1993) (appeal taken from Jam.).

184. Id. at 27.

185. Id. at 35.

186. Not until seven years later, after the denunciations had occurred, did the Privy Council acknowledge that "human rights bodies meet infrequently and are undermanned so that as things stand delays [beyond eighteen months] are almost inevitable." Lewis v. Attorney Gen. of Jam., [2001] 2 A.C. 50, 80 (P.C. 2000) (appeal taken from Jam.).

187. See Helfer & Slaughter, supra note 7, at 347–48; Cathleen Caron, News from the Inter-American System, 7 Hum. Rts. Brief 13, 13 (1999).

final decision on the merits.[188] In addition, the Privy Council failed to account for the fact that individuals can file petitions with the tribunals consecutively—by first petitioning the Inter-American Commission and, after it issues a decision, filing a second petition containing the same allegations with the Human Rights Committee.[189] Thus, even assuming one tribunal could complete its review within eighteen months, the Privy Council made no allowance for an appropriate period of delay for cases in which capital defendants petitioned both tribunals.

5. *The International Response to* Pratt. — Taken together, the Privy Council's unduly optimistic timetable for supranational review and its failure to consider the filing of petitions with both tribunals created hydraulic pressure on Commonwealth Caribbean governments. On the one hand, the petition procedures they ratified would be utterly meaningless if they did not delay carrying out executions until the tribunals had concluded their review.[190] On the other hand, by awaiting the tribu-

---

188. See Inter-Am. Comm'n on Human Rights, Non-Commuted Death Penalty Cases from the English-Speaking Caribbean: Statistics, at 2 n.5 (Jan. 2001) (on file with the *Columbia Law Review*) [hereinafter Inter-American Commission Death Penalty Statistics] (noting that Commission takes on average between twenty-four and thirty-six months to process petitions); Oldrich Andrysek, Gaps in International Protection and the Potential for Redress Through Individual Complaints Procedures, 9 Int'l J. Refugee L. 392, 403 (1997) (noting similar time periods for process petitions filed with Human Rights Committee). For a discussion of changing patterns of delay after *Pratt*, see notes 194–195 and accompanying text and Figure 3.

189. Pratt and Morgan had followed this very approach, extending the international review of their respective claims to a total of more than six years. Petitioning the tribunals in a different order is not permitted, however. See American Convention, supra note 26, art. 47(d), S. Exec. Doc. F, 95-2, at 54, 1144 U.N.T.S. at 156 (stating that Inter-American Commission "shall consider inadmissible any petition or communication . . . if . . . [t]he petition or communication is substantially the same as one previously studied by the Commission or by another international organization"). For a discussion of the different approaches to "successive petition forum shopping," see Helfer, supra note 1, at 306–07.

190. This is not to suggest that Caribbean governments habitually honored the tribunals' requests for interim measures seeking to prevent executions of defendants whose petitions were pending. To the contrary, the governments often refused to accede to the tribunals' requests for a stay and ignored their recommendations to commute death sentences. See Prince v. Trinidad & Tobago, Case 12.005, Inter-Am. C.H.R. 264, OEA/ ser.L/V/II.102, doc. 6 rev. 7–8 (1999), available at http://www.cidh.oas.org/annualrep/ 98eng/Admissibility/T&T%2012005.htm (on file with the *Columbia Law Review*) (noting the first instance in which Trinidad & Tobago complied with a request to stay an execution); Guerra v. Trinidad & Tobago, Communication Nos. 575 & 576/1994, U.N. GAOR, Hum. Rts. Comm., 50th Sess., Supp. No. 41, at 198–99, U.N. Doc. CCPR/C/57/1 (1996) (noting that government declined to give assurances that it would comply with Committee's request for interim measures not to execute defendant but stating that it was already bound by a domestic court's conservatory order preventing such execution); see also United Nations, Human Rights Committee, Consideration of Communications Under the Optional Protocol to the Covenant: Communication from Mr. Ashby, U.N. Doc. CCPR/C/SR.1352 (1996), available at http://www.unhchr.ch/tbs/doc.nsf/(Symbol)/ CCPR.C.SR.1352.En?Opendocument (on file with the *Columbia Law Review*) (noting Trinidad & Tobago's refusal to comply with request for interim measures not to execute defendant who had filed petition with the Committee, and noting that States parties had

nals' decisions, states risked running the five year clock and thus losing the ability to carry out any executions, even in cases where the tribunals' review ultimately disclosed no human rights violations.

This pressure was not lost on capital defendants and their council. As the following charts reveal,[191] the number of death row petitions increased markedly in the years following *Pratt*. As shown in Figure 1, the number of petitions grew from between three and fifteen per year between 1989 and 1993 to between twenty-two and twenty-eight per year between 1994 and 1999. This increase was not spread evenly across the two tribunals, however. The Human Rights Committee received the overwhelming majority of cases filed in 1995 and 1996, whereas the Inter-American Commission received the bulk of the cases filed between 1997 and 1999. In addition, as illustrated in Figure 2, Jamaica and Trinidad & Tobago—the Caribbean states with the region's largest death rows[192]—were the targets of the overwhelming majority of death row petitions both before and after the Privy Council's ruling.

Data concerning the time expended by the two tribunals to process death row petitions is also illuminating, particularly in light of the assertions by Trinidad & Tobago and Jamaica (discussed below) that the tribunals were dilatory in reviewing death row petitions. With respect to the Human Rights Committee, Figure 3 reveals that between 1989 and 1993 (the year of the *Pratt* ruling), the Committee took on average between forty-four and fifty-six months to review petitions from initial filing to a final decision on the merits. After *Pratt* was decided, the review period increased slightly to a peak of forty-six months for petitions filed in 1995, but declined sharply to twenty-five months for petitions filed in 1996, fifteen months for petitions filed in 1997, and nineteen months for petitions filed in 1998. In all but one instance, however, these time periods

complied with such requests in more than 100 cases of defendants under sentence of death); Follow-up Activities Under the Optional Protocol, U.N. GAOR, Hum. Rts. Comm., 50th Sess., Supp. No. 40 vol. 1, at 92, U.N. Doc. A/50/40 (1995), available at http://www.unhchr.ch/tbs/doc.nsf/898586b1dc7b4043c1256a450044f331/bbd592d8d48a76fec12563f000586adc/$FILE/N9602481.pdf (on file with *Columbia Law Review*) (noting Jamaica's explicit refusal to implement the Committee's recommendations in nine cases decided under the Optional Protocol).

191. These charts were generated from a database of information collected from 200 petitions filed by criminal defendants under sentence of death between 1989 and 1999, inclusive, against Commonwealth Caribbean states subject to the jurisdiction of the U.N. Human Rights Committee or the Inter-American Commission on Human Rights. See Database of Caribbean Death Row Human Rights Petitions (copy on file with author and with the *Columbia Law Review*). The database, which contains information current as of October 2001, includes petitions filed by defendants who received capital sentences that were later commuted. Information about the petitions in the database was obtained from published admissibility and merits decisions and from statistical information provided by the Inter-American Commission. Although case-specific information on unpublished decisions is confidential, inquiries made to the secretariats of both tribunals indicate that the number of unpublished decisions during this time period was extremely small.

192. See State Killing, supra note 156, at 3 (noting 2001 figures).

1876   *COLUMBIA LAW REVIEW*   [Vol. 102:1832

FIGURE 1

DEATH ROW PETITIONS FROM COMMONWEALTH CARIBBEAN NATIONS FILED
WITH HUMAN RIGHTS COMMITTEE (UNHRC) AND
INTER-AMERICAN COMMISSION (IACHR)

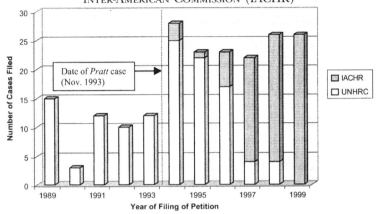

FIGURE 2

DEATH ROW PETITIONS FILED WITH HUMAN RIGHTS COMMITTEE
(UNHRC) AND INTER-AMERICAN COMMISSION (IACHR) BY
STATE AND TRIBUNAL

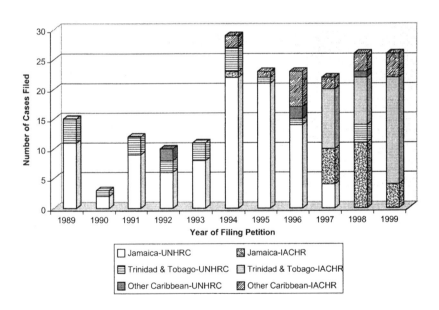

exceeded the eighteen months allocated by the Privy Council for the tribunal to review petitions.[193]

The limited number of death row petitions filed with the Inter-American Commission prior to 1996 makes it difficult to assess the changes in review times before and after the *Pratt* case. With respect to petitions filed in 1996 and later, however, Figure 3 shows a rapid decline in review periods both for admissibility and merits decisions.[194] In particular, the review period for decisions on the merits decreased from an average of thirty-six months for petitions filed in 1997 to fourteen months for petitions filed in 1999.[195] Again, only in 1999 did review times decrease below the Privy Council's eighteen-month estimate.

Another trend that co-varied with the rise in the number of petitions after the *Pratt* case was an increase in and changing composition of the representatives assisting death row defendants. As Figure 4 illustrates, of the fifty-one death row defendants petitioning the tribunals between 1989 and 1993, forty-six, or 90.1%, appear to have been assisted by a third-party representative. The information from this period is incomplete, however. Many cases either fail to state whether a defendant was represented (in which case it is assumed that the defendant represented himself) or state that a defendant was represented without providing additional information. Where a British law firm or the advocacy group Interrights appeared on behalf of the defendant, however, the decisions clearly note that fact.

The representation patterns changed significantly in the wake of *Pratt*. A large majority of the 149 petitioners (81.2%) during the period from 1994 to 1999 were represented by British law firms (often on a pro

---

193. The average review periods in Figure 3 for the Human Rights Committee's admissibility decisions includes only those petitions that the Committee declared inadmissible.

194. The dates on which the Commission decided the admissibility of petitions from death row defendants was not always made public in the case of petitions filed against Trinidad & Tobago that were later referred to the Inter-American Court. In such instances, the date on which the Commission requested that the Court adopt provisional measures directing the state not to execute a defendant was substituted for the date of the admissibility decision. However, because the Commission's request for provisional measures usually preceded its determination of a petition's admissibility, this substitution reduces the average review periods for the Commission's "decisions on admissibility" as reflected in Figure 3. As a result, the actual average review periods are likely to be somewhat longer than those indicated in Figure 3.

195. This data tracks statistics collected by the Inter-American Commission, which aggregates average review periods for both admissibility and merits decisions in noncommuted death penalty cases against Jamaica and Trinidad & Tobago. For Jamaica, the average review period declined from 27.5 months for petitions filed in 1997 to 10.5 months for petitions filed in 1998 and 7.6 months for petitions filed in 1999. For Trinidad, the average review period declined from twenty-three months for petitions filed in 1997 to fourteen months for petitions filed in 1998 and ten months for petitions filed in 1999. Inter-American Commission Death Penalty Statistics, supra note 188, at 2 n.5.

FIGURE 3

REVIEW OF PETITIONS TO HUMAN RIGHTS COMMITTEE (UNHRC) AND
INTER-AMERICAN COMMISSION (IACHR) FROM FILING TO DECISION
(ADMISSIBILITY AND MERITS)

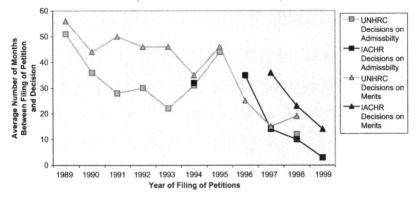

FIGURE 4

REPRESENTATION OF DEATH ROW DEFENDANTS IN PETITIONS FROM
COMMONWEALTH CARIBBEAN NATIONS FILED WITH
HUMAN RIGHTS TRIBUNALS

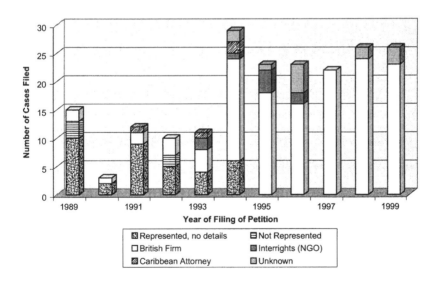

bono basis),[196] with a smaller number (4.7%) represented by Interrights. For those petitions for which information is available (136 of the 149 petitions), only two defendants were represented by Caribbean attorneys, and no defendants represented themselves.

6. *The Domestic Response to* Pratt. — When added together, the crowding of the tribunals' dockets and the delays in reviewing death row petitions often caused post-conviction review in capital cases to exceed the five-year execution window set in *Pratt.* Thus, simply by invoking domestic and supranational appellate review mechanisms, many capital defendants could effectively force Caribbean governments to commute their death sentences.[197] The result was a near de facto abolition of the death penalty in Caribbean states subject to the Privy Council's jurisdiction, even though neither the ICCPR nor the American Convention per se proscribes capital punishment.[198]

As the consequences of the *Pratt* ruling became clear, Caribbean governments and the Caribbean public began to perceive human rights tribunals as obstacles to imposing capital sentences and death row defendants as abusers of the tribunals' procedures.[199] In an effort to meet the Privy Council's five-year deadline, governments had sought to expe-

---

196. See Penal Reform Int'l, Assistance for Prisoners Under Sentence of Death in the Commonwealth Caribbean, available at http://www.penalreform.org/english/frset_region_en.htm (last visited Aug. 30, 2002) (on file with the *Columbia Law Review*) [hereinafter Assistance for Prisoners] (discussing pro bono assistance provided to death row defendants before Privy Council and human rights tribunals); O'Neill, supra note 152, at 196–97 (discussing letters sent by death row defendants to attorneys in the United Kingdom specializing in appeals before the Privy Council).

197. See Glenn McGrory, Reservations of Virtue? Lessons from Trinidad and Tobago's Reservation to the First Optional Protocol, 23 Hum. Rts. Q. 769, 778 (2001) (noting possibility of abolitionist lawyers "strategically seeking procedural delays" to commute death sentences for their clients).

198. See Scott Davidson, The Inter-American Human Rights System 267–74 (1997) (discussing circumstances under which the American Convention allows imposition of the death penalty); Natalia Schiffrin, Jamaica Withdraws the Right of Individual Petition Under the International Covenant on Civil and Political Rights, 92 Am. J. Int'l L. 563, 564 & n.5 (1998) (noting that ICCPR does not prohibit capital punishment); see also Frances Williams, Jamaica Quits UN Accord, Fin. Times (London), Oct. 27, 1997, at 3 (characterizing the *Pratt* decision as creating "a *de facto* abolition of the death penalty").

199. See Christof Heyns & Frans Viljoen, The Impact of the United Nations Human Rights Treaties on the Domestic Level, 23 Hum. Rts. Q. 483, 496 (2001) (noting that "official reason" for Jamaica's denouncement of the Optional Protocol was its frustration at delays in processing petitions by U.N. Human Rights Committee); Estrella Gutierrez, Rights-Americas: Trinidad and Tobago Stands Up to OAS, Inter Press Service, June 4, 1998, available at LEXIS, Inter Press Service File (on file with the *Columbia Law Review*) (reporting that Trinidad & Tobago foreign minister characterized filing of petitions with multiple tribunals as "death row prisoners . . . 'abusing' . . . recourse to human rights bodies"); Trinidad: Attorney-General Responds to Amnesty International's Charges, Cana News Agency, Apr. 18, 2000, available at LEXIS, BBC Worldwide Monitoring File (on file with the *Columbia Law Review*) (quoting Trinidad & Tobago Attorney General as stating that delay in reviewing claims by Human Rights Committee "has facilitated persons convicted of murder to escape the death penalty").

dite capital appeals in local courts. But they could not directly control the pace at which the tribunals reviewed international petitions.[200]

The governments initially sought relief from the Privy Council, arguing that the execution window set in *Pratt* was unreasonably short because "applications to the human rights bodies take on average two years."[201] The governments requested that "either the periods of time relating to applications to the human rights bodies should be excluded from the computation of delay or the period of five years should be increased to take account of delays normally involved in the disposal of such complaints."[202] The Privy Council categorically rejected this request, even in the face of a threat by Barbados to denounce the Optional Protocol if the court did not extend the time limits.[203]

Unable to ease the strictures of *Pratt* domestically, the two Caribbean governments with the largest death row populations next sought unilaterally to revise the tribunals' procedural rules to conform to the Privy Council's deadline. In August and October 1997, the Governors-General of Jamaica and Trinidad & Tobago promulgated "instructions" to both tribunals that sought to impose detailed and precise timetables for review of death row petitions.[204] According to the two governments, the instructions were an attempt "to co-operate with the international human rights institutions" while retaining the right to impose capital sentences within the time limits set in *Pratt*.[205] If the tribunals followed the instructions, the governments agreed not to carry out executions while a petition was pending. But the time allocated to each tribunal was extremely short. To allow for the possibility that defendants would petition both tribunals in succession, the instructions granted seven months to each tribunal to complete its examination, far less time than either body had taken to review petitions in the past. Perceiving the instructions as threats to their authority, both tribunals refused to follow the instructions,[206] and the Privy Council later invalidated them on constitutional grounds.[207]

---

200. McGrory, supra note 197, at 777; Schiffrin, supra note 198, at 566.

201. Bradshaw v. Attorney Gen. of Barb., [1995] 1 W.L.R. 936, 941 (P.C. 1995) (appeal taken from Barb.).

202. Id.

203. Id.

204. Government Notice, Miscellaneous No. 150, 120 Jam. Gazette (Extraordinary) 945 (Aug. 7, 1997) (on file with the *Columbia Law Review*); Instructions Relating to Applications from Persons Under Sentence of Death, 36 Trin. & Tobago Gazette (Extraordinary) 855 (Oct. 13, 1997) (on file with the *Columbia Law Review*).

205. Thomas v. Baptiste, [2000] 2 A.C. 1, 19 (P.C. 1999) (appeal taken from Trin. & Tobago).

206. See, e.g., United Nations, Human Rights Committee, Consideration of Reports Submitted by States Parties Under Article 40 of the Covenant: Concluding Observations of the Human Rights Committee: Jamaica, U.N. Doc. CCPR/C/79/Add.83 (1997) (refusing to follow Jamaica's attempt to "unilaterally impos[e] timetables" for review of petitions).

207. Lewis v. Attorney Gen. of Jam., [2001] 2 A.C. 50, 85 (P.C. 2000) (appeal taken from Jam.); *Thomas*, [2000] 2 A.C. at 21.

With their unilateral efforts to expedite review of death row petitions thwarted, Jamaica and Trinidad & Tobago denounced their treaty obligations. But their denunciations, as well as that of Guyana, did not eliminate all avenues of supranational review. On October 23, 1997, Jamaica denounced the ICCPR's First Optional Protocol, eliminating the right of individuals to petition the Human Rights Committee.[208] Jamaica did not, however, withdraw from the American Convention, thereby preserving the right of aggrieved individuals to file complaints with the Inter-American Commission. As Figure 2 above illustrates, death row defendants in Jamaica capitalized on this remaining avenue of review by filing an unprecedented number of petitions with the Commission. But because Jamaica had never accepted the jurisdiction of the Inter-American Court, those complaints could only result in recommendations by the Commission rather than legally binding judgments of the court.

Trinidad & Tobago's denunciations were more extensive. On May 26, 1998, the state denounced both the Optional Protocol and the American Convention.[209] On the same date, it reacceded to the Optional Protocol with a broad reservation that sought to preclude the Human Rights Committee from reviewing any petitions from capital defendants.[210] In a November 1999 decision, however, the Committee declared such a defendant's petition admissible, concluding that the reservation was incompatible with the object and purpose of the Optional Protocol and severable from the state's decision to reaccede to the treaty.[211] In response, Trinidad & Tobago denounced the Optional Protocol in its entirety on March 27, 2000.[212]

Guyana's response was more curious. As noted above, Guyana had eliminated appeals to the Privy Council in 1970 and thus was not bound by the *Pratt* case.[213] Its 1993 ratification of the Optional Protocol, in the year after its first free post-independence election, was motivated by the newly elected government's distrust of the local judiciary and its desire to make available to Guyanese an international body to review human rights

---

208. Optional Protocol Ratification Chart, supra note 138, at 226 n.1. Pursuant to Article 12 of the Optional Protocol, supra note 29, art. 12, Jamaica's denunciation became effective on January 23, 1998, three months after it was filed.

209. Pursuant to Article 12 of the Optional Protocol, supra note 29, art. 12, and Article 78 of the American Convention, supra note 26, art. 78, S. Exec. Doc. F, 95-2, at 61, 1144 U.N.T.S. at 161–62, the denunciation of the Optional Protocol took effect on August, 26, 1998 and the denunciation of the American Convention took effect on May 26, 1999, one year after it was filed.

210. The reservations prohibited the Human Rights Committee from receiving communications from "any prisoner who is under sentence of death in respect of any matter relating to his prosecution, his detention, his trial, his conviction, his sentence or the carrying out of the death sentence on him and any matter connected therewith." Optional Protocol Ratification Chart, supra note 138, at 229.

211. See Kennedy v. Trinidad & Tobago, Communication No. 845/1999, U.N. GAOR, Hum. Rts. Comm., 55th Sess., Supp. No. 40 vol. 2, at 266, U.N. Doc. A/55/40 (1999).

212. Optional Protocol Ratification Chart, supra note 138, at 231 n.3.

213. See supra note 147.

abuses.[214] Yet when in March 1998 the Human Rights Committee issued its first decision against Guyana, recommending that two Guyanese death row defendants be released from prison, government officials criticized the Committee for violating national sovereignty.[215] Guyana later denounced the Optional Protocol on January 5, 1999.[216] On the same date, Guyana reacceded to the treaty with a death penalty reservation identical to the one previously filed by Trinidad & Tobago.[217]

C. *Severing Links to the Privy Council and Creating a New Caribbean Court of Justice*

The denunciation of the human rights treaties and petition procedures by the three governments did not conclude the saga of the death row phenomenon in the Caribbean. Prior to May 26, 1999, the effective date of Trinidad's denunciation, thirty-two death row defendants in that country filed petitions with the Inter-American Commission.[218] Beginning on June 14, 1998, the Inter-American Court issued provisional measures directing the government not to execute these defendants pending a review of their claims by the Commission and the Court.[219] Trinidad

---

214. Bert Wilkinson, Rights-Caribbean: Another Government Withdraws from UN Body, Inter Press Service, Nov. 18, 1998, available at LEXIS, Inter Press Service File (on file with the *Columbia Law Review*) [hereinafter Wilkinson, Another Government Withdraws]; Bert Wilkinson, Rights-Guyana: Let Prisoners Go Free, U.N. Body Says, Inter Press Service, May 19, 1998, available at LEXIS, Inter Press Service File (on file with the *Columbia Law Review*).

215. Yasseen v. Guyana, Communication No. 676/1996, U.N. GAOR, Hum. Rts. Comm., Supp. No. 40 vol. 2, at 162, U.N. Doc. A/53/40 (1998); Wilkinson, Another Government Withdraws, supra note 214.

216. Optional Protocol Ratification Chart, supra note 138, at 228, 231 n.2; Bert Wilkinson, Rights-Guyana: On the Verge of Restoring Executions, Inter Press Service, Sept. 25, 1999, available at LEXIS, Inter Press Service File (on file with the *Columbia Law Review*).

217. Optional Protocol Ratification Chart, supra note 138, at 231 n.2. After the Human Rights Committee's decision in Kennedy v. Trinidad & Tobago, Communication No. 845/1999, U.N. GAOR, Hum. Rts. Comm., 55th Sess., Supp. No. 40 vol. 2, at 265-66, U.N. Doc. A/55/40 (1999), declaring Trinidad's death penalty reservation invalid, Guyana did not denounce the Optional Protocol entirely. Thus, all aggrieved individuals, including those on death row, may continue to file petitions with the Human Rights Committee. As of July 2002, seven petitions were pending against Guyana although their allegations are not publicly known. See Office High Comm'n Hum. Rts., U.N., Statistical Survey of Individual Complaints Dealt with by the Human Rights Committee Under the Optional Protocol to the ICCPR (2002), available at http://www.unhchr.ch/html/menu2/8/stat2.htm (on file with the *Columbia Law Review*).

218. See Hilaire v. Trinidad & Tobago, Inter-Am. Ct. H.R. at 3-5 (June 21, 2002), available at http://www.corteidh.or.cr/T_y_t/Serie_c_94_ing.doc (on file with the *Columbia Law Review*) (collecting thirty-two cases referred by Inter-American Commission prior to May 1999).

219. Press Release, Inter-Am. Ct. H.R., Provisional Measures James et al., CDH-CP9/98 English (Sept. 1998), available at http://www1.umn.edu/humanrts/iachr/pr8-98.html (on file with the *Columbia Law Review*); see also Press Release, Inter-Am. Ct. H.R., James et al. Provisional Measures CDH-CP6/99 English (June 9, 1999), available at http://

publicly flouted the court's orders by issuing death warrants and by carrying out executions of some of the defendants.[220]

In March 1999, however, the Privy Council issued a divided, controversial ruling in which it held that the government would violate the due process clause of Trinidad & Tobago's constitution if it executed defendants whose international petitions were still pending.[221] The Privy Council thus stayed their executions pending the outcome of their appeals before the Inter-American Court[222] (which, in June 2002, issued a judgment finding that Trinidad & Tobago had violated the defendants' rights under the American Convention[223]). In September 2000, the Privy Council applied the same reasoning to the Jamaican constitution in an

---

www1.umn.edu/humanrts/iachr/pr16-99.html (on file with the *Columbia Law Review*) (extending provisional measures to additional defendants on death row in Trinidad & Tobago). The Commission later found that the government had violated the defendants' rights under the American Convention, and it referred the cases to the Inter-American Court. Inter-American Commission Death Penalty Statistics, supra note 188, at 1 n.4 (noting referrals on May 25, 1999, Feb. 22, 2000, and Oct. 25, 2000). For a discussion of the court's judgment finding that Trinidad had violated the defendants' rights under the American Convention, see infra note 223.

220. See McGrory, supra note 197, at 773 & n.16 (discussing hangings in violation of Inter-American Court's orders); State Killing, supra note 156, at 22 (reporting that "Trinidad and Tobago has continued to execute defendants before the completion of the international judicial process" and refuting the state's denial that the executions are in violation of the Inter-American Court's orders); Trinidad: Attorney-General Rejects Inter-American No-Executions Order, Cana News Agency, June 25, 1998, available at LEXIS, BBC Worldwide Monitoring File (on file with the *Columbia Law Review*) (reporting statement by Attorney General of Trinidad & Tobago that "state does not plan to respond to a 'no-executions' order from the Inter-American Court on Human Rights").

221. Thomas v. Baptiste, [2000] 2 A.C. 1, 21–24 (P.C. 1999) (appeal taken from Trin. & Tobago).

222. Id. at 24, 29.

223. See Hilaire v. Trinidad & Tobago, Inter-Am. Ct. H.R. at 70–72 (June 21, 2002), available at http://www.corteidh.or.cr/T_y_t/serie_c_94_ing.doc (on file with the *Columbia Law Review*). The court found violations of, inter alia, the right to life, the right to be tried within a reasonable time, the right to an effective recourse, the right to humane treatment, and the right of all persons sentenced to the death penalty to apply for amnesty, pardon, or commutation of their sentence. Id. The court held that Trinidad was obligated, inter alia, to amend the Offences Against the Person Act to remove "the mandatory death penalty," to retry the defendants under the amended criminal code, to modify the conditions of its prisons to conform to international human rights standards, to commute the death sentences of those defendants who had not been executed, and to pay compensation with respect to one defendant. Id. at 39, 72–74. The Attorney General of Trinidad & Tobago has responded publicly to the judgment. Gov't Info Servs., Gov't of the Republic of Trin. & Tobago, The Attorney General Responds to the Ruling of the Inter American Court on Human Rights (July 10, 2002), at http://www.gov.tt/news/ AGHumaRightsResponse.asp (on file with the *Columbia Law Review*). She noted that the government will amend the Offences Against the Person Act and that the Privy Council's *Pratt* decision will eventually bar the defendants' executions. Id. It is unclear from her statement, however, what other measures, if any, the government will take to comply with the Inter-American Court's judgment. See id.

appeal brought by six death row defendants who had filed petitions with the Human Rights Committee and the Inter-American Commission.[224]

The pressure created by these decisions led Caribbean governments to cut their ties to the Privy Council. In February 2001, eleven Caribbean states finalized an agreement to replace the British court with a new Caribbean Court of Justice which will act as the region's highest court of appeal.[225] Pressure to ratify the agreement increased in the spring of 2002 after the Privy Council ruled that the mandatory imposition of death sentences for all murder convictions was unconstitutional.[226] Once the agreement enters into force, the link between the Commonwealth Caribbean and the Privy Council will be severed, and with it, many human rights advocates fear, the last bar to wholesale imposition of the death penalty in the Caribbean.[227]

D. *Caribbean Human Rights Protections in the Twenty-first Century*

In closing this Part, a brief review of the consequences of the Caribbean backlash against human rights seems warranted. Although the foregoing narrative has focused on issues relating to capital punishment, the impact of the governments' actions are in fact far broader and have left the regional legal landscape relating to human rights protection in a state of flux.

First, the backlash narrowed the opportunities for supranational review of human rights violations. Individuals in Jamaica and Trinidad & Tobago, the region's two most populous states,[228] can no longer petition

---

224. Lewis v. Attorney Gen. of Jam., [2001] 2 A.C. 50, 85 (P.C. 2000) (appeal taken from Jam.).

225. See Canute James, Controversial Caribbean Court Will Go Ahead, Fin. Times (International), Feb. 20, 2001, available at WL Fintimes Database (on file with the *Columbia Law Review*); Caribbean: Eleven Caribbean Leaders Sign Agreement to Set Up Caribbean Court of Justice, BBC Monitoring Summary of World Broadcasts, Feb. 17, 2001, at L/1 (agreement signed Feb. 15, 2001). The court will commence operations once three countries have ratified the agreement and deposited five years of dues in a special trust fund. See Owen Bowcott, Caribbean Severs Link to Privy Council, The Guardian (Manchester), Feb. 15, 2001, at 12. The court is "unlikely to sit before 2003. " Id.

226. See Reyes v. The Queen, Appeal No. 64 of 2001, ¶ 43 (P.C. Mar. 11, 2002) (appeal taken from Belize), available at http://www.privy-council.org.uk/files/pdf/2002_No.11.pdf (on file with the *Columbia Law Review*) (holding that mandatory death penalty for appellant's conviction of murder by shooting violates prohibition on inhuman or degrading punishment in Constitution of Belize); Canute James, Death Penalty Ruling Could Speed Up Plans for Caribbean-wide Court, Fin. Times. (U.S.), Mar. 15, 2002, available at WL Fintimes Database (on file with the *Columbia Law Review*) (stating that Caribbean governments are expected to speed up plans to establish Caribbean Court of Justice in wake of Privy Council's ruling).

227. See Bowcott, supra note 225, at 12 ("The decision to establish a shared Caribbean court of justice—advocated as a means of establishing full legal independence for the region and throwing off one of the last vestiges of colonialism—is likely to speed up the rate of hangings.").

228. The World Almanac and Book of Facts, at 867–68 (William A. McGeveran Jr. ed., 2002).

the Human Rights Committee regarding violations of any of the rights guaranteed under the ICCPR—including rights wholly unrelated to the criminal justice system.[229] If the demand for international review remains high, this may increase the workload of the Inter-American Commission, which retains the authority to review petitions alleging violations of the American Convention (in the case of Jamaica) or the nonbinding American Declaration of the Rights and Duties of Man (in the case of Guyana and Trinidad, which are parties to the OAS Charter but not to the American Convention).[230] Opportunities for supranational review in the remainder of the region are only slightly more promising.[231]

Second, the backlash fundamentally altered domestic judicial procedures for protecting human rights. Once the Caribbean Court of Justice commences operations, it will have the ultimate authority to interpret the region's constitutions. The new court will thus be empowered to decide whether to follow the Privy Council's precedents across a wide range of civil liberties issues, and whether to construe the bills of rights in Caribbean constitutions in harmony with international human rights standards. Although the Law Lords had begun to adopt broad and purposive

---

229. Guyana is still a party to the Optional Protocol because its reservation covering the death penalty is likely to be viewed as invalid by the Human Rights Committee. See supra text accompanying note 211 (describing the Committee's invalidation of Trinidad & Tobago's death penalty reservation, which is identical to Guyana's). All three states continue to be parties to the ICCPR, and thus are obligated to submit periodic reports to the Human Rights Committee on the measures they have taken to protect the rights in the Covenant. In practice, however, such reports are often late and only partly illuminate the human rights situation in a particular state. See Anne F. Bayefsky, The UN Human Rights Treaty System: Universality at the Crossroads 8, 21 (2000). It is for this reason that individual petition procedures are often seen as the most effective way to review compliance with human rights treaties. See Rein A. Myullerson, Monitoring Compliance with International Human Rights Standards: Experience of the UN Human Rights Committee, 1991–1992 Canadian Hum. Rts. Y.B. 105, 107 (1992) ("[I]t is only through the consideration of individual communications that complete conformity of national legislation and practice with the requirements of international law can be assessed.").

230. See Natasha Parassram Concepcion, Note, The Legal Implications of Trinidad & Tobago's Withdrawal from the American Convention on Human Rights, 16 Am. U. Int'l L. Rev. 847, 861–62 (2001) (noting that even after Trinidad & Tobago's denunciation of American Convention, individuals may still file petitions with the Inter-American Commission alleging violations of the American Declaration on the Rights and Duties of Man). The Commission's decisions interpreting the Declaration are not legally binding, however, and may not be referred to the Inter-American Court. Id. at 859–60.

231. Because all twelve states that comprise the Commonwealth Caribbean are members of the OAS, OAS Ratification Chart, supra note 139, the Inter-American Commission may receive communications alleging that these states have violated the nonbinding American Declaration. Concepcion, supra note 230, at 860. Of the twelve states, only Barbados is a party to both the American Convention and the ICCPR's Optional Protocol. St. Vincent & the Grenadines is also a party to the latter treaty. American Convention Ratification Chart, supra note 84; Optional Protocol Ratification Chart, supra note 138. Although Barbados threatened to denounce the American Convention after the *Pratt* case, see Gutierrez, supra note 199, neither it nor any other state in the region withdrew from their human rights treaty obligations.

constructions of the constitutions that considered international treaties and decisions as persuasive authorities,[232] it is unknown whether the Caribbean Court of Justice will continue this approach.

III. VIEWING THE CARIBBEAN BACKLASH THROUGH THREE OPTICS

What explains the actions of these Caribbean governments? The number and variety of state and nonstate actors involved in these events and the complexity of their interactions suggest that no single factor can be identified as the definitive cause of the backlash. It is possible, however, to achieve greater explanatory clarity by viewing the events through three different optics—one focused on the Caribbean backlash as a dispute over capital punishment, the second addressing the judicial imperialism of the Privy Council, and the third emphasizing the overlegalization of international obligations. Each of these optics emphasizes the causal contributions of a particular facet of the Caribbean case study. Filtering the denunciations through these three lenses reveals that although certain aspects of the backlash are unique to the region and unlikely to be replicated elsewhere, other features may prove informative for other treaty regimes and the ways in which those regimes might become overlegalized.

A. *The Caribbean Backlash as a Capital Punishment Dispute*

One optic focuses on the Caribbean treaty denunciations as principally if not exclusively caused by a dispute over the death penalty. Governments, legal elites, and the Caribbean public shared a strong preference for capital punishment as a way to deter the region's persistently high violent crime rate. According to one official (the Attorney General of Trinidad & Tobago), the legality of the death penalty was an essential condition of Caribbean participation in human rights regimes.[233] The

---

232. See Reyes v. The Queen, Appeal No. 64 of 2001, ¶¶ 17–24, 26, 40–42 (P.C. Mar. 11, 2002) (appeal taken from Belize), available at http://www.privy-council.org.uk/files/pdf/2002_No.11.pdf (on file with the *Columbia Law Review*) (stating that "[a] generous and purposive interpretation is to be given to constitutional provisions protecting human rights," and citing American Convention, European Convention, ICCPR, and decisions of Inter-American Commission, ECHR, and the Human Rights Committee as persuasive authority). For additional Privy Council decisions referring to international human rights sources, see Attorney Gen. of H.K. v. Lee Kwong-Kut, [1993] A.C. 951, 953, 967–68 (P.C. 1993) (appeal taken from H.K.) (citing decisions of ECHR and comments of Human Rights Committee); Vincent v. The Queen, [1993] 1 W.L.R. 862, 868 (P.C. 1993) (appeal taken from Jam.) (referring to decision of Human Rights Committee); Riley v. Attorney Gen. of Jam., [1983] A.C. 719, 720 (P.C. 1982) (appeal taken from Jam.) (citing to decision of ECHR); Ong Ah Chuan v. Pub. Prosecutor, [1981] A.C. 648, 651 (P.C. 1980) (appeal taken from Sing.) (citing decisions of ECHR); see also supra Part II.A.3 (discussing methodological approach of Privy Council to interpreting Caribbean constitutions).

233. Maharaj, supra note 177, at 150 ("It was on this basis that . . . Commonwealth Caribbean States organised their domestic legal and administrative procedures in capital cases and it was on this understanding that Trinidad and Tobago accepted the right of condemned prisoners to petition the international human rights bodies.").

evolution of capital punishment norms supports this claim. When Caribbean states first ratified human rights treaties, between the 1960s and the 1980s, the text of the treaties, the case law of the tribunals, and the judgments of the Privy Council all supported the view that death sentences and delays in executing them did not violate international or constitutional law. Restrictions on capital punishment existed, but moves toward abolition were only encouraged, not required.

The legal norms governing capital punishment shifted after the *Pratt* case, but the Caribbean preference for capital punishment did not. Initially, governments sought to reconcile their human rights commitments with their intent to carry out executions. But when faced with a perceived irreconcilable conflict between their domestic commitment to the death penalty and their international commitment to the human rights petition system, the governments chose exit—first from the tribunals' jurisdiction, and then, when that failed to ease constraints on executions, from the Privy Council. In the end, the regional preference for capital punishment was strong enough to outweigh the weaker preference for maintaining commitments to constitutional and human rights systems that effectively incorporated abolitionist norms. Supporting this conclusion is the fact that two of the three denouncing states immediately sought to reaffirm their treaty commitments for human rights unrelated to capital punishment.

Viewed as a story about the death penalty, the case study at first appears to have little resonance beyond its particular facts. Examined more broadly, however, the study provides evidence of how states may respond when international agreements expand into areas that clash with strongly held domestic preferences. Such norm shifts can create a form of overlegalization by increasing a treaty's levels of obligation and precision.[234] Norm shifts are particularly prevalent in the human rights arena, where treaties under the stewardship of international tribunals have been imbued with an inherently expansionist character.[235] But they are also plausible outcomes in areas as diverse as trade, intellectual property, arms control, or environmental law, where the consequences of treaty ratification become clear only after agreements are interpreted by international bodies or applied by the parties over time to a diverse series of factual settings.

The plausibility of an exit strategy in response to norm shifts will vary depending upon such variables as: (1) the mix of obligations and institutions a treaty contains; (2) the costs to a state's reputation and to the

---

234. See supra Part I.D.1 (describing overlegalization that changes initial treaty bargains).

235. See Laurence R. Helfer, Consensus, Coherence and the European Convention on Human Rights, 26 Cornell Int'l L.J. 133, 134 (1993) (analyzing ways in which ECHR has expanded the European Convention to keep pace with evolving legal standards).

credibility of its commitment to comply with other treaties;[236] and (3) the willingness of a state to eschew exit in exchange for a greater voice in shaping the regime's future.[237] Commitments negotiated as a "package deal," such as the WTO's family of agreements, are likely to be far stickier than single-subject treaties or treaties that permit issue-specific reservations ex ante.[238] But the Caribbean backlash demonstrates that the potential for exit is genuine, even for relatively robust treaty systems and states once committed to some form of international supervision.

B. *The Caribbean Backlash as a Consequence of Judicial Imperialism*

A second framing of the case study focuses on the Privy Council as an illegitimate legacy of colonialism. On this reading, the backlash achieved the judicial independence that was an inevitable, if delayed, consequence of earlier political independence. So long as the Privy Council's judgments were consonant with local values, the benefits of retaining appeals to London—free justice from learned jurists incorruptible by local politicians—outweighed the court's status as a vestige of colonial rule. But once the court began to articulate norms in conflict with local values, the court came to be perceived as engaging in a form of "judicial imperialism"[239] by "super-impos[ing] . . . Eurocentric notions and values" on the region.[240]

---

236. That Jamaica and Trinidad & Tobago believed that the credibility costs of exit were high is suggested by their efforts to remain as treaty parties after the *Pratt* decision. Rather than denouncing the treaties immediately, the governments first sought to convince the Privy Council and then the human rights tribunals to extend review periods in capital cases. See supra text accompanying notes 201–207.

237. See Weiler, supra note 14, at 2412, 2423, 2427 (arguing that members of the European Community began to exercise greater voice in EC's decisionmaking processes as their option to exit the Community diminished).

238. See Steve Charnovitz, Triangulating the World Trade Organization, 96 Am. J. Int'l L. 28, 31 (2002) (stating that negotiators of Uruguay Round trade agreements sought "a 'package deal' of interlocked commitments rather than a collection of stand-alone agreements"); Ernst-Ulrich Petersmann, Constitutionalism and International Organizations, 17 Nw. J. Int'l L. & Bus. 398, 442 (1996–1997) (characterizing agreements relating to services and intellectual property as part of "global package deals" negotiated within the GATT/WTO). In a sense, human rights treaties are also "package deals," a fact illustrated by the different sets of rights or different formulations of rights in agreements covering the same subject matter. See, e.g., Helfer, supra note 1, at 301–02 (comparing the civil and political rights provisions of the ICCPR and the European Convention). But such packages are restricted to the protection of individual liberties or group rights and are not linked to wholly unrelated subjects of international regulation. In addition, the WTO treaties do not permit state-specific reservations while human rights conventions usually do. See Final Act, supra note 18, art. XVI, para. 5.

239. Rose-Marie B. Antoine, Opting Out from the Optional Protocol—Is This Inhumane?, 3 Caribbean L. Bull. 28, 37 (1998) (noting claims by others that *Pratt* decision was an example of judicial imperialism).

240. Simmons, Death Penalty, supra note 176, at 10; see also Bryan, supra note 149, at 197–98 & nn. 129–130 (collecting statements by Caribbean judges that Privy Council's death penalty cases "did not conform to the judicial reality of the Caribbean region"); De

The explanatory power of this optic is uncertain, however. Had Caribbean states merely been seeking an excuse to generate the regional political support necessary to sever links to a court steeped in the values of the old empire, they could easily have done so immediately after the *Pratt* case. Guyana had already chosen this route, and proposals for other states to follow suit had been made repeatedly since the early days of independence.[241] Instead, they chose as a first best strategy to expedite petitions to the human rights tribunals but retain appeals to the court. By doing so, Caribbean governments acknowledged the Privy Council's legitimacy and signaled their willingness to persuade the Law Lords that *Pratt* was erroneous as a principle of Caribbean constitutional theory and unworkable as a rule of Caribbean criminal justice.

The judicial imperialism argument acquires greater force from the Privy Council's response to the governments' requests for accommodation. The court refused to acknowledge the clear evidence that *Pratt's* inflexibility had made it impossible for Caribbean states to permit human rights petitions to be heard within a reasonably deliberative period of time. Instead, it increased the strictures of its death row jurisprudence, invalidating the time limits the states had sought to impose on the tribunals and staying executions while petitions were pending. Far from adopting an incremental approach to introducing a new legal norm, the court's actions forced the norm upon a resistant legal and political culture. Even for established national courts, this approach might be criticized as politically inastute; but it was especially poor politics for a postcolonial court adopting a new rule that mapped perfectly onto a legal fault line dividing former colonies from the old empire.[242]

What predictive power does this imperial story have for relationships between national court judges and national political actors outside of the British Commonwealth? Given its sui generis postcolonial status, the Privy Council's role in promoting the backlash seems minimally relevant to national courts whose constitutional review functions are firmly anchored in their domestic political structures. There are, however, in the Privy Council's missteps important lessons for the increasing number of national courts engaging in a dialogue with foreign and international

---

La Bastide, supra note 150, at 407–08 (discussing effect of Privy Council rulings on Caribbean courts).

241. See supra notes 146, 148.

242. This analysis also implies that, whatever its formal powers, the Privy Council may in fact lie somewhere between a domestic court and a supranational tribunal. Its failure to perceive this hybrid status provides further insight into the causes of the backlash. The court's inflexible death row phenomenon rulings suggest that it viewed itself as a true domestic court with the ultimate power to say what the law is and to compel governments to act. A supranational tribunal would have been more circumspect, proceeding incrementally and flexibly because it could not assume compliance and had to rely instead on the persuasive power of its reasoning. The Privy Council's status is also relevant in assessing the case study's implications for international relations theory, a subject addressed in infra Part IV.C.

jurists over human rights and constitutional norms.[243] Courts participating in this growing trend toward "judicial globalization" permit their domestic jurisprudence to be shaped by outside influences and seek to harmonize—or at least reconcile—domestic, foreign, and international standards.[244] Although many judges and commentators have praised this development, others, most notably in the United States, have questioned its legitimacy.[245]

When courts incorporate international norms into their domestic law, either directly (by giving a treaty direct effect) or more obliquely (by interpreting domestic norms consistently with a state's international commitments or by engaging in a dialogue with supranational tribunals that review those commitments), they augment a treaty's delegation variable by establishing themselves as potential enforcers of treaty norms. As several international relations scholars have noted, governmental actions are most constrained when international agreements are highly "embedded" in domestic legal systems and can be enforced by autonomous national courts.[246] Sometimes governments acquiesce in this approach, in effect agreeing that domestic judges should serve as helpmeets for compliance. But where judges incorporate international norms on their own authority, the possibility of overlegalization increases.

---

243. See Claire L'Heureux-Dubé, The Importance of Dialogue: Globalization and the International Impact of the Rehnquist Court, 34 Tulsa L.J. 15, 16 (1998) (Justice of the Canadian Supreme Court stating that "[m]ore and more courts, particularly within the common law world, are looking to the judgments of other jurisdictions, particularly when making decisions on human rights issues"). For other examples of national courts in the Americas, Africa, and Asia following or carefully consulting the jurisprudence of human rights tribunals, see Slaughter, Judicial Globalization, supra note 16, at 1109–12 (European, South African, and Zimbabwean courts, and decision of Privy Council in Pratt); Developments in the Law—International Criminal Law, The International Judicial Dialogue: When Domestic Constitutional Courts Join the Conversation, 114 Harv. L. Rev. 2049, 2052–59 (2001) [hereinafter Developments in the Law] (Canadian, Indian, South African, and Zimbabwean courts). Somewhat ironically, these commentators cite the Privy Council's decision in the Pratt case as a salutary example of the ways in which judges consult foreign and international judicial decisions to interpret domestic laws. See Slaughter, Judicial Globalization, supra note 16, at 1110; Developments in the Law, supra, at 2054.

244. Slaughter, Judicial Globalization, supra note 16, at 1104.

245. Compare, e.g., Atkins v. Virginia, 122 S. Ct. 2242, 2250 n.21 (2002) (holding that the execution of mentally retarded defendants violates the Eighth Amendment of U.S. Constitution, and citing as persuasive evidence of a "consensus" against such executions the "overwhelming[ ] disapprov[al]" of "the world community"), with id. at 2254 (Rehnquist, C.J., dissenting) ("[I]f it is evidence of a *national* consensus for which we are looking, then the viewpoints of other countries simply are not relevant."); see also Knight v. Florida, 528 U.S. 990, 990–91 (1999) (Thomas, J., concurring in the denial of certiorari) (rejecting reliance by Justices Breyer and Stevens on foreign and international law sources to support defendant's claim that death row phenomenon violated Eighth Amendment's ban on cruel and unusual punishment).

246. Keohane et al., supra note 47, at 467.

   Although the case study confirms that it can be risky for judges to act as domestic "transmission belt[s]"[247] for international or foreign legal concepts, the risks will surely vary from jurisdiction to jurisdiction. In the case of the Commonwealth Caribbean, the risks were particularly great because of the Privy Council's colonial legacy and the potential for resistance to judicial rulings that domesticated legal concepts taken from the old empire. Similar concerns are likely to arise in dualist jurisdictions that strictly separate national and international law or limit the role of courts in enforcing international commitments,[248] even if they do not cause the kind of radical judicial restructuring that occurred in the Caribbean. Conversely, where judicial consultation of foreign and international legal sources is a constitutional mandate (as in South Africa[249]), resistance to a judgment that relies on those sources is likely to be weak. Perhaps the most delicate balancing will be required of courts in states transitioning toward greater permeability to international influence, as is now occurring in the United Kingdom after Parliament's enactment of legislation incorporating the European Convention into domestic law.[250]

C. *The Caribbean Backlash as Overlegalization of International Law*

   A third optic, one that draws upon but extends the insights of the previous two, concerns the Privy Council's overlegalization of Caribbean governments' treaty commitments. Consider first the effect of the court's death row rulings on each of the three legalization variables.[251] The court increased the *obligation* of the treaties in two ways: first by fixing a domestic constitutional standard—the five-year execution window—by reference to the international petition system, and later by prohibiting governments from executing defendants while their petitions were pending. It increased the treaties' *precision* by particularizing the content of the degrading punishment norm shared by both international and domestic instruments. And it enhanced *delegation* by urging states to respect the decisions of the human rights tribunals and encouraging capital defendants to file petitions with them, thereby increasing the likelihood

---

   247. Levit, supra note 58, at 329.

   248. See generally John H. Jackson, Status of Treaties in Domestic Legal Systems: A Policy Analysis, 86 Am. J. Int'l L. 310, 314–19 (1992) (exploring differing roles of treaties in monist and dualist legal systems).

   249. S. Afr. Const. ch. 2, § 39(1)(b) (directing courts and tribunals to "consider international law" when interpreting the Bill of Rights); see also id. ch. 14, § 233 (directing courts to interpret legislation consistently with international law whenever reasonably possible).

   250. See, e.g., Chris Ryan, Human Rights and Intellectual Property, 23 Eur. Intell. Prop. Rev. 521, 523–25 (2001) (discussing recent intellectual property decisions responding to Human Rights Act of 1998, which made the European Convention directly enforceable in courts in the United Kingdom).

   251. See supra Part I.A (explaining the three criteria—obligation, precision, and delegation—by which legalized characteristics of international agreements may be measured).

that those petitions would later result in commutation of their sentences. In each instance, the Privy Council expanded the legalized quality of the Caribbean governments' human rights obligations. What began as agreements with both hard and soft law elements became much harder law in practice. What were initially international recommendations with no binding force were transformed into decisions with practical binding effect.

The Privy Council's actions also engendered both types of overlegalization identified in this Article.[252] On the one hand, by effectively abolishing capital punishment where the treaties did not require abolition, the court altered the terms to which Caribbean nations had consented when they first ratified the treaties.[253] This change created significant domestic opposition to both the tribunals and the Privy Council and generated strong domestic pressures in favor of exit. On the other hand, the Privy Council engendered overlegalization by improving enforcement opportunities unrelated to capital punishment itself. Putting the death penalty and the death row phenomenon to one side, Caribbean governments were granting capital defendants fewer rights than the treaties required. These treaty breaches—relating to unfair or delayed trials and appeals and inadequate conditions of detention—were revealed in the numerous nonbinding decisions the human rights tribunals issued after reviewing petitions from capital defendants.[254] In many cases, the tribunals recom-

252. See supra Part I.D (discussing difference between overlegalization that changes initial treaty bargains and overlegalization that improves enforcement opportunities).

253. See supra Part III.A (discussing the Caribbean backlash as a capital punishment dispute).

254. See, e.g., Lamey v. Jamaica, Cases 11.826, 11.843, 11.846 & 11.847, Inter-Am. C.H.R. 996, 1071–72, 231–37, OEA/ser.L/V/II.111, doc. 20 rev. (2000), available at http://www.cidh.org/annualrep/2000eng/ChapterIII/Merits/Jamaica.11.826.htm (on file with the *Columbia Law Review*) (violations of Articles 5(1) and (2), and 1(1) of the American Convention based on mandatory nature of death penalty, delayed and unfair trial procedures, lack of legal aid, and conditions of detention on death row); Morgan v. Jamaica, Communication No. 720/1996, U.N. GAOR, Hum. Rts. Comm., 54th Sess., Supp. No. 40 vol. 2, at 221, U.N. Doc. A/54/40 (1998), available at http://www.unhchr.ch/tbs/doc.nsf/(symbol)/472d043ca55dd6b180256714004008e8?opendocument (on file with the *Columbia Law Review*) (finding violation of Article 10(1) of the ICCPR based on inadequate conditions of detention, including lack of medical treatment); Morrison v. Jamaica, Communication No. 635/1995, U.N. GAOR, Hum. Rts. Comm., 53d Sess., Supp. No. 40 vol. 2, at 123–25, U.N. Doc. A/53/40 (1998), available at http://www.unhchr.ch/tbs/doc.nsf/(symbol)/dbe98945ec059398802566d5003b510d?opendocument (on file with the *Columbia Law Review*) (violations of Article 9(2) and (3), Article 14(3)(c), Article 10(1), and Article 7(1) based on defendant not being informed of the charges against him until three or four weeks after his arrest, not being tried until two and a half years after arrest, and being ill-treated in custody); Smart v. Trinidad & Tobago, Communication No. 672/1995, U.N. GAOR, Hum. Rts. Comm., 53d Sess., Supp. No. 40 vol. 2, at 149, U.N. Doc. A/53/40 (1998), available at http://www.unhchr.ch/tbs/doc.nsf/(symbol)/1990c66b9a892223802566d4003cb607?opendocument (on file with the *Columbia Law Review*) (violations of Article 9(3) and Article 14(3)(c), based on two-year lag between arrest and trial). See generally Henry v. Jamaica, Communication No. 230/1987, U.N. GAOR, Hum. Rts. Comm., 47th Sess., Supp. No. 40, at 210, 218, U.N. Doc. A/47/40 (1991), available at

mended that the defendants' death sentences be commuted.[255] Prior to *Pratt*, Caribbean governments mostly ignored these recommendations.[256] After *Pratt*, the Privy Council required the governments to commute death sentences whenever appellate and international review procedures exceeded five years. By imposing the same remedy for domestic law violations of the degrading punishment ban that the tribunals had recommended for these other treaty breaches, the court effectively ended the governments' ability to shirk compliance with their human rights commitments.

As this discussion reveals, however, the overlegalization produced by the Privy Council's rulings occurred indirectly and thus requires a more nuanced analysis. Had the court sought to increase the legalized quality of the *obligation* and *delegation* variables in a straightforward way, it could have instructed Caribbean governments that the human rights tribunals' recommendations were henceforth to be treated as binding. Similarly, the clearest method for the court to increase the *precision* variable would have been to interpret the treaties as themselves requiring a definite time limit on death row detention.[257] The *Pratt* case adopted neither of these direct approaches. Instead, the Privy Council interpreted a parallel provision of *domestic law* in a way that indirectly augmented the treaties' legalization levels and allowed litigants and advocates to use the petition system strategically to effectively abolish capital punishment.

The Privy Council's indirect approach to legalization should hardly be surprising, however. As a formal matter, the court's interpretation of Caribbean constitutional texts rather than treaties conformed to the longstanding British rule that treaties can become binding as domestic law only through parliamentary enactments.[258] Any attempt by the court to disregard this settled rule and augment the tribunals' authority directly would have been politically unpalatable to Caribbean governments. But it would also have ceded to the tribunals control over how to interpret and apply the degrading punishment norm and diminished the court's

---

http://www.unhchr.ch/tbs/doc.nsf/(symbol)/91167d85d50848abc1256aaee0049fa3b? opendocument (on file with the *Columbia Law Review*) ("In capital punishment cases, the obligation of States parties to observe rigorously all the guarantees for a fair trial set out in article 14 of the Covenant admits of no exception.").

255. See, e.g., *Morgan*, U.N. Doc. A/54/40, at 222 (recommending commutation of death sentences); *Smart*, U.N. Doc. A/53/40, at 149 (same); *Lamey*, Cases 11.826, 11.843, 11.846 & 11.847, Inter-Am. C.H.R. at 1072, OEA/ser.L/V/II.111, doc. 20 rev. (same).

256. See supra note 190 (citing cases illustrating governments' refusal to comply with tribunals' recommendations or requests for interim measures).

257. Recall that in the decisions preceding the Privy Council's *Pratt* decision, the U.N. Human Rights Committee rejected the death row phenomenon as a violation of the ICCPR, whereas the Inter-American Commission appeared to treat it as a breach of the American Convention (although without indicating the maximum period of time that a defendant could be detained on death row). See supra Part II.B.2.

258. See Lewis v. Attorney Gen. of Jam., [2001] 2 A.C. 50, 83–84 (P.C. 2000) (appeal taken from Jam.).

ability to tailor the Caribbean legal landscape to its own conceptions of criminal justice.

The Privy Council's actions illustrate that the incorporation of international norms or international review procedures into domestic law is one important pathway by which national courts can increase a treaty's legalization levels. Although the Privy Council achieved this increase indirectly, the combined effect of its decisions fundamentally altered the legalized character of the treaties. And, unlike legalization trends elsewhere, Caribbean governments actively resisted an evolution limited to a single issue for which domestic opposition to change was exceptionally strong.

Equally important, the Privy Council mismanaged the integration of domestic and international legal systems that the *Pratt* case required. Instead of holding fast to a rigid rule, the court could have endorsed the death row phenomenon in principle on the egregious facts of *Pratt* but not imposed a five-year time limit for all future executions. In this way, the court could have fleshed out incrementally the contours of the degrading punishment norm in subsequent cases, tempering it to the realities of the region's criminal justice system and to a more realistic assessment of the review periods required by the human rights tribunals. Had the Privy Council adopted this course, it might have avoided the backlash altogether.

When filtered through this lens, the case study provides a cautionary lesson in the perils of overlegalization. It suggests that states intentionally design treaty regimes with both hard and soft law components precisely because they are wary of relinquishing their sovereignty and foresee advantages in retaining flexibility when unanticipated events occur.[259] Judges who modify these conscious regime design choices risk a backlash, particularly where they advance legalization too far or too fast, or without the tacit support of a state's political actors.[260] In short, regime design matters, and governments may actively resist efforts by international or national jurists to create more deeply legalized commitments or more stringent review procedures after they have signed on to a treaty.

IV. Assessing Competing International Relations Theories in Light of the Caribbean Treaty Denunciations

In addition to the insights generated by the three optics discussed in the previous Part, the Caribbean case study can be used to assess the realist, ideational, and liberal international relations theories identified in Part I. This Part first reviews the hypotheses that each theory would apply to evaluate the case study and then explores the extent to which those

---

259. See supra Part I.D.

260. Cf. Goldstein & Martin, supra note 20, at 621 ("If enforcement is too harsh, states will comply with trade rules even in the face of high economic and political costs, and general support for [trade] liberalization is likely to decline.").

hypotheses explain the events in the Commonwealth Caribbean. In assessing the predictive power of each theory, this Part portrays a richer and more nuanced picture than would a formal analysis of international legal rules alone. It thus adds to the broader debate between international legal scholars and political scientists over how the legalization of international norms affects states' conduct.

A. *Assessing Realist Theory*

Recall that realist theories of international relations emphasize the interests of powerful states in pressing weaker states for or against compliance with human rights norms. According to realists' focus on interstate bargaining power, both noncompliance with international commitments and exiting from a treaty are less likely if powerful nations actively oppose such conduct, and more likely if such states support or acquiesce in treaty-inconsistent behavior. In the Caribbean, the two powerful states able to influence the domestic policies of governments in the region are first, the United States, and second, the United Kingdom (and, more broadly, the European Union, of which it is a member). As is explained below, these states adopted divergent positions with respect to Caribbean human rights practices and Caribbean governments actively and successfully resisted any external pressures.

Consider first the United States. Although the United States exerts significant economic and political influence in the Caribbean,[261] in light of its domestic use of the death penalty and its opposition to international efforts to abolish capital punishment, it was hardly likely to challenge the Caribbean governments' denunciations.[262] Research for this Article has not revealed any attempt by the United States to oppose or protest Caribbean governments' treaty denunciations or their carrying out of death sentences. To the contrary, the State Department's country reports for Guyana and Trinidad & Tobago contain only short and uncritical descriptions of the denunciations—including the governments' justifications for their actions—and the report on Jamaica is silent on the matter.[263] Similarly, at a 1999 meeting of OAS government representa-

261. See Atkins, supra note 134, at 139–46, 166–67; Robert A. Pastor & Richard D. Fletcher, Twenty-first Century Challenges for the Caribbean and the United States: Toward a New Horizon, *in* Democracy in the Caribbean, supra note 120, at 255, 264–72.

262. See, e.g., EU Drops Divisive Death Penalty Resolution at the UN, Agence France Presse, Nov. 18, 1999, available at LEXIS, Agence France Presse File (on file with the *Columbia Law Review*) (noting successful opposition by United States to EU-sponsored resolution in U.N. General Assembly calling on all states to suspend use of the death penalty); cf. Schabas, supra note 160, at 262 (labeling Jamaica, Trinidad & Tobago, and United States "enthusiastic [death penalty] retentionist" states).

263. See 1999 Guyana Country Report, supra note 129; Bureau of Democracy, Hum. Rts. & Lab., U.S. Dep't of State, 1999 Country Reports on Human Rights Practices: Jamaica (Feb. 25, 2000), available at http://www.state.gov/www/global/human_rights/1999_hrp_report/jamaica.html (on file with the *Columbia Law Review*); Bureau of Democracy, Hum. Rts. & Lab., U.S. Dep't of State, 1999 Country Reports on Human Rights Practices:

tives commenting on Trinidad & Tobago's denunciation, the United States delegation did not issue a condemnation but focused instead on granting regional tribunals additional resources to process cases expeditiously.[264] The United States's position contrasts sharply with that of European governments, nine of which filed formal objections to the Caribbean denunciations of the Optional Protocal with the Secretary General of the United Nations.[265]

As for the United Kingdom, the Commonwealth Caribbean's close legal and political ties to that country allowed it to exert significant pressure on the region to abolish capital punishment.[266] For its five dependent territories in the Caribbean, Britain abolished capital punishment outright in 1991.[267] Such legislative action was not possible for independent Commonwealth members, but the British government used a variety of tools to urge Caribbean nations to halt executions.[268] As Foreign Secretary Robin Cook stated in the late 1990s, "'[w]e need to use our diplomatic clout, our technical assistance and our human rights projects to persuade other countries not to use the death penalty.'"[269] Additional pressure came from the European Union, which in June 1998 made the

---

Trinidad & Tobago (Feb. 2, 2000), available at http://www.state.gov/www/global/human_rights/1999_hrp_report/trinidad.html (on file with the *Columbia Law Review*).

264. OAS News, Ambassadors Stress Need to Strengthen Regional Human Rights System, Sept.–Oct. 1999, available at http://www.oas.org/OASNews/1999/English/September-Oct/art5.htm (on file with the *Columbia Law Review*) [hereinafter Ambassadors Stress Need].

265. Optional Protocol Ratification Chart, supra note 138 (noting objections of Denmark, Finland, France, Germany, Italy, the Netherlands, Poland, Spain, and Sweden).

266. The ties of the Commonwealth were not as strong as might be expected, however. In particular, the United Kingdom had little success after the Second World War in maintaining control over local political structures in its former colonies, including control over their human rights policies. See Krasner, supra note 3, at 187 (noting inability of United Kingdom to maintain influence over local political structures "by contracting with local leaders regarding constitutional arrangements").

267. Shelley Emling, As Crime Rises, Caribbean Governments Turn to Hanging, Flogging, Austin American-Statesman, Oct. 17, 1998, available at LEXIS-NEXIS Academic Universe, Austin American-Statesman File (on file with the *Columbia Law Review*); see also Jim Loney, Caribbean States Resent British Pressure Over Gays, AAP Newsfeed, Feb. 20, 1998, available at LEXIS, AAP Newsfeed File (on file with the *Columbia Law Review*) ("Britain is pressing its current and former overseas territories to amend laws that ban homosexuality and allow capital and corporal punishment through much of the region."). Those possessions are Anguilla, British Virgin Islands, the Cayman Islands, Montserrat, and the Turks & Caicos Islands.

268. Stephen Breen, Trinidad Begins Executing Killers, The Scotsman, June 5, 1999, at 12 (noting "strong pressure from Britain and Europe to abolish the death penalty"); Emling, supra note 267, at A23 ("For years, Britain has pressured [its] former colonies to abolish the death penalty, which the European Union has long opposed.").

269. See Maharaj, supra note 177, at 143 (quoting speech of British Foreign Secretary to Amnesty International).

worldwide abolition of capital punishment a foreign policy priority.[270] Under the new policy, EU officials expressed their opposition to the death penalty in demarches to Caribbean governments and allocated over half a million Euros for a legal assistance project to death row prisoners in the Caribbean.[271]

In response to these British and European pressures, Caribbean states were generally united in their resistance. The fifteen-member Caribbean Community (CARICOM) strongly opposed the EU's attempt to link the abolition of capital punishment to the provision of monetary aid, and Caribbean governments publicly defended the denunciations and use of capital punishment on sovereignty grounds.[272] For example, at the 1999 OAS meeting mentioned above, the Ambassador of Barbados expressed concern that "powerful countries [we]re beginning to abrogate the right to make laws and establish the way in which smaller countries should conduct their business."[273]

In sum, the case study supports the core realist claim that powerful states pressure weaker ones over the latters' compliance with international human rights commitments. In particular, the study illustrates that powerful states may increase pressure after weaker states have exercised their right to exit from a treaty. The efficacy of such coercive efforts is less certain, however. Although the precise pathways of power cannot be conclusively mapped, the case study suggests that coercion will fail where powerful states are divided and target states—even weak ones—unite in opposition. In the Caribbean, external pressure by European states was counterbalanced by tacit support of the United States and by a robust regional response that resisted conforming domestic criminal justice to international or foreign standards.

---

270. Council of the European Union, Guidelines to EU Policy Toward Third Countries on the Death Penalty, June 3, 1998, available at http://www.eurunion.org/legislat/DeathPenalty/Guidelines.htm (on file with the *Columbia Law Review*).

271. Eur. Comm'n, Commission Staff Working Document: Report on the Implementation of the European Initiative for Democracy and Human Rights in 2000, at 15, available at http://europa.eu.int/comm/external_relations/human_rights/doc/sec01_801.pdf (last visited Aug. 12, 2002) (on file with the *Columbia Law Review*) (noting financial support given to Penal Reform International to provide legal assistance to death row defendants in the Caribbean); Eur. Union, EU Annual Report on Human Rights 14, 60 (1999), available at http://europa.eu.int/comm/external_relations/human_rights/doc/report_99_en.pdf (on file with the *Columbia Law Review*) (noting diplomatic contacts with The Bahamas, Jamaica, and Trinidad & Tobago urging the abolition of capital punishment).

272. See Caribbean Community Rejects EU Link Between Aid and Ending Death Penalty, Cana News Agency, Feb. 27, 1999, available at LEXIS, BBC Worldwide Monitoring File (on file with the *Columbia Law Review*); see also Press Release, Organization of American States, Trinidad and Tobago Denunciation of OAS Human Rights Convention Effective Today, E-056/99ie (May 26, 1999), available at http://www.oas.org/oaspage/press2002/en/press99/0526991.htm (on file with the *Columbia Law Review*) (noting Trinidad & Tobago ambassador's defense of the death penalty as within states' domestic jurisdiction, a statement supported by ambassador from St. Vincent & the Grenadines).

273. Ambassadors Stress Need, supra note 264, at 2.

COLUMBIA LAW REVIEW

B. *Assessing Ideational Theory*

What lessons does the case study hold for ideational theory generally and the five-step spiral model of human rights change in particular?[274] In the 1980s, Commonwealth Caribbean states were far advanced along the spiral. They were (with the exception of Guyana and Granada) liberal democracies that had ratified one and often multiple human rights treaties, including individual petition procedures. Human rights norms were embedded in their domestic constitutions, judicial review of rights-limiting government actions was generally robust, and local NGOs engaged in human rights advocacy.[275] By the late 1990s, three Caribbean governments had denounced human rights petition procedures and all states in the region had resisted efforts by the Privy Council, European governments, and transnational advocacy networks to curtail or abolish their use of the death penalty.

Does the spiral model account for this sort of backlash? The model predicts that human rights changes are not always unidirectional, a hypothesis that the case study supports. But the model's creators also claim that most instances of repression or backlash will occur earlier in the spiral in states with far worse human rights records than those of the Commonwealth Caribbean.[276] More importantly, in light of the "norm shift" that occurred in the Americas and elsewhere in the 1980s and early 1990s, some ideational scholars have asserted that "human rights norms have reached consensual ('prescriptive') status on the international level by now," such that states will no longer invoke national sovereignty to oppose charges of rights abuses and will be hard pressed to engage in "norm denial" when interacting with other state and nonstate actors.[277]

As the case study reveals, however, Caribbean governments engaged in precisely such norm denial and invocations of sovereignty notwithstanding their prior commitment to human rights treaties and institutions.[278] This suggests that norm clashes (and even norm erosion) can occur at much later points in the spiral than ideationalists had predicted, well after a state has become a member of a human rights regime. More broadly, discursive efforts by state and nonstate actors to shame, cajole, and ultimately persuade Caribbean governments to comply with their treaty obligations were largely unsuccessful with respect to death penalty issues. To the contrary, support for capital punishment appears to have increased over time among both state actors and the public.

---

274. See supra Part I.C.1 (discussing the spiral model of human rights change).

275. See supra Part II.A.2.

276. See supra notes 64–65 and accompanying text.

277. See Risse & Ropp, supra note 62, at 266.

278. Larry Rohter, In the Caribbean, Support Growing for the Death Penalty, N.Y. Times, Oct. 4, 1998, at A14 (noting statements by Attorney General of Trinidad & Tobago that Inter-American Court's review of death penalty petitions was an "infringement of its sovereignty" and that "[t]he death penalty is not a human rights issue").

From an ideational perspective, what explains these events? Ideational studies note the existence of "blocking factors," domestic forces that prevent the spiral model from moving forward toward the final stage of rule-consistent behavior. These forces include "countervailing national norms and value structures which emphasize[ ] sovereignty and domestic cohesion more than human rights principles."[279] Governments violating human rights commitments consciously appeal to these national norms and values structures "to increase their own legitimacy and to orchestrate a nationalist response to the increasing transnational network pressures."[280]

Commonwealth Caribbean governments invoked two countervailing national norms in reaction to the flood of international petitions that followed the *Pratt* decision: (1) maintaining public order and security, and (2) upholding the domestic rule of law.[281] The first justification resonated strongly with the Caribbean public, given the continuing high crime rates in the region and the popularity of using capital punishment to deter crime.[282] The second justification resonated with legal elites, for it allowed governments to frame the issue as a binary choice between complying with the mandatory constitutional requirements of *Pratt* (itself grounded on the well-established human rights principle barring degrading punishment), or the practices of international tribunals alleged to be incompatible with those requirements.[283]

Invoking these countervailing norms allowed Caribbean governments not only to amass popular support for their actions, but also to shore up regional backing for capital punishment and resistance to external pressures. When faced with demands from state and nonstate actors, Caribbean governments publicly and collectively reaffirmed each others' right to impose the death penalty even if that required denouncing inter-

---

279. Risse & Ropp, supra note 62, at 261.

280. Id.

281. See Maharaj, supra note 177, at 152–53.

282. See supra note 158 and accompanying text.

283. In public statements that accompanied the denunciations, both Trinidad & Tobago and Jamaica justified their actions by reference to the domestic constitutional constraints imposed by the Privy Council. See Ministry of Foreign Affairs, Republic of Trinidad and Tobago, Notice to Denounce the American Convention on Human Rights (May 26, 1998), available at http://www.oas.org/juridico/english/Sigs/b-32.html (on file with the *Columbia Law Review*); see also Simeon C.R. McIntosh, Cruel, Inhuman and Degrading Punishment: A Re-Reading of *Pratt and Morgan*, 8 Caribbean L. Rev. 1, 4 (1998) ("The Jamaican Government has . . . explained its decision [to denounce the Optional Protocol] as one of 'agony' over how to respect Jamaica's various human rights treaty commitments, and yet, at the same time, have death penalty decisions carried out within five (5) years, as required by *Pratt and Morgan*."); Press Release, Organization of American States, Trinidad and Tobago P.M. Tells OAS That Death Penalty is Not a Human Rights Issue (Sept. 24, 1999), available at http://www.oas.org/OASpage/press2002/en/Press99/092399.htm (on file with the *Columbia Law Review*) (noting that treaty denunciations were required for continuing to impose capital punishment consistent with state's constitutional obligations).

national agreements. For example, in January 1999, attorneys general from twelve Caribbean states urged their governments to denounce the human rights agreements and reratify them with death penalty reservations.[284] Similarly, at a meeting of the OAS in June 1998, Caribbean foreign ministers broke from the rest of the OAS Assembly to express their unanimous support for Trinidad's decision to denounce the American Convention.[285]

These collective affirmations of regional autonomy fit with ideational theory, but in a strikingly different way than studies had predicted. Ideational scholars assert that the states "most susceptible to network pressures are those that aspire to belong [or already belong] to a normative community of nations,"[286] or "an emerging community of liberal states."[287] The Commonwealth Caribbean, a region of liberal democracies with a common political, legal, and historical identity, fits the definition of such a community. But unlike larger groupings of liberal states, Caribbean nations privileged a particular interpretation of human rights norms that excluded capital punishment. Ideationalists predicted that membership in a liberal or normative community would figure prominently in whether a state was susceptible to external pressure for human rights changes, and the case study supports this. But whereas ideationalists believed that such membership would *favor* compliance with international norms, the case study demonstrates that such membership can also weigh *against* compliance. Stated another way, membership in a normative community of Commonwealth Caribbean states reduced, rather than enhanced, states' vulnerability to external pressure and prevented them from being relegated to an "outgroup" of human rights violators.[288]

Two facets of the case study help to explain the strength of Caribbean resistance. The first relates to the contested and evolving nature of the human rights norms surrounding capital punishment. As explained above, a clear norm shift occurred in the years following Caribbean states' ratification of the human rights agreements.[289] Rather than challenging the death penalty directly, capital defendants reframed death row detention as a distinct human rights problem. Once the Privy Council accepted this argument, Caribbean states were forced to operate under constitutional time constraints in tension with allowing defendants to petition the human rights tribunals.

---

284. Amnesty International: USA Midnight Shame: USA Executes Child Offender, Feb. 5, 1999, available at LEXIS, M2 Presswire File (on file with the *Columbia Law Review*).

285. Caribbean: Caribbean States Support Trinidad and Tobago Human Rights Stance at OAS, BBC Monitoring Summary of World Broadcasts: Africa, Latin America and the Caribbean, June 6, 1998, at L/2; Row Over Decision to Quit Convention; Government Removes Obstacle to Death Penalty, Latin Am. Regional Rep., June 16, 1998, available at LEXIS, Latin American Newsletters File (on file with the *Columbia Law Review*).

286. Keck & Sikkink, supra note 54, at 29.

287. Risse & Sikkink, supra note 51, at 24.

288. Id. at 27.

289. See supra notes 223–224 and accompanying text.

Ideational studies predict that efforts to promote domestic change will depend upon the issues around which advocacy strategies coalesce. Although physical harm to vulnerable or innocent individuals is a compelling subject for transnational pressure, "what constitutes bodily harm and who is vulnerable or innocent may be highly contested."[290] The case study supports this issue-specific sensitivity. In particular, the sharp contestations over the human rights dimension of death row detention (and the Caribbean-European fault line around which divisions formed) allowed Caribbean states credibly to engage in norm denial after the norm shift occurred, and to use that denial to justify their withdrawal from the treaties.[291]

The second feature of the case study that implicates ideational theory concerns the pressure from nonstate actors. As the petition filing data described in Part II demonstrates, British law firms and organizations such as Interrights (both of which fit the definition of transnational advocacy networks) were especially active in bringing cases to the human rights tribunals following the *Pratt* decision.[292] Indeed, they were involved with a large majority of petitions filed by defendants on death row in the Caribbean. Not only were these petitions effective in delaying executions (often beyond the Privy Council's five-year window), but they also raised a slew of substantive challenges to capital sentences. Thus, nonstate actors imposed ample pressure on Caribbean governments "from above" to commute capital sentences in individual cases.

Pressure "from below" was inadequate, however. Although some Caribbean human rights organizations had forged links with transnational allies, local public opinion overwhelmingly favored capital punishment. Other than the Catholic Church, few domestic nonstate actors favored abolishing the death penalty.[293] The relatively thin support for abolition among domestic nonstate actors supports the core ideational claim that "[e]ffective [transnational advocacy] networks must involve reciprocal information exchanges, and include activists from target countries as well as those able to get institutional leverage."[294] In the absence of such local pressure, the boomerang pattern of influence—in which nonstate actors pressure governments from both above and below—is unlikely to emerge.

---

290. Keck & Sikkink, supra note 54, at 27.

291. Cf. Risse & Sikkink, supra note 51, at 24 ("[I]t is possible that denial and backlash is a normative phase particular to a period in which new international norms have emerged, but when they are still strongly contested internationally.").

292. See supra note 196 and accompanying text and Figure 4.

293. See O'Neill, supra note 152, at 194 (stating that Catholic church provided the only "visible dissent" to Caribbean death penalty policies); State Killing, supra note 156, at 5 ("The community working against the death penalty in the [English speaking Caribbean], while dedicated, is small and faces regular physical threats and vilification in the media."); see also supra note 158 and accompanying text.

294. Keck & Sikkink, supra note 54, at 28–29.

These two features—an increase in legalization focused solely on capital punishment and the absence of domestic groups favoring abolition—worked in tandem to remove pressures in favor of treaty compliance. Had the rise in legalization levels been distributed across a broad range of issues, local human rights advocates might have had stronger incentives to challenge the governments' actions. After all, a breach of one treaty right could have increased the risk that the governments would violate other rights. But the distinct treatment of capital punishment allowed the boomerang pattern of influence to break down and subjected the issue to blocking factors not applicable to human rights as a whole.

In sum, the case study's support for ideational hypotheses is equivocal. On the one hand, the mechanisms by which principled ideas are transmitted, including the role of transnational advocacy networks, the focus on norm evolution, and the tactics governments use to block human rights advances, provide important insights that help to explain the Caribbean backlash. Yet the case study calls into question the largely progressive and sanguine narrative of human rights change that ideational scholars have sketched. Ideational theory seems especially weak in its prediction that norm denial and rule violations are unlikely to occur among states that are fairly far advanced in the spiral of change. As the case study demonstrates, rights backlashes can occur even among liberal democracies that in the main are committed to protecting individual liberties and that are active players in human rights regimes.

C. Assessing Liberal Theory

To assess the case study's implications for liberal international relations theory, this Section first addresses liberal hypotheses regarding a state's regime type as an independent variable in predicting the nature of its relationships with international regimes. It then considers the case study's implications for liberal theories concerning compliance with treaty commitments and evolution of human rights regimes, including the critical variables of a treaty's incorporation into national law, the impact of supranational adjudication, and the role of private parties in enforcing international obligations.

1. *Differences in Regime Type as an Explanatory Variable.* — For liberal scholars, the regime type of a state is a critical predictor of how it will interact with international regimes.[295] At this level of analysis, the case study provides provocative, although ultimately inconclusive, new evi-

---

295. Some liberal scholars have asserted that liberal states are more likely than nonliberal states to comply with their international commitments. See, e.g., Simmons, Legalization, supra note 46, at 594–95 (summarizing theories regarding propensity of liberal democratic states to comply with their international commitments). Recent studies have become increasingly nuanced, however, using more fine-grained evidence to differentiate among different types of liberal states and among liberal democracies, rule of law societies, and nonliberal regimes. See supra notes 45–47. For a more detailed discussion of liberal theory, see supra Parts I.B, I.C.2.

dence. Jamica and Trinidad & Tobago—two of the three states that denounced human rights treaties and petition procedures—are liberal democracies, with long-standing commitments to liberal values, including independent judicial review and the protection of civil liberties. The third state, Guyana, is a regional outlier. It is a transitional democracy, struggling to overcome the consequences of its autocratic and socialist post-independence past, whose respect for liberal institutions and individual rights is only recently and shallowly entrenched.

Despite these differences in regime type, all three states denounced human rights treaties. Moreover, the two liberal governments denounced international regimes more comprehensively than did their nonliberal neighbor, and they were far more assertive in defending their actions domestically and internationally and in criticizing the tribunals.[296] These facts cut against the liberal claim that liberal democracies are more likely than other states to engage with international institutions and adhere to their international commitments.

Yet a contrary inference is also possible. Trinidad & Tobago and Jamaica could simply have ignored their treaty commitments in practice while nominally remaining parties to the treaties. By following the formal denunciation procedures that the treaties themselves authorized, the two governments demonstrated a form of respect for human rights regimes rather than the "[o]rganized [h]ypocrisy" that some international relations scholars have associated with insincere treaty ratifications.[297] In addition, the two liberal states had nonfacetious justifications for their actions, including the Privy Council's misperceptions about the time required to review death row petitions, the contested treatment of the death row phenomenon as a human rights issue, and the governments' attempt to expedite the tribunals' review periods prior to denouncing the treaties. Whatever one thinks of these rationales, they are far more persuasive than the justifications offered by nonliberal Guyana, which was not bound by the strictures of *Pratt* and which denounced the ICCPR's Optional Protocol after the Human Rights Committee issued its first unfavorable decision against it.[298]

This interpretation should not be overstated, however. Both Trinidad & Tobago and Jamaica often refused to implement the tribunals' recommendations even when they were parties to the treaties. And Trinidad openly flouted the internationally binding provisional measures orders of the Inter-American Court of Human Rights by hanging defendants who had filed petitions with the Inter-American Commission prior to

---

296. See supra Part II.B.6.

297. Krasner, supra note 3, at 32 (noting lack of correlation between human rights treaty ratifications and respect for human rights norms).

298. See supra notes 214–217 and accompanying text. Guyana's denunciation might also be viewed as an attempt to show solidarity with its two regional neighbors, with whom it had been actively promoting a new Caribbean Court of Justice. See supra notes 225–227 and accompanying text.

the effective date of the state's denunciation.[299] This behavior contrasts sharply with the practice of other liberal democracies, particularly in Europe, which are far more respectful of international human rights tribunals.[300]

When the Caribbean region is viewed as a whole, however, additional evidence supporting the liberal regime type hypothesis emerges. The nine other liberal democratic members of the Commonwealth Caribbean did not denounce human rights treaties, although they were equally bound by the time constraints of *Pratt* and their attorneys general had called for denunciations. And two states in the region ratified human rights instruments after the Privy Council issued its ruling in late 1993, including Barbados which was considering denouncing the American Convention.[301] Admittedly, the statistical evidence provided in Part II reveals that death row petitions filed against these other Caribbean nations were sparse, reducing the pressure to abrogate international review to meet the Privy Council's five-year timetable.[302] Nevertheless, when viewed in the aggregate, the case study supports the inference that most liberal democracies in a region under strong pressure to change domestic criminal justice policies refrained from abrogating (and in two cases extended) their treaty commitments.

Finally, an important cautionary note about the robustness of the foregoing conclusions is warranted. The case study involves an extremely small data set of twelve sovereign states, ten of which qualify as liberal democracies and only three of which actually denounced human rights treaties. In addition, Commonwealth Caribbean nations other than the Bahamas, Jamaica, and Trinidad & Tobago have small populations and even smaller death rows,[303] making comparisons among states in the region difficult. Similarly, generalizing about the conduct of nonliberal

---

299. See supra notes 218–220 and accompanying text.

300. See supra notes 17, 82–83 and accompanying text.

301. American Convention Ratification Chart, supra note 84 (noting June 4, 2000 acceptance of jurisdiction of Inter-American Court by Barbados); ICCPR Ratification Chart, supra note 84 (noting June 10, 1996 accession to ICCPR by Belize); see also Gutierrez, supra note 199 (reporting that Barbados may denounce American Convention).

302. See supra Figure 2.

303. See Michael Dorman, Caribbean Islands Battle Rising Crime, Newsday, Mar. 14, 1999, available at 1999 WL 8162017 (on file with the *Columbia Law Review*) (citing Amnesty International report stating that there are "nearly 250 prisoners on death rows in the Caribbean," of which 104 were incarcerated in Trinidad & Tobago, forty-seven were incarcerated in Jamaica, and forty were incarcerated in the Bahamas); Serge F. Kovaleski, Death Penalty Gaining Favor in Caribbean Isles; Rise in Violent Crime Sparks Public Outrage, Ft. Lauderdale Sun-Sentinel, Sept. 5, 1998, at 21A, available at 1998 WL 12827602 (on file with the *Columbia Law Review*) (citing Amnesty International report stating that twenty-four prisoners were on death row in Guyana and nine prisoners were on death row in Belize); Richards, supra note 158 (stating that St. Lucia, with a population of less than 150,000, had seven prisoners condemned to death); see also The World Almanac and Book of Facts, supra note 228, at 867–68 (listing populations of Commonwealth Caribbean nations).

states based solely on Guyana's conduct is problematic. That nation was the region's only long-standing nondemocracy, but it both ratified and withdrew from the Optional Protocol after a slow transition to democracy had commenced. Given these empirical limitations, it is impossible to determine with precision whether the case study supports or undermines liberal claims about the explanatory power of regime types.

2. *Incorporation and Supranational Judicial Review as Explanatory Variables.* — If the conclusions about the liberal regime type hypothesis are equivocal, the case study offers more definitive insights regarding the two variables of incorporation and supranational judicial review that liberal scholars (and others) have identified as central to promoting compliance with international commitments. As with the ECJ and ECHR, the critical interactions occurred among international tribunals, domestic courts, and private litigants, but the story that unfolded was far different from the one told in Europe. The puzzling question is why a de facto incorporation of international norms into domestic law and a domestic court's interactions with international tribunals produced not compliance but backlash.

The story begins with supranational judicial review, in which all three denouncing states had agreed to participate. That review, however, resulted in nonbinding recommendations by the two tribunals—recommendations that defending states often ignored. Supranational review (and the human rights violations it exposed) was thus only a weak constraint on governments seeking to impose death sentences, even if they did not always execute defendants while petitions were pending. Even in cases where states violated the treaties, governments could easily resist the tribunals' entreaties and ensure that their domestic laws remained unaltered.[304]

The *Pratt* case changed this legal landscape in crucial ways. First, it adopted a new human rights norm—the death row phenomenon—that was far more favorable to capital defendants than preexisting law and that imposed significant constraints on executions. Second, it signaled to Caribbean governments that the region's highest court considered supranational review to be a useful supplement to domestic appeals in capital cases, even while it acknowledged that the governments were not bound to commute death sentences if the tribunals so recommended. Third, the case publicized the existence of supranational judicial review to death row defendants and their advocates, raising hopes that the governments would give the tribunals' decisions the "weight and respect" the court believed they deserved.[305]

The most important aspect of *Pratt*, however, was its de facto incorporation of elements of international human rights regimes into domes-

---

304. See supra note 190 (discussing responses by Trinidad & Tobago and Jamaica to decisions and recommendations of human rights tribunals).

305. Pratt v. Attorney Gen. for Jam., [1994] 2 A.C. 1, 27 (P.C. 1993) (appeal taken from Jam.).

tic law. This incorporation had both substantive and procedural dimensions. Substantively, the Privy Council endorsed as a matter of domestic constitutional law a claim that international tribunals had been wrestling with as a matter of treaty construction for several years: that prolonged death row detention was degrading or inhuman. Indeed, the court used international decisions as persuasive support for its ruling. In the process, the Privy Council validated the tribunals' own efforts to limit states' authority in capital cases.

But the procedural incorporation aspect of the Privy Council's ruling was even more striking. *Pratt* expressly considered petitions to human rights tribunals when deciding how much of a delay in carrying out executions was constitutionally permissible. In effect, the Privy Council fixed a *domestic* constitutional standard by reference to the *international* petition system. The court's subsequent death row decisions confirmed and extended this approach, striking down the time limits Trinidad and Jamaica had sought to impose on the tribunals and barring executions while the defendants' international petitions were under review.[306]

Consider the effect of these rulings on the authority of the human rights tribunals and the treaties they interpret. Here was a domestic court that appeared to be entering into a partnership with the tribunals, validating their efforts, promoting the filing of new cases by private parties, and even authorizing a remedy (binding provisional measures) that the tribunals themselves were powerless to impose.[307] The practical effect of the court's rulings was to increase markedly the embeddedness of treaty rules and supranational review in domestic law. According to the liberal hypothesis discussed in Part I.C.2, this should have resulted in greater compliance with international commitments, especially in states with independent judiciaries and a strong commitment to protecting individual liberties. For a time, this proved to be true. But this increased compliance with international norms quickly backfired as governments sloughed off both their treaty obligations and the Privy Council's review.

Can liberal theory account for this behavior? On the one hand, recent liberal scholarship rejects the claim that international regimes have an inherently expansionist character that precludes backlashes.[308] It also asserts that governments do not always anticipate the domestic political consequences of participating in international regimes, particularly where such regimes include supranational tribunals to which private par-

---

306. Thomas v. Baptiste, [2000] 2 A.C. 1, 21, 24, 29 (P.C. 1999) (appeal taken from Trin. & Tobago); Lewis v. Attorney Gen. of Jam., [2001] 2 A.C. 50, 85 (P.C. 2000) (appeal taken from Jam.).

307. In the case of the American Convention, the Inter-American Commission had the authority to ask the Inter-American Court of Human Rights to issue provisional measures binding as a matter of international law on any state accepting the Court's jurisdiction. In the Commonwealth Caribbean, only Trinidad & Tobago (and, since June 2000, Barbados) could have been subject to such binding orders. American Convention Ratification Chart, supra note 84.

308. See Alter, supra note 16, at 512–13.

ties have access.[309] These factors suggest that the evolution of international regimes is often difficult to predict and that later iterations of a treaty system are not necessarily superior to earlier ones.[310] At the same time, however, scholars have asserted that high levels of incorporation and supranational judicial review "make it much more difficult for governments to retreat from their legalized commitments when the [unanticipated political] consequences become clear."[311] That result plainly did not occur in the Commonwealth Caribbean.

A related liberal hypothesis helps to explain why the treaty denunciations occurred notwithstanding the domestic incorporation of international norms. In explaining the success of the ECJ and ECHR in achieving increased levels of treaty compliance, liberal scholars have stressed the links between supranational tribunals, national courts, and the private litigants who use domestic and international litigation to press for legal and political change.[312] They have focused on how the incentives of each of these actors favored the forging of strong relationships between the judges, and how the mutual pursuit of self interest drove the expansion of the treaties.[313]

In the Commonwealth Caribbean, however, the self interest of each of these three actors was not mutually reinforcing. Instead, it exacerbated the clash between domestic and international legal systems and increased the political reaction against the supranational-domestic judicial partnership. Consider first the litigation incentives of capital defendants and their counsel. The timetable set by the *Pratt* case meant that death sentences could be overturned not only by convincing domestic courts that the government had violated a defendant's constitutional rights, but also by extending domestic and international review processes beyond the five-year window. Death row defendants and their counsel thus had strong incentives to file petitions with one or both tribunals and to convince the Privy Council to embed the international petition system in Caribbean domestic laws. The British law firms that represented the vast majority of Caribbean defendants before both the tribunals and the Privy Council were well situated to achieve these objectives.[314]

---

309. Keohane et al., supra note 47, at 477–78 (noting that state compliance with international commitments is enhanced where individuals and groups have direct access to international tribunals).

310. Cf. Goldstein & Martin, supra note 20, at 630 (arguing that earlier and less legalized GATT may have been superior at achieving progressive liberalization of international trade to later, more legalized WTO).

311. Kahler, supra note 53, at 682.

312. See supra notes 82–83 and accompanying text (discussing how European tribunals forged links with domestic courts and domestic litigants interested in seeking compliance with their rulings).

313. Burley & Mattli, supra note 82, at 60 (stating that "[t]he glue that binds this community of supra- and subnational actors is self-interest").

314. See Assistance for Prisoners, supra note 196 (discussing pro bono assistance provided to defendants in both judicial fora); see also supra Figure 4 (identifying

From the tribunals' perspective, the large number of death row petitions provided fresh opportunities to enhance their authority. The cases allowed the tribunals to clarify the scope and content of the treaties, to publicize the petition procedures, and to exert pressure on governments to alter their treaty-incompatible practices. But exercising these functions requires time and resources, and the tribunals had insufficient quantities of both to review cases within the eighteen-month window the Privy Council had set.[315] The result was that governments, rather than being shamed, cajoled, or persuaded into voluntarily implementing the tribunals' recommendations, strongly resisted the de facto partnership between the Privy Council and the tribunals that *Pratt* engendered.

The actions of the Privy Council also appeared to serve its rational self interest. During the 1980s and early 1990s, the court had begun to develop a more rights-protective jurisprudence and to engage in a dialogue with other national courts and supranational tribunals over the individual rights provisions common to both Caribbean constitutions and human rights treaties.[316] *Pratt* continued this trend and thus ensured that the Privy Council would remain an important player in policing Caribbean criminal justice systems through its powers of constitutional review. *Pratt* also came at a time when other British territories and members of the Commonwealth were severing their links with the Privy Council.[317] Given the active use of capital punishment in the Caribbean, accepting death row detentions as a form of degrading punishment ensured that the court would continue to have an active appellate docket and would not fall into desuetude.

In isolation, therefore, the behavior of each of these three actors appeared rational. Together, however, they made it impossible for Caribbean governments both to allow the international petition process to run its course and to carry out the executions that their citizens were clamoring for.

Two other aspects of the case study are relevant to this analysis of incentives. The first concerns whether the Privy Council should be treated as a domestic court. The Privy Council is nominally the Commonwealth Caribbean's highest court of appeal. But its location in London,

---

representation of Caribbean death row defendants by British law firms and advocacy groups).

315. This statement must be qualified for the Inter-American Commission, which expedited its review of Caribbean death row petitions filed in 1998 and 1999. See supra note 195 and accompanying text. The eighteen-month window would not, however, be adequate to permit defendants to petition two tribunals in succession. See supra note 189 and accompanying text.

316. See supra Part II.A.3 and note 232 (discussing evolution of Privy Council's jurisprudence and collecting cases discussing decisions of international human rights tribunals).

317. These include, during the 1990s, Australia, Fiji, Hong Kong, Malaysia, and Singapore. New Zealand is also considering abolishing appeals to the Privy Council. De La Bastide, supra note 150, at 402.

its staffing by British Law Lords, its colonial legacy, and the power of local governments to abolish appeals to it suggest that the Privy Council has a sui generis status somewhere between an international and a domestic court.[318] In Europe, the national courts that were essential players in expanding international commitments were accepted parts of the domestic legal order. The Privy Council, by contrast, was a distant judicial body steeped in different legal culture.[319] In this setting, it is not surprising that the Privy Council's death row rulings were perceived as externally imposed norms that did not receive the habitual acquiescence that even unpopular national court rulings receive in societies with independent judiciaries and commitments to the rule of law.

The second aspect of the case study that is relevant to actor incentives concerns the distributional effects of the *Pratt* decision and the international petitions it engendered. Liberal scholars have noted that the distribution of costs and benefits is relevant to how nonstate actors mobilize in the aftermath of supranational judicial rulings.[320] They have theorized that successful pressure for compliance with such rulings is more likely where their benefits fall on a narrowly defined group (particularly a group that has previously mobilized in favor of policy change) but their burdens are more widely distributed. Conversely, countermobilization against implementing judicial decisions is more likely if the costs of compliance are more narrowly focused.[321]

An analysis of the distributional effects of the Caribbean death penalty cases helps to explain the backlash, although the effects do not precisely track scholars' predictions. The benefits of the human rights tribunals' death row decisions flowed to a relatively small group of individuals (convicted criminal defendants), but a group that was a highly disfavored segment of Caribbean society with little if any political clout. The burdens of these decisions (that is, the effects of reduced criminal penalties) were widely distributed, but they were also deeply felt because of the popular belief that tough criminal sanctions deterred violent crime. To the extent that benefits also accrued to nonstate actors and legal counsel advocating criminal justice reform or abolition of the death penalty, most of those actors were located outside of the Commonwealth Caribbean, limiting the political pressure they could exert on governments to implement the tribunals' recommendations.

In sum, the case study provides important support for the liberal hypothesis that linkages among international tribunals, domestic courts, and private litigants are critical to determining compliance with international commitments. But where most liberal studies have focused on how

---

318. Cf. Barry Phillips, Pratt & Morgan v. Attorney-General for Jamaica, 88 Am. J. Int'l L. 775, 776 (1994) (Case Note) (stating that after *Pratt*, "the Privy Council could now be said to be developing into a human rights court for the British Commonwealth").

319. See supra Part III.B (discussing judicial imperialism by Privy Council).

320. See Alter, supra note 16, at 508.

321. Id.

these linkages can expand the legalized nature of treaty systems or enhance compliance, the Caribbean case study reveals how these interactions can also cause a counterreaction against further legalization and compliance.

V. CONCLUSION

The Commonwealth Caribbean backlash against human rights regimes at first appears puzzling. Why would three governments that generally respect the rule of law, protect individual liberties, and support international treaty regimes denounce human rights agreements and withdraw from the jurisdiction of human rights tribunals?

At least in part, the answer lies in the overlegalization of the human rights commitments that these three states had undertaken. Overlegalization can occur where a treaty develops higher levels of obligation, precision, and delegation than existed when a state first ratified the treaty. In its overlegalized form, a human rights treaty constrains a government's ability to balance the protection of individual liberties against other pressing social concerns, and thus generates domestic opposition to compliance or pressure to revise or denounce the treaty. In the Commonwealth Caribbean, the Judicial Committee of the Privy Council indirectly enhanced the legalization levels of the ICCPR and the American Convention when it interpreted domestic constitutional limitations on the maximum time defendants could spend on death row by reference to international human rights petition procedures. This interpretation effectively abolished the death penalty, a form of punishment that was overwhelmingly popular with the citizens of Guyana, Jamaica, and Trinidad & Tobago to combat high rates of violent crime in those countries. When the governments could not reconcile this strong domestic preference for capital punishment with their international commitment to allow defendants to petition the human rights tribunals, they withdrew from the treaties.

Additional insights into the causes of the backlash are found in three competing international relations theories that seek to explain why states enter into and comply with human rights agreements. Each of the three theories—realist, ideational, and liberal—helps to explain why Commonwealth Caribbean states acted as they did. But events in the region also provide important new evidence to assess claims made by international relations theorists, to question some of their assumptions, and to challenge accepted hypotheses. In particular, the Caribbean backlash provides an unusual opportunity to test in a non-European setting the explanatory power of such variables as external pressure from powerful states, the persuasive pull of the idea of human rights, the incorporation of international agreements into domestic law, links between national and international jurists, and the role of domestic interest groups and transnational advocacy networks as constituencies for or against treaty compliance.

Finally, if, as this Article suggests, the design of treaties matters to states and if treaties have a tendency to evolve toward higher levels of legalization or even overlegalization, scholars should broaden their scope of inquiry into the mix of hard and soft law elements that enhances states' compliance with their international commitments. In particular, scholars should consider when, how, and by whom legalization levels are modified, and the conditions under which linkages between domestic and supranational state and nonstate actors can expand compliance opportunities without eliciting hostile reactions from national governments.

[4]

The Origins of Human Rights Regimes: Democratic Delegation in Postwar Europe

Andrew Moravcsik

The fiftieth anniversary of the UN Universal Declaration on Human Rights marks an appropriate moment to reconsider the reasons why governments construct international regimes to adjudicate and enforce human rights. Such regimes include those established under the European Convention for the Protection of Human Rights and Fundamental Freedoms (ECHR), the Inter-American Convention on Human Rights, and the UN Covenant on Civil and Political Rights.

These arrangements differ from most other forms of institutionalized international cooperation in both their ends and their means. Unlike international institutions governing trade, monetary, environmental, or security policy, international human rights institutions are not designed primarily to regulate policy externalities arising from societal interactions across borders, but to hold governments accountable for purely internal activities. In contrast to most international regimes, moreover, human rights regimes are not generally enforced by interstate action. Although most arrangements formally empower governments to challenge one another, such challenges almost never occur. The distinctiveness of such regimes lies instead in their empowerment of individual citizens to bring suit to challenge the domestic activities of their own government. Independent courts and commissions attached to such regimes often respond to such individual claims by judging that the application of domestic rules or legislation violates international commitments, even where such legislation has been

For detailed suggestions and criticisms I am grateful to Gary Bass, George Bermann, Nancy Kokaz, Ronald Mitchell, Gerald Neuman, Daniel Nexon, Robert Paarlberg, Pasquale Pasquino, Kathryn Sikkink, Brian Simpson, and Henry Steiner, as well as Henning Boekle, John Ferejohn, Alexandra Filindra, Mary Ann Glendon, Virginie Guiraudon, John Ikenberry, Anne-Marie Slaughter, and participants in colloquia at Columbia University, Harvard University, New York University, the University of Oregon, the University of Pennsylvania, Princeton University, Rutgers University, and the 1999 Annual Convention of the American Political Science Association. I thank Jorge Dominguez, Stephen Holmes, and Richard Tuck for particular guidance, and Monique Hofkin, Alejandro Lorite, Alexandra Samuel, and Ilya Somin for able research assistance. Finally, I acknowledge financial and logistical support from the Weatherhead Center for International Affairs, the Center for European Studies at Harvard University, and the Center for European Studies at New York University. For an earlier version of this article with more detailed documentation, see Moravcsik 1998b.

enacted and enforced through fully democratic procedures consistent with the domestic rule of law. Arrangements to adjudicate human rights internationally thus pose a fundamental challenge not just to the Westphalian ideal of state sovereignty that underlies realist international relations theory and classical international law but also—though less-frequently noted—to liberal ideals of direct democratic legitimacy and self-determination. The postwar emergence of these arrangements has rightly been characterized as the most "radical development in the whole history of international law."[1]

Consider, for example, the ECHR, established under the auspices of the Council of Europe and based in Strasbourg, France. The ECHR system is widely accepted as the "most advanced and effective" international regime for formally enforcing human rights in the world today.[2] Since 1953, when the ECHR came into force, it has sought to define and protect an explicit set of civil and political rights for all persons within the jurisdiction of its member states, whether those individuals are aliens, refugees, stateless persons, or citizens. It initially established a Commission on Human Rights to review petitions.[3] The Commission could investigate the case, seek to settle it, or forward it under certain circumstances to a court of human rights, whose decisions governments are legally bound to follow. Two optional clauses of the ECHR, Articles 25 and 46, were subsequently adopted by all member states; they permit individual and state-to-state petitions and recognize the compulsory jurisdiction of the court. Many European governments have subsequently incorporated the convention into domestic law, directly or indirectly. For these reasons, the ECHR Court is right to proclaim the convention "a constitutional document of European public order."[4]

Over the last half-century, analysts agree, the legal commitments and enforcement mechanisms entered into under the ECHR have established "effective supranational adjudication" in Europe. Compliance is so consistent that ECHR judgments are now, in the words of two leading international legal scholars, "as effective as those of any domestic court."[5] In hundreds of cases where an explicit decision has been taken or a

---

1. See Humphrey 1974, 205, 208–209; Krasner 1995; and Falk 1981, 4, 153–83.

2. Petitions could be judged admissible if they meet several criteria, most importantly the prior exhaustion of domestic remedies. Henkin et al. 1999, 551. In this article I am not concerned with purely rhetorical human rights documents, such as the UN Universal Declaration, but solely with enforceable commitments. Rights imply remedies, without which the former are of little utility. Unsurprisingly, hypocrisy in signing declarations without mechanisms for direct enforcement appears to be without significant cost, regardless of a country's domestic policies. While liberal democracies may be more likely to sign such declarations, they are hardly alone in their willingness. At the height of the Cold War, the United States, the USSR, China, Iran, and dozens of other countries found ways to work around their differences and signed the wide-ranging UN Declaration on Human Rights. Some analysts conjecture that in the longer term such declarations help mobilize societal opposition to nondemocratic governments, for example, through the Inter-American and Helsinki CSCE–OSCE regimes. Yet it is telling that those interested in effective enforcement have consistently sought to establish mechanisms for raising and resolving disputes, as with the UN Covenants in the 1960s and the CSCE Vienna mechanism in 1989. Brett 1996.

3. See Janis, Kay, and Bradley 1995; Robertson and Merrills 1993; and van Dijk and van Hoof 1998. With reforms that came into effect in 1998, the commission was abolished and its activities turned over to the court itself, with similar criteria for admitting claims.

4. *Loizidou v. Turkey*, 310 Eur. Ct. *H.R.* (ser. A, 1995), 27.

5. Helfer and Slaughter 1997, 283, who draw on Shapiro 1981, 7, 26–36.

"friendly settlement" reached—including matters of criminal procedure, penal codes and the treatment of prisoners, vagrancy legislation, civil codes, systems of legal aid fees and civil legal advice, the rights of illegitimate children, military codes, expropriation policies, systems of awarding building permits, treatment of the mentally ill, reformatory centers, wiretapping, and censorship of the press—governments have amended legislation, granted administrative remedies, reopened judicial proceedings, or paid monetary damages to individuals whose treaty rights were violated.[6] When the court recently ruled that exclusion of homosexuals from the British armed forces violated the ECHR, the British government immediately announced its intention to comply. In countless additional cases, litigants have successfully pleaded the ECHR before domestic courts.[7]

There is a real theoretical puzzle here. Why would any government, democratic or dictatorial, favor establishing an effective independent international authority, the sole purpose of which is to constrain its domestic sovereignty in such an unprecedentedly invasive and overtly nonmajoritarian manner?

To answer questions such as this, political scientists tend to espouse either a realist or an ideational explanation for the emergence and expansion of formal human rights regimes. Democratic governments and transnationally active members of democratic civil societies either coerce other governments to accept human rights norms (the realist view) or persuade other governments to do so (the ideational view). Some scholars espouse both positions at once, arguing that powerful democracies are persuaded for essentially idealistic reasons to coerce others to respect human rights norms.

Such realist and ideational conjectures, though popular among scholars, rest on a remarkably thin empirical foundation. Historians have conducted almost no detailed case studies of the formation of international human rights regimes. Only the UN system—a notably weak regime—has been the subject of significant research, and this body of work focuses on rhetorical statements, such as the UN Declaration, rather than arrangements for adjudication and enforcement.[8] Such analyses, moreover, tend to accept uncritically the *ex post* conjectures of practitioners and commentators.

This article contains the first systematic empirical test of competing theories of the establishment of formal international human rights regimes. It does so by examining the negotiations to establish the ECHR in 1949–50. I argue that the primary proponents of binding international human rights commitments in postwar Europe were neither great powers, as realist theory would have it, nor governments and transnational groups based in long-established liberal democracies, as the ideational account would have it. Although established democracies supported certain human rights declarations, *they allied with dictatorships and transitional regimes in opposition to*

6. Carter and Trimble 1995, 309.
7. On domestic incorporation, see Polakiewicz and Jacob-Foltzer 1991; Drzemczewski 1983, 11–12; and Merrills 1993.
8. For the best of these, see Morsink 1999.

reciprocally binding human rights enforcement—a seldom-noted tendency for which realists and ideational theorists have no explanation. The primary proponents of reciprocally binding human rights obligations were instead the governments of newly established democracies.

This curious pattern is explicable only if we adopt a different theoretical starting point: the domestic political self-interest of national governments. Establishing an international human rights regime is an act of political delegation akin to establishing a domestic court or administrative agency. From a "republican liberal" perspective—one related to institutional variants of "democratic peace" theory as well as to the analysis of "two-level games" and public-choice theories of delegation—creating a quasi-independent judicial body is a tactic used by governments to "lock in" and consolidate democratic institutions, thereby enhancing their credibility and stability vis-à-vis nondemocratic political threats. In sum, governments turn to international enforcement when an international commitment effectively enforces the policy preferences of a particular government at a particular point in time against future domestic political alternatives.

I argue that governments will resort to this tactic when the benefits of reducing future political uncertainty outweigh the "sovereignty costs" of membership. It follows that "self-binding" is of most use to *newly established democracies*, which have the greatest interest in further stabilizing the domestic political status quo against nondemocratic threats. We should therefore observe them leading the move to enforce human rights multilaterally, whereas established democracies have an incentive to offer lukewarm support at best. In the case of the ECHR, this theoretical approach best explains the cross-national pattern of support for binding norms, the tactics governments employed, and the archival record of public rhetoric and confidential domestic deliberations.

The implications of this approach go well beyond postwar European human rights. The logic of "locking in" credible domestic policies through international commitments can be generalized to other human rights regimes—including the recent International Criminal Court—and unilateral human rights policies, not least the apparently anomalous behavior of the United States, as well as to other issue areas in world politics, regardless of whether their substantive content is "liberal." The latter include the stabilization of autocratic regimes under the Concert of Europe and Comintern, and the coordination of monetary and trade policies.

Existing Theories of International Human Rights Cooperation

Existing scholarship seeking to explain why national governments establish and enforce formal international human rights norms focuses on two modes of interstate interaction: coercion and normative persuasion. Respectively, these define distinctive "realist" and "ideational" explanations for the emergence of human rights regimes. Despite being widely viewed as theoretical antitheses, many empirical predictions of these two explanations converge.

Interstate Power: "For Countries at the Top, This Is Predictable"

Realist theories of international relations, and thus of the origin of human rights regimes, stress the distribution of interstate bargaining power. Governments accept international obligations because they are compelled to do so by great powers, which externalize their ideology—a prediction that follows equally from hegemonic stability theory and conventional realist bargaining theory.[9] All governments seek to maintain full domestic sovereignty wherever possible. With governments uniformly skeptical of external constraints, the major limitation on cooperation is the cost of coercion or inducement, which is inversely proportional to the concentration of power. Establishment of a binding human rights regime requires, therefore, a hegemonic ("k") group of great powers willing to coerce or induce recalcitrant states to accept, adjust to, and comply with international human rights norms. The greater the concentration of relative power capabilities, the greater the pressure on recalcitrant governments and the more likely is an international regime to form and prosper.

Precise formulations of the realist argument vary. E. H. Carr, Hans Morgenthau, and other classical realists maintain that governments employ liberal ideology, including support for human rights, to justify the pursuit of geopolitical interest.[10] Jack Donnelly writes of the Inter-American Convention on Human Rights that "much of the explanation [for] the Inter-American human rights regime . . . lies in power, particularly the dominant power of the United States. . . . [It] is probably best understood in these terms. The United States . . . exercised its hegemonic power to ensure its creation and support its operation."[11] John Ruggie uncharacteristically takes a similar line when he conjectures that human rights regimes will be weaker than nuclear nonproliferation regimes, because the former are of less concern to the core superpower security interests.[12] Kenneth Waltz asserts that powerful nations invariably seek to impose their views on other nations: "Like some earlier great powers, we [the United States] can identify the presumed duty of the rich and powerful to help others with our own beliefs . . . England claimed to bear the white man's burden; France had its *mission civilisatrice*. . . . For countries at the top, this is predictable behavior."[13] Alison Brysk links acceptance of human rights norms to the pressure by

9. Many analysts take the opposite view, namely that great powers tend to *oppose* strong human rights regimes. One might conjecture that large states have a commitment to sovereignty independent of the substantive issue at stake, or one might assume that great powers believe they can impose human rights on others unilaterally. This view is widely espoused as an explanation for the combined opposition during the 1950s of the United States, the United Kingdom, the USSR, and China to strong UN enforcement. Yet this consensus lacks theoretical underpinnings or empirical support beyond the casual impressions of a few participants. We shall see that the generalization is disconfirmed by the case of the ECHR negotiations. Compare Samnøy 1993, 76.

10. See Carr 1946; and Morgenthau 1960.

11. See Donnelly 1986, 625, also 637–38; and Ruggie 1983, 99.

12. Ruggie 1983, 104.

13. Waltz 1979, 200. See also Krasner 1992.

TABLE 1. *Establishing human rights regimes: Theories, causal mechanisms, and predictions*

	Realism	Ideational theory	Republican liberalism
Motivations and tactics	Great powers employ coercion or inducement to unilaterally extend national ideals derived from national pride or geopolitical self-interest. Smaller states defend their sovereignty.	Altruistic governments and groups in established democracies seek to extend perceived universal norms. Less-democratic states are socialized or persuaded through existing transnational networks (the "logic of appropriateness").	Governments seek to prevent domestic oppression and international conflict through international symbols, standards, and procedures that secure domestic democracy. They are constrained by fear that domestic laws might be struck down. International agreement reflects convergent interests.
Predicted national preferences on compulsory commitments	Supporters are led by democratic great powers. The weaker the state, the less support we observe.	Supporters are led by societal groups and governments in the most democratic states. The less established the democracy, the less support we observe.	Supporters are led by newly established democracies. Established democracies accept only optional or rhetorical commitments. Nondemocracies oppose.
Predicted variation in cooperation	Greater concentration of power in the hands of great power democracies More cost-effective coercion or inducement More cooperation.	More attractive norms, more salient, more legitimate exemplars, and the more established the transnational networks More powerful socialization effects More cooperation.	More immediate threats to democracy Greater desire to enhance domestic stability More cooperation.

international financial organizations such as the World Bank, backed by Western donor countries.[14] These predictions, and those of competing theories, are summarized in the first column of Table 1.

Normative Persuasion: "The Inescapable Ideological Appeal of Human Rights"

The most prominent ideational explanations for the emergence and enforcement of human rights regimes look to altruism and the persuasive power of principled ideas.

14. Brysk 1994, 51–56.

Such explanations rest, to that extent, on what used to be termed "utopian" or "idealist" foundations. The essence of such explanations lies in the prominence of idealistic or altruistic motivations for spreading liberal values.[15] Governments accept binding international human rights norms because they are swayed by the overpowering ideological and normative appeal of the values that underlie them. "The seemingly inescapable ideological appeal of human rights in the postwar world," writes Donnelly, who espouses a wide range of theories, "is an important element in the rise of international human rights regimes."[16]

Ideational arguments differ most fundamentally from realist arguments in their reliance on a distinctive conception of interstate interaction. They explicitly reject choice-theoretic foundations and instead stress the transformative power of normative moral discourse itself. In this view, a critical characteristic of political action in this area is that it is "principled"—that is, the altruistic and moral motives of actors have persuasive power in themselves. Accordingly, the most fundamental motivating force behind human rights regimes is not rational adaptation, let alone coercion, but transnational socialization—the "logic of appropriateness."[17] Many such explanations assert that transformations in actor identities occur though the impact of "principled" nongovernmental organizations (NGOs) on domestic and transnational opinion.[18] NGOs and publics within established democracies set up transnational networks, epistemic communities, and global discourses of human rights, dedicated to the advancement of a normative discourse of human rights. This in turn mobilizes domestic and transnational civil society at home and abroad, eventually socializing foreign and domestic leaders.[19]

Whence the ideological appeal of human rights? Some scholars look to human moral psychology, regional cultures, or salient historical events, but the most plausible explanation links support for international human rights protection to domestic democracy and commitment to the "rule of law."[20] In this view, which Thomas Risse terms "liberal constructivism," established democratic governments seek to extend their domestic values abroad and recognize others who do so. The more democratic they are, the more likely their espousal of human rights values.[21] Charles Kupchan and Clifford Kupchan conjecture that "states willing to submit to the rule of law and civil society are more likely to submit to their analogues internationally."[22] Similarly, Kathryn Sikkink points to the leading role of established democracies in promoting human rights, such as linking Scandinavian support for human rights enforce-

15. Keck and Sikkink 1998, chap. 1–3.
16. Donnelly 1986, 638. On soft power, see Nye 1990.
17. See Finnemore and Sikkink 1998; and Donnelly 1986.
18. See Sikkink 1993; Risse-Kappen 1994; and Finnemore 1996.
19. See, for example, Keck and Sikkink 1998; and Ramirez, Soysal and Shanahan 1997.
20. Russett 1993. For alternative views, see Keck and Sikkink 1998; Sikkink 1993; Sieghart 1983, 26–27; and Ando 1992, 171–72. See also Donnelly 1986; Whitfield 1988, 31, also 28–31; and Drzemczewski 1983, 220.
21. See Risse-Kappen 1996; and Moravcsik 1997. This view is related to the ideational variant of democratic peace theory, in which the democratic peace results from the tendency of liberal governments to externalize their domestic ideals. See Russett 1993.
22. Kupchan and Kupchan 1991, 115–16.

ment to the salience of social democratic values in their domestic politics.[23] Thomas
Franck asserts that compliance with international law is a function of the normative
acceptance of international rules, which in turn reflects (among other things) their
consistency with domestic values.[24] In sum, governments promote norms abroad
because they are consistent with universal ideals to which they adhere; governments
accept them at home because they are convinced doing so is "appropriate."

The desire to conform to shared ideas and norms of state behavior ("collective
expectations about proper behavior for a given identity"), in this view, does not
simply regulate state behavior, but constitutes and reconstitutes state identities.[25]
Such theories explicitly distance themselves from explanations that rely on instrumental calculations about the establishment of legitimate domestic governance.[26] Two
leading ideational theorists explicitly reject, for example, the argument I shall introduce later—namely, that governments support human rights regimes to advance partisan and public interest in preventing domestic violence and interstate warfare. In a
striking historical conjecture, these analysts assert that in the 1940s and 1950s governments could not possibly have sought human rights regimes to preserve the "democratic peace" because such founding moments "came well before the emergence of
the new social knowledge" that undemocratic regimes undermine peace—a collective belief they date to research by liberal international relations theorists in the early
1980s, led by Michael Doyle.[27] As we shall soon see, this equation of "social knowledge" with academic political science misstates the true origins of human rights regimes
because it underestimates the ability of nonacademics to generate a widely accepted, factually grounded—and ultimately accurate—consensus about world politics.

*The "New Orthodoxy": A Curious Convergence
of Realism and Idealism*

The study of human rights makes unlikely bedfellows. Although realist and ideational theories start from very different assumptions, their predictions about human
rights tend to converge. Most existing analyses of human rights regimes rest on an
uneasy synthesis of these two explanations. Realists cited earlier tend to argue that
human rights norms are expressions of domestic values, not simply propagandistic
justifications for the pursuit of national security interests.[28] Ideational theorists rarely
treat socialization (that is, transnational education, imitation, and fundamental norma-

23. Sikkink 1993.
24. Franck 1988.
25. Jepperson, Wendt, and Katzenstein 1996, 54.
26. Finnemore and Sikkink 1998. Thomas Risse has sought to take this further by drawing on Habermasian normative theory as a basis for positive analysis. See Risse 2000.
27. Keck and Sikkink 1998, 203. See also fn. 68 and accompanying text in this article. Compare Helfer
and Slaughter 1997, 331–35.
28. Even if this were the case, the argument would not be entirely realist, since the claim that democratic
governments are more likely to side with the West does not necessarily follow from realist theory. Even
self-styled realists increasingly concede that societal preferences play an important, often determinant role
in alliance formation. For a criticism of this type of realist degeneration, see Legro and Moravcsik 1999.

tive persuasion) as the sole (or even the primary) mechanism that induces governments to accept formal human rights guarantees. Donnelly argues, for example, that Gramscian "hegemonic ideas . . . can be expected to draw acquiescence in relatively weak regimes, but beyond promotional activities (that is, where significant sacrifices of sovereignty are demanded), something more is needed."[29]

Many in both schools therefore adopt what Robert Keohane has elsewhere termed the realist "fall-back" position: Public interest groups with idealistic values, perhaps transnationally organized, shape the underlying preferences of democratic great powers, which then deploy their preponderant power to construct and enforce international human rights norms. Idealism explains the position of great powers; realism explains the spread of norms.[30] In generalizing about human rights regimes, for example, Margaret Keck and Kathryn Sikkink focus extensively on the transcultural attractiveness of ideas and the density of transnational organization (ideational factors) *and* the vulnerability of targets to sanctions (a realist factor). As we have seen, they explicitly contrast this explanation, however, with an explanation that focuses on domestic institutional and material preconditions, which they reject outright (on theoretical, not empirical grounds) as at most only secondary.[31]

There is thus considerably more convergence in empirical predictions about the source of support for human rights regimes than broad theoretical labels might suggest (see Table 1). Most theories, whether realist or ideational, predict that governments, interest groups, and public opinion in established democratic states spearhead efforts to form and enforce international human rights regimes—and they induce, coerce, or persuade others to go join. Yet, as I discuss in more detail later, this is simply not the case. In postwar Europe, as in the UN during this period, established democracies consistently opposed reciprocally binding human rights obligations and neither coerced nor persuaded anyone else to accept them. Before moving on to the empirical analysis, it is therefore necessary to examine a third explanation for the formation of human rights regimes.

Republican Liberalism: Democratic Peace and Domestic Commitment

If realist and ideational explanations view the motivations for establishing human rights regimes as involving international coercion or persuasion, a "republican liberal" explanation views them as resulting from instrumental calculations about domestic politics.[32] In general, republican liberal theories stress the impact of varying

---

29. Donnelly 1986, 638–39.

30. Ruggie 1983, 98–99. On this sort of realist fall-back or two-step position more generally, see Legro 1996; Moravcsik 1997, 543; Keohane 1986, 183; and Legro and Moravcsik 1999.

31. Keck and Sikkink 1998, 201–209.

32. Liberal international relations theory focuses on state behavior driven by variation in the economic interests and conceptions of public goods provision on the part of societal groups, as well as by the nature of domestic political institutions. The republican liberal label is appropriate to international relations theory debates, though the concern about promoting democracy also has elements of ideational liberal-

domestic political institutions—in particular, the scope and bias of political representation—on foreign policy. The most prominent among such theories include institutional explanations of the "democratic peace," yet the family of republican liberal theories offers a far wider range of potential explanations, subsuming theories of the role of cartelized elites and independent militaries in provoking war, and of interest group capture (or the countervailing delegation of authority to strong executives) in foreign economic policy.[33] In contrast to the idealist theories considered earlier, which assume that social actors are responsive to external socialization and often altruistically motivated, republican liberal theories assume that states are self-interested and rational in their pursuit of (varying) underlying national interests, which reflect in turn variation in the nature of domestic social pressures and representative institutions.[34]

A useful republican liberal starting point for the problem at hand is to assume that international institutional commitments, like domestic institutional commitments, are self-interested means of "locking in" particular preferred domestic policies—at home and abroad—in the face of future political uncertainty. This presumption, which is not only consistent with republican liberalism but also draws on theories widely employed to explain domestic delegation to courts and regulatory authorities in American and comparative politics, treats domestic politics as a game in which politicians compete to exercise public authority.[35] Terry Moe observes that "most political institutions . . . arise out of a politics of structural choice in which the winners use their temporary hold on public authority to design new structures and impose them on the polity as a whole. . . . [Institutions are] weapons of coercion and redistribution . . . the structural means by which political winners pursue their own interests, often at the great expense of political losers."[36] Governments establish courts, administrative agencies, central banks, and other independent bodies as means by which the win-

---

ism—the strand of liberal theory based on the tendency to promote domestic provision of public goods (national identity, political institutions, and legitimate economic redistribution) preferred by domestic actors. (This differs from idealist theory in the minimal role it accords altruism or transnational socialization.) On the ideational strand of liberal theory, see Moravcsik 1997; and Van Evera 1990. In American or comparative politics, such an explanation might be thought of as drawing on public choice theory, institutionalist theory, constitutional theory, the theory of delegation, or theories of nested games.

33. For a discussion on the full range of potential liberal explanations, see Moravcsik 1997.

34. Liberal international relations theories assume that states behave as rational, unitary actors in the pursuit of their underlying preferences, though not in the definition of those preferences. Their theoretical distinctiveness lies in their consistent focus on variation in national preferences resulting from social pressures for particular material and ideational interests, as well as the way such interests are represented by state institutions. In this regard, institutional variants of democratic peace theory and theories of legislative-executive relations share common liberal theoretical assumptions. For an elaboration, see Moravcsik 1997; Doyle 1986; Russett 1993; Snyder 1991; Bailey, Goldstein, and Weingast 1997; Van Evera 1999; and Legro and Moravcsik 1999.

35. Moe 1990.

36. Ibid., 222, 213. In the domestic constitutional context, provisions are locked in by the fact that only a supermajority is typically able to amend it. Supermajorities bind subsequent majorities. The case we are analyzing here, like the case of administrative delegation, is more complex, since treaties are generally ratified by majority, and the nondemocratic opponents are constrained not by their majority but by the extent of their coercive power. Pasquino 1998.

ners of political conflict seek to commit the polity to preferred policies. From this perspective, a rational decision to delegate to an independent body requires that a sitting government weigh two crosscutting considerations: *restricting government discretion* and *reducing domestic political uncertainty.*

Consider first the surrender of national discretion, which in the international context might be termed the *sovereignty cost* of delegation to an international authority. All other things equal, governments in power prefer to maintain short-term discretion to shape collective behavior or redistribute wealth as they see fit. They are therefore inherently skeptical of delegation to independent judges or officials, since there is always some "agency cost" to the operation of central banks, administrative agencies, courts, and other quasi-independent political authorities. Judges, in particular, may seek to negate government actions by nullifying them outright or by failing to enforce them effectively. Legal scholars William Landes and Richard Posner observe that "the outcomes of the struggle can readily be nullified by unsympathetic judges—and why should judges be sympathetic to a process that simply ratifies political power rather than expresses principle?" They point to the sixty years preceding the New Deal in the United States, during which the federal judiciary obstructed reforms favored by Congress.[37]

In the international realm, the defense of governmental discretion translates into the defense of national sovereignty. All other things equal, the "sovereignty cost" of delegating to an international judge is likely to be even greater than that of delegating to a domestic judge. One reason is that cross-national variation in the precise nature, scope, application, and enforcement of human rights is likely to be greater than domestic variation. Any common international list of human rights is therefore likely to diverge further from individual national traditions and practices. In the most extreme cases, for example, Great Britain, international human rights regimes introduce an explicitly enumerated bill of rights for the first time. Many international human rights regimes establish, moreover, single, centralized institutional mechanisms for interpreting, enforcing, and balancing various rights. For such bodies to develop a coherent jurisprudence, they must override local particularities. Whereas judicially imposed harmonization may seem attractive to those who draft international covenants, it clearly imposes inconvenient constraints on individual national governments. Particularly for nations without a constitutional court—again, Britain is a striking example—the procedure marks a significant innovation.[38] These inconveniences may arise, moreover, not simply as a result of pressure from parochial special interests or unthinking adherence to tradition, but also through divergence in deeply rooted historical conceptions of the relationship between citizens and the state. From this perspective, the defense of "national sovereignty" is, in part, a legitimate defense of national ideals, political culture, and even democratic practices—a

---

37. See Landes and Posner 1975, 896; and Pasquino 1998, 49.
38. Drzemczewski 1983, 11.

228   International Organization

problem of which the framers of post–World War II human rights documents (and their academic advisers) were quite aware.[39]

Why would a national government, democratic or not, ever accept such external normative and institutional constraints on its sovereignty? The answer lies in the second major consideration that enters into a government's decision whether to delegate to an independent political body: reducing political uncertainty. In the republican liberal view, politicians delegate power to human rights regimes, such as domestic courts and administrative agencies, to constrain the behavior of future national governments. As Moe explains, a politician must always calculate that "while the right to exercise public authority happens to be theirs today, other political actors with different and perhaps opposing interests may gain that right tomorrow."[40] To limit the consequences of this eventuality, government authorities may thus seek to "lock in" favored policies in such a way, thereby insulating them from the actions of future governments.

From this perspective, human rights norms are expressions of the self-interest of democratic governments in "locking in" democratic rule through the enforcement of human rights. By placing interpretation in the hands of independent authorities managed in part by foreign governments—in other words, by alienating sovereignty to an international body—governments seek to establish reliable judicial constraints on future nondemocratic governments or on democratically elected governments that may seek (as in interwar Italy and Germany) to subvert democracy from within. In the language of international relations theory, this "two-level" commitment "ties the hands" of future governments, thereby enhancing the credibility of current domestic policies and institutions.[41] Salient and symbolic international constraints serve as signals to trigger domestic, and perhaps also transnational and international, opposition to any breach of the democratic order. Thus democratic regimes seek to prevent political retrogression or "backsliding" into tyranny.

The decision of any individual government whether to support a binding international human rights enforcement regime depends, in this view, on the relative importance of these two basic factors: Sovereignty costs are weighted against establishing human rights regimes, whereas greater political stability may be weighted in favor of it. If we assume that the inconvenience governments face is constant (or randomly distributed), it follows that a country is most likely to support a human rights regime when its government is firmly committed to democratic governance but faces strong internal challenges that may threaten it in the future. Its willingness to tolerate *sovereignty costs* increases insofar as the costs are outweighed by the benefits of reducing *domestic political uncertainty*.

If the republican liberal view is correct, *the strongest support for binding human rights regimes should come not from established democracies but from recently es-*

39. McKeon 1949.
40. Moe 1990, 227.
41. Evans, Putnam, and Jacobson 1993.

tablished and potentially unstable democracies. Only where democracy is established but nondemocratic groups (military officers, communists, fascists, and religious fundamentalists, for example) pose real threats to its future is the reduction of political uncertainty likely to outweigh the inconvenience of supranational adjudication.

It is obvious that opposition will come in part from *dictatorships* (or transitional regimes), since such governments both lack any interest in democracy and suffer particularly large inconveniences from persistent challenges to their (nondemocratic) domestic order.[42] (Governments striving to complete a transition to democracy through extralegal means are likely to be almost as skeptical.) Less obvious and in striking contrast to realist and idealist accounts, however, is the prediction that dictatorships will be joined in opposition to binding commitments by well-established liberal democracies. By accepting binding obligations, governments in established democracies incur an increased, if modest, risk of de facto nullification of domestic laws without a corresponding increase in the expected stability of domestic democracy, since the latter is already high. Such governments have good reason—indeed, a democratically legitimate reason—to reject any reciprocal imposition of international adjudication and enforcement of human rights claims.

This is not to say that established democracies never have an incentive to support international human rights instruments. According to republican liberal theory, established democracies have an incentive to promote such arrangements for others—which may involve some small risk of future pressure on established democracies to deepen their commitment—in order to bolster the "democratic peace" by fostering democracy in neighboring countries.[43] This is most likely to occur when democratization is expected to pacify a potentially threatening neighbor or solidify opposition to a common nondemocratic enemy. In such cases, established democracies can be expected to support rhetorical declarations in favor of human rights and regimes with optional enforcement that bind newly established democracies but exempt themselves. Yet there is little reason to believe that this concern will outweigh domestic interests; thus they are likely to remain opposed to reciprocally enforceable rules.[44] Further observable implications concerning national tactics and confidential discussions are developed in the next section.

---

42. Governments must of course have sufficient freedom at the current time to act—a point stressed by Moe. It would therefore be somewhat surprising to see a democratic government that requires nondemocratic means to stay in power—for example, a government under heavy military influence or engaged in a civil war—take such a step. For this reason such transitional regimes—Greece in the immediate post–World War II period or Russia today are examples—may remain skeptical of enforceable commitments.

43. Russett 1993. This argument is liberal rather than realist, since for realists the domestic governance of states should make no difference in the perception of threat, whereas for democratic peace theorists, it does.

44. In theory, one might argue that the incomplete adherence of established democracies could be expected to undermine the international regime, which could in turn destabilize newly established democracies and thereby create threats to established democracies. Yet in practice the signaling function of international norms in any given country does not appear to depend on the adherence by others to enforcement clauses; certainly this conjecture seems to have played an unimportant role in British or European deliberations.

Testing the Theories: The Negotiation of the ECHR

What light does the negotiating history of the ECHR cast on the power of these three competing theories? The negotiation of the ECHR took place between 1949 and 1953 under the auspices of the Council of Europe. At the first session of the Council of Europe's Consultative Assembly in September 1949, its legal committee under the chairmanship of the Frenchman Pierre-Henri Teitgen recommended that an organization be created to ensure adherence to human rights in Europe. Extended meetings of governmental committees and consultations with the assembly itself through the first half of 1950 led to the signing of the ECHR, which came into force three years later.

Realist, ideational, and liberal institutional theories all offer prima facie explanations for the general form and timing of the ECHR's establishment. For realists, this period marked the dawning of an "American century" and a moment in which the West became embroiled in a bipolar conflict with the Soviet Union. For ideational theorists, it immediately followed the Holocaust, a salient historical event of considerable moral force, and occurred immediately after the rise to salient Western leadership of two long-established democratic exemplars, the United States and the United Kingdom.[45] During the immediate postwar period, republican liberals might observe, a wave of new liberal democracies emerged (or reemerged) across Western Europe. Nondemocratic institutions were widely viewed as a source of both World War II and the Cold War, and, accordingly, the democratization of Germany, Italy, and other West European nations was seen as a guarantee against both a revival of fascism and the spread of communism.

To assess the relative importance of these three plausible theories, we therefore require more fine-grained evidence than a simple coincidence of timing or the existence of occasional public rhetorical justification. I consider three types of evidence: the cross-national pattern of national positions, the process of international negotiation, and the direct documentary record of national motivations. What does the historical record reveal?

Cross-National Variation in National Preferences

We have seen that both realist and ideational theories predict that the most firmly established and committed democracies (or democratic great powers)—in short, the major Western powers led by the United States and the United Kingdom—would have been the primary supporters of binding international human rights norms. On the contrary, the historical record strongly supports the republican liberal theory, which predicts that newly established democracies will spearhead support for binding international human rights guarantees, whereas long-established democracies will support only rhetorical or optional commitments—and even these only where needed to bolster the "democratic peace." Dictatorships or governments that have not completed the transition to democracy will be opposed outright.

45. For a more solidly grounded view, see Helfer and Slaughter 1997, 331–35.

We can measure the willingness of governments to accept binding obligations by examining their position on two related elements of the institutional design of the ECHR—both essential to the future effectiveness of the regime.

- *Compulsory jurisdiction*: Should the regime mandate that member states recognize the jurisdiction of an independent international court, as opposed to a body of foreign ministers?

- *Individual petition*: Should the regime mandate that member states grant private individuals and groups standing to file cases?

Since both mandatory binding jurisdiction *and* individual petition are required to render a system of international human rights adjudication effective, a vote for both is defined as support for a reciprocally binding regime, whereas a vote against either marks opposition.[46] Positions on these two issues generated parallel (if not precisely identical) coalitions among national governments, suggesting that they tap a single underlying dimension of state preference.[47]

To investigate the relationship between democratic governance and support for binding regimes, we also require a measure of how stable a democracy is expected to be.[48] European political systems involved in the negotiations can be divided into three categories. The first category, "established democracies," contains those systems that had been continuously under democratic rule since before 1920 and remained so thereafter: Belgium, Denmark, Luxembourg, Netherlands, Norway, Sweden, Netherlands, and the United Kingdom. (Occupation is not coded as a suspension of domestic democracy, but the establishment of a nondemocratic domestic regime is—for example, Vichy France) The second category, "new democracies," contains

46. Sikkink suggests a less satisfactory coding, one which conflates the domestic and external concerns of governments in such a way as to greatly exaggerate the relative importance of the latter. Sikkink 1993. In fact only a miniscule set of ECHR cases have been brought by one state against another.

47. Council of Europe 1975, IV/248–52, also 132ff, 242–96, also I/xxiv, 10–24, 296ff; passim, and V/68–70. By the time the member states negotiated individual petition, underlying positions were harder to make out, since it was becoming increasingly clear that such provisions will be optional. Austria, Belgium, France, Germany, Iceland, Ireland, and Italy supported creation of a court of human rights and mandatory jurisdiction, whereas Denmark, Greece, Luxembourg, the Netherlands, Norway, Sweden, Turkey, and the United Kingdom were opposed to anything except a court with optional jurisdiction. On the question of whether the right of individual petition should be automatic, there was slightly more ambivalence, but Britain, Greece, and perhaps also the Netherlands remained the most skeptical. On the question of the scope of the rights to be protected under the regime, a similar cleavage emerged, with advocates of a strong system, such as Teitgen, supporting an open-ended grant of institutional authority. See Council of Europe 1975, I/276. More skeptical countries, such as Britain, the Netherlands, Sweden, and Denmark, sought a more precise and narrower enumeration of rights and warned against an ambitious, open-ended system. Council of Europe 1975, I/80–82, 88–90; III/254–56, but 268.

48. Conventional political science measures of "democracy" are inappropriate, since such measures assess institutions' levels of democracy, not future expectations of democratic stability. The length of continuous democratic rule is a conventional measure in the literature on the democratic peace and elsewhere for the depth of commitment to democracy. See, for example, Russett 1993. As a more problematic check on the measure, one might also consider whether the regime remained a liberal democracy after 1950. Such *ex post* coding is problematic, though not entirely inappropriate, since what we seek to measure is not how democratic a state is, but how stable its democracy is perceived to be. In any case, the two measures are closely correlated.

those that were firmly established during the negotiations and remained so thereafter, but only since a point between 1920 and 1950: Austria, France, Italy, Iceland, Ireland, and West Germany. The third category, "semidemocracies and dictatorships," contains the two governments that were not fully democratic by 1950, because of civil war or internal repression (and did not remain so thereafter), namely Greece and Turkey. Spain and Portugal, though not involved in the negotiations, also belong in this category.[49]

Turning to the findings, we see little evidence of the positive correlation between support for binding regimes and power or length of democratic rule predicted by realist and idealist theory. Instead, we observe the inverse-U-shaped relationship between the stability of democracy and support for binding human rights commitments predicted by republican liberal theory. Table 2 summarizes the findings. All six new democracies (plus one of the ten long-established democracies, Belgium) support binding human rights guarantees. In contrast, six of the seven established democracies join the four transitional governments and nondemocracies in opposing one or both such guarantees (or, in the case of Luxembourg, abstaining). Even the sole exception, Belgium, is not fully disconfirming, since Belgian representatives originally sided with the other established democracies against binding guarantees, shifting their position only late in the negotiations.[50] The correlation is so strong that even recategorization of borderline cases—France and Turkey, say—would not undermine the striking relationship.

A number of ad hoc conjectures suggested by historians, legal academics, and common intuition about postwar European politics also fall by the wayside. Opposition appears to be uncorrelated with the possession of colonies.[51] Among major colonial powers, Britain and the Netherlands are skeptics, whereas France and Belgium are supporters. Among countries without colonies, Germany and Italy are supporters, whereas the Scandinavian countries (Iceland excepted) are opponents.

Opposition is similarly uncorrelated with the existence of a strong domestic tradition of parliamentary sovereignty, as some analysts of Britain conjecture. Many strong supporters—France, Belgium, Italy, Germany, Austria, Iceland, and Ireland—shared an equally deep tradition of parliamentary sovereignty. Any imputation of causality from the correlation between *postwar* support for domestic judicial review and international enforcement of human rights (say, in the cases of Italy, Germany, and Austria), furthermore, is very likely to be spurious. Postwar Germany contemporaneously adopted systems of constitutional judicial review, thereby shifting political weight away from a traditionally sovereign parliament toward a separation of powers involving an independent judiciary. In Italy, Christian Democrats fearing the advent of a Socialist-Communist majority placed a constitutional court in the postwar constitution. It is far more plausible that these countries adopted both domestic *and* international judicial review because of a strong desire to bolster the democratic

---

49. For a further discussion of this coding, see the notes to Table 2.
50. Council of Europe 1975, I/80–82, 88–90, III/254–56, but 268.
51. This is the factor most often mentioned in the secondary literature.

TABLE 2. *Stability of democratic governance and national positions on the European Convention on Human Rights*

	Unstable or non-democracies (stable democracy not yet clearly established by 1950)	*New democracies (continuous democracy only since a date between 1920 and 1950)*	*Established democracies (continuous democracy since a date before 1920)*
Supports enforcement (individual petition and compulsory jurisdiction mandatory)	—	Austria, France, Italy, Iceland, Ireland, Germany[b]	Belgium[c]
Opposes enforcement (individual petition and/or compulsory jurisdiction optional or absent)	Greece,[a] Turkey[a] (Portugal,[d] Spain[d])	—	Denmark, Sweden, Netherlands, Norway, United Kingdom, Luxembourg[e]

[a]Greece and Turkey are characterized as unstable, whereas Austria, France, Italy, Iceland, Ireland, and Germany are characterized as new, because (1) it had been less than a year after conclusion of the bloody Greek civil war, and extra-legal measures were still in force; and (2) Greek and Turkish democracy were widely viewed as limited by the role of the military and incomplete judicial autonomy. It is also worth noting that both governments would subsequently slip back into dictatorship. This coding is consistent with the general literature on delegation, which notes that governments must have sufficient power to put institutions in place. Governments unable to rule by established democratic means belong in the nondemocratic category.

[b]Germany, not yet a member of the Council of Europe, did not have voting rights, but participated actively in the negotiations.

[c]Belgium initially hesitated, supporting the convention only with optional clauses, but then came to favor mandatory enforcement.

[d]Spain and Portugal, both dictatorships, were not members of the Council of Europe. Yet, in striking contrast to Germany (also not a member), they showed little independent interest in participating informally, nor were they invited to do so.

[e]In some cases, Luxembourg abstained on, rather than opposed, enforcement measures.

order, not that the inclusion of a constitutional court in the postwar constitution had immediate implications for the national position on the ECHR.[52] In sum, the establishment of domestic constitutional review, like the establishment of international human rights guarantees, is a postauthoritarian phenomenon. National positions are uncorrelated with support for European federalism: the Netherlands and Luxembourg opposed mandatory enforcement, whereas Austria, Ireland, and Iceland favored it. More consistent with the republican liberal view is the conjecture that both support for Europe (in this very early period, this meant support for the Council of Europe and the European Coal and Steel Community) and support for a binding ECHR reflect (in this period but not later) the influence of a third factor—say, demo-

52. See Ackerman 1997, 773; and Pasquino 1998, 39, 44–48. There is no evident correlation between support and the existence of civil or common-law traditions, or monist or dualist legal systems.

cratic stability and security threats.[53] Finally, the experience of being invaded by
Germany during World War II seems to explain little. The French and Belgians
favored mandatory enforcement, whereas the Dutch, Danes, and Norwegians
opposed it.

Republican liberal theory also seems to offer the most accurate account of the
instrumental attitude governments adopted toward more detailed provisions of the
ECHR. Should the convention create, governments asked themselves, an independent court, a quasi-judicial body of government representatives, or no central institution at all? Cleavages around this issue were similar to those around compulsory
jurisdiction and individual petition, with opponents of effective enforcement opposing the court.[54] Governments favorable to binding human rights adjudication proposed that the members of the intermediary Commission on Human Rights be nomi-
nated by the court—a clear effort to render international institutions more
independent—whereas more skeptical governments favored granting power of nomi-
nation to the intergovernmental Committee of Ministers.[55]

Similar cleavages formed around the enumeration of rights. Some skeptics considered delaying the proceedings, as well as limiting future uncertainty, by pressing for
a precise enumeration of rights or transferring the issue to the less-effective UN
Commission on Human Rights.[56] In the end, the precise enumeration of rights, which
was considerably narrower than that granted by any member state with such a constitutional enumeration, resulted from a careful calculation of instrumental, self-
regarding considerations.[57] Representatives of right- and left-wing parties were concerned about the status of particular laws favored by their constituencies. Social
Democratic representatives assured that social welfare rights were not threatened and
that property rights did not restrict state intervention. Christian Democratic representatives assured that rights of private familial, educational, and religious choice were
maintained, while opposing any right to redistribution of property.[58] The final docu-

---

53. See Glendon 1998a, 1170–72. See also Slaughter, Stone Sweet, and Weiler 1998.

54. Council of Europe 1975, IV/248–50.

55. Council of Europe 1975, III/268–70.

56. Council of Europe 1975, III/268, 304, 306, IV/178, also 106–108.

57. For the most plausible argument for the impact of the UN Declaration, see Teitgen 1988, 481, 490.
The enumeration of rights also did not simply conform to a focal point established a few years before in
the UN Declaration—the sort of transnational dynamic of standard-setting many ideational theorists stress.
Despite similarities in wording, advocates saw the European system in this respect not simply as a continuation of the UN system, but also as a pragmatic *reaction* to it. The UN system was widely viewed as too
broad to be effective; the ECHR system was designed to be potentially enforceable, which required that
the scope of rights be narrowed considerably. Indeed, the principal author of the UN Declaration, the
Frenchman Réne Cassin, overtly opposed the creation of the ECHR. Finally, even the enumeration of
rights in the UN Declaration was drawn not from proposals of activists per se, but primarily from systematic and scholarly analyses of comparative law (such as from the American Law Institute and UN officials)
as well as international documents (such as the Pan American Declaration), then whittled down through
intergovernmental negotiation. Glendon 1998a; Glendon 1998b, chap. 3; Humphrey 1984, 31–32; Teitgen
1988, 489–92; and Morsink 1999.

58. For reports of debates on marriage, education, and property, see Council of Europe 1975, I/166–86,
242–64; II/48–132. For a response to the possible objection that these rights were controversial because
they are intrinsically more difficult to define, see ibid., V/304–14.

ment offended neither side, because it was constrained to include only the least controversial among basic political and civil rights.[59]

The Domestic and International Decision-making Process

Realism, ideational theory, and republican liberalism also generate distinctive predictions about the tactics likely to be most salient in interstate negotiations. Realist theory, with its stress on interstate power and deep conflicts of interest, leads us to expect to observe attempts by great powers to coerce or bribe weaker states to change their policies. Ideational theory, by contrast, leads us to expect to observe attempts by governments or transnational groups in civil society to engage in transnational persuasion. Such persuasion may suffice in itself or may be a prelude to subsequent coercive tactics. For liberal theorists, by contrast, there is little reason to expect governments to alter their views on fundamental issues such as the nature of constitutional adjudication in light of threats, promises, or normative persuasion by other democratic governments. The interest of established democracies in the stability of neighboring, less-established democracies is surely less intense than the domestic self-interest of new democracies; hence established democracies cannot easily be induced to accept domestic constraints in order to make the regime work—particularly when the option of creating optional enforcement mechanisms exists.[60]

Published documents contain very little direct confirmation of either the realist or ideational predictions. No great power or long-standing democracy appears to have made threats or offered inducements to secure stronger commitments. The most important powers engaged in Western Europe at the time, the United States and the United Kingdom, were respectively absent or opposed. Ideational theorists might point out that the "European Movement," working through the Assembly of the Council of Europe, was engaged in transnational discussion and mobilization. Certainly many leading advocates of the convention were European federalists and viewed the ECHR as a step toward European integration.[61] Yet there is little evidence that a shared transnational discourse influenced the positions of parliamentary politicians in the assembly, let alone representatives of national governments. There is, we have seen, little correlation between national positions on the ECHR and positions on European integration. Indeed, we observe little shift in national positions at all, let alone influence wielded by established democracies, as predicted by ideational theory. Although we cannot entirely exclude the possibility that subtle forces of transnational persuasion and mobilization played a modest role in organizing the forum for discussion, they were surely not decisive in defining the positions of the participating governments.

---

59. Teitgen 1988, 480.

60. Liberal theory predicts that interstate bargaining outcomes are a function of the relative intensity of national preferences. Governments that strongly seek a particular cooperative outcome will concede more in order to achieve it. Moravcsik 1997.

61. Some Jewish parliamentarians and law professors were also prominent and may have been influenced by their experiences and beliefs.

Instead the preponderance of evidence concerning negotiating tactics confirms republican liberal predictions. Rather than seeking to coerce or persuade one another, or mobilizing groups in civil society, national governments conducted a classical international negotiation. Governments focused primarily on practical compromises that would assure that the system functioned to assure each state its preferred level of sovereign control. New institutions were modified to a compromise close to the lowest common denominator, with no government forced to accept immediate constraints on its own policies significantly greater than those it ideally sought. Where there was discord, optional clauses afforded governments flexibility. The real explanation of the outcome, as liberal theory predicts, lies in the pattern of underlying national preferences.

Domestic Deliberation and Public Justification

The final type of evidence consists of the records of confidential deliberations and public justifications by national decision-makers, drawn from debates in the Parliamentary Assembly of the Council of Europe, negotiating sessions among the national governments, and the documentary record of confidential deliberations in one critical country where such documents are available, namely the United Kingdom. What do these reveal?

Let us begin by noting a salient fact. Not a single piece of documentary evidence in the sources I have been able to consult supports the realist prediction that governments impose international human rights norms through threats of external coercion or inducement. At no point do we observe governments weighing the costs and benefits of coercion, concerning themselves with the distribution of power capabilities, or mentioning foreign or military aid.

There is slightly more evidence for the ideational view, but not enough to establish any confidence in its veracity. At most, NGOs and public opinion appear to have played a secondary, even insignificant, role.[62] The rhetoric of politicians in the European Assembly, as well as some interest groups, invoked moral considerations. Yet for the ideational theory to be confirmed, such statements must be designed to socialize or persuade national governments by appealing to respect for human rights as an end in itself, rather than as an instrument to promote concrete ends of enduring interest to member governments—the prevention of tyranny, genocide, and aggression. There is no evidence of this; positions, as we have seen, do not change. In Britain, we observe officials in occasional meetings with NGOs. A 1951 Colonial Office draft circular blandly recalled "in deciding to sign the Convention, His Majesty's Government took into account the importance attached to it by public opinion both in and outside this country."[63] Yet, although NGOs were relatively well developed in Britain (perhaps more so than anywhere else) and made salient contributions

62. For a similar conclusion regarding the abolition of the slave trade, see Kaufman and Pape 1999.
63. Marston 1993, 824. Some British officials attributed the support of other governments for a human rights court to their desire to assert the symbolic significance of the council vis-à-vis the claims of Communist governments and parties. Marston 1993, 809.

to the specific form of the final document, the British government paid little heed to their pleas to accept mandatory enforcement. The issue was neither debated in Parliament nor mentioned in election campaigns. British public opinion, like public opinion elsewhere, took relatively little note of the ECHR negotiations.

The overwhelming bulk of the documentary evidence confirms instead the republican liberal account. By far the most consistent public justification for the ECHR, to judge from debates in the Council of Europe Constituent Assembly, was that it might help combat domestic threats from the totalitarian right and left, thereby stabilizing domestic democracy and preventing international aggression. (It is helpful to remember that both Hitler and Mussolini came to power, at least initially, by constitutional means.) Teitgen, the chief French advocate of the ECHR in the assembly, considered "Fascism, Hitlerism, and Communism" as the major postwar threats to democracy.[64] Governments, Teitgen argued, should seek to "prevent—before it is too late—any new member who might be threatened by a rebirth of totalitarianism from succumbing to the influence of evil, as has already happened in conditions of general apathy. It is not enough to possess freedom; positive action must be taken to defend it. . . . Would Fascism have triumphed in Italy if, after the assassination of Matteoti, this crime had been subjected to an international trial?"[65] Yet postwar human rights regimes were a response not simply to the recent fascist past but also to the prospect of a Communist future. The latter was mentioned just as often. In this period, we must recall, the French Communist Party enjoyed plurality electoral support. Teitgen spoke of the "abominable temptation" to "exchange . . . freedom for a little more bread."[66]

Such concerns were linked explicitly to the shared belief that nondemocratic states tend toward international aggression as well as domestic oppression. Teitgen's motivation was, at least in part, to assure the stability of *German* democracy and thereby the security of France. None other than Konrad Adenauer told Teitgen in 1949 that integration was needed to restrain postwar Germany, not just the Soviet Union. Teitgen reports he "needed no more" to convince him to work for the Council of Europe.[67] Such arguments were advanced by the ECHR's advocates in the assembly far more often than any others. This clearly refutes the conjecture—which, as we have seen, Sikkink and Keck treat as an essential piece of evidence for ideational theory— that few analysts before the 1980s could possibly have been aware of a link between democracy and peace. In many ways the democratic peace proposition, which dates from the eighteenth century, was a central tenet, arguably *the* central tenet, of postwar Western planning, as it had been in the thinking of Woodrow Wilson and other liberal statesmen a generation before.[68]

Yet domestic self-interest dominated. The most explicit justifications for the ECHR as a bulwark against future tyranny were advanced not by representatives from coun-

---

64. Council of Europe 1975, I/40–42.
65. Council of Europe 1975, I/192, 120, 64, also 60–64, for statements by others, I/66, 84, 120ff, 192–94, 276, 278–80, 292.
66. Council of Europe 1975, I/40–42.
67. Teitgen 1988, 476.
68. Keck and Sikkink 1998, 203. Compare footnote 27. See Moravcsik 1992 and 1997.

tries with the longest democratic heritage but, as republican liberal theory predicts, by those from newly established democracies. Among the most persistent advocates of this position were Italian and German representatives. (Germany was not a formal member of the Council of Europe but enthusiastically sought to participate, in striking contrast to the disinterest shown by Spain and Portugal.) The Italian representative to the assembly who advanced perhaps the most extensive proposal for centralized institutions, one Mr. Benvenuti, stressed the need to prevent totalitarian movements—a problem, he argued, particularly important in nations where democracy is not yet firmly established. Another Italian representative affirmed "the principle of the joint responsibility of democratic states."[69] A German representative went further, proposing a treaty obliging all member states to come to each other's aid, apparently with force, if domestic freedom were threatened.[70]

Yet the primary expectation was not that the regime would strengthen democracy by mobilizing intervention by foreign governments to enforce human rights norms, as realist and some ideational theory might lead us to expect. Nor did governments stress active transnational mobilization. Most participants appear to have felt that domestic politics would remain the primary site of enforcement—all members were to be democracies, at least formally—with international controls serving as an external signaling device to trigger an appropriate domestic response.[71] The ECHR was intended primarily to strengthen existing domestic institutions of judicial review, parliamentary legislation, and public action, not to supplant them. Even skeptical British officials voiced little fear of direct foreign intervention on domestic politics, fearing instead the mobilization of domestic groups.

Critics in the assembly often asked why an arrangement was required at all, if its scope was restricted to existing democracies. Nowhere was republican liberal logic clearer than in the responses given by advocates. The arrangement was primarily a means to prevent backsliding by new democracies. As Sir David Maxwell-Fyfe of the United Kingdom put it: "In answer to the criticism that, as signatories will be limited to democratic states the Convention is unnecessary . . . our plan has the advantage of being immediately practicable; it provides a system of collective security against tyranny and oppression."[72]

Unlike the UN system, the ECHR was designed to be enforceable—a goal, Maxwell-Fyfe argued, that was realistic only because all of its members already shared an essentially democratic political culture.[73] Among skeptics, the primary focus of criticism was, as republican liberal theory predicts, the fear that the application of domestically legitimate national laws might be declared in violation of the convention. The compatibility of the ECHR with existing domestic legal practices dominated discussion—a fact suggesting also that decision-makers took the commitment seriously.[74]

69. Council of Europe 1975, II/142.
70. Ibid., V/328–30, 336–40.
71. Lester 1994, 4–5. See also Teitgen 1988, 482.
72. Council of Europe 1975, I/120.
73. See ibid., I/50–52; and Teitgen 1988, 488.
74. Council of Europe 1975, II/246ff, also 148–87; I/54; also I/64–68.

On this point it is instructive to examine more closely the contrary position of one government, namely that of the United Kingdom. From a methodological perspective the United Kingdom is a critical case. Opposition by the oldest and most firmly established democracy in Europe constitutes a particularly striking disconfirmation of realist and ideational theory.[75] The British, as we have seen, supported international declaratory norms but firmly opposed any attempt to establish binding legal obligations, centralized institutions, individual petition, or compulsory jurisdiction.[76] As W. E. Beckett, legal advisor to the Foreign Office and the initiator of the British government's participation, put it, "We attach the greatest importance to a well-drafted Convention of Human Rights but we are dead against anything like an international court to which individuals who think they are aggrieved in this way could go."[77] Even Beckett conceded the existence of "overwhelming objections" to any strong means of enforcement in Britain involving the individual right of petition and an independent tribunal—despite his efforts to work with British NGOs on specific proposals.

What issues were raised in confidential British deliberations? The secondary literature on British human rights policy makes much of two British concerns: the fear that residents of British colonies and dependencies might invoke the ECHR, and aversion to European federalism. To judge from confidential discussions, however, neither appears to have been a dominant concern. To be sure, Colonial Secretary Jim Griffiths was concerned that "extremist politicians" among "politically immature" colonies would exploit the document.[78] Yet overall there is surprisingly little discussion of colonial implications in the deliberations—certainly far less than purely of domestic considerations. Colonial Office concerns appear to have been isolated and intermittent. In any case, a colonial clause in the ECHR would limit any such claims, and consideration of such a clause did not blunt British opposition.[79] Nor, despite the fact that the Council of Europe Assembly was the locus of European federalist activity, do British government officials often mention the connection between human rights and European federalism. The British government resisted efforts to make international human rights law directly enforceable in this way, regardless of whether its forum was European or not—and continued to do so for some time thereafter.[80]

Confidential domestic deliberations suggest instead that British opposition reflected what A. Maxwell, permanent secretary to the Home Office, described as "grave apprehension about what might happen at home."[81] When the issue finally reached the Cabinet, the attention of ministers—after brief mention of colonial and economic

---

75. The UK position was also viewed as decisive. See, for example, Paul-Henri Spaak, cited in Teitgen 1988, 478. Britain is also a country for which we have a wealth of reliable archival documents and oral histories. I have restricted myself here to materials found in published sources.

76. Marston 1993, 799–800.

77. Marston 1993, 804.

78. Lester 1984, 50. See also Lester 1994, 2; and Marston 1993, 812.

79. Marston 1993, 806–807, 809–10, 812, 816. In 1953 the British government voluntarily extended the Convention to the forty-two overseas territories for whose international relations they were responsible.

80. See Lester 1984, 55; and Lester 1994, 3.

81. Marston 1993, 813.

concerns—seems to have focused on domestic application. Precisely as republican liberal theory predicts, the primary concern was not the vulnerability of the overall British record on human rights. As Parliamentary Secretary for Foreign Affairs Hector McNeil observed in a 1947 memo to Prime Minister Clement Atlee, Britain had an "extremely good record." British decision-makers appear sincerely to have believed that Britain would be less inconvenienced by reciprocal commitment than other member governments. The definition of rights in the convention was, so the Foreign Office memo to the Cabinet in 1950 concluded, "consistent with our existing law in all but a small number of comparatively trivial cases."[82]

Nor did ministerial apprehension result from major public policy considerations. Most such concerns—such as the belief of some in the Labour Party, led by Chancellor of the Exchequer Sir Stafford Cripps, that the convention might restrict government intervention in the economy, including entry of government inspectors into private homes—were shared with similar political groups in other countries and were therefore handled effectively by narrowing and qualifying the explicit rights enumerated in the convention to exclude constraints on economic policy, education, and political institutions.[83]

Instead British officials and politicians—most notably in Cabinet discussions—dwelled primarily on the fear that the convention would threaten idiosyncratic (but not unambiguously undemocratic) political practices and institutions in the United Kingdom.[84] Yet when pressed in confidential discussions to make their concerns explicit, the examples cited by British opponents seem either absurdly vague or comically trivial.

The defense of British institutional idiosyncrasy elicited the most violent rhetoric from British politicians and officials. Lord Chancellor Jowitt's official paper criticized the draft convention, largely the work of two distinguished former British officials, as

> so vague and woolly that it may mean almost anything. Our unhappy legal experts . . . have had to take their share in drawing up a code compared to which . . . the Ten Commandments . . . are comparatively insignificant. . . . It completely passes the wit of man to guess what results would be arrived at by a tribunal composed of elected persons who need not even be lawyers, drawn from various European states possessing completely different systems of law, and whose deliberations take place behind closed doors. . . . Any student of our legal institutions must recoil from this document with a feeling of horror.[85]

A common complaint was that judicial review would undermine parliamentary sovereignty. Beckett wrote: "It seems inconceivable that any Government, when

---

82. Marston 1993, 811. With a lack of modesty about their domestic political institutions characteristic of this period, British officials and politicians also sometimes cited the need to set a good example for foreign countries as a reason for Britain to take an active role in the negotiations.

83. See Lester 1984, 50–52; and Lester 1994, 2. The British position did not change under the subsequent Conservative government of Anthony Eden.

84. Lester 1984, 54–55.

85. Ibid., 52.

faced with the realities of this proposal, would take the risk of entrusting these unprecedented powers to an international court, legislative powers which Parliament would never agree to entrust to the courts of this country which are known and which command the confidence and admiration of the world."[86] "Our whole constitution," a government document intoned, "is based on the principle that it is for the Parliament to enact the laws and for the judges to interpret the laws."[87] The British government even opposed a clause protecting rights to "free elections" and "political opposition," apparently because they believed that their distinctive "first past the post" unique electoral system might be challenged.[88]

The specific issue cited most often by the government's legal authorities was the British policy toward political extremists. A ministerial brief referred to a "blank cheque" that would "allow the Governments to become the object of such potentially vague charges by individuals as to invite Communists, crooks, and cranks of every type to bring actions."[89] Lord Chancellor Jowitt's complaint was that "the Convention would prevent a future British government from detaining people without trial during a period of emergency . . . or judges sending litigants to prison for throwing eggs at them; or the Home Secretary from banning Communist or Fascist demonstrations."[90]

Yet it would be misleading to argue that British institutional idiosyncrasy *caused* British opposition. Every established democracy, after all, has its treasured idiosyncrasies, and British leaders sincerely believed that, as the cradle of rule-of-law governance, they would suffer least.[91] In comparative perspective, many general concerns—government intervention in the economy, the challenge to colonial rule, concern about political extremism, skepticism of courts, a tradition of insular nationalism, and parliamentary sovereignty—hardly distinguished Britain from France, Italy, and many other continental supporters of the convention. Many of these fears—including those concerning colonies and electoral rules—could have been and were addressed by restricting the document.[92] For British decision-makers, the decisive point was not the nature of these concrete objections but *the utter absence in the British domestic context of any countervailing self-interested argument in favor of membership.*

The quaint scenarios of extremist threats raised by British officials demonstrate this. They arose not because extremist groups in Britain were particularly strong but because, in comparison with the Continent, they were so weak. Whereas French, German, and Italian officials viewed the ECHR as a check on the potential triumph of

---

86. Ibid., 803.
87. Ibid., 799.
88. Council of Europe 1975, III/182, 264.
89. Marston 1993, 806.
90. Lester 1994, 2.
91. It is possible they were wrong. One intriguing conjecture is that the longer a democratic form of government is in place, the more attached to its idiosyncrasies citizens and elites are likely to grow, and the further from the norm of international constitutionalism its practices are likely to become. Hence we would expect countries such as Britain, the Netherlands, Sweden, and the United States to become particularly attached to their idiosyncratic national systems. If correct, this would mean that established democracies not only reap fewer benefits from international human rights enforcement but also bear greater costs.
92. Samnøy 1993, 46–47.

popular extremist parties, British officials saw it only as a hindrance to a defense of the political system against agitation by isolated individuals. British internal debates and external statements were utterly devoid of any recognition of the advantages of collective security against domestic extremists—advantages central to continental arguments for the ECHR. Whereas the French were concerned that the Communist Party might take power electorally and have to be checked by the ECHR, the British were concerned that isolated radicals might file suit under the ECHR. In this context, marginal inconveniences overridden elsewhere in the interest of bolstering democratic stability became fundamental obstacles to the acceptance of binding international human rights norms.

For these reasons, the British government long considered opposing the convention altogether. Yet, in the words of an internal Foreign Office paper, "The alternative, namely refusal to become a party to a Convention acceptable to nearly all the remaining States of the Council of Europe, would appear to be almost indefensible. . . . Political considerations, both domestic and foreign, compel us now to bring ourselves to accept" an (optional) right of individual petition.[93] What blunted British opposition to any postwar European human rights regime was, above all, the fear of resurgent totalitarianism abroad that might pose an eventual military threat to the United Kingdom—precisely as republican liberal theory predicts.[94] This fear reflected not just a concern with a resurgence of Fascism, but also a turnaround in British foreign policy in 1948 in response to the perceived rise of the Communist threat in Western Europe. The West, the government argued, needed not only to maintain the military balance but also to strengthen continental democracies. For these purposes, the propaganda battle against Communism was critical. Such concerns had led Britain and France to help form the Council of Europe a few years earlier.[95]

In the minds of British officials, however, the primacy of domestic sovereignty over collective defense of the democratic peace remained unchallenged. The cabinet mandated efforts to water down the force of any agreement in Britain. British representatives sought to limit the potential risk of open-ended jurisprudence by calling for the careful enumeration and definition of human rights before agreeing on any enforcement mechanism. The expectation was that governments would not be able to agree on a list both extensive and precise.[96] Acting on Prime Minister Clement Atlee's direct instruction, the British delegation successfully pressed to place the right of individual petition and the jurisdiction of the court into optional clauses.[97] Foreign Minister Ernest Bevin himself instructed British negotiators to veto any mandatory right of individual petition "even if it [means] being in a minority of one."[98] With

93. W. E. Beckett, Legal Advisor to the Foreign Office, April 1947 Foreign Office meeting, cited in Marston 1993, 798, 811, also 798–804.
94. Note that this differs from the realist account in that the threat is not, in the first instance, a function of military power, but of political and ideological difference.
95. Simpson 1998, 15–19, 37–38.
96. Marston 1993, 808. See also Council of Europe 1975, III, especially 182, 280, 304.
97. Marston 1993.
98. Marston 1993, 814. Britain withdrew its similar intention to veto over the issue of colonial dependencies.

Cabinet approval, Britain pursued a similar policy with respect to the negotiation of UN human rights commitments.[99]

Having secured these concessions, which essentially rendered the convention unenforceable in Britain, the cabinet unanimously accepted the desirability of signing it. Ratification proceeded without difficulty. Subsequently, the Atlee government treated the ECHR as a declaratory document and made no effort to introduce implementing or incorporating legislation. Yet even this outcome—one with no immediate concrete consequence—was viewed among British leaders as second best. They were fully aware that once the document was signed, future domestic political pressure might well arise to incorporate the treaty or to accept its optional clauses. Foreseeing that a future government, as the lord chancellor put it, "might be forced to concede" the jurisdiction of the court, the British government sought also to include a provision permitting any state to withdraw from the ECHR on six months' notice.[100]

To judge from their voting record and their contributions to the assembly debates—given the absence, for the moment, of more detailed documentary research—the attitude of British politicians appears typical of attitudes in other recalcitrant countries, such as Sweden, Norway, Denmark, the Netherlands, and Luxembourg. Governments and publics in these countries appear to have been, on balance, more firmly committed to democracy, more altruistically inclined, and sometimes even (subsequent experience within the regime suggests) more willing to use coercion to spread human rights norms than the governments and publics of countries that favored binding commitments.[101] Yet, given the high level of certainty about the future political stability of these democratic systems and the immediate benefits of sovereignty for ruling parties and government officials, there was little self-interested reason to accept compulsory and enforceable international commitments in the area of human rights. Accordingly they refused to do so.

Generalizing the Argument: Human Rights and Beyond

We have seen that the origins of the ECHR, the most successful international human rights adjudication and enforcement regime in the world today, lies not in coercive power politics or socialization to idealistic norms, as contemporary international relations theories predict. Instead its origins lie in self-interested efforts by newly

---

99. Foreign Secretary Herbert Morrison, in his 1951 memorandum to the cabinet on the UN Covenant, wrote, "As the United Kingdom government has always played a leading part in promoting [human rights in the UN], it would be difficult to draw back at this stage. In these circumstances, the prudent course might be to prolong the international discussions, to raise legal and practical difficulties, and to delay the conclusion of the Covenant for as long as possible." Lester 1984, 55.

100. Lester 1984, 53–54. See also Marston 1993, 824–26. This clearly disconfirms the conjecture that future evolution was an entirely unforeseen, path-dependent consequence of earlier commitments.

101. On the subsequent willingness of Sweden, Norway, Denmark, and the Netherlands, as well as France and Austria, to pressure foreign states, see Sikkink 1993. On Sweden, see Council of Europe 1975, III/262, 264.

established (or reestablished) democracies to employ international commitments to consolidate democracy—"locking in" the domestic political status quo against their nondemocratic opponents. This empirical finding has three broader implications for future research on domestic politics and international relations.

The Origin and Evolution of Human Rights Regimes

The first implication of the theoretical argument is that the tendency of states to enhance the credibility of domestic policies by binding themselves to international institutions may help explain the origins and evolution of human rights enforcement regimes more generally. In negotiations to create the Inter-American Convention on Human Rights, the UN Covenants, and the emergent African human rights system, we should expect to see a similar pattern of support from new democracies, suspicion from established democracies, and hostility from dictatorships.[102] In the following overview I highlight suggestive evidence and propose areas for future research.

The negotiation of the UN Covenant on Civil and Political Rights appears to illustrate the dynamics of democratic commitment. At the height of the Cold War, in the early 1950s, the most stable among modern democracies, including the United States and the United Kingdom, allied with authoritarian and totalitarian states like the Soviet Union, China, South Africa, and Iran, in opposition to the inclusion of compulsory, enforceable commitments. The alliance in favor of such commitments, as republican liberal theory predicts, included recently established democracies in continental Europe, Latin America, and Asia.

Republican liberal theory also explains a troubling anomaly for scholars and activists alike, namely, the consistent unwillingness of the United States to accept multilateral constraints on its domestic human rights practices under the Inter-American and UN systems. This unwillingness is generally attributed to ad hoc, idiosyncratic factors: the United States' superpower status (as is often said of its opposition to binding UN obligations), its uniquely segregated southern states (as is often said of support for the Bricker Amendment in the early 1950s), or its unique political institutions (federalism and supermajoritarian treaty ratification rules). From the republican liberal perspective, in contrast, U.S. skepticism is the norm, not the exception, among established democracies—a norm related to the relatively low level of offsetting domestic benefits in an established, self-confident democracy, not the nature of American objections per se.[103]

The positions of the established democracies in recent years concerning the creation of war crimes tribunals offer at least partial confirmation of republican liberal

---

102. For an overview, see Robertson and Merrills 1996.

103. An intriguing parallel example is the recent refusal of the European Community's European Court of Justice (ECJ) to permit the EU to adhere collectively to the ECHR without a treaty amendment, noting that (1) there is no express human rights commitment in the Treaty of Rome, hence no legal justification for adherence, and (2) human rights already "form an integral part of the general principles of law whose observance the [ECJ] ensures." See ECJ, I-1789. Adherence would, of course, undermine the ECJ's own authority in this area.

theory. Established democracies had little difficulty accepting tribunals with jurisdiction over the former Yugoslavia and Rwanda, where their own policies would not be implicated. Yet where commitments were (de facto) reciprocally binding—namely, in open-ended institutional commitments involving countries that actually engage in foreign intervention—established democracies, confident that they maintain adequate domestic safeguards against domestic atrocities, hesitated to accept international constraints. In the recent International Criminal Court negotiations, three established democracies with a recent history of intervention abroad (the United States, France, and Israel) posed the greatest difficulties. After fighting to dilute the obligations of the treaty, the United States and Israel joined China and highly repressive Middle Eastern and North African states in opposition, while France was the very last major power to lend its support to the treaty.[104]

What about the development of human rights regimes over time? An understanding of major human rights regimes does not end with their founding. We have seen that the ECHR, like other major human rights instruments, created a number of optional clauses on individual petition and compulsory jurisdiction of the court. In some cases, early opponents of an enforceable convention remained exceptionally recalcitrant.[105] Yet over the subsequent five decades, all West European governments progressively adopted such clauses and in many cases incorporated the ECHR into domestic law.

Much of this accords with republican liberal theory. We observe a strengthening of commitments during and immediately after "democratic waves"—as hit Latin America and Central Europe during the 1990s. Such efforts are strongly favored by new democracies.[106] In Europe, the most important reform in the history of the ECHR, for example, was launched in the early to mid-1990s. "Protocol 11," opened for signature in May 1994, permits the ECHR Court to assume the functions of the commission and compels all new signatories to accept compulsory jurisdiction and individual petition—practices already universal among the original members. Leading legal academics argue that the most important impetus for Protocol 11 was "the widening . . . to include [states] that have had little domestic, much less international, experience in the legal protection of human rights."[107] The first three countries to ratify Protocol 11 were three transitional democracies: Bulgaria, Slovakia, and Slovenia. The governments of some new democracies in Central and East Europe were similarly quick to accept minority rights obligations as a means of locking in domes-

104. For a general treatment of war crimes tribunals demonstrating the unwillingness of established democracies to pay high costs, see Bass 1999.

105. Sweden and the Netherlands are among the handful of countries that have been specifically ordered by the ECHR to allow more effective domestic judicial review of human rights claims; many have argued that Britain should be on the list as well. Lester 1994.

106. Huntington 1991. Consider, however, former British colonies, which on gaining independence adopted explicit bills of rights and constitutional review—some on their own, some with the encouragement of the British government. Many were patterned after the European Convention, but the underlying impetus stems, republican liberal theory argues, from their status as emerging postauthoritarian democracies. Some of the most stable of these, such as those in the Caribbean, rejected international obligations.

107. Janis, Kay, and Bradley 1995, 88–89, 113–18.

tic democracy.[108] In the Americas, acceptance of compulsory jurisdiction by the Inter-American Court has occurred over the past two decades—a period in which domestic constitutional review also became nearly universal. In contrast, human rights norms remain weak in those regions where new democracies are few, as in Africa or the Middle East.

Despite these important insights, however, the determinants of the evolution of human rights regimes are unlikely to be identical to the determinants of their founding and are therefore unlikely to be explained entirely by republican liberal theory. The ECHR deepened over a period during which European governments grew more confident about the stability of domestic democratic governance. Hence the theory advanced here cannot be the sole, or even the major, explanation for the subsequent deepening of the regime. A social process intervenes between original intent and ultimate evolution—a process, we have seen, of which governments were quite aware in 1950. British officials believed that the ECHR would alter domestic political arrangements so as to encourage the mobilization of new social demands for human rights enforcement. Republican liberal theory would suggest that such new demands reflect new opportunities for representation of social interests once a nation joins a regime; broader liberal theory would stress changes in social ideas and interests. Further research is required to clarify the precise dynamics of such long-term trends.[109]

Generalizing the Theory to Other Issue Areas

A second direction for future research is to extend the theory to cooperation in other issue-areas. Despite the "republican liberal" label, the theoretical distinctiveness of the explanation advanced here is only incidentally connected to the liberal content of the philosophy embodied in human rights regimes. In other words, the argument is *theoretically* rather than substantively liberal.[110] Distinct to republican liberal theory is the decisive role of domestic political representation in world politics and, by extension, the possibility that international institutions, like their domestic counterparts, can enhance the credibility of domestic political commitments, thereby "locking in" current policies. Whether or not governments are "liberal," international institutions may "strengthen the state" domestically by expanding its domestic control over initiative, information, ideas, and institutions.[111] Compared with more conventional "functional" theories of international regimes, which stress reciprocal commitments to manage transnational societal transactions, this analysis points to a more purely domestic or "two-level" motivation for establishing international institutions.[112]

Under what general conditions should we expect to observe international commitments of this kind? Republican liberal theory suggests three conditions: (1) govern-

108. See Manas 1997; and Wippman 1999.
109. Moravcsik 1995.
110. Moravcsik 1997.
111. Moravcsik 1994.
112. Putnam 1988.

ments fear future domestic political uncertainty, (2) the position of the national government is supported by a consensus of foreign governments, and (3) international cooperation helps induce domestic actors to support the maintenance of current policies.

Where else in world politics might these three conditions be met? Two types of examples must suffice. Where nondemocratic governments cooperate to enhance their domestic credibility, a mirror image of human rights institutions may arise. Stephen David argues that "weak and illegitimate" leaders of developing countries often view internal enemies as more dangerous than external ones and are therefore likely to select international alliances that undermine domestic opponents.[113] The Holy Alliance is a nineteenth-century example of international cooperation designed to block the seemingly inevitable spread of domestic liberalism and nationalism— inside and outside its membership. A century later, ruling Communist governments in Eastern Europe, fearing for their domestic legitimacy, supported membership in the Warsaw Pact; their comrades worldwide cooperated through Comintern.

Further examples of efforts to use international regimes to bolster domestic policy credibility are found in international trade and monetary policy.[114] Mexico, for example, in exchange for its commitment to the North American Free Trade Area (NAFTA), gained relatively few economic concessions from the United States and Canada. This has led many analysts to argue that NAFTA should be seen less as a quid pro quo and more as a means of establishing the credibility of the Mexican commitment to trade and economic liberalization against the future potential of backsliding.[115] Mexican reform within NAFTA was just such a case where the three conditions were met: policy credibility was questionable, the consensus among foreign governments (the United States and Canada) was closer to the views of the domestic (Mexican) government than those of Mexican protectionists, and the costs of unilateral defection were perceived as large.

The process of European integration rested similarly on centralizing power in national executives, who consistently employed "foreign policy" decision-making institutions to handle issues traditionally decided in "domestic" forums.[116] In this regard, the European Union has played the role in postwar European integration that a strong presidency and "fast track" institutions have played in securing postwar U.S. support for multilateral trade liberalization. In European monetary cooperation, weak-currency countries like France and Italy have been among the strongest proponents of deeper exchange-rate cooperation—often with the intention of using external policy to stabilize domestic macroeconomic policy and performance. As predicted, these examples tend to be cases in which a government whose views are relatively closer to those of the regional consensus employs international cooperation to "lock in" cooperation. This process is facilitated also by the independent ideological value of "Europe" in the minds of the Italian electorate, for example, and by the

113. David 1991.
114. Rodrik 1989.
115. For example, Haggard 1997.
116. See Moravcsik 1994; and Goldstein 1997.

perception that monetary cooperation is linked to trade and agricultural cooperation—both of which shifted the perceived costs of defection.[117]

Realism and Idealism in International Relations Theory

The third and broadest implication of this analysis is that it counsels caution about the uncritical acceptance of certain ideational explanations for the emergence of international norms. Recent scholarship has been quick to assume that if realist (or regime) theory fails to explain international cooperation—say, in areas like human rights and environmental policy—the motivation for cooperation must lie in ideational socialization to altruistic beliefs. This assumption, once termed "idealist" or "utopian," seems plausible at first glance. The realist explanation for the emergence of human rights norms is manifestly weak. In a modern world increasingly dominated by liberal democratic practice, human rights seem salient and attractive ideals. Political action to protect them, moreover, clearly requires mobilizing a diffuse constituency in favor of the provision of what is in fact a public good, which in turn often requires that political actors issue strong normative appeals. Ideational theorists have little trouble finding public professions of moral conviction to support their view.

Yet scholars should not jump too quickly to the conclusion—as many recent studies of foreign aid, arms control, slavery, racism, and human rights invite them to do—that altruism must motivate the establishment of morally attractive international norms.[118] The tendency to jump to this conclusion demonstrates the danger of conducting debates about world politics around the simple dichotomy of realism versus idealism (or realism versus constructivism), as seems the current norm.[119] Presumptive evidence for the importance of altruistic or "principled" motivations vis-à-vis a realist account may melt away, as we have seen, as soon as the underlying theory is tested against more sophisticated rationalist, yet nonrealist (in this case, liberal) theories of self-interested political behavior. Moreover, to establish methodologically the existence of altruistic motivations and socialization processes, rather than alternative liberal theories, one must do more than cite public professions of idealism, document the actions of moral entrepreneurs, or invoke the desirability of the ultimate end. Talk and even mobilization are often cheap and often redundant or futile; accordingly, such evidence is often misleading. Cross-national comparison and primary-source documentation of decision making are the critical tests.

In the case of the establishment of the ECHR, the proper theory and method reverses an idealist conclusion that might appear to offer a plausible alternative to realism.[120] What seems at first to be a conversion to moral altruism is in fact an instrumental calculation of how best to lock in democratic governance against future

---

117. See Frieden 1993; Collins 1988; Moravcsik 1998a, chap. 4, 6; and Krugman 1994, 189–94.

118. What drives cooperation is prior domestic institutional convergence. Hence the nature of domestic regimes is not an intermediate variable between fundamental socialization and state behavior but the critical variable that determines the nature of interdependence in the first place.

119. This is a view ideational theorists are coming to accept. Finnemore and Sikkink 1998, 916–17.

120. For example, Legro and Moravcsik 1999.

opponents—a practice hardly distinct from similar practices in the most pecuniary areas of world politics, such as trade and monetary policy. I am not denying, of course, that ideas and ideals matter in foreign policy; I am challenging only a particular idealist argument. Surely some domestic support for democratic governance may be ideological, even idealistic, in origin. But if we can learn a single lesson from the formation of the world's most successful formal arrangement for international human rights enforcement, it is that in world politics pure idealism begets pure idealism—in the form of parliamentary assemblies and international declarations. To establish binding international commitments, much more is required.

References

Ackerman, Bruce. 1997. The Rise of World Constitutionalism. *Virginia Law Review* 83 (4):771–97.

Ando, Nisuke. 1992. The Future of Monitoring Bodies—Limitations and Possibilities of the Human Rights Committee. In *1991–1992 Canadian Human Rights Yearbook*, 169–175. Toronto: Carswell.

Bailey, Michael A., Judith Goldstein, and Barry R. Weingast. 1997. The Institutional Roots of American Trade Policy: Politics, Coalitions, and International Trade. *World Politics* 49 (3):309–38.

Bass, Gary. 1998. Judging War: The Politics of International War Crimes Tribunals. Ph.D. diss., Harvard University.

Brett, Rachel. 1996. Human Rights and the OSCE. *Human Rights Quarterly* 18 (3):668–93.

Brysk, Alison. 1994. *The Politics of Human Rights in Argentina: Protest, Change, and Democratization.* Stanford, Calif.: Stanford University Press.

Carr, E. H. 1946. *The Twenty Years' Crisis 1919–1939.* 2d ed. London: Macmillan.

Carter, Barry E., and Phillip R. Trimble. 1995. *International Law.* 2d ed. Boston: Little, Brown.

Collins, Susan M. 1988. Inflation and the EMS. In *The European Monetary System*, edited by Francesco Giavazzi, Stefano Micossi, and Marcus Miller, 112–39. Cambridge: Cambridge University Press.

Costello, Declan. 1992. Limiting Rights Constitutionally. In *Human Rights and Constitutional Law: Essays in Honour of Brian Walsh*, edited by J. O'Reilly, 177–87. Dublin: Round Hall Press.

Council of Europe. 1975. *Recueil des Travaux Préparatoires.* 6 vols. Strasbourg: Council of Europe.

David, Stephen R. 1991. Explaining Third-World Alignment. *World Politics* 43 (2):233–56.

Dijk, Pieter van, and G. J. H. van Hoof. 1998. *Theory and Practice of the European Convention on Human Rights.* 3d ed. Hague: Kluwer.

Donnelly, Jack. 1986. International Human Rights: A Regime Analysis. *International Organization* 40 (3):599–642.

Doyle, Michael W. 1986. Liberalism and World Politics. *American Political Science Review* 80 (4): 1151–69.

Drzemczewski, Andrew Z. 1983. *The European Human Rights Convention in Domestic Law: A Comparative Study.* Oxford: Clarendon Press.

European Court of Justice. 1996. Opinion Pursuant to Article 228 of the Treaty. Opinion 2/94 (29 March): I/1763–I/1790.

Evans, Peter B., Harold K. Jacobson, and Robert D. Putnam. 1993. *Double-Edged Diplomacy: International Bargaining and Domestic Politics.* Berkeley: University of California Press.

Falk, Richard A. 1981. *Human Rights and State Sovereignty.* New York: Holmes and Meier.

Finnemore, Martha. 1996. *National Interests in International Society.* Ithaca, N.Y.: Cornell University Press.

Finnemore, Martha, and Kathryn Sikkink. 1998. International Norm Dynamics and Political Change. *International Organization* 52 (4):887–917.

Franck, Thomas M. 1988. Legitimacy in the International System. *American Journal of International Law* 82 (4):705–59.

250 International Organization

Frieden, Jeffry A. 1993. Making Commitments: France and Italy in the European Monetary System, 1979–1985. Working Paper Series 1.14. Berkeley, Calif.: Center for German and European Studies.

Glendon, Mary Ann. 1998a. Knowing the Universal Declaration of Human Rights. *Notre Dame Law Review* 73 (5):1153–90.

————. 1998b. The Universal Declaration of Human Rights. Unpublished manuscript, Harvard Law School, Cambridge, Mass.

Goldstein, Judith. 1996. International Law and Domestic Institutions: Reconciling North American "Unfair" Trade Laws. *International Organization* 50:541–64.

Haggard, Stephan. 1997. The Political Economy of Regionalism in Asia and the Americas. In *The Political Economy of Regionalism*, edited by Edward Mansfield and Helen Milner, 20–49. New York: Columbia University Press.

Helfer, Lawrence, and Anne-Marie Slaughter. 1997. Toward a Theory of Effective Supranational Adjudication. *Yale Law Journal* 107 (2):273–391.

Henkin, Louis, Gerald L. Neuman, Diane F. Orentlicher, and David W. Leebron. 1999. *Human Rights*. New York: Foundation Press.

Humphrey, John P. 1974. The Revolution in the International Law of Human Rights. *Human Rights* 4:205–16.

————. 1984. *Human Rights and the United Nations: A Great Adventure*. Dobbs Ferry: Transnational Publishers.

Huntington, Samuel. 1991. *The Third Wave: Democratization in the Late Twentieth Century*. Norman: University of Oklahoma Press.

Janis, Mark W., Richard S. Kay, and Anthony W. Bradley. 1995. *European Human Rights Law: Text and Materials*. Oxford: Clarendon Press.

Jepperson, Ronald L., Alexander Wendt, and Peter J. Katzenstein. 1996. Norms, Identity, and the Culture of National Security. In *The Culture of National Security: Norms and Identity in World Politics*, edited by Peter J. Katzenstein, 33–75. Ithaca, N.Y.: Cornell University Press.

Kaufman, Chaim D., and Robert A. Pape. 1999. Explaining Costly International Moral Action: Britain's Sixty-Year Campaign Against the Atlantic Slave Trade. *International Organization* 53 (4):631–68.

Keck, Margaret E., and Kathryn Sikkink. 1998. *Activists Beyond Borders: Advocacy Networks in International Politics*. Ithaca, N.Y.: Cornell University Press.

Keohane, Robert O. 1986. Theory of World Politics: Structural Realism and Beyond. In *Neo-Realism and Its Critics*, edited by Robert O. Keohane, 158–203. New York: Columbia University Press.

Krasner, Stephen D. 1992. Sovereignty and Intervention. Unpublished manuscript, Stanford University, Stanford, Calif.

————. 1995. Compromising Westphalia. *International Security* 20 (3):115–51.

Krugman, Paul R. 1994. *Peddling Prosperity: Economic Sense and Nonsense in the Age of Diminished Expectations*. New York: Norton.

Kupchan, Charles A., and Clifford A. Kupchan. 1991. Concerts, Collective Security, and the Future of Europe. *International Security* 16 (1):114–61.

Lake, David A. 1993. Leadership, Hegemony, and the International Economy: Naked Emperor or Tattered Monarch with Potential? *International Studies Quarterly* 37 (4):459–89.

Landes, William M., and Richard A. Posner. 1975. The Independent Judiciary in an Interest-Group Perspective. *Journal of Law and Economics* 18 (3):875–901.

Legro, Jeffrey W. 1996. Culture and Preferences in the International Cooperation Two-Step. *American Political Science Review* 90 (1):118–37.

Legro, Jeffrey W., and Andrew Moravcsik. 1999. Is Anybody Still a Realist? *International Security* 24 (2):5–55.

Lester, Anthony. 1984. Fundamental Rights: The United Kingdom Isolated? In *1984 Public Law*, edited by Graham Zellick, 46–72. London: Stevens and Sons.

————. 1994. Taking Human Rights Seriously. *King's College Law Journal* 5:1–15.

Manas, Jean E. 1996. The Council of Europe's Democracy Ideal and the Challenge of Ethno-National Strife. In *Preventing Conflict in the Post-Communist World: Mobilizing International and Regional*

Organizations, edited by Abram Chayes and Antonia Handler Chayes, 99–144. Washington, D.C.: Brookings Institution Press.

Marston, Geoffrey. 1993. The United Kingdom's Part in the Preparation of the European Convention on Human Rights, 1950. *International and Comparative Law Quarterly* 42 (4):796–826.

McKeon, Richard. 1949. The Philosophic Bases and Material Circumstances of the Rights of Man. In *Human Rights: Comments and Interpretations*, edited by UNESCO, 35–46. New York: UNESCO.

Merrills, J. G. 1993. *The Development of International Law by the European Court of Human Rights*. 2d ed. Manchester, U.K.: Manchester University Press.

Moe, Terry. 1990. Political Institutions: The Neglected Side of the Story. *Journal of Law, Economics, and Organization* 6 (1):213–53.

Moravcsik, Andrew. 1992. Liberalism and International Relations Theory. Center for International Affairs Working Paper Series 92-6. Cambridge, Mass.: Harvard University.

———. 1994. Why the European Community Strengthens the State: International Cooperation and Domestic Politics. Center for European Studies Working Paper Series No. 52. Cambridge, Mass.: Harvard University.

———. 1995. Explaining International Human Rights Regimes: Liberal Theory and Western Europe. *European Journal of International Relations* 1:157–89.

———. 1997. Taking Preferences Seriously: A Liberal Theory of International Politics. *International Organization* 51 (4):513–53.

———. 1998a. *The Choice for Europe: Social Purpose and State Power from Messina to Maastricht*. Ithaca, N.Y.: Cornell University Press.

———. 1998b. The Origin of Human Rights Regimes: Liberal States and Domestic Uncertainty in Postwar Europe. Working Paper No. 98/17. Cambridge, Mass.: Weatherhead Center for International Affairs, Harvard University.

Morsink, Johannes. 1999. *The Universal Declaration of Human Rights*. Philadelphia: University of Pennsylvania Press.

Morgenthau, Hans J. 1960. *Politics Among Nations: The Struggle for Power and Peace*. 3d ed. New York: Alfred Knopf.

Nye, Joseph S., Jr. 1990. *Bound to Lead: The Changing Nature of American Power*. New York: Basic Books.

Pasquino, Pasquale. 1998. Constitutional Adjudication and Democracy: Comparative Perspectives— USA, France, Italy. *Ratio Juris* 11:38–50.

Pierson, Paul. 1996. The Path to European Union: A Historical Institutionalist Analysis. *Comparative Political Studies* 29 (2):123–63.

Polakiewicz, Jörg, and Valérie Jacob-Foltzer. 1991. The European Human Rights Convention in Domestic Law: The Impact of Strasbourg Case Law in States Where Direct Effect Is Given to the Convention. *Human Rights Law Quarterly* 12:65–85, 125–142.

Putnam, Robert D. 1988. Diplomacy and Domestic Politics. *International Organization* 42 (3): 427–61.

Ramirez, Francisco O., Yasemin Soysal, and Suzanne Shanahan. 1997. The Changing Logic of Political Citizenship: Cross-National Acquisition of Women's Suffrage Rights, 1890–1990. *American Sociological Review* 62 (5):735–45.

Risse, Thomas. 2000. Let's Argue! Communicative Action and International Relations. *International Organization* 54 (1):1–39.

Risse-Kappen, Thomas. 1994. Ideas Do Not Float Freely: Transnational Coalitions, Domestic Structures, and the End of the Cold War. *International Organization* 48 (2):185–214.

———. 1996. Collective Identity in a Democratic Community: The Case of NATO. In *The Culture of National Security: Norms and Identity in World Politics*, edited by Peter J. Katzenstein, 357–99. New York: Columbia University Press.

Robertson, A. H., and J. G. Merrills. 1993. *Human Rights in Europe: A Study of the European Convention on Human Rights*. 3d ed. Manchester, U.K.: Manchester University Press.

———. 1996. *Human Rights in the World: An Introduction to the International Protection of Human Rights*. 4th ed. Manchester, U.K.: Manchester University Press.

Rodrik, Dani. 1989. Credibility of Trade Reform: A Policy Maker's Guide. *World Economy* 12 (1):1–16.

Ruggie, John Gerard. 1983. Human Rights and the Future International Community. *Daedalus* 112 (4):93–110.

Russett, Bruce. 1993. *Grasping the Democratic Peace: Principles for a Post–Cold War World*. Princeton, N.J.: Princeton University Press.

Samnøy, Åshild. 1993. *Human Rights as International Consensus: The Making of the Universal Declaration of Human Rights, 1945–1948*. Bergen: Michelsen Institute.

Shapiro, Martin. 1981. *Courts: A Comparative and Political Analysis*. Chicago: University of Chicago Press.

Sieghart, Paul. 1983. *The International Law of Human Rights*. Oxford: Clarendon Press.

Sikkink, Kathryn. 1993. The Power of Principled Ideas: Human Rights Policies in the United States and Western Europe. In *Ideas and Foreign Policy: Beliefs, Institutions, and Political Change*, edited by Judith Goldstein and Robert O. Keohane, 139–70. Ithaca, N.Y.: Cornell University Press.

Simpson, A. W. Brian. 1998. Short History of the European Convention on Human Rights. Unpublished manuscript, University of Michigan Law School, Ann Arbor.

Slaughter, Anne-Marie, Alec Stone Sweet, and Joseph H. H. Weiler, eds. 1998. *The European Court and National Courts: Doctrine and Jurisprudence*. Oxford: Hart Publishing.

Snyder, Jack. 1991. *Myths of Empire: Domestic Politics and International Ambition*. Ithaca, N.Y.: Cornell University Press.

Teitgen, Pierre-Henri. 1988. *Faites entrer le tèmoin suivant 1940–1958: de la résistance à la Ve République*. Rennes, France: Ouest-France.

Van Evera, Stephen. 1990. Primed for Peace. *International Security* 15 (winter):7–57.

———. 1999. *The Causes of War: Power and the Roots of Conflict*. Ithaca, N.Y.: Cornell University Press.

Waltz, Kenneth N. 1979. *Theory of International Politics*. Reading, Mass.: Addison-Wesley.

Wippman, David. 1999. Practical and Legal Constraints on Internal Power Sharing. In *International Relations and Ethnic Conflict*, edited by David Wippman, 170–88. Ithaca, N.Y.: Cornell University Press.

Whitfield, John H. 1988. How the Working Organs of the European Convention Have Elevated the Individual to the Level of Subject of International Law. *ILSA Journal of International Law* 12:27–53.

Part II
Human Rights Discourse
and Domestic Norms

[5]

The Constitutionalization of Human Rights in Argentina: Problem or Promise?

Janet Koven Levit[*]

Argentina incorporated several international human rights treaties into its Constitution in 1994, uniquely importing international law into its domestic legal system. While recent scholarship links internalization of international law to obedience, the Argentine experiment highlights that naked constitutionalization will not necessarily enhance compliance with international law. After analyzing the Constitutional Assembly's debates and the ensuing fate of the freshly constitutionalized human rights treaties in domestic courts, this Article concludes that the problems and the incipient promises of Argentina's constitutionalization experiment may be traced to the identity, enthusiasm, and cohesiveness of the transnational actors that coalesced to drive the internalization strategy. Furthermore, in countries like Argentina, where the rule of law is not firmly anchored, an internalization strategy that centers on law, and law alone, is unlikely to succeed. A successful internalization strategy must be a dynamic, multifaceted process that engages a myriad of transnational actors from social, political, as well as legal, spheres.

* Assistant Professor of Law, University of Tulsa College of Law (on leave 1998-1999). Attorney Advisor, Export-Import Bank of the United States. A.B., Princeton University, 1990; M.A., Yale Graduate School, 1994; J.D., Yale Law School, 1994. The Author wishes to thank the University of Tulsa College of Law for its financial support of this project. The Author is grateful to Martín Abregú, Martin Böhmer, Carlos Rosenkrantz, and Roberto Saba for helping in the collection of Argentine sources. The Author sends thanks to Professor Harold Koh and Professor Michael Reisman for sparking my interest in human rights. The Author sends special thanks to Professor Robert Burt and Professor Owen Fiss for inspiring this piece and fueling my interest in Argentina. Finally, to my husband, Kenny Levit, thank you for pushing me to finish this piece; and to my son, Nathan, thank you for filling my days and nights with smiles.

I.   INTRODUCTION

International law is as potent as nations' proclivities to obey. For hundreds of years, international relations and legal scholars have asked why nations follow international norms. Recent scholarship recognizes that internalization, or domestication, of international norms enhances compliance. While the internalization of international law is international legal scholars' vogue mantra, these scholars have not delved sufficiently into the process by which international law is drawn into domestic systems. This Article will use a recent experiment in internalization of international law as a window into its process and limits.

Unlike many Latin American constitutions, the core of Argentina's Constitution had not been significantly altered since 1853. As part of the democratization process following the military dictatorship, Argentina engaged in a major constitutional reform effort, incorporating, by reference, nine prominent human rights treaties into its Constitution. Thus, Argentina presents scholars with an ostensibly prototypical example of legal internalization—internalization of international law via constitutionalization.

Argentina's Constitution provides a glimpse at the dynamic process by which nations internalize international norms. Argentina's experiment, while young, has thus far produced rather limited results in terms of compliance because it failed to empower, mobilize, and create synergistic relationships among a diverse panoply of transnational actors —individuals, politicians, non-governmental organizations ("NGOs"), governmental entities and supranational bodies—that straddle Argentina's legal, political and social spheres. Thus, the problems and the promise of Argentina's constitutionalization experiment may be traced to the identity, enthusiasm, and cohesiveness of the transnational actors that coalesced to drive Argentina's internalization strategy.

II.   COMPLIANCE, OBEDIENCE AND TRANSNATIONAL LEGAL PROCESS

Internationalists in the legal community as well as the political science community have long searched for answers to the "compliance question"—why do nations comply with international law?—and its derivatives: if we understand why nations comply with international law, can we predict when they will comply and when they will disregard international law? Or, can we structure rules and/or political relationships that maximize compliance?

While the international law theoretical landscape evolved significantly during the postwar years, the search for an answer to the "compliance question" remained a constant thread. Classic rationalists believe that nations comply with international law when the perceived

284   *COLUMBIA JOURNAL OF TRANSNATIONAL LAW*   [37:281

benefits outweigh the perceived costs.[1] Rationalists have refined their
approaches, creating sophisticated game theory-inspired models
rearticulating their time-worn proposition: states abide by international
law when it is in their self-interest to do so.[2] The New Haven School
links compliance to a communicative process of authoritative decision-
making on a domestic level which strives to maintain a world public
order of "human dignity."[3] Regime theorists link compliance to
dispute-settlement mechanisms, information gathering mechanisms, and
concomitant retaliatory actions.[4] Liberal theorists link compliance to
"liberal" political and economic structures.[5] Liberal states and

---

1. Rationalists, sometimes referred to as interest theorists, believe that states comply with
international law when it suits their interests, primarily defined in terms of wealth and power.
The theory is systemic, resting on nation-states as the primary actors, and has been used
extensively in the arms control and trade contexts. For the classic rationalist approach, see
generally LOUIS HENKIN, HOW NATIONS BEHAVE (2d ed. 1979).

2. For modern examples of the rationalist approach, see generally John K. Setear, *An
Iterative Perspective on Treaties: A Synthesis of International Relations Theory and
International Law*, 37 HARV. INT'L L.J. 139, 142-47 (1996); Kenneth W. Abbott, *'Trust but
Verify': The Production of Information in Arms Control Treaties and Other International
Agreements*, 26 CORNELL INT'L L.J. 1 (1993); Kenneth W. Abbott, *Modern International
Relations Theory: A Prospectus for International Lawyers*, 14 YALE J. INT'L L. 335 (1989);
Kenneth W. Abbott, *The Trading Nation's Dilemma: The Functions of the Law of International
Trade*, 26 HARV. INT'L L.J. 501 (1985); Duncan Snidal, *Coordination Versus Prisoner's
Dilemma: Implications for International Cooperation and Regimes*, 79 AM. POL. SCI. REV. 923
(1985); Duncan Snidal, *The Game Theory of International Politics*, 38 WORLD POL. 226 (1985).

3. *See* MYRES S. MCDOUGAL, INTERNATIONAL LAW, POWER, AND POLICY: A
CONTEMPORARY CONCEPTION 8 (1954); W. Michael Reisman, *International Lawmaking: A
Process of Communication*, 75 AM. SOC'Y INT'L L. PROC. 101, 107, 113 (1981) (describing the
New Haven School as a "communications model" which sees the legal process as comprising
three communicative streams—"policy content, authority signal and control intention"—which
thereby "liberates the inquirer from the . . . distorting model of positivism, which holds that law
is made by the legislature," in favor of the notion that "any communication between elites and
politically relevant groups which shapes wide expectations about appropriate future behavior
must be considered as functional lawmaking."). *See generally* Richard A. Falk, *Casting the
Spell: The New Haven School of International Law*, 104 YALE L.J. 1991 (1995); Symposium,
McDougal's Jurisprudence: Utility, Influence, Controversy, 79 AM. SOC'Y INT'L L. PROC. 266
(1985) (remarks of Oscar Schacter); Myres S. McDougal & W. Michael Reisman, *The World
Constitutive Process of Authoritative Decision*, 19 J. LEGAL EDUC. 253 (1967). For an excellent
description of the New Haven School, see Anne-Marie Slaughter Burley, *International Law and
International Relations Theory: A Dual Agenda*, 87 AM. J. INT'L L. 205, 209-11 (1993)
[hereinafter *A Dual Agenda*].

4. *See generally* ORAN R. YOUNG, INTERNATIONAL COOPERATION: BUILDING REGIMES
FOR NATURAL RESOURCES AND THE ENVIRONMENT (1989); Robert M. Axelrod, *An Evolutionary
Approach to Norms*, 80 AM. POL. SCI. REV. 1095 (1986); ROBERT O. KEOHANE, JR., AFTER
HEGEMONY: COOPERATION AND DISCORD IN THE WORLD POLITICAL ECONOMY (1984); ROBERT
M. AXELROD, THE EVOLUTION OF COOPERATION (1984); ORAN R. YOUNG, COMPLIANCE AND
PUBLIC AUTHORITY: A THEORY WITH INTERNATIONAL APPLICATIONS (1979).

5. *See* Anne-Marie Slaughter, *International Law in a World of Liberal States*, 6 EUR. J.
INT'L L. 503, 511 (1995) [hereinafter *International Law: Liberal States*]. *See generally A Dual
Agenda, supra* note 3; Anne-Marie Burley, *Law Among Liberal States: Liberal Internationalism
and the Act of State Doctrine*, 92 COLUM. L. REV. 1907 (1992). Liberal theorists are sometimes
referred to as "identity" theorists.

transnational actors therein comply with international agreements with other liberal states because of a mutual perception that liberal legal structures, primarily an independent judiciary, will foster compliance and constrain deviation from an international norm.[6] International society theorists believe that the "norms, values, and social structure of international society"[7] condition compliance, particularly because transnational actors have a "longer-term interest in the maintenance of law-impregnated international community."[8]

Professor Harold Koh, in a recent series of articles,[9] asks a slightly more nuanced and robust question—why do nations obey (rather than comply with) international law?[10] The difference between compliance and obedience is rather subtle. Compliance is norm-conforming behavior conditioned by exogenous forces, that is, the desire to reap certain benefits or avoid punishment;[11] while obedience is endogenous, the voluntary accession to a norm incorporated into internal value systems. Compliance is contingent, dependent on the consequences of non-compliance (I will comply because I want X or do not want Y), while obedience is a non-contingent embodiment of a rule or a norm. While compliance may be begrudging, obedience is habitual, almost instinctual. Through obedience, international norms become an embedded part of a nation's legal fabric.[12]

Then, how do nations come to obey, rather than merely comply with, international law? Koh's answer: transnational legal process.[13]

---

6. *See International Law: Liberal States, supra* note 5, at 532-33. *See generally A Dual Agenda, supra* note 3.

7. Harold Hongju Koh, *Why Do Nations Obey International Law?*, 106 YALE L.J. 2599, 2634 (1997) (reviewing ABRAM CHAYES & ANTONIA HANDLER CHAYES, THE NEW SOVEREIGNTY: COMPLIANCE WITH INTERNATIONAL REGULATORY AGREEMENTS (1995); THOMAS M. FRANCK, FAIRNESS IN INTERNATIONAL LAW (1995)).

8. *Id.* (quoting Andrew Hurrell, *International Society and the Study of Regimes: A Reflective Approach*, in REGIME THEORY AND INTERNATIONAL RELATIONS 49, 59 (Volker Rittberger ed., 1993)).

9. *See generally* Koh, *supra* note 7; Harold Hongju Koh, *Transnational Legal Process*, 75 NEB. L. REV. 18 (1996).

10. *See* Koh, *supra* note 7, at 2603 & n.13; *see generally* SECURING COMPLIANCE: SEVEN CASE STUDIES (Martin L. Friedland ed., 1990).

11. *See, e.g.*, Charles O'Reilly III & Jennifer Chatman, *Organizational Commitment and Psychological Attachment: The Effects of Compliance, Identification, and Internalization on Prosocial Behavior*, 71 J. APPL'D PSYCHOL. 492, 493 (1986) (noting that compliance is "instrumental involvement for specific, extrinsic rewards").

12. *See* Koh, *supra* note 7, at 2654.

13. Koh admits that transnational legal process presents little that is new. *See id.* at 2659 ("This Review Essay has demonstrated that, far from being novel, domestic obedience to internalized global law has venerable historical roots and sound theoretical footing."). Koh recognizes that transnational legal process is the descendant of the International Legal Process movement. *See id.* at 2620-24 (discussing the International Legal Process School and the New Haven School as predecessors to transnational legal process). Koh also recognizes that Henry

Transnational legal process links obedience to a complex, multidimensional process of interaction, interpretation and internalization.[14] Like many modern international legal theorists, Koh recognizes that states do not constitute the universe of transnational actors—individuals, corporations, non-governmental entities, public-interest organizations, sub-governmental entities, regional organizations, and international bodies play decisive roles in transnational legal processes.[15] These transnational actors are the engines of compliance, and later, obedience. According to Koh, transnational legal process involves three integrally-intertwined sub-processes: 1) interaction among transnational actors generates international norms; 2) further interaction in national and supranational fora leads to interpretation of norms; and 3) concomitant internalization of international norms into domestic legal systems results in compliance and, if the internalization strategy is effective, ultimate obedience.[16] Transnational actors' repeated norm-producing interaction and norm-illuminating interpretations foster entrenchment of international law into domestic legal systems, causing international norms to become "sticky" and ultimately breeding not mere compliance, but rather, habitual

---

Steiner and Detlev Vagts pioneered the study of transnational legal process. *See id.* at 2626 (discussing HENRY STEINER & DETLEV VAGTS, TRANSNATIONAL LEGAL PROBLEMS (1968) (now HENRY STEINER, DETLEV VAGTS & HAROLD HONGJU KOH, TRANSNATIONAL LEGAL PROBLEMS (4th ed. 1994)). He further admits that transnational legal process is an amalgamation of several strands of international legal theory: (1) interest [*see supra* notes 1-2 and accompanying text]; (2) identity [*see supra* notes 5-6 and accompanying text]; (3) constructivist [(constructivists believe that international norms play a significant constitutive role in defining national interests and identities) (*see* Ngaire Woods, *The Uses of Theory in the Study of International Relations,* *in* EXPLAINING INTERNATIONAL RELATIONS SINCE 1945, at 26 (Ngaire Woods ed., 1996); Alexander Wendt, *Constructing International Politics,* 20 INT'L SECURITY 71 (1995); Alexander Wendt, *Collective Identity Formation and the International State,* 88 AM. POL. SCI. REV. 384 (1994))]; and (4) international society [*see supra* notes 7-8 and accompanying text]. Yet, for Koh, these roots strengthen, rather than diminish, the theoretical value of transnational legal process. *See* Koh, *supra* note 7, at 2634.

14. *See* Koh, *supra* note 7, at 2645-58.

15. *See id.* at 2626 (transnational actors include "nation-states, international organizations, multinational enterprises, nongovernmental organizations, and private individuals . . .").

16. *See id.* at 2602-03, 2646 ("[Transnational legal process] can be viewed as having three phases. One or more transnational actors provokes an *interaction* (or series of interactions) with another, which forces an *interpretation* or enunciation of the global norm applicable to the situation. By so doing, the moving party seeks not simply to coerce the other party, but to *internalize* the new interpretation of the international norm into the other party's internal normative system. The aim is to 'bind' that other party to obey the interpretation as part of its internal value set . . . . The transaction generates a legal rule which will guide future transnational interactions between the parties; future transactions will further internalize those norms; and eventually, repeated participation in the process will help to reconstitute the interests and even the identities of the participants in the process.").

Koh explores isolated examples of "transnational legal process" in action. For Koh's discussion of the Anti-Ballistic Missile Treaty Reinterpretation Debate, see *id.* at 2646-48. For his discussion of the Middle East peace process, see *id.* at 2651-54. For his discussion of the Haitian refugee interdiction policy, see Koh, *supra* note 9, at 196-99.

obedience.[17] Thus, transnational legal process is a robust theory that emanates descriptive, prescriptive, and predictive energy.

While the ultimate bridge to obedience is internalization of international law, transnational legal process envisions internalization processes that are necessarily fluid, loosely defined by transnational actors' interests, which may respond to and be reconstituted as a result of transnational processes. In his work, Koh suggests that internalization strategies may involve social,[18] political,[19] and/or legal[20] mechanisms; he also offers several illustrative glimpses of these internalization processes at work.[21] Yet for all of its energy and all of its dynamism, transnational legal process theory's treatment of its crucial and defining link—international law's penetration into domestic systems—is rather thin. Transnational legal process thus beckons scholars to take a deep, exploratory dive into the dynamics of internalization processes or, as Koh phrases it, the nature of the "transmission belt."[22] Koh implicitly admits this, concluding his piece with a plea to the international legal and scholarly communities to develop strategies for internalization.[23] This Article, which explores one particular internalization strategy—internalization via constitutionalization—is a response to his plea.

III. CONSTITUTIONALIZATION OF HUMAN RIGHTS IN ARGENTINA: THE CONTEXT

A. *Argentina's Constitutional Reform*

Unlike many Latin American constitutions, Argentina's Constitution was a portrait of longevity, dating from 1853.[24]

---

17. *See* Koh, *supra* note 7, at 2646, 2649, 2651, 2655.

18. *See id.* at 2656 ("Social internalization occurs when a norm acquires so much public legitimacy that there is widespread general obedience to it.").

19. *See id.* at 2656-57 ("Political internalization occurs when political elites accept an international norm, and adopt it as a matter of government policy.").

20. *See id.* at 2657 ("Legal internalization occurs when an international norm is incorporated into the domestic legal system through executive action, judicial interpretation, legislative action, or some combination of the three.").

21. *See supra* note 16 and accompanying text.

22. Koh, *supra* note 7, at 2651.

23. *See id.* at 2656-59.

24. *See* CONST. ARG. (1853) 9-49 (Editorial Universidad, 1990) (translations of the 1853 Argentine Constitution are by the Author). Although the core of Argentina's Constitution has remained constant since 1853, there have been several amendments since 1853. For example, in 1860 the *Convención Nacional* bolstered the powers of the federal government vis-à-vis the provinces, abolished slavery, and limited the government's power to restrict individual liberties, including freedom of the press; in 1866 the *Convención Nacional* constitutionalized several federal taxes; in 1898 the *Convención Nacional* changed the representation in the *Cámara de*

Argentina's Constitution largely echoed the U. S. Constitution, especially regarding separation of powers and federalism.[25] The 1853 Constitution did not explicitly address human rights treaties, or even international law in general. Like the U.S. Constitution, the 1853 Constitution divided power over international treaties among the three independent branches: "The Congress shall approve or disapprove of treaties concluded with other nations";[26] the Executive shall conclude and sign treaties with foreign powers and receive their ministers;[27] and the federal courts shall have jurisdiction over matters pertaining to international treaties.[28]

From 1976 through 1983, Argentina suffered a brutal military dictatorship, during which thousands "disappeared."[29] These severe

---

Diputados (House of Representatives); and in 1957 the *Convención Nacional* added a provision that enhanced the rights of workers. *See id.* at 55-67. *See also* Larry Rohter, *In Latin America, 'The Constitution is What I Say It Is,'* N.Y. TIMES, Aug. 30, 1998, at 1 (noting the tendency of many Latin American countries to edit their constitutions frequently).

25. *See* CONST. ARG. (1853) at 22-49 (Second Part: National Authority). In fact, the Argentine Supreme Court frequently cites U.S. Supreme Court decisions as authoritative. *See generally* Jonathan M. Miller, *Judicial Review and Constitutional Stability: A Sociology of the U.S. Model and its Collapse in Argentina*, 21 HASTINGS INT'L & COMP. L. REV. 77 (1997); Jonathan M. Miller, *The Authority of a Foreign Talisman: A Study of U.S. Constitutional Practice as Authority in Nineteenth Century Argentina and the Argentine Elite's Leap of Faith*, 46 AM. U. L. REV. 1483 (1997).

26. *See* CONST. ARG. (1853) art. 67(19).

27. *See* CONST. ARG. (1853) art. 86(14) (the President shall have the power to "conclude and sign treaties regarding peace, commerce, navigation, alliance, neutrality, accords, and other negotiations required for the maintenance of good relations with foreign powers, as well as receive their ministers and admit their consuls.").

28. *See* CONST. ARG. (1853) art. 100 ("The Supreme Court and the inferior federal tribunals shall have jurisdiction over all causes of action regarding . . . treaties with foreign nations.").

29. Following violence and political polarization that occurred during the mid-1970's, a junta of military dictators—General Videla, Admiral Massera, and Brigadier Agosti—took control of Argentina's government. Engaged in a war against "subversion" and in the name of "national security," the junta suspended civil liberties and imposed a state of siege. *See* CARLOS SANTIAGO NINO, RADICAL EVIL ON TRIAL 53-54 (1996). National security forces abducted those who were engaged in "subversive" activities, brought them to clandestine detention centers, tortured and interrogated them, and frequently killed them. *See id.* at 54. Recent confessions on the part of ex-military officials reveal that the military threw many prisoners from airplanes over the Atlantic Ocean. *See* Laurie Goering, *Argentine 'Dirty War' Informer Vilified: Ex-Navy Officer Details Killings in '70s Oppression*, CHI. TRIB., Dec. 7, 1997, at 6. For a haunting discussion of the *modus operandi* of the military, including a description of torture techniques and detention centers, see COMISIÓN NACIONAL SOBRE LA DESAPARACIÓN DE PERSONAS (CONADEP), NUNCA MAS (1985) (truth commission's accounting of dirty war atrocities). While the official estimates are that 10,000 "disappeared," most human rights groups believe that the number is closer to 30,000. *See Argentina to Release List of 'Disappeared,' Human Rights Groups Call for More Details from 1970s 'Dirty War,'* CHI. TRIB., Mar. 26, 1995, at 10; David Chrieberg, *'I Can't Erase This,'* NEWSWEEK, Mar. 27, 1995, at 38.

The military dictatorship remained strong from 1976 to 1980, but began to falter thereafter for several reasons. First, the Inter-American Commission on Human Rights, coupled with the pro-human rights stance of President Jimmy Carter, turned international opinion against the military dictatorship. *See* NINO, *supra,* at 60. Second, Britain defeated Argentina's

human rights abuses were the backdrop to subsequent democratization efforts and, ultimately, the 1994 constitutional reform. When President Raúl Alfonsín, a member of the Radical Party, ushered in democracy in the wake of the military dictatorship, he promised to fight human rights abuses prospectively, principally through prophylactic legislative action.[30] Toward this end, he convoked *El Consejo para la Consolidación de la Democracia* (the Advisory Commission for the Consolidation of Democracy, or Advisory Commission)[31] and included in the group's charge a study of a major constitutional reform initiative.[32] After extensive consideration, the Advisory Commission recommended that the President convene a Constitutional Assembly to undertake the first comprehensive constitutional reform since 1853 and highlighted several substantive issues for reform.[33] With regard to human rights, the Advisory Commission implored any constitutional assembly to "amplify and strengthen" individual rights and, under no circumstances, diminish or limit such rights.[34] The Advisory

---

military with great speed and ease during the Falklands War, thus discrediting Argentina's military. *See id.* at 60-61. Third, non-governmental organizations, most prominently the *Madres de Plaza de Mayo*, began to publicize the disappearances. *See id.* at 59. Fourth, the economy declined. *See id.* at 60.

There is a vast literature on Argentina's military dictatorship, referred to as the "dirty war." For a representative sample, see NINO, *supra*, at 41-104 (describing Argentina's history, from the dirty war through democratization); ALISON BRYSK, THE POLITICS OF HUMAN RIGHTS IN ARGENTINA: PROTEST, CHANGE, AND DEMOCRATIZATION (1994); MARTIN E. ANDERSON, DOSSIER SECRETO: ARGENTINA'S *DESAPARECIDOS* AND THE MYTH OF THE "DIRTY WAR" (1993); IAIN GUEST, BEHIND THE DISAPPEARANCES: ARGENTINA'S DIRTY WAR AGAINST HUMAN RIGHTS AND THE UNITED NATIONS (1990); Alejandro M. Garro, *Nine Years of Transition to Democracy in Argentina: Partial Failure or Qualified Success?*, 31 COLUM. J. TRANSNAT'L L. 1 (1993); Carlos S. Nino, *The Duty to Punish Past Abuses of Human Rights Put Into Context: The Case of Argentina*, 100 YALE L. J. 2619 (1991); LAWRENCE WESCHLER, A MIRACLE, A UNIVERSE: SETTLING ACCOUNTS WITH TORTURERS (1990).

30. *See* NINO, *supra* note 29, at 67-73. President Alfonsín also attempted to impose "retroactive justice" through domestic criminal trials of the military junta. For a description and assessment of these trials, see generally *id.* President Menem ultimately pardoned all those who were convicted in these trials. *See id.* at 103-04.

31. *See* EDITORIAL UNIVERSITARIA DE BUENOS AIRES, REFORMA CONSTITUCIONAL: DICTAMEN PRELIMINAR DEL CONSEJO PARA LA CONSOLIDACIÓN DE LA DEMOCRACIA 7 (1986).

32. *See id.* at 8, 13-14.

33. The Advisory Commission believed such reform was necessary for the following reasons: 1) the executive had neutralized or nullified the effects of prior reform (amendment) efforts; 2) structural and substantive constitutional defects had limited the previous Constitution's force and effectiveness; 3) the political philosophies upon which the original Constitution rested had shifted; 4) while there was robust political debate on many issues, there was broad social consensus regarding the need for structural reform in the wake of the dictatorship; and 5) while some argued that the constitutional reform effort should await a period of calm, the Advisory Commission believed that some of the most profound constitutional moments followed a period of significant unrest and upheaval. *See id.* at 23-30.

34. *Id.* at 39 (noting in particular that the following articles of the 1853 Argentine Constitution should not be limited or circumscribed: Article 14 (rights of labor); Article 15 (abolition of slavery and the prohibition thereof); Article 16 (abolishing nobility); Article 19 (right to privacy); and Article 20 (equal rights of foreigners)).

290   *COLUMBIA JOURNAL OF TRANSNATIONAL LAW*   [37:281

Commission made several suggestions regarding the constitutional status of international law: 1) grant Congress the power to delegate certain functions to supranational entities; 2) make all international treaties self-executing[35] upon congressional ratification; and 3) establish the superiority of international treaties over domestic law.[36]

Despite the meticulous and painstaking work of the Advisory Commission, the constitutional reform project languished with the Alfonsín government.[37] The reform project was not to be revived until 1993, when, following extreme animosity and partisanship between President Menem (the Peronist Party) and the discredited Radical Party, the two camps agreed to proceed with the constitutional reform.[38] The public viewed the agreement, known as the "Pacto de Olivos," as shrouded in a cloak of partisan suspicion, seeing it as a mere opportunity for the Peronists to consolidate and extend their power and for the Radical Party to create an institutional and programmatic space for themselves in the wake of its discredited government.[39] The ensuing law divided the substantive reform effort into two components: a nucleus of mandatory reforms[40] and a peripheral group of themes for possible consideration.[41] Congress did not include human rights *per se*

---

35. A self-executing treaty is one that is enforceable law without enabling legislation. Likewise, a non-self-executing treaty is unenforceable absent legislative action. *See* RESTATEMENT (THIRD) OF THE FOREIGN RELATIONS LAW OF THE UNITED STATES § 111 (1986) [hereinafter RESTATEMENT].

36. *See* EDITORIAL UNIVERSITARIA DE BUENOS AIRES, *supra* note 31, at 82-83.

37. President Alfonsín's constitutional reform efforts were impeded by an economic crisis due to such factors as an inflated public sector and massive foreign debt. *See* Lita Olbrich, *Only Economic Restructuring Can Save Argentina*, DALLAS MORNING NEWS, July 16, 1989, at 31A. Nevertheless, Alfonsín remained tireless in his efforts to consolidate democracy. *See generally* NINO, *supra* note 29, at 99-104. In addition to the severe military crisis, President Alfonsín faced threats of military coup and political unrest. *See id.* at 90-104; Jill Smolowe, *Caught in a Revolving Door: Alfonsín's State of Siege is Hobbled by the Courts*, TIME, Nov. 11, 1995, at 53.

38. President Menem hoped to amend the Constitution to enable him to remain in office beyond the constitutionally circumscribed term. In exchange for Radical Party (Alfonsín) support for this amendment, President Menem agreed to comprehensive constitutional reform. *See* Christopher M. Nelson, *An Opportunity for Constitutional Reform in Argentina: Re-Election 1995*, 25 U. MIAMI INTER-AM L. REV. 283, 294 (1994); Juan C. Vega, *Contexto Social y Político de la Reforma Constitucional de 1994* in JERARQUÍA CONSTITUCIONAL DE LOS TRATADOS INTERNACIONALES 1, 2-3 (Juan Carlos Vega & Marisa Adriana Graham eds., 1996) (translations by the Author). The text of the agreement became Law No. 24,309 (on file with Author). *See also infra* notes 165-70 and accompanying text.

39. *See* VEGA, *supra* note 38, at 2-5.

40. This nucleus included the following issues: Presidential reelection; reduction of the Presidential term to four years; lengthening of the annual legislative session; direct election of the Mayor of Buenos Aires; limitation on the President's power to act via executive decree; and auditing of the federal coffers. *See id.* at 9-10.

41. The list of peripheral themes included: strengthening of the federal government; municipal autonomy; popular initiatives and consultations; updating of Congressional and Executive functions; investigative and enforcement powers of Congress; institutions dealing

in either group, although it included issues concerning international treaties in the latter and created a committee within the Constitutional Assembly, the *Comisión de Integración y Tratados Internacionales* (Commission on Integration and International Treaties, or Treaty Commission), to study the status of international treaties and create mechanisms to further regional integration efforts.[42]

While post-1994 provisions regarding executive and judicial power vis-à-vis international treaties remained highly reminiscent of the 1853 Constitution,[43] Article 75(22) of the 1994 Constitution, ostensibly concerning legislative powers, dramatically altered the Argentine Constitution's substantive treatment of human rights, as well as the legal status of international human rights treaties. The new provision specifies the following: 1) Congress will approve or reject treaties concluded with other nations, with international organizations, and with the Holy See; 2) all international treaties (currently ratified, as well as those that Argentina may ratify in the future) are superior to domestic laws; 3) several human rights treaties enjoy constitutional status;[44] 4) none of these treaties may limit any of the rights granted in the first part of the Constitution;[45] 5) human rights treaties may be renounced by the

---

with integration and international treaties; the defense of democracy; the preservation of the environment; an executive commission to investigate economic/social issues; indigenous communities; consumer rights; and habeas corpus/direct constitutional appeals. *See id.* at 10.

    42. *See* id. at 11-12.

    43. *See supra* notes 26-28 and accompanying text. *See also* CONST. ARG. (1994). Article 99(11) regarding executive power over international treaties in the 1994 Constitution is similar to Article 86(14) in the 1853 Constitution. Article 116 regarding judicial power over international treaties in the 1994 Constitution is identical to Article 100 in the 1853 version.

    44. The following treaties have constitutional standing: American Declaration of the Rights and Duties of Man, *signed* May 2, 1948, OEA/Ser.L./V./I.4, rev. 6 (1965); American Convention on Human Rights, Nov. 22, 1969, 9 I.L.M. 673 (1970) [hereinafter American Convention]; Universal Declaration of Human Rights, *adopted* Dec. 10, 1948, G.A. Res. 217(III)A, U.N. Doc. A/810, at 71 [hereinafter Universal Declaration]; International Covenant on Economic, Social, and Political Rights, *concluded* Dec. 16, 1996, 993 U.N.T.S. 4 (entered into force Jan. 3, 1976); International Covenant on Civil and Political Rights, *concluded* Dec. 16, 1966, 999 U.N.T.S. 171 (entered into force Mar. 3, 1976) [hereinafter International Covenant]; Optional Protocol to the International Covenant on Civil and Political Rights, *concluded* Dec. 16, 1966, 999 U.N.T.S. 171, 302 (entered into force Mar. 23, 1976); Convention on the Prevention and Punishment of the Crime of Genocide, *concluded* Dec. 9, 1948, 78 U.N.T.S. 227 (entered into force Jan. 12, 1951); International Convention on the Elimination of All Forms of Racial Discrimination, *concluded* Dec. 21, 1965, 660 U.N.T.S. 195 (entered into force Jan. 4, 1969); Convention on the Elimination of All Forms of Discrimination Against Women, *concluded* Dec. 18, 1979, 1249 U.N.T.S. 13 (entered into force Jan. 4, 1969); Convention Against Torture and Other Cruel, Inhuman, Degrading Treatment or Punishment, G.A. Res. 39/46, Annex, U.N. GAOR, 39th Sess., Supp. No. 15, at 197, U.N. Doc. A/39/51 (1985); Convention on the Rights of the Child, G.A. Res. 44/25, Annex, U.N. GAOR, 44th Sess., Supp. No. 49, at 166, U.N. Doc. A/44/49 (1990).

    All other international treaties are superior to domestic statutes but inferior to the Constitution. *See infra* notes 181-84 and accompanying text.

    45. *See* CONST. ARG. (1994) arts. 1-42 (Declarations, Rights, and Guarantees; New Rights and Guarantees).

executive, with the prior approval of two-thirds of both houses of the legislature, a procedure similar to that required for constitutional amendments;[46] and 6) other human rights treaties and conventions, approved by Congress, require a two-thirds vote of both houses of the legislature in order to endow them with constitutional standing.[47] The Constitutional Assembly also included a new provision promoting regional integration.[48]

B. Human Rights and South American Constitutions

As the following perusal of South American constitutions[49] demonstrates, Argentina's constitutionalization of human rights was a unique development in the region. Substantively, while international human rights norms infiltrate national constitutions to greater or lesser degrees, Argentina's Constitution is a unique, verbatim replica of these treaties. In terms of status, Argentina is the only country that grants human rights treaties constitutional standing. The following section groups South American constitutions along these two comparative axes —substance and status—illustrating that Argentina's Constitution is a lone outlier. This section merely attempts to classify constitutions vis-à-vis their treatment of international human rights norms and/or treaties; it does not assess the relative effectiveness of different constitutional approaches in the protection of human rights.

---

46. *See id.* art. 30. (setting forth the procedures for amending the Constitution: "The Constitution may be amended entirely or in any of its parts. The necessity of amendment must be declared by the Congress by a vote of at least two-thirds of the members; but it shall not be effected except by a convention called for the purpose.").

47. For the full text of Article 75(22), see CONST. ARG. (1994).

48. *See* CONST. ARG. (1994) art. 75(24) (Congress shall have the power to "approve integration treaties which delegate competences and jurisdiction to interstate organizations concerned with reciprocal and equal conditions and which respect the democratic order and human rights. Any standards dictated pursuant thereto supersede the laws."). *See also infra* note 243 and accompanying text.

49. This Author chooses to limit her comparison to South American constitutions for the following reasons: 1) most, if not all, have been rewritten, or significantly revised in the post-World War II period; 2) the region has shared a recent history of human rights abuses and thus shares a desire to combat future human rights abuses; and 3) the geographical and cultural proximity to Argentina.

1.   Substantive Incorporation of Human Rights Norms

Many modern constitutions[50] incorporate human rights norms, borrowing from international and regional human rights treaties. While many human rights treaties could serve as comparative reference points, this Article selects the International Covenant on Civil and Political Rights (the "International Covenant")[51] and the American Convention on Human Rights (the "American Convention")[52] because they comprehensively attempt to address and redress the most heinous of the civil and political rights abuses that became commonplace in South America during the military dictatorships.[53]

---

50. For human rights purposes, a modern constitution is one that post-dates World War II; for prior to World War II, international law did not recognize the human being—the individual—as an international actor who bears international rights. *See* LOUIS HENKIN, THE RIGHTS OF MAN TODAY 18 (1978); IAN BROWNLIE, PRINCIPLES OF PUBLIC INTERNATIONAL LAW 323-45 (4th ed. 1990); Steven R. Ratner, *The Schizophrenias of International Criminal Law*, 33 TEX. INT'L L.J. 237, 242 (1998); Tom Farer, *Introduction* to INTER-AMERICAN COMMISSION ON HUMAN RIGHTS: TEN YEARS OF ACTIVITIES 1971-1981 v-vi (1982). *See also* The London Charter, Charter of the International Military Tribunal (IMT), Agreement for the Prosecution and Punishment of the Major War Criminals of the European Axis, Aug. 8, 1945, 58 Stat. 1544, 82 U.N.T.S. 280. The London Charter is the document that constituted the Nuremberg Tribunal, christened the modern human rights era, and delineated the causes of action for which the allies intended to try the Nazi defendants, including crimes against humanity—"murder, extermination, enslavement, or any other inhumane act committed against any civilian population before or during the war, as well as persecution based on political, religious, or racial grounds . . . regardless of whether the accused had violated the domestic law of the countries where the deeds had been committed." *Id.* art. 6. Through its definition of crimes against humanity, the London Charter recognized and legitimized the two salient features of modern international human rights law: 1) the individual is the beneficiary of the rights; and 2) certain rights are universal, superior to the dictates of national law.

Also following World War II, the international community joined to create an international body, the United Nations, that would presumably forestall the type of international "meltdown" that had ripened into such a devastating war. The United Nations Charter lists promotion of and respect for "human rights and for fundamental freedoms" among its primary animating purposes. U.N. CHARTER art. 1, para. 1. Beyond flagging human rights as a preeminent concern, the Charter did not specifically contemplate any substantive rights. Instead, the United Nations General Assembly adopted the Universal Declaration, providing all individuals with the rights to equality; life; liberty; travel; privacy; participation in government through election or otherwise; protections during criminal trials; and freedom of thought, religion, and assembly. In addition, the Universal Declaration sets forth several economic- and social-oriented rights, including the rights to work; social security; rest and leisure; a "standard of living adequate for the health and well-being of himself and of his family"; education; and participation in cultural life. *See generally* Universal Declaration, *supra* note 44. While the Universal Declaration is not a treaty, nor is it legally binding on states, many of its provisions have become embedded in customary and/or conventional international law, and thus, have arguably become binding on states.

51. *See* International Covenant, *supra* note 44.

52. *See* American Convention, *supra* note 44.

53. In choosing to focus on the International Covenant and the American Convention, this Author by no means implies that the rights contained in other human rights treaties (most notably those delineated *supra* note 44) are any less significant. However, the political and civil rights contained in the International Covenant and the American Convention contain the building blocks of international human rights law and hence are often called the "first

The survey revealed that South American constitutions fall into one of two broad groups.[54] The first group includes constitutions that incorporate the "spirit" of human rights treaties.[55] In general, these constitutions are skeletal reflections of international human rights treaties, incorporating many core rights—core ideas—but lacking the flesh to make these rights as robust as their treaty-based counterparts. The second group, on the other hand, incorporates the texture and nuances of international treaty-based rights.

Constitutions in the first group frequently are "missing" several rights found in the international treaties, leaving conspicuous gaps in the constitutional treatment of human rights. None of the constitutions in this group contain the following rights: the right to self-determination;[56] an explicit gender equality provision;[57] a provision for the minimum due process rights for aliens facing expulsion;[58] a prohibition on traffic in women;[59] or the right to recognition as a person before the law.[60] Most constitutions in this group lack a provision promising prisoners "humane" treatment, including segregation of convicted criminals from those criminal defendants awaiting trial and segregation of juveniles from adults;[61] granting ethnic or religious minorities the right to enjoy their culture and group identity;[62] prohibiting war propaganda and advocacy of racial, national or religious hate;[63] and prohibiting imprisonment for contractual debt.[64] A few of the constitutions have some dramatic omissions. The Venezuelan and Uruguayan

---

generation" of human rights. *See generally* Louis B. Sohn, *The New International Law: Protection of the Rights of the Individual Rather than States*, 32 AM. U. L. REV. 1, 17-32 (1982).

54. For a comprehensive comparison of South American constitutions, please refer to Table 3: Constitutional Treatment of Human Rights in South America, which is appended to this Article.

55. *See* CONST. BOL. (1967, amended 1995); CONST. CHILE (1980, amended 1989); CONST. PERU (1993); CONST. URU. (1967, reinstated 1985); CONST. VENEZ. (1961, amended 1983).

56. *See* International Covenant, *supra* note 44, art. 1.

57. *See id.* art. 3.

58. *See id.* art. 13; American Convention, *supra* note 44, art. 22(6).

59. *See* American Convention, *supra* note 44, art. 6.

60. *See* International Covenant, *supra* note 44, art. 16; American Convention, *supra* note 44, art. 3.

61. *See* International Covenant, *supra* note 44, art. 10; American Convention, *supra* note 44, art. 5. Chile's Constitution provides for segregation of convicted and arrested prisoners but does not provide for segregation of juveniles from adults. *See* CONST. CHILE art. 19(7)(d). Thus, this constitutional provision is narrower than the international counterparts.

62. *See* International Covenant, *supra* note 44, art. 27. *But see* CONST. PERU art. 2(19).

63. *See* International Covenant, *supra* note 44, art. 20; American Convention, *supra* note 44, art. 13(5). *But see* CONST. VENEZ. art. 66.

64. *See* International Covenant, *supra* note 44, art. 11; American Convention, *supra* note 44, art. 7(7). *But see* CONST. PERU art. 2(24)(c); CONST. URU. art. 52.

Constitutions contain no clause prohibiting slavery and slave trade.[65] Chile's Constitution contains no prohibition on torture or other cruel, inhumane or degrading treatment.[66] Uruguay's Constitution does not proscribe the use of *ex post facto* laws[67] and does not grant citizens freedom of thought, conscience or religion.[68] While the American Convention also excludes some of these rights,[69] the aforementioned constitutions are striking in their omission of several rights in addition to those that the American Convention chose not to codify.

Those rights that the constitutions include tend to be skeletal replicas of the rather developed rights found in the International Covenant and the American Convention.[70] Other rights are significantly less expansive in scope. For example, criminal defense rights are

---

65. *See* International Covenant, *supra* note 44, art. 8; American Convention, *supra* note 44, art. 6.

66. *See* International Covenant, *supra* note 44, art. 7; American Convention, *supra* note 44, art. 5(2).

67. *See* International Covenant, *supra* note 44, art. 15; American Convention, *supra* note 44, art. 9.

68. *See* International Covenant, *supra* note 44, art. 18; American Convention, *supra* note 44, art. 12.

69. The American Convention does not include the following: the right to self-determination [*see* International Covenant, *supra* note 44, art. 1]; an explicit gender equality provision [although the American Convention has a generic equal protection clause, (*see* American Convention, *supra* note 44, art. 24), it does not explicitly provide for gender equality (*see* International Covenant, *supra* note 44, art. 3)]; and the right of ethnic and religious minorities to enjoy their culture and group identity [*see* International Covenant, *supra* note 44, art. 27]. See also Table 2 in the Appendix for a comparison of the International Covenant and the American Convention.

70. For example, the International Covenant states in Article 21: "The right of peaceful assembly shall be recognized. No restrictions may be placed on the exercise of this right other than those imposed in conformity with the law and which are necessary in a democratic society in the interests of national security or public safety, public order, the protection of public health or morals or the protection of the rights and freedoms of others." International Covenant, *supra* note 44, art. 21. Likewise, Article 22 states: "1. Everyone shall have the right to freedom of association with others, including the right to form and join trade unions for the protection of interests. 2. No restrictions may be placed on the exercise of this right other than those which are prescribed by law and which are necessary in a democratic society in the interests of national security or public safety, public order, the protection of public health or morals or the protection of the rights and freedoms of others. This article shall not prevent the imposition of lawful restrictions on members of the armed forces and of the police in their exercise of this right." International Covenant, *supra* note 44, art. 22. The American Convention provides for similar rights. *See* American Convention, *supra* note 44, arts. 15, 16. In contrast, Bolivia merely grants each person the right "[to] assemble and to associate for lawful purpose." CONST. BOL. art. 7(c). Venezuela merely grants each person the "right of association for lawful ends" and the "right to meet with others, publicly or privately without previous permission, for lawful ends and without arms." CONST. VENEZ. arts. 70, 71. In addition, the international instruments' family rights provisions (*see* International Covenant, *supra* note 44, art. 23; American Convention, *supra* note 44, art. 17), which not only highlight the preeminence of the family but which further grant the right to consensual marriage and equality of spouses during marriage and upon dissolution, give way to simplistic proclamations that "[t]he family is the basis of our society," (CONST. URU. art. 40), and that "[t]he family is the basic core of society" (CONST. CHILE art. 1).

296   *COLUMBIA JOURNAL OF TRANSNATIONAL LAW*   [37:281

generally sparse, granting many fewer protections than those granted in the International Covenant and American Convention.[71] The freedom of conscience and religion clauses in some constitutions are rather narrow.[72] As opposed to the approach in the international treaties, many constitutions' "right to life" provisions do not evince discomfort with

---

71. *See* International Covenant, *supra* note 44, art 14; American Convention, *supra* note 44, art. 8. See also Table 2 in the Appendix for a delineation of the rights of criminal defendants in the International Covenant and the American Convention, and Table 3 in the Appendix for a comparison of South American constitutions vis-à-vis these rights.

The Constitution of Bolivia merely includes protection from self-incrimination, a presumption of innocence, a general right to a defense, and the right to be assisted by a defense attorney. *See* CONST. BOL arts. 14, 16.

The Constitution of Peru only provides for a few criminal defense protections, namely the presumption of innocence and a prohibition on the admissibility of coerced statements (which is not explicitly set forth in the International Covenant or American Convention), and lacks most of the other rights found in the International Covenant and American Convention. *See* CONST. PERU arts. 2(24)(e), 2(24)(h).

The Constitution of Venezuela provides for some criminal defense rights, but it does not provide for a right to defense counsel, a right to an interpreter, a right to prepare a defense, or a right to appeal. *See* CONST. VENEZ. art. 60.

The Constitution of Chile, in its delineation of criminal defense rights, includes provisions regarding the following: adequate time for the preparation of defenses, a prohibition on double jeopardy, the right to an interpreter, and the right to be informed of the charges pending against the criminal defendant. *See* CONST. CHILE arts. 19(3), 7.

Uruguay's criminal rights provisions lack the right to be informed of charges; the right to a defense lawyer; the right to an interpreter; a prohibition on placing a criminal defendant in double jeopardy; and the right to an appeal. *See* CONST. URU arts. 12, 20-22.

72. For example, the Constitution of Bolivia contains a rather narrow freedom of thought and freedom of religion clause. The International Covenant provides that "Everyone shall have the right to freedom of thought, conscience and religion. This right shall include freedom to have or to adopt a religion or belief of his choice, and freedom, either individually or in community with others and in public or private, to manifest his religion or believe in worship, observance, practice and teaching." International Covenant, *supra* note 44, art. 18(1). The American Convention provides, "Everyone has the right to freedom of conscience and of religion. This right includes freedom to maintain or to change one's religion or beliefs, and freedom to profess or disseminate one's religion or beliefs either individually or together with others, in public or in private." American Convention, *supra* note 44, art. 12(1). The Constitution of Bolivia states, "The State recognizes and upholds the Roman Catholic Apostolic Religion. It guarantees the public exercise of any other worship." CONST. BOL. art. 3. Bolivia merely guarantees the public, not the private, exercise of worship, and does not explicitly protect freedom of thought or conscience; nor does Bolivia's Constitution fully develop the right in terms of choices and dissemination of ideas.

the death penalty.[73] Constitutional clauses regarding torture appear thin when juxtaposed with international analogs.[74]

Some constitutional provisions in this group ostensibly mimic international treaties but carve elastic exceptions that envelop the substantive right. Some constitutions exclude entire groups of people from constitutional protections.[75] Frequently, "state of emergency" provisions, which allow the executive (usually with some type of nodding acquiescence from the legislature) to suspend certain rights in the face of an extreme crisis, are artfully drafted to create gaping loopholes that detract from the potency of many rights. Sometimes the triggering event—the emergency—is defined in such broad, catch-all terms that the executive could "legitimately" invoke the "state of emergency" clause in a wide range of situations.[76] The International

---

73. The International Covenant and the American Convention strongly disfavor the death penalty's use in their "right to life" provisions. *See* International Covenant, *supra* note 44, art. 6; American Convention, *supra* note 44, art. 4. These instruments support the abolition of the death penalty [*see* International Covenant, *supra* note 44, art. 6(6); American Convention, *supra* note 44, art. 4(3)], and, at a minimum, proscribe countries from imposing the death penalty for anything but the most serious crimes [*see* International Covenant, *supra* note 44, art. 6(2); American Convention, *supra* note 44, art. 4(2)], and from extending the death penalty "to crimes to which it does not presently apply" [American Convention, *supra* note 44, art. 4(2)]. Peru's "right to life" provision does not bar or curtail the death penalty's use but merely states that "Every person has the right to life, to his identity, to his moral, spiritual, and physical integrity." CONST. PERU art. 2(1). Chile's "right to life" provision does not disapprove of or strongly disfavor the death penalty, stating, "The Constitution guarantees to all persons the right to life and to the physical and psychological integrity of the individual . . . . The death penalty may only be instituted for a crime considered in law approved by a qualified quorum." CONST. CHILE art. 19(1).

74. The International Covenant and the American Convention respectively state that no one "shall be subjected to torture or to cruel, inhumane, or degrading punishment or treatment." International Covenant, *supra* note 44, art. 7; American Convention, *supra* note 44, art. 5(2). The Constitution of Venezuela states that "No one may be . . . subjected to torture or to other proceedings which cause physical or moral suffering." CONST. VENEZ. art. 60(3). This phrasing is conspicuously distinct and appears to be narrower than the International Covenant or the American Convention. The Constitution of Uruguay prohibits brutal treatment in prisons but does not prohibit such treatment outside of prisons, nor is it clear that brutal treatment encompasses all instances when the proscription on "torture or other cruel, inhuman or degrading treatment" may apply. CONST. URU. art. 26.

75. For instance, Peru's constitutional provision regarding "personal freedom and security" contains many of the same protections found in Article 9 of the International Covenant and in Article 7 of the American Convention—no arbitrary arrest, right to be informed about the reasons for the arrest, prompt recourse to judicial scrutiny of legality of custody—but suspends these very protections when suspected drug traffickers, terrorists, or spies are under scrutiny. *See* CONST. PERU art. 2(24)(f).

76. Certain rights may only be suspended under the International Covenant "[i]n time of public emergency which threatens the life of the nation." International Covenant, *supra* note 44, art. 4(1). The American Convention's "state of emergency" provisions may only be invoked "[i]n time of war, public danger, or other emergency that threatens the independence or security of a State Party." American Convention, *supra* note 44, art. 27(1).

Peru's Constitution sanctions usage of the "state of emergency" clause "in case of a disturbance of the peace or of the internal order, catastrophe, or grave circumstances affecting

Covenant and American Convention do not allow derogation of certain rights, even when a "state of emergency" is in effect.[77] Most constitutions, like the International Covenant and the American Convention, limit the number of rights/prohibitions that the executive and/or legislature may curtail. This list, however, is frequently shorter than the International Covenant and the American Convention, meaning that the number of suspendable rights is somewhat greater.[78] In providing for basic core rights, these constitutions are true to the "spirit" of the international human rights treaties but do not mirror their nuances, depth, or texture.

The second group of constitutions[79] integrates not merely the spirit, but also the letter, of international human rights treaties. These constitutions emulate, or even surpass, international treaties in scope and breadth. In this group, international treaties conspicuously infiltrate national constitutions, serving as models for the content and scope of constitutional rights.

In general, the constitutions in the second group contain most of the rights enumerated in the International Covenant and the American Convention.[80] Constitutional provisions tend to mirror international

---

the life of the nation." CONST. PERU art. 137(1). Venezuela's "state of emergency" clause covers internal or external conflicts, "disorder that may disturb the peace," or "grave circumstances that affect economic or social life." CONST. VENEZ. arts. 240-41. Under Chile's state of emergency provision, enumerated rights may be suspended during "foreign or internal war, internal disturbances, emergency, and public calamity." CONST. CHILE art. 39.

77. The International Covenant and the American Convention do not permit suspension of the following rights/prohibitions: right to life [*see* International Covenant, *supra* note 44, art. 6; American Convention, *supra* note 44, art. 4]; freedom of thought [*see* International Covenant, *supra* note 44, art. 18; American Convention, *supra* note 44, art. 13]; torture [*see* International Covenant, *supra* note 44, art. 7; American Convention, *supra* note 44, art. 5(2)], slavery [*see* International Covenant, *supra* note 44, art. 8; American Convention, *supra* note 44, art. 6], imprisonment for contractual liability [*see* International Covenant, *supra* note 44, art. 11; American Convention, *supra* note 44, art. 7(7)]; *ex post facto* laws [*see* International Covenant, *supra* note 44, art. 15; American Convention, *supra* note 44, art. 9]; and recognition as a person before the law [*see* International Convention, *supra* note 44, art. 16]. In addition, the American Convention does not allow derogation from the following rights: right to judicial personality [*See* American Convention, *supra* note 44, art. 3]; right to family [*see id.* art. 17]; children's rights [*see id.* arts. 17(5), 18, 19, 20]; and the right to participate in government [*see id.* art. 23].

78. For example, Venezuela apparently permits the suspension of most rights. *See* CONST. VENEZ. arts. 240-42, 244. Similarly, Uruguay allows the derogation of all rights related to individual security in order to apprehend "guilty parties," presumably including the right to life, the prohibition on torture, and the prohibition on punishment for contractual liability. *See* CONST. URU. art. 31.

79. *See* CONST. BRAZ. (1988); CONST. COLOM. (1991); CONST. ECUADOR (1979, amended 1992); CONST. PARA. (1992).

80. The Constitution of Brazil is the most stunning, at least touching upon all of the rights except for one: the right to recognition as a person. The Constitution of Colombia is only missing three rights: the right to self-determination (which is not included in the American Convention); an explicit provision regarding segregation of different types of prisoners; and a prohibition on war propaganda and advocacy of racial, national or religious hate. The

rights;[81] other provisions, most notably constitutional protection of criminal defendants,[82] are significantly more robust than those developed in the international instruments.[83] Some constitutions expand the scope of various rights.[84] Other constitutional rights are more potent

---

Constitution of Ecuador lacks four rights: an explicit provision regarding segregation of different types of prisoners; a provision regarding due process rights for aliens facing expulsion; the right to recognition as a person; and a prohibition on war propaganda and advocacy of racial, national or religious hate. The Constitution of Paraguay is missing the right to self-determination, the right to recognition as a person, prohibition of war propaganda, and basic children's rights.

81. For example, the International Covenant and the American Convention mandate State Parties to segregate certain classes of prisoners from other classes: juveniles must be segregated from adults, and those accused should be segregated from those convicted. *See* International Covenant, *supra* note 44, art. 10; American Convention, *supra* note 44, arts. 5(3), 5(4). Most of the constitutions in the first group omit this right all together. *See supra* note 61 and accompanying text. Paraguay's Constitution not only includes this right but echoes the international instruments—also demanding that juveniles and adults, as well as the accused and the convicted, should be separated. *See* CONST. PARA. art. 21.

The American Convention provides generically that no one shall be imprisoned for failure to pay a debt, yet further specifies that this provision does not apply for orders issued for "nonfulfillment of duties of support." *See* American Convention, *supra* note 44, art. 7(7). Brazil similarly draws an exception to the general rule for "defaults on an alimony obligation." CONST. BRAZ. art. 5(LXVII).

82. See *supra* note 71 and Table 2 in the Appendix for the international instruments' treatment of criminal defense rights. In Paraguay's Constitution, the "personal liberty and security" provision, covering arrest procedures, provides for all the rights granted in international treaties but also explicitly grants criminal defendants the right to have family members or other designated individuals informed of the arrest; the right to engage an interpreter as soon as the detention begins; and the right to remain silent. *See* CONST. PARA. arts. 12(2), 12(4), 12(1). Paraguay's criminal defense rights, covering the trial itself, are also significantly enhanced, including the right to have copies of all relevant documents; the right "to offer, produce, check, and reject evidence"; and the right "to have the court dismiss any evidence produced or proceedings carried out in violations of legal provisions." CONST. PARA. arts. 17(7), 17(8), 17(9). Brazil's Constitution also expands criminal defense rights: the arrest and place of detention shall be communicated to the detainee's family; the accused has the right to remain silent; the right to a jury; and illegal evidence will not be used in trial. *See* CONST. BRAZ. arts. 5(LXII), 5(LXIII), 5(XXXVIII), 5(LVI). Colombia's Constitution explicitly forbids use of illegally obtained evidence. *See* CONST. COLOM. art. 29.

83. The International Covenant and the American Convention set forth a basic right to freedom of association, including the right to join trade unions; but carve exceptions to this right in the name of "national security or public safety, public order, the protection of public health or morals or the protection of the rights and freedom of others"; and state that governments may lawfully restrict members of the armed forces and police in their exercise of this right. International Covenant, *supra* note 44, art. 22; American Convention, *supra* note 44, art. 16. The Brazilian Constitution provides for the following: "freedom of association for lawful purposes is complete, but any paramilitary association is prohibited"; "creation of associations and, as set forth in law, of cooperatives, requires no authorization, prohibiting state interference in their operations"; "associations may be compulsorily dissolved or have their activities suspended only by court decision; in the former case a final and unappealable decision is required"; and "no one can be compelled to join an association or to remain in one." CONST. BRAZ. arts. 5(XVII), 5(XVIII), 5(XIX), 5(XX). *See also* CONST. COLOM. arts. 38-39.

84. The international instruments provide for humane treatment of prisoners by mandating segregation of different groups of prisoners. *See* International Covenant, *supra* note 44, art. 10; American Convention, *supra* note 44, arts. 5(3), 5(4). The Brazilian Constitution enhances this right by providing for segregation with regard to age, sex, and criminal offense and further

because they are affirmative, creating state obligations.[85] Some constitutional rights are stronger because they eliminate encroaching exceptions.[86]

When substantive treatment of human rights norms is a comparative axis, constitutions split into two groups. However, these groups share two traits. First, international human rights treaties clearly provided a foundation—some type of model—for constitutional

---

providing that "female prisoners shall be assured conditions that allow them to remain with their children during the period of breast-feeding." CONST. BRAZ. arts. 5(XLVIII), 5(L).

Colombia's equal protection clause extends protection beyond the delineated categories to "those individuals who on account of their economic, physical, or mental condition are in obviously vulnerable circumstances." CONST. COLOM. art. 13.

85. For example, Paraguay's Constitution not only assures equality to "all residents as far as dignity and rights are concerned" (CONST. PARA. art. 46) and makes explicit equality assurances to men and women (*see id.* art. 48), but also creates potent, affirmative state duties: "The State will remove all obstacles and prevent those factors that support or promote discrimination," (*id.* art. 46); "The State will create conditions conducive to, and will create adequate mechanisms for, making this equality true and effective by removing those obstacles that could prevent or curtail this equality as well as by promoting women's participation in every sector of national life." (*id.* art. 48). While the International Covenant and the American Convention also impose obligations upon States Parties to assure that all persons have "free and full exercise" of rights in a non-discriminatory manner, the obligations imposed by Paraguay's Constitution are much more robust, requiring not only removal of obstacles impeding equality but also prevention of those factors that support or promote discrimination. *See* International Covenant, *supra* note 44, art. 2; American Convention, *supra* note 44, art. 1.

86. *See supra* notes 78-81 and accompanying text. The Constitution of Colombia does not allow suspension of any "human rights" or "fundamental freedoms" and provides that "[i]n all cases, the rules of international humanitarian law will be observed." CONST. COLOM. art. 214.

The international instruments' freedom of speech, religion, and association/assembly rights contain a strong exception: they may be restricted in the name of national security, public safety, public order, the protection of public health or morals, and in respect of the rights or reputations of others. *See* International Covenant, *supra* note 44, art. 18 (religion and conscience, excluding national security), art. 19 (expression and opinions), art. 21 (assembly); art. 22 (association). *See also* American Convention, *supra* note 44, art. 12 (conscience and religion, excluding reputation and national security), art. 13 (thought and expression), arts. 15, 16 (assembly and association, excluding reputation). However, the Constitution of Paraguay does not carve such exceptions for some of these rights, and for others it narrows the scope of the exception, thereby enhancing the breadth of the right. Article 26, concerning "freedom of expression and the press," does not carve any exceptions. CONST. PARA. art. 26. The right to assembly, Article 32, only carves exceptions in "areas of public traffic control, at certain hours, to preserve public order and the rights of others." *Id.* art. 32. Similarly, the Constitution of Brazil merely excepts meetings which "interfere with another meeting previously called for the same place" from its general freedom of assembly clause. "[P]rior notice to the proper authority" is an additional prerequisite to freedom of assembly. CONST. BRAZ. art. 5(XVI). Similarly, Brazil's freedom of association provisions do not carve out the same type of expansive exceptions, merely prohibiting "paramilitary association." *Id.* arts. 5(XVII-XX). The Colombian Constitution does not load its freedom of conscience, religion, and association provisions with restrictive exceptions. *See* CONST. COLOM. arts. 18, 19, 38-39. The Constitution of Ecuador does not place restrictions on the freedom of assembly or the freedom of association and limits exceptions for the freedom of opinion and expression provision by providing "[a]ny person who was affected by inaccurate statements or whose honor injured by the press or other means of social communication will have the right to have the corresponding rectification made by them free of charge." CONST. ECUADOR arts. 19(13), 31(h), 19(4).

development of individual rights.[87] Second, no constitution, not even those in the second group, contains all of the rights delineated in the international treaties. Those constitutions that incorporated most rights did not consistently emulate the scope and breadth of such rights, opting to curtail some rights while enhancing others. One can only speculate regarding the constitutional drafters' frame of mind at the inception of these constitutions. It is reasonable, however, to imagine a deliberative process that resulted in the inclusion of some rights, at the expense of others, as well as an attenuation of the scope of certain rights.

2.   Constitutional Status of Human Rights Norms

Many modern constitutions address the status of international human rights norms or, more generally, international law.[88] As in the previous section, this Article will focus on South American constitutions, and suggests the following broad groupings: 1) constitutions which place international treaties on a par with domestic law; 2) constitutions that deem international treaties superior to domestic law but inferior to the constitution; and 3) constitutions that do not explicitly (or implicitly) address the status of international law.

---

87.   *See, e.g.*, A.E. Dick Howard, *The Indeterminacy of Constitutions*, 31 WAKE FOREST L. REV. 383, 387 (1996).

88.   For a comprehensive survey of the constitutional treatment of international treaties, see Hurst Hannum, *The Status of the Universal Declaration of Human Rights in National and International Law*, 25 GA. J. INT'L & COMP. L. 287, 355 (1996) (Annex I: Constitutional Provisions Referring to the Status of International Law, Including References to the Universal Declaration of Human Rights).

While beyond the scope of this Article, the constitutional status of human rights treaties, principally the European Convention on Human Rights, has been a significant aspect of constitutional reform efforts in Central and Eastern Europe. *See* European Convention for the Protection of Human Rights and Fundamental Freedoms, *opened for signature* Nov. 4, 1950, Europ. T.S. No. 5, 213 U.N.T.S. 222 (entered into force Sept. 5, 1953). *See also* Howard, *supra* note 87, at 387-88; Eric Stein, *International Law in Internal Law: Toward Internationalization of Central-Eastern European Constitutions?*, 88 AM. J. INT'L L. 427 (1994); Wiktor Osiatynski, *Rights in New Constitutions of East Central Europe*, 26 COLUM. HUM. RTS. L. REV. 111, 161 (1994); Dalibor Jilek, *Human Rights Treaties and the New Constitutions*, 8 CONN. J. INT'L L. 407 (1993).

The following table sets forth the relevant constitutional provisions.

Table 1: South American Constitutions and the Status of International Law

Country	Constitutional Provisions
Bolivia (1967; 1995 amend.)	Art. 228: The Constitution of the State is the supreme law of the national juridical system. The courts, judges, and authorities shall apply it with preference over the laws, and the laws with preference over any other resolutions. Art. 96(2): The powers and duties of the President of the Republic are . . . to negotiate and conclude treaties with foreign nations; and to exchange them when ratified by Congress. Art. 59(12): The following are the functions of the legislative power . . . to approve international treaties, concordats and conventions.
Brazil (1988)	Art. 4: The international relations of the Federative Republic of Brazil are governed by the following principles: . . . prevalence of human rights. Art. 49 (I): The National Congress shall have exclusive powers to decide definitively on international treaties, accords or acts that involve serious changes or commitments on the national patrimony. Art. 84(VIII): The President of Brazil has the exclusive power to . . . enter into international treaties, conventions and acts, subject to the approval of Congress.
Chile (1980; 1989 amend.)	Art. 5: It is the duty of state agencies to respect and promote the rights guaranteed by this Constitution and by international treaties ratified by Chile and in force. Art. 32(17):[The President has the power to sign and ratify treaties, but they] must be submitted to the approval of Congress as prescribed for in Article 50, No. 1. Art. 50(1): The exclusive powers of Congress are: to approve or reject international treaties submitted by the President of the Republic prior to ratification thereof. The approval of a treaty shall be subject to the procedures prescribed by a law. The measures which the President of the Republic adopts or the agreements concluded by him or the fulfilment of a treaty in force shall not require new approval by the Congress, except in cases which constitute a matter of law.
Colombia (1991)	Art. 93: International treaties and agreements ratified by the Congress that recognize human rights and that prohibit their limitation in states of emergency have priority domestically. The rights and duties mentioned in this Charter will be interpreted in accordance with international treaties on human rights ratified by Colombia.

Ecuador (1979; 1992 amend.)	Art. 2: The primary function of the State is to strengthen national unity, ensure the effectiveness of fundamental human rights. Art. 44: The State guarantees to all individuals, male and female, who are subject to its jurisdiction, free and effective exercise and enjoyment of the civil, political, economic, social and cultural rights enunciated in declarations, pacts, agreements and other international instruments in force. Art. 137: The Constitution is the supreme law of the land . . . . Secondary norms and others of lesser importance must maintain conformity with constitutional precepts. Laws, decrees, ordinances, provincial, and international treaties or agreements that oppose the Constitution or modify its precepts in any way shall be void.
Paraguay (1992)	Art. 137: The Constitution is the supreme law of the Republic. The Constitution, the international treaties, conventions, and agreements that have been approved and ratified by Congress, the laws dictated by Congress, and other related legal provisions of lesser rank make up the national legal system. This listing reflects the descending order of preeminence. Article 141: International treaties that were properly concluded and approved by a law of Congress and the instruments of ratification which have been exchanged or deposited are part of the domestic legal system in keeping with the order of preeminence established under Article 137. Article 142: International treaties concerning human rights cannot be renounced, but must follow the procedure established herein for the amendment of this Constitution. Article 143: In its international relations, the Republic of Paraguay accepts international law and endorses the following principles: . . . 5) International human rights.
Peru (1993)	Art. 55: Treaties signed by the State and in force are part of national law. Art. 56: Treaties must be approved by the Congress before their ratification by the President of the Republic if they involve the following matters: 1) human rights; 2) sovereignty, dominion, or integrity of the State . . . . Art. 57: The President of the Republic may accept or ratify treaties without need for the prior approval of the Congress in matters not covered in the previous article. In all these cases, he must render an accounting to the Congress. When the treaty affects constitutional provisions, it must be approved by the same procedure that applies to amending the Constitution before being ratified by the President of the Republic. The denunciation of treaties falls under the authority of the President of the Republic who is responsible for rendering account to the Congress. In the case of treaties subject to the approval of the Congress, their denunciation requires its prior approval.

Uruguay (1967; reinstated 1995)	Art. 85(7): The General Assembly is competent . . . to declare war and to approve or disapprove, by an absolute majority of the full membership of both chambers, the treaties of peace, alliance, commerce and conventions or contracts of any nature which the Executive Power may make with foreign powers. Art. 85(20): The Executive shall . . . conclude and sign treaties, the approval of the Legislative Power being necessary to their ratification.
Venezuela (1961)	Art. 128: International treaties or conventions conducted by the National Executive must be approved by a special law in order to be valid, unless they concern the execution or completion of pre-existing obligations of the Republic, the application of principles expressed by it, the execution of ordinary acts in international relations, or the exercise of powers which the law expressly bestows on the National Executive.

The constitutions which place international law on a par with domestic law expose international norms to subsequent statutory invalidation.[89] International treaty norms thus become vulnerable and manipulable, depending on the sentiments and mood of transient legislatures. The Peruvian Constitution clearly states that treaties are a part of "national law."[90] The Venezuelan Constitution requires the legislature to pass laws validating all international treaties or conventions, relegating these international norms to the status of a domestic law.[91] Other constitutions do not explicitly address the status of international law, but divide power over international treaties among the executive, who concludes treaties, and the legislative branch, which ratifies treaties. Domestic constitutional law interpreting these provisions frequently relegates international treaties to the status of a domestic statute.[92]

---

89. In United States jurisprudence, this is known as the "last-in-time" rule. *See* RESTATEMENT, *supra* note 35, § 115(1), (2).

90. CONST. PERU art. 55. *See also* Table 1 *supra*.

91. *See* CONST. VENEZ. art. 128; Table 1 *supra*. Venezuela has determined, via its Constitution, that, for the most part, treaties will be non-self-executing, requiring domestic facilitating legislation prior to having legal effect. *See* RESTATEMENT, *supra* note 35, §§ 111(3), 111(4). Most commentators believe that non-self-executing treaties, once executed, are tantamount to domestic statutes. *See id.* § 111, cmts. (h), (i), reporter's notes 5, 6. *See also* Héctor Gros Espiell, *Los Tratados sobre Derechos Humanos y el Derecho Interno* in TEMAS DE DERECHO INTERNACIONAL: EN HOMENAJE A FRIDA M. PFIERTER DE ARMAS BAREA 61, 63 (R.E. Vineusa ed., 1989); MÓNICA PINTO, TEMAS DE DERECHOS HUMANOS 66 (1997) (stating that Venezuela's Constitution places international norms on a par with domestic law).

92. *See* CONST. URU. arts. 85(7), 85(20). *See also* Table 1 *supra*; Héctor Gros Espiell, *La Constitución y los Tratados Internacionales* (Ministerio de Relaciones Exteriores, Montevideo, 1997) (discussing Uruguayan constitutional jurisprudence interpreting these provisions and concluding that international law and domestic law share the same legal status); PINTO, *supra* note 91, at 66 (stating that Uruguay's Constitution places international norms on a par with domestic law). See also CONST. BOL. arts. 59(12); 96(2); 228; PINTO, *supra* note 91,

On the other hand, some constitutions explicitly elevate international norms, or a specific group of international norms. Paraguay's Constitution ranks sources of law, with international treaties and conventions falling below its Constitution but above "laws dictated by Congress."[93] Colombia's Constitution elevates international treaties that "recognize human rights and that prohibit their limitation in states of emergency."[94] Ecuador's Constitution is not explicit in its treatment of international human rights norms; it sanctifies "fundamental human rights"[95] and *guarantees* "free and effective exercise and enjoyment of the civil, political, economic, social and cultural rights enunciated in declarations, pacts, agreements and other international instruments in force,"[96] while it relegates international treaties or agreements to the status of a "secondary" or non-constitutional norm.[97] Juxtaposing these constitutional provisions, one can logically conclude that international treaty norms float somewhere between the Constitution and domestic law in Ecuador's domestic legal hierarchy.

Other constitutions leave the status of international norms ambiguous. Chile's Constitution, for example, mimics the constitutional division of power among the executive and the legislative branches found in the Uruguayan and Bolivian Constitutions,[98] suggesting that international norms would be on a par with domestic norms. Yet, a relatively recent amendment to Chile's Constitution charges state agencies with the duty "to respect and promote the rights guaranteed" in international treaties,[99] suggesting that such norms are cloaked with special domestic standing. Thus, Chile's Constitution is rather ambiguous regarding the precise status of international norms.[100]

The legal status of international treaties and conventions provides an additional axis for comparison of South American constitutions. Whether constitutions place international norms on a par with domestic law, above domestic law, or leave the issue unresolved, none of these

---

at 66 (arguing that Bolivia's Constitution places international norms on a par with domestic law).

93. CONST. PARA. art. 137. *See also* Table 1 *supra*; PINTO, *supra* note 91, at 64-65.

94. CONST. COLOM. art. 93. *See also* Table 1 *supra*; PINTO, *supra* note 91, at 69.

95. CONST. ECUADOR art. 2. *See also* Table 1 *supra*.

96. CONST. ECUADOR art. 44.

97. *See id.* art. 137.

98. *See* Table 1 *supra*.

99. CONST. CHILE art. 5. *See also* Table 1 *supra*.

100. *See* PINTO, *supra* note 91, at 69-70 (arguing that Chile's Constitution is ambiguous with regard to the status of international human rights norms).

Brazil's Constitution is similarly ambiguous. On one hand, the Brazilian Constitution lauds its commitment to human rights in its opening articles. *See* CONST. BRAZ. art. 4 (1988). On the other hand, it mirrors those constitutions which mechanically divide power among the executive and legislative branches. *See id.* arts. 49(I), 84(VIII); Table 1 *supra*; Espiell, *supra* note 91, at 63.

constitutions explicitly or implicitly place international law on par with
the constitution itself.[101]

C.   *Argentina's Constitution In Context: Pre-1994*

The previous section develops two axes upon which constitutions
may be compared vis-à-vis international human rights. In terms of
substance, some constitutions incorporate the skeletal spirit of
international human rights treaties, while others incorporate their
nuances and breadth. In terms of status, some constitutions place
international treaties on a par with domestic law, while others anoint
international norms with a status superior to domestic law. Argentina's
1994 constitutional reforms dramatically changed where its Constitution
falls on these two axes.

1.   Constitutional Status of Human Rights

Prior to 1994, Argentina's Constitution did not explicitly address
the status of international treaties. Similar to the Uruguayan, Brazilian
and Bolivian Constitutions,[102] Argentina's Constitution divided power
over international treaties among the three branches.[103] The
Constitution also stated in Article 31 that the Constitution, the laws that
are passed by Congress pursuant to the Constitution, and treaties with
foreign powers are the supreme law of the land; and that provincial
authorities are obliged to conform to this law[104]—suggesting some type
of parity between the Constitution and international treaties. On the
other hand, the Constitution provided in Article 27 that "[t]he federal
government will be charged with relations with foreign powers, through

---

101. *See* PINTO, *supra* note 91, at 66; Espiell, *supra* note 91, at 64.

While none of the South American constitutions place international norms on par with
constitutional norms, some European constitutions arguably elevate international norms to a
constitutional status. *Id.* at 64-65. *See also supra* notes 93-97 and accompanying text; CONST.
CZECH REP. art. 10 (Dec. 21, 1992)("Ratified and promulgated international treaties on human
rights and fundamental freedoms to which the Czech Republic is a party are directly binding and
take precedence over the law"); CONST. SLOVK. art. 1 (Sept. 8, 1992) ("International treaties on
human rights and basic liberties that were ratified by the Slovakia and promulgated in a manner
determined by law take precedence over its own laws, providing that they secure a greater extent
of constitutional rights and liberties"); CONST. HUNG. art. 7 (Dec. 31, 1990) ("The legal system
of the Republic of Hungary accepts the universally recognized rules and regulations of
international law, and harmonizes the internal laws and statutes of the country with the
obligations assumed under international law."). Constitutional jurisprudence in some Central
American countries, namely Nicaragua, Panama, and Costa Rica, suggests that some
international norms may have constitutional standing. *See* INSTITUTO INTERAMERICANO DE
DERECHOS HUMANOS, GUÍA SOBRE APLICACIÓN DEL DERECHO INTERNACIONAL EN LA
JURISDICCIÓN INTERNA 42 (1996).

102. *See supra* notes 92 & 105 and accompanying text.

103. *See supra* notes 26-28 and accompanying text.

104. *See* CONST. ARG. (1853) art. 31.

treaties that are in conformity with the public principles that are set forth in this Constitution,"[105] implying that international norms stand inferior to the Constitution. While many commentators interpreted Article 31 through a federalist lens, focusing on what it stated about province/federal government relations rather than what it stated about the status of international treaties vis-à-vis the Constitution,[106] the juxtaposition of these various provisions created some ambiguity regarding the precise status of international norms.[107]

Argentine constitutional jurisprudence resolved some of this ambiguity prior to the 1994 constitutional reform. The most significant case was *Ekmekdjián v. Sofovich*.[108] In this case, the petitioner sought to respond to some religiously "inflammatory" statements that the respondent read on television.[109] In support, the petitioner relied on the "right to reply" found in the American Convention.[110] Yet, domestic law also governed the "right to reply." In ultimately relying on the American Convention, the Court decided that an international treaty, properly ratified pursuant to the Constitution,[111] stands superior to

---

105. *Id.* art. 27.

106. *See* PINTO, *supra* note 91, at 65 (discussing Article 31 and comparing it to similar language in the U.S. Constitution, which sets forth the preeminence of federal law in the legal hierarchy); Espiell, *supra* note 91, at 62.

107. *See* Marisa A. Graham & Juan P. Cafiero, *Tratados sobre Derechos Humanos, in* JERARQUÍA CONSTITUCIONAL DE LOS TRATADOS INTERNACIONALES, *supra* note 38, at 27, 28-31.

Many of the members of the Constitutional Assembly discussed this ambiguity. *See* PROYECTOS INGRESADOS NO. 3, CONVENCION NACIONAL CONSTITUYENTE [Record of Constitutional Assembly] [hereinafter REC. CONST. ASSEMBLY], June 14, 1994, 10:00 P.M., at 547 (statement of Horacio Rosatti) (discussing the ambiguity that Article 31 creates); REC. CONST. ASSEMBLY NO. 19, June 17, 1994, 11:00 A.M., at 786 (statement of Guillermo E. Estevez Boero, Alfredo P. Bravo & Norberto L. La Porta) (same); REC. CONST. ASSEMBLY NO. 22, June 22, 1994, 1:00 P.M., at 888 (statement of Augusto J.M. Alasino) (same); REC. CONST. ASSEMBLY NO. 24, June 22, 1994, 5:00 P.M., at 1013 (statement of Alberto A. Natale, Pablo A. Cardinale & Carlos A. Caballero Martín) (same); REC. CONST. ASSEMBLY NO. 26, June 23, 1994, 1:30 P.M., at 1255 (statement of Juan C. Hitters) (discussing the conflict between Articles 27 and 31); REC. CONST. ASSEMBLY NO. 35, June 24, 1994, 5:30 P.M., at 1975 (statement of Alberto E. Balestrini) (discussing the tension between Articles 27 and 31 and the disparate views of the status of international treaties and conventions vis-à-vis the Constitution).

108. "Ekmekdjián," CSJN (1992), *reprinted in* JUAN ANTONIO TRAVIESO, JURISPRUDENCIA DE LOS TRIBUNALES ARGENTINOS SOBRE DERECHOS HUMANOS Y GARANTIAS 11 (1996) (concerning right to reply and freedom of speech) (translations of the case are by the Author).

109. *Id.* at 11.

110. *See id.* at 11. *See also* American Convention, *supra* note 44, art. 14(1) ("Anyone injured by inaccurate or offensive statements or ideas disseminated to the public in general by a legally regulated medium of communication has the right to reply or to make a correction using the same communications outlet, under such conditions as the law may establish.").

111. CONST. ARG. (1853) art. 86(14) (Executive concludes and signs treaties), art. 67(19) (Congress approves treaties).

domestic law.[112] Thus, as opposed to the practice in the United States,[113] a subsequent domestic law could not trump an international treaty provision, and Argentine domestic law could not constrict the scope or efficacy of international treaty provisions.[114] Furthermore, the Court concluded that an international treaty provision, properly ratified, is presumptively self-executing[115] as long as it is capable of "immediate operation, without additional institutions."[116] Thus, *Ekmekdjián* placed international treaties on a supra-statutory level and, by holding that they were presumptively self-executing documents, transformed them into a potent source of law which the Court itself harnessed to decide the case.

However, two subsequent Supreme Court opinions limited the reach of *Ekmekdjián*. In *Fibraca*, the Court examined a potential conflict between a treaty with the Holy See and the Constitution.[117] The Court refused to extend the holding of *Ekmekdjián* to the Constitution, stating that international treaties' supra-statutory status did not place them on a par with the Constitution.[118] The Court thereby underscored that the Constitution reigned supreme in the legal hierarchy. In *Hagelin*,[119] the lower court relied on the American Convention in granting the plaintiff indemnification for his daughter's illegal detention and subsequent disappearance, rather than a domestic indemnification law designed primarily as a remedy in light of Argentina's economic problems in the late 1980s.[120] While the Court reaffirmed the supremacy of international law over domestic law, it held that the former trumps the latter only in the face of a real legal conflict, such that the conflicting laws must be significantly, if not completely, congruent and the underlying purposes behind the laws must be similar.[121] Thus, if a domestic law is designed to deal with a specific problem, as the indemnification law in question, and an international norm deals more generically with a similar issue, the international norm is not deemed to

---

112. *See* Graham & Cafiero, *supra* note 107, at 28 (citing several lower court cases that support the legal conclusions in *Ekmekdjián*).

113. *See supra* note 89 and accompanying text (discussing the last-in-time rule in the United States).

114. *See* "Cafés la Virginia S.A.," CSJN [1995-I] J.A. 686 (holding that any administrative action in violation of international treaties violates the supremacy of those treaties over internal law).

115. *See supra* note 35 (discussing self-executing treaties).

116. "Ekmekdjián," CSJN (1992), at 16.

117. *See* "Fibraca Constructora, S.C.A.," CSJN 154 E.D. 164, 165 (1993).

118. *See id.* at 165.

119. "Hagelin, Ragnar," CSJN (1993), *reprinted in* TRAVIESO, *supra* note 108, at 37.

120. *See id.* at 37-38. *See also* American Convention, *supra* note 44, art. 5(1) ("Every person has the right to have his physical, mental, and moral integrity respected.").

121. *See* "Hagelin," CSJN (1993) at 39.

be in conflict and may not trump the domestic norm.[122] On the eve of the constitutional reform, Argentina's Constitution could be aligned with those constitutions that place international law somewhere between domestic law and constitutional norms.

2. Substantive Treatment of Human Rights

As far as substantive treatment of human rights, Argentina's pre-1994 Constitution was similar to those constitutions which are mere skeletal reflections of international human rights norms.[123] Admittedly, the core of Argentina's Constitution pre-dated the advent of international human rights; however, the last two constitutional amendments (1949 and 1957)[124] followed the United Nation's embracing of the Universal Declaration of Human Rights[125] and could have provided an ample and meaningful opportunity for substantive incorporation of human rights norms.

Argentina's pre-1994 Constitution[126] was "missing" several rights, most notably an equal protection-type clause,[127] a prohibition on imprisonment for debts,[128] the right to peaceful assembly,[129] and family/children's rights.[130] Of the fifteen rights that Argentina shared with the international instruments, twelve were rather minimal, mimicking only the spirit of international norms rather than their scope or depth.[131] In addition, Argentina's pre-1994 "state of emergency" provisions are classically expansive, providing the executive relatively unconstrained power to suspend constitutional guarantees in the face of an "internal disorder."[132]

---

122. *See id.*

123. *See supra* notes 56-81 and accompanying text.

124. *See* CONST. ARG. (amended 1949 and 1979).

125. *See* Universal Declaration, *supra* note 44.

126. See also Table 2: Argentina's Constitutional Treatment of Human Rights: Past and Present, in the Appendix, which compares Argentina's pre-1994 and post-1994 Constitutions in terms of human rights.

127. *See* International Covenant, *supra* note 44, art. 3; American Convention, *supra* note 44, art. 24.

128. *See* International Covenant, *supra* note 44, art. 11; American Convention, *supra* note 44, art. 7(7).

129. *See* International Covenant, *supra* note 44, art. 21; American Convention, *supra* note 44, art. 15.

130. *See* International Covenant, *supra* note 44, arts. 23-24; American Convention, *supra* note 44, arts. 17(5), 18-20.

131. Table 2 indicates that Argentina shares nineteen rights with the International Covenant and the American Convention. Table 2 also indicates with a "—" sign that eleven of these rights are significantly less robust than their treaty counterparts.

132. CONST. ARG. (1853) arts. 23-29.

D. Argentina's 1994 Constitution

Argentina's 1994 constitutional reform altered the Constitution's standing in terms of status and substance. Article 75(22) endowed nine international human rights treaties with constitutional standing,[133] and otherwise reaffirmed the Supreme Court's decisions[134] by providing all other international treaties with supra-statutory standing.[135] Thus, domestic law cannot trump an international norm, and certain international human rights norms, to be interpreted in harmony with the rest of the 1994 Constitution,[136] stand on par with the Constitution itself.

In terms of substance, it is important first to examine Argentina's new Constitution independent of Article 75(22), as set forth in the final column of Table 2 in the Appendix. Without Article 75(22), Argentina's Constitution remains highly reminiscent of its predecessor and similar to those constitutions that reflect the spirit, rather than the scope, of human rights treaties.[137] Significantly, in reforming the Constitution in 1994, Argentina left Chapter 1, "Declaration, Rights, Guarantees," almost untouched.[138] Chapter 2, "New Rights and Guarantees," a fresh addition to the 1994 Constitution, presented Argentina with the opportunity to "update" many rights, adding nuances to make its constitutional rights as robust as those in the international documents. Chapter 2, however, only nominally improved Argentina's substantive inclusion of human rights as set forth in the American Convention and International Covenant. The Constitution now provides explicitly for "equality of opportunity and treatment and the full exercise of rights recognized in this Constitution";[139] "real equality of opportunity between men and women in accessing elected and party

---

133. *See supra* note 44 and accompanying text.

134. *See supra* notes 108-22 and accompanying text (discussing recent Argentine Supreme Court decisions regarding status of international law).

135. *See supra* note 48 and accompanying text.

136. *See supra* note 46 and accompanying text. *See infra* note 242 and accompanying text.

137. *See supra* notes 55-78 and accompanying text.

138. Chapter 1 of the 1994 Constitution is identical to its 1853 predecessor. With the exception of some relatively minor changes in Article 22 (regarding the nature of representative government) and some mildly limiting language in the "state of emergency" provision ("Congress may not confer on the National Executive, nor the Provincial Legislatures or the Provincial Governors extraordinary powers, nor the whole of the public authority, nor grant them acts of submission or supremacy whereby the lives, honor or the property of Argentineans will be at the mercy of governments or any person whatsoever"), CONST. ARG. (1994) arts. 22, 29 (underlined language indicates 1994 amendments). *See also* Table 2 in the Appendix which shows that those rights which were "missing" from the pre-1994 Constitution are generally missing from the post-1994 Constitution.

139. CONST. ARG. (1994) art. 75(23). *See also* International Covenant, *supra* note 44, art. 2; American Convention, *supra* note 44 art. 1.

office";[140] habeas corpus;[141] ethnic and religious minority rights;[142] and somewhat veiled allusions to children's rights.[143] In addition, Chapter 2 begins with a reaffirmation of the Constitution and the democratic system.[144] Otherwise, Chapter 2 differs from the type of fundamental rights included in the International Covenant and the American Convention, addressing instead political corruption,[145] political parties,[146] environmental rights,[147] and consumer protection.[148] While these aforementioned rights, if implemented, will significantly improve the human rights situation in Argentina, Argentina's Constitution still lacks explicit reference to many rights, most notably, the right to peaceful assembly[149] and protection from imprisonment for debts.[150]

The Argentine Constitutional Assembly also failed to embrace the constitutional reform process as an opportunity to fortify those bare-bones rights which the 1853 Constitution listed. Protections for criminal defendants remain scant;[151] with the exception of the added

---

140. CONST. ARG. (1994) art. 37 ("This Constitution guarantees full enjoyment of political rights, in accordance with the principle of popular sovereignty and with laws dictated pursuant thereto. Suffrage is universal, equal, secret, and mandatory. Real equality of opportunity between men and women in accessing elected and party office is guaranteed through positive actions in the regulation of political parties and in the electoral system."). *See also* International Covenant, *supra* note 44, arts. 3, 25; American Convention, *supra* note 44 arts. 23-24.

141. *See* CONST. ARG. (1994) art. 43 ("When the right which has been harmed, restricted, altered, or threatened related to physical liberty or to a case of illegal worsening in the form or conditions of detention, or in the forced disappearance of persons, the writ of *habeas corpus* may be imposed by the affected person or by someone else to benefit him; the judge is to resolve the issue immediately, even while there is a state of siege."). Article 43 also provides for an *amparo*, which is a "quick, expedient action to protect himself, as long as no other more appropriate judicial means exist, against any act or omission of public authorities or any individuals, who actually or imminently, harm, restrict, alter or threaten rights and guarantees recognized by this Constitution." *Id. See* International Covenant, *supra* note 44, art. 9; American Convention, *supra* note 44 art. 7(1-6).

142. *See* CONST. ARG. (1994) art. 75(17) ("Congress shall have the power . . . [t]o recognize the ethnic and cultural pre-existence of indigenous Argentinean peoples."). *See also* International Covenant, *supra* note 44, art. 27.

143. *See* CONST. ARG. art. 75(23) ("Congress shall have the power . . . [t]o legislate and promote means of positive action that guarantee . . . the rights of children [and] women.").

144. *See id.* art. 36 ("This Constitution remains in power even when its observance is interrupted by acts of force against the institutional order and the democratic system. These acts are irredeemably null . . . .").

145. *See id.* ("Congress shall pass a law concerning public ethics for the exercise of that function . . . .").

146. *See id.* art. 38.

147. *See id.* art. 41.

148. *See id.* art. 42.

149. *See* International Covenant, *supra* note 44, art. 21; American Convention, *supra* note 44, art. 15.

150. *See* International Covenant, *supra* note 44, art. 11; American Convention, *supra* note 44, art. 7(7).

151. *See* CONST. ARG. (1994), art. 18. *See also* International Covenant, *supra* note 44, art. 14; American Convention, *supra* note 44, art. 8.

habeas corpus rights, the provisions for liberty and security of the person are thin;[152] and freedom of expression and religion clauses are generally narrower in scope than international counterparts.[153] In sum, of the nineteen rights that Argentina's Constitution now shares with the international instruments, eleven are significantly less "muscular" than the international norms, without the nuances, subtleties, and refinements included in the international instruments.[154] The "state of emergency" clause, which, despite being the target of constitutional reform, does not circumscribe the number or types of rights that may be suspended, potentially undermines the potency and scope of all constitutional protections.[155] Thus, Argentina's Constitution would have remained in first group of constitutions in terms of substance.

Now consider the effect of Article 75(22). The Argentine Constitution is no longer a succinct document containing 110 constitutional provisions but rather a compendium of the constitutional text and the nine human rights treaties which, by virtue of their constitutional status, are effectively incorporated into the constitutional text. Therefore, every right, every privilege, every guarantee, that the anointed human rights treaties grant are part of Argentina's Constitution. Whereas some constitutions merely incorporate the spirit of human rights treaties[156] and others more accurately reflect their scope and breadth,[157] Argentina's Constitution takes a further step: wholesale incorporation of the treaties themselves. The Constitution now mirrors these select human rights treaties, identical in scope, form, and substance. In this sense, Argentina's actions are unique in South America and, arguably, the world. The 1994 constitutional reforms thus forced a shift along both comparative axes, substance and status, leaving the Argentine Constitution unparalleled in South America.

---

152. *See* CONST. ARG. (1994), arts. 18, 43. *See also* International Covenant, *supra* note 44, art. 9; American Convention, *supra* note 44, art. 7(1-6).

153. *See* CONST. ARG. (1994), art. 14. *See also* International Covenant, *supra* note 44, art. 18; American Convention, *supra* note 44, art. 12.

154. See Table 2 in the Appendix. A comparison of Columns 1 and 2 with Column 4 shows that the Argentine Constitution shares nineteen rights with the international instruments. Of these nineteen rights, eleven have "—" signs indicating that they are less expansive than their international counterparts.

155. *See* CONST. ARG. (1994), arts. 23, 29. *See also* International Covenant, *supra* note 44, art. 4; American Convention, *supra* note 44, art. 8.

156. *See supra* notes 55-78 and accompanying text.

157. *See supra* notes 79-86 and accompanying text.

IV. ASSESSING THE INTERNALIZATION STRATEGY: A SCOREBOARD

Some human rights advocates laud Argentina's constitution-alization of human rights treaties as a bold step worthy of emulation.[158] On the "ground," however, Argentina's internalization experiment is nascent and virtually invisible. The Argentine government continues to violate human rights;[159] most lawyers have yet to unleash their new Constitution's potential; and the average individual is so skeptical of law and the possibility for law to vindicate any individual rights, let alone a new international human rights template, that the potential beneficiaries remain relatively ignorant of the constitutional changes. While Argentina internalized international law on paper, the nation clearly does not yet obey, let alone comply with, international human rights law.[160]

Why has this internalization strategy been largely ineffective? The answer lies, in great part, in transnational legal process theory, more specifically, with the transnational actors that drive transnational legal process. Transnational actors constitute and reconstitute interests, acting as antennae that reach into the depths of society, prodding corporal transformation. It is only logical that the number of transnational actors, or antennae, bears a direct relationship to the effectiveness of internalization strategies. Successful internalization

---

158. In particular, the *Centro de Estudios Legales y Sociales* (Center for Legal and Social Studies, or "CELS"), a leading Argentine human rights advocacy group, argues that Article 75(22) is a panacea to Argentina's human rights difficulties. *See* Interview with Martín Abregú, Director of CELS, in Buenos Aires, Arg. (June 24, 1997). *See also infra* notes 252-76 and accompanying text. In a series of lectures in June 1997, human rights advocates applauded the constitutionalization of human rights treaties. *See* Marcela Rodriguez, Woman's Rights Activist, Lecture to Summer Institute in International Law at Universidad de Palermo, Buenos Aires, Arg. (June 24, 1997) (describing Article 75(22) as a "good tool" for human rights activists); Raúl Alfonsín, Former President of Argentina, Lecture to Summer Institute in International Law at Universidad de Palermo, Buenos Aires, Arg. (June 25, 1997) (describing Article 75(22) as an "important" and "big step" and further describing Argentina's 1994 Constitution as the "Human Rights Constitution").

159. *See Argentina: Death and Corruption*, ECONOMIST, May 30, 1998, at 34 (discussing corruption, police brutality, and politicized judiciary); Calvin Sims, *Argentina's Bereft Mothers: And Now, a New Wave*, N.Y. TIMES, Nov. 18, 1997, at A4 (discussing the continuation of post-"dirty war" police violence and killings, and noting the rise in number of police brutality cases and recent condemnation by the United Nations Human Rights Committee for the continued use of torture in police stations and prisons, despite Argentina's ratification of the U.N. Convention Against Torture); *War on the Media in Argentina*, N.Y. TIMES, Sept. 16, 1997, at A30; Anthony Faiola, *Argentina Still Grappling with Oppressive Past*, WASH. POST, Oct. 15, 1997, at A25 (discussing Argentina's restrictions on press freedom, as well as police, governmental, and judicial corruption); Ivan Briscoe, *Argentine Murder Inquiry Points Finger at Police*, GUARDIAN, Apr. 9, 1997, at 7 (discussing linkage between the police and the Mafia in the murder of a noted photographer); Jonathan Friedland, *Police Give a Black Eye to Buenos Aires*, WALL ST. J., Apr. 1, 1997, at A15 (discussing police corruption).

160. *See supra* notes 9-12 and accompanying text for discussion of the distinction between compliance and obedience.

314   *COLUMBIA JOURNAL OF TRANSNATIONAL LAW*   [37:281

strategies—internalization strategies that breed a nation's desire to obey the law—are driven by the identity, enthusiasm, and relationships among transnational actors. Synergistic clusters of transnational actors—or epistemic communities[161]—are integral if international law is to permeate a nation effectively. Thus, a strategy that engages numerous transnational actors, from social, political and legal spheres, and that creates mutually reinforcing relationships between actors, is bound to affect a nation's psyche. Both the problems that Argentina's internalization strategy faces, and its incipient promises, may be traced to the extent to which various transnational actors participated in Article 75(22)'s epistemic community.

A.   *The Problems*

1.   The Constitutional Assembly: Where Are the Transnational Actors?

Some commentators argue that robust debate helps embed law in a nation's psyche.[162] In terms of transnational legal process, select transnational actors may stimulate discussion about an international norm, which in turn may spur debate, thereby animating new transnational actors and, whether intentionally or inadvertently, propagating an international norm. The Constitutional Assembly provided a potential focal point for such discourse, and yet several transnational actors, most notably the human rights community, stood on the sidelines as the Constitutional Assembly codified Argentina's internalization strategy. These transnational actors were relatively disinterested prior to the Constitutional Assembly because the politics surrounding the Pacto de Olivos contaminated its legitimacy. In addition, stifling procedures and dynamics during the Constitutional Assembly effectively excluded these transnational actors, who were

---

161. *See* Koh, *supra* note 7, at 2656; Peter M. Haas, *Introduction* to *Epistemic Communities and International Policy Coordination*, 46 INT'L ORG. 1, 3-4 (1992) ("An epistemic community is a network of professionals with recognized expertise and competence in a particular domain and an authoritative claim to policy-relevant knowledge within that domain or issue-area . . . . Members of transnational epistemic communities can influence state interests either by directly identifying them for decision makers or by illuminating the salient dimensions of an issue from which the decision makers may then deduce their interests. The decision makers in one state may, in turn, influence the interests and behavior of other states, thereby increasing the likelihood of convergent state behavior and international policy coordination, informed by the causal beliefs and policy preferences of the epistemic community."). *See also* Symposium, *International Law and International Relations Theory: Building Bridges*, 86 AM. SOC'Y INT'L L. PROC. 167, 171 (1992) (remarks by Kenneth Abbott).

162. *See generally* CARLOS SANTIAGO NINO, THE CONSTITUTION OF DELIBERATIVE DEMOCRACY 144-86 (1996) (discussing the legitimating merit of robust debate of legal, particularly constitutional, issues in Argentina and citing numerous political scientists who support his view).

already skeptical, from engaging in meaningful discourse. As a result, few transnational actors left the actual Constitutional Assembly with much energy or enthusiasm regarding Article 75(22).

a.   The Constitutional Assembly: the Prologue

The Constitutional Assembly arrived with little fanfare or advance billing.[163]   The newspapers tended to bury stories about the Constitutional Assembly.   Taxi drivers were unaware that the Constitutional Assembly was occurring. Many lawyers, including those involved in human rights issues, were skeptical and suspicious of the Constitutional Assembly and thus greeted its arrival in a nonchalant fashion.

Because of the fragility of law in Argentina,[164] legal reform efforts are generally regarded with skepticism and caution. Skepticism of the Constitutional Assembly, however, was justifiably more intense. The Constitutional Assembly grew out of the Pacto de Olivos,[165] which was little more than a political bargain: the Radical Party[166] agreed to support amendments to the Constitution which would allow President Menem to run for a second term, and, in exchange, the Peronists[167] supported broadening the scope of the reform effort.[168] Thus, the Constitutional Assembly was tainted with political compromise and bargaining, leaving many members of the human rights communities doubting whether the Constitutional Assembly would be a serious forum in which to broker positive legal changes.

Furthermore, the Pacto de Olivos delineated several issues which the Constitutional Assembly would definitely address, as well as several

---

163. Many of the statements contained herein are impressional.   The Constitutional Assembly began on May 25, 1994. I spent August 1994 in Argentina and attended some of the Constitutional Assembly's proceedings.

164. *See* NINO, *supra* note 29, at 47-48 (arguing that Argentina's disregard for the law has deep historical roots). For in-depth discussion of reasons for Argentina's lack of respect for the law, see generally CARLOS SANTIAGO NINO, UN PAÍS AL MARGEN DE LA LEY 53-136 (1992). *See also* Andrew Arato, *Forms of Constitution Making and Theories of Democracy*, 17 CARDOZO L. REV. 191, 199 (1995) ("[I]n Argentina . . . there is little constitutionalism."); Irwin P. Stotzky, *The Fragile Bloom of Democracy*, 44 U. MIAMI L. REV. 105 (1989).

For general discussion of the weak state of constitutionalism in Latin America, see Keith S. Rosenn, *The Success of Constitutionalism in the United States and Its Failure in Latin America: An Explanation*, 22 U. MIAMI INTER-AM. L. REV. 1 (1990); Keith Rosenn, *Federalism in the Americas in Comparative Perspective*, 26 U. MIAMI INTER-AM. L. REV. 1 (1994). *See also* Rohter, *supra* note 24, at 1.

165. *See supra* notes 37-42 and accompanying text.

166. The Radical Party is the more liberal of the two main parties. At the time, ex-President Alfonsín was at its helm. *See supra* note 30 and accompanying text.

167. The Peronist Party is now the more conservative of the two parties. President Menem is a member of the Peronist Party. *See supra* note 38 and accompanying text.

168. *See* Vega, *supra* note 38, at 2-5. As evidence of this political compromise, most of the topics included in the mandatory list of reforms concern executive powers and the length of the presidential term. *See supra* note 40.

areas which the Constitutional Assembly might address.[169] Human rights, however, was not on either list.[170] In the build-up to the Constitutional Assembly, there was little reason for the human rights community to become animated, for human rights were ostensibly outside the purview of constitutional reform.

b. The Constitutional Assembly Proceedings

During the Constitutional Assembly itself, the absence of human rights is striking. In the record, I expected to find passionate debate in support, fueled by the human rights community and the specter of the military's human rights abuses.[171] Instead, debate was flat and antiseptic, devoid of substantive discussion of human rights concerns.[172] I attribute this to the procedures and political dynamics of the Constitutional Assembly which exacerbated the human rights community's indifference by effectively constricting its discursive

---

169. *See supra* notes 40-42 and accompanying text.

170. Admittedly, a few of the issues on the "optional" list, *supra* note 41, tangentially broached particular human rights norms. For example, one issue on the "optional" list was *habeas corpus* and direct constitutional appeals, an area that would potentially bolster criminal defendant rights. Other issues for review were "indigenous communities" and "preservation of the environment." The former is a concern of the International Covenant. *See* International Covenant, *supra* note 44, art. 27. The latter is the subject of international treaties. *See, e.g.*, International Covenant on Economic, Social and Cultural Rights, *supra* note 44, art. 12(2)(b). However, there was no "human rights committee," where a full panoply of issues could be discussed, codified, and/or prioritized.

171. See *supra* note 29 and accompanying text for discussion of human rights abuses during the military dictatorship.

172. The Constitutional Assembly's limited discussion of the military's human rights abuses took place in rather guarded, controlled terms. Given the extent and horrific nature of the human rights abuses, one could imagine impassioned speeches about human rights and the need to take extraordinary measures to protect them. The Record of the Constitutional Assembly reveals that very few members even discussed Argentina's human rights record. Those that did were rather dispassionate in their discussions. *See, e.g.*, REC. CONST. ASSEMBLY No. 19, June 17, 1994, 11:00 A.M., at 784 (statement of Teresita B. Serrat) (veiled reference to the military's human rights abuses, while referencing democratic nation's duty to respect human rights); REC. CONST. ASSEMBLY No. 22, June 22, 1994; 1:00 P.M., at 930 (statement of Mabel G. de Marelli & Mario Dei Castelli) (proposed amendment to include executive oversight in response to "the historical experience of the Argentine people" that occurs when "the state does not promote as much respect for human rights"); REC. CONST. ASSEMBLY No. 26, June 23, 1994, 1:30 P.M., at 1255 (statement of Juan C. Hitters). Delegates did not delve into the substance of or reasons for human rights. Instead, they merely stated that human rights were "important" and that constitutionalization would showcase their import. *See, e.g.*, REC. CONST. ASSEMBLY No. 16, June 15, 1994, 3:00 P.M., at 611 (statement of Jorge D. Amena, Susana S. de De María, María C. Allenano & Augusto Acuña); REC. CONST. ASSEMBLY No. 19, June 17, 1994, 11:00 A.M., at 784 (statement of Teresita B. Serrat); REC. CONST. ASSEMBLY No. 20, June 21, 1994, 11:00 A.M., at 832 (statement of María Bercoff); REC. CONST. ASSEMBLY No. 21, June 21, 1994, 6:00 P.M., at 849 (statement of Rodolfo O. Ponce de León); REC. CONST. ASSEMBLY No. 21, June 21, 1994, 6:00 P.M., at 861 (statement of Hector J. Carattoli); REC. CONST. ASSEMBLY No. 31, June 24, 1994, 12:00 P.M., at 1701 (statement of Enrique de Vedia); REC. CONST. ASSEMBLY No. 33, June 24, 1994; 2:00 P.M., at 1840 (statement of Emilia Juañuk & Julio Humada).

space. Thus, the human rights community remained, for the most part, aloof and disinterested during most of the Constitutional Assembly.

The Constitutional Assembly charged the Treaty Commission with jurisdiction over human rights concerns.[173] The focus of this Commission was not human rights, but rather, the juridical status of international treaties[174] and Mercosur.[175] Human rights treaties gained special constitutional standing, not necessarily because of their substance, but because they were a symbolic break from the past and thus enhanced Argentina's reputation and standing vis-à-vis Mercosur and other economic integration efforts.[176] Thus, human rights issues arose incidental to these other concerns, woven into the Constitution

---

173. *See supra* note 43 and accompanying text. The Constitutional Assembly discussed the treaty issue at length in the following parts of the Constitutional Assembly's record: REC. CONST. ASSEMBLY, NOS. 3, 7, 10, 15, 16, 17, 19-22, 24-26, 28, 31, 33, 35 (1994).

174. As noted above, Argentina's pre-1994 Constitution was somewhat ambiguous with regard to the status of international treaties, particularly concerning the potential conflict between Article 27 and Article 31. *See supra* notes 102-07 and accompanying text. Many delegates viewed Article 75(22) as a mere opportunity to clarify this hyper-legal ambiguity. *See* REC. CONST. ASSEMBLY NO. 19, June 17, 1994, 11:00 A.M., at 786 (statement of Guillermo E. Estévez Boero, Alfredo P. Bravo & Norberto L. La Porta); REC. CONST. ASSEMBLY NO. 22, June 22, 1994, 1:00 P.M., at 88 (statement of Augusto J.M. Alasino); REC. CONST. ASSEMBLY NO. 24, June 22, 1994, 5:00 P.M., at 1013 (statement of Alberto A. Natale, Pablo A. Cardinale & Carlos A. Caballero Martín); REC. CONST. ASSEMBLY NO. 26, June 23, 1994, 1:30 P.M., at 1255 (statement of Juan C. Hitters); REC. CONST. ASSEMBLY NO. 35, June 24, 1994; 5:30 P.M., at 1975 (statement of Alberto E. Balestrini).

Other delegates argued that constitutionalization was necessary to comport with obligations assumed under the Vienna Convention on the Law of Treaties. *See* REC. CONST. ASSEMBLY No. 19, June 17, 1994, 11:00 A.M., at 786 (statement of Guillermo E. Estevez Boero, Alfredo P. Bravo & Norberto L. La Porta); REC. CONST. ASSEMBLY NO. 21, June 21, 1994, 6:00 P.M., at 848 (statement of Rodolfo O. Ponce de León); REC. CONST. ASSEMBLY NO. 21, June 21, 1994, 6:00 P.M., at 861 (statement of Hector J. Carattoli); REC. CONST. ASSEMBLY No. 31, June 24, 1994, 12:00 P.M., at 1701 (statement of Enrique de Vedia). *See also* Vienna Convention on the Law of Treaties, *opened for signature* May 23, 1969, art. 27, U.N. GAOR, 1st Sess., U.N. Doc. A/CONF.39/27 (1969) ("A party may not invoke the provisions of its internal law as justification for its failure to perform a treaty.").

Others believed that constitutionalization was necessary to comport with Article 2 of the American Convention, which requires that states conform domestic law to international obligations. *See* REC. CONST. ASSEMBLY NO. 21, June 21, 1994, 6:00 P.M., at 849 (statement of Rodolfo O. Ponce de León). *See also* American Convention, *supra* note 44, art. 2.

175. Mercosur is a common market among Argentina, Brazil, Paraguay and Uruguay, based on coordinated reductions in customs tariffs, elimination of non-tariff barriers, a common external tariff, and macroeconomic policy coordination. *See* Treaty Establishing a Common Market (Treaty of Asuncion), Arg.-Braz.-Para.-Uru., Mar. 26, 1991, 30 I.L.M. 1041 (1991); Additional Protocol to the Treaty of Asuncion on the Institutional Structure of Mercosur ("Protocol of Ouro Preto"), Dec. 17, 1994, 34 I.L.M. 1244 (1995) (creation of Mercosur's institutional structure, including Common Market Council, Common Market Group, Mercosur Trade Commission, Joint Parliamentary Commission, Economic and Social Consultative Forum, and Mercosur Administrative Secretariat); Protocol of Brasilia for the Settlement of Disputes, Dec. 17, 1996, 36 I.L.M. 691 (1997) (creation of a Dispute Settlement System). *See generally* Thomas Andrew O'Keefe, *An Analysis of the Mercosur Economic Integration Project from a Legal Perspective*, 28 INT'L LAW. 439 (1994).

176. For a thorough discussion of Mercosur's prominent role in the debates regarding Article 75(22), see *infra* notes 245-51 and accompanying text.

concomitant to more general consideration of international treaties. In a body charged with finding the proper status for international treaties, in particular integration treaties, human rights were an appendage. The human rights community, therefore, did not have a clear, uncluttered forum in which to debate substantive human rights issues. Whereas the human rights community could have been—should have been—Article 75(22)'s most vociferous ally, their spirit remained largely untapped because human rights themselves remained on the periphery of constitutional debate.

The mode of internalization—wholesale constitutionalization of entire human rights treaties—was perhaps the noxious by-product of the relegation of human rights concerns to a relatively disinterested committee. Recall that Argentina, as opposed to many South American countries,[177] did not borrow clauses from human rights treaties to develop and modernize the individual rights portion of its Constitution.[178] Instead, Argentina transplanted *in toto* entire human rights treaties, creating a type of mega-constitutional appendage. With the limited exception of delegates who championed women's rights,[179] delegates were not engaged in debate regarding particular individual rights, but rather, debated whether to annex entire treaties to the Constitution. The presumption throughout the Argentine Constitutional Assembly was "all or nothing"—either incorporation of all or none of the principles contained in any one, or several, human rights treaties.[180]

---

177. *See supra* notes 50-86 and accompanying text.

178. *See supra* notes 137-55 and accompanying text.

179. A few of the delegates focused on treaties dealing with women's/children's rights. *See* REC. CONST. ASSEMBLY NO. 3, June 3, 1994, 6:30 P.M., at 163 (concerned with equality, discrimination, and enhancing enforcement of rights found in the Convention on the Elimination of all Forms of Discrimination Against Women); REC. CONST. ASSEMBLY NO. 15, June 14, 1994, 10:00 P.M., at 575 (statement of Pedro Perette, Susana Melo, Humberto E. Salum & Luis M. Aguilar Torres); REC. CONST. ASSEMBLY NO. 17, June 15, 1994, 9:30 P.M., at 670 (statement of Cecilia Lipsyzc, Juan Schroeder, María Sanchez, Rina Leiva, Daniel García, Adriana Puiggrós & Ana M. Pizzurno) (proposed constitutionalization only of women's rights treaties); REC. CONST. ASSEMBLY NO. 19, June 17, 1994, 11:00 A.M., at 784 (statement of Teresita B. Serrat) (anti-abortion rhetoric veiled in discussion of importance of right to life and women's rights); REC. CONST. ASSEMBLY NO. 22, June 22, 1994; 1:00 P.M., at 910 (statement of María T. Méndez, Dora Rocha de Feldman, María L Casari de Alarcia & Elso G. González) (detailed discussion about the Convention on the Elimination of all Forms of Discrimination Against Women and the desire to constitutionalize this treaty).

Women's rights groups had a multi-issue agenda at the Constitutional Assembly, with their priorities being Article 37, which granted women the right to significant representation in political parties, and Article 75(23), which potentially could have banned abortions but instead set forth a comprehensive social security regime. Thus, women's groups' advocacy on behalf of Article 75(22) may have been incidental to these other concerns.

180. Of sixteen proposals to constitutionalize human rights treaties, fourteen even failed to differentiate among human rights treaties and recommended constitutionalization of all of them. *See* REC. CONST. ASSEMBLY NO. 16, June 15, 1994, 3:00 P.M., at 34; REC. CONST. ASSEMBLY NO. 17, June 15, 1994, 9:30 P.M., at 679-81 (statement of Eduardo S. Barcesat); REC. CONST. ASSEMBLY NO. 19, June 17, 1994, 11:00 A.M., at 779 (statement of María N. Meana García,

While this type of wholesale incorporation may have been the most efficient mode, it was not the most effective. Those few human rights discussions that did occur took place in undifferentiated terms. There was no discussion regarding the death penalty—discussion that could have prompted the support of criminal defendant rights groups; there was no discussion of the freedom of speech—discussion that could have motivated ACLU-like, individual liberties groups; and there was no discussion regarding the rights of indigenous populations—discussion that could have tapped into national and international non-governmental organizations. Different public interest groups may have been engaged if they had perceived an opening in the debate for prioritization, hierarchy, and differentiation among various rights. These groups could have become transformative transnational actors, entrenched in the ultimate success of Article 75(22). Instead, the human rights community, for the most part, remained aloof.

Nevertheless, Article 75(22) ultimately did differentiate among human rights treaties, granting some constitutional status while granting others mere supra-statutory status.[181] This differentiation, however, was not the result of meaningful prioritization of some human rights and thus did not transform potentially interested parties into engaged

---

Pablo Verani, Horacio Massaccesi & Santiago A. Hernandez); REC. CONST. ASSEMBLY NO. 20, June 21, 1994, 11:00 A.M., at 832 (statement of María Bercoff); REC. CONST. ASSEMBLY NO. 20, June 21, 1994, 11:00 A.M., at 835 (statement of Ana M. Dressino); REC. CONST. ASSEMBLY NO. 21, June 21, 1994, 6:00 P.M., at 848 (statement of Nilda Romero); REC. CONST. ASSEMBLY NO. 21, June 21, 1994, 6:00 P.M., at 876 (statement of Angel Prado); REC. CONST. ASSEMBLY NO. 22, June 22, 1994, 1:00 P.M., at 888 (statement of Augusto J.M. Alasino); REC. CONST. ASSEMBLY NO. 22, June 22, 1994, 1:00 P.M., at 898 (statement of Juan F. Armagnague); REC. CONST. ASSEMBLY NO. 22, June 22, 1994, 1:00 P.M., at 910 (statement of María T. Méndez, Dora Rocha de Feldman, María L Casari de Alarcia & Elso G. González); REC. CONST. ASSEMBLY NO. 24, June 22, 1994, 5:00 P.M., at 1071 (statement of Juan M. Pedersoli, Olga C. Abraham & Pascual A. Rampi); REC. CONST. ASSEMBLY NO. 25, June 22, 1994, 8:30 P.M., at 1120; REC. CONST. ASSEMBLY NO. 25, June 22, 1994, 8:30 P.M., at 1138 (statement of Alicia Oliveira & Eugenio R. Zaffaroni); REC. CONST. ASSEMBLY NO. 33, June 24, 1994, 2:00 P.M., at 1822 (statement of Enrique G. Cardosa); REC. CONST. ASSEMBLY NO. 33, June 24, 1994; 2:00 P.M., at 1840 (statement of Emilia Juañuk & Julio Humada).

The following proposals recommended constitutionalization of particular types of human rights treaties: *see* REC. CONST. ASSEMBLY NO. 17, June 15, 1994, 9:30 P.M., at 670 (statement of Cecilia Lipsyzc, Juan Schroeder, María Sanchez, Rina Leiva, Daniel García, Adriana Puiggrós & Ana M. Pizzurno) (only women's rights treaties); REC. CONST. ASSEMBLY NO. 19, June 17, 1994, 11:00 A.M., at 784 (statement of Teresita B. Serrat) (constitutionalization of any treaty including right to life provision and addressing discrimination).

181. *See supra* notes 44-48 and accompanying text. While nine human rights treaties are on par with the Constitution, other human rights treaties merely stand superior to domestic statutes but inferior to the Constitution. The constitutional provision granting all human rights treaties, at a minimum, supra-statutory status codifies the Supreme Court's decision in "Ekmekdijàn," CSJN (1992). Those human rights treaties which do not enjoy constitutional standing nonetheless further enforcement of human rights because, in standing superior to domestic law, they are not susceptible to abrogation by a subsequent statute. *See supra* note 89 and accompanying text for an explanation of the last-in-time rule. However, constitutional provisions could circumscribe and potentially nullify provisions in human rights treaties that do not enjoy constitutional standing.

transnational actors. After the Commission on Integration and International Treaties received recommendations and comments, it drafted a proposal which, reflecting the sentiments discussed above,[182] constitutionalized all the human rights treaties which Argentina had ratified.[183] Yet, Article 75(22) ultimately constitutionalized only nine

---

182. *See supra* note 180 and accompanying text for discussion of proposals regarding breadth of constitutionalization.

183. *See* CONVENCIÓN NACIONAL CONSTITUYENTE, DICTAMEN DE COMISIÓN DE INTEGRACIÓN Y TRATADOS INTERNACIONALES A LA COMISIÓN DE REDACCIÓN NO. 7 (July 13, 1994) [hereinafter DICTAMEN NO. 7] ("International treaties regarding human rights, that are ratified, enjoy constitutional standing, and the rights, liberties and guarantees that they sanctify are considered self-executing") (translations by the Author).

The Commission also listed all human rights treaties that Argentina had ratified, noting that the list was not exclusive and could be amended as Argentina ratified additional treaties. *See* CONVENCIÓN NACIONAL CONSTITUYENTE, DICTAMEN DE COMISIÓN DE INTEGRACIÓN Y TRATADOS INTERNACIONALES A LA COMISIÓN DE REDACCIÓN NO. 11 (July 13, 1994). The list, in chronological order of Argentine ratification, includes the following: Universal Declaration, *supra* note 44; American Convention on the Rights and Duties of Man, *supra* note 44; Convention on the Prevention and Punishment of the Crime of Genocide, *supra* note 44; Geneva Convention on International Humanitarian Law, *adopted* Aug. 12, 1949, 6 U.S.T. 3114, 3217, 3316, 3516, 75 U.N.T.S. 31, 85, 135, 287 (entered into force Oct. 21, 1950); Convention for the Suppression of the Traffic in Persons and of the Exploitation of the Prostitution of Others, *opened for signature* Mar. 21, 1950, 96 U.N.T.S. 271; Convention on the Status of Refugees, 189 U.N.T.S. 150 (entered into force Apr. 22, 1954); Convention on the Political Rights of Women, 193 U.N.T.S. 135 (entered into force July 7, 1954); Supplemental Convention on the Abolition of Slavery, the Slave Trade, and Institutions and Practices Similar to Slavery, 226 U.N.T.S. 3 (entered into force Apr. 30, 1957); Convention Against Discrimination in Education, 429 U.N.T.S. 93 (entered into force Dec. 14, 1960); International Convention on the Elimination of All Forms of Racial Discrimination, *supra* note 44; International Covenant (including Protocol), *supra* note 44; International Covenant on Economic, Social, and Cultural Rights, *supra* note 44; American Convention, *supra* note 44; Abolition of Forced Labor Convention, ILO No. 105, 320 U.N.T.S. 291 (entered into force Jan. 17, 1959); Convention on the Nationality of Married Women, G.A. Res 1040(XI), 11th Sess. (entered into force Jan. 29, 1957); Convention on Consent to Marriage, Minimum Age for Marriage, and Registration of Marriages, 521 U.N.T.S. 231 (entered into force Dec. 9, 1964); Declaration of the Rights of Disabled Persons, G.A. Res. 3447(XXX), U.N. GAOR, 30th Sess., Supp. No. 34, U.N. Doc. A/10034 (1975); Geneva Convention for the Amelioration of the Condition of Wounded, Sick and Shipwrecked Members of the Armed Forces at Sea, 6 U.S.T. 3217, 75 U.N.T.S. 85 (entered into force Oct. 21, 1950); Geneva Convention on the Treatment of Prisoners of War, 6 U.S.T. 3316, 75 U.N.T.S. 135 (entered into force Oct. 21, 1950); Geneva Convention Relative to the Protection of Civilian Persons in Times of War, 6 U.S.T. 3516, T.I.A.S. No. 3365, 75 U.N.T.S. 287 (entered into force Oct. 21, 1950); Protocol Additional to the Geneva Conventions of 12 August 1949 and Relating to the Protection of Victims of International Armed Conflicts, U.N. Doc. A/32/144, Annex I, 16 I.L.M. 1391 (entered into force Dec. 7, 1978); Convention between the American Republics regarding the Status of Aliens in their Respective Territories, *signed* Feb. 20, 1928, 46 Stat. 2753, T.S. No. 815, 132 L.N.T.S. 301; Convention on the Nationality of Women, *signed* Dec. 26, 1933, 49 Stat. 2957 (entered into force Aug. 29, 1934); Inter-American Convention on the Granting of Civil Rights to Women, Pan. Am. Union L. & Treaty Series No. 27; Inter-American Convention on the Granting of Political Rights to Women, *opened for signature* May 2, 1948, 27 U.S.T. 3301, T.I.A.S. No. 8365 (entered into force Mar. 17, 1949); International Convention on the Suppression and Punishment of the Crime of Apartheid, *opened for signature* Nov. 30, 1972, G.A. Res. 3068, U.N. GAOR, 28th Sess., Supp. No. 30, U.N. Doc A/9030 (1974) (entered into force July 19, 1976); International Convention on the Elimination of All Forms of Discrimination Against Women, *supra* note 44; Convention Against Torture and Other Cruel, Inhumane, Degrading Treatment or Punishments, *supra* note 44; Interamerican Convention for

human rights treaties.[184] What transpired to transform the Treaty Commission's inclusive proposal into the relatively restrictive text that became Article 75(22)? Finally, was there debate and discussion regarding prioritization of rights? We will never know and can only speculate. The Constitutional Assembly's *Comisión de Redacción* (Drafting Committee), comprised primarily of delegates from the "pactista" parties,[185] made final drafting decisions behind closed doors, imperviously sequestered from the influence or participation of any NGOs, including human rights organizations. In fact, the Drafting Committee itself grew from political compromise, designed to be the "true space for political and ideological control on the part of the 'pactista' parties."[186] While some commentators speculate on the rationale behind the Drafting Committee's substantial paring down of the proposal,[187] there is no record of its members' discussions and no hard evidence of their reasoning. At the moment when the Constitutional Assembly could have directed the debate on human rights from the generic to the specific, from a monolithic conception to a somewhat differentiated discussion of the merit of some treaties vis-à-vis the merit of others, from a sterile, nonengaging discourse to an animating, participation-invoking discussion, the debate became the exclusive realm of the Drafting Committee.

The Drafting Committee's closed door decisions also hindered Article 75(22)'s ability to tap transnational actors interested more generally in international law issues. The question of whether treaties are self-executing or non-self-executing is integrally related to the juridical status of such treaties.[188] Most countries resolve this issue in the domestic courts, as parties attempt to invoke rights or obligations

---

the Prevention and Punishment of Torture, *supra* note 44; and Convention on the Rights of the Child, *supra* note 44.

The minority proposal coming from the Treaty Commission was the following: "Once ratified and published, international treaties will prevail over the domestic laws of the Nation." DICTAMEN No. 7, *supra* note 183.

See also Graham & Cafiero, *supra* note 107, at 28 (discussing proposal emanating from Treaty Commission).

184. *See supra* note 44 and accompanying text.

185. "Pactista" references the parties to the Pacto de Olivos. *See supra* notes 37-39 and 165-67 and accompanying text.

186. *See* Vega, *supra* note 38, at 11.

187. *See* Graham & Cafiero, *supra* note 107, at 28 (suggesting that the Drafting Committee chose to constitutionalize those treaties that were universal, that bore particular significance to Argentina's recent history, and that came to the aid of those members of society that had been historically underrepresented).

188. *See supra* note 35 and accompanying text.

contained in various treaties.[189] Is Argentina required to enact enabling legislation, other than the ratification instrument, before international treaties, including those which enjoy constitutional status, are deemed operable law? Many delegates proposed explicit clarification of this issue in the Constitution itself.[190] Others viewed constitutionalization as tantamount to creating a group of self-executing treaties and thus proposed constitutionalization as a remedy to extant ambiguity.[191] The Treaty Commission's ultimate proposal explicitly granted self-executing status to the rights contained in the anointed human rights treaties.[192] The Drafting Committee, however, removed all references to the self-executing issue from the Constitution's text, thus leaving the new Constitution as ambiguous as the former.[193] While most commentators believe that the rights contained in constitutionalized treaties—indeed,

---

189. In the United States, "[w]hether an agreement is to be given effect without further legislation is an issue that a court must decide when a party seeks to invoke the agreement as law." RESTATEMENT, *supra* note 35, § 111 cmt. h. In *Asakura v. Seattle*, 265 U.S. 332 (1924), a Japanese alien challenged a city ordinance allowing only United States citizens to obtain pawnbroking licenses by invoking a provision of a treaty between the United States and Japan. The Court invalidated the ordinance on the grounds that the treaty was self-executing, noting that the treaty "operates of itself without the aid of any legislation . . . and it will be applied and given authoritative effect by the courts." *Id.* at 341. For an example of the Court's finding a treaty to be non-self-executing, see *Cameron Septic Tank Co. v. City of Knoxville*, 227 U.S. 39 (1913).

190. Many delegates submitted proposals which explicitly stated that human rights treaties bearing constitutional status would be self-executing. *See* REC. CONST. ASSEMBLY NO. 17, June 15, 1994, 9:30 P.M., at 654 (statement of Elisa M.A. Carrio); REC. CONST. ASSEMBLY NO. 20, June 21, 1994, 11:00 A.M., at 832 (statement of María Bercoff); REC. CONST. ASSEMBLY NO. 22, June 22, 1994, 1:00 P.M., at 898 (statement of Juan F. Armagnague); REC. CONST. ASSEMBLY No. 25, June 22, 1994, 8:30 P.M., at 1120 (statement of María Z.. Lucero); REC. CONST. ASSEMBLY NO. 33, June 24, 1994, 2:00 P.M., at 1822 (statement of Enrique G. Cardosa).

   Other delegates proposed that all international treaties are self-executing. *See* REC. CONST. ASSEMBLY NO. 19, June 17, 1994, 11:00 A.M., at 786 (statement of Guillermo E. Estevez Boero, Alfredo P. Bravo & Norberto L. La Porta).

191. *See* REC. CONST. ASSEMBLY NO. 21, June 21, 1994, 6:00 P.M., at 848 (statement of Rodolfo O. Ponce de León) (after reviewing Argentine, provincial, and international jurisprudence regarding self-executing/non-self-executing issue, concluding that there is a strong presumption that international treaties are self-executing, believes that constitutionalization bolsters this presumption, and further drafts a constitutional amendment that would embody this presumption); REC. CONST. ASSEMBLY NO. 31, June 24, 1994, 12:00 P.M., at 1701 (statement of Enrique de Vedia) (raising international treaties above domestic law will transform them into self-executing documents); REC. CONST. ASSEMBLY NO. 33, June 24, 1994, 2:00 P.M., at 1840 (statement of Emilia Juañuk & Julio Humada) (constitutionalization will make treaties self-executing).

192. *See* DICTAMEN NO. 7, *supra* note 183 ("International treaties regarding human rights, that are ratified, enjoy constitutional standing, and the rights, liberties and guarantees that they sanctify are considered self-executing".).

193. The current constitutional text does not make any reference to the self-executing/non-self-executing issue. *See supra* notes 44-47 and accompanying text. *See also* Graham & Cafiero, *supra* note 107, at 42-46 (noting that the Drafting Committee rejected the Treaty Commission's proposal).

in all human rights treaties—are self-executing,[194] the ambiguity remains left to the courts to resolve.[195]

What are the implications in terms of our transnational actor analysis? Numerous transnational actors care deeply about the self-executing/non-self-executing dichotomy. Virtually any person or entity with international contacts will have a position—a stake—in the resolution of the self-executing dilemma; any business person who has an interest in international commercial treaties, any exporter who has a stake in immediate enforcement of international trade agreements, and any prosecutor who would like immediate enforcement of Argentina's extradition agreements. The Treaty Commission hoped to entrench a partial solution in Article 75(22). This would have linked many of these generalized international interests to the ultimate fate of Article 75(22). Instead, the Drafting Committee sanitized the ultimate provision and thus left these potential transnational actors to fight their battles elsewhere, maybe in the courts or in the legislature, but definitely outside the epistemic space granted to Article 75(22).

The Constitutional Assembly—through its delegation of human rights issues to a committee dedicated generically to international treaties and integration, the concomitant presumption that human rights would be internalized in a wholesale manner, and the relegation of final decisions to a closed-door, non-participatory Drafting Committee—missed a ripe opportunity to create a loyal cadre of transnational actors from the human rights community, as well as from those with more generalized international law-related interests. Nevertheless, internalization of international law is a dynamic process. The disenfranchisement of the human rights community during the codification of Argentina's internalization strategy does not preclude them from entering Article 75(22)'s epistemic space at some point in the future. In fact, as will be discussed herein, human rights NGOs are currently working to anchor Article 75(22) in Argentina's legal discourse and practice. Nonetheless, Argentina's internalization strategy would have had powerful propagating momentum had the human rights community left the Constitutional Assembly as energized transnational actors.

---

194. *See* Graham & Cafiero, *supra* note 107, at 42-46 (arguing that the Drafting Committee did not materially alter the proposals of the Treaty Commission and that human rights treaties are self-executing).

195. *See, e.g.*, "Ekmekdjián," CSJN (1992) (stating that an international norm is self-executing when it does not require Congress to establish additional institutions to support the norm). *See also* Advisory Opinion OC-7/86, Inter-Am. C.H.R., ser. A, no. 7 (Aug. 29, 1986) (noting that Articles 1 and 2 of the American Convention, requiring states to recognize and guarantee all rights included therein, create a strong presumption that these rights are self-executing).

2.   The Domestic Courts in the Wake of the Constitutional Assembly: Passive Transnational Actors

The Argentine domestic court system is perhaps the essential link between the constitutional text and actual protection of human rights— between the domestic and international legal communities. To date, however, the Argentine courts have been relatively passive transnational actors, failing to harness the potency and breadth of international human rights law. The following section will trace the Supreme Court's, as well as some lower courts', use of their new constitutional tools (*i.e.,* human rights treaties) in deciding cases. The survey concludes that courts have not yet mobilized to become potent transnational actors in Article 75(22)'s epistemic community. Without energy, enthusiasm, activism, and creativity, the courts will not effectively absorb international law into Argentina's domestic legal community.

a.   The Supreme Court

In its initial confrontation with Article 75(22), the Court appears as an energetic soldier.   In *Giroldi,* the Court contemplated the constitutionality of appellate procedures in criminal courts.[196] The Court ultimately concluded that the procedures were unconstitutional pursuant to a provision of the American Convention which mandates that convicted criminal defendants have the right to an appeal.[197] By framing the case as one of constitutional import, yet relying on the American Convention for ultimate legal support, the Court consecrated the constitutional status of international human rights treaties.   More important, in relying on the American Convention as its legal crutch, the Court ruminated on the meaning of Article 75(22) and concluded that international jurisprudence, specifically the opinions of the Inter-American Court of Human Rights, "should serve as a guide for the interpretation" of the Convention's provisions.[198]   Thus, the Court concluded that the 1994 constitutional reform imported not only the text of several human rights treaties but also attendant interpretive jurisprudence.

While *Giroldi* suggests an active role for the Court, in its subsequent cases, the Supreme Court recoiled, becoming a rather

---

196.   *See* "Giroldi, Horacio David," CSJN (1995) (copy on file with Author) (translations of the case are by the Author).

197.   *See* American Convention, *supra* note 44, art. 8(h) ("During the [criminal] proceedings, every person is entitled, with full equality, to the following minimum guarantees: the right to appeal the judgment to a higher court.").

198.   "Giroldi," CSJN (1995), ¶ 11. In reality, the Court had been using international jurisprudence as an interpretive guide long before the *Giroldi* decision. *See, e.g.,* "Ekmekdjián," CSJN (1992), at 17. Thus, *Giroldi* is a reaffirmation of past practice in a post-constitutional reform climate.

passive, detached actor.[199] In these cases, the Court generally recognized the newly anointed position of human rights treaties.[200] While the Court cited international conventions, its decisions neither interpreted their meaning, pursuant to *Giroldi*, nor decisively relied on international law in reaching its conclusions[201]—instead, international law provided a mere cushion for the decision. In each instance, the Court could have animated international human rights treaties, interpreting relevant conventional law and catapulting that law into the forefront of constitutional jurisprudence. The Court, however, conservatively avoided this challenge. As a result, international human rights law lies more or less latent.[202]

---

199. *See* "H.C.S.," CSJN (1995) (copy on file with Author) (upholding the legality of forced blood samples to prove paternity); "Viaña, Roberto," CSJN (1995) (copy on file with Author) (granting *habeas corpus* petition after holding imprisonment of local legislator for defamatory statements to be illegal); "Gabrielli, Mario Carlos," CSJN (1996) (copy on file with Author) (translations of the case are by the Author) (upholding legality of discharge of soldier for failure to inform superiors of marriage pursuant to military law).

200. *See* "Gabrielli," CSJN (1996), ¶ 5 ("Besides, the 1994 Constitutional Reform has incorporated as part of the constitutional hierarchy . . . the rights consecrated in certain human rights treaties"); "H.C.S.," CSJN (1995), ¶ 13 (noting that Article 75(22) grants the Convention on the Rights of the Child constitutional hierarchy).

201. In *H.C.S.*, a case involving forced blood samples to prove paternity, the Court relied on three sources of law related to the right to privacy and the right against self-incrimination: 1) domestic statutes (the Court cites various provisions of the Penal and Civil Codes, especially those that concern intrusions on individual liberty and privacy, as well as those dealing with documenting birth and national identity); 2) relevant constitutional provisions (including Article 18, which protects individuals from forced self-incrimination, and Article 19, which states "The private actions of men that in no way offend public order or morality, nor injure a third party, are reserved only to God and are exempt from the authority of the magistrates"); and 3) Article 7 of the Convention on the Rights of the Child (stating that children have the right to know their parents and to be cared for by them). The Court expends little energy developing the Convention-based law, and the Convention is not a decisive arbiter of the Court's decision. *See* "H.C.S.," CSJN (1995).

In *Viaña*, a case dealing with the imprisonment of a local legislator for defamatory statements, the Court examines the law pertaining to freedom of expression. While the Court cites the American Convention (*see* American Convention *supra* note 44, art. 13), it relies on domestic statutes and the Constitution in reaching its decision to grant the habeas petition. *See* "Viaña," CSJN (1995).

In *Gabrielli*, a soldier was discharged under military law for failure to inform superiors of his marriage. The Court upheld the military code provision. While it lists the international treaties that grant individuals the right to marry (*see* Universal Declaration of Human Rights, *supra* note 44, art. 16(1); International Covenant, *supra* note 44, art. 23; American Convention, *supra* note 44, art. 17), the Court relies on limiting domestic case law and statutes that hold that the military law requiring soldiers to inform superiors of marriage is reasonable. *See* "Gabrielli," CSJN (1996).

202. One may counter that the U.S. Supreme Court explicitly avoids constitutional decisions and that the Argentine Supreme Court, in avoiding decisions based on international treaties (the Constitution), was merely following such practice. Yet, the United States is not haunted by a recent history of deprivation of fundamental rights, as Argentina is. The Argentine Supreme Court, if it had embraced the Constitution and human rights treaties, could have played an important role, not only in Article 75(22)'s epistemic community, but also in the consecration of fundamental rights that is crucial to Argentina's distancing itself from its past.

Worse, some recent opinions suggest that the Court may become a rogue member of Article 75(22)'s epistemic community. The Court has recently become more aggressive in its use of human rights treaties. In doing so, however, it has twisted international law against individual petitioners, hindering rather than helping compliance efforts. In *Bramajo*, the Court entertained the legality of a lengthy, pretrial preventative detention.[203] The American Convention grants individuals the right to "be brought promptly before a judge or other officer authorized by law to exercise judicial power and shall be entitled to a trial within a reasonable time . . . ."[204] Recognizing that the American Convention enjoys constitutional status and that *Giroldi* authorizes the Court to use international jurisprudence as an interpretational aid,[205] the Court relied on a 1989 Inter-American Commission on Human Rights opinion pertaining to the length of pretrial detention in Argentina.[206] According to the Commission, local judges should be the arbiters of the "reasonableness" of a pretrial detention.[207] Interpreting the Commission's decision as allowing "reasonableness" to be determined solely according to domestic standards, the Court relied on its own case law in upholding the lower court's decision to sanction the constitutionality of a three-year pretrial detention. Consequently, decisions of local judges remain impervious to international law.

In a subsequent case, *Chocobar*,[208] the Court contemplated the constitutionality of *post hoc* changes in Argentina's social security program. While the Court admitted that certain international human rights provisions, now enjoying constitutional status, could potentially undermine the legality of the state's actions,[209] it eschewed international law and instead rooted its decision in archaic Supreme Court decisions which interpreted the 1853 Constitution as granting the government *carte blanche* authority over the social security regime.[210] The Court justified its reasoning—its disregard of international law in the name of domestic law—with Article 75(22) itself: none of the international human rights treaty provisions should "curtail the rights or guarantees

---

203. *See* "Bramajo, Hernán Javier," CSJN (1996) (copy on file with Author) (translations of the case are by the Author).

204. American Convention, *supra* note 44, art. 7(5).

205. *See* "Bramajo," CSJN (1996), at 2. *See also supra* notes 193-95 and accompanying text.

206. *See* "Bramajo," CSJN (1996), at 2.

207. *Id.*

208. "Chocobar, Sixto C.," CSJN [1997-B] L.L. 240.

209. *See id.* at 243 (quoting Article 22 of the Universal Declaration, which guarantees all persons the "right to social security," and Article 26 of the American Convention, through which States parties promise to adopt internal measures that will further its economic obligations).

210. *See* "Chocobar," CSJN (1997), at 243-44.

provided for in the Constitution . . . and should be understood as complementing the rights and guarantees provided for therein."[211] The Court viewed its antedated decisions based on constitutional law as "rights or guarantees provided for in the Constitution," thus manipulating Article 75(22) to require international law to bow to these opinions. This formula—international human rights must harmonize with other constitutional rights, and the interpretation of those constitutional rights is governed by prior court decisions—creates a formidable and potent obstacle to the Court's exploration, activation, and unleashing of international human rights law. *Chocobar's* analysis allows the Court to remain a passive, if not an aberrant, transnational actor.

b. Lower Court Decisions

While a comprehensive review of post-1994 lower court decisions is beyond the scope of this Article, a representative survey from the lower federal courts based in Buenos Aires suggests that these courts are emulating the Supreme Court's passive approach.[212] In general, judges recognized that the 1994 Constitution incorporates select human rights treaties.[213] Most judges, however, merely listed international treaty provisions in conjunction with domestic statutes and decisions.[214] Thus,

---

211. CONST. ARG. (1994) art. 75(22).

212. *See, e.g.*, "Gonzalez, Juan Jose s/ if. ley 23.737," Buenos Aires, at 358 (Mar. 10, 1995) (myriad of criminal procedure violations, including forced confession outside presence of lawyer, illegal detention, and police brutality); "Astudillo Sanchez, Ramiro," Buenos Aires, at 442 (Mar. 22, 1995) (reasonable duration of imprisonment); "Pilade Fava L.M. s/ sobreseimiento," Buenos Aires (May 30, 1995) (imprisonment for repayment of debts); "Perasco, Luis C. s/ art. 1, ley 24.390," Buenos Aires (Feb. 13, 1996) (reasonable duration of imprisonment); "Blanco, R.A. s/ recusación," Buenos Aires, at 123 (Feb. 22, 1996) (right to impartial tribunal); "Bisbal de Haase, M. s/ cosa juzgada," Buenos Aires (Mar. 4, 1996) (protection from being placed in double jeopardy); "Furguielle, Silvio s/ sobreseimiento," Buenos Aires (Mar. 27, 1996) (reasonable length of pretrial detention); "Lescano, S.B. s/ nulidad," Buenos Aires (Aug. 22, 1996) (right to privacy, dignity of person, illegal search and seizure (vaginal drug searches)); "Paris, Alfredo Oscar s/ excarcelación," Olivos, at Part V (Nov. 1996) (preventative detention for sick detainee; right to health and right to be brought before a judge in reasonable time); "Cornador, Hernan Nicolas s/ internación," Olivos (Nov. 1996) (exploring constitutional rights of HIV-positive prisoners to special medical care); "Moreno Ocampo, L. s/ recusación," Buenos Aires, at 1498 (Nov. 22, 1996) (right to be adjudged before an impartial tribunal); "Cavallo, D.F. s/ excepción falta de acción y jurisdicción," Buenos Aires (Feb. 24, 1997) (right to equal protection before the law).

213. *See, e.g.*, "Pilade Fava," Buenos Aires (May 30, 1995) (stating that the American Convention now has constitutional standing as a result of Article 75(22)); "Perasco," Buenos Aires (Feb. 13,1996) (noting that the International Covenant is incorporated into the Constitution via Article 75(22)); "Furguielle," Buenos Aires (Mar. 27, 1996) (the court must interpret the reasonableness of pretrial detentions pursuant to the Constitution, which now includes international treaties); "Lescano," Buenos Aires (Aug. 22, 1996) (noting that international treaties now have constitutional standing).

214. *See, e.g.*, "Lescano," Buenos Aires (Aug. 22, 1996) (in case contesting the legality of vaginal searches for drugs, the court notes as relevant the right to be free from cruel, unusual and inhuman punishment and the right to personal dignity, listing, but not discussing the

as with much Supreme Court jurisprudence, international law provides additional, although non-critical, legal support for the judge's conclusions. With rather terse, fleeting treatment of international law, it is no surprise that few judges embrace *Giroldi* and engage in any interpretative analysis of international human rights law or peruse international jurisprudence.[215] This type of interpretation and analysis would undoubtedly and beneficially force judges to wrestle with international human rights law and mobilize the courts as fruitful transnational actors.

In merely listing international law along with domestic (constitutional and statutory) law, courts have not yet grappled with what it means for human rights treaties to have constitutional standing. Few judges differentiate human rights treaties' pre-1994 legal status from their post-1994 constitutional status,[216] and they generally do not harness the elevated constitutional status of human rights treaties. Beyond rotely stating that some human rights treaties have constitutional standing pursuant to Article 75(22),[217] judges have not invoked their special constitutional status in reaching decisions. Thus, the analytical rhythm changes little in post-1994 decisions. The year 1994 did not represent some magically-disjunctive moment in terms of the courts' analytic style, approach, or potency. From a functional-legal perspective, constitutionalization has proved rather redundant in that courts are not using international treaties differently than they did under *Ekmekdjián*.[218] The

---

substance of, select provisions of the American Convention and the International Covenant—ultimately resting its decision on domestic law); "Gonzalez," Buenos Aires (Mar. 10, 1995) (in case implicating right to counsel of choice, the court cites relevant provisions of the American Convention and the International Covenant; however, the court merely lists international sources of law and uses them to cushion its conclusion, which rests on criminal procedure codes in domestic law).

215. Some cases actually defy *Giroldi*. For example, in a case concerning the reasonableness of a three-year delay in presenting a case to a judge, the court cites Article 7(5) of the American Convention (which reads "Any person detained shall be . . . entitled to trial within a reasonable time or to be released without prejudice to the continuation of the proceedings"), yet the court looks toward domestic decisions for interpretive guidance in the face of compelling international jurisprudence. *See* "Furguielle," Buenos Aires (Mar. 27, 1996) (citing eight domestic decisions to interpret the meaning of "brought to trial within reasonable time"). Thus, the court flouts *Giroldi*'s instructions to use international jurisprudence in deciphering international law.

216. *See supra* note 102-22 and accompanying text.

217. *See* "Bramajo," CSJN (1996), at 2. *See also supra* note 213 and accompanying text.

218. For example, in a pre-constitutional reform case dealing with the right to a translator, the court relied in part on Article 8(2) of the American Convention in ordering one. *See* "Khalil H. Dib s/ desig. intérprete," Buenos Aires (July 25, 1994); American Convention, *supra* note 44, art. 8(2)(a) ("the right of the accused to be assisted without charge by a translator or interpreter, if he does not understand or does not speak the language of the tribunal or the court"). While the American Convention did not yet enjoy constitutional standing, Argentina's legislature had incorporated the American Convention into its statutory scheme, and the Supreme Court had endowed it with the ability to preempt conflicting statutes. *See* Law No. 23,054, Mar. 19, 1984 (copy on file with Author); "Ekmekdjián," CSJN (1992); *supra* notes

lower courts, like the Supreme Court, are latent, if not impotent, transnational actors.

3.   Transnational Actors in Potential Conflict: Argentina's Legal System vs. Inter-American Human Rights System

As transnational actors form "epistemic communities," their ability to reconstitute domestic interests to embrace an international norm increases exponentially. Argentina's internalization strategy failed to create an effective "epistemic community," not only because it failed to mobilize potential transnational actors, but also because it created competing rather than mutually-reinforcing relationships between two key transnational actors: Argentina's court system and the Inter-American human rights system.

While the Argentine courts are not currently meeting their potential,[219] they are the key domestic transnational actors and should serve as the crucial link between written, constitutional guarantees and the vindication of individual rights. They may invigorate human rights treaties and interpret international norms. They are, for all intents and purposes, the domestic "transmission belt,"[220] carrying international human rights norms to an individual level and thus transporting international law to the most fundamental unit in domestic society.

The Inter-American human rights system is also an important transnational actor. When Argentina incorporated the American Convention into its Constitution, it imported not only the rights contained therein but also the system which the Convention consecrates.[221] Argentina thus internalized and constitutionalized the entire regional system, comprised of an investigative/executive prong, the Inter-American Commission on Human Rights, and a judicial prong, the Inter-American Court of Human Rights.[222] One of these now-

108-16 and accompanying text. Thus, prior to constitutional reform, the Convention also served as a viable source of law that could invalidate official action.

219. *See supra* notes 199 and accompanying text.

220. Koh, *supra* note 7, at 2651.

221. The American Convention may essentially be divided into two parts. Part I delineates rights, including civil and political rights (Chapter II, Articles 3-25) and economic, social and cultural rights (Chapter III, Articles 26-31). Part II constitutes the Inter-American institutions, including the Inter-American Commission on Human Rights (Chapter VII, Articles 34-51) and the Inter-American Court of Human Rights (Chapter VIII, Articles 52-73). *See* American Convention, *supra* note 44.

222. Once a "person or group of persons, or any non-governmental entity legally recognized in one or more member states," exhausts domestic remedies, meets the six month statute of limitations, and proves that the subject of the petition is not pending in another international proceeding, the Commission shall consider complaints of violations of the Convention by States Parties. American Convention, *supra* note 44, arts. 44, 46(1). Assuming that the petition is admissible, the Commission then investigates the allegations and issues a confidential report to the States Parties. *See id.* arts. 48, 50(1). Within three months following the issuance of the

constitutionalized provisions requires that individuals seeking to vindicate rights before the Commission, and later the Court, exhaust domestic legal remedies, including the domestic court system.[223] Thus, Argentina's Constitution, albeit through the appendage of the American Convention, contains a provision which requires petitioners to utilize the domestic court system completely before tapping the Inter-American system.   Argentina's Constitution recasts the Inter-American Commission and Court as appellate-like tribunals, creating, in the words of one delegate, "a fourth and fifth" level of judicial review.[224]

This arrangement, with the Inter-American system constitutionally superimposed on the Argentine system like Russian stacking dolls, creates a zero-sum, highly-competitive relationship among these two transnational actors, undermining efforts to create a harmonious "epistemic community." Consider the following example.[225] Argentine non-profit law grants organizations serving the "public good" tax-exempt status. A public interest group, representing the interests of homosexuals and lesbians, asserts that it is an organization serving the "public good"

---

preliminary report, the Commission must either: 1) decide that the matter has been rectified; 2) submit the case to the Inter-American Court of Human Rights; or 3) issue a final report which includes recommendations and may be published. *See id.* art. 51. *See also* Advisory Opinion OC-13/93, Inter-Am. C.H.R., ser. A, no. 13 (July 16, 1993).

   If the Commission decides to submit the case to the Inter-American Court of Human Rights, it does so in a type of "solicitor general" capacity. The Court may only hear cases if the States Parties have agreed to its jurisdiction. *See* American Convention, *supra* note 44, art. 62. If the Court finds that a State Party violated the Convention, it may rule that "the injured party be ensured the enjoyment of his right" and may also receive "fair compensation." *Id.* art. 63(1). The Court may also adopt provisional measures, in "cases of extreme gravity and urgency." *Id.* art. 63(2).

   See also Holly Dawn Jarmul, *The Effect of Decisions of Regional Human Rights Tribunals on National Courts*, 28 N.Y.U. INT'L L. & POL. 311, 312-28 (1995-1996) (describing the Inter-American system); Thomas Buergenthal, *The Inter-American System for the Protection of Human Rights*, 1981 INTER-AM. Y.B. HUM. RTS. 80; Mary Caroline Parker, *"Other Treaties": The Inter-American Court of Human Rights Defines its Advisory Jurisdiction*, 33 AM. U. L. REV. 211(1983).

   223. *See* American Convention, *supra* note 44, art. 46(1)(a) ("Admission by the Commission of a petition or communication . . . shall be subject to the following requirements: a. that the remedies under domestic law have been pursued and exhausted in accordance with generally recognized principles of international law."). An applicant does not have to exhaust his remedies, however, if "(a) domestic legislation of the state concerned does not afford due process of law for the protection of the right or rights that have allegedly been violated; (b) the party alleging violation of his rights has been denied access to the remedies under domestic law or has been prevented from exhausting them; and (c) there has been an unwarranted delay in rendering a final judgment under the aforementioned remedies." *Id.* art. 46(2)(a).

   See also Jarmul, *supra* note 222, at 315 (exhaustion requirement not strictly enforced where petitioner was not afforded due process, was denied access to domestic remedies, or was subject to an unwarranted delay).

   224. *See* REC. CONST. ASSEMBLY NO. 35, June 24, 1994, 5:30 P.M., at 1975 (statement of Alberto E. Balestrini).

   225. This example is based on a live case. *See* "Comunidad Homosexual Argentina," CSJN 146 E.D. 228 (1991); "Comunidad Homosexual Argentina c/ Inspeción General de Justicia," CApel. CC, Buenos Aires (July 12, 1990) (copy on file with Author).

and that it should be granted tax-exempt status. The District Court disagrees, arguing that an organization serving homosexual interests does not serve the "public good." The Civil Court of Appeals agrees with the District Court, and the Supreme Court upholds the decisions of the lower courts. All Argentine courts interpret the American Convention's guarantee of equal protection of the laws in reaching their decision.[226] The public interest group then brings its case to the Inter-American Commission, arguing that Argentina's denial of tax-exempt status discriminates on the basis of sexual orientation, thus violating the American Convention. The claim is admissible because the public interest group has exhausted all domestic remedies.[227] The Commission issues a report that concludes that Argentina has violated the American Convention and asks Argentina to grant the petitioner-organization tax-exempt status.[228] Argentina does not respond to the Commission's report within the allotted time,[229] and the Commission then decides to bring the case to the Inter-American Court.[230] The Court hears the case and ultimately decides that Argentina did, indeed, violate the Convention by discriminating against the public interest group on the basis of sexual orientation.

Now what? If Argentina bends to accommodate the Inter-American Court's ruling, then it risks undermining the budding legitimacy of its own court system. As noted above, the domestic courts are the key transnational actors in Argentina's bid to internalize international law, and yet they have been notoriously weak, corrupt, and ineffective.[231]

---

226. *See* American Convention, *supra* note 44, art. 24 ("All persons are equal before the law. Consequently, they are entitled, without discrimination, to equal protection of the law.").

227. *See* American Convention, *supra* note 44, art. 46(1)(a).

228. *See id.* art. 50(1).

229. *See id.* art. 51(1).

230. *See id.*

231. The Argentine court system has been deemed to lack independence and to be relatively corrupt. *See* Tim Dockery, *The Rule of Law Over the Law of Rulers: The Treatment of De Facto Laws in Argentina*, 19 FORDHAM INT'L L.J. 1578, 1633 n.538 (1996) (citing public opinion polls demonstrating that Argentine citizens believe that the judiciary is corrupt and lacks independence from the executive); Garro, *supra* note 29, at 1. *See also* William C. Banks & Alejandro D. Carrio, *Presidential Systems in Stress: Emergency Powers in Argentina and the United States*, 15 MICH. J. INT'L L. 1, 37 (1993) (stating that the Argentine courts and Congress have done little to consolidate the rule of law in Argentina). *See also generally* Owen M. Fiss, *The Limits of Judicial Independence*, 25 U. MIAMI INTER-AM. L. REV. 57 (1993).

The 1994 bombing of a Jewish Community Center, killing ninety-nine people, provides a current example of an ineffective judiciary. *See* Kenneth J. Levit, *Terrorism, Democracy and the Jews of Argentina*, 22 HUM. RTS. 26, 1995. The investigation has proceeded at an extremely slow pace. *See* Katherine Ellison, *Jewish Center Bombing Probe Fails to Get Results*, HOUSTON CHRON., Dec. 15, 1995, at 27. Much evidence suggests that the Menem government itself, including the police, played a significant role in the bombing. *See* Sebastian Rotella, *Argentine Police Held in '94 Blast*, L.A. TIMES, Aug. 1, 1996, at A1. Despite weekly protests in front of the *tribunales* (courts), the courts have yet to conduct a meaningful, independent trial. Furthermore, violence against Jewish targets continues. *See* Calvin Sims, *Jewish*

Concomitantly, the rule of law has been problematic.[232] Most scholars agree that the rule of law and an independent judiciary are crucial to Argentina's attempt to fortify democracy,[233] perhaps the most important bulwark in the protection of individual rights. How, then, can a country's highest court effectively consolidate the rule of law when another court second-guesses its decisions? How can a court system build legitimacy and fortify its public image when a competing court system says, "almost, but not quite right"?   If domestic courts, particularly the Supreme Court, are to be effective "transmission belts," the public must perceive them as strong and legitimate. A contrary Inter-American Court decision that Argentina grafts onto its domestic system, however, reveals the vulnerability of the courts and the potentially ephemeral nature of their decisions—hardly legitimating and fortifying attributes.

What if Argentina ignores the Inter-American Court decision and the Supreme Court's decision rests? While Argentine courts might earn legitimacy, this move would undermine the legitimacy of the Inter-American system. It would also clash with efforts to consolidate the rule of law in Argentina itself. By virtue of the American Convention, the Inter-American human rights system is a part of the Constitution and the domestic legal fabric.[234] Thus, a dismissal of an Inter-American Court decision is tantamount to a dismissal of the Argentine Constitution. As Argentina attempts to consolidate the rule of law–one of the weakest links being adherence to constitutional norms–it must attempt to abide by, rather than deviate from, its own Constitution.

Argentina's internalization strategy has created a classic zero-sum game between two transnational actors, the Argentine courts and the Inter-American human rights system. To legitimize the domestic courts' decisions is to denigrate the legitimacy of the Inter-American system. On the other hand, to enhance the credibility of the Inter-American Commission and Court decisions is to detract from Argentina's efforts to bolster the image of its judiciary, as well as efforts to use the new Constitution as a vehicle to consolidate the rule of law.

This conundrum was not inevitable. If Argentina had internalized the substantive rights contained in human rights treaties rather than the entire treaties, then it would have reserved primacy for Argentine

---

Cemetery is Desecrated in Argentina, the Third this Year, N.Y. TIMES, Oct. 22, 1996, at A7.

232. *See supra* notes 164 and accompanying text.

233. For an in-depth look at the role of an independent judiciary in Argentina's transition to democracy, see the compendium of pieces in TRANSITION TO DEMOCRACY IN LATIN AMERICA: THE ROLE OF THE JUDICIARY (Irwin P. Stotzky ed., 1993). *See also* Stotzky, *supra* note 164 and accompanying text; Fiss, *The Limits of Judicial Independence, supra* note 231 and accompanying text; Carlos Santiago Nino, *Transition to Democracy, Corporation, and Constitutional Reform in Latin America,* 44 U. MIAMI L. REV. 129 (1989).

234. *See supra* notes 221-24 and accompanying text.

courts.[235] For the Constitutional Assembly, however, human rights treaties were hermetically-sealed, inseparable packages.[236] Instead, Argentina's Constitution now identifies two supreme arbiters of the law: the Supreme Court, as provided for in Article 116 of the Constitution[237] and, via the conduit of Article 75(22), the Inter-American Court, whose jurisdiction rests on the exhaustion of domestic remedies[238] and whose decisions are binding on States Parties.[239] Wholesale constitution-alization of the Inter-American system, as well as the rights contained in the American Convention, created this tug-of-war between the Argentine judiciary and the Inter-American Court.

In spite of its apparent commitment to the treaty-as-package-wholesale-incorporation process, the Constitutional Assembly could have anticipated the dilemma it was creating and neutralized this competitive, zero-sum relationship through artful drafting. However, only one delegate recognized the potential for competitive conflict between the Argentine judiciary and the Inter-American human rights system;[240] and a few other delegates recognized that by virtue of the constitutional amendments, Argentina was importing a new juridical system into its Constitution.[241] By stating that human rights treaties may

---

235. Prior to Argentina's constitutionalization of the American Convention, it was not clear what the domestic juridical effect of Inter-American Court decisions would be. While the American Convention provides that "[t]he States Parties to the Convention undertake to comply with the judgment of the Court in any case to which they are parties," there are no formal Inter-American mechanisms to ensure that States Parties enforce decisions. American Convention, *supra* note 44, art. 68(1). *See also* Jarmul, *supra* note 222, at 317. Nonetheless, political pressure from the Commission, the Organization of American States, or other countries frequently prods a country into compliance. *See id.* While States Parties assumed legal obligations vis-à-vis Article 68 of the American Convention, there was no practical enforcement mechanism other than political pressure. Furthermore, *domestic courts*, as opposed to legislatures or the executive, were not the primary compliance engines.

236. *See supra* notes 177-80 and accompanying text. A few delegates made proposals which included the constitutionalization of rights (along the lines of the constitutions discussed *supra* notes 55-86) rather than the entire treaties themselves. *See* REC. CONST. ASSEMBLY NO. 10, June 9, 1994, 3:30 P.M., at 394 (statement of Marta N. Martino de Rubeo); REC. CONST. ASSEMBLY NO. 26, June 23, 1994, 1:30 P.M., at 1255 (statement of Juan C. Hitters); REC. CONST. ASSEMBLY NO. 28, June 23, 1994, 7:00 P.M., at 1438 (statement of María C. Vallejos). However, neither the Treaty Commission nor the Drafting Committee appeared to entertain these proposals seriously.

237. CONST. ARG. (1994) art. 116.

238. *See supra* note 223 and accompanying text.

239. *See* American Convention, *supra* note 44, art. 62.

240. *See* REC. CONST. ASSEMBLY NO. 35, June 24, 1994, 5:30 P.M., at 1975 (statement of Alberto E. Balestrini) (recognizing that the Inter-American Court and Commission decide issues of law that will, by virtue of the constitutionalization of these institutions, stand above domestic constitutional decisions, thereby creating a fourth or fifth level of appeal).

241. *See* REC. CONST. ASSEMBLY NO. 19, June 17, 1994, 11:00 A.M., at 779 (statement of María N. Meana García, Pablo Verani, Horacio Massaccesi & Santiago A. Hernandez) (international and regional courts will make juridical pronouncements); REC. CONST. ASSEMBLY NO. 20, June 21, 1994, 1:00 A.M., at 832 (statement of María Bercoff) (individuals have the right to petition international and regional human rights systems to vindicate human rights);

not curtail or limit enumerated rights,[242] Article 75(22) clearly reveals that the Constitutional Assembly recognized the potential for conflict between substantive rights, as provided for in Titles I and II of the Constitution, and the panoply of substantive rights appended by virtue of constitutional incorporation of human rights treaties.[243] Just as the Constitutional Assembly resolved substantive conflicts, it could have resolved more procedural conflicts by drafting a provision that addressed the tension. For example, the Constitution could have stated the following: "Supreme Court decisions, granting due regard to extant international juridical pronouncements, are final and non-reviewable by any supranational institution," or, alternatively, "Supreme Court decisions are presumptively final but subject to the ultimate jurisdiction of the Inter-American Court." While the former may not enhance the legitimacy of the Inter-American system and the latter may not enhance the legitimacy of the Supreme Court, either option would have defined their relationship and preempted competitive and potentially destructive vying for power. Either option would have also defined a rule of law: either Supreme Court decisions are final or they are subject to review. Thus, abiding by that rule would have helped consecrate and consolidate the rule of law in a society where lawlessness and anomie have been prevalent.[244] Instead, we are left with two important transnational actors on a collision course.

B.   The Promises

Percolating below the surface are some nascent reasons for optimism. Prodded by energetic NGOs, some judges are beginning to

REC. CONST. ASSEMBLY NO. 20, June 21, 1994, 1:00. P.M., at 835 (statement of Ana M. Dressino) (human rights treaties, and their interpretation, should be subjected to the ultimate jurisdiction of supranational organizations); REC. CONST. ASSEMBLY NO. 22, June 22, 1994, 1:00 P.M., at 898 (statement of Juan F. Armagnague) (supranational organizations generate rules of law that Argentina must follow); REC. CONST. ASSEMBLY NO. 26, June 23, 1994, 1:30 P.M., at 1255 (statement of Juan C. Hitters) (recognizing that the Inter-American system has Commission and Court institutions and not only substantive rights).

242. CONST. ARG. (1994) art. 75(22) ("The rights granted in these treaties do not curtail the rights or guarantees provided for in the first part of the Constitution and should be understood as complementing the rights and guarantees provided for therein.").

243. Several delegates offered proposals regarding the potential conflict between written rights and appended rights. *See* REC. CONST. ASSEMBLY NO. 17, June 15, 1994, 9:30 P.M., at 670 (statement of Cecilia Lipsyzc, Juan Schroeder, María Sanchez, Rina Leiva, Daniel García, Adriana Puiggrós & Ana M. Pizzurno) (human rights treaties shall guide and condition the interpretation of domestic law); REC. CONST. ASSEMBLY NO. 19, June 17, 1994, 11:00 A.M., at 779 (statement of María N. Meana García, Pablo Verani, Horacio Massaccesi & Santiago A. Hernandez) (same); REC. CONST. ASSEMBLY NO. 26, June 23, 1994, 1:30 P.M., at 1255 (statement of Juan C. Hitters) (interpret the Constitution and internal law in conformity with the Universal Declaration and the American Convention); Rec. Const. Assembly No. 35, June 24, 1994; 5:30 P.M., at 1975 (statement of Alberto E. Balestrini) (same).

244. *See supra* notes 231-33 and accompanying text.

embrace international human rights law as a primary, if not the primary, source of individual rights. International human rights treaties are also slowly trickling toward untouched segments of society, and Article 75(22) may have some latent allies.

1. Unlikely Bedfellows: Potential Transnational Actors

Argentina's human rights internalization strategy may have some unexpected, yet largely untapped allies. Apparently, the impetus for constitutionalization of human rights treaties was not a magnanimous desire to sanctify human rights or a desire to repent for a dark past; it was instead an outgrowth of regional integration and regional trading blocks—namely Mercosur—and Argentina's desire to be a welcome and powerful member of such blocs.[245] In debate and public statements regarding Article 75(22), delegates incessantly referenced economic integration, and virtually all the delegates that spoke about the provision underscored its importance in terms of Mercosur and/or economic integration. For some delegates, sovereignty was the link: if sovereignty concerns had created resistance to human rights treaties and systems in the past, then Argentina's entrance into Mercosur, and its concomitant abdication of power to a supranational entity, neutralized these concerns.[246] Other delegates believed that if Argentina was going to make an honest attempt to join the international community, its joining a regional trade bloc was insufficient—Argentina also needed to participate in a multitude of international organizations, including those that promoted human rights.[247] As proof, many delegates referenced

---

245. *See supra* notes 173-76 and accompanying text.

246. *See* REC. CONST. ASSEMBLY NO. 20, June 21, 1994, 11:00 A.M., at 832 (statement of María Bercoff) (resigned to the fact that countries have ceded authority to supranational trading blocs, thus arguing that Argentina should not hesitate to cede authority in the human rights context); REC. CONST. ASSEMBLY NO. 20, June 21, 1994, 11:00 A.M., at 835 (statement of Ana M. Dressino) (regional integration demonstrates that countries can legitimately transfer authority and sovereignty to supranational entities).

247. *See* REC. CONST. ASSEMBLY NO. 16, June 15, 1994, 3:00 P.M., at 611 (statement of Jorge D. Amena, Susana S. de De María, María C. Allenano & Augusto Acuña; REC. CONST. ASSEMBLY NO. 19, June 17, 1994, 11:00 A.M., at 786 (statement of Guillermo E. Estevez Boero, Alfredo P. Bravo & Norberto L. La Porta) (in order to take advantage and participate in regional integration, it is necessary to participate in international organizations and therefore give more than lip service to international norms, among the most prominent being the Universal Declaration and the subsequent development of regional human rights system); REC. CONST. ASSEMBLY NO. 22, June 22, 1994, 1:00 P.M., at 898 (statement of Juan F. Armagnague) (discussing the European Union and the importance of creating international communities to nurture not only trade but also human rights); REC. CONST. ASSEMBLY NO. 24, June 22, 1994, 5:00 P.M., at 1013 (statement of Alberto A. Natale, Pablo A. Cardinale & Carlos A. Caballero Martín) (also discussing European Union)); REC. CONST. ASSEMBLY NO. 26, June 23, 1994, 1:30 P.M., at 1255 (statement of Juan C. Hitters) (international integration treaties, human rights treaties, and in fact all international treaties are integrated components of a new international world order); REC. CONST. ASSEMBLY NO. 28, June 23, 1994, 7:00 P.M., at 1438 (statement of María C. Vallejos) (international integration is socio-economic, and thus,

other countries who had constitutionally elevated the status of international human rights norms as part of a concerted effort to enhance the states' standing and prominence in the international community.[248]

The ultimate structure of Article 75 further illustrates the marriage between human rights and trading interests. Article 75 also provides the following: 1) Congress has the power to approve and disapprove of treaties regarding international/regional integration even if it involves delegating power to supranational entities; 2) these treaties enjoy a status superior to domestic law; and 3) approval of integration treaties with Latin American states only requires an absolute majority vote of both houses of the legislature.[249] In fact, most members of the Constitutional Assembly that proposed language concerning incorporation of international human rights norms concurrently proposed language concerning the approval and status of treaties regarding integration.[250]

Argentina must embrace human rights as well as regional trade); REC. CONST. ASSEMBLY NO. 31, June 24, 1994, 12:00 P.M., at 1701(statement of Enrique de Vedia) (building an international community requires rising to certain international standards, namely fundamental human rights standards); REC. CONST. ASSEMBLY NO. 33, June 24, 1994, 2:00 P.M., at 1840 (statement of Emilia I. Juañuk, Federico R. Puerta, Julio c. Humada & José D. Fabio) ("It is absolutely necessary that communities join to create conditions favorable to the utilization of progress, to open markets, to find peaceful solutions to conflicts. All in all, to improve the basic living standard and the quality of life."); REC. CONST. ASSEMBLY NO. 35, June 24, 1994, 5:30 P.M., at 1975 (statement of Alberto E. Balestrini) (building an international community requires protection of human rights).

248. *See* REC. CONST. ASSEMBLY NO. 17, June 15, 1994, 9:30 P.M., at 659-60 (statement of Marcelo Bassani) (focusing on regional integration and discussing the Constitutions of Uruguay, Brazil, Colombia, Paraguay; as well as European Union and the Treaty of Rome); REC. CONST. ASSEMBLY NO. 19, June 17, 1994, 11:00 A.M., at 786 (statement of Guillermo E. Estevez Boero, Alfredo P. Bravo & Norberto L. La Porta) (discussing Guatemala, Honduras, El Salvador, Panama, Costa Rica and Peru); REC. CONST. ASSEMBLY NO. 21, June 21, 1994, 6:00 P.M., at 848 (statement of Nilda Romero) (discussing Spain, France, Germany, and Brazil); REC. CONST. ASSEMBLY NO. 26, June 23, 1994, 1:30 P.M., at 1255 (statement of Juan C. Hitters) (discussing Spain and Portugal, as well as provinces); REC. CONST. ASSEMBLY NO. 35, June 24, 1994, 5:30 P.M., at 1975 (statement of Alberto E. Balestrini) (discussing Italy, France, Germany); REC. CONST. ASSEMBLY NO. 31, June 24, 1994, 12:00 P.M., at 1701 (statement of Enrique de Vedia) (discussing Germany, Spain, France, Italy and Belgium).

249. *See* CONST. ARG. (1994) art. 75(24) (Congress shall have the power to "approve or disapprove treaties regarding integration that delegate power and jurisdiction to supranational organizations, under conditions of equality and reciprocity and respecting the democratic order and human rights. These treaties shall have a status superior to domestic law. Approval of these treaties with Latin American countries shall only require an absolute majority of both houses of Congress . . . . The renouncement of these treaties will require the prior approval of an absolute majority of both houses of Congress.").

250. See the proposed constitutional provisions in REC. CONST. ASSEMBLY NO. 17, June 15, 1994, 9:30 P.M., at 654 (statement of Elisa M.A. Carrio); REC. CONST. ASSEMBLY NO. 20, June 21, 1994, 11:00 A.M., at 832 (statement of María Bercoff); REC. CONST. ASSEMBLY NO. 20, June 21, 1994, 11:00 A.M., at 835 (statement of Ana M. Dressino); REC. CONST. ASSEMBLY NO. 22, June 22, 1994, 1:00 P.M., at 898 (statement of Juan F. Armagnague); REC. CONST. ASSEMBLY NO. 24, June 22, 1994, 5:00 P.M., at 1013 (statement of Alberto A. Natale, Pablo A. Cardinale & Carlos A. Caballero Martín); REC. CONST. ASSEMBLY NO. 24, June 22, 1994, 5:00 P.M., at 1071 (statement of Juan M. Pedersoli, Olga C. Abraham & Pascual A. Rampi); REC. CONST. ASSEMBLY NO. 25, June 22, 1994, 8:30 P.M., at 1138 (statement of Alicia Oliveira

Human rights, international trade, and regional integration became a tightly knit package, and the Constitution reflects this interwoven relationship.

Those affiliated with trading interests and successful regional integration thus maintain a stake in the effective internalization of human right norms. As several delegates stated, Argentina's human rights record is a potent indicator of its ability to cooperate in regional economic relationships.[251] Among the Argentine business community, therefore, Article 75(22) may find engaged members of its epistemic community.

2. Mobilization of Key Transnational Actors: The NGOs

While the Argentine court system's failure to embrace international human rights norms has stymied compliance efforts, its reaction to the legal changes may be a result of benign ignorance rather than informed malevolence. Courts may not understand how to utilize human rights treaties or how such treaties fit into the legal hierarchy. Fortunately, through briefs and memorials, some NGOs are engaging in an instructive dialogue with courts.[252] In Argentina, NGOs played a prominent role in the 1970s in publicizing and, ultimately, curtailing human rights abuses.[253] Regarding enforcement of Article 75(22), the most active NGO is the *Centro de Estudios Legales y Sociales* (Center of Legal and Social Studies, or CELS).[254] With the assistance of a Ford Foundation grant, the CELS is engaged in a campaign to educate judges and

---

& Eugenio R. Zaffaroni); REC. CONST. ASSEMBLY NO. 26, June 23, 1994, 1:30 P.M., at 1255 (statement of Juan C. Hitters); REC. CONST. ASSEMBLY NO. 31, June 24, 1994, 12:00 P.M., at 1701 (statement of Enrique de Vedia); REC. CONST. ASSEMBLY NO. 35, June 24, 1994, 5:30 P.M., at 1975 (statement of Alberto E. Balestrini).

A few members did not link human rights and integration in their proposals. *See* REC. CONST. ASSEMBLY NO. 17, June 15, 1994, 9:30 P.M., at 659-60 (statement of Marcelo Bassani); REC. CONST. ASSEMBLY NO. 22, June 22, 1994, 1:00 P.M., at 88 (statement of Augusto J.M. Alasino); REC. CONST. ASSEMBLY NO. 26, June 23, 1994, 1:30 P.M., at 1193 (statement of María S. Farías, Federico P. Russo & Hebe A. Maruco); REC. CONST. ASSEMBLY NO. 28, June 23, 1994, 7:00 P.M., at 1438 (statement of María C. Vallejos); REC. CONST. ASSEMBLY NO. 33, June 24, 1994, 2:00 P.M., at 1840 (statement of Emilia I. Juañuk, Federico R. Puerta, Julio C. Humada & José D. Fabio).

251. *See supra* notes 246-47 and accompanying text.

252. For an excellent discussion of the importance of NGOs in enforcement of human rights norms, see Kathryn Sikkink, *Human Rights, Principled Issue- Networks, and Sovereignty in Latin America*, 47 INT'L ORG. 411, 415-23 (1993). *See also generally* NGOs, THE UNITED NATIONS, AND GLOBAL GOVERNANCE (Thomas G. Weiss & Leon Gordenker eds., 1996).

253. *See* Sikkink, *supra* note 252, at 423-28; Sims, *supra* note 159, at A4.

254. The CELS is recognized as a leading human rights advocacy group and think tank. *See* Faiola, *supra* note 159, at A25; Briscoe, *supra* note 159, at 7; Friedland, *supra* note 159, at A15.

practitioners regarding the post-1994 status of human rights treaties, highlighting their potency and import.[255]

It is one of CELS' self-professed missions to educate courts about "the State's international obligations," seeing as Argentina reaffirmed its commitment to "fulfill these obligations" during the 1994 constitutional reform process.[256] Through briefs and other pleadings, the CELS describes at length the elevated status of international human rights law and implores courts to respect treaties and to harness their potential. For example, in a case challenging the constitutionality of denying an AIDS patient new "cocktail" drugs that have proven effective in combating the onslaught of the disease, CELS sought to employ international law in support of its case. Instead of merely listing international treaties along with domestic sources of law, however, as many courts do,[257] the CELS engaged in a written lecture about the new status of international human rights law:

> The constitutional status of human rights treaties is not designed only to complement the dogmatic part of the Constitution but rather, and necessarily, to condition the exercise of all public power, including the exercise of judicial power, to respect and guarantee these international instruments. Given the constitutional hierarchy granted to the human rights treaties, their violation constitutes not only an assumption of the State's international responsibilities but also a violation of Argentina's own Constitution. On an internal level, the failure to apply these treaties on the part of domestic tribunals could result in the adoption of arbitrary decisions by ignoring norms with constitutional status.
>
> The domestic tribunals are the entities that can assure that all international obligations regarding human rights assumed by the State . . . are entirely respected and guaranteed by other powerful entities within the State. According to one scholar, 'The state has the right to delegate the application and interpretation of treaties to the judicial power. Nonetheless, if the tribunals commit errors in their work or decide not to give

255. The project is referred to as *Programa sobre Aplicación del Derecho Internacional de los Derechos Humanos por los Tribunales Locales* (Programa DIDH) [Program Regarding the Application of International Human Rights Law by Local Courts].

256. Memorial en Derecho, en Calidad de Amici Curiae, del Centro de Estudios Legales y Sociales (CELS), y el Center for Justice and International Law (CEJIL) s/ Libertad de Expresión y Calumnias e Injurias a Funcionarios Públicos (amicus curiae brief submitted by CELS and CEJIL), "Eduardo G. Kimel," Buenos Aires (Mar. 1996) (translations by the Author).

257. *See supra* notes 200-01 and 213-18 and accompanying text.

effect to the treaties, . . . then, through their decisions, the State violates the treaties.'[258]

The CELS repeats this "lecture" frequently, reinforcing to courts their responsibilities and the import of breeding Argentine compliance with human rights law.[259]

Some courts have internalized this message, regurgitating similar language in many of their opinions. For example, two judges who included in their opinions a discussion on the status of international treaties, chose language highly reminiscent of the CELS "lecture":

> The constitutional status of human rights treaties conditions the exercise of all public power, including the exercise of judicial power, to respect and guarantee these instruments. If courts do not apply these treaties, it could signify the adoption of arbitrary decisions by ignoring norms with constitutional status. The courts carry the burden of assuring that all international obligations assumed by Argentina with regard to human rights, are entirely respected and guaranteed; if the tribunals commit errors in the application or interpretation of treaties, their decisions will impose on the State a violation of the same treaties and responsibility before the international community.[260]

Through crafted brief writing, the CELS is successfully educating judges. While these opinions represent only a few isolated examples, they may be cause for cautious optimism regarding the ability of courts, when guided, to harness human rights treaties' invigorated potential.

---

258. Acción de Amparo Contra Instituto de Servicios Sociales para Jubilados y Pensionados, (Martín Abregú & Victor E. Cosarin, attorneys) (photocopy on file with Author) (quoting LORD MCNAIR, THE LAW OF TREATIES 346 (1961) (translations by the Author).

259. *See* Human Rights Watch/Americas & Centro por la Justicia y el Derecho Internacional, Memorial en Derecho Amicus Curiae, "Mignone, Emilio F. s/ presentación," *reprinted in* 33 EL DERECHO 8834 (Sept. 14, 1995) (using identical language as that quoted above in explaining the status of international human rights treaties) (photocopy on file with Author); Centro de Estudios Legales y Sociales (CELS), Memorial sobre el Derecho Internacional de Los Derechos Humanos Relativo a las Condiciones de Detencion de Los Enfermos con HIV y a la Restrictividad con que Debe Aplicarse la Prision Preventiva, "Sterla, Silvia s/ Interrupción de la Prisión Preventiva" [hereinafter CELS MEMORIAL] (Sept. 1996) (using identical language as that quoted above in explaining the status of international human rights treaties) (photocopy on file with Author) (translations by the Author); Promueve Amparo, "Mariela Cecilia Viceconte" (Martín Abregú & Victor Cosarin, attorneys) (same) (photocopy on file with Author); Promueve Demanda de Amparo, "Sofía Tiscornia" & "Emilio Fermin Mignone" (Gastón Chillier & Victor Cosarin, attorneys) (same) (photocopy on file with Author).

260. "Paris, Alfredo Oscar s/ excarcelación," Olivos, at V (Nov. 1996) (constitutionality of prison conditions for prisoner who is chronically ill) (translations of the case are by the Author). *See also* "Cornador, Hernan Nicolas s/ internación," Olivos, at I (Nov. 1996) (constitutionality of prison conditions for HIV positive prisoners) (translations of the case are by the Author). While this passage is a translation, the original Spanish version is a verbatim copy of the Spanish version cited *supra* note 258 and accompanying text.

The CELS, however, is not merely conditioning judges by feeding useful language. It is also implicitly teaching judges how to improve the analytic depth of their opinions through the use of *Giroldi*-approved sources.[261] For example, in a memorial concerning prison conditions, particularly those for prisoners who tested positive for HIV,[262] the CELS cited the typical panoply of sources, including the International Covenant on Civil and Political Rights,[263] the International Covenant on Economic, Social, and Political Rights,[264] the Universal Declaration,[265] and the American Convention on Human Rights.[266] In addition, the CELS cites some "non-traditional," interpretive sources pursuant to *Giroldi*'s admonition to employ international jurisprudence in aid of judicial interpretation: the Committee on Economic, Social and Cultural Rights, in interpreting the state's obligations with regard to the right to health;[267] the UN Commission on Human Rights reports with regard to state obligations in the face of the AIDS epidemic;[268] and the European Commission on Human Rights and the Inter-American Commission on Human Rights with regard to the meaning of "inhumane treatment."[269] These interpretive sources have seeped into the responsive judicial opinions, frequently mirroring the brief's citation and language.[270] The CELS' mode of analysis, citing human rights treaties with constitutional standing and then exploring international jurisprudence as an interpretive aid, indisputably shaped the courts' analyses, lending variety and depth to the courts' opinions and instructing courts on the power of *Giroldi*.[271]

---

261. *See supra* notes 196-98 and accompanying text.

262. *See supra* note 260 and accompanying text and *infra* note 273 and accompanying text.

263. *See* International Covenant, *supra* note 44.

264. *See* International Covenant on Economic, Social and Political Rights, *supra* note 44.

265. *See* Universal Declaration on Human Rights, *supra* note 44.

266. American Convention, *supra* note 44

267. See "Cornador," Olivos (Nov. 1996), at 8.

268. *See id.* at 10.

269. *Id.* at 17, 20.

270. For example, one judge cites the Committee on Economic, Social and Cultural Rights for the proposition that states' ratification of the Covenant on Economic, Social and Cultural Rights obliges States Parties to guarantee the right to health, in a non-discriminatory manner, to all, including those who are HIV-positive. See "Cornador," Olivos (Nov. 1996), at I. The CELS MEMORIAL states, "The Committee on Economic, Social and Cultural Rights, the organ charged with enforcing the Pact [the International Covenant on Economic, Social and Cultural Rights] . . . imposes two obligations with immediate effect: first, states promise to guarantee that the pertinent rights will be exercised without any discrimination (Art. 2.2), logically including those who are HIV-positive. The second obligation having immediate effect is to adopt means to assure [the previous obligation], whether legislative, judicial, administrative, or of any other type." CELS MEMORIAL, *supra* note 259, at 8-9. *See also* "Paris," Olivos, (Nov. 1996) at I (in case about preventative detention for those who are ill, quoting the same language).

271. These interpretive sources are slowly finding their way into other opinions. A few judges have cited the U.N. Commission on Human Rights (*see* "Paris," Olivos (Nov. 1996), at VIII; "Cornador," Olivos (Nov. 1996)), as well as the European Court on Human Rights (*see* "Moreno Ocampo, L." Buenos Aires (Nov. 22, 1996), at 1499.

With courts enhancing their understanding of the constitutional status of human rights and their ability to employ varied interpretive sources, human rights law appears to be slowly assuming a more prominent role in judicial decisions, thus portending an increased and more efficient use of international human rights treaties. Whereas some courts passively enlisted international law to support conclusions following constitutional reform,[272] a few courts, with the ostensible prompting of CELS, have begun to use international law as a primary decision-making engine. In two notable cases concerning health issues, one dealing with treatment for prisoners with AIDS[273] and another dealing with the legality of preventative detention for those who are ill,[274] as well as one case concerning recusal of a biased judge,[275] the courts, while discussing domestic law, mobilized international norms as their primary analytic tool. With the prodding of dedicated and relentless NGOs, Argentine courts, in an isolated and haphazard manner, are becoming more active transnational actors. Time will tell whether the courts will drive Argentina to compliance and ultimate obedience.

3.   Empowering Transnational Actors: The Individual

The constitutionalization of human rights treaties enhanced public access to international human rights norms. In Argentina, law is notoriously difficult to find. There is no Argentine form of Westlaw; there is no Argentine Lexis; there is no current, computerized access to Supreme Court decisions. The law library at the Universidad de Buenos

---

272.   *See supra* notes 212-17 and accompanying text.

273.   In *Cornador,* the court addresses the constitutionality of prison conditions for prisoners with AIDS, ultimately concluding that certain prison conditions implicate several constitutional and statutory rights, including, but not limited to, the right to health (under the Universal Declaration and the International Covenant on Economic, Social and Cultural Rights); the right to personal integrity (under the International Covenant and the American Convention); and the right to humane treatment while detained (under the American Declaration on the Rights and Duties of Man). *See* "Cornador," Olivos (Nov. 1996), at 8.

274.   In *"Paris,"* the court explores the legality of preventative detention for prisoners who are chronically ill. The court concludes that preventative detention for such prisoners is illegal, ultimately resting its decision on two rights—the right to health and the right to be brought before a judge within a reasonable period of time—and concluding that the primary legal sources of these rights are the Universal Declaration, the International Covenant, the International Covenant on Economic, Social and Cultural Rights, and the American Convention. *See* "Paris," Olivos (Nov. 1996).

275.   The court in *Moreno Ocampo* examined the denial of a request for judicial recusal. The appellant, Luis Moreno Ocampo, is a popular media personality who exposes corruption among politicians and members of the judiciary. In a case in which Moreno Ocampo was a party, he was assigned to a judge who had been a target of one of his exposes. The judge denied the motion to recuse, and Mr. Moreno Ocampo appealed. The court reversed the denial of the motion to recuse, reasoning that the judge denied Moreno Ocampo the right to an impartial tribunal, citing the American Convention, the American Declaration on the Rights and Duties of Man, and the International Covenant on Civil and Political Rights, as primary legal support. *See* "Moreno Ocampo, L." Buenos Aires (Nov. 22, 1996).

Aires is little more than a card catalog. The private universities' collections are better, but do not closely approximate U.S. standards. To find the Supreme Court opinions discussed in this Article, the Author engaged in a multi-day, multi-step process that culminated at the Supreme Court itself. Even finding a courtroom in the maze labeled *Los Tribunales* is a herculean task. In a society where the search for the law is so cryptic, those who are not trained to access the law, or those who cannot afford to hire someone so trained, stand highly disenfranchised–unable to negotiate through the dense web of rights.[276]

The Argentine Constitution is one exception to this rule. Newsstands adorn the streets of Buenos Aires. Along with the papers, tabloids, Harlequin novels, and soap opera digests, many vendors sell a copy of the "Constitución de la Nación Argentina." As a result of Article 75(22), this popular copy of the Constitution now includes the following: the American Declaration on the Rights and Duties of Man; the American Convention on Human Rights; the Universal Declaration; the International Covenant on Economic, Social, and Political Rights; the International Covenant; the Convention on the Prevention and Sanction of the Crime of Genocide; the International Convention on the Elimination of all Forms of Racial Discrimination; the Convention on the Elimination of all Forms of Discrimination against Women; the Convention against Torture and other Forms of Cruel, Inhuman, and Degrading Punishment; and the Convention on the Rights of the Child. While the non-lawyer may not herself be able to vindicate her rights, the popularization and access-granting effect of constitutionalization enhances the non-lawyer's ability to identify and claim ownership of rights. Until a large coterie of public interest lawyers develops in Argentina,[277] the common person's ability to vindicate human rights violations may be somewhat limited. Supply frequently follows demand, however, and the first step in creating demand for such a coterie is to grant a broader segment of the population access to their panoply of rights. The constitutionalization of human rights treaties, at a minimum, creates such access and thus empowers individuals as the ultimate beneficiaries of such rights.

---

276. For an enlightening discussion of public interest law in Argentina and the virtual disenfranchisement of individuals, see Martin F. Böhmer, On the Inexistence of Public Interest Law in Argentina, Address at Semiario de Latinoamerica sobre Temas Constitucionales (Aug. 17, 1996) (copy on file with Author).

277. *See id.*

V. IMPLICATIONS FOR TRANSNATIONAL LEGAL PROCESS: THE LIMITS OF THE LAW

Argentina's experiment is young and dynamic. At the time of the writing of this Article, international human rights treaties continue to seep into the Argentine legal landscape. Just as courts, with the prodding of CELS, became more receptive to international law, other transnational actors may similarly ignite processes that breed compliance and, ultimately, obedience. Thus, any conclusions one may draw from the Argentine experience are necessarily premature. Nonetheless, the first round of lessons from Argentina's internalization of international law—its limits and its latent promises—may help countries craft more potent internalization strategies.

Argentina's experience demonstrates how to build an epistemic community that will effectively propel an internalization strategy. Transnational actors are the constituents of epistemic communities. The number of transnational actors that support an internalization strategy, as well as their enthusiasm and mutual relationships, will determine the relative success or failure of such strategies.

In the Argentine case, the internalization strategy fell relatively flat because it did not engage, energize and create synergistic relationships among transnational actors. The Constitutional Assembly debated the incorporation of human rights treaties in rather generic, undifferentiated terms; in fact, most debate concerned regional economic integration, with human rights treaties a mere afterthought. Thus, the constitution-alization process failed to enlist numerous members of the human rights community. Constitutionalization ordained the Argentine courts as the transnational actors responsible for the vindication and protection of international human rights; yet, the courts, thus far, have been passive actors. Furthermore, incorporation of entire treaties—treaties which constitute regional human rights systems—created a competitive, zero-sum relationship between the Argentine courts and the Inter-American human rights system. Rather than synergistically entering Article 75(22)'s epistemic community, the Argentine courts and the Inter-American Commission and Court may vie, in a potentially counterproductive manner, to be the final arbiter of international human rights.

The glimmer—the incipient promise—in Argentina's internalization experiment may also be traced to the identity and enthusiasm of various transnational actors. By publicizing international human rights, Article 75(22) may transform the bearers of those rights—individuals—into transnational actors. While linking Article 75(22) to the creation of a fertile legal climate for regional economic integration effectively removed human rights from debate and discussion, it also created potential allies among the trade and business communities. Finally, the energy and enthusiasm of NGOs, who themselves are members of Article 75(22)'s epistemic community, are helping transform passive transnational actors—the courts—into active, energetic transnational actors. Both the problems and the promises in Argentina's internalization strategy suggest that a large coterie of energetic and cooperative transnational actors create the "transmission belt" necessary to propel nations not only toward compliance, but also toward obedience of international norms.

Furthermore, the nature of the internalization strategy may determine its ultimate effectiveness. In describing transnational legal process, Professor Koh notes that internalization may take place via legal, political *or* social means.[278] Argentina's experience suggests that in countries where the rule of law and the judiciary have historically been weak, internalization *must* be multifaceted, including legal, political, *and* social strategies. On its face, Article 75(22), a constitutional amendment, is a prototypical example of legal internalization. It strives to harness law to drive internalization of international norms. Law, however, is one of the weaker Argentine institutions and, within law, the Constitution is perhaps the weakest.[279] While a naked law, especially in a country like Argentina, will not significantly further obedience, it may animate political and social actors who, in turn, may further obedience. In antiseptically removing "human rights" from debate and effectively treating Article 75(22) as an afterthought—an appendage necessary to facilitate economic integration efforts—the members of the Constitutional Assembly missed an opportunity to transform much of the human rights community into effective social and political actors with a stake in successful internalization of human rights law. Legal internalization did not trigger concomitant social and political internalization processes. And law alone is rather hollow in Argentina. Argentina now faces a challenge: it must transform a legal gesture into concrete, programmatic change.

---

278. *See supra* notes 18-20 and accompanying text.

279. *See supra* notes 164, 231-33 and accompanying text.

Appendix

Table 2: Argentina's Constitutional Treatment of Human Rights: Past and Present[280]

International Covenant	American Convention	Argentina (1953 & amend.)	Argentina (1994)
Art. 1: Right to self-determination	N/A		
Art. 2: State obligation to respect the rights and ensure the rights "without distinction of any kind, such as race, colour, sex, language, religion, political or other opinion, national or social origin, property, birth or other status."	Art. 1: Race, color, sex, language, religion, political or other opinion, national or social origin, property, birth or any other social distinction.	Art. 16 — (Article 16 does not list categories, rather it merely states "All its inhabitants are equal before the law.")	Art.16/Art.75(23) 0 Art. 75(23) (Guarantees equal opportunity as provided for in international treaties)
Art. 3: Equal rights of men and women	Art. 24: General equal protection clause with no explicit reference to sex discrimination		Art. 37 — (Equal rights for men and women to hold political office)

---

280. Table 2 compares Argentina's 1853 and 1994 Constitutions, and then compares both to the International Covenant and the American Convention. Column 1 delineates the rights in the International Covenant. Column 2 lists the analogous rights in the American Convention, noting, where appropriate, the differences between the two international instruments. Columns 3 and 4 compare the Argentine Constitutions to these instruments. If a constitutional provision is analogous to a provision in one of the international documents, the Table notes the article's number. Furthermore, the Table indicates whether the constitutional provision is similar to (0), less expansive in scope than (-), or more expansive in scope than (+), the international instruments. The Table indicates, in bold, those places where the 1994 Constitution enhances the rights provided for in the 1853 Constitution.

International Covenant	American Convention	Argentina (1953 & amend.)	Argentina (1994)
Art. 4[281]: Public emergency allows suspension of rights; however no derogation from rights to life, prohibition on torture, slavery, punishment for contractual liability, *ex post facto* laws, recognition as a person, and freedom of thought & conscience	Art. 27: Allows derogation from rights during times of war, public danger, or other emergency. No derogation from the following: right to juridical personality; right to life; rights to human treatment; prohibition on slavery, *ex post facto* laws; freedom of conscience; right to family; right to name; rights of child; right to nationality; right to participate in government	Art. 23 Art. 29 — (In event of internal disorder, unlimited power to suspend Constitution to arrest, but not punish, individuals, or transfer individuals to different part of nation)	Art. 23 Art. 29 —/0 (Same, except Congress cannot confer upon Executive "extraordinary powers" or "the whole of public authority" whereby "lives, the honor, or the property" of Argentines shall be affected)
Art. 6: Right to life; death penalty only for the most serious crimes, right to amnesty or pardon	Art. 4	Art. 18 — (No death penalty for political crimes; no explicit right to life)	Art. 18 — (Same)
Art. 7: No one subject to torture or other cruel, inhuman or degrading treatment	Art. 5(2)	Art. 18 — (No torture or whipping)	Art. 18 — (Same)
Art. 8: No slavery or slave trade	Art. 6: Includes trafficking in women	Art. 15 0	Art. 15 0

---

281. The state of emergency provisions are exceptions to the rights granted in international instruments and constitutions. Thus, a state of emergency provision that permits curtailment of many rights under many circumstances circumscribes fundamental rights. The more expansive the state of emergency provision, the less expansive other rights. Thus, a broad state of emergency provision that allows many derogations receives a " — ," while a narrower state of emergency provision that allows few derogations receives a " + ."

International Covenant	American Convention	Argentina (1953 & amend.)	Argentina (1994)
Art. 9: Liberty and security of the person; no arbitrary arrest; informed of the charges and the reason for the arrest; prompt recourse to judicial process; right to go to court to determine lawfulness of detention	Art. 7(1-6)	Art. 18 — (Warrant)	Art. 18 (Warrant) Art. 43 (Habeas corpus) —
Art. 10: All those detained shall be treated with humanity; accused shall be segregated from convicted and juveniles segregated from adults; focus will be on rehabilitation and reformation	Art. 5	Art. 18 — (Provides for clean and safe prisons designed for security and not punishment.)	Art. 18 — (Same)
Art. 11: No one imprisoned merely because they cannot pay debts	Art. 7(7)		
Art. 12: Liberty to move within a country and to leave the country, except for restrictions provided by law in order to protect national security, public order, public health, morals or the rights and freedoms of others; no one arbitrarily denied the right of entry to own country	Art. 22: Includes right to asylum; may restrict these rights "to the extent necessary in a democratic society to prevent crime or to protect national security, public safety, public order, public morals, public health, or the rights or freedoms of others."	Art. 14 — ("Entering, remaining in, traveling through and leaving Argentine territory")	Art. 14 — (Same)
Art. 13: Can only expel an alien in accordance with law and alien shall be able to express reasons against expulsion	Art. 22(6)		

International Covenant	American Convention	Argentina (1953 & amend.)	Argentina (1994)
Art. 14: Core criminal defendant rights: equal before the courts, presumption of innocence, informed of the nature of the charge, adequate time to prepare defense, no undue delay, tried in presence, right to defense lawyer and right to have one appointed by the court if "interests of justice so require," cross examination, free assistance of interpreter, protection from self-incrimination, prohibition against double jeopardy, right to appeal, right to be compensated if illegally detained	Art. 8: In addition, confession is only valid if made without coercion	Art. 18 — (Right to trial protection against self-incrimination right to defense)	Art. 18 — (Same)
Art. 15: Prohibition on *ex post facto* laws, except if benefits the defendant	Art. 9	Art. 18 — (Defendant does not receive benefit of subsequent favorable law)	Art. 18 — (Same)
Art. 16: Everyone has the right to recognition as a person	Art. 3		
Art. 17: No one subjected to arbitrary or unlawful interference with privacy, family or home	Art. 11: Also includes correspondence and unlawful attacks on "honor and reputation"	Art. 18 0 (Home and personal correspondence is inviolable)	Art. 18 0 (Same)

International Covenant	American Convention	Argentina (1953 & amend.)	Argentina (1994)
Art. 18: Freedom of thought, conscience and religion. Can restrict right to manifest religious beliefs only as necessary to protect public safety, order, health and morals or fundamental rights	Art. 12: Conscience and religion	Art. 14 — (Right "to freely profess one's creed")	Art. 14 — (Same)
Art. 19: Freedom of expression & right to hold opinions. Right to expression may be restricted in respect of the rights or reputations of others or for protection of national security or public order or public health or morals	Art. 13: Thought and expression. Also prohibits prior censorship, excluding censorship aimed at children; and prohibits government manipulation of radio waves	Arts. 14 & 32 — ("[T]o publish ideas in the press without prior censorship" & "Federal Congress shall not enact laws that restrict freedom of the press or that establish federal jurisdiction over it")	Arts. 14 & 32 — (Same)
Art. 20: Prohibition on war propaganda and advocacy of racial, national or religious hate	Art. 13(5)		
Art. 21: Right to peaceful assembly, restrictions in the name of national security, public safety, public order and the protection of public health or morals	Art. 15		
Art. 22: Freedom of association and to join trade/labor unions; restrictions in the name of national security, public safety, public order and the protection of public health or morals	Art. 16: Includes restrictions on police and armed forces ability to form associations	Art. 14 (1957 amend) — / 0 ("[T]o associate for useful ends" and labor union rights)	Art. 14 (1957 amend) — / 0 (Same)

International Covenant	American Convention	Argentina (1953 & amend.)	Argentina (1994)
Art. 23: Preeminence of the family; right to marry; need consent of spouses	Art. 17		
Art. 24: Basic children's rights to equal protection; nationality; and registration	Art. 18: Right to a name Art. 19: Right to legal protection Art. 20: Right to nationality Art. 17(5): Equal protection for those born in and out of wedlock		Art. 75(23) 0 (Women & children rights)
Art. 25: Equal opportunity to partake in public affairs and engage in public service; right to vote	Art. 23: Specifies that the law can regulate rights only in the name of age, nationality, residence, education, civil & mental capacity		Art. 37 0
Art. 26: Standard equal protection clause, including same protected classes as those listed in Article 2	Art. 24: Does not list the protected classes	Art. 16 —	Art. 16 —
Art. 27: Right of ethnic or religious minorities to enjoy their culture and group identity.	N/A		Art. 75(17) 0

Table 3: Constitutional Treatment of Human Rights in South America[282]

International Covenant	American Convention	Bolivia (1967/ 1995 Amend.)	Venezuela (1961/ 1983 amend.)	Chile (1980/ 1989 amend.)	Paraguay (1992)	Uruguay (1967/ 1985 reinstated)	Peru (1993)	Brazil (1988)	Colombia (1991)	Ecuador (1979/ 1992 amend.)
Art. 1: Right to self-determination	N/A							Art. 4(III) 0		Art. 4 0
Art. 2: State obligation to respect the rights	Art. 1: State obligation to respect the rights	Art. 60 0	Art. 61 —	Art. 19(2) —	Art. 47 —	Art. 8 —	Art. 2(2) 0	Art. 5 0	Art. 13 +	Art. 19(5) 0
Art. 3: equal rights of men and women	Art. 24: General equal protection clause				Art. 48 +			Art. 5(I) 0	Art. 43 +	Art. 44 0
Art. 4: Public emergency allows suspension of rights	Art. 27: Allows derogation of rights during times of war/ emergency	Art. 112 +	Arts. 240-42 Arts. 244 —	Art. 39 Art. 41 0/—	Art. 288 +	Art. 31 Art. 168(17) —	Art. 137 0	Art. 136 Art. 139 0	Art. 214 +	Art. 78 0/—

282.   This Table surveys South American constitutions, comparing them to the International Covenant on Civil and Political Rights and the American Convention on Human Rights. Column 1 lists the rights as set forth in the International Covenant. Column 2 delineates the rights in the American Convention, noting where, appropriate, the differences between the two international instruments. Columns 3-11 compare domestic constitutions to the international instruments. If a particular constitution contains a provision that is analogous to the rights provided for in the international instruments, the Table notes the constitution's article number. Furthermore, the Table indicates whether the constitutional provision is similar to (0), less expansive in scope (—), or more expansive in scope (+).

International Covenant	American Convention	Bolivia (1967/1995 Amend.)	Venezuela (1961/1983 amend.)	Chile (1980/1989 amend)	Paraguay (1992)	Uruguay (1967/1985 reinstated)	Peru (1993)	Brazil (1988)	Colombia (1991)	Ecuador (1979/1992 amend)
Art. 6: Right to life	Art. 4	Art. 7(a) Art. 17 0	Art. 58 0	Art. 19(1) —	Art. 4 0	Art. 7 Art. 26 0	Art. 2(1) —	Art. 5 (intro) Art. 5 (XLVII) 0	Art. 11 0	Art. 19(1)/0
Art. 7: No torture	Art. 5(2)	Art. 12 0	Art. 60(3) Art. 60(7) —		Art. 5 0	Art. 26 —	Art. 2(24)(h) 0	Art. 5 (III) Art. 5 (XLVII) 0/+	Art. 7 0	Art. 19(1) 0
Art. 8: No slavery or slave trade	Art. 6: Includes trafficking in women	Art. 5 0		Art. 19(2) —	Art. 10 0		Art. 2(24)(b) —	Art. 5 (XLVII) —	Art. 17 0	Art. 19(11) Art. 19(17) 0
Art. 9: Liberty and security of the person	Art. 7(1-6)	Art. 9 Art. 11 Art. 18 0/—	Art. 60 —	Art. 19(3) & (7) —	Art. 9 Arts. 11-12 Art. 39 +	Art. 7 0	Art. 2(24) —	Art. 5 (LIV, LXI, LXII, LXIII, LXIV, LXV-VI, LXVIII) +	Art. 28 Art. 30 0/—	Art. 19(17) 0
Art. 10: Detained treated with humanity	Art. 5			Art. 19(7)(d) —	Art. 21 0	Art. 43 —		Art. 5 (XLVIII-L) +	Art. 28 0	
Art. 11: No one imprisoned because they cannot pay debts	Art. 7(7)				Art. 13 0	Art. 52 0	Art. 2(24)(c)	Art. 5 (LXVII) +		Art. 19(17)(b) 0
Art. 12: Liberty to move within a country and to leave country	Art. 22: Includes right to asylum:	Art. 7(g) —	Art. 64 Art. 116 0	Art. 19(7)(a) 0	Art. 41 Art. 43 0	Art. 37 —	Art. 2(11) Art. 2(21) 0/—	Art. 5 (XV) 0	Art. 24 Art. 36 0	Art. 17 Art. 19(9) +

International Covenant	American Convention	Bolivia (1967/1995 Amend.)	Venezuela (1961/1983 amend.)	Chile (1980/1989 amend.)	Paraguay (1992)	Uruguay (1967/1985 reinstated)	Peru (1993)	Brazil (1988)	Colombia (1991)	Ecuador (1979/1992 amend.)
Art. 13: Can only expel an alien in accordance with law and alien shall be able to express reasons against expulsion	Art. 22(6)				Art. 41 0/—			Art. 5 (LII) —	Art. 35 Art. 100 0/—	
Art. 14: Core criminal defendant rights (See Table 2 supra)	Art. 8: In addition, confession is only valid if made without coercion	Art. 14 Art. 16 —	Art. 60(4-8) —	Art. 19(3) & (7) —	Arts. 16-18 +	Art. 12 Arts. 20-25 —	Art. 2(24)(e-h) —	Arts. 5 (LIII-LX, LXIII, LXXIV, LXXIV) +	Art. 29 Art. 31 Art. 33 0/+	Art. 19(17) 0/—
Art. 15: Prohibition on ex post facto laws	Art. 9	Art. 16 Art. 33 0	Art. 60(2) Art. 44 0	Art. 19(3) 0	Art. 14 0		Art. 2(24)(d) 0	Art. 5 (XL) 0	Art. 29 0	Art. 19(17) (c) 0
Art. 16: Everyone has the right to recognition as a person	Art. 3								Art. 14 0	
Art. 17: No arbitrary or unlawful interference with privacy or family or home	Art. 11: Also includes correspondence and unlawful attacks on "honor and reputation"	Art. 20 Art. 21 —	Art. 59 Arts. 62-63 0	Art. 19(5) 0	Arts. 33-34 Art. 36 0	Art. 11 Art. 28 —	Art. 2(6-7)& (9) 0/+	Arts. 5 (X-XII) 0	Art. 15 Art. 28 0	Art. 19(2, 7, 8) 0
Art. 18: Freedom of thought, conscience and religion.	Art. 12 Conscience and religion	Art. 3 —	Art. 65 —	Art. 19(6) 0	Art. 24 0		Art. 2(3) 0/+	Arts. 5 (VI, VIII) 0/+	Art. 18 Art. 19 +	Art. 19(6) 0

International Covenant	American Convention	Bolivia (1967/1995 Amend.)	Venezuela (1961/1983 amend.)	Chile (1980/1989 amend.)	Paraguay (1992)	Uruguay (1967/1985 reinstated)	Peru (1993)	Brazil (1988)	Colombia (1991)	Ecuador (1979/1992 amend.)
Art. 19: Freedom of expression & right to hold opinions.	Art. 13: Thought and expression --	Art. 7(b) —	Art. 66 0/ —	Art. 19(12) +	Arts. 25-26 +	Art. 29 0	Art. 2(4) & (8) +	Arts. 5 (VIII-IX) 0	Art. 20 +	Art. 19(4) +
Art. 20: prohibition on war propaganda and advocacy of racial, national or religious hate	Art. 13(5)		Art. 66 —					Art. 5 (XVII) Art. 5 (XLII) 0		
Art. 21: Right to peaceful assembly	Art. 15	Art. 7(c) —	Art. 71 0	Art. 19(3) +	Art. 32 +	Art. 38 0	Art. 2(12) 0	Art. 5 (XVI) +	Art. 37 0/ +	Art. 19(13) +
Art. 22: Freedom of association	Art. 16: Includes restrictions on police and armed forces ability to form associations	Art. 222 —	Art. 70 —	Art. 19(15) 0	Art. 42 0	Art. 39 0	Art. 2(13) —	Arts. 5 (XVII-XXI) +	Art. 38 Art. 39 +	Art. 19(13) Art. 31(h) +
Art. 23: Preeminence of the family; right to marry; need consent of spouses	Art. 17	Art. 194 —	Art. 73 —	Art. 1 —	Ch. 4, generally 0/ —	Art. 40 —		Art. 226 0/ —	Art. 42 +	Arts. 22-23 0
Art. 24: Basic children's rights	Art. 18: Right to a name Art. 19: right to legal protection Art. 20: right to nationality Art. 17(5): equal protection for those born in and out of wedlock	Art. 193 Art. 195 Art. 199 0	Arts. 74-75 0/ —			Arts. 40-42 0		Art. 227 0	Art. 42 0/ —	Arts. 24-25 0

International Covenant	American Convention	Bolivia (1967/ 1995 Amend)	Venezuela (1961/ 1983 amend)	Chile (1980/ 1989 amend)	Paraguay (1992)	Uruguay (1967/ 1985 reinstated)	Peru (1993)	Brazil (1988)	Colombia (1991)	Ecuador (1979/ 1992 amend)
Art. 25: Equal opportunity to partake in public office	Art. 23: Law can regulate rights in the name of age, nationality, residence, education, civil & mental capacity	Art. 40 —	Arts. 110-11 —	Arts. 16-18 —	Arts. 117-26 0/—	Art. 77 0	Art. 2(17) —	Arts. 12, 14-16 0	Art. 40 0/+	Arts. 32-33 0
Art. 26: Standard equal protection clause	Art. 24: Does not list the protected classes	Art. 6 0	Art. 61 —	Art. 19(2) 0/—	Art. 46-47 +	Art. 8 0/—	Art. 2(2) 0	Art. 5 (intro) 0	Art. 13 0	Art. 19(5) 0
Art. 27: Right of ethnic or religious minorities to enjoy their culture and group identity.	N/A				Ch. V 0		Art. 2(19) 0	Art. 215 Art. 231 0	Art. 70 —	Art. 1 Arts. 26-28 0

[6]

The Justice Cascade:
The Evolution and Impact of Foreign Human Rights Trials in Latin America

Ellen Lutz* and Kathryn Sikkink**

I. Introduction

During the Falklands/Malvinas War of 1982, the British captured Argentine Navy Captain Alfredo Astiz. Non-governmental human rights organizations accused Astiz, a notorious figure during Argentina's "dirty war," of involvement in the disappearance of two French nuns, the arrest and killing of a Swedish girl, and the interrogation, torture, and disappearance of hundreds of Argentines at the Naval School of Mechanics in Buenos Aires.[1] After his capture, France and Sweden asked to question Astiz concerning their nationals, and the British transported him to London for that purpose. Astiz, availing himself of the protections afforded by the Geneva Convention on Prisoners of War, refused to answer. Although there was substantial evidence against him and the Geneva Conventions do not shield prisoners of war from prosecution for human rights crimes, neither country sought his extradition, nor did Britain entertain trying him in the United Kingdom.[2] Instead, he was repatriated to Argentina.

Seventeen years later, the British government arrested Chilean General and former President Augusto Pinochet on a Spanish extradition warrant for torture and other human rights crimes. This time, the British courts assiduously considered the jurisdictional issues posed by the Spanish request and determined that the Spanish courts had jurisdiction to try Pinochet for crimes committed in Chile over a decade before. Although British authorities ultimately allowed Pinochet to return to Chile, finding that he was too incapacitated to stand trial, the events in Europe had

---

* Executive Director of the Center for Human Rights & Conflict Resolution, Fletcher School of Law and Diplomacy, Tufts University.

* Executive Director of the Center for Human Rights & Conflict Resolution, Fletcher School of Law and Diplomacy, Tufts University.
** Professor of Political Science at the University of Minnesota. The authors greatly appreciate the insights, shared knowledge, and assistance of Naomi Roht Arriaza, Timothy J. Buckalew, Anthony Pereira, Maria Florencia Belvedere, and David Weissbrodt.

1. Tina Rosenberg, *Children of Cain: Violence and the Violent in Latin America* 79–141 (William Morrow 1991).
2. Nigel S. Rodley, *The Treatment of Prisoners Under International Law* 125–27 (Clarendon 2d ed 1999).

Chicago Journal of International Law

important political repercussions in Chile that are now rippling across Latin America and the rest of the world. Taking a lesson from Spain, a Netherlands court has determined that under a theory of universal jurisdiction it can try former Surinamese military dictator Desi Bouterse for human rights crimes committed in Suriname in 1982.[3]

From a political point of view, it would have been easier to try Astiz in 1982 than Pinochet in 1999. Astiz was a mid-level naval officer of a country then at war with Britain. Trying him for human rights violations would have given substance to the British government's rhetoric about the repressive nature of the Argentine regime. Pinochet was a former head of state and current senator-for-life of a country that had supported Great Britain during the Falklands/Malvinas War. This Article examines what changed between 1982 and 1999 that made Pinochet's arrest in Britain possible. We address two main questions: (1) why, in the last two decades of the 20th century, was there a major international norms shift towards using foreign or international judicial processes to hold individuals accountable for human rights crimes; and (2) what difference have foreign judicial processes made for human rights practices in the countries whose governments were responsible for those crimes.

A. THE IMPETUS FOR THE "JUSTICE CASCADE"

We argue that the surge of foreign judicial proceedings was neither spontaneous, nor the result of the natural evolution of law in the countries where the trials occurred. Rather, it was the result of the concerted efforts of small groups of activist lawyers who pioneered the strategies, developed the legal arguments, often recruited the plaintiffs and/or witnesses, marshaled the evidence, and persevered through years of legal challenges. These groups of lawyers resemble an *advocacy network*, in that they are interconnected groups of individuals bound together by shared values and discourse who engage in dense exchanges of information and services.[4] The transnational justice network was atypical, however, because its membership was confined to a handful of groups of lawyers with appreciable technical expertise in international and domestic law who systematically pursued the tactic of foreign trials. In this sense, the transnational justice network resembles what political scientists call an *epistemic community*—a network of professionals engaged in a common policy enterprise with recognized expertise and competence in the particular domain and an authoritative claim to policy-relevant knowledge in that issue or domain.[5] In other ways, however, the transnational justice network differs from a typical epistemic community. According to the epistemic community literature, states turn to epistemic

---

3.   Marlice Simons, *Dutch Court Orders an Investigation of '82 Killings in Suriname*, NY Times 12 (Nov 26, 2000).

4.   Margaret E. Keck and Kathryn Sikkink, *Activists Beyond Borders: Advocacy Networks in International Politics* 2 (Cornell 1998).

5.   Peter Haas, *Introduction: Epistemic Communities and International Policy Coordination* 46 Intl Org 1 (1992).

communities in situations of complexity and uncertainty for information to help them understand the situation and their interests. But states did not turn to the transnational justice network for expertise in a situation of complexity. Instead, the transnational justice network independently pursued justice for human rights violations often in the face of governmental indifference or recalcitrance. The transnational justice network thus blends characteristics of advocacy networks and epistemic communities. Like advocacy networks, it is motivated by shared principled ideas. Like epistemic communities, it is a network of professionals with recognized expertise and competence, and an authoritative claim to policy relevant knowledge.

The transnational justice network did not operate in a vacuum. It was part of a broader human rights advocacy network working in the context of a broad shift in international norms towards greater protection for human rights.[6] At times, key members of the transnational justice network were simultaneously leaders in the broader human rights network.

In a previous article we explored what prompted Latin American states to shed dictatorial regimes that routinely engaged in serious human rights abuses and replace them with elected regimes that for the most part comply with fundamental international human rights norms. We concluded that this transformation was best explained by a broad norms shift between the late 1970s and the mid-1990s that led to increased regional consensus concerning an interconnected bundle of human rights norms, including the norms against torture and disappearance and the norm for democratic governance. The popular, political, and legal support and legitimacy these norms now possess is reinforced by diverse legal and nonlegal practices fashioned to implement and ensure compliance with them. We found this transformation to be consistent with what legal scholars at the University of Chicago, describing rapid, dramatic shifts in the legitimacy of norms and action on behalf of those norms, call a "norms cascade."[7]

There are not yet precise definitions or standard ways of showing the operation of a norms cascade.[8] Because most of the work on norms cascades has been done by legal theorists interested in domestic norms, there have not been efforts to model what

---

6. See Ellen L. Lutz and Kathryn Sikkink, *International Human Rights Law and Practice in Latin America*, 54 Intl Org 633, 654–57 (2000).

7. Cass R. Sunstein, *Free Markets and Social Justice* 36–38 (Oxford 1997); Randal C. Picker, *Simple Games in a Complex World: A Generative Approach to the Adoption of Norms*, 64 U Chi L Rev 1225 (1997); see also Martha Finnemore and Kathryn Sikkink, *International Norm Dynamics and Political Change*, 52 Intl Org 887, 902–04 (1998).

8. See Sunstein, *Free Markets and Social Justice* at 32–69 (cited in note 7); Picker, 64 U Chi L Rev 1225 (cited in note 7). Picker presents a fascinating computer simulation model of norms cascades, but also does not define or show how norms cascades operate in the real world. See also Finnemore and Sikkink, 54 Intl Org at 902–04 (cited in note 7).

an international norms cascade would look like. We suggest that norms cascades are collections of norm-affirming events. These events are discursive—they are verbal or written statements asserting the norm. We are careful to define a norms cascade as something different from changes in actual behavior, because we are interested in exploring the impact that norms have on behavioral change.

In Latin America during the last two decades of the 20th century there was a rapid shift toward recognizing the legitimacy of human rights norms and an increase in international and regional action to effect compliance with those norms. The "justice cascade" has occurred in the context of that larger human rights norms cascade. This phenomenon can be likened to the aftershock of an earthquake. While its genesis is the larger norms transformation, its independent impact is significant and produces its own set of consequences. Moreover, those consequences are not limited to Latin America. They are reverberating internationally and contributing to a transformation in international norms reflected in the creation of such new international bodies as the International Criminal Court ("ICC"), and changing popular and political expectations regarding the treatment of perpetrators of human rights abuses in other parts of the globe, including greater judicial acceptance of the principle of universal jurisdiction.

The justice norms cascade is being operationalized through a series of norm-affirming events including the decisions of foreign courts to try cases involving violations of international human rights, the active participation of non-governmental organizations ("NGOs") and governments in the process of establishing the ICC, and the willingness of states to ratify the ICC treaty. Even cases like *Pinochet*, in which a foreign court recognized the legitimacy of a third country's jurisdiction but ultimately did not take steps to ensure the trial of the perpetrator, can be seen as norm-affirming events.

B. HOW FOREIGN JUDICIAL PROCESSES HAVE IMPACTED HUMAN RIGHTS PRACTICES IN LATIN AMERICA

The transnational justice network operates by enabling individuals whose access to justice is blocked in their home country to go outside their state and seek justice abroad. This dynamic is similar to the primary mechanism of other transnational advocacy networks. Foreign court rulings against rights-abusing defendants have the effect of putting pressure "from above" on the state where the rights abuses occurred. Increasingly, this pressure serves to open previously blocked domestic avenues for pursuing justice. Looking at other advocacy networks, Keck and Sikkink have called this dynamic a "boomerang pattern"—domestic activists bypass their states and directly search out international allies to bring outside pressure on their states.[9] Thus,

---

9. Keck and Sikkink, *Activists Beyond Borders* at 12 (cited in note 4).

to understand the domestic impact of transnational justice network activity, we must look at the interaction of both domestic and international judicial and political processes. *Pinochet* is a model for this type of complex interaction. For domestic political reasons, almost all human rights trials were blocked in Chile prior to Pinochet's arrest in Great Britain. But the decision of the British House of Lords that Spain had jurisdiction to try him for human rights abuses had the effect of opening judicial space for the human rights trials now underway in Chile.

Such boomerangs have not worked in all the cases we explore in this Article. The domestic impact of foreign judicial processes has depended on other factors as well— specifically in the amount of publicity those processes received, the parallel development of more general international human rights law, the receptiveness of domestic legal and political systems in the target states, and a change over time in regional attitudes with respect to human rights. In order to document these conclusions, we turn to a chronological description of key foreign human rights cases, and examine their evolution and impact. First, we briefly contrast our theoretical approach with alternative theoretical explanations.

II. ALTERNATIVE THEORETICAL APPROACHES TO EXPLAIN THE EMERGENCE AND EFFECTIVENESS OF A JUSTICE NORMS CASCADE[10]

The approach adopted here is an "ideational" approach to the emergence and effectiveness of justice norms. An ideational approach suggests that the origins of many international norms lie not solely in preexisting state or societal interests but in strongly held principled ideas (ideas about right and wrong). These ideas are fundamental for shaping a state's perceptions both of its interests and its identity, which in turn determine state policies. Ideational theorists view the international system as a society made up not only of states, but also of non-state actors that may have transnational identities and overlapping loyalties. In such a society, states change their behavior not only because of the economic costs of sanctions, but because of changing models of appropriate and legitimate statehood, and because the political pressures of other states and non-state actors affect their understanding of their identity and their standing in an international community of states. International law and international organizations are the primary vehicles for expressing community norms and for conferring collective legitimation. Human rights norms are particularly important because a good human rights performance signals to other members of the society that the state belongs to the community of democratic states.[11] In the language

---

10. This section draws on some ideas from a forthcoming review article by Hans Peter Schmitz and Kathryn Sikkink, *Human Rights and International Relations Theory*, in Walter Carlsneas, Thomas Risse, and Beth Simmons, eds, *Handbook of International Relations* (forthcoming Sage 2002).

11. This is the approach in Thomas Risse, Stephen Ropp, and Kathryn Sikkink, eds, *The Power of Human Rights: International Norms and Domestic Change* (Cambridge 1999); Kathryn Sikkink, *The Power of Principled*

Chicago Journal of International Law

of international relations theory, human rights practices have become "constitutive" of the identity of a democratic state.

The ideational perspective assumes that the institutionalization of human rights norms independently influences state actors to comply with them. In this sense it resembles the "managerial" approach to norm compliance discussed by such legal theorists as Thomas Franck and Abram and Antonia Chayes.[12] We maintain that state actors are drawn towards the rhetorical acceptance of human rights norms not only by virtue of their intrinsic appeal, or as the result of discussion and jawboning at international conferences, but also because active human rights pressures and sanctions by state and non-state actors contribute to processes of socialization and emulation. Ideational theorists are still grappling to satisfactorily explain which norms are most likely to be intrinsically appealing to states, and under what conditions are they likely to have an influence. This Article continues to explore these issues.

The main alternatives to the ideational approach are the realist approach associated with the work of Stephen Krasner, and a "republican liberal" approach put forward by Andrew Moravcsik.[13] Realists argue that international norms emerge and gain acceptance when they are embraced and espoused by the hegemon.[14] Conversely, realists argue that powerful hegemonic states can block any progress on human rights. This theory has some initial plausibility for explaining the justice cascade when we consider that the earliest foreign human rights trials began in US courts. But it does not explain why the US cases have been less effective, while the cases in Spain (clearly not a hegemon) have been much more effective. Nor does this approach explain why certain human rights initiatives proceeded when hegemons were followers, not leaders, or when hegemons actively opposed them. Consistent with the realist approach, US leadership was important for setting up the international tribunals for Rwanda and the former Yugoslavia. But the process of establishing the ICC treaty is going ahead in the face of active US opposition. Finally, realist theorists do not provide a convincing explanation for why and when hegemonic states are willing to begin pursuing human

Ideas: Human Rights Policies in the United States and Western Europe, in Judith Goldstein and Robert Keohane, eds, *Ideas and Foreign Policy: Beliefs, Institutions, and Political Change* 139–72 (Cornell 1993); Keck and Sikkink, *Activists Beyond Borders* (cited in note 4).

12. See Thomas M. Franck, *Fairness in International Law and Institutions* (Clarendon 1995); Thomas M. Franck, *The Emerging Right to Democratic Governance*, 86 Am J Intl L 46 (1992); Abram Chayes and Antonia Handler Chayes, *The New Sovereignty: Compliance with International Regulatory Agreements* (Harvard 1995). For a survey of approaches, see Harold Hongju Koh, *Why Do Nations Obey International Law?*, 106 Yale L J 2599 (1997).

13. These three approaches are also discussed by Andrew Moravcsik, *The Origins of Human Rights Regimes: Democratic Delegation in Postwar Europe*, 54 Intl Org 217, 225–26 (2000).

14. Stephen D. Krasner, *Sovereignty, Regimes and Human Rights*, in V. Rittberger and P. Mayer, eds, *Regime Theory and International Relations* 139-167 (Oxford 1993); John G. Ikenberry and Charles Kupchan, *Socialization and Hegemonic Power*, 44 Intl Org 283–315 (1990).

rights norms, when they did not do so before. What triggered US court willingness to consider international human rights cases in the 1980s and 1990s? Why was Britain willing to find Pinochet extraditable to stand trial for human rights crimes in 1998, but not willing to take action with respect to Astiz in 1982?

When liberal theory is used to explain the adoption of human rights norms, regime type is a crucial factor. Moravcsik argues that states accept binding human rights treaties mainly as a means of political survival—for example, newly democratizing states are most likely to ratify legal human rights instruments to protect still unstable democratic regimes from opponents who might attempt to overthrow them. He provides convincing evidence from Europe that the earliest supporters of binding human rights treaties were newly democratizing states, while the more well-established democracies initially failed to support the treaties, or even worked to weaken them. Hence, Moravcsik argues, the emergence and evolution of human rights institutions is mainly a function of newly democratic governments' perceptions of domestic threat, rather than the result of outward-projected activities by the established and most powerful democracies in the international system. Where realists emphasize coercion, liberals claim voluntary, self-interested, and rational behavior of state actors in accepting long-term limits to sovereignty.

Evidence from the Americas does not clearly confirm the liberal or realist theories. In the Americas, established democracies (except for the United States) have supported regional and global human rights systems from the start.[15] But after the regional wave of re-democratization between 1978 and 1991, the newly democratizing countries rapidly ratified international and regional human rights treaties. We do not know with certainty what motivated them. Along the lines of liberal theory suggested by Moravcsik, it is likely that part of the motivation was the need to protect their democracies against the danger of being overthrown. However, these ratifications were also intended to signal the countries' newly reestablished democratic identity and their reentry into the community of democratic states. In some cases domestic policy makers who believed in the human rights ideals were the driving force behind the ratifications. Thus, the record provides evidence for both liberal and ideational perspectives. Realism also is relevant to the Americas. US foreign policy was extremely active in promoting its own vision of human rights and democracy throughout the region. Though that policy was often contradictory and inconsistent, the United States has exercised active hegemonic leadership with regard to human rights in the region.

---

15. Costa Rica, Colombia, Uruguay, and Canada ratified early the Optional Protocol to the International Covenant on Civil and Political Rights; and Costa Rica and Venezuela were the first two countries to accept compulsory jurisdiction of the Inter-American Court.

III. Events Contributing to the Justice Cascade

A. The US Cases

The practice of "borrowing" foreign judicial systems to seek justice for past human rights abuses began in the United States in 1979 with the path-breaking *Filartiga v Peña-Irala*,[16] and the family of cases that followed. The US cases differed from the later Spanish cases in that they were civil instead of criminal, and they required as a basis for jurisdiction that the defendant be physically present in the United States. An interconnected group of lawyers pursued these cases, each learning from and building upon previous efforts.

Since the mid 1970s, human rights NGOs in Chile, Argentina, Guatemala, and elsewhere, to the extent their governments allowed them to operate at all, dedicated themselves to protesting and documenting human rights violations and ensuring that the evidence they uncovered was protected. This served multiple functions. It served as a clearinghouse of information that domestic attorneys could use when demanding information about the whereabouts of a disappeared person or seeking the release of a political prisoner. It preserved a record that could one day be used to hold perpetrators accountable and ensure that history was accurately recorded. Finally, it aided international human rights groups by providing accurate evidence of violations that they could use when appealing to other governments and inter-governmental organizations to exert pressure to stop the violations. Latin American human rights advocates actively cooperated with international human rights organizations to ensure that governments and international organizations used the provided information for this purpose.

As awareness of human rights violations in Latin America filtered north, human rights lawyers in the United States sought ways to help heighten pressure on Latin American governments. A creative group of lawyers at the New York-based Center for Constitutional Rights ("CCR") uncovered a little used jurisdictional statute called the "Alien Tort Claims Act" which provides: "The district courts shall have original jurisdiction of any civil action by an alien for a tort only, committed in violation of the law of nations or a treaty of the United States."[17] In 1979, these lawyers got their first opportunity to test whether this jurisdictional basis could be used to sue a foreigner in a US court for money damages for violations of human rights that occurred abroad. The plaintiffs, Dr. Joel Filartiga and his daughter Dolly, filed suit in federal district court for the torture and murder of their seventeen-year-old son and brother Joelito. The defendant, Americo Norberto Peña-Irala, was the former Police Inspector of Asunción, then illegally residing in New York. The Filartigas alleged that he kidnapped and killed Joelito to pressure Dr. Filartiga to end his political activities.

---

16.   *Filartiga v. Peña-Irala*, 630 F2d 876 (2d Cir 1980).

17.   28 USC § 1350 (1994) (originally drafted in 1789).

The Second Circuit Court of Appeals decision in *Filartiga* broke new ground. It declared that torturers, like pirates and slave traders before them, were "enemies of all mankind" who could be tried wherever they were found.[18] After the Second Circuit rendered its ruling in 1980, Peña-Irala was deported and defaulted. The district court awarded the Filartigas $10 million in compensatory and punitive damages to "make clear the depth of the international revulsion against torture" and in the hope that it would deter other would-be torturers from engaging in similar conduct.[19]

The success of *Filartiga* provided US human rights lawyers with a new avenue for striking back at perpetrators of human rights abuses and the means to offer some satisfaction to individuals who had suffered. A network of US lawyers mobilized to take on these cases and before long the nuances of the legal theories first raised in *Filartiga* were being tested in the courts. Many of the lawsuits involved victims and perpetrators of human rights abuses from Latin America. The cases we discuss here are representative of this trend.

In January 1987, human rights advocates discovered Carlos Guillermo Suarez-Mason, former Commander of Argentina's First Army Corps, living clandestinely outside of San Francisco, California. The First Army Corps had jurisdiction over the city and province of Buenos Aires and was purported to be responsible for as many as half of all disappearances, deaths, torture, and prolonged arbitrary detentions during Argentina's dirty war during the mid- to late-1970s. Immediately three overlapping teams of lawyers, including lawyers working on behalf of CCR, Americas Watch, and the American Civil Liberties Union of Southern California, filed suit in US federal court in San Francisco. Their clients were half a dozen Argentine victims who were tortured, imprisoned, or disappeared during Suarez-Mason's rule. Although three separate lawsuits were filed, the pro bono lawyers coordinated their litigation strategies (one lawyer, Juan Mendez, the Executive Director of Americas Watch, was part of the legal team in each of the three cases) and default judgments were entered against Suarez-Mason in all three suits.[20] One case set an important legal precedent: until that time, federal courts had been willing to find defendants liable for torture and murder, but were reluctant to find that "disappearances" were "torts . . . in violation of the law of nations." In a moving self-reversal, District Judge Jensen concluded in *Forti v Suarez-Mason* that there existed a "universal and obligatory international proscription of the tort of 'causing disappearance.'"[21] Like Peña-Irala,

18. *Filartiga*, 630 F2d at 890 (cited in note 16).
19. *Filartiga v Peña-Irala*, 577 F Supp 860, 866 (E D NY 1984).
20. *Forti v Suarez-Mason*, 672 F Supp 1531 (N D Cal 1987); *Martinez Baca v Suarez-Mason*, No C-87-2057 (N D Cal April 22, 1988); *de Rapaport v Suarez-Mason*, No C-87-2266 (N D Cal April 11, 1989).
21. *Forti v Suarez-Mason*, 694 F Supp 707, 711 (N D Cal 1988). The Court ruled that this tort had two essential elements: "(1) abduction by state officials or their agents; followed by (2) official refusals to acknowledge the abduction or to disclose the detainee's fate." Id.

Suarez-Mason, after failing to defeat the court's jurisdiction, refused to defend himself in the US civil litigation. Each of the plaintiffs received a six-figure default judgment that included compensatory and punitive damages.

In June 1991, nine Guatemalans and one US citizen filed suit in the US district court in Boston against former Guatemalan Minister of Defense General Hector Gramajo. Gramajo was served with process while attending his commencement from the John F. Kennedy School of Government at Harvard University. This case was spearheaded by the CCR in cooperation with the Lowenstein International Human Rights Clinic at Yale Law School and El Rescate Legal Services in Los Angeles. The plaintiffs, Kanjobal Indians and a missionary who worked with them, alleged they were forced to flee Guatemala as a direct result of abuses inflicted upon them or their families by Guatemalan military forces who ransacked their villages and brutalized them. Some of the plaintiffs were subjected to torture and arbitrary detention. Others were forced to watch as family members were tortured to death or summarily executed. One plaintiff's father disappeared. The plaintiffs maintained that in his roles as Vice Chief of Staff and Director of the Army General Staff, commander of the military zone in which the plaintiffs resided, and Minister of Defense, Gramajo was personally responsible for ordering and directing the implementation of the program of persecution that caused their suffering. Gramajo refused to defend himself and voluntarily returned to Guatemala. A default judgment of $47.5 million was entered against him in 1995.

B. THE EUROPEAN CASES

Latin American human rights advocates also collaborated with their counterparts in Europe to apply outside pressure on their governments to bring rights violators to justice. In Europe they did this, not by filing civil lawsuits, but by pushing European courts to criminally try, in Europe, alleged perpetrators of rights violations that took place in Latin America. This was possible for two reasons. First, many European countries, unlike the United States, recognize the passive personality basis for criminal jurisdiction in which a state may exercise criminal jurisdiction over anyone who injures one of their nationals, no matter where the crime occurred. Second, the Southern Cone countries were populated by Spaniards, Italians, and others of European descent, and many of these European countries recognize as nationals their children and even subsequent generations. As a result, transnational justice network lawyers were able to convince European judges that they had jurisdiction to criminally try Latin American perpetrators of rights abuses for the torture, disappearance, or murder of their nationals.

The most prominent early case of this type involved Alfredo Astiz, alleged to be responsible for the torture and presumed murder in Argentina of two French nuns, Alice Domon and Leonie Duguet, among other crimes. Their lawyers, supported by human rights advocates that were part of the transnational justice network, pressed a

French court to take up his case. In March 1990, that court tried Astiz in absentia for these crimes, found him guilty, and sentenced him to life in prison. This, apparently, was the first time a French court had convicted a foreigner in absentia for crimes committed against its citizens on foreign soil. France then asked Argentina to extradite Astiz. Consistent with its legal position that Astiz was protected from trial for the nuns' deaths by the *Punto Final* measure,[22] and by its across the board refusal to submit its citizens to stand trial abroad for crimes committed in Argentina, Argentina refused. But by doing so, Argentina jeopardized its relations with France. France objected, in 1995, when the Argentine Naval Command announced that Astiz was to receive a promotion, and that promotion was stopped. In 1996, before Argentine President Carlos Menem went to France to present Argentina's credentials to join the Organization for Economic Cooperation and Development, Astiz was removed from active duty with the Argentine Navy.[23]

In 1998, the normally press-averse Astiz, who though "retired" from the Navy remained under military discipline and enjoyed full privileges including a pension, access to health care, and the right to wear a uniform, gave an interview to *Tres Puntos*, an Argentine periodical.[24] In the interview he described his actions in kidnapping during the dirty war and boasted that he did his duty and felt no remorse. He also bragged that the Navy was protecting him and ensuring his comfortable retirement, and he threatened journalists who wanted to know more about the fate of the disappeared that he and his former colleagues were "trained to kill." Responding immediately, the naval command placed him under a sixty day arrest; when President Menem proclaimed that he had brought the Navy into disrepute, Astiz was sacked. He also was criminally charged for offenses including justifying crime, attacking the constitutional order, and threatening behavior, though after a trial in early 2000 he was sentenced to a mere three month suspended sentence.

France was not the only European country interested in trying Astiz. Sweden sought him for the murder of one of its nationals, Dagmar Hagelin, a teenager who was arrested and murdered in Buenos Aires, probably as a result of mistaken identity, and put out an international warrant for his arrest. Spain also sought his arrest.

Astiz's case was included in an orchestrated effort by Argentine exiles living in Spain to convince a Spanish court to file criminal complaints against Argentine military junta leaders for human rights crimes in Argentina between 1976 and 1983. On March 28, 1996, an association of Spanish prosecutors (*Unión Progresista de*

---

22. The *Punto Final* Law, adopted by the Argentine legislature in late 1986, set a sixty day limit on the filing of new criminal complaints against anyone for crimes committed during Argentina's dictatorship. Americas Watch, *Truth and Partial Justice in Argentina: An Update* 48 (April 1991).

23. *Menem bids on OECD Status*, Latin America Regional Reports: Southern Cone (March 14, 1996).

24. Gabriela Cerruti, *Interview with Alfredo Astiz*, Tres Puntos (Marko Miletich, trans), reprinted in *Harper's* 25 (April 1998); *Astiz speaks out of turn about killings, Menem sacks officer for damaging navy's image*, Latin American Regional Reports: Southern Cone Report (Feb 3, 1998).

Fiscales) formally triggered proceedings before Spain's "National Audience" Investigatory Court for alleged crimes against humanity including genocide and terrorism. *Izquierda Unida*, the third largest political party in Spain, working with SERPAJ, the Argentine human rights NGO headed by Nobel laureate Adolfo Perez Esquivel, filed a subsequent private criminal action (*acción popular*). On June 28, 1996, Judge Baltazar Garzón asserted that his court had jurisdiction to investigate the Argentine case.[25]

Around the same time, Chilean exiles in Spain adopted a similar strategy and filed the first of two cases against the Chilean military junta. That case similarly was succeeded by a private criminal action by private groups and individuals including the Salvador Allende Foundation, the *Unión Progresista de Fiscales*, and a number of Chilean citizens. On July 25, 1996, Judge Manuel Garcia Castellon accepted jurisdiction over the Chilean case and began an investigation.[26]

In October 1998, upon learning that Pinochet was in England, the *Unión Progresista de Fiscales* asked Judge Garzón to request the opportunity to interrogate Pinochet about his role in "Operation Condor," a multinational intelligence network that operated in the Southern Cone in the 1970s that was implicated in the disappearance and killing of Argentine dissidents. When the United Kingdom refused to allow the interrogation without an arrest warrant, Judge Garzón formally requested Pinochet's extradition to Spain. Around the same time, the *Agrupación de Familiares de Detenidos y Desaparecidos de Chile* (Chilean Group of Relatives of Detained and Disappeared People) requested that Pinochet and other junta members be charged with genocide, terrorism, and torture. With Pinochet as the nexus, the Spanish judicial system consolidated the Argentine and Chilean cases before Judge Garzón, whose case was the former in time. On October 30, the National Audience affirmed Spain's jurisdiction over the Argentine and Chilean cases and, on November 3, Judge Garzón issued a request of extradition against Pinochet. Garzón's 285-page indictment against Pinochet was issued on December 10, 1998. In it he charged Pinochet with genocide for designing and implementing a plan, coordinated down to the smallest detail, to eliminate a sector of the Chilean population. He also charged Pinochet with terrorism and torture.[27]

---

25. F. Javier Leon Diaz, 'The 'Pinochet Case,' From the Spanish Perspective* (on file with authors); Richard J. Wilson, *Spanish Criminal Prosecutions Use International Human Rights Law to Battle Impunity in Chile and Argentina*, available online at <http://www.Derechos.org/koaga/iii/5/wilson.html?pinochet+extradition> (visited Mar 25, 2001), originally published in ACLU Intl Civ Lib Rep (Jan 1997).

26. Id.

27. Id.

C. Transnational Justice Network Steps to Strengthen the Principle of Universal Jurisdiction

The transnational justice network did not limit its work to bringing cases in foreign courts. It also was pro-active in pushing for changes in international law that would strengthen its capacity to bring cases. Jurisdiction in the US civil cases discussed above was founded not on a treaty but on customary international law and narrow US jurisdictional statutes. But by accepting jurisdiction, the US courts effectively declared that states had at least a permissive right to assert universal jurisdiction over human rights crimes that violated customary international law. While reliance on the universality principle of jurisdiction had been used in the past for such acts as piracy, slave trading, and violence against ambassadors, *Filartiga* (albeit a civil lawsuit) was the first case to apply the principle in a non-wartime human rights case.

Prior to the late 1970s, international norms proscribing the most heinous war crimes, crimes against humanity, and genocide were well established as a matter of customary international law and were embedded in widely ratified treaties. These treaties underscored both the criminality of these acts and the legal principle that persons alleged to have committed these crimes, by virtue of the fact that they are crimes against the international community, can be tried by any state whenever the alleged offender is found within that state's territory.[28] Factors such as where the acts occurred, the identity of the victims, or the extent of contacts with the forum state are not barriers to the principle of universal jurisdiction.

As a matter of practice, universal jurisdiction was rarely relied on as a basis for trying persons accused of heinous human rights crimes. Countries that tried persons accused of war crimes or crimes against humanity usually had more traditional bases for asserting jurisdiction to do so: the acts occurred on that state's territory (territorial basis for jurisdiction); the defendant was a national of the trying state (the nationality principle of jurisdiction); or the victim was a national of the trying state (the passive personality principle of jurisdiction).[29] The most prominent exceptions were the Nuremberg Trials after World War II[30] and the Adolf Eichmann trial in Israel, in

---

28. Consider the Convention on the Prevention and Punishment of the Crime of Genocide, 78 UNTS 277 Art 6 (1948). Note that Article 6 of the Genocide Convention provides that "persons charged with genocide or any of the other acts enumerated in article III shall be tried by a competent tribunal of the State in the territory of which the act was committed, or by such international penal tribunal as may have jurisdiction" but commentators and courts have interpreted this provision as one that does not exclude the universal basis of jurisdiction, at least on a permissive basis. See Rodley, *The Treatment of Prisoners* at 102 (cited in note 2).

29. See generally, Jordan J. Paust, et al, *International Criminal Law: Cases and Materials* 95–107 (Carolina 1996).

30. *Demjanjuk v Petrovsky*, 776 F2d 571, 581–83 (6th Cir 1985).

which, in addition to the universal basis of jurisdiction, the Israeli court relied on a uniquely Israeli basis for jurisdiction: crimes against the Jewish people.[31]

By the late 1970s, the principal international human rights treaties, including the ICCPR, the American Convention on Human Rights, and the European Convention on Human Rights were in force. These treaties prohibited conduct such as summary execution, torture and other cruel, inhuman or degrading treatment or punishment, prolonged arbitrary detention, and so forth, and required ratifying states to take measures to ensure that victims of such acts had enforceable remedies. But they did not specify the criminal elements of these acts nor did they require states to try persons alleged to be responsible for them. The transnational justice network, led by lawyers working under the auspices of Amnesty International, many of whom also were involved in the human rights lawsuits described above, pushed hard for the adoption of additional international treaties that would define, criminalize, and clarify the full scope of states' obligations with respect to violations of many of the rights protected generally under these treaties. They won early support from key European governments that collaborated with the NGOs to press for their adoption, and lobbied other states to support provisions binding ratifying states to treat such conduct as criminal.

In the most pronounced example, during the drafting the United Nations Convention Against Torture and Other Cruel, Inhuman or Degrading Treatment or Punishment, the transnational justice network and its government supporters pushed hard to ensure that the treaty required states to criminalize torture and establish jurisdiction to try torturers, not only under traditional bases of jurisdiction, but also under the universality principle of jurisdiction. The latter proved to be one of the most controversial proposals before the working group assigned by the United Nations Human Rights Commission to prepare the treaty, and it was not until the working group's final session in 1984 that the matter was resolved.

The transnational justice network prevailed and the text of the treaty, which was adopted by the General Assembly in December 1984, provides, "Each State Party shall [. . .] take such measures as may be necessary to establish its jurisdiction over such offenses in cases where the alleged offender is present in any territory under its jurisdiction and it does not extradite him."[32] The Organization of American States ("OAS") took this same approach to universal jurisdiction the following year when it adopted the Inter-American Convention to Prevent and Punish Torture. The subsequent wide ratification of these treaties contributed to fortifying the means for states to try or extradite individuals responsible for torture or similar heinous crimes.

---

31. Hannah Arendt, *Eichmann in Jerusalem: A Report on the Banality of Evil* 5 (Penguin rev and enlgd ed 1994).
32. Convention Against Torture and Other Cruel, Inhuman, or Degrading Treatment or Punishment, 24 ILM 535, Art 5 para 2 (1985).

The turning point for application of the universality principle of jurisdiction came in *Pinochet* when Judge Garzón asserted Spain's competence to try Pinochet on the principle of universal jurisdiction for certain international crimes recognized under Spanish law. Because of the double criminality rule,[33] and the fact that British law does not give British courts as broad a jurisdiction over international crimes as Spanish law affords Spanish courts, the House of Lords was unwilling to extradite Pinochet for all the crimes for which he was indicted by Judge Garzón. But, relying on Britain's implementation of the Convention Against Torture, a treaty to which both Britain and Spain are parties, the House of Lords determined that Pinochet could be extradited to Spain to stand trial for torture that had occurred in Chile.[34]

D. REGIONAL EVENTS THAT CONTRIBUTED TO THE JUSTICE CASCADE

While the cases described above and a handful of other human rights cases were proceeding through US courts, events in Latin America were not stagnant. The unprecedented wave of repression and human rights abuses that inundated the region in the 1970s and 1980s gave way by the early 1990s to the restoration of electoral democracy and human rights improvements in a majority of countries in the region. This transformation was interwoven with increased regional consensus and adherence to international and regional instruments that codified states' obligations to protect human rights and ensure democratic participation in government. Between 1976 and 1978 the most important international human rights treaties relevant to Latin America—including the ICCPR and the American Convention on Human Rights— entered into force. Probably in response to pressure from the Carter administration and the international bandwagon effect accompanying these treaties' entry into force, a handful of Latin American countries ratified the major human rights instruments between 1977 and 1981. But after 1985 ratifications surged. This can only be explained by the occurrence of a genuine norms shift that rippled through the region. Torture, disappearance, extrajudicial executions, and government violations of other basic civil and political rights were no longer regarded as legitimate tactics of regimes trying to preserve national security. Instead, they came to be viewed as crimes.

Argentina carried the idea of criminal responsibility the farthest when it tried nine former junta members for human rights crimes during the 1976-83 dictatorship. In Argentina, and elsewhere, this produced a clamor for amnesty or other forms of immunity from prosecution from military personnel and others who were responsible

---

33. Under this rule, which is embedded in most international agreements addressing the subject of extradition, a person cannot be extradited to stand trial for a crime that is not recognized by the state to which the request for extradition is submitted.

34. *R v Bow Street Metro Stipendiary Magistrate and Others, ex parte Pinochet Ugarte*, 1 AC 147 (House of Lords 1999).

for such past crimes and their supporters. In many cases these officers believed they were shielded from prosecution by self-amnesty laws that they passed prior to leaving power. In others, the question of amnesty did not arise until negotiations leading to civilian rule. In both cases, military officers threatened to topple fragile new democracies if protection from judicial sanctions was not ensured.

Throughout the region, amnesty laws impeded prosecutions, but did not squelch demands for justice. To the contrary, these demands grew louder with the passage of time and the consolidation of democracy throughout the region. Military threats to undermine democracy unless individual officers were protected from prosecution had the unintended consequence of contributing to a regional norms shift with respect to electoral democracy. In most Latin American countries, a return to military rule was politically unacceptable. Thus, while elected governments acquiesced to demands for legal protections from prosecution for those responsible for past rights abuses, governments, individually and collectively, focused on ways to shore up democracies so that they would be able to resist threats to popular electoral sovereignty. At the national level, many newly elected governments downsized military forces and rapidly promoted unimplicated junior officers who saw their role as serving a democratically elected regime; senior officers who participated in prior military regimes were retired.

At the international level, states cooperated through the OAS to adopt specific norms promoting democracy. In 1991, the OAS General Assembly adopted a resolution on democracy in the Americas called the Santiago Commitment to Democracy and the Renewal of the Inter-American System.[35] The OAS General Assembly also established a process for convening an ad hoc meeting of the region's foreign ministers in the event of any sudden or irregular interruption of democratic governance by a member state.[36] The following year, members of the OAS strengthened this regional commitment to democracy when they amended the OAS Charter with the Protocol of Washington. That Protocol provides that two-thirds of the OAS General Assembly may vote to suspend a member state whose democratically elected government has been overthrown by force.[37] The Santiago Declaration and the Protocol of Washington have provided the procedural basis for many regional actions supporting democracy in Latin America during the 1990s.

---

35. Resolution adopted at the Third Plenary Session (June 4, 1991), reprinted in Viron P. Vaky and Heraldo Muñoz, *The Future of the Organization of American States* 103–106 (Twentieth Century 1993).

36. AG/RES 1080 (XXI-0/91), Representative Democracy, Resolution adopted at the Fifth Plenary Session (June 5, 1991), reprinted in Vaky and Muñoz, *The Future of the Organization of American States* at 107–08 (cited in note 35).

37. 1-E Rev OEA Documentos Officiales OEA/Ser.A/2 Add 3 (SEPF), signed December 14, 1992, entered into force September 25, 1997.

E. INTERNATIONAL EVENTS PROPELLING A DEMAND FOR JUSTICE

Internationally, events were changing as well. The Cold War ended and with it the potential for proxy wars in Latin America and elsewhere diminished. Broader international consensus in favor of liberal democracy was accompanied by a greater international political willingness to allow institutions like the OAS and the United Nations to achieve agreement on how to respond to new crises than had been possible during the Cold War. In the case of Haiti, the United Nations Security Council broke new ground when, at the behest of the United States, it approved Resolution 940 which called on member states to "use all necessary means to facilitate the departure from Haiti of the military leadership." This was the first time the Security Council legitimized the use of force in defense of democracy.[38]

Haiti turned out to be the exception. Lacking an international military force or the funds necessary to recruit state military forces to serve the interests of international peace on behalf of the United Nations, the UN Security Council often found itself searching for alternative measures, short of the use of troops, to intervene to stop bloodshed or inhumanity. One such measure was the establishment of criminal tribunals for the purpose of trying individuals responsible for such crimes.

In 1993, in response to widespread and systematic murder, rape, and "ethnic cleansing" of civilians in Bosnia, the UN Security Council, acting under the peace enforcement provisions of the UN Charter (Chapter VII), established the Ad Hoc Tribunal for the Prosecution of Persons Responsible for Serious Violations of International Humanitarian Law Committed in the Territory of the Former Yugoslavia since 1991 ("ICTY"). Eighteen months after the establishment of the ICTY, the Security Council established a similar court to prosecute genocide and other systematic, widespread violations of international humanitarian law in Rwanda ("ICTR"). Although both tribunals got off to rocky starts, as of October 2000 the ICTY was actively prosecuting 38 of 65 indictees accused of atrocities in connection with the conflict in the former Yugoslavia, had sentenced four, and acquitted one. The ICTR had convicted eight and had forty-three others in detention. As judicial institutions, the ICTY and ICTR are increasingly respected for their independence and their decisions are setting international precedents concerning some of the most important legal questions of our time. For example, in 1998 the first conviction by an international tribunal of an individual charged with genocide occurred when the ICTR found Jean-Paul Akayesu, the political leader in Rwanda's Taba commune, guilty of genocide. The tribunal further held that rape and sexual violence constitute genocide if committed with the specific intent to destroy a targeted group.

---

38. Robert A. Pastor, *More and Less than it Seemed: The Carter-Nunn-Powell Mediation in Haiti, 1994*, in Chester A. Crocker, Fen Osler Hampson, and Pamela Aall, eds, *Herding Cats: Multiparty Mediation in a Complex World* 507–525 (US Inst of Peace 1999)

The institutionalization of the two ad hoc tribunals reinvigorated international interest in establishing a permanent international criminal court. After the Nuremberg Trials, the newly formed United Nations took up the task of planning for a permanent international criminal court to try war criminals and perpetrators of human rights. But the Cold War, and its attendant stalemate at the United Nations, disrupted serious efforts in this regard. Renewal of these efforts in the mid-1990s was spearheaded by a coalition of actors including the lawyers who had worked on the human rights litigation in US courts, NGOs, such as Human Rights Watch, the Lawyers Committee for Human Rights, and Amnesty International, that had long pushed for trials of perpetrators and other forms of accountability in the wake of gross violations of human rights, and governments, particularly in Europe, that had internalized the international justice ethic. Such a court would redress the chief complaint concerning the two ad hoc tribunals—that they were arbitrary because they were created in response to events in two countries, whereas no similar court was available to prosecute those responsible for similar tragedies elsewhere.

In the summer of 1998, the United Nations sponsored an international diplomatic conference in Rome to draft a statute for an International Criminal Court ("ICC"). In Rome a group of some sixty "like minded" countries and hundreds of NGOs propelled the process and achieved consensus or compromise to achieve a comprehensive 128-article statute. Several Latin American states, including Argentina, Brazil, Chile, Costa Rica, and Venezuela were among the key players in the "like minded" group; Argentina and Venezuela played particularly active roles.

A treaty enabling states to participate in the ICC is now open for signature; the ICC will be created once sixty nations ratify it. The Rome Statute describes in extensive detail every aspect of the ICC's operation and functioning, but further refinement is ongoing. As of January 1, 2001, 139 countries had signed and twenty-seven had ratified the treaty.

The Rome Statute is a major accomplishment that provides a workable starting point for a court that could make a lasting difference. Objectively, its success will be measured by the number of states that ratify the treaty and join the Assembly of States Parties, the adequacy of funding provided to ensure that once it is established it is a viable court, and by the degree to which, because it exists, those who hold power and would abuse that power by committing terrible abuses of human rights, are deterred by the knowledge that they will be held accountable law for their crimes in an international court of law. Subjectively, it already is a success. The Rome Statute underscored international commitment to the rationale for universal jurisdiction— that some crimes are crimes not only against the people and states in which they occur, but against the international community as a whole. This, in turn, boosted the confidence of national judiciaries to prosecute or respond favorably to other country's requests to extradite persons accused of human rights crimes, no matter where those crimes took place.

IV. THE IMPACT OF THE US AND EUROPEAN CASES ON THE VICTIMS AND IN THE COUNTRIES WHERE ABUSES OCCURRED

Turning now to the impact of the US and European cases on the victims and in the countries where the human rights violations occurred, we examine two types of impact: (1) direct impact on individuals; and (2) indirect impact altering societal or institutional perceptions or practices. Direct impact fosters change in how actors who care about or are involved with these issues feel and act. For senior political leaders it is reflected in what policies they call for or promote. For military or police officials and others involved in perpetrating past abuses, it is reflected in the level of contrition they display, as well as their attitudes about future involvement in the political arena. For human rights organizations it is measured in their sense of how much progress has been made on the human rights front. For victims and their families, it is measured by the degree to which they feel that justice has been served and the extent to which it enables them to leave the past in the past and move forward with their lives.

Indirect impact occurs where foreign trials have an effect on political processes and institutions in the country where the abuses occurred that in turn have implications for perpetrators and victims of human rights abuses. These can be either perceptual changes, which occur when non-governmental actors are emboldened to seek political change as a result of an external judicial process, or actual changes in institutional practice effected by governmental organs in response to external events.

In the United States, the transnational justice network lawyers dedicated hundreds of hours of volunteer time to the civil lawsuits discussed above. They received substantial support from all the leading international human rights organizations. Their efforts led to US federal court judgments on behalf of the plaintiffs. But other than having the defendants declared "enemies of all mankind," or the equivalent, the plaintiffs received little direct benefit. Moreover, the impact on the human rights situations in the countries where the abuses occurred was minor.

In Paraguay no court was willing to enforce the default judgment awarded in *Filartiga*, thus the family was never compensated. A decade after the decision, Dolly Filartiga told a newspaper reporter that "little has changed in her native Paraguay . . . [and that] she still dares not return for fear of reprisal because of her role in exposing Joelito's murderer."[39]

Little changed in Paraguay during the years Peña-Irala was in the United States. Paraguay still endured the dictatorship of General Alfredo Stroessner, who held power from 1954 to 1989. Torture and prolonged arbitrary detention of opponents of the regime were routine occurrences throughout the Stroessner years, and all efforts to develop democratic institutions and civil society were stifled. In an interview, Dr.

---

39.   Kenneth R. Clark, *Murder in Paraguay: HBO Docudrama Tells Frustrating Tale of Family's Fight for Justice*, Chicago Tribune C15 (April 18, 1991).

Filartiga stated that his case made very little impact in Paraguay and did not lead to an improvement in human rights there. "Here, nothing happened. They didn't even know about [the Filartiga case]. They treated me as an anti-Paraguayan. No information on the case was published. Here it was all a dead-end street."[40] Former US Ambassador to Paraguay Robert White reported some nervousness at the highest levels of the Paraguayan government after the decision was rendered: "'After the case was decided in favor of Dr. Filartiga one of the people closest to General Stroessner told me that I just had to do everything possible to get this decision reversed. . . . [N]o Paraguayan government figure would feel free to travel to the United States if this judgment was upheld because . . . they would feel that they would be liable to arrest.'"[41] But even if nervousness in fact inhibited the travel plans of key Paraguayan political figures, it did not alter their behavior in Paraguay, nor did the lawsuit have any impact on human rights policies or practices in the country. The Filartiga family got some sense of justice when a foreign court pronounced Peña-Irala liable, but this satisfaction was overshadowed by the complete lack of response in Paraguay.[42]

Similarly in the lawsuit against Suarez-Mason, none of the plaintiffs collected on their judgments. The plaintiffs in one of the lawsuits, Deborah Benchoam and Alfredo Forti, are still attempting to collect on their judgments in Argentina, but so far have been unsuccessful. Two of the *Rapaport v Suarez-Mason* plaintiffs, the widowed mother and sole surviving sibling of a disappeared youth, reported that the suit's most significant benefit was family reunification. Before the lawsuit, the elderly mother was denied permission to travel to the United States to visit her exiled daughter because US Immigration and Naturalization Service ("INS") officials feared that she would remain and become a burden on the United States. Only after the district court judge ordered her appearance in connection with the case did INS relent and grant her a visa.

But unlike Peña-Irala, Suarez-Mason returned to a political climate in Argentina that was fundamentally different from when he commanded the First Army Corps in Buenos Aires. After the armed forces' humiliating defeat in the Falklands/Malvinas War in 1982, and the restoration of democracy the following year, judicial accountability for past human rights abuses became a national obsession. Revulsion at the abuses perpetrated by the military on thousands of Argentine citizens during the dirty war created sufficient political space for newly elected President Raul Alfonsin's government to try nine former junta members in 1985; five were convicted and sentenced to time in prison.

---

40.   Interview with Dr. Joel Filartiga, Asunción, Paraguay, January 2, 1996 (on file with authors).

41.   Richard P. Claude, *The Case of Joelito Filartiga in the Courts* 328, 336, in Richard Pierre Claude and Burns H. Weston, eds, *Human Rights in the World Community: Issues and Action* 336, 328–339 (Pennsylvania 2d ed 1992).

42.   Filartiga interview (cited in note 40).

Among the leaders of Argentina's military dictatorship, Suarez-Mason was among the most radically anti-democratic, anti-Semitic, and anti-communist. In 1984, before President Alfonsin had secured legislation to try his predecessors for human rights abuses, a federal judge issued a warrant for Suarez-Mason's arrest in a case involving the disappearance of a scientist in 1978. Suarez-Mason, who announced he would not be a scapegoat, immediately left the country. No other Argentine military officer fled Argentina rather than face trial and, for doing so, he was held in contempt by his military comrades-in-arms. When he refused to appear before the court, they stripped him of rank and expelled him from the Army. After human rights activists discovered that he was living in the United States and filed civil lawsuits against him, the government of Argentina requested his extradition to stand trial for hundreds of human rights crimes. Extradition for thirty-nine murders was approved and he was returned to Argentina where he immediately was arrested. Because of his military seniority and the early date on which charges were brought against him, he was not subject to either of two amnesty measures introduced in the latter years of the Alfonsin administration to appease military officers who were hostile to continued trials for rights abuses during the dirty war—the due obedience law and the *Punto Final*. But criminal proceedings against him languished and in December 1990 he benefited from the second of two pardons offered by President Menem to military officers who remained indicted or convicted of human rights crimes during the dictatorship.

Suarez-Mason's encounters with the Argentine judicial system did not end with his pardon. In December 1996 he was charged by an Argentine court with making an anti-Semitic remark in violation of Argentine law and $1,500 of his assets were frozen.[43] In December 1999 he was arrested again for human rights crimes, this time for the theft of children of Argentina's "disappeared," suppression of their identities, illegal custody and concealment.[44] Meanwhile, in December 1997, Spanish judge Baltasar Garzón, the judge who indicted Pinochet, indicted Suarez-Mason for the disappearance of Spanish citizens in Argentina. He also was convicted in absentia by an Italian court for kidnapping and murdering eight Italian citizens during the dirty war.

By publicizing Suarez-Mason's whereabouts, the US civil litigation had the direct impact of prodding the Argentine government into seeking his extradition and continuing judicial proceedings against him in Argentina. But his case was exceptional. Although the military opposed trials of military officers for their conduct during the dictatorship, they did not oppose trying Suarez-Mason because of his cowardice in fleeing the country, which they regarded as an act of dishonor. Yet, the fact that by the time he was pardoned he had not yet been tried is evidence of political

---

43. *Ex Military Chief Charged for Antisemitic Comments*, Agence France Presse (Dec 4, 1996).
44. Marcela Valente, *Rights—Argentina: Arrests of Military Officers Continue*, Inter Press Service (Dec 6, 1999).

ambivalence about trying him and how little indirect impact his case had on political decision-making at the time.

For the *Gramajo* plaintiffs, the process similarly has been frustrating and has stirred up painful memories. They have not been compensated nor have they experienced any sense that justice has been done. Their only satisfaction is knowing that Gramajo was found liable by a US court.[45] The lawsuit apparently has had an impact on General Gramajo. In the early 1990s, Gramajo was particularly well regarded in some US political circles; they saw him as a key mediator between the Guatemalan military and the country's political sector.[46] A *Washington Post* article in 1992 claimed that many expected Gramajo to win the next presidential elections in Guatemala in 1995.[47] But the tide turned quickly. A month before the court's decision was handed down, then-US Congressman Robert Torricelli accused the Central Intelligence Agency ("CIA") of being implicated in human rights abuses in Guatemala. A week before the court issued its decision, the Clinton administration decided to cut off covert CIA aid to Guatemala, which had continued despite Congress' 1990 decision to end military aid. In that week's edition of *The Nation*, US journalist Allan Nairn specifically accused Gramajo of being one of the "CIA's men" in Guatemala.[48] Gramajo defended himself in a Guatemalan radio broadcast by asserting that he worked "with the CIA" and not "for the CIA."[49] On the heels of these events the US court found that "plaintiffs have convincingly demonstrated that, at a minimum, Gramajo was aware of and supported widespread acts of brutality committed by personnel under his command resulting in thousands of civilian deaths. . . . [and that he] refused to act to prevent such atrocities."[50]

After this confluence of bad publicity, Gramajo's cordial relations with influential political groups in the United States were severed. Apparently in response to the lawsuit, US military officers distanced themselves from him and the US government withdrew his invitation to speak at a military conference in Miami.[51] Possibly due to this loss of external sponsorship, his political fortunes in Guatemala also faded. He received a tiny fraction of the presidential vote in the 1995 elections and since that time human rights activists in Guatemala and the United States have

45. Telephone interview with Alice Zachmann, December 22, 2000 (on file with authors).

46. *Human Rights Causes Row between the US and Guatemala*, in Latin American Regional Reports: Mexico and Central America Report (March 29, 1990).

47. Shelley Emling, *Guatemala's Possible Future President*, Wash Post (Foreign Journal) A13 (Jan 6, 1992).

48. Allan Nairn, *CIA Death Squads*, The Nation 511–13 (April 16, 1995).

49. Fabiana Frayssinet, *Guatemala: Gramajo Case Sheds Further Light on CIA Intervention*, Inter Press Service (April 18, 1995).

50. *Xuncax v Gramajo*, 886 F Supp 162, 172–73 (D Mass 1995).

51. Colum Lynch, *US backs away from Guatemala general*, Boston Globe 9 (April 15, 1995).

lost sight of him. He plays no role in public life in Guatemala and nothing about him appears in the news.[52]

The impact of the European cases turned out to be more significant. The turning point was *Pinochet*. Although most of those indicted or charged with human rights crimes have, until now, evaded punishment, momentum for such trials has built and more and more cases are moving forward. The Argentine and Chilean cases before Judge Garzón, though initially brought on behalf of only a handful of victims, have swelled to include hundreds, and international arrest warrants have been issued for dozens of former junta members and military officers from those two countries.

In Italy, a criminal case against Suarez-Mason, Omar Santiago Riveros, and five other Argentine military defendants for the murder of eight Argentines of Italian descent including one infant went to trial after a sixteen-year investigation. On December 6, 2000, after a fourteen month trial, the Court found all seven guilty. Suarez-Mason and Riveros were sentenced, in absentia, to life imprisonment; the remaining defendants were each sentenced, in absentia, to twenty-four years in prison.[53]

Another Italian judicial proceeding occurred with respect to retired Argentine Army Major Jorge Olivera. Olivera was arrested in August 2000 while in Rome with his wife celebrating their silver wedding anniversary. His arrest was based on a French warrant charging him with participation in the kidnapping, torture, and disappearance of Marie Anne Erize Tisseau, a French citizen who lived in Argentina during the dictatorship. Olivera's defense attorney produced Erize's death certificate, which prompted the Italian court to conclude that the crimes with which he was charged could not be tried in Italy. Consequently, Italy was barred from extraditing him to France. Olivera was released and immediately returned to Argentina. Upon his return, Argentina charged him with forging the documents that won his release.[54]

The impact of the European cases has even reached Latin America. In August 2000, Mexico arrested retired Argentine Navy Captain Miguel Cavallo as the plane on which he traveled from Mexico City to Buenos Aires stopped to refuel in Cancún. In November 1999, Spanish Judge Baltasar Garzón filed charges against Cavallo for torturing Thelma Jara de Cabezas, a Spanish woman living in Buenos Aires in the late 1970s, and the murder of Monica Jurequi and Elba Delia Aldaya, two other Spaniards. Judge Garzón issued an international warrant for his arrest. Cavallo was in Mexico because an Argentine company he heads had obtained a contract to operate Mexico's newly privatized National Registry of Vehicles. The Mexican newspaper *Reforma* received complaints from Mexican drivers about arcane vehicle registration

---

52. Zachmann Interview (cited in note 45).
53. *Tribunal Penal de Roma*, Sentence of Dec 6, 2000.
54. *Ex-Argentine Officer Charged with Forgery for Papers That Won Him Jail Release*, Deutsche Presse-Agentur (Sep 23, 2000).

requirements, and asked its correspondent in Buenos Aires to investigate. The reporter uncovered Cavallo's past and the international warrant for his arrest, and *Reforma* passed the information on to Mexican authorities. Cavallo is now in jail in Mexico awaiting the outcome of Spain's request for his extradition.[55]

V. NATIONAL RESPONSES IN LATIN AMERICA TO INTERNATIONAL EVENTS PROPELLING THE JUSTICE CASCADE

In Chile, the arrest of Pinochet appears to have lifted psychological, political, and juridical barriers to justice by weakening the powerful forces blocking such trials in Chile since the return to democracy. International pressures bolstered by routine retirement and replacement in the Chilean judiciary and military have yielded a more liberal judiciary and a younger, less implicated military officer corps. The longer Pinochet's detention in Britain continued, and the more legal decisions that accumulated justifying his arrest, the more significant the domestic impact appeared to be. While political and military leaders, and human rights organizations and victims, disagreed about whether Pinochet should be tried at all, most agreed that if he was tried the trial should take place in Chile. This consensus was founded on both ideological and practical concerns. Although temporarily weakened during the dictatorship, Chileans have a long tradition of pride in their judicial system, which has a reputation for impartiality, fairness, and effective administration of justice. They also have a high level of national pride and confidence in their capacity to solve domestic problems without external interference. In addition, Chileans agreed that the fairest trial would occur where all the witnesses and evidence were located, and where people of Chile, of all political persuasions, could closely observe the proceedings.

Since Pinochet's arrest, twenty-five Chilean officers have been arrested on charges of murder, torture, and kidnapping. In an interview, Defense Minister Edmundo Perez Yoma discussed a "new attitude" emerging among the military high command: "You deal with it or it will never go away. You have to confront it—that's the changed attitude."[56] In July 1999, Chile's Supreme Court upheld a lower court decision that the amnesty law was no longer applicable to cases in which people had disappeared. Until the bodies of the victims were located, the crime was not murder but kidnapping, meaning the crime was a continuing event beyond the 1978 amnesty deadline.

When British authorities allowed Pinochet to return to Chile after determining that his ill health prevented him from standing trial, many feared that these legal advances in Chile would be reversed. But, despite a hero's welcome, and his surprising vigor on the Santiago tarmac, New York Times reporter Clifford Krause's description

---

55. Bruce Zagaris, *Mexico Detains Argentine on Spanish Extradition Request for "Dirty War" Atrocities*, 16 Intl Enforcement Law Rep 960 (Oct 2000).

56. Clifford Krause, *Chilean Military Faces Reckoning for its Dark Past*, NY Times 1 (Oct 3, 1999).

of Pinochet as "a real nowhere man" most accurately reflects his current position.[57] His return sped up negotiations between military and civilian officials on a human rights accord that created a mechanism to uncover what happened to approximately 1,200 people who disappeared during Pinochet's dictatorship. On June 5, 2000, a Santiago appeals court ruled, by a vote of thirteen to nine, that Pinochet could be stripped of his lifetime immunity from prosecution and could be tried for the disappearance of at least nineteen people in October 1973. Two months later, the Chilean Supreme Court affirmed the lower court's ruling. In December 2000, Pinochet's case was once more in the news: a Chilean prosecuting judge ordered Pinochet to stand trial for human rights crimes.

The European cases against the Argentine military officers had the unanticipated effect of spurring change in Argentina's willingness to try human rights cases. The decision by the Argentine government to imprison Admiral Massera and General Videla pending trial apparently was a preemptive measure in response to the Spanish judge's international arrest warrants.[58] Argentina has even extended its judicial reach transnationally; albeit in a case in which the events took place in Argentina. In November 2000, a former Chilean secret police agent was sentenced to life in prison in Argentina for his role in the assassination of former Chilean General Carlos Prats and his wife, Sofia Cuthbert. Prats was Chile's Army Commander in Chief during the administration of Salvador Allende and fled to Argentina when Allende was overthrown. Prats and his wife were killed in a car bomb in Buenos Aires on September 30, 1974. The Argentine court has formally requested the extradition of Pinochet to stand trial in Argentina for his role in the Prats murder. The first judge to receive the extradition request in Chile recused himself citing "pressure from the right."[59] A new judge was appointed and is considering arguments concerning Argentina's request.[60]

The Spanish court cases have raised the hopes of human rights activists throughout Latin America that justice for rights abuses in their countries is possible. Following the lead of Argentine and Chilean human rights activists, Guatemalan Nobel Peace Prize winner Rigoberta Menchu filed a case in the Spanish court against three former Guatemalan presidents and military leaders, Romeo Lucas García, Oscar Mejía Victors, and Efrain Ríos Montt, currently president of the Chamber of Deputies, and five lower ranking officials, for murders and other crimes that she asserts amount to genocide against Guatemala's indigenous Mayan population. Lawyers for the defendants have counterattacked by filing a suit against Menchu in

57. Clifford Krause, *Pinochet at Home in Chile: A Real Nowhere Man*, NY Times 12 (Mar 5, 2000).
58. Interview with Dr. Martin Abregu, Director of the *Centro de Estudios Legales y Sociales* ("CELS"), Buenos Aires, July, 1999 (on file with authors).
59. *Former Chilean agent sentenced to life in prison*, Agence France Presse (Nov 21, 2000).
60. *Judge rejects Pinochet's defense against extradition*, UPI (Dec 1, 2000).

Guatemalan courts charging her with treason, sedition, and violation of the constitution for filing charges in a foreign court. In December 2000, the Spanish court dropped the indictments saying the case should be brought before the courts in Guatemala, but left open the possibility that the Spanish courts could provide jurisdiction if the political pressure or legal restrictions impede the case from going forward there. Guatemala never had a blanket amnesty law as did Chile and Uruguay, nor a statute of limitations for human rights violations that effectively served as an amnesty as did Argentina. Thus numerous human rights cases have moved forward in Guatemalan courts, but because these cases are plagued by death threats and intimidation of witnesses, political interference, and scores of procedural flaws, few have led to convictions.

Meanwhile, *Pinochet* and the efforts of Menchu to bring former Guatemalan dictators to account in Spain have contributed to an aura of contrition among Guatemala's senior policymakers. In August 2000, Guatemalan President Alfonso Portillo admitted government responsibility for atrocities committed during the country's thirty-six-year civil war and pledged to investigate massacres, prosecute those responsible, and compensate the victims. Moreover, in a show of good faith, President Portillo signed an agreement with the Inter-American Human Rights Commission ("IACHR") that affirms Guatemala's institutional responsibility for war crimes and empowers the IACHR to monitor the actions of the Guatemalan government in light of its new promises to redress those past wrongs.[61] In December 2000, the Inter-American Court found that the Guatemalan government had killed Efrain Bamaca Velasquez, a rebel leader, and the husband of human rights activist Jennifer Harbury. It is still too soon to know the impact of the Inter-American Court's decision on domestic legal processes in Guatemala.

Elsewhere on the continent, hopes are rising that more trials of high-ranking officials accused of human rights abuses will occur. In June 2000, Congressman Marcos Rolim, who heads the Human Rights Commission in Brazil's Chamber of Deputies, asked President Fernando Henrique Cardoso to strip former Paraguayan dictator Alfredo Stroessner of his political asylum. Once it is lifted he plans to ask Brazilian prosecutors to charge the former dictator with human rights violations during his nearly thirty-five-year rule in neighboring Paraguay. Congressman Rolim agreed that his trial in Paraguay would be preferable but argued that in light of the recent failed military coup and the continuing ties many current political actors in Paraguay still have to Stroessner, a trial in Paraguay could generate further political unrest. In his view, "Brazil, by giving asylum and protection to Stroessner, has

---

61. Jan Mcgirk, *Guatemalan Leader Admits Civil War Atrocities: Human Rights President Promises To Compensate Those Who Lost Relatives at the Hands of Military Government During Bloody 36-Year Conflict*, The Independent 12 (Aug 11, 2000).

responsibility for his destiny."[62] In December 2000, a Paraguayan court requested Stroessner's extradition from Brazil to stand trial for the 1977 disappearance of Paraguayan physician Agustin Goiburu, who was living in exile in Argentina when he disappeared in 1977.

In Haiti, democratically elected President Aristide's return was accompanied by a clamor for justice encouraged by Aristide and his successor, President Rene Preval. In November 2000, a court tried fifty-eight former military leaders and other lesser players in the 1991 coup that drove President Aristide from power. The case focused on the April 1994 massacre at the Raboteau shanty town in the coastal city of Gonaives in which approximately a dozen people were murdered and thrown into the sea, and many other residents were beaten or had their houses burned. For Haitians, although the trial focused on one human rights criminal event, it was symbolic of all the human rights crimes that occurred during the three-year Cedras regime. In the first phase of the trial, sixteen former soldiers and their henchmen who were arrested in Haiti were convicted; six others were acquitted. The convicted soldiers were sentenced to life imprisonment; the others received sentences between four and nine years. In the second phase, thirty-seven senior military officials, including former coup leader Raoul Cedras who in return for giving up power received a comfortable exile in Panama, were convicted of premeditated voluntary homicide and sentenced in absentia to life imprisonment.

Latin American countries also have enthusiastically supported efforts to establish the ICC. As of December 2000, Argentina, Bolivia, Brazil, Chile, Colombia, Costa Rica, Ecuador, Haiti, Honduras, Mexico, Panama, Paraguay, Peru, and Uruguay had signed the ICC treaty and were taking steps towards ratification. Three countries, Belize, Venezuela, and Uruguay, had ratified it. The Latin American embrace of an international court to try perpetrators of human rights is closely linked with the region's determination to promote and protect democracy, and countries' recognition that the rule of law and an effective independent judiciary are crucial elements of any functioning democracy. Contrary to Moravcsik's liberal republican theory, both old and new democracies in the region have moved quickly to sign and ratify the treaty. The Rome Statute gives preeminence to national judiciaries and state sovereignty by limiting the ICC's jurisdiction to situations where a state that has jurisdiction is unable or unwilling to investigate the matter, or to prosecute it if the outcome of an investigation determines prosecution is appropriate.[63] Thus in supporting the establishment of an international criminal court, Latin American democracies feel no

---

62. *Trial Sought for Long-Ruling Dictator*, St. Petersburg Times 10A (June 10, 2000) (quoting Brazilian Congressman Marcos Rolim).

63. Rome Statute of the International Criminal Court, Art 17, available online at <http://www.un.org./icc> (visited Mar 25, 2001).

threat to their sovereignty because criminal cases over which their national tribunals have jurisdiction will not end up before a world court.

VI. A CAUTIONARY TALE

Through the process of "borrowing" foreign judicial systems to seek justice for past human rights abuses, the justice network and human rights victims have had to face the limits of the process they have sought so fervently. The "successful" US civil cases, that produced little more than symbolic benefit for the plaintiffs, were prescient shadows of what could occur.

In November 2000, jurors in a federal court in Miami, Florida absolved two El Salvadoran generals, José Guillermo García, who was El Salvador's Minister of Defense, and Carlos Eugenio Vides Casanova, former director of El Salvador's National Guard, of civil liability for the abduction, rape and murder of four American churchwomen by National Guardsmen in 1980. Five enlisted National Guardsmen were convicted in El Salvador in 1984 of the crimes and were sentenced to thirty-years imprisonment. During their criminal trials, they asserted that they had acted on superior orders.

After listening to many days of testimony concerning the violence, chaos, and gross violations of human rights during El Salvador's twelve-year civil war, the jury concluded that the situation was so chaotic and command so decentralized that the generals lacked sufficient command over and control of their troops to be responsible for their conduct. The verdict, which was rendered after only eleven hours of deliberation, dismayed family members of the four churchwomen who had presented days of testimony about human rights abuses during the civil war that claimed 75,000 lives.

Trial observers asserted that the trial was closely watched by military officers in El Salvador, Guatemala, and elsewhere who were concerned that although they received amnesties they could yet be prosecuted.[64] During the trial, prosecutors in El Salvador sought to reopen the case of six Jesuits who were slain, along with their housekeeper and her daughter, in 1989. They were rebuffed by a Salvadoran court which ruled that the prosecutor's request was "without legal substance."[65] It bears noting that neither El Salvador nor Guatemala have yet signed the ICC treaty.

The lesson of the El Salvador case is that even the fairest trial does not always result in the outcome the transnational justice network seeks. Courts can achieve justice only to the extent the evidence to secure a conviction or civil finding of liability is available. Unfortunately, in human rights cases the evidence needed to support a

---

64. David Gonzalez, *Trial of Salvadoran Generals in Nuns' Deaths Hears Echoes of 1980*, NY Times A8 (Oct 21, 2000).

65. *New Charges Barred in Salvador Killings*, NY Times A12 (Oct 24, 2000).

judgment in a court of law often is controlled by those involved in human rights abuses who have reason to destroy it or otherwise ensure that it is never produced for use against them. Sovereignty concerns also may play a role. Thus, even if a government is willing to investigate, prosecute, or allow human rights trials to proceed in its courts, it may be unwilling to cooperate with a foreign court to accomplish the same purpose. Evidence also may be diluted by non-political factors such as the passage of time, the death of key witnesses, insufficient resources, or even immigration decisions that restrict the ability of parties to be present to press their claims in foreign courts.

Moreover, judicial systems are human institutions; individual attitudes and biases can insinuate themselves into even the fairest of processes. In the Salvadoran generals' case, jurors interviewed after the conclusion of deliberations said that notwithstanding the evidence to the contrary presented by the human rights NGOs representing the plaintiffs, they were persuaded that the generals had done what they could to curb abuses given the tumult of the era and a lack of resources to conduct effective investigations or to discipline their troops.[66]

VII. CONCLUSION

We have argued that a justice cascade is underway in Latin America today. This norms cascade was the result of the concerted efforts of a transnational justice advocacy network, made up of connected groups of activist lawyers with expertise in international and domestic human rights law. The justice cascade, in turn, is part of a larger human rights norms cascade in Latin America, and its success is very much connected to the larger progress of human rights and democracy norms and practices in the region. This explanation primarily reflects an ideational theory of international relations, that stresses the effects of ideas and norms on social life. We do not expect ideas, in and of themselves, to have a compliance pull. Rather, we argue that ideas are influential because of the actions, pressures, and sanctions of state and non-state actors aimed at promoting human rights norms. Aspects of both "liberal" and "realist" approaches are also relevant to understanding the justice cascade. Some of the most enthusiastic supporters of the justice cascade in Latin America have been newly democratizing states that are concerned about the stability of their new democracies. The position of the hegemonic US government at times plays an important role in supporting the justice cascade. Backtracking on human rights by the new US administration would, without doubt, slow down or even temporarily stall its progress. But, contrary to realist thought, lack of support from the hegemon will not decisively block the justice cascade, as the progress on the ICC Statute's ratification in

---

66.   David Gonzalez, 2 Salvadoran Generals Cleared by US Jury in Nuns' Deaths, NY Times A3 (Nov 4, 2000).

the region suggests. A full explanation of the justice cascade must include attention to the power of the principled ideas that undergird it, and the activism of states and NGOs that support and sustain it.

Although we do not yet know the full scope and extent of the justice cascade in Latin America, there is no doubt that a significant norms transformation has occurred, and that the process is ongoing. Twenty years ago trials of human rights perpetrators in foreign courts had little domestic impact on either individuals or policy. The victims got little more than the nominal benefit of having a judge—albeit a foreign judge in a foreign court—declare that the person they blamed for their suffering was indeed legally responsible. Today the domestic response to extranational trials and international efforts to establish an international criminal court is transforming the behavior of political leaders and military and police officers, heightening victims' and victims' family members' sense that justice is being served, and even changing the agendas of human rights organizations. Because of positive governmental responsiveness, many human rights NGOs in Argentina, Chile, and other Latin American countries are able to turn their attention to human rights issues other than the quest for justice for past human rights abuses. In some countries, policy and institutional changes have occurred in all branches of government, from courts, which have found ways to obtain jurisdiction over perpetrators of past abuses, to legislatures and executive branches of government. The latter have legislated or decreed human rights polices aimed at redressing past abuses, or have stood aside when their national judiciaries have moved ahead with judicial proceedings against past perpetrators.

The certainty that these events constitute a justice cascade and not merely opportunistic reaction to isolated external events is reinforced by the pervasive change in values in the region. Certainty also is evident in the willingness of governments to act to ensure its continuation, such as taking steps to prosecute past perpetrators when there was no immediate likelihood of their trial in a foreign court, as Haiti did, or signing an agreement with the IACHR to monitor compliance with promises to prosecute and redress past abuses, as President Portillo of Guatemala did. Thus the move towards justice is driven as much by policymakers' changing principles as by their pragmatic concerns, as the ideational approach would suggest. But pragmatic concerns are not absent here. The transnational justice network has used a "boomerang" dynamic similar to that used by other transnational advocacy networks. Domestic human rights groups have cooperated with international groups of lawyers to bring pressure from outside to bear on their governments and their courts. Where they have succeeded, it probably is a blend of principle and pragmatism that leads governments and militaries to conclude that if they are going to face trials, it is preferable to face them in their own country than abroad.

The consequences of this justice cascade are far reaching. With respect to the perpetrators, even if they never face punishment, or even trial, they are finding themselves "landlocked." Even where their own government is willing to protect them from the reach of foreign courts, they dare not travel abroad for fear that the country they travel to will extradite them to a country seeking to try them. This pressure is felt not only by those who know they are under indictment, but those who have reason to fear they might be indicted abroad.

The much bigger casualty seems to be the amnesty decrees that past Latin American dictators gave themselves before leaving office, or post-dictatorship democratic regimes gave their predecessors in exchange for their allowing democracy to flourish by not seizing power again. Old amnesties are not bearing up well against current national sovereignty concerns. Latin America's democracies care deeply about their international reputations and seem prepared to sacrifice former perpetrators' immunity if the alternative is an infringement of sovereignty resulting from having their former political leaders tried in a foreign court. No Latin American country, particularly those with rapidly consolidating democracies, wants to foster the perception that its courts lack the competence, capacity, or independence necessary to effectively try its own nationals. Moreover this view is shared not only by elected governmental officials, but by the armed forces that previously had insisted on amnesties, and by the non-governmental human rights organizations that consistently has demanded trials.

Still, there is plenty of evidence that in Latin America the justice cascade is far from complete. In countries that have not yet faced the possibility that foreign judiciaries will try their nationals, policy-makers have had far less enthusiasm for trials even though they find the *Pinochet* precedent worrisome. Thus Uruguay has taken steps to restrict the foreign travel of its nationals who were implicated in past abuses of human rights, while at the same time stepping up other initiatives, such as the establishment of a national commission to investigate the disappearances of Uruguayan nationals during the period when Uruguay and its neighbors all lived under military regimes. Even in countries where internalization of the justice cascade is more advanced, it is far from fully realized. Thus in Argentina, where there has been substantial progress with respect to conducting trials, there is far less movement when it comes to executing judgments for civil damages in human rights trials that occurred abroad. The inability of most plaintiffs to collect damages on their judgments suggests that the application of the rule of law to achieve justice for victims in non-criminal cases has not yet been swept up by the justice cascade.

We conclude that in Latin America, while the justice cascade is in progress, the extent of its realization in each country depends on numerous factors including: (1) the degree of consolidation of that country's democracy and legal system, (2) whether that country has directly faced the possibility that one of its former senior political figures would be tried abroad, (3) the amount of publicity and support foreign judicial processes have received, (4) the intensity of the determination of domestic human rights advocates and victims, amply supported by their international counterparts, to pressure their government to realize justice for past wrongs, (5) the degree to which each country feels it will bear some embarrassment or other international consequence for not conducting trials that is not outweighed by domestic political pressures exerted by the supporters of those it would try, and (6) the extent to which those now in power have internalized the justice norm and believe that trying past perpetrators is the right thing to do.

The consequences of the justice cascade, including its manifestation in Latin America, reach far beyond the region. Earlier we noted some of the efforts being taken by European states to bring to justice those from other countries responsible for egregious past violations of human rights. But the norms cascade is beginning to penetrate non-European regions as well. In February 2000, a group of Chadian rights activists and victims convinced a Senegalese court to indict former Chadian dictator Hissene Habre and four collaborators. Habre has lived in luxurious exile in Senegal since 1990, and Senegal was the first country to ratify the ICC treaty. Political events in Senegal have subsequently waylayed the process. In April, Senegal's new president, Abdoulaye Wade, appointed Habre's main attorney as his special legal adviser, and, in June, President Wade abruptly removed the judge who had indicted Habre from the case. In July a new judge found that Senegal did not have jurisdiction for the torture charges brought against Habre and dismissed the case. Meanwhile human rights activists in Chad, invigorated by the possibility that Habre might be prosecuted, filed suit in Chadian courts against their torturers. Chadian President Deby, sensitive to the international exposure his country is receiving as a result of Habre's indictment in Senegal, and to the heightened efforts of domestic human rights advocates to achieve redress for past crimes, met for the first time with human rights victims and told them that "the time for justice has come." President Deby promised them he would fire all former officials still serving in government who were involved in past abuses. He also promised that he would reopen the files of an investigatory commission that documented some 4000 killings and other human rights crimes during the Habre regime. The Commission's findings had been locked away by the Deby government and until now ignored.

While we cannot predict how widespread the justice cascade will be or how deeply it will penetrate, we can suggest some benchmarks that will help observers measure the depth of that penetration. Objective indicators include: (1) the number of trials held in countries where human rights abuses took place, (2) legislative changes in those countries that allow trials where none were permitted before, and (3) judicial decisions by domestic courts and perhaps by international bodies such as the Inter-American Court of Human Rights, that certain crimes are not included in amnesties. Subjective indicators include: (1) the career trajectories of individuals accused of human rights abuses, (2) the level of satisfaction of human rights victims involved in both foreign and domestic lawsuits or who were victims of or witnesses in criminal trials of human rights perpetrators, and (3) policy changes (and even political conversations about policy changes) relating to the prosecution of those responsible for human rights abuses in countries that have not yet been impacted by the possibility of a foreign human rights trial of one of their nationals. Studying these indicators over time will enable researchers to more fully evaluate the domestic impact of foreign human rights trials.

[7]

Justice, Accountability and Social Reconstruction: An Interview Study of Bosnian Judges and Prosecutors

By
The Human Rights Center and the International Human Rights Law Clinic, University of California, Berkeley, and the Centre for Human Rights, University of Sarajevo

I.

PREFACE

This study of judges and prosecutors in Bosnia and Herzegovina (hereinafter "BiH") is the first report in a multi-year study undertaken by the University of California, Berkeley, Human Rights Center regarding the relationship between justice, accountability and reconstruction in the former Yugoslavia.[1] The Human Rights Center conducts interdisciplinary research on emerging issues in international human rights and humanitarian law. The International Human Rights Law Clinic at the University of California, Berkeley School of Law (Boalt Hall) and the Centre for Human Rights at the University of Sarajevo collaborated with the Human Rights Center to conduct this study. The International Human Rights Clinic engages law students in projects designed to promote and strengthen human rights protections in national, regional and

---

1. This study is part of Communities in Crisis, an interdisciplinary, multi-institutional project of the Human Rights Center, University of California, Berkeley that is examining the relationship between the pursuit of international justice and local approaches to social reconstruction in the aftermath of genocide in Rwanda and the former Yugoslavia. Communities in Crisis seeks the following policy outcomes:

- To provide national and international policy makers, including those associated with the *ad hoc* tribunals and the International Criminal Court, with the first transnational study of the relationship between the pursuit of justice by international tribunals and local efforts at social reconstruction;
- To encourage transnational coalition building among university researchers and activists on issues of justice, development, and reconstruction;
- To broaden conceptions of accountability so as to foster community-based projects that combine advocacy for human rights with economic, social, and development programs; and
- To support the active participation of communities in researching their needs and developing programs.

international fora. The Centre for Human Rights seeks to build capacity within BiH to conduct human rights research as well as to integrate the study of human rights into university curricula.

Clinical Professor Harvey Weinstein, Associate Director of the Human Rights Center, Lecturer-in-Residence Laurel Fletcher, Associate Director of the International Human Rights Clinic and Ermin Sarajlija, then Acting Director of the Centre for Human Rights directed this project with the participation of Clinic interns Damir Arnaut, Daska Babcock-Halaholo, Kerstin Carlson, Brian Egan, Anne Mahle, Joyce Wan and Nazgul Yergalieva as well as Bosnian law students Edisa Peštek, Gordan Radić and Tamara Todorović. Professor Zvonko Miljko, University of Mostar (West), Assistant Elmedin Muratbegović, Univesity of Sarajevo and Professor Rajko Kuzmanović, University of Banja Luka served as faculty liaisons to the researchers during the field work portion of the study. The report was written by Professors Fletcher and Weinstein and Clinic interns Arnaut, Babcock-Halaholo, Carlson and Mahle. The researchers gratefully acknowledge the significant contribution of the staff of the Centre for Human Rights in Sarajevo, Acting Director Dino Abazović, Librarian and Archivist Saša Madackić and Progamme Officer Aida Mehiević.

II.

EXECUTIVE SUMMARY

This report describes the findings from an interview study conducted in June, July and August of 1999, of a representative sample of thirty-two Bosnian judges and prosecutors with primary or appellate jurisdiction for national war crimes trials. The purpose of this study was to assess the understanding of attitudes among these legal professionals towards the International Criminal Tribunal for the former Yugoslavia (hereinafter "ICTY" or "Tribunal") and prosecution of war crimes. We sought to clarify objections and resistance to the ICTY by examining: (1) the acceptability of international justice; (2) the factors that may contribute to misunderstandings or non-acceptance of international criminal trials; and (3) the perceptions of the relationship between criminal trials and social reconstruction. Based on our analysis of the findings we offer recommendations to strengthen the relationship between the Tribunal and the Bosnian legal community.

Our findings suggest that across national groups, participants supported the concept of accountability for those who committed war atrocities. Yet, the extent of support for the ICTY varied by national group. Participants generally lacked a clear understanding of the procedures of the Tribunal and were poorly informed about its work. However, all desired impartial information about the Tribunal with legal content, since judges and prosecutors had limited or no access to legal publications from or about the ICTY. A universal criticism of the ICTY by legal professionals was that they perceived their sporadic contact with the Tribunal as a sign of disrespect. Moreover, they expressed several areas of concern with the ICTY: its unique blend of civil and common law procedures; the way in which cases are selected; the way in which indictments are issued –

particularly sealed indictments; the length of detention and trials; and the evidentiary rules applied by the Tribunal. In some of these areas, participants of particular national groups expressed reservations unique to that national group. For example, the Bosnian Serb and Bosnian Croat participants disapproved of or questioned the use of sealed indictments. Further, virtually all participants in these two groups expressed concern that the ICTY was a "political" organization; in this context, "political" meant biased and thus incapable of providing fair trials.

Several themes and topics emerged on which participants across all national groups expressed consistent views, including:

Professionalism: Participants consistently emphasized their strong adherence to high professional standards, and associated professionalism with the strict application of legal rules to a particular case.

Justice: Participants supported the principles of justice and the impartial application of the law, even in instances in which the judicial verdict ran counter to public opinion.

Western European Legal Tradition: Participants viewed the Bosnian legal system as part of the Western European legal tradition and supported reform of the legal code to make it consistent with that of the developed European democracies.

Corruption and Decline in Standards: Participants denounced corruption – which they defined narrowly as bribery – in the legal profession in general and emphasized that they and their immediate colleagues did not engage in corrupt practices. Nevertheless, judges and prosecutors expressed grave concern about the impact on the legal profession of the loosening of professional standards during the war and the decline in the social status of the profession.

Politics: Participants cited financial dependence on the legislature as the primary threat to the independence of the judiciary. Judges and prosecutors denounced the destructive effects of political parties on the judicial system.

International Community: Participants supported efforts of the international community to strengthen the independence of judges and prosecutors. However, legal professionals criticized international organizations operating in BiH, commenting that international representatives frequently were unfamiliar with the Bosnian legal system and acted arbitrarily to impose external rule on the country and its legal institutions.

The impact of national identity clearly became evident as participants discussed their views regarding national groups; the role of the State; responsibility and accountability for the war; genocide; the role of the ICTY and the future of BiH. For example, with regard to genocide, Bosniak participants primarily believed that Serb forces had committed acts of genocide against Bosniaks while Bosnian Serb legal professionals generally stated either that they did not have sufficient information to give an opinion or that genocide was committed by all three sides. As well, most Bosnian Croat participants stated that acts of genocide occurred on "all three sides."

The implications of these findings are considered in Discussion (§ V). Based on our findings and analysis we recommend that the appropriate authorities:

- *enact* legislation that ensures the independence of the judiciary in both entities in BiH;
- *institutionalize* regular and sustained professional contact between legal professionals in each entity;
- *adjudicate* war crimes trials in each entity by a panel of three judges, one of whom should be a judge who is not a citizen of BiH or of any of the states of the former Yugoslavia;
- *pursue* the option of conducting ICTY trials on the territory of BiH supported by a rigorous protection program for witnesses, judges and legal professionals;
- *amplify* the ICTY outreach program;
- *examine* a range of alternatives to criminal trials to promote social reconstruction through the organization of an inter-entity council sponsored by the Office of the High Representative ("OHR"); and
- *incorporate* appropriate International Criminal Court (hereinafter "ICC") mechanisms to ensure transparency and accessibility with attention paid to the needs and concerns of the directly affected communities and their legal practitioners.

III.
INTRODUCTION

"The court was formed in Nuremberg where the war criminals were tried, and after that and despite that, the war criminals appeared throughout the world. And it will be so in the future. They cannot be deterred."

Bosnian Judge

"The Hague Tribunal doesn't serve justice. Look at that war criminal, Erdemović, who received five years for killing over seventy people. It is unjust that he should receive such a light sentence."

Woman of Srebrenica

"You cannot correct The Hague when it was planted and rooted badly. It was wrong in how it was established, structured, and funded. We want to relieve [former ICTY Prosecutor, Louise] Arbour and have them tried here – but in what courts? They would be obstructed by the entire structure."

Bosnian Journalist

"People do not have confidence in the Tribunal. But it is the only light at the end of the tunnel. Without it, there would be no justice and this would be the final betrayal."

Bosnian Magazine Editor

106   *BERKELEY JOURNAL OF INTERNATIONAL LAW*   [Vol. 18:102

The purpose of this study was to examine issues raised in four distinct areas:

(1) Is international justice acceptable to judges and prosecutors who work within a national framework?

(2) What factors contribute to misunderstandings or non-acceptance of international criminal trials?

(3) How do judges and prosecutors in Bosnia and Herzegovina perceive the relationship between criminal trials and social reconstruction?

(4) What processes can be put into place to facilitate the acceptance by the national legal system of an international court?

A. The Problem

This report is part of a larger study examining traditional assumptions regarding justice, accountability, and reconstruction in the aftermath of mass violence and genocide. Although the international community has paid much attention to conflict resolution and diplomatic mechanisms of violence prevention, it has devoted less attention to identifying the necessary aspects of the process of rebuilding a country torn apart by sectarian strife.[2] After initial humanitarian intervention has provided the necessities for survival, long-term development traditionally has focused primarily on economic factors while ignoring the social and psychological issues that precipitated the violence or arose as its consequence. How postwar societies understand the past, assign responsibility for atrocities committed and struggle to reconstruct divided communities is a multifaceted process about which there are many opinions but little understanding. Further, although conventional wisdom holds that criminal trials promote several goals, including uncovering the truth; avoiding collective accountability by individualizing guilt; breaking cycles of impunity; deterring future war crimes; providing closure for the victims and fostering democratic institutions, little is known about the role that judicial interventions have in rebuilding societies.[3]

In May 1993, the United Nations Security Council created an ad hoc international tribunal to try alleged perpetrators of war crimes committed since 1991 in territory the former Yugoslavia.[4] As noted in an ICTY document, one of its goals is to serve "as a means to assist in reconciliation and to prevent a recurrence of conflict."[5] However, unlike the Nuremberg and Tokyo tribunals, the ICTY is not the product of "victor's justice." The Tribunal, established under the auspices of the international community, has been charged with the prosecution of war crimes committed by all parties to the conflict. Nevertheless, as we

---

2. CARNEGIE COMMISSION ON PREVENTING DEADLY CONFLICT, PREVENTING DEADLY CONFLICT (Dec. 1997).

3. MARK OSIEL, MASS ATROCITY, COLLECTIVE MEMORY, AND THE LAW 6-10 (1997).

4. S.C. Res. 808, U.N. SCOR, 48th Sess., 3175th mtg., U.N. Doc. S/RES/808 (1993); S.C. Res. 827, U.N. SCOR, 48th Sess., 3217th mtg., U.N. Doc. S/RES/827 (1993).

5. International Criminal Tribunal for the former Yugoslavia, Office of the President, Outreach Program Proposal (1999) (unpublished report, on file with the *Berkeley Journal of International Law*)[hereinafter Outreach Program Proposal].

will indicate, many Bosnian Croat and Bosnian Serb legal professionals – members of national groups whose armed forces the international community has condemned as carrying out massive war atrocities – have dismissed the ICTY as a "political" court. Thus, the ICTY is plagued by a crisis of legitimacy in Bosnia.

Citizens of BiH from all national groups express ambivalence towards the ICTY. Many see the Tribunal as a critical step towards justice, while others see it as a manifestation of outside interference.[6] Coupled with this concern, many Bosnians and international organizations question the ability of the national judiciary, both in the Federation of Bosnia and Herzegovina (hereinafter "Federation") and in the Republika Srpska (hereinafter "RS"), competently to prosecute war criminals in a non-partisan manner. Finally, since the recently-established ad hoc Tribunals (the ICTY and the International Criminal Tribunal for Rwanda) are holding the first international trials since the Second World War, yet take place in a radically different context, their effect on domestic war crimes trials and their relationship to the domestic judiciary has still yet to be fully understood.

The ICTY procedures and rules of evidence were patterned primarily after the common law system, one unlike the civil law tradition of BiH. The international tribunals at Nuremberg and Tokyo created procedural rules that borrowed from the civil and common law systems. In contrast, the ICTY adopted a "largely adversarial" approach to its proceedings.[7] As the first president of the Tribunal explained, the judges wanted to remain "as neutral as possible" and therefore rejected most aspects of the civil law system, a system that allocates to the judge the primary task of investigating allegations and gathering the necessary evidence.[8] We postulated that the choice of procedural rules might have important implications for how accessible the Tribunal appeared to Bosnian judges and prosecutors. Yet there has been little systematic study on the impact that the choice of the rules of evidence and procedure has had on the perceptions of the international body by Bosnian legal professionals.

Despite the challenges posed by international criminal tribunals, United Nations support for international criminal prosecutions is growing, as demonstrated by the recent creation of the statute for a permanent International Criminal Court.[9] The involvement of the international community in the recent wars in the Balkans marks an important shift toward international intervention in con-

---

6. The Human Rights Center at University of California, Berkeley, conducted an informal survey of nongovernmental organizations (hereinafter "NGO's"), journalists, academics, survivors and representatives of international organizations in BiH in the summer of 1998 that defined the scope and nature of this project.

7. Antonio Cassese, President of the International Criminal Tribunal for the Former Yugoslavia, Summary of Rules of Procedure of the International Criminal Tribunal for the Former Yugoslavia, Address at a Briefing to Members of Diplomatic Missions (Feb. 11, 1994) *in* VIRGINIA MORRIS & MICHAEL P. SCHARF, AN INSIDER'S GUIDE TO THE INTERNATIONAL CRIMINAL TRIBUNAL FOR THE FORMER YUGOSLAVIA 650-51 (1995).

8. *Id.*

9. Rome Statute of the International Criminal Court, U.N. Doc. A/CONF.183/9 (1998); also available at <www.un.org/law/icc/index.htm>.

flicts based on humanitarian reasons. Indeed, subsequent interventions in Kosovo and East Timor are recent examples of further erosion of the traditional impunity offered by state sovereignty. The question remains on what basis and where the world community will intervene, but it is apparent that state sovereignty no longer provides the shield against outside intervention that it once did.

International intervention in armed conflict has been linked increasingly to international prosecution for humanitarian law violations committed during such episodes. In addition, the opinion of world leaders and diplomats has coalesced around the idea that international criminal prosecutions are integral to the process of reconciliation in a country that has been torn apart by violence.[10] Comments by Tribunal officials and legal scholars indicate that they too have embraced this larger aspiration – an attribution of the influence of the court that moves beyond the narrowly focused legal mandate of adjudicating criminal trials.[11] Seven years after the inception of the ICTY, much and little has changed. Despite the continuing resistance of some countries and politicians to cooperate with the Tribunal, the number of arrests has increased and with additional resources, the Tribunal is now firmly established. This is an opportune time to reexamine the policies and practices instituted when the Tribunal was established in the midst of war.

B.   *The Bosnian Judicial System and the ICTY*

The ICTY has primary jurisdiction for war crimes prosecutions. Nevertheless, a well-functioning national judicial system in Bosnia is critical to any widespread and systematic effort to prosecute accused war criminals. The sheer

---

10.   Upon the conviction of Jean-Paul Akayesu, the Office of the Press Secretary at the White House stated: "Reconciliation, security, and regional development will take hold . . . only when the cycle of violence has been broken and accountability established." Office of the Press Secretary, The White House (Sept. 3, 1998) (visited May 9, 2000) <http//:www.pub.whitehouse.gov/>; "Reconciliation cannot begin when justice is delayed for the guilty. As long as justice remains fleeting, the perception of guilt will remain and the difficult process of national reconciliation will end before it has a chance to begin." U.S. Ambassador to the United Nations, Bill Richardson, *No Peace Without Justice*, report from the Diplomatic Conference of Plenipotentiaries for the Establishment of an International Criminal Court, Rome, Italy (July 15-17, 1999); M. Cherif Bassiouni, *Searching for Peace and Achieving Justice*, 59 Aut Law & Contemp. Probs. 9, 23 (1996). *See also* M. Cherif Bassiouni, *The Commission of Experts Established pursuant to Security Council Resolution 780: Investigating Violations of International Humanitarian Law in the Former Yugoslavia*, 5 Crim. L. F. 279, 339 (1994); Peter Burns, *An International Criminal Tribunal: The Difficult Union of Principle and Politics*, 5 Crim. L. F. 341, 344, 374 (1994).

11.   Gabrielle Kirk McDonald, former President of the ICTY stated: "[T]hrough this process, it is our hope that we will deter the future commission of crimes and lay the groundwork for reconciliation. I do not expect the Tribunal to . . . somehow magically create reconciliation, but at least we can lay the groundwork." Interview by Eric Stover and Christopher Joyce, with Judge McDonald in The Hague, The Netherlands (July 26, 1999); "This judicial process is essential for reconciliation to begin." Richard Goldstone, *Ethnic Reconciliation Needs the Help of a Truth Commission*, Int'l Herald Trib., October 24, 1998. In addition, the UN Legal Counsel and Under-Secretary General for Legal Affairs Carl-August Fleichhauer stated: "These three important goals [ending war crimes, holding perpetrators accountable and breaking the cycle of ethnic violence and retribution] are intertwined in the fundamental reason for the establishment of this Tribunal . . . ." *quoted in* Peter Burns, *An International Criminal Tribunal: The Difficult Union of Principle and Politics*, 5 Crim. L.F. 341, 374 n.137 (1994). *See* Theodore Meron, *Answering for War Crimes, Lessons from the Balkans (ICTY)*, Foreign Aff., Jan./Feb. 1997 at 2-8.

numbers of potential defendants and the resources needed to conduct such trials would overwhelm the capacity of the ICTY. Consequently, accountability for large numbers of war crimes violations will require the active participation of the national courts in BiH.[12] Yet many Bosnians and representatives of international organizations ask whether the national judicial system is able to meet this challenge.

Complicating this task is the 1996 agreement between the three signatories of the Dayton Peace Agreement (Bosnia-Herzegovina, Croatia, and the Federal Republic of Yugoslavia) titled the "Rome Agreement" or the "Rules of the Road."[13] According to this document, Bosnian authorities must submit case files of accused war criminals to the ICTY Office of the Prosecutor (hereinafter "OTP") for review and approval before proceeding with the arrest and trial of such persons. Initially, due to lack of funding, the OTP did not have the resources to conduct an expeditious review of files. As a result, Bosnian judges and prosecutors initiating war crimes trials confronted exasperating delays. At the time of this study, the review process remained a sensitive issue. The initiation of national war crimes trials is an area in which the BiH legal system and the ICTY intersect. Given the tension surrounding this procedure, we hope to shed light on the manner in which Bosnian judges and prosecutors perceive this institutional arrangement.

Concerns about the Bosnian judicial system have come from such diverse sources as the United Nations Mission in Bosnia and Herzegovina (hereinafter "UNMIB"),[14] the International Crisis Group (hereinafter "ICG"),[15] OHR,[16] the Judicial System Assessment Programme of the United Nations (hereinafter "JSAP")[17] and the European Stability Initiative (hereinafter "ESI").[18] Criti-

---

12. Neil J. Kritz, *Coming to Terms with Atrocities: A Review of Accountability Mechanisms for Mass Violations of Human Rights*, 59-AUT LAW & CONTEMP. PROBS. 127, 133-34 (1996).

13. The Rome Agreements were signed on Feb. 18, 1996 in Rome, Italy. They can be found at <http://www.nato.int/ifor/rome/rome2.htm>.

14. In July 1999, Elizabeth Rehn was reported as saying that Bosnia was becoming: "An El Dorado of organized crime." She indicated her belief that judges were corrupt, prosecutors afraid and witnesses intimidated. RFE/RL NEWSLINE July 26, 1999. <http://www.rferl.org/newsline/1999/07/260799.html>.

15. INTERNATIONAL CRISIS GROUP, RULE OVER LAW: OBSTACLES TO THE DEVELOPMENT OF AN INDEPENDENT JUDICIARY IN BiH, ICG Report No. 72 (1999) [hereinafter ICG REPORT RULE OVER LAW]; INTERNATIONAL CRISIS GROUP, RULE OF LAW IN PUBLIC ADMINISTRATION: CONFUSION AND DISCRIMINATION IN A POST-COMMUNIST BUREAUCRACY, ICG Balkans Report No. 84 (1999).

16. *Report of the High Representative for Implementation of the Bosnian Peace Agreement to the Secretary-General of the United Nations*, Office of the High Representative, para. 65 (March 14, 1996); para. 113 (April 14, 1997); para. 92 (July 11, 1997); para. 69 (Jan. 16, 1998); para. 81, 82 (April 9, 1998); para. 99, 100 (July 14, 1998); para. 83 (Oct. 14, 1998); para. 68 (Feb. 12, 1999); para. 64, 68, 100 (May 7, 1999); para. 43, 48, 49 (July 16, 1999); para. 56, 57, 59, 61, 65 (Nov. 11, 1999).

17. UNITED NATIONS MISSION IN BOSNIA AND HERZEGOVINA [hereinafter UNMIB], JUDICIAL SYSTEM ASSESSMENT PROGRAMME [hereinafter JSAP], REPORT FOR THE PERIOD NOVEMBER 1998 TO JANUARY 1999 (1999); UNMIB, JSAP, THEMATIC REPORT III: ON ARREST WARRANTS, AMNESTY AND TRIALS *In Absentia* (December 1999); UNMIB, JSAP, COMMENTS ON THE INDEPENDENCE OF THE JUDICIARY (February 2000).

18. EUROPEAN STABILITY INITIATIVE, RESHAPING INTERNATIONAL PRIORITIES IN BOSNIA AND HERCEGOVINA: PART ONE, BOSNIAN POWER STRUCTURES (1999).

cisms have focused on lack of judicial accountability; corruption of judges and judicial ministries; intimidation by nationalist political parties and criminal elements; lack of enforcement of judicial decisions by police; political resistance to a unified judicial system in the Federation; poor inter-entity cooperation; financial dependence of judges on the political system; politically-influenced judicial appointments; inexperienced judges; lack of resources for efficient management and poor distribution of relevant legal material. These problems reflect the transition from the Communist system based on patronage and control as well as the profound effects of the war that damaged infrastructure and economic stability. These observations suggest that there are vulnerabilities within the Bosnian legal system that influence its relationship to the Tribunal.

Attempts to address these identified problems have been undertaken by several international organizations such as JSAP, OHR, the Council of Europe, the Central and Eastern European Law Initiative of the American Bar Association (hereinafter "ABA/CEELI"), and the International Human Rights Law Group. These initiatives have focused on education of judges on the European Convention on Human Rights and international human rights and humanitarian laws as well as monitoring of trials to assess whether they meet international standards. The success of these efforts has not been evaluated. More importantly, there has been no formalized attempt to ascertain the views of Bosnian legal professionals regarding the professional capacity and/or problems of the Bosnian judicial system, or their impressions of the educational interventions undertaken by the international community. This study represents the first attempt to gather systematic data on these important issues.

C.   The ICTY Outreach Program

Effective collaboration between a national judiciary and an international tribunal depends in part on the integrity of each judicial institution and on the mechanisms of communication established between the two structures. Beginning in 1997, Judge Gabrielle Kirk McDonald, then President of the ICTY, became increasingly concerned about the gap that existed between the Tribunal and those most affected by its decisions: the peoples of the former Yugoslavia. With the realization that the Tribunal was viewed negatively by many in the Balkans, President McDonald invited a group of legal professionals to The Hague in October 1998, to observe the Tribunal and its workings first-hand.[19]

Further, in November 1998, President McDonald sent a group of ICTY staff to Bosnia to assess the problem of a lack of understanding of the Tribunal among the people. The mission members reported a "strong desire" for information and direct involvement with representatives from the Tribunal and they proposed the creation of an Outreach Program located within the Office of the Registrar and urged that the capacity of the Public Information Unit be enhanced. With a focus on disseminating accurate information and increasing dialogue, the program is "intended to engage existing local legal communities and

---

19.   Outreach Program Proposal, *supra* note 5.

non-governmental organizations, victims' associations, and educational institutions."[20] In 1999, the Outreach Program opened offices in Zagreb, Croatia and Banja Luka, BiH.

The Outreach Program has the potential to ameliorate the schism in understanding between the ICTY and the people of the former Yugoslavia. In light of the critical role that the national legal system plays in the internationalized framework for criminal justice, it will be necessary to win the support of Bosnian judges and prosecutors. This project was undertaken, in part, to strengthen this objective.

D. Methodology

The project employed qualitative methods to allow the judges and prosecutors to discuss their views in response to a series of open and closed-ended questions. Qualitative research uses methods including observation, study and analysis that can illuminate experience in ways that surveys or more quantitative approaches do not. Data is gathered through interviews, focus groups, field observations, participant observation and analysis of published sources of information. The advantage of the approach is the richness of the information obtained; the principal disadvantage is that the sample is non-random and that careful attention must be paid to such issues as validity and bias.

(1) **Study Design**: The field research consisted of in-depth, semi-structured interviews of thirty-two judges and prosecutors during June, July and August of 1999, in BiH. The length of the interviews ranged from two to six hours. Trained teams of researchers conducted the interviews. There were three teams, each consisting of two researchers (one from the United States, one from BiH) and a faculty liaison. One team, based in Sarajevo, primarily interviewed participants in the Bosniak-majority areas of the Federation (the "Sarajevo Group"). The Bosnian researcher and faculty liaison were Bosniaks. Another team, based in Banja Luka, interviewed participants exclusively in the Republika Srpska and in Brčko (the "Banja Luka Group"). The Bosnian researcher and faculty liaison were Bosnian Serbs. The final team, based in Mostar, primarily interviewed participants in the Bosnian Croat-majority areas of the Federation (the "Mostar Group"). The Bosnian researcher and faculty liaison were Bosnian Croats. Faculty liaisons were recruited from the universities of Sarajevo, Banja Luka and Mostar (West).

(2) **Sample**: Criteria were developed to ensure a representative sample of judges and prosecutors. These criteria included:

(a) *Jurisdiction*: For the Sarajevo Group, of the twelve interviews, seven were with judges in cantonal courts, courts of first instance for war crimes trials; two with judges from the Federation Supreme Court, which has appellate jurisdiction for such cases and one with a judge from the Federation Constitutional Court. The final two interviews were with prosecutors with jurisdiction to seek indictments for war

---

20. *Id.*

crimes. For the Banja Luka Group, of the ten interviews, three were with judges in the basic courts, courts without jurisdiction for war crimes cases; three were with judges in district courts, courts which have jurisdiction for war crimes cases; and two were with judges from the RS Supreme Court. The final two interviews were with prosecutors; one had jurisdiction to seek indictments for war crimes and one did not. For the Mostar Group, of the ten interviews, four were with judges in the basic court, courts of first instance for war crimes trials in the region; four were with judges in the cantonal courts, courts with appellate jurisdiction of war crimes trials in the region; and the final two were with prosecutors, one of whom had jurisdiction to seek war crimes indictments and the other was a cantonal prosecutor who represented the state in appellate review of such trials.

(b) *Geographic Distribution*: Judges and prosecutors were selected from the various regions of BiH.

(c) *Demography*: Age, level of experience and gender were considered in selection of judges. Membership in a particular national group was not a selection criterion. Nevertheless participants belonged overwhelmingly to the national group that constituted a majority in that particular area.

(3) Questionnaire: The researchers created a semi-structured questionnaire of forty-five items.[21] The items were translated into the appropriate languages and then back translated to ensure accuracy. The questionnaire was reviewed by all team members and was pre-tested. Topic areas included:

(a) Demographics: education and legal experience; personal background; national background and the impact of the war;

(b) Role of the judge/prosecutor and courtroom process in BiH;

(c) Domestic effects of the ICTY: legal definitions of accountability and the rule of law; social reconstruction and war crimes; genocide; the role of the Dayton Accords and international law; and perceptions of the ICTY, including its goals, choice of those indicted, knowledge of specific trials and Rules of the Road, sources of information about the ICTY, and its effects on the participant's legal practice as well as on the country as a whole;

(d) Domestic war crimes trials, including procedures, personal experience with war crimes trials and the effects of such trials; and

(e) Hopes for the future.

We were concerned that the sensitive nature of some of the questions would hinder open and honest responses. Therefore interviewees were assured of confidentiality in their answers and all members of the research team, including translators, signed pledges of confidentiality. Interviews were carried out in the privacy of the participants' offices except where the judge or prosecutor preferred another setting. Furthermore, we have not identified the sources of

---

21. *See* Appendix A.

any quotations used in this report to protect the confidentiality of the participants.

(4) Study Limitations: As a qualitative study, the data may be limited by the small size and non-random nature of the sample. The trade-off is the depth of the information reflected in almost 150 hours of transcribed interview material. By establishing clear criteria, every effort was made to assure that the sample was representative. Since the faculty liaisons contacted the interviewees, it is possible that selection bias was present. Other possible threats to validity include the small number of women interviewed, the need to work through interpreters, as well as the possible need of the legal professionals to present themselves in a favorable light to Western researchers. Cultural and national biases of interviewers, interpreters and the researchers must always be kept in mind when these data are analyzed. Since most of the legal professionals were male and five of the six interviewers were female, gender bias may have influenced the interviewee responses. The accuracy of the translation of the participants' comments was improved by the presence of a Bosnian researcher and an interpreter in every interview. Further, all taped interviews were reviewed by a native speaker to assure accuracy of translation.

(5) Analysis: Each interview was taped, transcribed and checked for accuracy. Field observations were noted and recorded. Within each team, every interview was reviewed separately by each team member and coded according to key concepts developed by the research group. In addition, the University of California project directors and a member of each team reviewed the interview transcripts of all three teams. Team members reviewed their coding together and finally, cross-team comparisons were conducted.

IV.

FINDINGS[22]

Our sample consisted of twenty-six judges and six prosecutors.[23] They were predominately of middle age and had occupied their positions for several years prior to the onset of the war. For the judges, the median number of years on the bench was 13.5. The prosecutors had occupied their positions for a median of seventeen years. Nine of the participants were Bosnian Serb, twelve were Bosnian Croat and eleven were Bosniak. The principal limitation of the study was the small number – only six – of female participants. Among the judges, forty-two percent lost their housing and seventy-three percent reported that a relative had been injured or killed during the war. Thirty-three percent of the prosecutors had lost their homes and a similar percentage indicated injury or death of relatives.

---

22. We have attempted to describe accurately the significant themes that emerged among participants. Where it is helpful to illustrate important differences of perception, we have provided precise numerical data regarding the responses.

23. *See* Appendix B, Tables 1 and 2.

A. Common Themes Among Participants in the RS and in the Federation

1. Participants Identify as Professionals

All participants highlighted the importance of professionalism. This theme, commonly found among participants in both entities, is an important finding because it was one of the few areas on which all agreed. Participants equated professionalism generally with pride in work, strict adherence to legal rules, impartiality, objectivity and the independence of the judiciary. Participants also used the term "professionalism" to refer to a duty to support, uphold and enforce the rule of law as well as the social norms of fairness and equity. Further, the interview data suggest that these aspirations for their professional role were intimately bound up with participants' social status and self-definition.

The judges and prosecutors described their work as involving the strict and objective application of legal rules to a particular case. Participants explained that the primary role of the judge and prosecutor in the civil law system was to determine which provision of the legal code applied to the case at hand. Judges and prosecutors frequently referred to the legal code as the basis of legal authority which they were duty-bound to apply. Thus, they viewed the essence of their professional competence as the ability solely to select and apply the appropriate law.

One example that demonstrates how judges and prosecutors understood the limits of their professional roles lies in the area of refugee returns. Participants made a clear distinction between the prerogatives of politicians to define the conditions under which refugees could return and their own roles in applying property rights for returning refugees as defined in the legal code. No participant indicated that a judge was empowered to interpret the law beyond that which was written in the code. For example, when asked what role a judge might play in facilitating refugee returns, one participant responded: "The court is an independent body and has no active role in the return of refugees. But it does have a role in the case of disputes of which I mean, personally, I can only speed up the process of bringing a person's case to court, that is all I can do."[24]

Participants defined professional status to include their external presentation and professional conduct. The role of a legal professional in the community was defined by how and where one is seen in public, adherence to high standards of morality and conduct and professional dignity. For example, several participants remarked that judges must choose "with care" the restaurants they frequented since their appearance in public reflected their degree of professionalism.

Participants also were concerned about the moral and ethical standards that enhanced the dignity of the profession. Participants described the importance of professional integrity and each averred that they met their own high standards of judicial professionalism. Participants identified lack of impartiality, corruption, lower expectations for newcomers to the legal profession, and political pressures

---

24. The quotes provided may have been modified through correction of grammar in order to make the meaning clear.

leading to a lack of independence on the part of legal professionals as unacceptable characteristics and problem areas in the Bosnian judiciary.

2. Belief in the Principles of Justice

All participants valued the ideal of justice. Many reported that the Bosnian legal system supported this principle. As proof, participants pointed to the legal code as the embodiment of this normative value. Participants generally equated justice with the equal application of law. In accordance with the principles of professionalism, they stated that the personal beliefs, attitudes or morals of the individual judge or prosecutor were irrelevant to the administration of justice. As one participant stated: "The judge acts only according to law. Only." Participants further described that the purpose of the judicial system was to promote specific and general deterrence of criminal conduct, inculcate normative values and rectify inequities. As one judge noted: "A judicial decision can effect or change people's behavior. The court has a role to prevent future behaviors."

Participants saw their capacity to be objective as paramount to the administration of justice. They saw their own opinions as objective, honest and correct. For example, when asked about genocide, one judge stated: "When you look objectively, that's [genocide] that happened." In addition, another participant noted: "[A] judge shouldn't have any complex that he is infallible. He should stand with his feet on the ground. He shouldn't have any prejudice if he is a real judge. . . . A judge should be an honest man." Other participants agreed that "good" and "correct" decisions promoted justice.

While noting the value of objectivity, participants agreed that justice was also a function of perception. Participants were aware that those affected by their decisions did not always see the outcomes as just. Or, as another participant put it: "I think our courts conduct fair trials here. However, there are many of our verdicts with which everyone is dissatisfied." Despite the fact that parties to a dispute as well as the public might disagree with a judicial outcome, participants were convinced that if they applied the law strictly to the facts, the public would perceive the judicial system as trustworthy and fair. As one participant stated: "If a judicial decision is made according to the law, this can impart a feeling of righteousness to the parties, no matter if the decision is positive or negative for them." Nevertheless, another participant noted that publicity surrounding court decisions increased public pressure on judges.

Finally, participants acknowledged that in certain cases, impartial application of the appropriate legal rule did not produce justice. Nevertheless, legal professionals reported they were constrained by their professional obligations to apply the law in these instances. As one prosecutor stated: "You always have to stick to the legal solution. The fact is that although something is legal does not mean that it is just." Another judge echoed this sentiment: "Sometimes people think that we are doing our job wrong, but we only do our work as it is prescribed by the law."

3. *Participants Identify with the Western European Legal Tradition*

Participants from all three national groups highlighted the significance that Western European culture and legal traditions have had on their work. Participants were aware that the social and economic conditions resulting from the war have increased the disparity between Bosnia and Western Europe. However, participants expressed a strong desire to integrate with Western Europe, to move toward a more Western European ideal. Participants made frequent comparisons between Bosnia and countries in Western Europe, suggesting it was not simply legal integration they desired but also the Western European standard of living. For some, such integration required changes internal to Bosnia. As one participant stated: "We can't go to Europe in peasant shoes." Clearly, it was important to these legal professionals that Bosnian laws are either integrated with, or comparable to, the laws of Western Europe.

Several participants spoke of the importance of human rights protections. Additionally, some spoke of the integration of European and international treaties into Bosnian law through the Dayton Agreement and one judge discussed the need for his colleagues to study the European Convention on Human Rights (hereinafter "European Convention") and its application to domestic criminal procedures. Another saw the incorporation of expanded due process rights in the Federation's new Criminal Code as evidence that Bosnia's legal system was rising to the standards of Western Europe: "It's a degree of a developed civilization that protects the rights of indicted or accused persons; democratic rights are the very rights of accused persons."

Participants also cited the abolition of the death penalty – brought about as a result of the application of the European Convention to BiH through the Dayton Agreement – as an example of legal reform. However, participants differed in their assessment of this development. Some who favored abolition of the death penalty welcomed the change. However, others characterized the new rule as an intrusion by the international community into domestic affairs, whether or not they supported the death penalty.

4. *Decline in Status and Professional Standards*

The once privileged status of Bosnian legal professionals is in decline. Participants acknowledged informal rules and customs in pre-war Yugoslavia that conferred influence, social status, privileges and obligations which the judges and prosecutors readily accepted. In fact, many participants reported that they had chosen the legal profession because of the social status associated with it. However, some criticized the special treatment that judges who were active members of the Communist Party received in pre-war Yugoslavia: "There was a lot of 'party' in the Party meetings! They didn't do work." Nevertheless, participants believed it remained the responsibility of the State to provide adequate material support for judges and prosecutors. "The state, the government, must provide elementary conditions. First of all, an adequate salary, an apartment, so the judge doesn't have to think about those problems. So his basic problem can be how, in the most successful way, to perform his function."

In addition to unpaid salaries, benefits once provided by the State such as apartments for judges and prosecutors are fast disappearing and frequently those provided were seen as substandard. Thirteen participants – almost half – were displaced by the war. Several others expressed two concerns. First, they were frustrated and angry that they had been unable to reclaim their former apartments. One participant, who was living in a rented apartment, explained that he was forced to do so because he could not regain possession of his former apartment which was also located within the city in which he worked: "I have a three bedroom flat . . . which is a hundred meters away from here. And in my apartment are people who are not refugees or displaced persons." Second, participants who had been given state-owned apartments were dissatisfied with the quality of their current housing. One participant reported that he lived separately from his family because his government-provided one-room apartment was too small – thirty-eight square meters (approximately 350 square feet).

Legal professionals reported dissatisfaction with the impact of the post-war economy on their social status. For example, one participant stated: "You have people [like legal professionals] who have studied all their life . . . but their salaries are incredibly small, unlike the salaries of the people who have no schooling whatsoever, they're earning millions of marks. These are the absurdities." One participant reported that a one-night stay in a hotel in Vienna cost the equivalent of one month's salary, highlighting the discrepancy between the standard of living for legal professionals in Bosnia and those in Western Europe. In particular, two participants explicitly reported that the diminution of status, salary and benefits has led them to consider other job opportunities. One veteran legal professional stated: "This is only a transitional period for me. Most probably, I will start working as a lawyer." The other explained that being a judge in Bosnia is "not the same job that it is in the West, as it should be" and stated he might become an attorney "because it's a better-paid job, nothing more."

The war has brought significant changes to the profession, such as the impact of the decline in professional standards during the war. The qualifying test for judicial candidates reportedly was easier in the midst of the conflict. One participant reported that judges elected during the war did not have to pass the judges' examination at all.[25] Many participants reported that this loosening of requirements had denigrated the profession.

Participants stressed the importance of well-educated and well-informed legal professionals, and they equated legal experience with competence. As one judge stated: "I think it would be a good thing if more judges were more educated, had more life and work experience. This might require that they work as lawyers before becoming a judge." Many participants suggested that declining salaries and benefits attracted fewer promising candidates. In addition, partici-

---

25. This participant indicated that during the war the authorities sought to address the shortage of judges by passing a special law that allowed individuals to become judges with only a law degree. He stated that this practice was discontinued after the war.

pants emphasized the importance of judges serving as mentors to develop the skills of newcomers to the judiciary and noted that the loss of experienced judges since the war has decreased the number of senior judges available to perform this role. Participants also cited the migration and subsequent loss of so many experienced legal professionals due to the war as a contributing factor both to the diminished competence and lessened status of the profession. As one legal professional remarked: "There are some judges in lower courts who are just there by accident." Many participants believed that unqualified judges should be removed to maintain high standards of judicial professionalism.

5. Corruption

Participants questioned the accusations of corruption that had been leveled against the Bosnian judicial system by the international community. Participants appeared to define corruption narrowly – as taking money in exchange for a particular outcome, i.e., bribery. Using this definition, participants frequently stated that they and their immediate colleagues did not engage in corrupt practices. For example, in discussing the issue of corruption one lower court president stated simply: "not in my court."

Other participants, however, alluded to corruption around them: "I am a professional, but I cannot speak to the professionalism of my colleagues." In response to the question: "Is a fair trial possible in Bosnia?" one participant thoughtfully stated: "I don't know. There's a different person sitting behind every desk. As far as [my city] and my authority go, everything is in order. The first time it is out of order, I won't work."

Participants speculated on the impact of low or unpaid salaries for judges and prosecutors. Many participants discussed the fact that judges and prosecutors were prohibited from accepting employment outside their profession, even to augment their low state salaries. Participants related the need for adequate salaries to an independent judiciary and suggested that some colleagues engaged in outside employment, possibly compromising professional duties. One described behavioral changes that indicated to him that the professional integrity of his colleagues possibly had been compromised by accepting outside work: "They are less interested in their daily job duties; they are often absent." Another stated: "You need to . . . make a judge independent in every way. Because if you have to beg in other ways – to make money privately from a friend – it's different, there are consequences."

Several Bosniak participants noted that the objectivity of legal professionals also was compromised by threats to their personal security and that of their families. As one participant explained: "It's not easy for judges to make a judgment if before the trial they get a threat that their family will be killed." Another observed that such threats, when issued with impunity, had a chilling effect on both the targeted judges and their colleagues.

6. Politics

All participants used the term "politics" or "political" primarily to distinguish between a legal process – a process governed by a fixed set of rules that can be applied in a neutral manner – and a process by which decision-makers exercise discretion to achieve a particular policy goal or desired outcome. Frequently, judges and prosecutors adamantly reiterated the distinction between themselves, as legal professionals, and politicians. In addition, participants repeatedly expressed their personal distaste for politics and politicians and vigorously criticized the overt and indirect influence of political parties on the legal system.

Participants equated politics with bias. Participants felt that politicians operated for corrupt, personal reasons, against the interests of the populace and without transparency. As one judge stated:

> I do not trust the politicians that much. A person who is applying the law should believe in the other parts of government. But considering how many of them just came to the top and made so much money, I am afraid that there are not that many who honestly believe in the rule of law. Because if they had that honest belief, then we would not have so many problems.

Politics and political decisions were declared by some participants to be defined by nationality. One participant stated that all political parties were connected to a national group, and that the lack of a political party not tied to a nationality "forces" people into political parties according to nationality. Virtually all participants agreed that politicians played a destructive role in the war and agreed that politicians brought a war no one wanted. As one participant stated: "Who ordered this war? Who is accountable for it? It was politicians." Furthermore, participants saw the on-going political problems of the State as a reflection of the parochialism of the political parties.

Judges and prosecutors frequently declined to respond to questions regarding their personal views of the judicial system and its application of laws, stating that those were "political questions." Participants also responded to questions regarding controversial issues such as genocide or the creation of a State Supreme Court of Bosnia and Herzegovina by noting that these too were "political" questions.[26]

In pre-war Yugoslavia, virtually all judges were members of the Communist Party, including most of the legal professionals in this study. However, participants reported varied levels of more recent involvement in political parties and structures. For example, many participants served as military judges and prosecutors during the war. Others were directly involved in political structures. One participant actively supported the military efforts of the Croatian Defense Council (hereinafter Hrvatsko Vijeće Obrane or HVO). Another assisted in the formation of and served in institutional arrangements that were established to govern a portion of the Republika Srpska. Finally, others served in judicial leadership positions within the transitional government and quasi-governmental

---

26. *See* §§ IV, and V and Appendices D and E.

structures between 1992 and 1995. While these participants described their involvement or action in support of political parties during the war, none identified their activities as political.

Under current law, judges and prosecutors are prohibited from membership in political parties. Participants supported this rule and agreed that political involvement might compromise the objectivity of a judge or prosecutor. As one participant stated: "If you become a member of a political party, it's a matter of time before you become an object of manipulation." Participants stated that currently they were not politically active. Only one participant expressed any personal sympathy for a particular political party.

Participants deplored being targets of political influence and many felt that the independence of judges and prosecutors was undermined by the power that political parties exerted on the judicial system. One participant observed: "the judicial system is in the hands of the political oligarchy" and said, "as long as the people who are guilty and responsible for the war remain in positions of power, there will never be an adequate application of the law the way we want." A few participants stated that politicians did not want a truly independent judiciary because it did not benefit them: "Politicians don't care about us, to have the rule of law, an independent judicial system, because if these existed they could not do what they wanted to do." Some participants specifically commented on politicians' lack of education and capability. One legal professional derisively remarked that he thought a top local official "did not finish college."

Many participants often spoke emphatically about their resistance to attempts at political interference and their own resolve to apply the law. "I can certainly vouch that this court does all the things in a very professional manner. But I do have information that in other parts of the country, nationality of a party sometimes matters. But I cannot speak about that, it's just what I heard." Another stated his resolve to remain impartial: "You're always under some influence from the politics, the politicians, the parties. And we are here to be professionals, to proceed according to the law as it should be and that's difficult and hard."

Sources of pressure included government officials and international monitors. "If there is political pressure, it's coming from the cantonal or federal ministry of justice – someone who is in the government." A judge stated that he felt international monitors had sought to influence him improperly by suggesting at the close of a proceeding, but prior to the verdict, that the evidence was insufficient to convict and the judge should release the accused. Another form of political pressure cited by others was the failure of Ministry of Justice officials to support the judiciary after nationalist groups or the international community criticized Bosnian judges.

Participants specifically cited control of the legislature over judicial budgets as an essential factor that contributes to political interference in judicial matters. Many tied financial dependence to corruption. One participant observed that since the judicial budget is controlled by the legislators "of course, they can affect the work of the court."

7. Attitudes Towards the International Community

On the whole, study participants used the term "international community" broadly to refer to the United Nations, foreign governments and international governmental and non-governmental organizations. This terminology reflected a homogenization of foreign actors as well as a recognition of the power differential between Bosnian nationals and representatives from foreign-based organizations. Generally, participants expressed ambivalence toward the involvement of the international community in BiH. On the one hand, participants welcomed the role of international institutions and organizations in strengthening Bosnian governmental structures and promoting economic growth. On the other hand, they often perceived the manner in which those interventions took place to be demeaning.

Participants in each national group agreed that involvement of the international community was necessary to prevent further war, to stimulate the economy, to ensure fairness and accountability in judicial proceedings and to prosecute war criminals. Some expressed concern that in the case of national war crimes trials, judges in Bosnia might be biased or politically pressured to render a particular verdict.

Citing political pressures, participants also favored international involvement to promote an independent judicial system. In particular, participants supported the efforts of groups like OHR to secure enactment of legislation to promote the independence of the Bosnian judiciary. However, some prosecutors expressed concerns that not enough international attention had been paid to the need to strengthen prosecutorial independence and suggested that broader powers for prosecutors should be included in the criminal code.

Participants expressed mixed reactions to the legal training for judges and prosecutors provided by international organizations. Many reported that the training was not well planned, that those conducting sessions were not familiar with Bosnian legal structures and that the training covered too many topics in a limited time. One stated: "You cannot expect a seminar to be organized and in two days to know all European laws." Some reported that international seminars were not particularly relevant to their work because the trainers and attendees frequently came from different legal systems.

However, other participants noted that the value of the seminars lay less in their content than in the opportunity to renew contacts with colleagues across national lines. Judges and prosecutors reported sporadic communication with colleagues outside their area and welcomed the opportunity to reestablish professional relationships in the other entity. One participant who attended an international seminar noted its main significance as "the first meeting of judges and prosecutors from all around Bosnia-Herzegovina." Participants considered selection to participate in such meetings a professional distinction and some raised the concern that the selection process for the seminars was not transparent.

Participants expressed criticism of international organizations operating within Bosnia. Opinions varied toward international organizations such as OHR, United Nations and the ICTY[27] as well as international non-governmental organizations. Participants frequently commented that the representatives of international organizations lacked knowledge about Bosnia and seemed unprepared and uncommitted. One participant described international monitors as people without "good wishes" who were only interested in living in a foreign country for awhile. Another experienced as personally adversarial the comments of an international monitor who also was a judge: "He wanted to irritate me." This same judge described his other experiences with international visitors to his courtroom as pointless "because all trials in Bosnia are public. I was curious why they came. It's of little value."

Some participants perceived international involvement in Bosnia as an unwelcome intrusion into the country's legal system. One participant stated that he would prefer that the international community focus on assisting Bosnia in creating its own institutions rather than intervening in routine matters. Another reported that the representatives of international community within Bosnia lacked knowledge of, and respect for, the Bosnian legal system and he complained that he had to spend "half my time explaining basic laws and rules we apply here, sometimes it's boring."

In particular, participants expressed positive and negative attitudes toward OHR. Some viewed it as a thoroughly political institution and expressed frustration with OHR's changing of the laws. Nevertheless, many felt that OHR ensured political stability. One participant who criticized certain OHR actions also noted that without it "we would still be arguing about the size of the letters on passports." Another attributed judicial independence to OHR, stating:

> Fortunately we do have the OHR, which is the only body in this region that can say: "Hey, prosecutor, you are not a good prosecutor, you have done such and such." Without OHR, you would have totally dependent judges and prosecutors, because the political parties would want to make agreements and that would make judges and prosecutors dependent.

Two Bosniak participants were appalled by the comments made by the UN Special Representative in Bosnia, Elizabeth Rehn, in which she criticized the judiciary as corrupt.[28] These judges felt that Rehn's blanket criticisms unfairly damaged the credibility of the judiciary. "Mrs. Rehn openly said that the courts are corrupt. I don't think that she talks for nothing. But it would be good if she could offer concrete evidence. There are many good judges who are far from that categorization." The other judge asserted that such comments put an "enormous burden on all judges" since the judicial system was unable to initiate removal proceedings without allegations against specific judges, and thus the accusations encouraged those dissatisfied with a court judgment to claim it was the result of corruption.

---

27. The opinions regarding the ICTY are addressed separately, in § IV(C), below.

28. *See supra* note 14.

8. National Consciousness and Allegiance to State Structures

Although self-identification with a national group contributed significantly to participants' national consciousness, e.g., "I am Serb, I cannot be anything else," or, "I am a Bosniak. Because I feel that way," many participants expressed the idea that nationalism is anathema to the legal profession. As one participant noted, legal professionals "are not burdened with national tensions, or they shouldn't be." Some participants suggested that they, as professionals, combated tensions between national groups and did not contribute to the war: "We judges are professionals, and we did not cause this conflict."

Nonetheless, the theme of national identity, citizenship and allegiance was evident in the interviews. Participants' attitudes toward national identity were influenced by their political views. One participant expressed regret at no longer having the option to identify as a "Yugoslav." Another spoke nostalgically about the time before the war when one's identification with a national group was a private matter. A Bosnian Croat participant expressed his view with a caustic comment regarding the "so-called Herceg-Bosna" State. Other Bosnian Croat participants however, referred to the army of Bosnia-Herzegovina during the war as the "so-called BiH Army." A Bosniak participant reflected on the impact the war has had on national consciousness: "Well, before the war . . . Bosnian people were the people that were Yugoslavs. Because we felt Yugoslavia was our country. . . . [W]e had different identifications with national groups, and it was less important which group you were in . . .. [T]hat wasn't important before."

Participants spoke at great length about issues regarding the role of the State, the question of national boundaries and allegiance to State structures. Their responses revealed ambivalence towards the Dayton Agreement and its consequences for the country. These perceptions appeared to be influenced by membership in a particular national group. Therefore, we examine these responses according to the region of the country in which the participant was interviewed.

Many participants were grappling with how to reconcile nationalism with the political structures established by the Dayton Agreement. One Bosnian Croat participant discussed the relationship of the constitutions to reconstruction and reconciliation and noted: "In no State do you have two entities, three nations, four constitutions, cantonal constitutions. How can you realize the rights? It is a forest of rules that no expert can go around in." Two other participants believed that the constitutions adversely affected the rights of national minorities in Bosnia. One stated with respect to minorities such as Hungarians: "The constitution does not guarantee rights to all nations, which needs to be changed." The other observed: "I know my friends, Serbs who are natives of Sarajevo, and they feel not as a minority but as second class citizens in the territory of the Federation. They don't feel comfortable in such a legal system."

National divisions were noteworthy among the responses to questions regarding the supreme law of Bosnia and whether a Supreme Court of BiH should be created. The Dayton Agreement established that the constitution of the State, which was an annex to the Agreement, was the supreme law of the country. Virtually all Bosniak participants reported that the Constitution of the State of Bosnia and Herzegovina was the highest source of legal authority, while virtually all Bosnian Serb participants stated that the highest authority was the Constitution of the Republika Srpska or both the constitutions of Bosnia and Herzegovina and the Republika Srpska. Only one Bosnian Serb legal professional stated unequivocally that the Constitution of Bosnia and Herzegovina was the supreme law of the land. The answers of Bosnian Croat participants were divided between the State constitution and Federation constitution.[29]

Responses similarly were divided regarding the need for a State Supreme Court with jurisdiction to hear disputes involving State laws. Currently there is no court with the ability to adjudicate such matters.[30] Bosniak legal professionals uniformly supported this proposal, while with two exceptions, Bosnian Serb participants opposed it. Bosnian Croat participants were ambivalent and gave the proposal qualified approval.[31]

In general, Sarajevo Group participants (including non-Bosniaks) expressed the desire for the re-creation of a unified and diverse Bosnia. This sentiment was illustrated by one judge who described pre-war Bosnia as a country in which "people lived together for thousands, thousands of years" and thirty percent of marriages in Sarajevo were mixed. Another spoke passionately about his beliefs in a diverse Bosnia: "Bosnia is . . . her structure, by her nature, she is really multi, multi, multi. And always we cared about that and now we also do care. And is has to be that way in Bosnia. But if it's not so then we have a problem."

Mostar Group participants were tentative in their support of a unified State. Eight qualified their opinion that it would be possible for people of different national groups to live together by noting that because of the war it would take time to achieve a multi-national state. As one described: "I think that it is possible, provided punishment of war criminals and the organization of a state, a normal state, not what we have now." Another who stated that life together was possible qualified his statement by noting that the pre-war political parties that initiated this "horrible war" remained in power. Thus, there was "no more trust" that the political process would result in normalization of relationships across national lines. However, one participant who agreed that Bosnians could live together so long as the international community was present, also advocated the further division of BiH: "I think that there should be three entities . . . . Rela-

---

29. For a comparison by national group of responses to the question: "What do you consider the highest law of the land?" see Appendix C.

30. The BiH Constitution does not provide for any court of general jurisdiction at the State level. The primary function of the Constitutional Court is to adjudicate disputes regarding whether entity laws violate the BiH constitution. Art. IV (3)(a). Thus, there is no State court with jurisdiction for individual violations of State laws. *See* ICG REPORT RULE OVER LAW, *supra* note 15.

31. For a comparison by national group of responses to the question: "Should a Supreme Court of Bosnia-Herzegovina be created?" see Appendix D.

tions between people would be much cleaner." Another participants said people could live "side by side," but that life together "all mixed up" was impossible.

Six Bosnian Serb participants stated that life together was possible, but their answers ranged from qualified support to outright skepticism. They said that the process would take time. As one stated: "It is possible, but we have to take time, lots of time. Hopefully life will be as it used to be. But I think that lots of time should pass." One participant stated that life *next* to one another was possible, but also circumscribed his answer:

> It's possible to create conditions, to live peacefully one beside each other, one next to each other. And to agree and solve what is common to us, and mutual to us. And to get used to it in the course of time. To change people and politics because if we could live for seventy years in Yugoslavia all together, why can't we live 1000 next to each other. But the international community contributed to all that because of their interfering with the conflict.

Two from this group of Bosnian Serb participants, while suggesting that life together might be possible in concept, noted that a unified state was impossible to achieve through external pressure. One stated: "There are a lot of common things between both of these entities" but continued that life together was not possible "if we are forced." The other discussed the challenges of refugee returns, both on a practical and a political level, and stated that it might not be practicable to implement the right of return guaranteed in the Dayton Accords given the horrors that people experienced during the war. Finally, two stated that life together was not possible. As one put it:

> It is a problem of the antagonism between Christianity and those other ones, between all three parties. The differences are too high, too great, the best solution is this one, one living next to the other for the future of children that are to be born. Who will guarantee that if we are living mixed that there would not be a war again?

It was significant that despite the variety of and often-contradictory statements among participants regarding national identity, there appeared to be a consensus among all participants that any continuation of war would be the worst thing to happen to BiH. As captured by one participant: "I am conscious that war cannot bring good to anyone. And war is the worst evil that can happen to people. Nothing can be worse than that." Another legal professional reflected on the lasting impact of the war on the judiciary:

> We have lived through a hard period, three or four years is a lot for an individual; for a nation it is only a moment. You have to understand that our judicial decisions are still connected to war, but I think that things have improved, people are and will learn about the consequences of war and everything that happened during the war. Every war is evil, and this one that took place here [was as well], however, regardless of things I am hopeful.

B. Factors That Contribute to Resistance Among Participants to International Criminal Trials and Accountability for War Crimes

Several factors emerged that contributed to reluctance of these Bosnian legal professionals to support the work of the ICTY wholeheartedly. While many accepted the Tribunal in concept, participants generally lacked clarity about its goals. In particular, the responses of Bosnian Serb and Bosnian Croat participants indicated they did not share the goals of the ICTY as they understood them. The Security Council resolution creating the ICTY,[32] and subsequent annual reports[33] reflect the goal of the international community to create a judicial body to hold accountable those responsible for war atrocities and to promote a "sustainable peace" among the peoples of the former Yugoslavia. The participants were asked specifically on whom the ICTY should focus and whether a connection existed between the work of the ICTY and the processes of social reconstruction and reconciliation. The responses indicated a lack of consensus among participants of the differing national groups as well as within national groups. In addition, there was a gap between the expectations of Bosnian legal professionals and the goals of the international community.

Further, proximity to violence and physical destruction of the community exerted a critical influence. Participants from areas untouched by the fighting, primarily Bosnian Croats, were prepared to put the past behind them. They focused on economic reconstruction as a mechanism for social reconstruction and less on the contribution of war crimes trials to this process. In marked contrast, those participants who lived in areas of heavy fighting emphasized the atrocities of the war and questions of individual responsibility and accountability.

There was a divergence of opinion as to who was responsible for the war and who should be held accountable. This divergence was also reflected in differing opinions about individual and collective responsibility and accountability for war crimes and genocide.[34] However, at least one participant in all three national groups identified the international community as responsible for the war. They believed that the world community did nothing to stop the war, even after atrocities were discovered, resulting in an extended conflict.

Nevertheless, the divergence of perspectives regarding responsibility and accountability for the war was largely consistent among participants of the same national group. However, the views of Bosniak, Bosnian Serb and Bosnian Croat legal professionals on these topics were inconsistent among the groups and often contradictory. Since three different versions of these themes emerged,

---

32. *See supra* note 4.

33. *Report of the International Tribunal for the Prosecution of Persons Responsible for Serious Violations of International Humanitarian Law Committed in the Territory of the Former Yugoslavia Since 1991,* U.N. GAOR, 54th Sess., Agenda Item 53 at 3, U.N. Doc. A/54/187; *See also: Fifth Annual Report of the International Tribunal for the Prosecution of Persons Responsible for Serious Violations of International Humanitarian Law Committed in the Territory of the Former Yugoslavia Since 1991,* <http:www.un.org/icty/rapportan/rapport5-e.htm>; *Third Annual Report of the International Tribunal for the Prosecution of Persons Responsible for Serious Violations of International Humanitarian Law Committed in the Territory of the Former Yugoslavia Since 1991,* <http:www.un.org/icty/rapportan/thir96tc.htm>; *First Annual Report of the International Tribunal for the Prosecution of Persons Responsible for Serious Violations of International Humanitarian Law Committed in the Territory of the Former Yugoslavia Since 1991,* <http:www.un.org/icty/rapportan/first-94.htm>.

34. A comparison of the responses by national group to the question: "In your legal opinion, did genocide happen anywhere in Bosnia-Herzegovina? Against whom did these acts of genocide occur?" are contained in Appendix E.

we will describe separately how each of these perspectives influenced resistance to the ICTY.

Finally, participants reported misunderstanding regarding and disagreement with the decisions by the international community regarding the location of the ICTY as well as the rules of evidence and procedure governing its work.

1. The Bosniak Perspective

All Sarajevo Group participants stated that Bosniaks were the victims of Serb aggression. They identified Slobodan Milošević, president of Yugoslavia and Radovan Karadžić, former president of the self-proclaimed Bosnian Serb Republic as those responsible for the war. Two of the Sarajevo Group – both of whom lived in areas of heavy fighting between Bosniak and Bosnian Croat forces – included Croatia as a belligerent state, and specifically named Franjo Tuđman, now-deceased president of Croatia, as the initiator of these actions. One participant reinforced the notion of individual accountability as follows:

> Believe me that I am telling you what I feel because I was here during the war and I survived with my family . . . . And I am telling you now as a human that people responsible, accountable and guilty for all those crimes should be accountable for those crimes, because people need that.

Half of the Sarajevo Group focused on the events in Srebrenica as epitomizing the aggression against, and genocide of, the Bosniaks. For example, one participant, when asked against whom genocide occurred stated: "We all know and considering Srebrenica, and starting with Srebrenica, we all know against whom." Another stated:

> If you start from the definition of genocide used by The Hague Tribunal I think that in relation to Bosniaks the genocide did happen, especially in certain parts. Especially in thinking about the Podrinje, because the Muslims – Bosniaks – were a majority in all the municipalities before the war there except in Foča. And in Foča there was a really slight majority of Serbs in relation to Bosniaks. And the war was conducted there; you had civilians, the destruction of whole Islamic monuments, mosques, mass killings of people, showing that the real goal of this was ethnic cleansing, actually, genocide. The identical of this situation was in the [Bosnian] Krajina, region.

Two Sarajevo Group participants stated that the Bosnian Croats were also victims of genocide, while one participant stated that "genocide occurred on all three sides" and another alluded to "genocide in a couple of directions."

Nearly all Sarajevo Group participants believed that there should be differing accountability for those in command responsibility and those in lower positions. They affirmed that those in command positions should be held accountable for the acts of their subordinates and cited specific examples from the ICTY trials or war anecdotes.

Sarajevo Group participants believed that the ICTY was a neutral and fair court in which to try indicted war criminals, especially those of highest rank. No one described the work of the ICTY – including the selection of indictees – as "political." All affirmed their support for its existence, while recognizing the challenges that it faced. As one stated: "I think that the ICTY is very correct. I know it has some difficulties, some technical problems. . . . I am for that court to be stronger and to be permanent." Another felt that those who critiqued the work of ICTY did so from a nationalist perspective: "All complaints about the work of the ICTY are mostly of a political nature. . . . I want it to work, and to try everybody, not just certain people." Most of the Sarajevo Group participants agreed with one judge who stated that he believed the "ICTY is rooted in justice."

Many Sarajevo Group participants believed that the main objective of the ICTY should be to prosecute and judge those individuals responsible for carrying out the war in Bosnia. They expressed a belief that the ICTY should focus its energies on those "most responsible" or "most guilty," and that the Tribunal would be more effective if this were done. However, three participants also expressed concern that the international community lacked the "political will" to arrest the "biggest fish."

Some Bosniak participants specifically expressed relief that the ICTY assumed jurisdiction for the cases involving the most serious war crimes. One stated that the trials of the "most accountable" war criminals, those who committed the most serious crimes and who still wield tremendous power, were the ones in which the involvement of the international community was most necessary. Another stated that despite the best intentions of a good judge, it would be difficult to conduct a fair trial of such cases in Bosnia because of political pressures. By the term "political pressure" he was referring specifically to inappropriate attempts at influence from various sources such as the Ministries of Justice, individual politicians, or criminal gangs. A Bosniak judge denied any "unprofessional" aspects of the judiciary but said the ICTY was needed because it used different "standards." In contrast to this view, another judge expressed his frustration with the ICTY and suggested that the Bosnian judiciary was better able to adjudicate war crimes trials: "The ICTY is still running away from genocide. And we who are here, we know why somebody was killed. Somebody was not killed because he was a civilian, he was killed because his last name belonged to a certain [national group]." Other than this critique, Bosniak participants saw the location of the ICTY as an advantage.

Sarajevo Group participants, in general, resisted assigning collective responsibility to "all Serbs" or "all Croats." Further, participants rejected the principle that an entire national group should be held accountable for the actions of their leaders. When asked specifically about accountability for war crimes, respondents stated that "those who organized the crimes should be held accountable" and tended to reject the assignment of accountability to anyone other than specific individuals.

Sometimes, these comments regarding collective accountability were tied to reconciliation in Bosnia. Sarajevo Group participants made a connection between trials of accused Serb war criminals and the alleviation of condemnation of the "whole people," as one participant stated:

> I think that the trials like those can build some new relations between the people.
> I think that is making a more clear situation between people. If he is guilty he

should be responsible for those acts. So less the whole culture be suspected for the one man's act. Every criminal act is done by an individual or many of them in a group. But never a people, whichever it is. Some punishment for those crimes can bring reconciliation and normal life in Bosnia.

Another echoed this belief, stating:

I think there is no making up without punishing the guilty. I think it is very important that nobody's guilt is collective guilt, every guilt is individual. And because of the removing the burden of collective guilt, meaning for example, the guilt of the Serbian people, it is in their interest that accused war criminals from their ranks be punished so it is known that not the whole people as it happened committed the war crimes. And the same of course applies to the other two peoples.

The belief that reconciliation and reconstruction depended upon the successful prosecution of war criminals is most characteristic of the Sarajevo Group. Some Bosniak judges felt that the ICTY contributed to reconciliation because it lay outside the influence of domestic political structures. Some of these participants saw value in the international community's ability to name perpetrators of war crimes and to facilitate discussion of the war in Bosnia. Many thought that the prosecution of war criminals by the ICTY would contribute to reconciliation in Bosnia. Others, however, suggested that even if the ICTY did not facilitate reconciliation it served to acknowledge their status as victims in the war. Some judges said that the longer the major war criminals – such as Karadžić and General Ratko Mladić, former head of the Bosnian Serb forces – remained free, the less likely reconciliation would result from their eventual prosecution. As one judge indicated, the faster the resolution of these significant cases, the more their outcome would contribute to the process of reconciliation.

2. The Bosnian Serb Perspective

Universally, Bosnian Serb participants viewed the conflict as a civil war; while only three specifically referred to the war as a "civil war," none referred to it as a war of aggression or an international war. As one participant stated: "Here in Republika Srpska, we consider that it was a civil war. The other side thinks we were aggressors. How can we be aggressors in our own country?" One participant stated that the Bosnian Serbs fought to maintain Yugoslavia as a unified state and to "prevent a centralized state [in Bosnia] where one nationality would be dominant." Another participant unequivocally stated: "This was a religious civil war." This perspective contrasts sharply with that of participants of other national groups.

Dominant themes in the Banja Luka Group were that the onset of the war was inevitable, inexplicable, or that the war was due to factors beyond the control of Bosnian Serbs. "The war just had to happen. As soon as the break up of Yugoslavia took place, Bosnia-Herzegovina could not stay intact. The war was inflicted upon the Serbs. There was no aggression from any side." Two Bosnian Serb participants stated that they could not attribute responsibility for the war to anyone in particular. As one put it, this was "because we do not know the background of the war itself, or the real cause of all this." Participants framed their understanding of the consequences of the war in terms of inexplicable events. For example, one participant termed the loss of the Muslim population in the area as "migration." He wondered what had happened to his legal colleagues: "Many of them I cannot even say where they are now. Some of them were just gone when the war happened. Many abandoned these areas. Some citizens from this area left."

Four of the nine Bosnian Serb participants stated that they did not believe or did not have sufficient evidence to confirm that genocide occurred during the conflict. "Did genocide happen? I think not. I am not aware of those facts." Or as another stated: "I don't have any evidence and information whether it happened. In our area, I have no information." Four observed that genocide was carried out by all three sides. As one remarked: "It happened throughout Bosnia. . . . To all three peoples." One legal professional declined to respond.

For the most part, Bosnian Serb participants did not assign responsibility to specific individuals for initiating the war. Rather, they assigned responsibility to larger categories, including "the people," the international community, politicians and national parties. Others responded by saying that they did not know, refusing to answer or as noted above, that the war was inevitable.

Like their Bosniak and Bosnian Croat colleagues, Bosnian Serb participants emphasized individual accountability for all who committed war crimes. As one participant stated: "I chase criminals" regardless of nationality. Another emphasized that "a war crime is a war crime no matter from which side it arises." Seven of the participants were asked specifically about command responsibility; of those, four acknowledged that commanders should be held accountable for the actions of their subordinates. Only one participant mentioned a specific individual – General Tihomir Blaškić[35] when discussing this concept. This lack of specificity mirrored responses to the question of accountability for the war for which participants named no individuals. Those who discussed this topic emphasized not rank, but bringing to justice anyone who committed war crimes.

Along with Bosniak and Bosnian Croat legal professionals, Bosnian Serb participants rejected the concept of collective accountability for war crimes. In contrast to their resistance to holding individuals responsible for the war, Bosnian Serb participants insisted that only individuals could be held accountable for war crimes. In discussing genocide, one participant stated that "genocide was done by individuals or small groups of individuals, not by a whole nation." However, even here, some participants also rejected the principle of collective responsibility of political leaders. While one Bosniak and a few Bosnian Croat

---

35. On March 3, 2000, Blaškić was sentenced by the ICTY after the court found him guilty crimes against humanity, war crimes and grave breaches of the Geneva Convention of 1949. The sentenced followed a 25-month trial with testimony from 158 witnesses and approximately 30,000 pages of evidence. Blaškić, 39, was commander of Croat fighters in central Bosnia during the war. He was held responsible for attacks across the Lasva River Valley that left hundreds of Bosniaks dead and sent thousands more fleeing the area. In particular, the court held that Blaškić ordered a April 1993 attack on the village of Ahmici in which more than 100 men, women and children were killed.

participants were willing to hold political leaders accountable for the war – including their own – Bosnian Serb participants were unwilling specifically to name Bosnian Serb political leaders among those responsible for the war. In fact, two participants stated that political leaders should not be held accountable because their policies reflected the will of the people. While some did blame the war on politicians, none named specific leaders of any national group, and one specifically stated that Milošević wasn't "guilty."

While few Bosnian Serb participants mentioned the international community in connection with the war in Bosnia, those who did were vehement in their opinions. Generally, they believed that the international community was unfair to the Serbs or that it did not understand what happened in Bosnia during the war. One participant characterized the opinion of Serbs by the international community as: "Serbs are the bad guys. But I think it's the reverse." This sentiment was echoed by another: "We are satanized in the world, and we are not like they said, we are an old Christian, civilized people. We are not the monsters we are presented in the media." Another participant stated: "It seems to me that many representatives of international organizations, a great number of them, are always in a trance. Maybe there wasn't an opportunity for them to learn, or maybe they gained their information from different sources, about what really happened here."

Three Bosnian Serb participants saw the actions of the international community toward them as hypocritical and openly expressed hostility toward NATO bombing of Serbia and Kosovo. They complained about the "double standard" of accountability – Bosnian Serbs were being held accountable for war crimes committed in Bosnia, while leaders of countries participating in the bombing were not held accountable although these Bosnian Serb participants saw the bombing as a violation of international law. One referenced the United States bombings of Yugoslavia and Vietnam to illustrate the hypocrisy of the international community. The other two participants supported this concept by pointing out that NATO had violated the principle of state sovereignty by initiating the bombing of Serbia.

Using this same argument, Bosnian Serb participants were highly critical of the ICTY. Many disparaged the ICTY for its apparent lack of impartiality and independence, qualities that underlie their definition of professionalism. As one participant stated: "I think that court is not a real court. I think that my court is more mature in its proceedings, and more expert and diligent in the conduct of trials." All criticized the ICTY and international organizations operating within Bosnia for being influenced by politics. "The international court in The Hague is discussed too much. It is too artificial a court and it is under the jurisdiction of powerful societies. There is no justice in that court." In addition, many stated that they did not understand the court and its workings because it is "nothing like a court we have here." The one Bosnian Serb who supported the ICTY suggested that it should "organize a round table for every judge and prosecutor who is willing to come to meet and to get familiar with The Hague Tribunal. . . .

To have an explanation why it is good for someone and not for someone else [to be indicted]. Not to be closed."

In general, participants viewed the Tribunal as a political body that was an instrument of Western influence rather than an independent judicial institution. One Bosnian Serb participant asserted that public international law has no place in courts because it concerns violations by states of their international obligations rather than individual liability. Two participants pointed to the fact that only Western judges served on the Tribunal and that no judges from the national group of the accused sat in judgment of their own.

When Bosnian Serb judges and prosecutors were asked on whom the ICTY should focus its energy, the responses were general in nature. Almost universally, they stated that the ICTY should deal with "all of those who committed war crimes" or that "all should be held accountable." When asked how the ICTY should allocate its scarce resources, participants reiterated their initial responses. For example, one Bosnian Serb judge stated: "I would choose the persons who committed war crimes." When asked to be more specific, this judge took out the Criminal Code of the Republika Srpska and proceeded to show the interviewers the provision regarding war crimes. Another participant, when asked whether the ICTY should focus on leaders, such as Milošević, responded: "I won't answer. On the persons, that's politics, and I don't want to interfere with that topic. I think that my answer is sufficient, that everyone who committed a war crime should be tried." However, one Bosnian Serb judge explicitly stated that the ICTY should focus "on those who established . . . the conditions for the war."

Many participants expressed the view that the ICTY was biased against the Serb people. Six Bosnian Serb participants stated that the ICTY only targets Serbs or that the actions of the ICTY are only focused on "one people." As one participant described: "There are some rules created in [the] world that only Serbs are criminals." In addition, two specifically mentioned that, during the course of a NATO Stability Force (hereinafter SFOR) action to arrest the former Prijedor police chief, he was killed. They described the SFOR arrest as a kidnapping and they saw this as a flagrant disregard of the judicial process. Three felt that there was "no justice" or "no righteousness" in the ICTY. Another participant raised the example of the linkage between economic assistance and cooperation with the ICTY as additional evidence for the politicization of the ICTY. Paradoxically, while all but one of the Bosnian Serb legal professionals criticized the ICTY as unfair, only two believed that it should be abolished.

Bosnian Serb participants were dubious about the impact of the ICTY on social reconstruction. Six stated that they did not believe that the ICTY and the process of social reconstruction were linked. Participants illustrated their lack of confidence in the ICTY's contribution to social reconstruction by noting "the future of the people in this area is not dependent upon the ICTY. The ICTY is not significant for the life of those people here." One participant, who was particularly vehement in this view, reasoned from his own feelings about the impact that the successful prosecution of those who burned down his house would have on him: "It would not change [my feelings about social reconstruction]. I don't have any hope for [a multi-ethnic state] actually happening. If they were caught and tried I would have no satisfaction in that." The five other participants stated that the ICTY played no role in reconstruction because reconciliation was an extra-judicial process: "When someone wants to forgive somebody, he'll do it without a court. . . . The fate of those people here is not a matter of nationality or interest, it is not dependent upon some court. . . . If we are human, we don't need a court."

In fact, two Bosnian Serbs suggested that the ICTY and its slowness and inefficiency might be widening the gap between the peoples in Bosnia. Another described this belief more starkly, stating that the ICTY had a negative influence upon people and increased the "antagonism" between them. However, two others believed that the ICTY could, if it were more "efficient and fair," contribute to the process of reconciliation. Another stressed that it would take time to overcome their mistrust of the ICTY: "Maybe we're still under the influence of the war." Finally, one felt that economic development, and not the ICTY, would trigger social reconstruction.

Bosnian Serb participants were resistant to the Tribunal and to its primary jurisdiction for war crimes. According to the Rome Agreement, Bosnian prosecutors must seek permission from the ICTY before initiating arrest and prosecution of war criminals. Although the Bosnian Serb participants did not explicitly comment on the location of the Tribunal, nearly all stated that they did not see why war crimes trials could not be held in Bosnia. One participant suggested that the ICTY conduct its proceedings in Bosnia. Eight Bosnian Serb participants believed that national courts were competent to conduct trials of accused war criminals. Of this group, two believed that the trials should only be held in the areas where the crimes were committed. Two implied that national courts were on par with the ICTY and could conduct fair trials, but one suggested that it would be good for internationals to conduct trials in Bosnia.

3. The Bosnian Croat Perspective

Virtually all Mostar Group participants perceived the war as an act of the Yugoslavian People's Army (hereinafter Jugoslovenska Narodna Armija or JNA) and Serb aggression, and many specifically named Milošević and Karadžić as responsible. As one stated: "The politics of Slobodan Milošević and Serb nationalism, those started the war, others just accepted it." Mostar Group participants did not differentiate between the Yugoslav national army and the Bosnian Serb forces. "In Bosnia-Herzegovina there was Serbian aggression by Serbia and Montenegro." Another participant assigned responsibility for the war by sharing an anecdote. Prior to the war, he was in Serbia on business and saw on a kiosk a map that appeared to show Yugoslavia. On closer inspection, the map was labeled "Greater Serbia" and much of Bosnia was included in this territory. Another stated: "I think it was the policy of Slobodan Milošević. He did not understand that these countries could separate peacefully." Finally, another described the events leading up to the war: "We all voted on two options.

Becoming a state or staying in Yugoslavia. We voted for independence of Bosnia-Herzegovina. The Serbs would not abide by such decisions and so they
started the war."

Many participants stated that the actions of the HVO were simply a response to the aggression of the Serbs and that the Bosnian Croats were the only
ones who were ready to defend themselves:

> There were many victims except on the Croat side because people prepared to
> defend themselves. . . . Herzegovina knew what would happen because they saw
> an example of it in Croatia. The Croats in Herzegovina stopped the Serbs. While
> Croats were fighting the Serbs who were trying to capture Konjic, the Muslims
> were sitting in the cafes.

Although Bosnian Croat participants did not specifically discuss the alleged
atrocities committed by the HVO, they defended their tactics by asserting that
every party to the conflict, including the HVO, needed to "play by the Serbs'
rules" and thus followed the lead of the Bosnian Serb forces.

Six Bosnian Croat participants stated that genocide occurred against all
three peoples in Bosnia. One stated that the JNA/Serb aggression against the
Bosniaks and Croats was an act of genocide; however genocide by the other
sides was not as clear-cut. One Bosnian Croat judge explicitly acknowledged
that Croat forces committed genocide, stating: "Genocide took place on all
sides. But, as Croats, there are fewer Croat perpetrators but it seems as though
they are the ones that are caught. But that does not undermine the percent of
responsibility, their accountability, the very numbers are the evidence." Other
participants had different views: "I don't think there was a real genocide anywhere in Bosnia-Herzegovina. In some ways there was a genocide, in others not
actually, you didn't have one nation actually completely wiped out." One Bosnian Croat refused to answer the question. Interestingly, none of the Mostar
Group participants talked about the collective accountability of any of the national groups involved in the war.

Mostar Group legal professionals adhered to the concept of individual accountability. However, their acceptance of the principle of command responsibility was more ambiguous. As an example, two Bosnian Croat judges referred
specifically to the Blaškić trial and expressed skepticism about his control of the
forces under his command. In contrast to this view, one participant believed in
the application of command responsibility. "Because it is difficult to establish
who murdered, the commanders of military units that did commit these crimes
should be responsible, should be accountable." The lack of clarity around this
issue was illustrated by a statement made by another Bosnian Croat judge. He
claimed that in order to determine responsibility for war crimes, one needs to
ascertain who was in control of the geographic region at the time. This contradicted his earlier statement questioning the concept of command responsibility.

Like their colleagues in the Sarajevo Group, Bosnian Croat participants
expressed concerns regarding the acquiescence of the international community
in the face of atrocities. As one Bosnian Croat observed: "If the international
community wanted to prevent the wars, they would have prevented it. In 1992,

in 1991." Another pointed to the international arms embargo: "When Bosnia-Herzegovina was attacked, the international community imposed an embargo and allowed the Serbs to kill some three or four hundreds of thousands of people so the international community is directly responsible for it." Finally, one Bosnian Croat participant went so far as to suggest that the Dutch battalion in Srebrenica should be held accountable for the massacre of Bosniaks there.

Several Bosnian Croat participants also criticized the ICTY and international organizations operating within Bosnia as thoroughly political bodies. And one participant criticized the Federation's choice of liaison to the ICTY as politically motivated and unrepresentative of the interests of Bosnian Croats. A third described the international community as following its own agenda, yet working to promote fairness and accountability in the domestic judiciary.

Mostar Group participants had specific ideas regarding how the ICTY should focus its resources. Many argued that the ICTY should indict and try those of the highest rank, specifically Karadžić, Mladić and Milošević. A common theme among Bosnian Croat participants, frequently associated with an expression of frustration or anger, was the belief that only Croats were held in custody in The Hague. Although they never explicitly denied the culpability of Bosnian Croat indictees, many expressed concern that no indictments had been issued by the ICTY for atrocities committed in pre-war Croat-majority towns: "I think you know that no one from the army of Bosnia and Herzegovina is accused of crimes, only Croats. In places where the BiH Army operated, murders occurred, in Prusina, in Grabovica, and in Doljani. Nobody has answered for those crimes." Three participants referred to these murders and indicated that requests to arrest those involved had been sent to the ICTY in accordance with the Rules of the Road but no further action had resulted. Many of the Bosnian Croat participants expressed concern that the international community pressured Croatia to turn over its indictees or lose valuable economic assistance. However, one participant was pleased that the Croatian government had complied with ICTY requests to deliver Croatian accused war criminals to The Hague.

In addition to the criticism that Bosnian Croats were selectively prosecuted by the ICTY, participants reported concern about the way in which cases sent by Bosnian Croat authorities to the ICTY had been handled. These cases alleged war crimes against Bosnian Croats by members of the BiH army. When the ICTY returned the cases to Bosnia for trial, they were assigned to the Sarajevo Cantonal Court rather than the courts with original jurisdiction. Although the assignment of cases was not the responsibility of the ICTY, but rather that of the Federation Supreme Court, Bosnian Croat participants conflated these two mechanisms, assuming that the reassignment decision reflected the political priorities of the ICTY.

Bosnian Croat participants gave varied responses regarding the influence of the Tribunal in post-war Bosnia. Like Sarajevo Group participants, many believed that over time the work of the Tribunal could play an important role in reconciliation and reconstruction. As one participant stated: "I think that the ICTY is part of everything that has happened here," and that its work has allowed "people to talk about things more openly and more honestly." Still, two others expressly stated that the ICTY had no impact on reconciliation or reconstruction and that economic development was critical to a reconstructed society: "Our people care to buy medicine and to survive. That is the answer." Or as another participant stated: "I would not ever, personally, ever connect these ideas: social reconstruction, economic reconstruction, as far as I am concerned, they have nothing to do with those who committed war crimes." However, all believed – despite the reservations of some – that the ICTY and its work ultimately would be important to the country.

Like their counterparts among the Sarajevo Group, Mostar Group legal professionals questioned why more indictees had not been arrested and called for greater SFOR action. Many believed that the lack of arrests – especially of Bosnian Serb leaders – demonstrated a lack of political will on the part of the international community.

Similar to the Sarajevo Group, Mostar Group legal professionals believed that it was important for the ICTY to conduct its work in The Hague. Six participants stated that the trials should be held in The Hague, implying that judges in Bosnia would be subject to political pressures that would compromise their ability to guarantee fair trials. Two others proposed that the more important trials be held in The Hague while those of lesser rank be tried in national courts to speed up the process and reduce costs. In addition, participants believed that the country could not withstand the instability that would be a consequence of such trials.

However, some suggested that the ICTY would be more accessible to the people if it conducted trials in Bosnia, provided that international judges adjudicated the cases. Three expressed concerns that the location of the Tribunal was a hardship for the families of those awaiting trial in terms of the emotional burden, financial cost and the difficulty to meet with the attorney for their relative. Moreover, these same three participants were concerned that no compensation was paid to those acquitted by the ICTY. As one stated: "We have the situation where some people from the community, who have spent several months there, were actually freed in the end. I don't think it's fair that [they] do not have any right to compensation."

C. Participants' Perceptions of Practices and Procedures of the ICTY

Across national groups, participants generally lacked a clear understanding of the procedures of the ICTY. They expressed several areas of concern: its unique blend of civil and common law procedures; how cases are selected; how indictments are issued – particularly sealed indictments; the length of detention and trials; and the evidentiary rules applied by the ICTY.

Judges and prosecutors across national groups reported that they did not understand how the blend of common law and civil law traditions impacted the work of the ICTY. A Bosniak judge acknowledged that this structural hybrid made it difficult for judges in Bosnia to understand the procedures of the ICTY. As one Bosnian Croat judge stated: "None of us knows the rules according to which they work. Only a few people who have any contact with such a court know something about it, but the rest of us [do] not." In sum: "These rules are a bit foreign to us."

Participants also did not understand how the ICTY set priorities for investigations and prosecutions. Instances in which ICTY indictments did not conform to participants' expectations led them to conclude that the Tribunal and its processes were unfair. As one Bosniak judge explained his frustration with the process: "I can tell you that, as a citizen, if you have a United Nations resolution then you know who was the aggressor, then you can tell who is politically and militarily accountable, but probably the ICTY has its own way to work."

When asked about the practice of issuing sealed indictments, participants' responses fell into one of two categories. Bosnian Serb and some Bosnian Croat participants understood the practice of sealed indictments as a political tool to keep people "afraid" and to pressure politicians into desired behaviors, whereas most Bosniaks and many Bosnian Croat participants generally found the use of sealed indictments acceptable.

Bosnian Serb participants expressed concern that sealed indictments constituted an abuse of the indictee's rights, demonstrated the lack of transparency of the ICTY and were unnecessary. They asserted that war criminals could not evade justice forever. Another Bosnian Serb judge criticized the use of sealed indictments because he believed that innocent people would turn themselves in to the ICTY. However, he later noted that war criminals would not "accidentally run into SFOR soldiers." Finally, one judge noted that the lack of transparency in the indictment process creates fear among army veterans who worry that army service in this period might constitute a war crime.

Legal professionals in the Sarajevo Group generally found the sealed indictments acceptable. They recognized that under usual circumstances such procedures might violate the rights of the accused. However, in the present circumstances, they believed that the apprehension of serious war criminals warranted this deviation. One accepted the practice of sealed indictments as necessary because Bosnia was "totally undemocratic" and otherwise the capture of war criminals would be more difficult. Another stated that sufficient safeguards existed to make the use of sealed indictments acceptable. Finally, a Bosniak prosecutor saw them as necessary to bring those accused before the Tribunal. This prosecutor noted that if the procedures for sealed indictments were "written in their rules, that's okay."

Some Bosnian Croat participants echoed the views of their Bosnian Serb and Bosniak counterparts. Two stated that sealed indictments were necessary, at least temporarily: "It's okay if it will help to apprehend a criminal." Three others said that the sealed indictments were used by the ICTY "so they can manipulate" and maintain fear among the people. One Bosnian Croat prosecutor demonstrated ambivalence about sealed indictments by stating that they could be "justified" but "it is also about the political pressure."

While participants in the Sarajevo Group made no comments about pre-trial detentions, their colleagues complained that the detentions of accused war criminals were too lengthy. Across national groups participants decried the length of the ICTY trials. As one prosecutor noted: "Is it fair to keep someone waiting for four years if he's accused of war crimes, to keep him waiting for his verdict to be announced, guilty or not guilty? The Hague Tribunal has to be more efficient, and faster." When considering the ICTY trials, participants compared the length of trials at the ICTY with those conducted in BiH, where criminal trials are generally shorter. They associated fair trials with speed and "efficiency" of the court process. "You can have justice if someone could be . . . brought to trial in a very short time. Everything that has been dragged on has a negative effect. I am not saying that anybody should be amnestied because the time has passed, but I am saying the effectiveness of a sentence [is less]." Sarajevo Group participants echoed this concern.

Several participants criticized the efficiency of the ICTY. A Bosnian Serb participant remarked: "That's so much talk and fuss about [the ICTY] and little work done. They'll fill all those prisons and they're not doing anything." Many Bosnian Croat participants and one Bosniak specifically cited the multi-year trial of General Blaškić as an example of the excessive length of trials at the ICTY. When asked what the priorities of the ICTY should be given limited resources, a Mostar Group participant questioned the limited nature of the ICTY's resources in light of the length of the trials and number of witnesses called to testify.

In contrast, a Bosnian Croat judge averred that: "Justice may be slow, but it is available." And one judge who had visited the ICTY acknowledged the competence and diligence of the ICTY staff. However, he recognized that the Tribunal and its staff required time to understand the region, its history and the various political and military organizations. Similarly, one Bosnian Croat judge suggested that the ICTY has slowed itself down by accepting "small cases" rather than focusing on the most serious war crimes. This same judge supported others' concerns that the length of the trials was costly for defendants and their families, noting further that families turned to charitable organizations for financial support.

The use of expert witnesses by the ICTY provoked strong opinions among Mostar Group and Banja Luka Group participants. For example, one Bosnian Serb participant criticized the ICTY's reliance on an historian to determine the genesis of the conflict. This participant stated that he did not understand the relationship between such general information and a particular crime. He labeled expert testimony as "unreliable statements" that had "no relation" to a criminal case and concluded that the work of the ICTY involved "imagination." He reiterated that: "My job is based on the specific case, specific acts." He was supported by a Bosnian Serb colleague who stated that the ICTY "issued decisions without real evidence. I would never try a case like that."

Bosnian Croat participants also questioned the testimony of a history professor as an expert witness. As one noted: "He might never have been to Bosnia-Herzegovina. He was explaining the history of Bosnia, and the relationship between the three nations, which had nothing to do with the Blaškić case. But if judges want to know about Bosnia, they needed to educate themselves, like myself: take books and read." Two Bosnian Croat judges asserted that only "direct" evidence of a particular crime should be admitted in court, as is the case in Bosnia.

On the other hand, only one Sarajevo Group participant commented upon the use of expert witnesses. This judge, who had visited the ICTY, looked more favorably upon the use of expert testimony and saw expert witnesses as advantageous because they were neutral, were not involved in the war, and offered "the highest scientific dignity."

The participants raised additional concerns about the quality and quantity of evidence. For example, a Bosnian Croat judge suggested that there should be more evidence at trial. Another viewed the release of evidence to the ICTY as dependent on internal political forces within Bosnia. In contrast, another Bosnian Croat legal professional felt that there were too many irrelevant witnesses called to testify in the Blaškić case: "There were two or three hundred witnesses there in The Hague who really didn't have anything to do with it, no connections with the case."

Four Bosnian Serb participants questioned the Tribunal's use of evidence. And others generally questioned the role of the ICTY in the collection of evidence within the RS.

D.   Participants' View of Their Treatment by the ICTY

Across national groups, legal professionals perceived their sporadic contact with the ICTY as a sign of disrespect. Bosniak and Bosnian Croat judges and prosecutors reported periodic visits from ICTY officials to collect files regarding suspected war criminals. Those participants with experience presiding over or prosecuting domestic war crimes cases reported awareness of and compliance with the Rules of the Road procedures. However, ICTY officials failed to keep their Bosnian colleagues informed of the status of the investigations, even in response to direct inquiries. As one judge explained: "They came here at the end of 1995. They took the cases with them, and said that the criminals would be brought to justice, but nothing has happened." A judge reported that after having submitted twenty-five cases and waiting eight months, the ICTY had not responded. Other judges and prosecutors stated that they too had submitted files several years before and had received no communication. A Bosnian Serb participant expressed similar frustration. He reported that ICTY investigators never responded to an indictment he submitted for approval in mid-1997. These professionals viewed the ICTY as unresponsive and detrimental to the ability of Bosnian courts to conduct national war crimes trials.

Some who interacted with representatives of the ICTY wanted to be respected in their own right as legal professionals. However, their attitude toward the ICTY was ambivalent and influenced by the status they believed they occupied in relation to the international community. Participants across national groups reported they perceived that the international community saw them as intellectual inferiors who did not understand the relevant law. As one participant remarked: "When all these people come from outside they think that we absolutely do not have any knowledge; they have certain biases already when they come in." One judge remarked upon the power differential that exists between the ICTY and the Bosnian judicial system. However, one Bosnian Serb judge expressed pride in the approval by the ICTY of the legal work he had performed noting that: "Everything I did was accepted by the Tribunal with no objections." Even in instances in which the ICTY approved of their performance, the power of the Tribunal to validate Bosnian legal competence was clear.

E.   *Gaps in Communication Identified by Participants*

With two exceptions, Bosnian legal professionals were poorly informed about the work of the ICTY. A Bosnian Serb participant questioned whether the Tribunal had ever issued a verdict. Another wondered whether it was founded on a statute. Some participants expressed concern that the information they had received had been distorted by the media. Despite this lack of information, participants did not report any self-initiated study of war crimes or the ICTY.

Legal professionals across national groups reported that virtually all the information about the ICTY they received came from the local sources. Participants in the RS and the Federation recognized that the limited source of information was problematic because of the nationalist slant of the communication industry in BiH. One Bosnian Serb legal professional noted the influence of politics on media reports stating: "There is mostly news with political features, not professional." A Bosnian Croat participant stated: "Every side gets its own version of the story." A Bosniak prosecutor remarked that Bosnian newspapers were "short on news." Another criticized the accuracy of reporting about the ICTY, stating: "nothing can be lied about too much."

Across all national groups, participants desired impartial information about the ICTY with legal content as they had limited or no access to legal publications from or about the ICTY.[36] One judge reported that he was unable to locate a copy of the Tadić judgment which he remarked was critically influential in a "legal and political sense." Two judges reported that they periodically received computer disks from the ICTY with bulletins about the Tribunal's recent work. Others cited informal "exchange of opinions" with colleagues as an additional source of information.

Participants offered suggestions to improve communication with the ICTY. One suggested that the ICTY regularly distribute its reports directly to judges and prosecutors. Another believed that more judges and prosecutors should visit the Tribunal. In addition, a judge encouraged visits by the highest officials from the ICTY to meet members of the local judiciary.

---

36.   The ICTY website, <http://www.un.org/icty/index.html>, had not included documents in the local languages of BiH until after the survey was completed.

V.
DISCUSSION

The purpose of this study was to assess the perceptions and consequent attitudes of Bosnian judges and prosecutors involved in the adjudication of war crimes. The following discussion offers some interpretations of the major themes that emerged. In so doing, our goal is to offer a richer understanding of the impact of international criminal trials on a national judicial system. The survey results suggest that those international institutions that interact or are involved with the Bosnian legal system should take seriously the problems and resistances articulated by the study participants in formulating future directions. In addition, these perceptions may offer lessons about the ICTY's effect on Bosnian legal professionals that can be applied to the process of establishing an International Criminal Court. The findings suggest that it is essential to incorporate a context-specific understanding of an affected country and its judicial processes in order to enhance cooperation with and decrease resistance to institutions of international criminal justice.

A. Context

The legal professionals who participated in this survey were surprisingly open and candid in the interviews. However, it was apparent that certain topics provoked a significant emotional response, most clearly in the areas of war crimes and genocide. Across the board, participants avoided provocative questions that addressed the relationship of law to justice. For example, in response to questions regarding their role in refugee returns, the creation of a State supreme court for BiH or the prosecution of political leaders for war crimes, participants frequently resorted to the evasive statement that the question was "political" and therefore inappropriate. This response may reflect the traditional and narrowly defined role of the judge in a civil law system or participants' perspective on the role of law in a Communist society. It may also reflect their caution in making statements that may expose them to retaliation or retribution by the legislative and executive branches of government which wield tremendous power over the judiciary.

In addition, there was a strong association between the emotional response to particular topics and the participant's national origin. It was interesting that participants expressed few reservations regarding the confidential nature of the interview, despite the caution they displayed in answering certain questions. In fact, it became evident that a few had discussed their participation with colleagues. The researchers feel that, despite the difficult context in which these judges and prosecutors operate, their answers reflected an honest attempt to grapple with the issues raised.

B. Professional Identity

Given the ongoing criticism of the Bosnian legal system by members of international organizations such as UNMIB, JSAP and OHR, we were surprised to observe the extent to which the notion of "professionalism" dominated the views of the participants in this study. While the international community has considered Balkan politics primarily in terms of conflict between national groups, it has paid too little attention to other factors that may influence attitudes and behaviors, like professional identity. The judges and prosecutors in the sample reported that they maintained high ideals of integrity and respect for the rule of law. These precepts were accompanied by reverence for codified law that reflect the civil law tradition. In this system, there is no concept of judicial activism. While recognizing that injustice may be caused by political decisions, judges and prosecutors did not see themselves as empowered to use the law to ameliorate the negative consequences of these decisions. It is also possible that some legal professionals may have relied on the formal structure of the civil law tradition to mask their personal support for the goals of the politicians in power, particularly since they were communicating to an international audience.

Further, the participants reported anger and confusion over the criticisms by international lawyers who did not appear to understand the legal tradition of civil law countries or, if they did, were perceived as showing disrespect for the judicial system to which Bosnian legal professionals were devoted. These attitudes, coupled with the decision of the ICTY to combine common and civil law to the great confusion of our participants, may lead to a pervasive sense of being practitioners in a second-rate system. Judges and prosecutors therefore find themselves on the defensive, powerless in the face of an international community that rejects their beliefs. Prior to the war, judges and prosecutors were people of stature – community leaders with means and position. Having lost their homes, family members, and friends, these Bosnian professionals appeared to cling to their professional identities. Unfortunately, participants perceived international criticism of the Bosnian legal system as an attack on their professional identity. This perception by participants indicates that efforts by international organizations to enhance the professionalism of Bosnian judges and prosecutors should be designed with this vulnerability in mind. If Bosnian legal professionals experience educational interventions as denigrating their competence, such well-meaning programs run the risk of promoting resistance to, rather than cooperation with, international groups.

These findings do not tell the whole story. These legal professionals are beleaguered: not only are they criticized by those outside the country but they are under pressure from those within, particularly politicians and criminal elements who act with impunity. Since they are dependent on legislative and executive branch officials for fiscal and other resources, they are pressured to render decisions that are favorable to these authorities. Compounding this, threats to them or to their families, evidenced by abductions or beatings, place them in positions of great vulnerability with minimal protections. Given these pressures, it is significant that this sample of judges and prosecutors insisted on their integrity and consistently advocated independence of the judiciary. We must also emphasize that they recognize what needs to be rectified in their system if positive change is to occur – decent salaries paid regularly, protection from harm, competent judges, transparent decision-making and non-interference by politicians. Although they recognized that corruption (defined as bribery) was possible and perhaps even likely among some of their colleagues, they traced this to the poor pay and diminished quality of life. Further, they supported the law that prohibits judges from joining political parties.

There appears to be a disconnect between the views of Western legal experts and those of Bosnian legal professionals in this study. It centers on the question of influence or the appearance of influence on judicial and prosecutorial activities. Although it is not clear to what extent improprieties exist, the reports of such have been cited as justifications for large-scale reform of the Bosnian legal system. In order to promote an effective dialogue between these groups, Western experts need to acknowledge the expertise and strengths of Bosnian legal professionals. In addition, international representatives must articulate the justifications for the new professional standards that the international community seeks to inculcate within the national legal system.

Like the rest of the country's institutions, the legal system is coping with the transition from the pre-war Communist era. Our study suggests that the judges are open to change but the modifications required must occur within the larger context of transformation of the political system. Moreover, the influx of international lawyers and others who are perceived as promulgating a foreign system of law disempowers Bosnian professionals, heightens their ambivalence and potentially mitigates the positive effects that could result from the international presence.

There is no question that disparities in power color this process of evolution. Our findings suggest that the Western legal community may not be sufficiently sensitive to these issues in their concern to implement a "modern" system of law. Although international organizations have Bosnian nationals on staff, this level of integration is insufficient to overcome the perception among the Bosnian legal professionals we interviewed that the international community is imposing foreign values upon them. We suspect that the desired changes will require many years to implement fully. It is likely that a systematic and well-paced process – one that more completely involves the Bosnian legal community in design of training, modifications of the law and which respects the integrity of the Bosnian legal tradition – will have a more profound and sustained impact on the legal system. Power disparities generate ambivalence, and attention to the resistances that reflect this ambivalence will further the goals of a truly independent and stable judicial system.

Finally, the rejection of the political process by members in our study of this professional class is disturbing. Since the members of our sample were highly educated and relatively well informed, their rejection of the political process has implications for the development of democracy in BiH. For many, "political" has come to be reflective of nationalism and war. If these judges and prosecutors see the need to withdraw from political participation, there is a danger that legal professionals will be further disempowered as they eschew the democratic process. If other educated individuals feel similarly, this will not augur well for an active citizenry fully engaged in democratic decision-making.

C. Participants' Perceptions of the International Community and the ICTY

We have described how our sample views the international community. These views influence their perspective on the ICTY as well. The international community responded to war crimes and genocide in Bosnia by establishing the first international war crimes tribunal since Tokyo. The difficulties in establishing the ICTY are well documented and include its inception in the midst of a war and a lack of financial and human resources as well as ambivalent support from world leaders. In the early years of the Tribunal its work suffered from lack of cooperation from authorities in Bosnia. Additionally, the narrow mandate of the international troops stationed as peacekeepers in Bosnia inhibited arrest of indicted war criminals. In the seven years since its creation, significant positive changes have taken place as financial support has increased, countries with peacekeeping troops on the ground have improved cooperation with ICTY prosecutors and the ICTY has clarified its practices and procedures. This study provides the opportunity to re-evaluate the practices and institutional arrangements of the ICTY in order to lessen resistance and encourage collaboration between these judicial entities.

The participants perceived the following areas of concern: location of the ICTY; judicial appointments; criticisms by international organizations of the Bosnian legal system; a misunderstanding of the hybrid nature of ICTY judicial procedures; the inherently political nature of a United Nations-sponsored ad hoc tribunal; and the lack of communication between Bosnian and Tribunal legal professionals. This constellation of factors has coalesced around a perception by Bosnian judges and prosecutors we interviewed that the ICTY, as well as those international legal organizations working in Bosnia, have contributed to the marginalization of Bosnian legal professionals. While most participants continued to support the concept of the ICTY, these concerns have placed them on the defensive and led to skepticism that undermines their support of the Tribunal.

Mass accountability for Bosnian war criminals necessarily requires the active participation of the Bosnian legal system because of the sheer numbers of suspects involved. Currently, because the ICTY assumes primary jurisdiction for war crimes, the Bosnian legal system largely has been bypassed or reduced to a subsidiary role in this process. The skeptical, even negative, attitudes of participants that we have described pose a significant risk to the long-term development of the Bosnian legal system and its integration into Western Europe. The findings indicate that current efforts of the ICTY and international institutions working to promote the Bosnian legal system have yet to overcome this negative perception. Five years after the signing of the Dayton Accords, the persistence of this skepticism is of grave concern. Greater attention needs to be paid not only to the political and financial limits on the Bosnian legal system but also to the more subtle psychosocial factors that sabotage professional identity and commitment to positive change.

In 1993, when the ICTY was created in the midst of active conflict, important choices were made regarding the location and structure of the Tribunal. At that time, it was not possible to locate the Tribunal in the Balkans or to include participation by the Bosnian judiciary in trials. Participants' concerns about marginalization lead to the question of whether the original decision regarding the location of the ICTY and the exclusion of Bosnian legal professionals in its judicial ranks should be reconsidered. These tactical decisions, taken at the Tribunal's inception, are examples of choices made in the context of armed conflict that now might be revisited.

In the findings, we have described a series of factors that have contributed to resistance to the ICTY. The synergistic effect of these factors requires closer examination. The Bosnian legal system has been under intense international scrutiny particularly since the end of the war. Bosnian legal professionals have received contradictory signals from the ICTY and international organizations. For example, under the Rome Agreement, Bosnian authorities lawfully can arrest and prosecute alleged war criminals only subject to ICTY approval. At the same time, international organizations like UNMIB, JSAP and OHR continue to criticize the Bosnian judicial system for its lack of independence, incompetence and corruption. These evaluations send the message to Bosnian judges and prosecutors that fair war crimes trials are impossible in their own country. On the one hand, international organizations have reported that local justice is vulnerable to influence; some judges may be corrupt, incompetent, and/or influenced by nationalist politics. On the other hand, this is not universal. The net effect of these mixed messages may be to amplify the negative overtones of these signals. Thus, the overwhelming impression that Bosnian legal professionals have of the ICTY and international organizations in Bosnia is that these institutions, with few exceptions, have little respect for the Bosnian legal system. In pursuing their own predetermined agendas, without meaningful input from Bosnian legal professionals, international organizations run the risk of undermining the very goals they are trying to achieve.

Moreover, many Bosnian legal professionals perceive the ICTY and its procedures as indicating that the Bosnian legal system is substandard. Bosnian judges and prosecutors perceive the choice of a hybrid set of procedures that embody primarily common law as a negative evaluation of the civil law system and a challenge to the precepts of Bosnian legal professionals. Each of these legal systems has a distinct culture. The structure of a civil law system results in a more rapid trial, fewer witnesses and the role of the judge is more narrowly defined.[37] For many Bosnian legal professionals, the common law system is inaccessible and, by extension, the ICTY.

Bosnia is a virtual protectorate of the international community. Across national groups, participants perceived that they occupied a diminutive status in this arrangement. It became clear among our sample that they did not consider themselves to be co-equal partners in the design and implementation of many of

---

37. *See* MIRJAN R. DAMAŠKA, THE FACES OF JUSTICE AND STATE AUTHORITY 19, 51-3 (1986).

the programs intended to rebuild their legal system and their country. The attitudes toward the international community were multifaceted and strongly colored participants' views of the ICTY: some were grateful to the world community for ending the war; others were angered by the time that it took for intervention to occur; and still others resented the support for a multicultural, unified Bosnia. Against the backdrop of the helplessness engendered by severe personal loss, the lack of information about the ICTY may compound the implicit message that the Bosnian judiciary and its prosecutors are at best, barely acceptable, and at worst, irrelevant. Bosnian legal professionals have lost status and their social contribution has been denigrated as a result of the war. Compounding the powerlessness that results from these losses, they now find themselves sidelined in the process of reconstruction. In response, nationalist perspectives are supported, myths about the ICTY's bias are perpetuated and its positive contributions are minimized.

The findings suggest that national identity influences the participants' opinions regarding the ICTY. For example, those Bosnian Croat and Bosnian Serb participants characterizing the ICTY as a "political" body simultaneously delegitimize the Tribunal and bolster their own integrity as legal professionals. Thus, to label the ICTY as "political" enables these participants to dismiss its judgments as the result of a legal charade and to reaffirm their own fealty to the principles of neutral adjudication and professionalism. Moreover, this labeling also may serve to mask the political biases of the participants and avoid acknowledgment of the consequences of their political choices. Further, it is essential that we recognize the ICTY as a political body in its inception, judicial selection and in the rules and procedures it promulgates.[38] Moreover, its activities and decisions have far-reaching effects within each national group and within the state as a whole. The absence of a frank discussion between the ICTY and Bosnian legal professionals regarding the perceived political dimensions of the ICTY may have served indirectly to enhance resistance to the Tribunal within Bosnia.

It is abundantly clear that Bosnian legal professionals did not have accurate information about the ICTY. At best, this confusion has generated misunderstanding on the part of those legal professionals who supported the ICTY. At worst, the absence of correct information has fueled suspicion and hostility among those Bosnian Croat and Bosnian Serb participants who viewed the ICTY as the authoritative and critical voice of the international community. For these, the ICTY contradicted their own understanding of the role their national group played in the war relative to that of other groups. However, all participants, even those who displayed outward hostility toward the ICTY, expressed genuine interest in receiving more and direct communication from the Tribunal.

---

38.   Former President of the ICTY, Gabrielle Kirk McDonald, has acknowledged the political nature of the Tribunal: "First of all, we are a political court. We were established by the Security Council and that makes us political because the Security Council is a political body. And as President, I have acknowledged that. That does not mean that we act in a political way. The judges are independent." Interview with Gabrielle Kirk McDonald, *supra* note 11.

The few participants who have had personal exposure to the ICTY came away with a deep respect for the Tribunal and the professional integrity of its staff, regardless of their national identity. Their experiences provide reason to believe that negative attitudes of some Bosnian legal professionals may be changed by increased exposure to the Tribunal.

D. Accountability, Responsibility and Genocide

Participants hold strong views regarding who is responsible and who should be held accountable for atrocities committed during the conflict.[39] The cohesion of views among participants of the same national group again indicates that war experiences of participants, their self-identification with a particular national group and their exposure to dominant narratives about the role of their national group in the conflict exert a profound impact. The willingness of participants to demand accountability for particular individuals varied substantially with national group – Sarajevo Group participants being most specific. It is noteworthy that participants – Bosniaks and Bosnian Croats – who refer to atrocities that have been corroborated by international human rights groups and United Nations-sponsored bodies appear more likely to demand international accountability for the perpetrators of these crimes. Other participants – predominately Bosnian Serb – claim victimhood and yet describe no specific atrocities or war crimes. For them, accountability seems to be an abstract concept.

All participants seek to present the war experience of their national group as that of victims. However, the international community sees Bosnian Serb and Bosnian Croats as aggressors. This disparity in viewpoints may explain the responses that were defensive or evasive. The insistence of these legal professionals on recognition of the suffering or misunderstanding of their national group may have been used to deflect unspoken or presumed criticism by the researchers. While the experience of each national group provides a unique perspective on the conflict, the lack of a public discussion within each national group critical of the war atrocities carried out in the name of that national group solidifies and privileges one "truth" at the expense of all others. Although the findings indicate this pattern is observed in response to questions about accountability and responsibility in general, nowhere is it more pronounced than in the responses to the topic of genocide.

When asked their legal opinion about the occurrence of genocide during the war, participants responded by recounting the politically accepted version of events from the perspective of their national group. Bosniak participants were unequivocal and consistent in their statements that genocide against Bosniaks occurred during the war, while Bosnian Serb participants tended to state that genocide occurred against all three sides, that they had no knowledge of any acts of genocide or that genocide did not occur at all. Bosnian Croat legal profes-

---

39. In the local language participants spoke during the interviews, the word for "responsibility" is the same as "accountability." Nevertheless, it was possible to distinguish these two concepts based on the context in which the word was used.

sionals were willing to state that genocide occurred, but if so, that all three sides had suffered it. The statement that genocide occurred on all three sides serves indirectly to acknowledge that the armed forces of the participant's national group had committed mass war crimes while allowing the speaker to claim the status of victim for his or her national group. The diffusion of responsibility that characterized this opinion is ominous.

There are two immediate consequences to turning each national group into co-equal victims of genocide. First, it ignores the historical record that indicates that some suffered more than others. For example, this opinion implicitly trivializes events like the Srebrenica massacre. In addition, the ideal of co-equal accountability obfuscates the facts and recapitulates the pernicious historical revisionism following World War II that has haunted the former Yugoslavia. Second, this idea has radical implications for international war crimes prosecutions. If all sides to the conflict are equally guilty, then the ICTY should indict and try equal numbers of Bosniak, Bosnian Serb and Bosnian Croat war crime suspects – an expectation articulated by many Bosnian Croat and Bosnian Serb legal professionals. This perspective also acknowledges that the judges and prosecutors themselves understand the significant political ramifications of the trials. The disdain for the "political nature" of the ICTY reflects the reality that the Tribunal's prosecutorial choices validate one version of events over others. The principle of proportional prosecution, suggested by some of the participants, would lead to under-prosecution of Bosnian Serb perpetrators of war crimes and/or over-prosecution of Bosniaks and Bosnian Croats since there is a disparity in atrocities committed by members of particular national groups. Therefore, equal numbers of prosecutions do not produce equal justice.

The divergence among the groups is particularly striking considering that we asked participants to state their *legal opinion* as to whether genocide occurred. Yet, with few exceptions, participants did not refer to a legal definition of genocide. Rather their responses suggested that participants used the term "genocide" to refer generally to war atrocities. As noted, we view this generalization of the use of the term genocide as a mechanism to diffuse responsibility for the war. Their interpretation demonstrated how identity and national consciousness can color legal reasoning. The lack of legal precision in their responses may have indicated that it was difficult for participants to remain objective when they discussed this controversial issue.

The difficulty that participants had in discussing responsibility and accountability for the war raises serious implications for the ability of Bosnian legal professionals to conduct impartial trials of accused war criminals. Participants prided themselves on their objectivity and their ability to adjudicate matters before them impartially. To the extent that they expressed reservations about conducting national war crimes trials, they stated that political pressures may corrode due process protections. However, the strong association between the "legal" opinion offered on genocide and the national group identity of participants indicates that Bosnian legal professionals may not be neutral on issues regarding accountability for war crimes and genocide. These attitudes are cause for concern. At the time of this study, there existed a gross disparity in the numbers of war crimes trials held in the Federation and the RS (where virtually none had taken place). While we recognize that war crimes trials require the active participation of police and government structures, we share the concern expressed by many participants that the Bosnian judicial system may not be prepared fairly to adjudicate the trials of those accused of war crimes.

E.   Social Reconstruction and Reconciliation

The concept of reconciliation in post-war societies remains elusive. Further, the positive contribution of international criminal trials to this process, while widely and uncritically accepted, remains an empirical question.[40] Materials produced by the ICTY and comments by its supporters reiterate the importance of war crimes trials to the process of national reconciliation.[41] Generally, reconciliation refers to a process by which peoples who were formerly enemies put aside their memories of past wrongs, forego vengeance and give up their prior group aspirations in favor of a commitment to a communitarian ideal. Since "reconciliation" has theological overtones that reflect the Christian religious tradition, we have chosen to use the term "social reconstruction" to describe the evolution of social institutions, economic development, community-building and person-to-person connection that may underlie the commitment of people to live together.

Reconstruction is a contested notion. Our study suggests that the widely held belief that war crimes trials – which individualize accountability – contribute to social reconstruction may reflect more of an aspiration than a reality. In fact, our findings indicate that many Bosnian Croat and Bosnian Serb legal professionals do not view criminal trials as integral to social reconstruction. An analysis of the responses of our participants suggests that social reconstruction may not occur when people are faced with judicial decisions that do not correspond to their perceptions of what happened, i.e., their "truth." Evidence that is sufficient to produce a verdict in a court of law may not be sufficient to override solidified national group perspectives among the ranks of some legal professionals. These narratives that reflect national or "ethnic" history, whether contemporary or ancient, profoundly influence how our sample viewed individual verdicts. The participants in this study operate within a political context in which national identities are inscribed. It is possible that transformation toward a more open and democratic society will enable these judges and prosecutors to separate themselves from national group allegiances and to articulate thinking that is different from the current national stories about the war. Thus, our study highlights how war experiences and national group narratives may work in tandem to isolate and increase political distance among national groups.

---

40. *See* MICHAEL IGNATIEFF, THE WARRIOR'S HONOR: MODERN CONSCIENCE 164-90 (1997). Ignatieff describes the "articles of faith" that underlie the commitment of the world community to international trials for war crimes. He asks: "What does it mean for a nation to come to terms with its past?"

41. MORRIS & SCHARF *supra* note 3; Outreach Program Proposal *supra* note 5; Kritz, *supra* note 12 at 128-29. *See also supra* note 11.

For example, responses to the question of the relationship between war crimes trials and social reconstruction once again reflected national group perspectives. For Bosniak judges and prosecutors, the widely held belief that social reconstruction follows from individualizing guilt was a valid construct. However, Bosnian Serb legal professionals saw no relationship between trials and social reconstruction. In fact, they focused primarily on living amiably next door to their Bosniak and Bosnian Croat brethren but not in one geographical space. They seemed more interested in promoting the regional governmental structures that were established at Dayton within the RS rather than in strengthening the State institutions. Thus, the ICTY was perceived as irrelevant while issues of economic reconstruction and job creation were critical.

Our sample of Bosnian Croats participants showed more variation in their responses. Most were positive about the feasibility of a unified state but qualified their remarks by indicating that such a process would take many years. Two advocated a three-entity solution, living side-by-side. Most felt that the ICTY over time would contribute to the political stability of the country. While some focused on acknowledgement of their victimhood and retribution as the next step, others emphasized the importance of economic development. As the recent ESI and ICG reports suggest, the existence of the shadow state of Herceg-Bosna under the aegis of the Croatian Democratic Union (hereinafter Hrvatska Demokratska Zajednica or HDZ) has led to a de facto separation that OHR seeks to eradicate. How the judges and prosecutors see their roles in this shadow state was not apparent, although they articulated support for the full integration of the judicial systems, especially in Mostar. It is too soon to evaluate the impact of the death of Croatian president Tudman and the defeat of the HDZ party in the recent elections, although the apparent rigidity of the HZD in Herzegovina suggests that significant changes will not occur in the immediate future.

Only a minority of Bosnian legal professionals in our sample believed that war crimes trials were a vehicle for social reconstruction. Diplomats, world leaders, ICTY officials and human rights proponents may be advocating that the ICTY achieve an objective – reconciliation – for which there is no broad-based acceptance among our participants. The data suggest that Bosnian legal professionals do not necessarily aspire to a future that is a reconstruction of pre-war social arrangements. Therefore, the contribution of the ICTY to social reconstruction is in question since it may resonate only with the beliefs of a minority of the legal profession.

Many legal commentators have urged the ICTY to use its judgments to promulgate an authoritative historical record of the conflict in the former Yugoslavia that will serve as the basis for social reconstruction.[42] In recent years,

---

42.   Payam Akhaven, *Justice in the Hague, Peace in the Former Yugoslavia? A Commentary on the United Nations War Crimes Tribunal*, 20.4 HUM. RTS. Q. 737, 782-85 (1998); Aryeh Neier, *Rethinking Truth, Justice, and Guilt after Bosnia and Rwanda*, in HUMAN RIGHTS IN POLITICAL TRANSITIONS: GETTYSBURG TO BOSNIA 39, 49 (Carla Hesse & Robert Post eds.,1999) [hereinafter HUMAN RIGHTS IN POLITICAL TRANSITIONS]; Ruti Teitel, *Bringing the Messiah Through the Law*, *id.* at 177-90; Naomi Roht-Arriaza, *The Need for Moral Reconstruction in the Wake of Past Human Rights Violations: An Interview with Jose Zalaqett, id.*, at 195-209. *See also supra* notes 10, 11;

there has been considerable debate over the necessity of a public accounting for past human rights abuses to promote the rule of law and a strong and democratic society.[43] Traditionally, this debate has been framed as choice between extremes: utter impunity v. individual trials. The dilemma is how to respond to past gross abuses in a manner that allows multiple communities with varied needs and goals to learn to live together again. Ultimately, while justice and accountability may be significant contributors to the process of social reconstruction, our findings indicate that war crimes trials should be conceptualized as but one aspect of a larger series of possible interventions.

This study underscores the need to attend to the competing claims of national groups, whether they are victims or aggressors. It is critical to reexamine the assumption that remembrance – in the form of legal record – is the foundation for social reconstruction. For some groups, forgetting may be the only avenue to community building. For others, acknowledgement of past suffering may be the cornerstone of social repair. However, our findings indicate that differing responses to the war create competing needs for avenues for recovery. In the aftermath of mass violence, there may not be a consensus about who were victims and who were perpetrators. Although international trials render verdicts based on an examination of "facts," the responses of our participants indicate that their perception of truth may outweigh the facts as determined by an international body. Consequently, for Bosnian Serb and some Bosnian Croat legal professionals, international trials were construed as privileging the needs of some voices over others.

Across national groups, participants in this study believed that all who were responsible for war crimes must be held accountable. Nevertheless, the findings suggest that the ingredients and priorities for social reconstruction are influenced by whether an individual is a member of a national group that is perceived by the international community as a victim or a perpetrator. In addition, we suggest that those who are members of victimized national groups have a different timeframe for initiation of war crimes trials from those whose political leaders initiated the war but who themselves did not directly commit atrocities. For the former, individual criminal trials are an immediate and overriding goal; for the latter, social reconstruction is a long-term process that may not involve criminal trials. We must honor the needs of victims of gross human rights abuses. However, our findings suggest that if social reconstruction is a worthwhile objective, it is important to achieve it in a framework that engages those who, while not directly acting as perpetrators, supported the aims of those who promulgated crimes of war and genocide. For the international community the question is what are the limits of amnesia.

Martha Minnow, Between Vengeance and Forgiveness: Facing History After Mass Genocide (1998).

43. Diane F. Orentlicher, *Settling Accounts: The Duty to Prosecute Human Rights Violations of a Prior Regime*, 100 Yale L.J. 2537. *See* Carla Hesse & Robert Post, *Introduction*, to Human Rights in Political Transitions, *supra* note 42, at 13-31; Ken Roth, *Human Rights in the Haitian Transition to Democracy*, *id.* at 93-127.

VI.

RECOMMENDATIONS

These findings indicate needed improvements in the areas of judicial and prosecutorial independence, continuing education, and improved communication and collaboration among legal professionals across national groups. In addition, the findings suggest that there are several areas in which changes could be made to enhance the acceptability of international criminal trials to Bosnian legal professionals. To these ends, we make the following recommendations:

1. We support legislation that ensures the independence of the judiciary in both entities in BiH. In particular, we encourage action to establish appropriate salaries – timely paid – and adequate security measures.

2. We support the institutionalization of regular and sustained professional contact between legal professionals in each entity. In particular:

   a. continuing education programs for Bosnian legal professionals should be expanded and should include discussions of war crimes trials, international humanitarian law and international human rights standards;

   b. continuing education programs should be conducted by international professionals who have a sound knowledge of the Bosnian legal system and tradition; and

   c. continuing education programs should be conducted as soon as possible by Bosnian legal professionals and/or professionals with a thorough grounding in the civil law tradition.

3. We support the strengthening of the independent legal associations recently established. These associations should continue to promote review, development and dissemination of ethical and professional standards for lawyers and judges.

4. We strongly encourage the Tribunal to pursue the option of conducting trials on the territory of BiH.[44] We suggest that such trials be held in the region in which the alleged incidents occurred.

5. We suggest that war crimes trials in each entity be conducted by a panel of three judges, one of whom one should be a judge who is not a citizen of BiH or of any of the states of the former Yugoslavia. Appellate review of such trials should also be conducted by a three-judge panel, one of whom should be a judge who is not a citizen of BiH or of any of the states of the former Yugoslavia. Such measures are warranted because the majority of war crimes trials will be held in the domestic courts of BiH and the vulnerabil-

---

44. In establishing the ICTY, the Security Council, pursuant to Resolution 827, stated that "The Tribunal may sit elsewhere [outside of the Netherlands] when it considers it necessary for the efficient exercise of its functions," *supra* note 4.

ity of Bosnian judges and prosecutors to improper political influences will continue for the foreseeable future.

6. We strongly support a rigorous protection program for witnesses, judges and legal professionals involved in war crimes trials held on the territory of BiH. Adequate protection necessarily must be offered during the investigation, trial and appellate proceedings. The offer of meaningful resettlement must be offered in appropriate instances. Such a program may require the financial support and active participation of the international community.

7. We support the concept of an ICTY outreach program. This program should pay particular attention to communication with Bosnian legal professionals in the local language. In particular, the program should:

   a. establish an advisory council of Bosnian legal professionals to determine the information needs of the legal community and to cooperate with the ICTY to address those needs;

   b. focus on the on-going and rapid dissemination of accurate information regarding ICTY activities. This information should be disseminated in the local language through print, computer and videotape;

   c. offer seminars and, preferably, other forms of face-to-face interaction with legal professionals and officials of the ICTY to address areas of misunderstanding, ignorance and concern. These fora may be live or conducted through the medium of telecommunications;

   d. rotate Bosnian legal professionals through the ICTY in The Hague to provide first-hand observation of facilities, procedures and judicial processes. The criteria for selection should be transparent;

   e. emphasize content that addresses such issues as the priorities of indictments for the court, explanation of the hybrid nature of the procedures, limitation of the court's purview and the intended impact of the court's decisions in Bosnia.

8. We recommend that communication between the ICTY and the people of BiH be enhanced. Communications should be in the local language and all branches of the media should be utilized. Civil society should be encouraged to include representatives of the ICTY at community-sponsored events including professional conferences and nongovernmental organizations' meetings and events. Although press conferences are useful, officials from The Hague visibly should be present at such activities.

9. We suggest that opinion leaders and service providers such as educators, health professionals, journalists, leaders of Bosnian nongovernmental organizations, representatives of civil society, social

service providers and writers also should be rotated through the ICTY or brought together from both entities to meet in The Hague to address areas of misunderstanding, ignorance and concern. The criteria for selection should be transparent.

10. We urge the ICTY to convene and visibly be present at periodic community meetings in BiH. These meetings should be held in various locations throughout the country and include towns and villages outside of the larger cities.

11. We strongly encourage OHR to undertake the organization of an inter-entity council to examine a range of alternative mechanisms to promote social reconstruction. Since Bosnian legal professionals do not uniformly connect war crimes trials to social reconstruction, such a council should analyze and make recommendations to promote democratization, open communication and a free press, cross-entity small business development, and religious and cultural tolerance. Members of this council should reflect a balance with respect to gender and national origin and include representatives from academia, primary and secondary education, the media, nongovernmental organizations, professional associations, and the religious communities.

12. We suggest that the findings of this study may offer insights that enhance the effectiveness of the International Criminal Court. In the institutional structures and arrangements – yet to be created – procedures, positions and resources should be established and devoted to maximize the impact and understanding of the trials within the directly affected communities. In particular, procedures and programs should address the following issues:

    a. the trials should be located on or as near as possible to the territory in which the alleged incidents occurred;

    b. the goals, objectives, judicial selection, priorities for indictment and other mechanisms of the ICC should be transparent and communicated effectively in the local language of the country in which the alleged incidents occurred;

    c. the rules of evidence and procedure governing the ICC should take into account the major legal traditions. To the extent that there is flexibility in the rules, their application should be responsive to the legal culture of the country in which the alleged incidents occurred;

    d. the procedures governing the investigation, trial and appellate phases should be communicated effectively in the local language to members of the legal profession in the country in which the alleged incidents occurred;

e. innovative ways of including representatives of the affected country's judiciary in the adjudicative process should be explored; and

f. additional interventions that are different from, but complementary to trials, such as facilitating culturally accepted mechanisms of justice, should be considered.

APPENDIX A

Justice, Accountability, and Reconstruction in the Former
Yugoslavia:
An Interview Study of Bosnian Judges and
Other Key Informants[45]

Question coding:

Questions in plain text: demographic information.

Questions in italics: How does the work of an international war crimes tribunal
contribute to local efforts at social reconstruction?

Questions in bold type: How do war and changes in identity influence the
administration of justice?

QUESTIONS IN SMALL CAPS: WHAT IS THE ROLE OF JUSTICE AND THE LEGAL SYS-
TEM IN SOCIAL RECONSTRUCTION?

Interview Code # _____
Disclosure Read _____ Y _____ N
Subject Agreed _____ Y _____ N

I.

DEMOGRAPHICS

A. Experience

How did you become a judge?

Where were you educated?

Have you ever been educated outside Yugoslavia?

How long have you been a judge?

Why did you become a judge? (motivation)

What do your professional contacts with judges in the other entity consist of?

B. Personal background

When were you born?

Where have you lived and during what time periods?

II.

ROLE OF THE JUDGE

What do you see as the judge's most important role?

-Inside the courtroom?

-Outside the courtroom?

How has the 1992-1995 war affected your motivations for being a judge?

How has it affected your career path?

Are the national identities of the parties in your courtroom proportionately different than they were before the war?

---

45. This questionnaire was translated into the three local languages of BiH.

Is the national identity of parties included in courtroom records?

Has that changed since the war?

Do you believe that judicial decisions can play a role in changing people's attitudes? Can you give us any examples where this has happened?

In your opinion, how has law and its application changed since the war?

What is the role of the judge with respect to the return of refugees? (Should judges apply a strictly legal analysis to the return of refugees to their homes, or should they allow for the fact that there is a housing shortage and the return of refugees could produce a domino effect?)

III.
IDENTITY OF AND IMPACT OF THE WAR UPON THE JUDGE

A. National background

With which national groups do you identify and why?

With which groups do (did) your parents identify?

Before the war, did you identify with a different national group?

B. Impact of the war

What has been the most significant change in your life since the war broke out?

Has your health been affected by the war?

Did any of your family or friends die or disappear or become injured during the war?

Were you ever in any army? If so, when?

Did you serve as a military judge in the 1992-1995 war?

Have you ever been a member of a political party?

Are you politically active now?

IV.
DOMESTIC EFFECTS OF THE ICTY

A. Legal definitions

HOW DO YOU DEFINE RULE OF LAW?

WHO IN BOSNIA-HERZEGOVINA TODAY BELIEVES THAT THE RULE OF LAW IS THE BEST WAY TO RESOLVE DISPUTES? JUDGES? ATTORNEYS? THE PUBLIC? POLITICAL LEADERS?

HAS THIS CHANGED SINCE THE WAR?

DO YOU VIEW THE JUDICIAL SYSTEM IN BOSNIA-HERZEGOVINA AS AN EFFECTIVE WAY TO RESOLVE CONFLICTS?

IF YES, IS THIS TRUE FOR DISPUTES BETWEEN PERSONS OF DIFFERENT NATIONAL GROUPS?

IF NO, WHY NOT, AND IS IT DIFFERENT FOR DISPUTES BETWEEN PERSONS OF DIFFERENT NATIONAL GROUPS?

DO YOU THINK THAT YOUR COLLEAGUES (IN YOUR CANTON/REGION) CAN PROVIDE A FAIR TRIAL UNDER THE CURRENT, DIFFICULT CONDITIONS?

How would you explain legal accountability?
How does accountability influence your decisions in court?
Should individuals be held more or less accountable for their actions during periods of warfare?
- If so, how? If not, why not?
What do you think the relationship is between ensuring the widespread accountability of war criminals and social progress and economic development in Bosnia-Herzegovina?

B.   Dayton Accords and formal structures

WHAT ROLE DO THE ENTITY CONSTITUTIONS OF THE RS AND THE FEDERATION PLAY IN RECONCILIATION AND SOCIAL RECONSTRUCTION?
DOES INTERNATIONAL LAW IMPACT YOUR COURTROOM? IF SO, HOW?
WHAT DO YOU CONSIDER THE HIGHEST LAW OF THE LAND?
SHOULD A SUPREME COURT OF BOSNIA-HERZEGOVINA BE CREATED?

C.   Concepts of accountability

In your legal opinion, did genocide happen anywhere in Bosnia-Herzegovina?
Against whom did these acts of genocide occur?
Do you hold anyone accountable for the war?
Do you think that bringing war criminals to trial can deter future war crimes?

D.   Knowledge of the ICTY

What do you think about the ICTY?
What would you like to see the ICTY accomplish?
What changes would you make to the current processes or structure of the ICTY?
Who should the ICTY focus upon? The persons of the highest rank, like Milošević, or anybody who participated in war crimes?
What do you think others (your neighbors, friends, colleagues) would like to see them do?
Where should war crimes trials be held?
What do you think of the practice of sealed indictments?

How does the ICTY affect life in Bosnia-Herzegovina?
Do you think that citizens of Bosnia-Herzegovina are interested in the activities of the ICTY? Should they be?
Does the ICTY affect the process of "making up"?
Does it affect the process of reconstruction and redevelopment?
Do you think the ICTY affects people's perceptions of accountability regarding the war in Bosnia-Herzegovina?
What cases have you been following at the ICTY?
How do you get your news regarding the ICTY?
How has the ICTY affected proceedings in your courtroom?
Have you sent a case to the ICTY?

2000] *JUSTICE, ACCOUNTABILITY AND SOCIAL RECONSTRUCTION* 159

Been asked for evidence from the ICTY?

How do the Rules of the Road impact your courtroom?

Do other actions of the ICTY, such as decisions, indictments, and appeals, play a role in your own decision-making process?

V.
DOMESTIC WAR CRIMES TRIALS

WHAT IS A WAR CRIMES TRIAL WHEN CONDUCTED WITHIN BOSNIA-HERZEGOVINA? HOW DO YOU IDENTIFY SUCH A TRIAL?

DO DOMESTIC WAR CRIMES TRIALS HAVE AN EFFECT ON SOCIAL RECONSTRUCTION?

CAN YOU GIVE US EXAMPLES OF ANY OF THESE?

[Provide closure for people and their communities; stimulate recovery and reconciliation, reconstruction; deter future war crimes]

HAVE YOU HAD A WAR CRIME TRIAL IN YOUR COURTROOM?

IN YOUR COMMUNITY?

>   PLEASE TELL US ABOUT THAT TRIAL. (WHAT WAS THE RESULT OF THE TRIAL? WHAT WERE THE EFFECTS ON YOUR COURTROOM? WITHIN YOUR COMMUNITY?)

HOW WAS THAT TRIAL DIFFERENT FROM OTHER TRIALS IN YOUR COURTROOM?

[IF THE DECISION WAS NOT MADE BY THIS JUDGE. . .] WAS IT A TYPICAL RESULT? IN YOUR OPINION, WAS THIS RESULT THE BEST ONE POSSIBLE?

IF NOT, WHAT ARE THE SPECIFIC CONDITIONS THAT WOULD HAVE MADE IT A FAIR TRIAL?

WHAT DID/DO YOU/WOULD YOU DO TO ENSURE A WAR CRIMES TRIAL WOULD BE FAIR?

IS LIFE TOGETHER IN BOSNIA-HERZEGOVINA POSSIBLE?

IN CLOSING:

Do you have any questions that you would like to ask us?

Are there any questions that we should have asked you that we have not?

Thank you / Hvala!

APPENDIX B

TABLE 1

DEMOGRAPHICS OF SAMPLE—JUDGES

PERSONAL AND PROFESSIONAL BACKGROUND OF JUDGES

	Number	Percentage
Number of Judges	26	100%
Median Age	48.5	—
Median Years as Judge	13.5	—
Female	4	15%
Male	22	85%
Bosnian Serb	8	31%
Bosnian Croat	10	38%
Bosniak	8	31%

WARTIME EXPERIENCE		
Lost Housing	11	42%
Relative Injured or Killed	19* (one judge was not asked)	73%

TABLE 2

DEMOGRAPHICS OF SAMPLE—PROSECUTORS

PERSONAL AND PROFESSIONAL BACKGROUND OF PROSECUTORS

	Number	Percentage
Number of Prosecutors	6	100%
Median Age	49.5	—
Median Years as Prosecutor	17	—
Female	2	33%
Male	4	67%
Bosnian Serb	1	17%
Bosnian Croat	2	33%
Bosniak	3	50%

WARTIME EXPERIENCE		
Lost Housing	2	33%
Relative Injured or Killed	2	33%

APPENDIX C

What is the Supreme Law of the Land?[46]

BOSNIAK	CROAT	SERB
BiH Constitution	Federation of BiH Constitution	RS Constitution
The Constitution	The Constitution	RS Constitution
BiH Constitution	Federation of BiH Constitution	RS Constitution
BiH Constitution	Federation of BiH Constitution	RS Constitution
BiH Constitution	BiH Constitution	RS and BiH
BiH Constitution	BiH Constitution	BiH Constitution
BiH Constitution	BiH Constitution	RS Constitution
BiH Constitution	BiH Constitution	RS or BiH Constitution
BiH Constitution	The Constitution	RS Constitution
BiH Constitution	Federation of BiH Constitution	
BiH Constitution	BiH Constitution	

---

46.   Thirty-one out of 32 participants responded to this question.

APPENDIX D

Should the Supreme Court of Bosnia-Herzegovina be created?[47]

BOSNIAK	CROAT	SERB
YES	"Political question"	NO
YES	YES	NO
YES	"under certain conditions"	NO
YES	YES	NO
YES	YES	NO
YES	YES	YES
YES	YES	NO
YES	YES	YES
YES	NO	NO
YES	NO	
	YES	

---

47. Thirty out of 32 participants responded to this question.

APPENDIX E

1. In your legal opinion, did genocide happen anywhere in Bosnia-Herzegovina?[48]
2. To whom/Against whom?

BOSNIAK	CROAT	SERB
YES "In this country there was too much genocide." "Aggression on BiH as recognized by Security Council resolution."	YES "Against all three nations."	YES "To all three peoples."
YES "Against Muslim and Croat peoples, the non-Serb peoples."	DO NOT KNOW ". . .I am talking about legal assessments of certain acts, and I can't give only approximate judgments."	PROBABLY "I think it was done by all to everybody"
YES ". . .personally I don't' have any information so I can't tell you where that happened and what happened."	YES ". . .against all three people, against all three nations."	YES "What I have heard is that there was genocide everywhere."
YES "It was not 'ethnic cleansing.' It did happen on all sides, but you cannot compare the examples. There is Srebrenica."	YES "Against everybody. It all depends on who happens to be in what kind of situation at the time. . . It's only the question of possibility."	NO
YES "I think that genocide occurred against Bosniak people."	YES ". . .Serb aggression was surely genocide against the Bosniak and Croat people." "I am positive that it was first created against Bosniak and Croat people, I really don't know if genocide occurred on Serb[s]."	NO "In the area of my supervision I think not."

---

48. Thirty-one out of 32 participants responded to this question.

BOSNIAK	CROAT	SERB
YES "It is a well known fact." "We all know, and starting with Srebrenica we all know against whom." "Well, there was some genocide against Croats."	YES "Genocide took place on all sides."	YES "Against all ethnic groups."
YES "Here, the most against Muslim people." "Mostly, mostly against Muslims."	"That's a political question."	I DO NOT KNOW
YES ". . .a horrible one." "School example of genocide in Srebrenica." "Against Bosniaks." "Against others, only murders, but not genocide."	YES "Against all three peoples. All of them committed genocide, some more, some less, but all three sides committed genocide."	"I do not want to speak about it."
YES "If you start from the definition of genocide used by the. . .Tribunal, I think that in relation to Bosniaks, the genocide did happen, especially in certain parts."	YES ". . .everywhere, all three sides." ". . .certain sides had more power. . ." "And as usual, people who are least ready suffer the most."	NO "I don't have any evidence and information whether it happened somewhere. In our area, I have no information."
YES "I don't even want to talk about Bosnia-Herzegovina. In this town, in ten days over 3,000 people were killed. If that's not genocide, I don't know what is." "Here, against Bosniaks."	MAYBE "I don't think there was a real genocide anywhere in BiH, the full one. In some ways, there was a genocide, in others not actually, you didn't have one people actually completely wiped out."	
YES "[A]gainst Bosniaks in Visegrad . . . Mass slaughters, mass killings. Expulsions, rapes. And all done along strictly ethnic lines, without any reason, any logical reason . . . [A]gainst everybody else was much, much smaller in scale."	YES ". . .on Bosniak people that happened." "You just have as example Srebrenica. And other places similar to Srebrenica."	

[8]

INTERNATIONAL CRIMINAL COURT

Complementarity in Practice: The International Criminal Court as Part of a System of Multi-level Global Governance in the Democratic Republic of Congo

WILLIAM W. BURKE-WHITE[*]

Abstract

This article asserts the emergence of multi-level global governance through an analysis of the relationship between the International Criminal Court and the Democratic Republic of Congo. The article suggests a far deeper set of influences than previously anticipated, presenting research on how the ICC is directly influencing Congolese domestic politics and how some actors within the Congo are seeking to manipulate the Court for their own political benefit. Further, the article considers the self-referral by the Congolese government, the early impact of complementarity, and efforts at judicial reform in the Congo. In the process the article develops a set of criteria to evaluate the 'total or substantial collapse' provisions of the complementarity regime.

Key words

International Criminal Court; complementarity; Democratic Republic of Congo; global governance; Joseph Kabila

The entry into force of the Rome Statute of the International Criminal Court in July 2002 marked a major milestone in the process of ensuring accountability for international crimes. The complementarity provisions of the Rome Statute highlight the Court's role as a backstop to national jurisdictions.[1] The logic of complementarity expressed at Rome was that the Court, where seized of jurisdiction, would merely step in where national courts fail to act.[2] The ICC, it was thought, would provide a simple

---

[*] Assistant Professor of Law, University of Pennsylvania School of Law. The author wishes to thank the members of the research team who made this project possible: Yuriko Kuga, Mariyan Zumbulev, Dawn Hewett, Jordan Tama, Leslie Medema, Barbara Feinstein, Adrian Alvarez, Christopher Broughton and Francis Hartwell. In addition the author thanks Luis Moreno-Ocampo and all those in the Democratic Republic of Congo who assisted with this research.

1. See Rome Statute of the International Criminal Court, at Art. 17. See also J. Holmes, 'The Principle of Complementarity', in R. Lee (ed.), *The International Criminal Court, The Making of the Rome Statute: Issues, Negotiations, Results* (1999), 41; J. Holmes, 'Complementarity: National Courts versus the ICC', in A. Cassese (ed.), *The Rome Statute of the International Criminal Court: A Commentary* (2002), 667 (noting that 'Ironically, however, the provisions of the Rome Statute itself contemplate an institution that may never be employed').
2. See Holmes, 'Complementarity: National Courts versus the ICC', *supra* note 1, at 667 (noting: 'Of course, in reality there is a need for the ICC, since States may be unwilling to exercise jurisdiction over international crimes').

substitution of an international forum for a domestic one. The first investigation by the ICC in the Democratic Republic of Congo suggests, instead, a much deeper and more complex interplay between national and international law and politics, best captured by the concept of multi-level global governance.

The idea of multi-level global governance draws on the works of scholars such as James Rosenau, who sought to identify and apply international structures that reach beyond states and to proscribe transnational solutions for global problems.[3] In so doing, they identified new kinds of interaction between national and international institutions and structures. Rosenau recognized a shift away from hierarchical organization generated by the distribution of power in the international system toward 'spheres of authority' in which states and non-state actors alike collectively utilize their authority to achieve shared goals.[4] The concept of multi-level global governance goes a step further, suggesting that international and domestic governance structures (such as courts) are engaged in deeply interconnected governance efforts whereby each level of authority continuously cross-influences, reshapes, and, ideally, reinforces activities at other levels of governance.

As the first investigations by the ICC have begun to unfold, what has emerged begins to look far more like the complex sharing of authority and multi-dimensional influences between national and international structures suggested by the global governance literature than the simple substitution of an international court initially anticipated by the Rome Statute. Understanding this interaction requires shifting our mental maps of complementarity from the substation model to one which sees the ICC and national governments as two distinct layers of governance authority engaged in political and legal interactions whereby each level is continuously responding to and impacting actions at the other level. These interactions include everything from the political posturing of national officials and the reform of domestic courts to the application of the complementary criteria by international officials.[5]

The first investigation launched by the ICC, the situation in the Democratic Republic of Congo, offers a powerful example of the multi-level global governance model of interaction between the Court and national governments created by the complementarity regime.[6] This article argues that the relationship between the ICC and the Democratic Republic of Congo is far deeper and more complex than the simple substitution model of complementarity and that the theoretical framework

---

3.   This new scholarship can largely be traced to the writings of James Rosenau's seminal work in 1992. See J. Rosenau, 'Governance, Order, and Change in World Politics', in *Governance Without Government: Order and Change in World Politics* (1992) 1, at 4. Elements of global governance thinking can be found in the earlier writings of the English School in political science. See generally, H. Bull, *The Anarchical Society* (1977). The growing scholarship in the field of global governance led to the foundation of a new journal in the mid-1990s entitled *Global Governance*, which has been the focal point of writings on the topic.

4.   J. Rosenau, *Along the Domestic–Foreign Frontier: Exploring Governance in a Turbulent World* (1997), at 45.

5.   In the global governance literature, such interactions are said to occur along a governance frontier. Rosenau suggests that the frontier is 'space in which world affairs unfold . . . the arena in which domestic and foreign issues intermesh'. Rosenau, *supra* note 4, at 5.

6.   On 8 September 2003 Prosecutor Louis Moreno-Ocampo announced that the situation in the Ituri region of the Democratic Republic of Congo would be the first 'which merits to be closely followed by the Office' of the Prosecutor. Luis Moreno-Ocampo, Second Assembly of States Parties to the Rome Statute of the International Criminal Court Report of the Prosecutor of the ICC, Mr Luis Moreno-Ocampo, 8 September 2003, available at http://www.icc-cpi.int/otp/030909_prosecutor_speech.pdf.

of multi-level global governance best captures four distinct but interrelated influences between the international Court and the target state of investigation. First, the existence of the ICC has offered a politically expedient solution for the Congolese president to deal with potential electoral rivals, resulting in the somewhat surprising referral of the situation to the Court by the Congolese government itself. Second, the complementarity regime has divided elements within the Congolese government, such that those factions opposed to international prosecutions have sought to strengthen the hand of the domestic judiciary in order to exercise primacy over the ICC. Third, the requirements of complementarity are providing important, but incomplete, guidelines for the reform of the Congolese domestic judiciary. Finally, the threat of international prosecution may already be providing a deterrent effect on rebel leaders within the Congo.

Moving from a simple substation model of complementarity to a multi-level global governance model has profound implications for understanding international judicial institutions such as the ICC. In the multi-level global governance model, the ICC itself becomes a participant in the domestic process, altering political as well as legal outcomes. Similarly, the international Court itself may become an instrument of actors at the domestic level. National and international officials alike must recognize and adapt to this more expansive role of the ICC. If the Court's broader role is used wisely, it may well promote domestic reform, good governance, and accountability. If ignored, however, the Court's position in a system of multi-level global governance may well invite dangerous political manipulation.

This article begins by briefly discussing the methodology of the in-depth case study research utilized herein. Part 2 sketches a short but critical history of the Congo conflict. Part 3 addresses the ways in which the ICC has reshaped the incentives of actors within the Congolese domestic government and seeks to explain the surprising decision by President Kabila to refer the Congolese situation to the ICC. Part 4 examines how the complementarity regime has divided the Congolese domestic government and is catalyzing judicial reform efforts in Congo. Part 5 considers the Rome Statute's partial, but insufficient, guidelines for the reform of domestic judiciaries, proposes a more detailed set of criteria for the ability of a state to prosecute, and argues that presently the Congo must be deemed 'unwilling or unable' to prosecute international crimes. Finally, Part 6 analyzes the ways in which international justice efforts may already be having a deterrent effect on rebel leaders in Congo.

1. RESEARCH AND METHODOLOGY

This article is based on an in-depth evaluation of the situation in the Democratic Republic of Congo and draws heavily on interview research in the Congo and elsewhere in the fall of 2003 and throughout 2004. The general methodology employed is that of qualitative case-study research.[7] Such a research methodology is particularly

---

7. For a general discussion of such research, see D. Silverman (ed.), *Qualitative Research, Theory, Method and Practice* (2004).

useful when there is little, if any, quantitative data available and the focus is on 'the process by which events and actions take place' and the causal relationships among observed phenomena.[8] The overall goal of this study is to examine the nature of interaction between the ICC as an institution of supranational governance and the domestic governmental structures in the Congo. Qualitative research provides unique insight into the processes and causal relationships at work in these interactions.

The primary data analyzed herein derive from numerous interviews conducted over the past two years. In October and November 2003 a ten-person research team conducted field interviews in the Democratic Republic of Congo (Kinshasa, Kisangani, Bukavu and Goma), Rwanda (Kigali), Uganda (Kampala), France (Paris), Belgium (Brussels) and the Netherlands (The Hague and Amsterdam). Over 100 interviews were conducted with government officials, judicial personnel, local and international NGOs, and rebel leaders.[9] These interviews are supported by documentary analysis, such as the consideration of court documents, governmental communiqués, and NGO reports, where available.[10]

Interviewees were selected for this study based on three main characteristics: their position in governmental or non-governmental organizations with direct bearing on the issues in hand, their particular expertise or knowledge on these issues, and/or their first-hand observation of the phenomena under consideration. Such selection is generally referred to as 'purposeful sampling' in the qualitative research literature.[11] In purposeful sampling, interviewees 'are selected deliberately in order to provide important information that can't be gotten as well from other choices'.[12]

Interviewees were contacted in advance (usually via telephone) and asked to participate in a conversation with an academic research team from Princeton University in the United States. They were not provided with questions in advance and their responses were spontaneous. Similarly they were given no incentives, financial or otherwise, for their participation. They were told that the interview team had no particular political motivations and, where requested, anonymity was granted. Most interviews were tape recorded, though hand notation was offered as an alternative when subjects were uncomfortable with an audio recording being made.

In any such qualitative research project a number of biases are possible. First, there may be a selection bias inherent in the choice of interviewees. Despite efforts to select interview participants for purposive reasons, issues of availability, access and fear of reprisals for participation may result in a skewing of interview subjects. Second, a key information bias may be present, whereby major parts of the data may

---

8.   J. Maxwell (ed.), *Qualitative Research Design: An Interactive Approach* (1996), 19–20.
9.   For a discussion of the basic techniques used in qualitative interview analysis, see J. Miller and B. Glassner, 'The "inside" and the "outside": Finding realities in interviews', in Silverman, *supra* note 7, at 125–35; J. Morse, 'Emerging from the Data: The Cognitive Process of Analysis in Qualitative Inquiry', in J. Morse (ed.), *Critical Issues in Qualitative Research Methods* (1994) 44, at 56.
10. For a consideration of documentary analysis in qualitative research see 'Analyzing Documentary Realities', in Silverman, *supra* note 7, 56 at 56–76.
11. M. Patton, *Qualitative Evaluation and Research Methods* (1990), 169.
12. See Maxwell, *supra* note 8, at 70–2.

come from a small number of individuals.[13] Third, an inherent political bias may exist, in that respondents may have had a particular political motive in structuring their answers. Throughout the research, a range of techniques has been employed to limit the danger of such biases in research methodology. These include triangulation, rich data, comparison, and documentary corroboration.[14]

The result of this research project is an original analysis of the relationship between the ICC and the DR Congo. The data analyzed herein provides clear evidence of the operation of multi-level global governance in international law enforcement. This study is not intended to be, nor do the research methods employed herein allow it to provide, concrete proof of the relationships suggested between national and international actors. Some areas of consideration remain speculative. Yet, as a preliminary investigation, it is intended to offer a compelling picture of a far more complex relationship between the ICC and national governments than was heretofore understood.

2. HISTORY AND CONTEXT OF THE CONGO WAR AND PEACE PROCESS

Understanding the operation of multi-level global governance in the enforcement of international criminal law in the DR Congo requires reference to the historical context and present circumstances of government in the country. The International Rescue Committee, which has conducted the most thorough studies of mortality rates in Congo, found that 3.3 million people have died during the past decade in Congo from war-related famine and disease, international crimes, and war.[15] The Congo war and the horrible death toll associated therewith can largely be divided into four separate, but interrelated, conflicts. First, beginning in 1996, Laurent Kabila, with the backing of Rwanda and Uganda staged a revolt and led a military drive toward Kinshasa against the forces of then ailing President Mobuto, leaving a trail of largely civilian blood.[16] On 17 May 1997 Kabila took Kinshasa and established a new government.[17]

After Kabila distanced himself from his Tutsi supporters in Rwanda and Uganda in 1998 and 1999, military forces in both those countries entered and occupied large portions of Eastern Congo.[18] While the ostensible justification for this intervention was to prevent military action by Hutu Interahamwe groups then residing in Eastern Congo, both Rwanda and Uganda also sought to lay claim to vast natural resources

---

13. For a discussion, see ibid., at 73.
14. For a consideration of how these techniques can be employed to enhance the validity of qualitative research results, see ibid., at 90–5.
15. International Rescue Committee, 'Mortality in the Democratic Republic of Congo: Results from a Nationwide Survey', Conducted September–November 2002, Reported in April 2003, at i, (noting that 'Based on past and current IRC data, it is estimated that 3.3 million people have died as a result of this war').
16. R. Edgerton, *The Troubled Heart of Africa: A History of the Congo* (2002), at 218–21. Reports suggest that during this drive for power, Kabila's army murdered thousands – if not tens of thousands – of Hutu militiamen and their supporters. Edgerton, *supra*, at 229.
17. Edgerton, *supra* note 16, at 221, 223–7.
18. Ibid., at 229.

in the region including gold, diamonds and coaltan.[19] Throughout 2000 and 2001 various foreign militaries engaged in fierce combat in the region surrounding the central Congolese city of Kisangani, again killing countless civilians and pillaging villages for resources, food, and sexual services.[20]

In the third aspect of the conflict, rebel groups in the eastern half of Congo, namely the Congolese Rally for Democracy (RCD) and the Movement for the Liberation of Congo (MLC), revolted against the Kabila regime and established what was effectively a separate state in Eastern Congo from 2000 to 2002.[21] All commerce, trade, and transport between the eastern and western portions of the country were stopped. During this period of a divided state, the RCD and MLC inflicted a systematic campaign of terror against local civilians, demanding food and resources as well as kidnapping local women.[22]

Finally, in the decade from 1994 to 2004, a range of ethnic groups in Eastern Congo also committed serious inter-ethnic crimes including murder and rape. At various times these crimes have been perpetrated by and directed against the Hema, the Lendu, the Mai-Mai and the Pygmies. For example, after the occupation of Eastern Congo by Rwanda and Uganda, Hutu loyalists 'unleash[ed] a bloody pogrom' against Tutsi civilians in the region.[23] Most recently, these crimes have been rampant in the Ituri region of Eastern Congo, with reports of widespread killing and cannibalism.[24]

In December 2002, the various parties involved in the Congo conflict reached an 'all inclusive peace agreement' during a meeting at Sun City, South Africa.[25] This agreement, which serves as the basis of the current transitional government, creates a power-sharing arrangement among the former government, the RCD, the MLC, and the unarmed opposition.[26] Substantial progress toward a lasting peace has been made since the transitional government took power in July 2003. While the country

---

19. See ibid., at 230. For a discussion of Rwanda's motivations for action in Congo, see T. Longman, 'The Complex Reasons for Rwanda's Engagement in Congo', in J. Clark (ed.), *The African Roots of the Congo War* (2002), 128, at 136 (noting 'opportunity for both personal and national enrichment'). Rwanda's previously non-existent exports of coaltan rose to US$20 million per month after the occupation. Similarly, diamond exports rose from 166 carats per year in 1998 to 30,500 carats in 2000. Longman, *supra*, at 136. Coaltan is a valuable and scarce mineral used in the production of cell phones and other electronic devices. For a discussion of Uganda's motivations, see J. Clark, 'Museveni's Adventure in the Congo War', in *supra*, at 145–165.

20. Human Rights Watch, Democratic Republic of Congo: War Crimes in Kisangani: The Response of Rwandan-backed Rebels to the May 2002 Mutiny 5. See Edgerton, *supra* note 16, at 230–2.

21. Human Rights Watch, *supra* note 20, at 5.

22. Edgerton, *supra* note 16, at 230.

23. Ibid., at 229.

24. For a discussion of these crimes in Ituri, see 'Ituri: Covered in Blood: Ethnically Targeted Violence in Northeastern DR Congo', *Human Rights Watch Report* (July 2003) (noting that 'Human Rights Watch estimates that at least 5,000 civilians died from direct violence in Ituri between July 2002 and March 2003. These victims are in addition to the 50,000 civilians that the United Nations estimates died there since 1999). See also, D. Bergner, 'The Most Unconventional Weapon', *The New York Times Magazine*, 26 October 2003.

25. This framework is memorialized in the Global Inclusive Agreement which concluded the Inter-Congolese Dialogue. See 'Accord Global et Inclusif sur la Transition en République Démocratique du Congo', 17 décembre 2002, adopted at Sun City, South Africa, 1 April 2003, reprinted in *Journal Officiel de la République Démocratique du Congo*, 44 année, 5 April 2003.

26. See Accord Global et Inclusif sur la Transition En République Démocratique Du Congo, *supra* note 25, at Art. 1 (providing: 'Les Parties au présent Accord et ayant des forces combattantes, a savoir le Gouvernement de la RDC, le RCD, le MLC, le RCD-ML, le RCD-N, et les Mai Mai renouvellent leur engagement, conformément a l'accord de Lusaka … de cesser les hostilités et de rechercher une solution pacifique et équitable à la crise que traverse le pays').

is still highly unstable, the transitional government has effectively reunified eastern and western Congo and relative peace has been restored in much of the country. Based on the framework agreed to at Sun City, the government's current focus is on preparations for forthcoming elections.

Despite the Sun City Agreement in December 2002 and the installation of the transition government in July 2003, international crimes have continued in the regions of Ituri and South Kivu – located in North-West Congo.[27] These include a systematic campaign of cannibalism against local Pygmies as well as more conventional attacks on civilian populations throughout the region.[28] In June 2003, the International Crisis Group observed that Ituri 'has been the theatre of spiraling violence bordering on genocide'.[29] With some support from Rwanda and Uganda, two ethic groups turned militias – the Hema and the Lendu – have committed numerous international crimes since the Rome Statute came into force.[30] For example, in August 2003 hundreds of civilians were massacred near the town of Songolo[31] and in October 2003 the bodies of 16 women and children were found in a fresh mass grave in the village of Ndunda.[32] Even as recently as June 2004, rebel leader General Laurent Nkunda seized the city of Bukavu in South Kivu, leading to looting, plunder and rampant attacks on civilian populations.[33] These continuing crimes in eastern Congo are the likely target of any ICC prosecutions as they fall within the temporal and territorial jurisdiction of the ICC.[34] As of mid-2005, the situation remains unstable, violence continues and it is unclear whether elections will occur in the next year as planned.

3. THE CONGOLESE REFERRAL: THE ICC AND THE ALTERATION OF NATIONAL PREFERENCES IN THE DR CONGO

A first incidence of the operation of multi-level global governance in the working of the ICC is the decision of Congolese President Joseph Kabila to refer the situation in the Congo to the ICC.[35] This move was greeted with some surprise internationally given that, during the negotiation of the Rome Statute, most commentators assumed

27. See generally, Bergner, *supra* note 24.
28. See generally, ibid.; 'Ituri: Covered in Blood', *supra* note 24.
29. International Crisis Group, 'Congo Crisis: Military Intervention in Ituri', 13 June 2003, ICG Africa Report No. 64, at i.
30. Ibid., at 1.
31. See 'Ituri: Covered in Blood', *supra* note 24.
32. 'World Briefing Africa: Congo: U.N. Finds New Massacre', *The New York Times*, 11 October 2003.
33. 'DR Congo Slams Rwandan Invasion', *BBC News*, 3 June 2004, available at http://news.bbc.co.uk/1/hi/world/africa/3771729.stm.
34. The Rome Statute limits the jurisdiction of the ICC to crimes committed after the entry into force of the Statute in July 2002.
35. On 19 April 2004, the ICC Prosecutor received a formal referral of the situation in the Congo from Joseph Kabila, President of the Democratic Republic of Congo. Press Release: 'Prosecutor receives referral of the situation in the Democratic Republic of Congo', 19 April 2004, available at http://www.icc-cpi.int/newspoint/pressreleases/19.html. A similar referral by the national state has been made by Uganda with respect to crimes committed in Uganda. See Press Release: President of Uganda refers situation concerning the Lord's Resistance Army (LRA) to the ICC, 29 January 2004, availabe at http://www.icc-cpi.int/newspoint/pressreleases/16.html. Likewise, the Central African Republic has referred the situation on its territory to the Court. See 'Prosecutor Receives Referral Concerning Central African Republic',International Criminal Court Press Release, 7 January 2005, available at http://www.icc-cpi.int/press/pressreleases/87.html.

situations would be referred by third states[36] or would be initiated under the *proprio motu* powers of the Prosecutor.[37] Yet Congolese President Kabila himself chose to refer the situation in his own country to the Court, even though such a referral could not be limited only to rebel groups and the ICC investigation might eventually turn against the very government that referred the situation in the first place. This section offers an explanation of the Congolese referral through the lens of multi-level global governance. In short, it argues that the existence of the Court sufficiently shifted the incentive structure for the national government such that President Kabila perceived it to be in his own interests to refer the case.

Viewing the ICC as engaged in a dynamic legal and political interplay with the Congolese government offers the necessary perspective to explain President Kabila's referral. This move requires disaggregating the state – peering into the 'black box' of the nation state and examining the interests of various actors within the state and the interaction between these sub-state elements and the ICC itself.[38] The new transitional government that took power in Kinshasa in July 2003 is based on a power-sharing agreement among the four parties to the Inter-Congolese Dialogue – the government, the unarmed opposition, the RDC and the MLC.[39] The transitional government is led by President Joseph Kabila, son of Laurent Kabila, who rode the 1996 rebellion into power. Under Kabila are four vice presidents, one from each of the primary factions to the Congolese civil war.[40] Each of the vice presidents has a range of ministries under his authority. Those ministries are led, in turn, by ministers appointed by a different party to the peace agreement. This produces a situation in which former enemies directly report to one another, often resulting in political maneuvering and dangerous infighting. Under the transitional constitution, this power-sharing government is scheduled to remain in place until new elections, originally slated for summer 2005, but now postponed till 2006.[41]

Within this framework, during the short time period before national elections, the primary political actors have a strong incentive to position themselves for

---

36. Article 14 of the Rome Statute grants any state party the power to refer a case within the jurisdiction of the Court to the Prosecutor. It was initially assumed that most such referrals would involve a state party on whose territory the crime did not occur referring the situation in another state to the Court. See P. Kirsch, 'Referral by States Parties', in Cassesse, *supra* note 1, at 619.

37. Article 15 of the Rome Statute gives the Prosecutor the authority to 'initiate investigations *proprio motu* on the basis of information on crimes within the jurisdiction of the Court' if the Pre-Trial Chamber 'considers that there is a reasonable basis to proceed with an investigation'. Rome Statute, Article 15. See also P. Kirsch and D. Robinson, 'Initiation of Proceedings by the Prosecutor', in Cassesse, *supra* note 1, at 657.

38. Such an approach is largely based on liberal international relations theory. For a discussion of this approach, see A. Moravcsik, 'Taking Preferences Seriously: A Liberal Theory of International Politics', (1997) 51 *Int'l Org.* 513.

39. This framework is memorialized in the Global Inclusive Agreement which concluded the Inter-Congolese Dialogue. See Accord Global Et Inclusif sur la Transition en République Démocratique du Congo, *supra* note 25.

40. Constitution De La Transition, *infra* note 84, at Art. 83 (according to which 'Les Vice-Présidents sont issues respectivement des Composantes Gouvernement de la République Démocratique du Congo, le Rassemblement Congolais pour la Démocratie (le RCD), le Mouvement de Libération du Congo (MLC) et l'opposition politique').

41. See Accord Global et Inclusif sur la Transition en République Démocratique du Congo, *supra* note 25, at Art. IV (providing that 'Les élections se tiennent dans les 24 mois qui suivent le début de la période de transition'). The elections were originally scheduled for July 2005 but it now seems inevitable that a one-year extension provided for in the Constitution will be exercised.

electoral victory by undermining the position of other parties to the peace agreement. Given that many of the key political actors are implicated in international crimes, criminal justice offers a powerful mechanism to discredit enemies and reshape the domestic political landscape. The potential implications of a criminal indictment by national or international courts are significant.[42] If a senior government official were indicted or prosecuted, that individual might be unable to effectively compete in the upcoming balloting or might already be in The Hague facing prosecution. If used strategically, this could greatly enhance the electoral prospects of unindicted opponents.

For President Kabila, the ICC thus has the potential to serve as a political weapon in the forthcoming national elections. Kabila is unlikely to be the subject of any ICC investigation, yet two of his potential electoral opponents – Vice Presidents Jean Pierre Bemba of the MLC and Azarias Ruberwa of the RCD – are among those most likely to be the subject of any early investigation. Though Kabila's hands are not clean, it is unlikely that he has committed significant crimes within the jurisdiction of the ICC. He was a relative newcomer on the political scene when his father died in January 2001 and has not been directly involved in the ongoing conflict in Ituri and South Kivu.[43] Any crimes against humanity committed by Kabila likely occurred prior to 1 July 2002 and, as yet, there is little evidence that he has been directly involved in any of the major massacres in Congo within the Court's temporal jurisdiction. As a UN Mission in Congo (MONUC) official observes, one would expect Kabila, therefore, to support a tribunal with jurisdiction over 'genocide and war crimes'.[44]

Kabila's chief political rivals, however, were more directly involved in ongoing crimes in eastern Congo and could well find themselves the targets of international investigations, in turn strengthening Kabila's political hand in the transitional government and forthcoming elections. While an ICC investigation may only implicate a select few in the transitional government who have been involved in Ituri, both Bemba and Ruberwa are likely to be among them. Various reports to the Prosecutor have implicated Bemba personally in war crimes and crimes against humanity in the Ituri region.[45] Apparently he is sufficiently concerned by such potential prosecution that he keeps a fuelled helicopter next to his office for quick escape should it become necessary.[46] Similarly, the RCD Vice President Azarias Ruberwa is also implicated in numerous crimes during the period of RCD rule in Eastern Congo,

---

42. Though the actual implications of such an indictment or prosecution in the DR Congo remain to be seen, the impact on governmental officials, such as Slobodan Milošević and Charles Taylor, are already evident. For a discussion with respect to Milošević, see A. Danner, 'Enhancing the Legitimacy and Accountability of Prosecutorial Discretion at the International Criminal Court', (2003) 97 AJIL 510, at 544 (asking if 'the Prosecutor [should] worry about the risks of destabilizing delicate political situations through the publicizing of investigations or the bringing of charges' and discussing the implications of the Milošević indictment). See also P. Akhavan, 'Beyond Impunity: Can International Criminal Justice Prevent Future Atrocities', (2001) 95 AJIL 7, at 9 (suggesting that 'the ICTY helped to delegitimize Milosevic's leadership').

43. See Edgerton, *supra* note 16, at 231.

44. Malik Dechambenoit, MONUC Political Officer, Personal Interview, Kinshasa, DR Congo, 28 October 2003 (interview conducted by Adrian Alvarez, Yuriko Kuga and Leslie Medema).

45. J. Astill, 'Congo Cannibalism Claim Provides First Challenge', *Guardian*, 11 March 2003.

46. M. Lacey, 'Hope Glimmering as War Retreats from Congo', *The New York Times*, 21 October 2003.

including Ituri.[47] The possible connections between Vice-Presidents Ruberwa and Bemba and crimes within ICC jurisdiction is not surprising, considering that both men were in direct control of rebel forces alleged to have committed war crimes and crimes against humanity in eastern Congo up to the mid-2003 peace settlement. A third vice president, Abdulaye Yerodia Ndombasi, though technically a Kabila ally as the 'government's vice president, could potentially pose an electoral threat to Kabila in 2005. He too might be the subject of ICC investigation and was previously indicted in Belgium for 'serious violations of international humanitarian law'.[48]

Even if an ICC investigation and prosecution were limited to warlords in eastern Congo outside the current government, Kabila could stand to benefit. Such prosecutions might well reveal information about crimes committed by Kabila's opponents or strengthen the hand of the sitting government vis-à-vis rebel groups.

Observers on the ground in Congo echo this analysis of the present political situation. As one MONUC official notes, 'transitional justice is more in the interest of President Kabila than others because he has the lightest balance sheet'. Speaking to audiences in the US and Europe, Kabila has called for an international criminal tribunal for Congo, in hopes of reaching an even wider set of potential rivals and political spoilers than might be subject to ICC prosecution.[49] These calls may be but political grandstanding to western audiences, but may also reflect strategic political calculations.[50]

Given the advantages prosecutions may offer Kabila, one might expect him to initiate domestic investigations of his potential electoral rivals. Domestic prosecutions, however, are not politically viable and the Congolese judiciary presently lacks the capacity to undertake the necessary investigations. The transitional government represents a precarious balance of interests between the government and the former rebel groups and any serious prosecutions launched by the government itself would likely destabilize the ongoing peace process.[51] Moreover, the capacity limits of the current Congolese judiciary make national prosecutions nearly impossible. As

---

47. J. Astill, 'Fighters Now Hold Their Punches in Muhammad Ali's Congo Hotel', *The Guardian*, 25 September 2003 (noting that Ruberwa is 'the former leader of a brutal Rwandan-backed rebel group' and perhaps the most loathed man in Congo').

48. *Case Concerning the Arrest Warrant of 11 April 2000 (Congo v. Belgium)*, Merits, 2002, at para 10. The proceedings against Ndombasi were stopped by the decision of the International Court of Justice in *Congo v. Belgium*, which held that the prosecution of Ndombasi violated the principle of sovereign immunity as he was then sitting foreign minister of Congo. Ibid.

49. J. Kabila, 'Intervention du Président de la République Démocratique du Congo a la 58ème session de l'Assemblée Générale des Nations Unies', New York, 24 September 2003 : 'Sur le plan international, nous pensons que le principal objectif en cette matière est, à titre de rappel, l'établissement, avec l'assistance des Nations Unies, d'un Tribunal Pénal International pour la République Démocratique du Congo, pour connaître des crimes de génocide, des crimes contre l'humanité, y compris les viols utilisés comme armes de guerre, et de violations massives des Droits de l'Homme. Par ailleurs, en vue d'assurer une couverture optimale en matière de protection des droits de l'homme ainsi que des droits humanitaires, la République Démocratique du Congo a ratifié plusieurs conventions internationales dont le Statut de Rome instituant la Cour pénale internationale'.

50. It is worth noting that, at home, Kabila has been largely silent on these issues, possibly due to the potential destabilizing effects international prosecution could have on the transitional government.

51. For discussions including the implications of such prosecutions as part of a transitional justice programme see generally M. Minow, *Between Vengeance and Forgiveness* (1999); R. Teitel, *Transitional Justice* (2002).

discussed in part 4 below, the Congolese judiciary is extremely weak and likely unable to mount a serious investigation of sitting government leaders.

Viewing the ICC as part of a system of multi-level global governance in international law enforcement offers a theoretical explanation for Kabila's decision to refer the case to the Court. Where the ICC is viewed as a simple substation mechanism for failed national prosecutions, decisions by the national government to act occur largely in isolation from international institutions. In the global governance model, however, the Court can be seen as shifting the incentives facing domestic actors, in this case by offering Kabila an alternative to national prosecutions – namely a referral to the Court. Such a referral serves Kabila's interests by possibly resulting in an investigation of his rivals while shifting the political costs of prosecution away from the weak national government and onto the ICC itself. In short, by referring the case to the ICC, Kabila can let the international community do his bidding, without bearing the domestic political costs of prosecution.[52] The interaction between the ICC and the Congo produces a heretofore impossible outcome – the threat of investigation by an international body without the same dangerous political repercussions for the national government.

The theory of multi-level global governance further suggests that these political dynamics at the national level may be altering the policies of the ICC itself. Kabila's referral may well be indicative of a broader phenomenon of weak states self-referring situations to the ICC, when sitting governments can benefit from prosecutions but the political costs of prosecuting at home are too great to allow domestic action. This is, apparently, the case in Congo and, arguably, in Uganda as well. The ICC has recognized the opportunity presented by such self-referrals and built them into its own operational strategy as a means of overcoming the inherent weaknesses of the Court. A recent policy memorandum from the Office of the Prosecutor outlines a strategy of co-operative complementarity. 'Where the Prosecutor receives a referral from the State in which a crime has been committed, the Prosecutor has the advantage of knowing that that State has the political will to provide his Office with all the co-operation within the country that it is required to give under the Statute'.[53] The obvious benefits for the ICC in such cases are the lack of challenges to admissibility and the co-operation of the national government.

While there are benefits, co-operative complementarity also carries with it significant difficulties, namely that the ICC may alter a delicate domestic political balance. The ICC must recognize that it is part of a system of global governance in international law enforcement, that its policies will alter incentives at the national level, and that in responding to actions by national governments it may be engaging in a potentially dangerous political game. The Prosecutor has noted that: 'Groups bitterly divided by conflict may oppose prosecutions at each others' hands and yet

---

52. For a discussion of political cost externalization in the context of international criminal prosecutions see W. Burke-White, 'A Community of Courts: Toward a System of International Criminal Justice', (2003) 24 *Mich. J. Int'l L.* 1, at 39–40, 47–54.

53. Annex to the 'Paper on Some Policy Issues Before the Office of the Prosecutor': Referrals and Communications, available at http://www.icc-cpi.int/library/organs/otp/policy_annex_final_210404.pdf.

agree to a prosecution by a Court perceived as neutral and impartial.'[54] Yet, at least in the Congo case, it seems likely that all groups may not necessarily support ICC involvement. The danger in such cases is that the Prosecutor will unwittingly or unintentionally play into the hands of the national government, and alter the political dynamic within the target state in favour of one particular side.

While the ICC's goal, as articulated in the Rome Statute, is to 'put an end to impunity',[55] the powers of prosecutorial discretion give the Prosecutor the ability to take into account the impact of his prosecutorial strategy on domestic political outcomes. Article 53(1)(c) of the Rome Statute allows the Prosecutor to consider whether 'Taking into account the gravity of the crime and the interests of victims, there are nonetheless substantial reasons to believe that an investigation would not serve the interests of justice'.[56] While there are considerable limitations on the Prosecutor's decisions to initiate a case, and strict review by the Pre-trial Chamber the Prosecutor has considerable leeway to decide that a prosecution would not serve the interests of justice.[57] Given that the Court is part of a larger system of global governance through which decisions at the international level have profound implications for domestic outcomes and vice-versa, the Prosecutor ought to consider carefully how his policies will effect decision-making at the domestic level. Where externalizing the political costs of domestic prosecution supports a legitimate peace process or helps a democratic law-abiding government, this may be a win-win situation and the Prosecutor should proceed. But, where the ICC becomes an implement of a potentially despotic national government whose own hands may not be clean, the Prosecutor might be well advised to encourage national prosecutions that fully account for the political costs of justice or to delay international investigation until his actions are less likely to alter domestic political outcomes.

4. THE COMPLEMENTARITY REGIME AND DOMESTIC JUDICIAL REFORM

The complementarity regime of the Rome Statute also serves as a catalyst for domestic judicial reform. The simple substitution model of complementarity suggests that the ICC will merely step in when domestic courts are unable or unwilling to act.[58] The multi-level global governance model instead recognizes that international and domestic institutions are engaged in complex interactions whereby the international level, and particularly the ICC's complementarity regime, may catalyze changes at the national level. This section examines the nature of these interactions, suggests that the complementarity provisions of the Rome Statute are,

---

54. Paper on Some Policy Issues Before the Office of the Prosecutor, September 2003 at 5, available at http://www.icc-cpi.int/library/organs/otp/030905_Policy_Paper.pdf.
55. 1998 Rome Statute of the International Criminal Court, at Preamble.
56. Ibid., at Art. 53(1)(c).
57. See A/CONF.183.C.1/SR.7, Rome Conference Travaux, 183; G. Turone, 'Powers and Duties of the Prosecutor', in Cassese, *supra* note 1, at 1137, at 1142.
58. For a commentary on the complementarity provisions of the Rome Statute based on this substation model, see Holmes, 'Complementarity: National Courts versus the ICC', *supra* note 1. See also F. Lattanzi, 'The International Criminal Court and National Jurisdictions', in M. Politi and G. Nesi (eds.), *The Rome Statute of the International Criminal Court* (2001) at 177.

in fact, facilitating reform of the Congolese domestic judiciary, and provides a political account of this catalytic effect based on changes to structural incentives created by complementarity.

One way for a state to avoid an ICC investigation is to utilize its own national judiciary to prosecute in an exercise of primacy. For states with failed domestic institutions, such an assertion of primacy will often involve significant domestic reform. The suggestion that complementarity might be fostering domestic judicial reform in Congo as a means of asserting primacy seems to be in irreconcilable tension with Kabila's referral of the situation to the ICC. If the Congolese government did not desire ICC involvement in the first place, why refer the case at all and, if it does seek ICC action, there is no need to reform the judiciary in an attempt to assert primacy. However, the Congolese government – like any government – does not always act as a unified whole, but rather consists of a number of factions and elements with different spheres of authority and power. While President Kabila was able to refer the situation in Congo to the ICC largely on his own authority, his main political rivals, who are significantly more threatened by an ICC investigation, have powerful influence over domestic judicial reform. Vice Presidents Bemba and Ruberwa, among others, have been extremely active in attempting to enhance the capacity of the national judiciary so as to exercise primacy over the ICC should that become necessary.

Bemba and Ruberwa are among the most likely to be investigated or implicated by ICC action and their rational preference is to keep the ICC out of Congo at all costs. They control a number of key governmental portfolios including Justice, Finance, Budget, Foreign Affairs, and Defense, Demobilization and Demilitarization,[59] giving them authority over domestic judicial reform and potential leverage points to control domestic prosecutions.

As part of a global governance system, the ICC has again shifted the incentives for domestic actors. Were it not for the ICC, Bemba, Ruberwa and others would seek to keep national courts weak so as to avoid prosecution. Given the existence of the ICC and the operation of the complementarity regime, however, their incentives change in favour of strengthening the national judiciary. National prosecutions may seem a far lesser threat than those by the ICC. After all, it is likely that senior governmental officials would have sufficient control over such proceedings to minimize political damage. Though the ICC could still act if a strengthened national judiciary refused to investigate a case or undertook a sham prosecution to shield a particular suspect,[60] challenges to admissibility would likely delay any such trials until after the forthcoming elections.[61] As the ICC has shifted the incentives of domestic actors

---

59. For a breakdown of these portfolios, see *Balancing Peace, Justice, and Stability: A Special Tribunal for the Democratic Republic of Congo*, Woodrow Wilson School of Public and International Affairs (2004) at Appendix B (on file with author). Though Minister of Justice Ngoy is himself from the Unarmed Opposition, he reports directly to Vice President Ruberwa of the RCD. Ibid.

60. See 1998 Rome Statute of the International Criminal Court, at Art. 17(2).

61. See ibid., at Art. 17. The legal proceedings required to determine admissibility where the national state seeks to assert primacy involve a full review by the Pre-Trial Chamber, likely taking a considerable period of time. Article 18 requires the prosecutor to defer a case for six months when the national state claims it is investigating the matter. Similarly, Article 18 grants the national state a right to appeal a decision of

in favour of a stronger national judiciary, Bemba, Ruberwa and others threatened by international prosecution have sought to enhance the standing of the Congolese courts.

Since the Prosecutor's September 2003 announcement that he would closely follow the situation in the Congo,[62] elements within the Congolese government have responded by launching reforms of the national judiciary and establishing a Truth and Reconciliation Commission.[63] Immediately after the Prosecutor's announcement, key Congolese government figures sought to make a case for the assertion of primacy over the ICC. In late September 2003, a series of senior Congolese officials appeared on local TV and radio to argue that 'Congo is competent to try these cases'.[64] This proposition has been frequently repeated in Congolese media and governmental circles. Minister of Justice Honorius Kisimba-Ngoy argues: 'For crimes committed by Congolese, we will hold them accountable in national courts. For crimes committed by international actors, we will hold them accountable in international courts.'[65] In other words, Congolese citizens should be tried in Congo and the ICC should only be involved in prosecutions of Rwandan rebels active in eastern Congo. A human rights advocate in Kinshasa suggests that the minister is not alone in taking this stance: 'there will be no end of Congolese saying they are perfectly competent to try the case themselves'.[66]

Many in Congo recognize that any primacy claims over the ICC will fall on deaf ears in The Hague unless significant progress is made to enhance judicial capacity at home. Minister of Justice Ngoy's first efforts in this vein have focused on reunifying the judiciary, which had effectively been divided into totally separate eastern and western regions during the period of civil war. A conference of the entire judiciary is being planned in Kinshasa in 2005 to accomplish this task.[67] Similarly, a conference on the relationship between the ICC and domestic courts involving international advisors and government officials is to be held in early 2006.[68] Likewise, a number of commissions have been established to begin work on judicial and legislative reform. According to the Director of the Cabinet to the Minister of Human Rights, one 'local commission [is] studying how to adapt the ICC to the DRC'.[69] Similarly, 'a permanent committee within the Ministry [of Justice has been established] for reforming the

---

admissibility by the Pre-Trial Chamber to the Appeals Chamber. Even if heard on an expedited basis, such proceedings could well continue through the election period.

62.   Luis Moreno-Ocampo, Second Assembly of States Parties to the Rome Statute of the International Criminal Court Report of the Prosecutor of the ICC, Mr Luis Moreno-Ocampo, 8 September 2003, available at http://www.icc-cpi.int/otp/030909_prosecutor_speech.pdf.

63.   For a discussion of how an enhanced judiciary could serve this purpose, see Holmes, 'Complementarity: National Courts versus the ICC', *supra* note 1.

64.   Joe Wells, International Human Rights Law Group, Personal Interview, Kinshasa, 27 October 2003 (interview conducted by Yuriko Kuga, Leslie Medema and Adrian Alvarez).

65.   Honorius Kisimba-Ngoy, Minister of Justice, Personal Interview, Kinshasa, 29 October 2003, (interview conducted by Yuriko Kuga, Leslie Medema and Adrian Alvarez).

66.   Joe Wells, International Human Rights Law Group, Personal Interview, Kinshasa, 27 October 2003 (interview conducted by Yuriko Kuga, Leslie Medema and Adrian Alvarez).

67.   Honorius Kisimba-Ngoy, Minister of Justice, Personal Interview, Kinshasa, 29 October 2003 (interview conducted by Yuriko Kuga, Leslie Medema and Adrian Alvarez).

68.   Report of the University of Amsterdam – No Peace Without Justice Experts Meeting, October 2004.

69.   Olela Okondji, Director of the Cabinet to the Minister of Human Rights, Personal Interview, Kinshasa, DR Congo, 29 October 2003 (interview conducted by Yuriko Kuga, Leslie Medema and Adrian Alvarez).

domestic law' and is 'learning how to implement the ICC' crimes into domestic law.[70] This committee has been responsible for draft legislation to formally implement the Rome Statute. The so called *Project de Loi de Mise en Oeuvre du Statut de la Cour Penale Internationale* was drafted in July 2003 and is currently under review by the Ministry of Justice and the transitional parliament.[71] As of late 2004 a draft law was under consideration but had yet to be passed by the National Assembly. While the establishment of such commissions and the preparation of legal drafts is only a first step toward meaningful domestic judicial reform, it is a preliminary indication that national reform efforts are under way.

Similarly, in the eastern provinces, officials at all levels of government expressed strong desires to enhance the capacity and effectiveness of the domestic judiciary. The Prosecutor General of Kisangani, for example, observes the current weakness of the domestic judiciary: 'The underpaid and politically weak Supreme Court, under the current conditions, will not be able to prosecute a major political leader'.[72] He is simultaneously committed to improving judicial capacity, noting, 'Priority should be given to strengthening the power of the Supreme Court'.[73] Similarly, the Chief Prosecutor of the South Kivu Province comments: 'Currently our courts are very weak, but we want to improve them quickly'.[74] In fact, judicial officials in the East claim to be taking particularly aggressive steps to improve domestic judicial capacity, even in the face of serious resource constraints. As South Kivu provincial prosecutor Mirindi notes, 'even before Kinshasa takes real action, we are already trying to do much to improve here in Bukavu. We have been collecting books and materials, trying to be sure we have the most up-to-date legal codes. And we are all helping to train younger lawyers so we can handle more cases'.[75] Again, these may be small steps but, to the degree they are occurring across the country and eventually will be backed by politicians in Kinshasa and international donors,[76] they have the potential to result in substantial change.

---

70. The Commission's formal name is the *Commission Permanente de Reforme du Droit Congolais*. Personal Interview, Director of the Cabinet to the Minister of Human Rights, Ms Olela Okondji, Kinshasa, 29 October 2003 (interview conducted by Yuriko Kuga, Leslie Medema and Adrian Alvarez).

71. See 'Democratic Republic of the Congo: Confronting Impunity', Human Rights Watch Briefing Paper, January 2004, at VI(b). The draft law 'provides a comprehensive definition of war crimes, crimes against humanity, and genocide'. In addition, it pledges the DRC to 'work with the ICC to prosecute such crimes'. Finally, it expands the jurisdiction of civilian courts to try soldiers accused of war crimes and crimes against humanity. Ibid.

72. Procureur of Kisangani, Personal Interview, 30 October 2004, Kisangani DRC (interview conducted by Christopher Broughton and Mariyan Zumbulev).

73. Ibid.

74. M. Mirindi, Prosecuting Magistrate, Personal Interview, Bukavu, DR Congo, 29 October 2003.

75. Ibid.

76. Significant international involvement in Congolese judicial reconstruction is already under way. Since 2001, the EU has had in place a multi-year €28 million judicial assistance programme and is currently considering plans to expand that programme. See Personal Interview, Emmanuel Altit, 8 December 2003 (interview by Jordan Tama). Under these auspices, an EU judicial assessment team visited Congo in late 2003 and is preparing an 'Organizational Audit of the Democratic Republic of Congo justice system'. See 'Democratic Republic of the Congo: Confronting Impunity', *supra* note 71, at l. In addition, human rights and the rule of law are one of the five strategic priorities of MONUC. According to William Swing, the Special Representative of the Secretary General in Congo, MONUC is in the process of establishing a Rule of Law Task-Force that will 'bring together many stakeholders including magistrates, NGOs, law enforcement officials'. Personal Interview, William Lacy Swing, Special Representative of the Secretary General, Kinshasa, DR Congo, 31 October 2003 (interview conducted by Yuriko Kuga, Leslie Medema and Adrian Alvarez). Swing further

Efforts have also been undertaken to enhance the capacity of the domestic police authority so as to be able to apprehend those suspected of serious crimes. Though the Congolese police force still remains weak, special police units have been established for the apprehension of serious crimes suspects. In March 2005, for example, Thomas Lubanga, the leader of the Congolese Patriotic Union, and Floribert Ndjabu, a rebel leader from Ituri, were arrested in Kinshasa.[77]

Throughout the country, both political and judicial officials attributed many of these reform efforts to the complementarity regime. The Governor of the South Kivu province observes: 'many horrible crimes were committed here in South Kivu. I want them prosecuted here in our courts. I am putting pressure on our courts to do a better job.'[78] Upon inquiry, the Governor was familiar with the concept of complementarity: 'I have heard that if our courts are good enough, the ICC will not be able to prosecute here. That is why we need to make these changes quickly'.[79] The general prosecutor of the South Kivu, as well as other judicial officials, had at least basic understandings of complementarity and expressed a desire to ensure that domestic courts function well enough that the ICC 'will not be able to try our people, but only the foreigners who are guilty'.[80]

Beyond reforming the domestic judiciary, the Congolese government is also act-ively pursuing the creation of a Truth and Reconciliation Commission (TRC). Al-though the TRC itself may not appear directly related to the complementarity regime, there is a widely held belief in Congo that a TRC investigation can prevent ICC action. TRC Chairman, Dr Jean-Luc Kuye Ndondo, asserts that the TRC can prevent the ICC from investigating low-level crimes by granting amnesty to perpetrators. He notes that 'for big crimes as crimes against humanity, it is better to go to international courts, for lesser crimes the TRC should take priority'.[81] The Rome Statute is silent on the question of whether a TRC-granted amnesty would be a bar to prosecution and the issue was 'evaded at the Rome Conference itself'.[82] Some authors contend that a legitimate amnesty along the lines of the South African model should be respected,

---

notes that MONUC wants to 'build judicial capacity and that means improving and increasing the police force, reforming the structure, repairing courts, building prisons and jails'. Ibid. Consideration is being given to the creation of a special mobile investigative unit to address serious crimes. For a discussion of this proposal, see 'Democratic Republic of the Congo: Confronting Impunity', *supra* note 71, at V(a). In Bunia, the major city in the Ituri region, MONUC is in the final stages of constructing a new expanded prison facility. MONUC is also supporting the creation of the Truth and Reconciliation Commission, particularly the implementation of an Organic Law for the Commission, though Swing cautions that the TRC can only be effective 'if the right people are in place'. Personal Interview, William Lacy Swing, Special Representative of the Secretary General, Kinshasa, DR Congo, 31 October 2003 (interview conducted by Yuriko Kuga, Leslie Medema and Adrian Alvarez). Another proposal recently presented to the US Department of State would establish a special tribunal along the lines of that operating in Sierra Leone to prosecute a small group of those most responsive for atrocities since 1996 and involve a mix of foreign and local judges. See *Balancing Peace, Justice, and Stability: A Special Tribunal for the Democratic Republic of Congo*, Woodrow Wilson School of Public and International Affairs (2004), at 24 (on file with author).

77.   'Another Key Ituri Leader Arrested', *Integrated Regional Information Networks*, 22 March 2005; 'Warlord Arrest for Killings', BBC News, 1 March 2005, available at http://news.bbc.co.uk/2/hi/africa/4308583.stm.
78.   Xavier Ciribanya, Personal Interview, Bukavu, DR Congo, 30 October 2003.
79.   Ibid.
80.   M. Mirindi, Prosecuting Magistrate, Personal Interview, Bukavu, DR Congo, 29 October, 2003.
81.   Dr Kyue-Ndondo, President of the Truth and Reconciliation Commission, Personal Interview, Kinshasa, DR Congo, 27 October 2003.
82.   J. Dugard, 'Possible Conflicts of Jurisdiction with Truth Commissions', in Cassesse, *supra* note 1, at 700. See also M. Scharf, 'The Amnesty Exception to the Jurisdiction of the ICC', (1998) 32 *Cornell Int'l L. J.* 507.

while others suggest that 'the establishment of the ICC testifies to the judgment on the part of the international community' that 'justice ... must take priority over peace and national reconciliation' and hence an amnesty should not bar ICC action.[83] While the effect of a TRC-granted amnesty remains an open question, the fact that it is perceived as a bar to prosecution in the Congo is sufficient to link the attention presently being paid to the TRC to the Rome Statute's complementarity regime.

The Congolese TRC grew out of the Inter-Congolese Dialogue and is written into the interim constitution.[84] The Constitution dictates the TRC be composed of eight parties: the government, the unarmed opposition, civil society, the RCD-Goma, the MLC, the Mai-Mai, the RCD-National and the RDC-KML.[85] In addition to the TRC Chairman, each of the eight parties has chosen one member of the Commission. After a long-delayed review process,[86] a February 2004 meeting of stakeholders in the TRC process held in Kinshasa brought the parties closer to an agreement on a draft text, but failed to produce a final result.[87] The organic law of the Congolese Truth and Reconciliation Commission was eventually adopted on 30 July 2004. Given concerns over the composition of the Commission appointed by the warring factions, the Organic Law provides for the appointment of an additional 13 members from 'religious institutions, academic institutions, associations of women and other associations whose activities are related to the objective of the TRC'.[88]

As mentioned earlier, although early drafts suggested that the TRC would only have the authority to amnesty low-level crimes,[89] the July 2004 law anticipates a broader amnesty grant by the national legislature and provides that the Commission will have the power, 'Under reserve of the amnesty law which will be voted by the National Assembly, [to] propose to the competent authority to accept or refuse any individual or collective amnesty application for acts of war, political crimes and crimes of opinion'.[90] As it stands, the current version of the law would allow the TRC to grant amnesties for crimes within the jurisdiction of the ICC that, at least in the view of Congolese officials, could in turn block ICC action. In addition, the Commission has the authority to offer reparations to the victims, though the source of funds for any reparations remains unclear.[91]

---

83. Dugard, *supra* note 82, at 702.
84. Constitution De La Transition, Journal Officiel de la République Démocratique du Congo, 44 année, 5 April 2003, at Art. 154 (noting: 'Les Institutions d'appui a la démocratie sont: ... La Commission vérité et réconciliation').
85. Dr Kyue-Ndondo, President of the Truth and Reconciliation Commission, Personal Interview, Kinshasa, DR Congo, 27 October 2003.
86. See 'Truth Commission to be Established in Kinshasa', AFOL News, 19 February 2004, available at http://www.afrol.com/articles/11310.
87. See Y. Kabamab, 'National Consultations on DRC Truth and Reconciliation Commission', 19 February 2004, MONUC Press Release, http://www.monuc.org/news.aspx?newsID=1952. See also, 'Truth Commission to be Established in Kinshasa,' *AFOL News*, 19 February 2004, available at http://www.afrol.com/articles/11310.
88. Organic Law, 30 July 2004, cited in 'A First Few Steps: The Long Road to a Just Peace in the Democratic Republic of Congo', *International Center for Transitional Justice Occasional Paper*, October 2004 at 39–40, available at http://www.ictj.org/downloads/ICTJ.DRC.Eng.pdf.
89. For a discussion of the appropriate range of powers for such a TRC, see W. W. Burke-White, 'Reframing Impunity', (2002) 42 *Harv. J. Int'l L.* 467. For a discussion of similarly situated TRCs, see P. Hayner *Unspeakable Truths: Confronting State Terror and Atrocity* (2001).
90. Organic Law, *supra* note 88, at 43. It is worth noting that this amnesty provision has changed several times in the drafting process.
91. Organic Law, *supra* note 88, at Art. 41.

The government's efforts to create a TRC have been greeted with much scepticism by Congolese and foreign observers alike. The Commission's structure – with its members drawn from the warring factions – undermines much of its legitimacy. One senior US government official who spoke on grounds of anonymity observes: 'The TRC has been completely politicized, and many of the nominees have been authors of war crimes themselves'.[92] A second major failing of the TRC, according to representatives of victims' groups is that the membership of the commission and the lack of any witness protection may result in victims being unwilling to testify.[93] As it stands today, while the TRC has been a focus of the government's domestic judicial reform, it seems unlikely to develop into a successful and legitimate body.[94] Yet it is hardly a surprising response from a government that is internally divided and unsure whether it really wants an ICC investigation. The ambignity of the status of a TRC in the Rome Statute means that most domestic actors can support a TRC without having to confront its real implications for an ICC prosecution.

While efforts at judicial reform and the development of the Congolese TRC remain too preliminary to prove that complementarity has been a catalyst for reform, there are strong indications that the ICC, as a supranational layer of governance authority, is altering incentives at the national level and catalyzing reform efforts. As the Special Representative to the Secretary General William Swing observes: 'The ICC is ... one piece in the mosaic. It can be used as a means to put pressure on the people.'[95] Many Congolese officials are familiar with the concept of complementarity and, for political reasons, some are eager to exercise primacy vis-à-vis the ICC. Their actions to encourage reform of the domestic judiciary and the establishment of the TRC seem closely linked to this desire to keep prosecutions domestic. Clearly, both resources and political capital are sufficiently limited that reform may be far slower and less comprehensive than judicial officials anticipate. But the ICC appears to be playing a part in spurring on those efforts.

5. COMPLEMENTARITY AS A BENCHMARK FOR JUDICIAL EFFECTIVENESS: EVALUATING THE CONGOLESE JUDICIARY IN LIGHT OF ICC ADMISSIBILITY

A third means through which the ICC is emerging as part of a system of multi-level global governance in the Congo is by providing a set of benchmarks for judicial effectiveness. In the simple substation model of complementarity, Article 17 of the Rome Statute merely delineates the limits on admissibility of cases before the Court. Article 17 specifies that a case will not be admissible if it is being investigated or prosecuted by a national court, unless the proceedings were undertaken for 'the

---

92.   Personal Interview, Kinshasa, DR Congo, 26 October 2003.
93.   Round Table with Victims Groups, Personal Interview, Bukavu, South Kivu, 30 October 2003.
94.   For a more general critique of the Commission, see 'A First Few Steps: The Long Road to a Just Peace in the Democratic Republic of Congo', *International Center for Transitional Justice Occasional Paper*, October 2004, at 39–40, available at http://www.ictj.org/downloads/ICTJ.DRC.Eng.pdf.
95.   William Lacy Swing, Special Representative of the Secretary General, Personal Interview, Kinshasa, DR Congo, 31 October 2003 (interview conducted by Yuriko Kuga, Leslie Medema and Adrian Alvarez).

purpose of shielding the person concerned from criminal responsibility', there has 'been an unjustified delay in the proceedings', or the proceedings were not 'conducted independently or impartially'.[96] Further, in cases of judicial collapse, Article 17(3) of the Rome Statute instructs the Court to consider 'whether, due to a total or substantial collapse or unavailability of its national judicial system, the State is unable to obtain the accused or the necessary evidence and testimony or otherwise unable to carry out its proceedings'.[97]

Approaching these limitations from the perspective of multi-level global governance engages the ICC and its potential jurisprudence in a set of iterative interactions with national judicial systems. In this model, national governments may be seen as responding to the complementarity provisions of Article 17 in shaping their own judicial reform efforts. The basic provisions governing admissibility of cases before the Court simultaneously serve as benchmarks for the effectiveness of national judiciaries. Where national courts fail to meet these standards, they are deemed so ineffective that the ICC can intervene to replace the national judiciary. The incentive structure in this circumstance is such that national governments seeking to avoid ICC action will endeavour to meet the minimum benchmarks of effectiveness embedded in the complementarity regime. The Court and the Rome Statute can then be seen as guiding national governments in undertaking 'genuine' prosecutions.[98]

Admittedly, the admissibility criteria of the Rome Statute provide but a thin set of guidelines or a skeletal framework for national judiciaries. Commentators have sought to add substance to these criteria. John Holmes suggests that the goal at Rome was to offer a set of criteria as 'objective as possible' and that the use of the term 'genuine' in the Statute instructs the Court to consider whether the national government has acted 'in good faith'.[99] In assessing the inability of a state to prosecute, Holmes notes that the discussion in Rome included a consideration of 'the extent to which the State was exercising effective control over its territory, the existence of a functioning law enforcement mechanism, ... whether the State was able to secure the accused or the necessary evidence, ... the extent and scope of the crimes committed,' and the ability of the state to give 'full respect of the rights of the accused'.[100] Despite efforts to expand on the criteria developed at Rome, the Statute leaves much for the Court to specify in early cases testing admissibility.[101]

If the ICC is envisioned as part of a system of multi-level global governance and engaged in a kind of conversation with national judiciaries, a more detailed

---

96. 1998 Rome Statue of the International Criminal Court, at Art. 17(2).
97. Ibid., at Art. XVII (3).
98. The word 'genuine' was chosen in a compromise to avoid seemingly more intrusive scrutiny by the ICC under the proposed language of an 'effective' investigation or prosecution. At the very least, a genuine investigation or prosecution seems to be one that is undertaken with some diligence and could, potentially, lead to the criminal liability of the accused. See OTP Informal Expert Paper: The Principle of Complementarity in Praxis (2003) 8 para. 22. On this matter, cf. J. Holmes, 'The Principle of Complementarity', *supra* note 1, at 49.
99. Holmes, 'Complementarity: National Courts versus the ICC', *supra* note 1, at 674.
100. Holmes, 'The Principle of Complementarity', *supra* note 1, at 49.
101. The Pre-trial Chamber will make apply the complementarity provisions to make determinations of admissibility. For a discussion, see Lattanzi, *supra* note 58, at 49 (observing: 'it is always up to the Court to decide on issues of complementarity').

specification of the complementarity criteria is essential. Such specification would provide national governments, particularly those emerging from a total or substantial judicial collapse, more specific benchmarks for their reform efforts and would offer important guidance to judges and jurists alike as to the necessary components of judicial effectiveness. While the Pre-Trial Chamber will, hopefully, provide such standards in its early decisions on admissibility challenges, the Office of the Prosecutor may be well served to develop and publicize a set of criteria that it will look to when deciding to proceed with an investigation. A more detailed set of criteria, even if not the operative law of the Pre-Trial Chamber, could more effectively catalyze judicial reform efforts by providing substantive guidance for national governments.

This section proposes a more detailed set of criteria to evaluate the ability of a national government to undertake genuine prosecutions, particularly in the wake of a total or substantial collapse of the national judiciary. Further, the section evaluates the Congolese judiciary in light of the criteria developed. Given the desire of some Congolese leaders to assert primacy over the ICC,[102] should national prosecutions be initiated in the Congo, the ICC may well be required to make a determination of admissibility.[103] The discussion that follows provides a preliminary analysis of the present ability of the Congolese judiciary to undertake genuine prosecutions.

Four key analytical factors can be derived from Article 17 of the Rome Statute, their commentaries, and a range of international agreements and instruments addressing judicial 'best practices' to judge the effectiveness of judicial systems in states recovering from a total or substantial judicial collapse. These include the availability of experienced and unbiased judicial personnel, the presence of a viable legal infrastructure, the existence of adequate operative law, and a sufficient police capability to undertake arrest and investigation. These factors are crucial to a genuine investigation and prosecution as they address the ability of the national government to apprehend suspects, collect evidence, provide security to victims and witnesses, and undertake unbiased adjudication.

This analysis suggests that presently the Congolese domestic judiciary is unable to undertake genuine investigations or prosecutions. On each factor in the proposed test, the Congolese government currently falls short. As a February 2004 Human Rights Watch briefing paper concludes: 'The DRC's national justice system is in a state of disarray ... It will likely take years to establish a functioning, independent, impartial and fair judiciary'.[104] The sections that follow develop each of the four prongs of the proposed test in more detail and apply them to the DRC.

5.1. Judicial personnel

The adequacy and independence of judicial personnel is an essential component of a state's genuine willingness and ability to prosecute international crimes. As

---

102. See text *supra* parts 3 and 4.
103. Article 17 of the Rome Statute starts from the presumption that cases are admissible before the ICC. The Court is instructed to deem the case inadmissible if it is 'being investigated or prosecuted by a State which has jurisdiction over it, unless the State is unwilling or unable genuinely to carry out the investigation or prosecution'.
104. 'Democratic Republic of the Congo: Confronting Impunity', *supra* note 71, at IV.

one commentator on the Rome Statute observes: 'the absence of sufficient qualified personnel to effect a genuine prosecution could be a determining factor in judging admissibility.'[105] Judges must have adequate training and experience, guarantees of personal safety, and both financial and political independence to act as impartial arbiters in any dispute. The International Covenant on Civil and Political Rights, for example, requires that 'everyone shall be entitled to a fair and public hearing by a competent, independent and impartial tribunal established by law'.[106] Similarly, Transparency International's Bangalore Principles of Judicial Conduct make clear that 'Judicial independence is a pre-requisite to the rule of law'. More specifically, addressing the question of financial independence, the Principles expound: 'judge[s] ... shall neither ask for, nor accept, any gift, bequest, loan or favour in relation to anything done or to be done or omitted to be done by the judge in connection with the performance of judicial duties.'[107] In short, the Court must determine whether the national state has a sufficient number of competent lawyers and judicial officials who are free from political or financial bias to undertake an investigation and prosecution.

The DRC currently lacks adequate and independent judicial personnel to undertake investigations or prosecutions that meet the genuineness test under Article 17 of the Rome Statute. On one level Congo is blessed with a wealth of educated lawyers. One report suggests that there are at least 1,500 lawyers and 700 other judicial officials in the country.[108] While the actual number of judges may be small, for an extremely poor African state, Congo has a respectable enough pool of lawyers to operate a judiciary. At universities in Kinshasa and Bukavu, criminal and international law are regularly taught and law students are relatively familiar with international crimes.[109] Moreover, a number of judges have received international graduate training, particularly in Belgium and France.[110] Compared to other states such as East Timor, where international criminal tribunals have been established using national personnel, Congo is far better equipped with trained lawyers.[111] With additional training, the existent personnel pool could presumably provide an effective basis for the reform of the Congolese judiciary.

There are, however, significant problems with judicial independence. Judges often lack both political independence and financial impartiality. A recent report by the

---

105. Holmes, 'Complementarity: National Courts versus the ICC', *supra* note 1, at 678.
106. International Covenant on Civil and Political Rights, at Art. 14. For a more detailed discussion of judicial independence see, e.g., S. Shetreet and J. Deschenes (eds.), *Judicial Independence: The Contemporary Debate* (1985).
107. Transparency International, 'The Bangalore Principles of Judicial Conduct', available at http://www.transparency.org/building_coalitions/codes/bangalore_conduct.html.
108. Dominique Kamuandu and Theo Kasonga, Avocates Sans Frontières, Personal Interview, Kinshasa, DR Congo, 28 October 2003 (interview conducted by Adrian Alvarez and Yuriko Kuga. Human Rights Watch confirms that 'the latest figures released by the Ministry of Justice show that as of 1998, there were only 1448 judges and prosecutors in the entire country'). See 'Democratic Republic of the Congo: Confronting Impunity', *supra* note 71, at IV(b).
109. Dean of the Faculty of Law, University of Kinshasa, Personal Interview, Kinshasa, DR Congo, 27 October 2003. M. Mirindi, for example, completed an LL.M. at the Free University of Brussels.
110. M. Mirindi, Prosecuting Magistrate, Personal Interview, Bukavu, DR Congo, 29 October, 2003.
111. For a discussion of the problems with finding adequately trained judicial personnel in East Timor, see Burke-White, *supra* note 52, at 61–75.

Syndicat Autonome des Magistrats de la République Démocratique du Congo notes that 'the judges of our country have been wrongly and unjustly reduced to the rank of simple public functionaries of the state'.[112] The Congolese President has largely unchecked authority over the appointment of judges.[113] On this matter, Human Rights Watch suggests 'the constantly growing power of the executive since the mid-1970s has resulted in the *de facto* subordination of the judiciary to the executive branch'.[114] The problems of judicial independence are highlighted by the ongoing operation of the *Cour de Sûreté de l'Etat*, 'a special tribunal established in the 1970s to prosecute political offences', which is known to lack independence and find in favour of the government.[115]

Financial independence may be of even greater concern. Many judges in Congo have not been paid regularly in more than five years.[116] Particularly in the eastern part of the country, where most crimes have occurred, judges have simply not received compensation from the state. Even when paid, government salaries of no more than US $50 per month are wholly inadequate to prevent an overwhelming temptation for abuse and corruption.[117] Congolese judges are frequently seen travelling in chauffer-driven BMWs, clearly beyond the means of their salaries. These same unpaid judges often supplement their income with payments from the parties before them.[118] Rumour has it that for roughly US$1000, the official police and judicial apparatus can be purchased to assure the arrest and incarceration of an individual.[119]

Unpaid judges or those paid directly by the parties cannot be independent and are therefore unable to carry out genuine investigations and prosecutions. Unless the judges for any domestic accountability process receive adequate compensation such that they need not depend on pay-offs from the parties, Congo will likely remain unable to undertake a genuine judicial process. These problems could, however, be overcome through either outside financial assistance or the commitment of greater domestic resources to judicial salaries and serious anti-corruption efforts.

5.2. Infrastructure

A second necessary prong of the test of a state's ability and willingness to prosecute is the existence of sufficient judicial infrastructure to undertake international prosecutions. Article 17(3)'s reference to the 'total or substantial collapse or unavailability of its national judicial system' as grounds for ICC admissibility implies the necessity

---

112. *Memorandum du Syndicat Autonome des Magistrats de la République Démocratique du Congo*, Kinshasa, 25 August 2003, cited in 'Democratic Republic of the Congo: Confronting Impunity,' *supra* note 71, at IV(a).
113. 'A First Few Steps: The Long Road to a Just Peace in the Democratic Republic of Congo', *supra* note 88, at 24.
114. 'Democratic Republic of the Congo: Confronting Impunity', *supra* note 71, at IV(a).
115. Ibid., at IV(d).
116. M. Mirindi, Prosecuting Magistrate, Personal Interview, Bukavu, DR Congo, 29 October 2003; Personal Interview, Chief of the Cabinet of the Judiciary, Bukavu, DR Congo, 29 October 2003.
117. Dominique Kamuandu and Theo Kasonga, Avocats Sans Frontières, Personal Interview, Kinshasa, DR Congo, 28 October 2003 (interview conducted by Adrian Alvarez and Yuriko Kuga). See also Personal Interview, Luc Heymans, Director, UN Office of the Coordination of Humanitarian Affairs, Kinshasa, Congo, 25 October 2003.
118. M. Mirindi, Prosecuting Magistrate, Personal Interview, Bukavu, DR Congo, 29 October 2003.
119. Jo Wells, Human Rights Law Group, Personal Interview, Kinshasa, Congo, 25 October 2003 (interview conducted by Yuriko Kuga and Leslie Medema).

of some existent national infrastructure.[120] In the terms of the Statute, without some minimal infrastructure, a state is 'unable to otherwise carry out its proceedings'.[121] At the negotiations in Rome, the example of the Rwandan judiciary in the mid-1990s, which lacked any infrastructure whatsoever after the genocide, was often cited as an example of substantial collapse.[122] John Holmes, in a commentary to the Statute, notes the necessity of a 'functioning law enforcement mechanism' as a prerequisite to an effective prosecution.[123] Moreover, to meet minimum international standards, facilities are required to ensure security for victims, witnesses, judges and defendants.[124] Finally, some prison facilities are needed to ensure that those convicted of international crimes can be incarcerated.

Applying this infrastructure prong of the test for an effective judiciary to the DRC, the question becomes whether the Congolese judicial infrastructure has experienced a total and substantial collapse such that no genuine trial would be possible. Courts in the national capital of Kinshasa look and act like many of their counterparts in failed states – they operate in a general state of disarray.[125] However, despite the often limited resources and apparent chaos, some courts in Congo may be able to undertake genuine investigations and prosecutions.[126] The Congolese Supreme Court heard approximately 180 cases in 2003 and has two hearing rooms that appear to be used with some frequency.[127] While filing rooms at the Supreme Court in Kinshasa were subject to frequent leaks and flooding, often leading to the loss of documents, records were, at the very least, kept. Similarly, while courtrooms often lacked recording equipment or other modern conveniences, in Kinshasa adequate facilities do exist for some trials.[128] Research facilities were minimal, at best, but judges had office space and some law books on Congolese, Belgian and French law.[129] While the situation in the capital is better than in the rest of the country, only one serious prosecution for international crimes or human rights abuse has been undertaken since the transitional government came to power.[130] In early 2005, a number of rebel leaders were arrested, but prosecutions have yet to be initiated.

Despite the apparent viability of the judiciary in Kinshasa, the eastern part of the country suffers from a serious collapse of infrastructure. As one human rights

---

120. 1998 Rome Statute of the International Criminal Court, at Art. 17(3).
121. Ibid.
122. Holmes, 'Complementarity: National Courts versus the ICC', *supra* note 1, at 677.
123. Holmes, 'The Principle of Complementarity,' *supra* note 1, at 49.
124. For a discussion of the evaluation of judicial infrastructure and capacity in EU member states, which obviously requires a higher standard than what could be expected in post-conflict states in Africa, see EUMAP Monitoring on Judicial Capacity (2002), available at http://www.eumap.org/topics/judicial.
125. For a general discussion on the role of courts in Africa, see J. Widner, *Building the Rule of Law: Francis Nyalali and the Road to Judicial Independence in Africa* (2001).
126. Personal visit and interview, Supreme Court of the Democratic Republic of Congo, Kinshasa, 25 October 2003.
127. Yenyi Olungu Victor, Premier Avocat Général de la République, Personal Interview, Kinshasa, DR Congo, 29 October 2003 (interview conducted by Leslie Medema, Yuriko Kuga and Adrian Alvarez).
128. It seems most unlikely that the available facilities are sufficient to support comprehensive judicial activities for a country of 56 million. See *CIA World Fact Book: Democratic Republic of Congo*, available at http://www.cia.gov/cia/publications/factbook/geos/cg.html.
129. M. Mirindi, Prosecuting Magistrate, Personal Interview, Bukavu, DR Congo, 29 October 2003.
130. The case, being tried in a military, rather than a civilian court, involves 22 individuals suspected of serious human rights violations in Ankoro, Katanga Province. See 'A First Few Steps: The Long Road to a Just Peace in the Democratic Republic of Congo', *supra* note 88, at 18–20.

advocate in Kinshasa put it, 'there is no [judicial] capacity' in Eastern Congo.[131] Effective courts are only operating in three major cities – Bukavu, Kisangani and Goma.[132] In the entire Oriental Province, an area approximately the size of France, there is only one operational court.[133] To reach a functioning court and file a complaint or appear as a witness requires, for the vast majority of Congolese, a multi-day walk along often flooded 'roads' through dangerous territory. Even when they reach a major city, Congolese citizens are not guaranteed that courts will be functioning or will operate without bribes. As one recent study found, less than 20% of the Congolese population has access to any courts at all.[134] For the purposes of domestic prosecutions of international crimes, it is particularly problematic that the judicial infrastructure does not reach out into provinces where key evidence is likely to be found. Investigation of such crimes is thus extremely difficult, if not impossible. In many communities, the only available justice is the local *Baraza* system, in which community elders adjudicate petty crimes – a system largely unable to deal with the more serious international crimes.[135] The Congolese Minister of Justice sums up the problems in the east: 'in general the [judicial] situation is very bad'.[136] Similarly, a 2004 report by the International Center for Transitional Justice concludes: 'The infrastructure of the judicial system has all but collapsed; judges and prosecutors lack copies of basic laws and are in dire need of training or re-training'.[137]

Even in the major cities of eastern Congo – Bukavu, Kisangani or Goma – courts are only semi-operational. As one magistrate judge in Bukavu noted, 'everything is missing for us to do our work: money, buildings, even typewriters'.[138] These courts have no formal judicial library and many lack even copies of relevant statutory law. While the Bukavu Municipal Court has managed to hear approximately 500 cases in the past year, it has few if any records and only operates when the parties can bear the costs.[139] Moreover, the effective partition of Congo over the past few years has meant that these courts in Eastern Congo had no contact with the Supreme Court or Ministry of Justice in Kinshasa, preventing appellate review or national harmonization.[140]

---

131. Jo Wells, Human Rights Law Group, Personal Interview, Kinshasa, DR Congo, 25 October 2003 (interview conducted by Yuriko Kuga and Leslie Medema).

132. M. Mirindi, Prosecuting Magistrate, Personal Interview, Bukavu, DR Congo, 29 October 2003.

133. Procureur of Kisangani, Personal Interview, 30 October 2004, Kisangani DR Congo (interview conducted by Christopher Broughton and Mariyan Zumbulev).

134. Only 54 of the 180 'Tribunaux de Paix' were established by May 2004. See 'A First Few Steps: The Long Road to a Just Peace in the Democratic Republic of Congo', *supra* note 88, at 24.

135. Personal Interview, John Meyers, UN Office of Community and Humanitarian Affairs, Bukavu, DR Congo, 28 October 2003. Many of the problems with *Baraza* stem from its exclusion of women and ethnic minorities from deliberation proceedings. Personal Interview, PAIF, Promotion et Appui aux Initiatives Feminines, Goma, DR Congo, 31 October 2003 (interview conducted by Dawn Hewett and Barbara Feinstein).

136. Honorius Kisimba-Ngoy, Minister of Justice of DR Congo, Personal Interview, Kinshasa, DR Congo, 29 October 2003 (interview conducted by Leslie Medema, Adrian Alvarez and Yuriko Kuga).

137. See 'A First Few Steps: The Long Road to a Just Peace in the Democratic Republic of Congo', *supra* note 88, at 24.

138. M. Mirindi, Prosecuting Magistrate, Personal Interview, Bukavu, DR Congo, 29 October 2003.

139. Chief of the Cabinet of the Judiciary, Personal Interview, Bukavu, DR Congo, 29 October 2003.

140. Luc Heymans, Director, UN Office of the Coordination of Humanitarian Affairs, Personal Interview, Kinshasa, DR Congo, 25 October 2003.

A final area in which Congolese infrastructure has collapsed is the prison system. Prisons are, obviously, required to incarcerate those convicted of international crimes, but also to protect defendants from retribution before and during trials. Visits to prisons in Kisangani and Goma demonstrated the overwhelming insufficiency of resources. In Goma, men, women and even children were being housed in common facilities.[141] According to one observer in Kisangani, the local warden is unpaid and takes regular bribes from prisoners, while sexually transmitted diseases and other contagious illnesses are rampant.[142] Food and medical services were often available only when provided by families on the outside. One 2002 NGO report on prisons in Kinshasa describes the situation as nothing less than a 'catastrophe'.[143] While MONUC is in the process of building new prison facilities in Ituri and elsewhere, at present Congo lacks the facilities to imprison even a fraction of those who likely bear the greatest responsibility for serious international crimes.[144] In sum, Congo has undergone and still suffers from a significant collapse of domestic judicial infrastructure.

5.3. Legal framework

A third area relevant to the ability of domestic judicial mechanisms in a post-conflict state to undertake prosecution of international crimes is the legal framework for such prosecutions. The legal authority of the national government to prosecute an international crime can derive from two principle sources – domestic law or international law directly applicable in the state in question. Generalizing this prong of the test of a state's ability to prosecute is difficult as each state has its own legal and constitutional order governing both crimes punishable under international law and the domestic effect of international law. For a state to undertake a genuine prosecution of the crimes proscribed by the Rome Statute, those crimes must either be included in domestic penal legislation or the international legal proscriptions must have direct domestic effect. As Flavia Lattanzi notes in a commentary on the Statute: 'The lack of implementation in domestic legal orders of applicable international standards ... could lead to the Court's decision of the admissibility of a case, as a consequence of the 'incapacity' of the national jurisdictions to provide justice in the case.'[145]

Determining whether a state has a sufficient legal framework to prosecute raises a further question as to whether the state's ability to prosecute the constituent elements of crimes defined in the Rome Statute, rather than the crimes themselves, would meet the tests of complementarity. For states that have not incorporated the

141. Personal visit, Goma Provincial Prison, 31 October 2003.
142. Father Giovanni, Kisangani Catholic Parish of the Sacred Heart, Personal Interview, 30 October 2003, Kisangani, DR Congo (interview by Christopher Broughton and Mariyan Zumbulev).
143. Prisons in the Democratic Republic of Congo: A Series of Reports Commissioned by the Refuge Documentation Center Ireland 5 (2002) available at http://www.ecoi.net/pub/sb47/rdc-cod-prison0502.pdf. A 1994 report by Human Rights Watch reached a similar conclusion. See 'Prison Conditions in Zaire', Human Rights Watch Report (1994).
144. Luc Heymans, Director, UN Office of the Coordination of Humanitarian Affairs, Personal Interview, Kinshasa, DR Congo, 25 October 2003. For reference to minimum international standards of detention, see International Covenant on Civil and Political Rights, at Art. 10.
145. Lattanzi, *supra* note 58, at 181.

Rome Statute and in which international law does not have direct effect, national law may only address certain lesser included acts of international crimes (for example, murder as a lesser included offence of a crime against humanity). It remains an open question whether the investigation and prosecution of the included acts of an international crime would be sufficient to deny admissibility. Article 17 of the Rome Statute specifies that a case shall be deemed inadmissible if 'the case is being investigated or prosecuted by a state which has jurisdiction over it'.[146] The use of the word 'case' appears broad enough to include the investigation and prosecution of lesser offences. This would, however, be a sub-optimal result for a number of reasons. Such a prosecution would not respect the particularly heinous nature of the crimes in question, it may not provide for appropriate punishments, and it might allow for various domestic defences not available in international law. Where a state chooses to prosecute an accused of minor crimes or crimes which provide for only very light sentences,[147] Article 20 of the Statute would allow the ICC to retry the individual for the international offence if the domestic prosecution 'was inconsistent with an intent to bring the person concerned to justice'.[148] For the purposes of determining the state's ability to undertake a genuine prosecution, the existence of a legal framework allowing for the prosecution of the actual offences enumerated in the Rome Statute appears essential.

A final aspect of the statutory basis for prosecution is whether there exist any bars to domestic prosecution such as national amnesties or statutes of limitations in domestic law. While a Truth and Reconciliation Commission investigation followed by a narrowly tailored amnesty might meet the tests of complementarity,[149] a blanket amnesty denying domestic courts jurisdiction would result in the inability of national courts to investigate or prosecute.[150] Although statutes of limitations generally do not apply to international crimes such as those included in the Rome Statute,[151] they may well apply under national law to the prosecution of lesser included offences. In determining whether the national judiciary has the requisite legal framework to prosecute, it is necessary to ensure that there are no statutory bars to prosecution that would deprive national courts of jurisdiction.

Applying these criteria to the Congo situation requires first a determination of whether the crimes proscribed in the Rome Statute have been implemented into domestic law. Congo inherited its legal system from the Belgians upon independence in 1960. The system is split into military and civilian courts, with members of the

---

146. 1998 Rome Statute of the International Criminal Court, at Art. 17(1)(a).
147. An example of this that may eventually lead to an admissibility test before the ICC is a new Columbian law providing extermely light sentences for those convicted of international crimes, possibly as a way of shielding the accused from more serious punishment by an international court.
148. 1998 Rome Statute of the International Criminal Court, at Art. 20.
149. See generally, Dugard, *supra* note 82.
150. Examples of such blanket amnesties denying national courts jurisdiction over particular offences include Law of Amnesty, No. 2.191 (18 April 1978) (Chile) reprinted in *Americas Watch, Human Rights and the 'Politics Of Agreements': Chile During President Aylwin's First Year* (1991) 32; First Amnesty Law of 14 June 1995, No. 26479 (1995) (Peru). Such an amnesty could also be a strong indication of the unwillingness of the state to investigate or prosecute crimes within the Court's jurisdiction.
151. See 1998 Rome Statute of the International Criminal Court, at Art. 29.

armed forces tried before military courts, and others in civilian courts.[152] None of the international crimes proscribed in the Rome Statute have been implemented into the civilian penal code.[153] An update to the military penal code in 2002 has expanded the coverage of international crimes so as to penalize genocide and war crimes, yet these definitions still fall 'short of the elements of these crimes under both the Rome Statute and the Geneva Conventions'.[154] While the Congolese legislation implementing the Rome Statute will rectify many of these shortcomings, it has yet to be passed and will not apply retroactively. As a result, Congolese civilian courts are unable to prosecute the crimes in the Rome Statute and military courts, where they have jurisdiction, may not be able to prosecute 'genuinely'.

Reliance on the military penal code poses a further legal challenge in that the revisions of the military penal code of 2002 were adopted while the country was partitioned during the civil war. Congolese legal scholars differ on whether the amended military penal code has the force of law in the eastern half of the country, which was not subject to Kinshasa's rule at the time of enactment.[155] Although this could easily be remedied by a repassage of the law in the newly unified parliament, this has yet to be done.

To the degree that Congolese domestic law provides an insufficient legal basis for prosecution, it is necessary to consider whether international law can be invoked directly in Congolese courts. As Congo follows the monist legal tradition inherited from Belgium, international law can, theoretically at least, have direct effect, without the need for national implementing legislation. Congolese courts, however, have been reluctant to rely on international law in the absence of implementing legislation.[156] One Congolese legal scholar suggests that the Genocide Convention and the Rome Statute may have direct effect without the need for implementing legislation.[157] Moreover, there is no precedent in Congolese law for the direct application of customary international law.[158]

Finally, it is necessary to consider amnesties or other statutory bars to prosecution in Congolese law. On 15 April 2003, a presidential decree granted amnesty, pending adoption of an amnesty law by the National Assembly, for 'acts of war, political crimes and crimes of opinion committed during the period from 2 August 1998 and

---

152. Apparently any crime involving a firearm tends to end up in the military system. Personal Interview, Dominique Kamuandu and Theo Kasonga, Avocates Sans Frontières, Kinshasa, DR Congo, 28 October 2003 (interview conducted by Adrian Alvarez and Yuriko Kuga).
153. 'A First Few Steps: The Long Road to a Just Peace in the Democratic Republic of Congo', *supra* note 88, at 20.
154. 'Democratic Republic of the Congo: Confronting Impunity,' *supra* note 71, at VI(a); Personal Interview, Dominique Kamuandu and Theo Kasonga, Avocates Frontières, Kinshasa, DR Congo, 28 October 2003 (interview conducted by Adrian Alvarez and Yuriko Kuga). See also, 'A First Few Steps: The Long Road to a Just Peace in the Democratic Republic of Congo', *supra* note 88, at 20 (suggesting that the definitions of crimes in the military penal code 'do not conform to international definitions and are, at best, ambiguous').
155. ASADHO Organization, Personal Interview, Kinshasa, DR Congo, 28 October 2003 (interview conducted by Adrian Alvarez and Yuriko Kuga).
156. 'A First Few Steps: The Long Road to a Just Peace in the Democratic Republic of Congo', *supra* note 88, at 21. This view was also expressed by the Congolese office of Avocates Sans Frontières. Personal Interview, Dominique Kamuandu and Theo Kasonga, Avocates Sans Frontières, Kinshasa, DR Congo, 28 October 2003 (interview conducted by Adrian Alvarez and Yuriko Kuga).
157. Dean of the Faculty of Law, University of Kinshasa, Personal Interview, Kinshasa, DR Congo, 28 October 2003. M. Mirindi, for example, completed an LL.M. at the Free University of Brussels.
158. 'A First Few Steps: The Long Road to a Just Peace in the Democratic Republic of Congo', *supra* note 88, at 21.

4 April 2003 ... excluding war crimes, genocide and crimes against humanity'.[159] As a national amnesty law has yet to be passed by the Assembly, the Presidential Amnesty Decree does not appear to bar prosecution of crimes within the jurisdiction of the ICC, though it might bar prosecution of lesser included offences by national courts. A ten-year statute of limitations for most serious crimes may further hinder the prosecution of lesser included offences in domestic law.[160]

At present, the ability of the Congolese government to undertake genuine prosecutions depends largely on whether judges are willing to directly apply international legal instruments in domestic law. To the degree that they are willing to set new precedent and do so, Congo may well have the necessary legal framework to act. Nonetheless, this framework would be infinitely strengthened by the passage of the implementing legislation for the Rome Statute which would provide sufficient authority and clarity for meaningful prosecutions by national judicial institutions.

5.4. Policing and investigation

The fourth relevant area of enquiry necessary to establish the ability of a state to undertake genuine prosecutions is the policing capacity of the national government. The language of the Rome Statute suggests the critical importance of policing when it calls on the ICC to evaluate, in the case of state collapse, the ability of the state 'to obtain the accused or the necessary evidence and testimony' in making admissibility determinations.[161] Effective police power and investigatory mechanisms are essential components to the apprehension of suspects and the collection of evidence. Commentators on the Statute note the importance of the state's ability to 'secure the accused' in determining admissibility.[162] While the police capacity of the state need not reach the levels of the most developed states, at a minimum it must be sufficient to allow the capture of suspects, the acquisition of relevant evidence, and the protection of victims and witnesses.[163]

To date there has not been a systematic study of the policing capacity of the new transitional government. However, a number of reports and recent events suggest the inadequacy of the police force at maintaining rudimentary order, much less collecting evidence or apprehending war criminals. In May 2002, for example, upwards of 100 Congolese police officers simply disappeared during a revolt in Kisangani.[164] Other reports suggest that a group of Congolese police officers in the Ituri region was ambushed by rebel forces and left naked and weaponless. One MONUC official in the eastern part of the country observes: 'Civilian police have no

---

159. Presidential Decree no. 03-001 of 15 April 2003, on amnesty for acts of war, political crimes and crimes of opinion, Art. 1.
160. Article 24 of the Congolese Criminal Code stipulates a ten-year statute of limitations for crimes punishable by a jail sentence of more than five years. See 'A First Few Steps: The Long Road to a Just Peace in the Democratic Republic of Congo', *supra* note 88, at 22.
161. 1998 Rome Statute of the International Criminal Court, at Art. 17(3).
162. Holmes, 'The Principle of Complementarity', *supra* note 1, at 49.
163. An important, but open, question is whether the presence of an international peacekeeping force in the national state – such as KFOR in Kosovo or MONUC in Congo – should be considered part of the national judicial capacity in these cases.
164. 'DR Congo Police Officers "Missing"' BBC News, 21 May 2002, available at http://news.bbc.co.uk/2/hi/africa/1999902.stm.

pay, authority, or training to conduct proper arrests. Their role is currently limited to directing traffic.'[165] Although MONUC has begun police training programmes and is presently training 250 new Congolese officers, MONUC officials have questioned the capability of the government to provide anything resembling adequate policing.[166] Arrests of two key rebel leaders in early 2005 suggest that the policing capabilities of Congo may be improving, but they remain woefully inadequate given the number of suspects at large.[167]

Moreover, the investigative powers of Congo are extremely limited. Police or investigative teams are often unable to reach or operate in remote areas where crimes have occurred. Even if they are able to do so, there are neither facilities for, nor expertise in, war crimes investigation, criminal forensics, or evidence collection.[168] Human Rights Watch notes that 'criminal cases are in general poorly handled'.[169] In most cases, both the state and the defence lack the resources to undertake meaningful investigations. Even when one side is able to do so, there are no procedures in place to ensure some semblance of equality of arms or disclosure to the opposing party.[170]

Beyond Congolese government police forces, MONUC does have its own policing capability on the ground in Congo. MONUC's Civilian Police Component (CIVPOL) was established by the Security Council in 2001 and expanded numerous times.[171] It is charged with, *inter alia*, providing assistance to the Congolese police, assisting with security arrangements, and training local police officers.[172] Yet CIVPOL consists of only 182 police officers from 18 countries[173] – hardly adequate for a country of 2.3 million square kilometres.[174] The CIVPOL presence equates to four officers responsible for a territory the size of the Netherlands. On the positive side, however, MONUC's CIVPOL capacity is backed up by military forces numbering a total of 8,700 that have been given the expanded authority to use force as necessary to secure the peace, thereby enhancing the policing ability of CIVPOL.[175] Yet these forces are still regularly attacked and have yet to create real peace or stability in the Ituri region of north-eastern Congo.[176]

---

165. Marie France, MONUC Kisangani Political Affairs Director, Personal Interview, 29 October 2003, Kisangani, DR Congo (interview conducted by Mariyan Zumbulev and Christopher Broughton).
166. Nishkala Suntharalingam, MONUC Political Officer, Personal Interview, Kinshasa, DR Congo, 26 October 2003.
167. See 'Another Key Ituri Leader Arrested', Integrated Regional Information Networks, 22 March 2005; 'Warlord Arrest for Killings', BBC News, 1 March 2005, available at http://news.bbc.co.uk/2/hi/africa/4308583.stm.
168. For a discussion of the standard contingent of a war crimes investigation team as early as the Second World War, see T. Borek, 'Legal Services During War', (1998) 120 *Mil. L. Rev.* 19, at n. 90.
169. Ibid., at IV(c).
170. See 'Democratic Republic of the Congo: Confronting Impunity', *supra* note 71, at IV(c).
171. See UNSCOR 1355 (2001).
172. See MONUC CIVPOL Mandate, available at http://www.monuc.org/Civpol/.
173. See MONUC CIVPOL Strength and Structure, available at http://www.monuc.org/Civpol/Strength.aspx.
174. *CIA World Fact Book, supra* note 128. That works out to approximately one police officer per 12,000 sq. km.
175. See UNSCOR 1493 (2003) (authorizing MONUC to 'take all necessary measures' to 'contribute to the security conditions').
176. See 'DRC: MONUC Investigators Attacked in Ituri', *The East African*, 5 February 2004, available at http://allafrica.com/stories/200402050162.html (reporting a 5 February attack by unidentified gunmen on UN investigators). Notably, even with its enhanced authority MONUC failed to repel a recent rebel advance on the city of Bukavu. See 'UN Troops Open Fire in Kinshasa', BBC News, 3 June 2004, available at http://news.bbc.co.uk/2/hi/africa/3773629.stm.

It seems fairly clear that the Congolese government presently lacks the ability to apprehend suspects and collect evidence in much of eastern Congo. Although, with MONUC support, Congo might arguably be deemed to meet a bare minimum of police capability to undertake genuine prosecutions, even this policing ability remains too weak to offer widespread accountability.

The proposed framework for evaluating the ability of a post-conflict judiciary to undertake genuine investigations and prosecutions suggests that Congo has experienced the very type of total or substantial collapse envisioned in the Rome Statute. Without adequately paid personnel, a minimal judicial infrastructure, sufficient legal authority or the ability to apprehend suspects, Congo is unable to investigate or prosecute. While Congo might come close to meeting some aspects of the test – for example legal authority or police capacity with the assistance of MONUC – taken as a whole, Congo is presently genuinely unable to investigate or prosecute international crimes.

Admittedly, many of these shortcomings can be rectified with sufficient attention from the national government, international financial assistance, and deeper co-operation with MONUC. If such efforts are undertaken, it seems quite possible that a small group of effective courts could be established in key areas. In cities such as Goma, Bukavu and Kisangani, sufficient funding, training, assistance and legal reform could allow the Congolese government to make a plausible case for the assertion of primacy over the ICC.

Recognition that the ICC is part of a system of multi-level global governance highlights the importance of more fully articulating the standards for genuine prosecutions by national governments. As states seek to meet the complementarity criteria, they will look to the Court for clarification on the specific requirements for an effective judiciary. As part of a global governance system, the ICC has an opportunity to offer invaluable guidance to national governments on where to channel available resources and attention to meet the test of effectiveness. Through an analysis of the Congolese judiciary, the preceding section has sought to begin this process by giving greater depth and substance to the criteria articulated in Article 17 of the Statute. The Office of the Prosecutor in its policy statements and the Pretrial Chamber in its early jurisprudence must further clarify the standards.

6. A DETERRENT EFFECT IN CONGO?

Conceiving of the ICC as part of a system of multi-level global governance further suggests that the Court will alter the incentives not just of government officials but also of the perpetrators or potential perpetrators of international crimes within its jurisdiction. The iterative interactions between the Court as a supranational governance organ and the state (or its citizens) should produce an observable effect on the behaviour of would-be criminals. The ICC and the larger project of international criminal accountability have been much lauded as a means of deterrence as well as retribution.[177] To date, however, there has been no systematic

---

177. See, e.g., Akhavan, *supra* note 42, at 7.

study of the deterrent effect of international justice and, despite the rise of international criminal law over the past decade, international crimes have continued.[178] The recent experience of Congo suggests – at least in a very preliminary and anecdotal way[179] – that the ICC may well be serving as a deterrent to further international crimes. This is not to claim that the investigation in Congo has brought about an end to international crimes in the region. Nonetheless, interviews with high-level suspects of crimes in Ituri do suggest that the ICC investigation is altering the thinking and possibly the behaviour of criminal actors.

Thomas Lubanga is one of the most notorious warlords of Eastern Congo.[180] He is President of the Congolese Patriotic Union,[181] a rebel group in the Bunia region, is reported to have upwards of 12,000 men in his private army,[182] and is suspected of systematic campaigns of cannibalism against civilians in the region. In late October 2003, approximately 45 days after the Prosecutor's announcement of his plans to investigate Ituri, an extensive interview with Lubanga indicated that he was aware of the ICC and concerned by the prospect of a possible indictment. Lubanga was subsequently arrested in March 2005 by government forces and awaits potential trial in Kinshasa.[183]

For the 2003 interview, Lubanga arrived at the Grand Hotel Kinshasa with his lawyer, a local Congolese-trained former judge. In the conversation, Lubanga argued that the ICC must stay out of Congo, as any prosecutions would break the fragile peace. But he went on to request a copy of the Rome Statute in French, observing that he had yet to see its specific provisions.[184] In consultation with his lawyer, he carefully analyzed both the jurisdiction of the Court and the legal requirements for crimes against humanity. Though protesting his own innocence and asserting that the ICC could have little effect on him or his organization, Lubanga noted the Court's potential power: 'the Court has been a pressure on the political actors who were killing people ... these people are very afraid today to commit such slaughter'.[185] He went on to note that with the Prosecutor's announcement, 'there is a palpable pressure not to do certain things' and 'those responsible are now very worried'.[186] Whether Lubanga was obliquely referencing his own behaviour or merely reporting his observations of the Court's effect in Ituri is unclear. However,

178. Congo provides an all-too graphic example of how these types of crime have continued even in the face of international criminal law.
179. The methodological problems with such a claim are myriad. First, only a very few interview subjects are available as many perpetrators are inaccessible or refuse to talk to outsiders. Moreover, interviewees have a strong incentive to alter their responses given the potential prosecutions that many ensue, despite the non-judicial nature of such interviews. Finally, the potential causal variables of a reduction in crime are numerous – economic improvement, a new peace process, better policing, lower crime reporting, etc. With the available data, it is impossible to isolate a causal variable or even provide statistically meaningful evidence as to whether the ICC has had a direct effect. It is nonetheless interesting and arguably useful to observe the correlation between decreasing crime rates and statements by perpetrators that the ICC has been causal of their behaviour change.
180. 'Democratic Republic of Congo', 2004 *Economist Intelligence Unit Report*, at 14.
181. For more information on the Congolese Patriotic Union (UPC) see the group's website: www.upc-rp.info.
182. See http://observer.guardian.co.uk/print/0,3858,4735034-110490,00.html, 17 August 2003. See also http://news.bbc.co.uk/1/hi/world/africa/3025031.stm, 12 May 2003.
183. 'Another Key Ituri Leader Arrested', Integrated Regional Information Networks, 22 March 2005.
184. Personal Interview, Thomas Lubanga, Kinshasa, DR Congo, 26 October 2003.
185. Thomas Lubanga, Personal Interview, Kinshasa, DR Congo, 26 October 2003.
186. Thomas Lubanga, Personal Interview, 26 October 2003, Kinshasa, DR Congo.

for one of the principle suspects of international crimes in the region to be actively interested in the text of the Rome Statute and to claim the Court was altering the behaviour of suspected criminals is, at the very least, noteworthy.

Lubanga was not alone among Congolese warlords to recognize the ICC's possible deterrent effect. Similarly, Xavier Ciribanya, governor of Congo's South Kivu Province until 2004, indicated the ICC was having an effect on the behaviour of criminal actors in the region. Ciribanya is a noted former rebel leader of the RCD-Goma,[187] suspected of a range of crimes against civilians in both the Kivus and Ituri. He has also been sentenced to death in absentia by a court in Kinshasa for his alleged role in the assassination of former President Laurent Kabila.[188] In February 2004, the government in Kinshasa suspended Ciribanya from his post as governor, after his bodyguards clashed with government troops in Bukavu following the discovery of a large arms cache at one of his residences.[189]

Like Lubanga, Ciribanya was well aware of the ICC and noted that the Court could prosecute new crimes committed in Ituri. According to Ciribanya, 'many here in the East are afraid the Court will come. I hear they will go to Bunia [Ituri] first'.[190] Moreover, Ciribanya noted a possible deterrent effect: 'We all now are thinking twice. We do not know what this Court can and will do'.[191] That said, he remained sceptical of the ICC's enforcement powers: 'We do not know if this Court will be stronger than [the government in] Kinshasa. But there are many here who still have weapons'.[192] His veiled threat to the Court seems particularly apt in light of the recent firefight between Ciribanya's bodyguards and government troops.[193]

Congolese government and civil society leaders as well as MONUC officials likewise suggested the deterrent force of the ICC may already be felt. The Congolese Advocate General, Victor Yenyi Olungu, noted that the ICC 'is for everyone', suggesting that all those involved in international crimes have something to fear.[194] Marie-Madeleine Kalala, the Congolese Human Rights Minister, observed in January 2004 that the ICC 'has had a pronounced deterrent effect on armed groups in the strife-torn northeast'.[195] Raphael Wakenge, the Director of the Congolese Initiative for Justice and Peace in Bukavu claimed that individuals possibly as high up as Vice President Bemba are now asking 'maybe me too'.[196] Roberto Ricci of MONUC's

---

187. See Daily Press Briefing by the Office of the Spokesman for the Secretary General, 10 February 2003, available at http://www.un.org/News/briefings/docs/2004/db021004.doc.htm.
188. For a discussion of this death sentence, see *Democratic Republic of Congo News*: 28 February 2003, available at http://www.genocidewathc.org/congofebruary282003.htm.
189. See T. Tshibangu, 'Monitoring DRC', MONUC Briefing, 9 February 2004, available at http://www.monuc.org/News.aspx?newsID=1880; see also 'Xavier Chiribanya ou le sommet visible de l'iceberg, nkoko-mboka.com – hebo', 10 February 2004, available at http://www.nkolo-mboaka.com/Xavier-CHIRIBANYA-02.html. This was the same residence a which the interview was conducted.
190. Xavier Ciribanya, Personal Interview, Bukavu, DR Congo, 30 October 2003.
191. Ibid.
192. Ibid.
193. See Tshibangu, *supra* note 189.
194. Victor Yenyi Olungu, Premier Avocat Général de la République, Personal Interview, Kinshasa DR Congo, 30 October 2003 (interview conducted by Yuriko Kuga, Adrian Alvarez and Leslie Medema).
195. A. Deutch, 'Congolese Human Rights Minister: New Criminal Court Deters Tribal Warfare', The Associated Press, 22 January 2004, available at http://www.ictj.org/news.asp.
196. Raphael Wakenge, Initiative Congolaise du Justice et Paix, Personal Interview, Bukavu, DR Congo, 30 October 2003.

human rights division noted that the significant attention being paid to the ICC was having a deterrent effect in Ituri.[197] Moreover, the Court is empowering MONUC in its dealings with rebel groups by providing a new threat to use in negotiations. William Swing, the Special Representative of the Secretary General in Congo and the head of MONUC, observes: 'I certainly use it [the ICC] as a threat each time I speak to suspected war criminals. I tell them that they will be brought to justice.'[198] It seems the rebels may, in fact, be listening.

Since the establishment of the ICC, many rebel leaders have left the field and joined the peace process in Kinshasa, Congo's capital. Though crime statistics are imperfect and often unavailable, anecdotal evidence suggests that violence in the Ituri province has decreased since 2003. Admittedly, crimes have not ceased altogether and war criminals still live in impunity. But a sense of change is afoot. It may never be possible to show a causal relationship between the Court and decreased violence, but the comments of Lubanga, Ciribanya and others suggest the ICC may be playing an important part in this process.

Again, if the Court views itself as part of a system of multi-level global governance and recognizes that its interactions with domestic governance layers can alter the incentives of national actors and even potential criminals, there is much more it could do to enhance its deterrent effect beyond just prosecutions. Iterative interactions between the Court and potential criminals may well alter the preferences, actions and policies of the likes of Lubanga and Ciribanya.[199] Specifically, this vision of the Court suggests a need for greater emphasis on outreach programmes and the provision of information about the ICC in target regions.

7. CONCLUSION

This article has sought to provide an alternate means of conceptualizing the role of the ICC as part of a system of multi-level global governance. In this model, international institutions interact with and respond to governance structures at the national level, altering preferences, catalyzing domestic activity, guiding reform efforts, and possibly even deterring acts by potential individual criminals. As part of a global governance system, the ICC is not merely a significant new international mechanism for accountability. Nor are the complementarity provisions of the Rome Statute merely means for determining when cases will be admissible before the Court. Rather, the ICC and the complementarity regime are embedded in a system of interactions with national institutions that have the potential to collectively

---

197. Roberto Ricci, MONUC, Personal Interview, Kinshasa, DR Congo, 28 October 2003 (interview conducted by Adrian Alvarez, Yuriko Kuga and Leslie Medema). Notably, not all MONUC officials interviewed agreed with this position. Some suggested that 'many warlords don't know about [the ICC] yet. Only folks in Bunia do'. Personal Interview, Bukavu, DR Congo, 29 October 2003.

198. William Lacy Swing, Special Representative of the Secretary General, Personal Interview, Kinshasa, DR Congo, 31 October 2003 (interview conducted by Yuriko Kuga, Leslie Medema and Adrian Alvarez)

199. This process involves both changes to rational interest calculation and identity perceptions. For a discussion of the latter in the context of the transnational legal process, see H. Koh, 'Transnational Legal Process', (1996) 75 *Nebraska Law Rev.* 181.

enhance the prospects for accountability and good governance at the national as well as supranational levels.

Through an analysis of the role of the ICC in the Congo, the article has identified four key areas of interaction where the ICC is already having or can easily have a pronounced effect beyond serving as a direct mechanism of prosecution: altering the preferences and policies of the national government catalyzing reform efforts; offering benchmarks for judicial effectiveness; and providing a deterrent from future crimes. From a theoretical standpoint, these or similar forms of interaction are likely to be present in the ICC's relationship with other states in the future, particularly those states recovering from a total or substantial collapse of domestic institutions. While the specific factors at play may vary from country to country, the global governance model indicates a far larger role and broader effect for the ICC and complementarity than previously envisioned.

As applied to the Congo, this alternative model helps answer a number of key questions. The Court's ability to alter the incentives of domestic actors helps explain President Kabila's decision to self-refer the situation in Congo. The complementarity provisions of the Rome Statute have provided incentives for Bemba, Ruberwa and others to strengthen the national judiciary should it become necessary to assert primacy over the ICC. Likewise, the criteria for admissibility of cases before the ICC may be serving as a benchmark for national judicial reform efforts, offering the Court significant leverage in guiding such reforms. Finally, the interactions of the ICC and the Rome Statute with potential perpetrators of international crimes may offer the first causal links between the ICC and deterrence.

If the ICC is to fulfil its mission in the broadest sense – 'to put an end to impunity'[200] – the Court and its senior personnel must recognize its larger place in a system of global governance. In so doing, the Office of the Prosecutor ought to be aware of the effects and incentives it creates for national governments. Where these incentives can benefit the larger mission of accountability, the Court should take full advantage of them. Where, however, national governments which themselves have unclean hands seek to use the Court as a political tool, caution must be exercised. Similarly, the ICC has an opportunity to use its position of leverage to enhance judicial reform efforts through a clearer set of principles for effective prosecutions and to promote deterrence through better outreach and information in target states. The fact that the ICC is embedded in a system of global governance gives the Court far-reaching powers to alter outcomes at the national level, leverage it has yet to fully recognize and use. The Congo situation offers the ICC an opportunity both to learn how it can be used by a national government and, in turn, to provide incentives and guidance to that government to further the quest for domestic and international accountability.

---

200. 1998 Rome Statute of the International Criminal Court, at Preamble.

[9]

Reconciliation and Revenge in Post-Apartheid South Africa

Rethinking Legal Pluralism and Human Rights[1]

by Richard A. Wilson

Human rights are a central element in the new governmental project in the new South Africa, and this article traces some of the specific forms of connection and disconnection between notions of justice found in townships of the Vaal and rights discourses as articulated by the Truth and Reconciliation Commission. The introduction of human rights in post-apartheid South Africa has had varied social effects. Religious values and human rights discourse have converged on the notion of reconciliation on the basis of shared value orientations and institutional structures. There are clear divergences, however, between human rights ideas and the notions of justice expressed in local *lekgotla*, or township courts, which emphasize punishment and retribution. The article concludes that the plurality of legal orders in South Africa results not from systemic relations between law and society but from multiple forms of social action seeking to alter the direction of social change in the area of justice within the context of the nation-building project of the post-apartheid state.

RICHARD A. WILSON is Senior Lecturer in Social Anthropology at the University of Sussex (Falmer, Brighton BN1 6SJ, U.K. [R.Wilson@sussex.ac.uk]). Born in 1964, he was educated at the London School of Economics and Political Science (B.Sc., 1986; Ph.D., 1990). He has been Lecturer in Latin American Studies at the University of Essex (1990–94) and Visiting Associate in the Department of Social Anthropology at the University of the Witwatersrand (1995–97) and has done fieldwork in Guatemala and in South Africa. He is the author of *Maya Resurgence in Guatemala: Q'eqchi' Experiences* (Norman: University of Oklahoma Press, 1995) and the editor of *Human Rights, Culture, and Context: Anthropological Perspectives* (London and Chicago: Pluto Press, 1997) and (with B. Gills and J. Rocamora) *Low-Intensity Democracy* (London and Chicago: Pluto Press, 1993). The present paper was submitted 16 XII 98 and accepted 11 V 99.

1. This research was funded by the Economic and Social Research Council (U.K.), Ref. R000222777. Versions of this paper were given during 1998–99 at the London School of Economics, the University of the Witwatersrand in Johannesburg, the School of Oriental and African Studies, and Queen's University, Belfast. I thank the participants in those seminars for their valuable comments. I also benefited from discussions with Jocelyn Alexander, Marie-Bénédicte Dembour, Saul Dubow, Sakkie Niehaus, and Fiona Ross. All errors are my own responsibility.

In a street-theatre performance sponsored by the South African Council of Churches, a black minister presents a white Afrikaans-speaking policeman to his congregation. The policeman confesses to the daughter and widow of a dead African man that he was present at the torturing and murder. The policeman says, "I'm sorry. I was afraid. I would like to seek to reconcile with you." The women react angrily, and the mother shouts, "You are a bastard, and you deserve to die." The minister puts himself between the two parties and protects the policeman. An old man, also a relative of the deceased, enters and quotes Genesis. He says that he forgives the policeman. "I forgive, but I won't forget. I want to build a new South Africa." The pastor extols his virtue, saying, "You have set an example for the others." He sends the two women to a trauma counselor.

Duma Khumalo had been sentenced to death with five others in 1986 for the murder of a local Vaal councilor that he claimed he had not committed. The "Sharpeville Six" became a cause célèbre, a case which was taken to the United Nations and became an international symbol of the lack of justice for blacks under apartheid. When Duma was released in 1993 after seven years on death row, he demanded a retrial but was ignored. He staged a sit-in at the Sharpeville police station for 27 days in November 1995. In December the police took him to meet with the chief prosecutor and white magistrate in Vereeniging, who said that he had no case because there was no new evidence. On January 5, 1996, Duma hid an axe in his coat, entered the Vereeniging court while it was in session, and went berserk. The prosecutor cowered under his desk and shrieked, "Don't kill me!" As others fled screaming, Duma, an imposing figure at over 6 feet tall and weighing over 200 pounds, swung the axe at desks, chairs, furniture, and the court's public-address system. He attacked no one, and when armed police arrived he put his axe down calmly and put his hands in the air. In minutes he had created pandemonium, wreaked $15,000 worth of damage, and hewn a large pile of expensive teak firewood. Interviewed in late 1996, he said, "I just wanted justice."[2]

South Africa's first post-apartheid government, led by the African National Congress (ANC), has embarked

2. The first of these vignettes comes from a performance at Johannesburg's Central Methodist Church during a meeting of the Khulumani Support Group (a victims' organization) on September 21, 1996. The second is based upon my own interviews in 1996–97 with Duma Khumalo, Father Patrick Noonan, and members of the Vaal Legal Aid Centre, who provided Khumalo's legal defense. Khumalo later testified at the Human Rights Violations hearings in the Vaal and became a fieldworker for the Khulumani Support Group.

76 | CURRENT ANTHROPOLOGY *Volume 41, Number 1, February 2000*

upon a nation-building project consciously predicated upon the creation of a "culture of human rights." This has involved a number of classic liberal institutional reforms such as the incorporation of international human rights law into the Bill of Rights of the 1996 Constitution and the setting up of an array of new bodies such as the Human Rights Commission and the Truth and Reconciliation Commission (TRC). This article evaluates the manifold consequences of state formulations of human rights in African townships by looking at local responses to the view of reconciliation commonly espoused during TRC Human Rights Violations hearings.[3] It attempts to answer questions such as How does transnational human rights talk relate to everyday moralities and normative understandings of justice? Do human rights concepts have any purchase in areas affected by political violence, and, if so, then how and why?

Over the past 15 years, there has been a lively dialogue between anthropologists and colonial historians regarding the relationship between state law and informal moralities and mechanisms of adjudication which are sometimes referred to as "customary law." A key and contested notion in this debate has been "legal pluralism," a descriptive term and analytical concept which attempts to address the existence of more than one legal system in a single political unit. In general, anthropologists have found the term useful, whereas historians of colonialism have objected to it. This article asks whether the idea of legal pluralism is valuable for thinking about legal consciousness in the unique historical phase of the dismantling of apartheid, an institutionalized regime of racial segregation and dominance.

Legal pluralism originated in antipositivist legal philosophy in the early 20th century as a reaction to an exclusionary state centralism which regarded only state law as law (see Santos 1995, Teubner 1997). In reality, argued pluralists, state law was far from absolute and in many contexts was not particularly central to the normative ordering of society. Against legal monism, Malinowski (1926) asserted that social norms in non-state societies perform the same regulatory functions as legal norms, thus raising uncodified social rules to the status of law. The insight that law does not have absolute privilege in dealing with conflict was an important one (see

Strathern 1985 and Vincent 1990), even though it came with normative functionalist assumptions about organic stability and stasis.

Legal pluralists such as Jane Collier (1975) and Sally Engle Merry (1988) reinforced Malinowski's stance by conceptualizing legal and social norms as equivalent and mutually constitutive. Judicial rules and extra-state norms (e.g., found in customary or community courts) are both "law" in that both are codes of social thought expressing moralities and social identities.[4] The legal and the nonlegal relate to each other as competing normative discourses, and there is no inherent *categorical* hierarchy between them (although the state usually enjoys an institutionalized dominance over private moralities).[5]

However, the emphasis on the importance and autonomy of social norms rather than positivized rules often entailed a neglect of the colonial state in the writings of midcentury legal anthropologists of Africa such as Schapera (1938). Legal anthropology in the colonial context often characterized state law and informal law as coexisting but unconnected spheres of authority and adjudication which employed different procedures embedded in distinct moralities. Discussions of the relationship between state and informal law often portrayed the two systems as static and isolated, thus fueling parallel debates about universalism and cultural relativism in the area of human rights.

In South African legal anthropology, an isolationist perspective is adopted in Comaroff and Roberts's (1982) influential book *Rules and Processes*. This characterized Tswana law as a forum for individual negotiation separate from the interventions of colonial and postcolonial legal regimes. Although the authors have moved on to look in greater depth at the place of customary law within colonial policy (Roberts 1991), others have maintained a view of it as fundamentally controlled at the level of local communities and culture rather than by colonial and postcolonial states. Gulbrandsen (1996:125), for one, argues that the colonial encounter did not erode the local political-juridical bodies of the Northern Tswana of the Bechuanaland Protectorate (now Botswana), which were able to safeguard a "genuinely Tswana normative repertoire." The stress in Gulbrandsen's study is upon the preservation of "cultural integrity" and the "autonomy of Tswana jurisprudence" (p. 128) according to culturally specific ideas about gender, hierarchy, and space, to the detriment of a thoroughgoing

---

3. My 12 months' research in South Africa took place over a four-year period; in 1995, before the TRC began functioning, in 1996–97, while it was in full swing, and in late 1998 after the main regional offices had been closed. I attended three weeks of Human Rights Violations hearings in Klerksdorp, Tembisa, and Kagiso and three weeks of amnesty hearings for Northern Province security policemen in Johannesburg. I interviewed nearly half of the TRC commissioners and many staff workers, such as lawyers, researchers, and investigators in the Johannesburg office. Much of my research took place outside of the TRC process and in the Vaal, where I made regular trips from my base in Johannesburg. In the Vaal I engaged in in-depth interviews over a four-year period with dozens of members of the Khulumani Support Group, as well as local ministers, political leaders, legal personnel, and former policemen. Few "perpetrators" were open about their involvement in acts of violence, but I did interview three Inkatha Freedom Party (IFP) members who had been convicted in the courts for their participation in the 1992 Boipatong massacre.

4. See Guillet (1998) for a thorough discussion of new developments in legal pluralism in relation to law-and-economics studies.

5. More recently, this approach has found favor within postmodernist jurisprudence, which challenges legal positivist claims of doctrinal unity. For the Derridean legal scholar Davies (1996:7) "law" is not to be confined to positive law. Echoing the distant anthropological voices of Llewellen and Hoebel (1941) in *The Cheyenne Way*, she writes that "law is everywhere—in our metaphysics, our social environment, our ways of perceiving the world, the structure of our psyche, language, the descriptive regularities of science, and so on." Legal pluralism and postmodernist legal theory converge primarily upon the (problematic) Geertzian premise that "law is culture" (Geertz 1983).

analysis of the transformation of customary law by successive states.

The anthropological consensus on legal pluralism was directly challenged in the mid-1980s by legal centralist critiques to the effect that collapsing legal and social norms into the same category mistakenly turns all social norms and values into "law." This move makes defining law problematic in that every norm is defined as "legal." Legal pluralism, it is argued by legal theorists such as Brian Tamanaha (1993), loses sight of how the rules of state law are created by specialists within state institutional structures and backed by a monopoly on means of physical coercion. Legal rules and social norms are constructed through quite different processes: positivized, written legal rules are generated by specialists within rationalized bureaucratic structures. Moreover, Tamanaha correctly points out that legal anthropologists never formulated a cross-cultural definition of law that did not somehow rely upon the state (see also Dembour 1990).

The primacy that anthropologists give to Africans' juridical autonomy has recently been subjected to a critique by colonial historians, who generally take the view that customary law was utterly transformed by, controlled, and integrated within the administrative apparatus of the colonial state (see Mann and Roberts 1991: 9; Chanock 1985; Klug 1995). Instead of legal pluralism in Africa, there was only "a single, interactive colonial legal system" (Mann and Roberts 1991:9). The most influential and consistent advocate of the centralist approach to African legal history has been Martin Chanock (1985, 1991a), whose work focuses primarily on the place of the legal regime in the policies of colonial states. He asserts that legal ideology has been a central part of the domination of society by the state. In his materialist reading, colonial and customary law were welded into a single instrument of dispossession and were part of a wider administrative policy of creating and maintaining a particular type of peasantry (Chanock 1991a:71). Rather than being the product of immutable tradition, "custom" was manufactured as a legitimating device for maintaining the status quo after dispossession by reinforcing the position of the chieftaincy. Pluralism is but a legal fiction, a part of the ideology of British indirect rule in African and Indian colonial territories. According to Chanock (1991a:81), "An indigenous system of land tenure did not exist under colonial conditions, but its shadow was summoned into existence by both colonial and postcolonial states, essentially to retard the establishment of freehold rights for Africans."

In evaluating this debate, my sympathies are broadly with the legal pluralists, since the above centralist critiques have not fully taken into account more recent studies which conceptualize the relationship between state and non-state legalities in increasingly sophisticated ways. We are not forced to choose between the insights of legal pluralists and those of legal centralists, who have been moving closer to each other's position in recent years to look at the interplay between state law and local ideas and institutions of justice. Because of the

way the question is formulated (What is the relationship between law and society?), neither tradition is wholly indispensable. Legal pluralism provides an important descriptive model of society as made up of a diversity of modes of conflict resolution, shattering the myth of state law's unchallenged empire.[6] At the same time, the centralist argument has identified a logical contradiction: when the domains of the legal and nonlegal are fused,[7] the category of "law" becomes meaningless, as it includes everything from table manners to national constitutions and transnational covenants of rights. Further, centralists remind us of the Weberian maxim that law is a semiautonomous discourse created by bureaucratic officials for the purposes of legal domination. Law's norms are positivized ones, often far removed from though not wholly unrelated to the lived norms of existential experience.

It is possible to take a more synthetic view of the creative tension between anthropologists and colonial historians and build up a version of legal pluralism that is useful for thinking about the interactions between state officials advocating new human rights ideas and practices and local moralities and legal institutions in African communities. There has been excellent work by social historians on the interactions between Africans and European colonial administrators, each pursuing their own interests, with the result being a "complex patchwork of overlapping legal jurisdictions" (Mann and Roberts 1991:16).[8] The work of Sally Falk Moore (1978, 1986) provides a useful starting point, as she has maintained a legal pluralist perspective while keeping the state firmly within the scope of the analysis. In Moore's view, "customary law" is the product of historical competition between local African power holders and central colonial rulers, all trying to maintain and expand their domains of control and regulation. Law is imposed upon semiautonomous social fields with uneven and indeterminate consequences. We must not overestimate the power of law, as the connection between native courts on Kilimanjaro and the British colonial high court was "nominal rather than operational" (1986:150). Moore takes us away from a static view of plural legal systems to look at the historical transformations of regulatory practices, and her work oscillates between small-scale events (individual court cases) and large-scale social processes (colonialism, decolonization, etc.). Moore largely accepts Chanock's portrayal of the profound transformation of customary law by colonial rule, yet her more interactionist focus upon the Habermasian "life world" and more specifically upon the kinship basis of Chagga society means that she allows more room for local strategizing in pursuit of greater political autonomy. She

6. This can also be done within a state-discourse-centered approach such as that of Fitzpatrick (1987), who analyzes how law operates without having to adopt an approach outside of state law. I thank Marie-Bénédicte Dembour for this observation.

7. As they are in Foucault's writings and those of postmodern legal theorists such as Davies (1996) and Santos (1995).

8. See also Charles van Onselen's work (1982) on vigilantes on the Witwatersrand at the turn of the 20th century.

78 | CURRENT ANTHROPOLOGY *Volume 41, Number 1, February 2000*

concludes in one essay (1991:125) that "local law cases reflect the local history of African peoples rather than the history of the Europeans who ruled them."

Yet there is still some work to do on the notion of legal pluralism in order to replace the stark dualism of pluralism versus centralism by a redefinition of the subject matter. Instead of adopting oversystematizing theories which construct the "legal" and the "societal" as two total and coherent cultural systems with distinct logics (see Santos 1995:116), we must analyze how adjudicative contexts are transformed over time by the social actions of individuals and collectivities within a wider context of state regulation and discipline. In any locale there are a variety of institutions and competing value orientations which have emerged via a long process of piecemeal aggregation, rupture, and upheaval and continue to be transformed by social action.

In a revised view of legal pluralism, the question to be answered is how social actors (encompassing both individuals and collectivities) have contested the direction of social change in the area of justice and what the effects of this are for state formation and the legitimation of new forms of authority. This is a legal pluralism of action, movement, and interaction between legal orders in the context of state hegemonic projects. In post-apartheid South Africa this involves looking at how state officials, township courts, and Anglican ministers combine transnational human rights talk, religious notions of redemption and reconciliation, and popular ideas of punishment and revenge in an effort to control "historicity" (i.e., the direction of social change, in the formulation of Alain Touraine [1971; 1995:219, 368]).[9] The struggle over historicity in post-apartheid South Africa presents itself as a struggle over how to deal with the political crimes of the apartheid past—to construct discontinuities with the past and in so doing to reconfigure legal authority in the present. The plurality of legal orders therefore exists within a context of remarkably rapid movement in the production of norms and values.

Legal institutions, be they local township fora, magistrates' courts, or human rights commissions, are simultaneously subjected to *centralizing* and *pluralizing* discourses and strategies. At different historical moments, one set of strategies may exercise dominance over another and become hegemonic. In the mid-1980s, as the internal anti-apartheid movement led by the United Democratic Front reached its crescendo and "popular courts" punitively enforced counterhegemonic values and political strategies, the dominant tendencies in the area of justice were fragmenting, decentering, and pluralizing (see Lodge and Nasson 1992). Since the post-apartheid elections of 1994, the main direction of legal change has been towards greater centralization as state officials attempt to restore the legitimacy of state legal

institutions. Government officials such as Minister of Justice "Dullah" Omar have sought to integrate certain non-state structures (armed units of the liberation movements and the Inkatha Freedom Party [IFP]) into the police service and exclude others such as township courts. Part of my general thesis about the South African Truth and Reconciliation Commission (TRC) is that it represents one effort on the part of the new regime to reformulate "justice" and establish a unified and uncontested administrative authority. This is a common strategy of regimes emerging from authoritarianism, which seek to unify a fragmented legal structure inherited from the ancien régime. The notion of "reconciliation" found in human rights talk is the discursive linchpin in the centralizing project of post-apartheid justice. The idea of human rights performs a vital hegemonic role in the democratizing societies of Africa and Latin America, one which compels social conformity, guiding the population away from punitive retribution by characterizing it as illegitimate mob justice.[10]

The new values of a human rights culture are formulated primarily by intellectuals and lawyers representing a new political elite which has sought to superimpose them upon a number of semiautonomous social fields. These values engender new discursive and institutional sites of struggle, and their impact is uneven and emergent, raising questions for research such as Has the centralizing project as pursued through the TRC altered the terms of the debate on post-apartheid justice, and, if so, how? How can we more precisely conceptualize the specific continuities and discontinuities between normative codes? In what areas of social life are human rights ideas and practices resisted, when are they appropriated, and when are they simply ignored (for earlier discussions see Wilson 1997a, c)?

In post-apartheid South Africa there are various competing discourses and systems of values around justice and reconciliation. Christian discourses on forgiveness advocated by TRC officials often swayed individuals at hearings, but they clashed with the retributive notions of justice which are routinely applied in local township and chiefs' courts. In thinking about how to understand the complex negotiations around the TRC's redemptive concept of reconciliation, I eschew categories of "law" and "society" in order to examine two forms of connection and disconnection between the TRC and its urban African constituency: (1) *adductive affinities*, the close associations between the TRC's understanding of reconciliation as forgiveness and the religious values of victims and local churches, and (2) *relational discontinuities*, the divergence of human rights ideas from local court formulations of justice, which emphasize vengeance and punishment. If reconciliation is the key category of the new state's centralizing project, then vengeance is the main concept around which pluralizing notions of justice coalesce.

These two categories are not static and mutually ex-

---

9. Touraine, it must be acknowledged, defines "historicity" in different ways—as the direction of social change and as a cultural model of knowledge production. I am using it in the former sense, which portrays social life as a set of relations between the social actors of change (Touraine 1995:219).

10. On the limitations of human rights in Latin American democratization processes, see Panizza (1995).

clusive, and writers such as Minow (1998) and Jacoby (1983) have asserted that retribution need not entail vengeance and that vengeance and forgiveness can converge.[11] In the South African instance, these categories of justice are reformulated with respect to one another by different social actors. Paying attention to the unintended consequences of moral categories alerts us to the slippage between reconciliation and vengeance. Ironically, the threat of punishment through local institutions can facilitate the results which human rights commissions seek, namely, coexistence of former pariahs and their neighbors in the townships.

The Truth and Reconciliation Commission

Along with the Guatemalan Historical Clarification Commission, the South African Truth and Reconciliation Commission (1996–98) is the latest of more than 15 truth commissions in the world during the past two decades. Truth commissions, set up to investigate certain aspects of human rights violations under authoritarian rule, have become standard institutions in democratizing countries (see, e.g., Ensalaco 1994, Hayner 1994, Huyse 1995). It is argued that they will revitalize citizens' respect for the rule of law and promote a new culture of human rights.

In South Africa, the 1994 Promotion of National Unity and Reconciliation Act mandated the TRC to investigate "gross violations of human rights," defined as "the killing, abduction, torture or severe ill treatment of any person" between March 1, 1960 (the Sharpeville massacre), and December 5, 1993 (see Krog 1998; Sarkin 1998; Wilson 1996, 1997b).[12] The terms of reference allowed the possibility of including high-ranking intellectual authors of atrocities, as they referred to "any attempt, conspiracy, incitement, instigation, command or procurement to commit an act." This was the widest mandate of any truth commission to date, but it did not include the banality and technicality of apartheid segregation policies. Detentions without trial, forced removals, and "Bantu" education policy, all legal under apartheid, were not included under the terms of the Act,[13] although they were seen by many as human rights violations. The work of the TRC was divided into three committees: the Human Rights Violations Committee, the Reparations and Rehabilitation Committee, and the Amnesty Committee.

Throughout 1996 and 1997, the Human Rights Violations Committee held 80 hearings in town halls, hospitals, and churches all around the country to which thousands of ordinary citizens came and testified about past abuses. This process received wide national media coverage and brought ordinary, mostly black, experiences of the apartheid system into the national public space

11. For an examination of the place in punishment in legal and political philosophy, see Pauley (1994).
12. This cutoff date was later shifted to May 10, 1994, because of pressure from the far-right Freedom Front.
13. Unless, in extreme cases, the commissioners decided to include specific cases under the rubric of "severe ill treatment."

in a powerful way. The South African TRC took more statements than any previous truth commission in history (over 21,000), and the Human Rights Violations Committee faced the daunting task of checking the veracity of each account, choosing which would be retold at public hearings, and passing along verified cases to the Reparations and Rehabilitation Committee. The TRC also took on a limited investigative role, and by issuing subpoenas and taking evidence *in camera* it constructed a fragmented picture of the past. In its final report, published in October 1998, it produced findings on the majority of the 21,298 cases brought before it and named 400 perpetrators of violations. The "truth" of the TRC lay mostly in its officially confirming and bringing into the public space what was already known.

The efforts of the Reparations and Rehabilitation Committee to facilitate reconciliation represented the weakest of the three committees' activities. Part of the problem lay in the fact that the TRC had no money to disburse to survivors; it could only make nonbinding recommendations to the President's Fund. The TRC made it abundantly clear that victims should expect little from the process and only a fraction of what they might have expected had they prosecuted for damages through the courts. In the end, it recommended that those designated "victims" should receive approximately US$3,500 per year over a six-year period. It remains to be seen whether the reparations process, a key element of reconciliation, will even begin to address the needs and expectations of survivors.

Finally, the TRC was unique in incorporating an amnesty process, which elsewhere had always been a separate judicial mechanism. The final deadline for amnesty applications was September 30, 1997, and the TRC was overwhelmed with over 7,000 applications. To receive amnesty the applicant had to fulfil a number of legal criteria, including convincing the panel that the crime was political, not committed for personal gain, malice, or spite. Crucially, the applicant had to disclose all that was known about the crime and its political context, including the chain of command which authored the act. If amnesty was refused or if it was later found that not all material evidence had been fully disclosed, the applicant could be prosecuted.

In amnesty hearings, former members of the security police divulged information never made public before, such as the existence of a covert body called Trewits which drew up lists of activists to be "eliminated" (killed). Amnesty applicants also confirmed much of what was suspected, for instance, that in 1989 President P. W. Botha had ordered the bombing of Khotso House, the national office of the South African Council of Churches. The amnesty hearings were a theatricalization of the power of the new state, which compelled key actors in the previous political conflict to confess when they would rather have maintained their silence. Perpetrators were compelled to speak the new language of human rights and in so doing to recognize the new government's power to admonish and to punish.

This theatricalization of power is a clue to why de-

80 | CURRENT ANTHROPOLOGY *Volume 41, Number 1, February 2000*

mocratizing governments set up truth commissions rather than relying upon the existing legal system: truth commissions are transient politico-religious-legal institutions which have much greater symbolic potential than dry, rule-bound, technically obsessive courts of law. The TRC's legal status was ambiguous: on the one hand, it was not a court of law which could prosecute or sentence, but on the other it was administered by the Ministry of Justice and had powers of subpoena, seizure, and the granting of legal indemnity from prosecution. The South African truth commission inhabited a liminal space between state institutions, and this liminality granted it a certain freedom from both the strictures of legal discourse and the institutional legacy of apartheid. National legal discourse did not contain the language with which to undertake its own rehabilitation, and the liminality of the TRC allowed it to plagiarize from a religious idiom. The TRC's position as a quasi-judicial institution allowed it to mix genres—of law, politics, and religion—in particularly rich ways, and this makes it an interesting case study for understanding how human rights ideas interact with wider moral and ethical discourses.

Reconciling Races?

The dominant view on reconciliation in the TRC was created through an amalgam of transnational human rights values and a Christian ethic of forgiveness and redemption. It was propagated through dozens of Human Rights Violations (HRV) hearings in which selected victims spoke of the violations which they or relatives had suffered. In the HRV hearings, commissioners would lay a redemptive template across testimonies as they responded to victims' stories, which conjoined individual suffering and a narrative of nation building. Commissioners' responses were formulaic and predictable, regularly containing the following stages: a recognition of suffering, the moral equalizing of suffering, the portrayal of suffering as a necessary sacrifice for the liberation of the nation, and finally the forsaking of revenge by victims. There was a progressive movement built into these stages, from individual testimony towards the collectivity and the nation and finally back to the individual, all in order to facilitate forgiveness and reconciliation.

RECOGNIZING AND COLLECTIVIZING SUFFERING

The first stage involved expressing an appreciation of the evidence and sympathy for the witness. The individual circumstances were given recognition and value. From the idiosyncratic individual circumstances, commissioners quickly moved to the universal aspects of suffering under apartheid. When Peter Moletsane (Klerksdorp, Monday, September 23, 1996), recounted how he was tortured in police custody in 1986 after he had protested the killing of his uncle, TRC Chairperson Desmond Tutu replied, "Your pain is our pain. We were tortured, we were harassed, we suffered, we were oppressed." Tutu

was not claiming that he had been actually tortured like Moletsane. Instead, he was constructing a new political identity, that of "national victim," a new South African self which included all the dimensions of suffering and oppression. Thus, individual suffering, which ultimately is always unique, was brought into a public space where it could be collectivized and shared by all and merged into a wider narrative of national redemption. At ritualized HRV hearings, suffering was lifted out of the mundane world of individuals and their profane everyday pain and made sacred in order to construct a new national collective conscience (Buzzoli 1998; see also, on the self and suffering, Das 1987, 1994; Hamber and Wilson 1999; Scarry 1985; and Kleinman, Das, and Lock 1996).

THE MORAL EQUALIZING OF SUFFERING

In the HRV hearings, commissioners repeatedly asserted that all pain was equal, regardless of class or racial categorization or religious or political affiliation. Whites, blacks, ANC comrades, IFP members, and others all felt the same pain. No moral distinction was drawn on the basis of what actions a person was engaged in at the time. Whether they were informing to the police or placing explosives for the Azanian People's Liberation Army (APLA), the fact that they suffered was enough. For instance, Susan van der Merwe (Klerksdorp, September 23, 1996) told of how her husband, a white Afrikaner farmer, had been killed by MK (umKhonto we Sizwe, the armed wing of the ANC) guerrillas whom he had picked up hitchhiking along the border with Botswana. His vehicle had been found, but his body remained missing, hidden somewhere in the scrub brush of the desert. Archbishop Tutu responded to the story by saying, "I hope that you feel that people in the audience sympathize with you. Our first witness this morning [an African man, Gardiner Majova, whose son had disappeared in 1985] also spoke of getting the remains of a body back. It is wonderful for the country to experience that—black or white—we all feel the same pain."

This moral equalizing is a common strategy adopted by reconciling postwar regimes to avoid public identification with one side in the conflict. Eric Santner (1992:144) writes how in Bitburg, Germany, in 1985 at a public ceremony of reconciliation there was a "sentimental equalization of all victims of war," which he understands as part of a wider rehabilitation of the SS within a narrative of "Western" resistance to Bolshevism. Public rituals such as the TRC hearings in South Africa and the Bitburg memorial service in Germany are complex mnemonic readjustments designed to defuse political discord by denying the ideological reasons for the conflict.[14]

14. The final report judged that a just war had been fought against the apartheid regime, confirmed as a crime against humanity. Yet in the body of the report all abuses regardless of motivation were subsumed under the same blanket category of "human rights violations," which made no such moral distinctions.

LIBERATION AND SACRIFICE

The embedding of an individual's account in an allegory of liberation began immediately after the testimony. The first question by the commissioner leading the cross-examination was almost always about the context of the township or area at the particular time, not the individual event or unique circumstances of the victim. In this way, individual events were sutured to a social context of chaos, resistance, rioting against police, and rent and school boycotts and therefore part of a wider liberation struggle. "Sacrifice" provided the main symbolism for grafting individual pain onto wider political narratives and social processes, providing new meaning for death by creating a heroic figure of self-sacrifice in a new mythology of the state. Meaning was attached to the death by a process of teleologizing—of mapping onto the experiences of the dead and the survivors a narrative of destiny which portrays an inexorable progression towards liberation and the place of the specific individuals within it. This teleologizing of loss and pain is a common feature of "survivor's syndrome" and has been documented for the Holocaust (Bettelheim 1952) and Argentina (Suarez-Orozco 1991).

The message was that people had died not in vain but for the liberation of the nation. Commissioners often referred to victims as "heroes." The history of the new South Africa is a history of suffering which was necessary for its liberation and redemption. A clear link was forged between religious interpretations of suffering emphasizing sacrifice and martyrs and a more secular liberation narrative, with its imagery of national heroes. A unifying symbol which brought these two narratives together in a particularly powerful way was the figure of the black-consciousness leader Steve Biko. It emerged in the testimony of a security policeman applying for amnesty that Biko had been chained to a gate in the crucifix position before he died (*The Guardian* [Manchester and London], March 31, 1998), turning him into a symbol as a Black Christ of the oppressed African nation.

Benedict Anderson (1991) has drawn our attention to how nations are imagined through their war dead, focusing upon cenotaphs and tombs of the unknown soldier, which are filled with the ghostly imaginings of the nation. On certain memorial days, the whole nation participates in a simultaneous event to memorialize its dead. Similarly, HRV hearings often ended with the chair's asking the audience to stand and observe one minute's silence for the new nation's fallen heroes. This has been institutionalized in South Africa with a Day of Reconciliation on December 16, ironically also the day on which the ANC celebrates the initiation of the armed struggle in 1961 and Afrikaner nationalists celebrate the Day of the Covenant in memory of the white settlers' defeat of 12,000 Zulu warriors at the Battle of Blood River in 1838. This is the day on which the TRC started its work in 1995.

REDEMPTION THROUGH FORSAKING REVENGE

Explaining why he had gone to such lengths to allow Winnie Madikizela-Mandela the opportunity to apologize, TRC Chairperson Desmond Tutu said, "I believe that we all have the capacity to become saints" (*Weekly Mail and Guardian* [Johannesburg], December 23, 1997).

In the final stage of the process, the spiritual recompense for the loss of a family member was accentuated in the hope that it would preclude any need for individual acts of retaliation. The experience of the TRC was to heal wounds and smooth over resentments. Once individual suffering was valorized and linked to a national process of liberation, commissioners urged those testifying to forgive perpetrators and abandon any desire for retaliation against them. Commissioners never missed an opportunity to praise witnesses who did not express any desire for revenge. When Desmond Tutu replied to a case of murder in which the body was not found, he gave out clear signals about his views on retaliation. In the case of Susan van der Merwe, who had lived in relative penury after her husband's disappearance, Tutu said, "It is good to see that you are not bearing any grudges. You state that your story of pain is but a drop in the ocean, but it is still pain that happened to you. I hope that God will anoint your wounds with the Holy Spirit and heal them." The hearings were structured in such a way that any expression of a desire for revenge would seem out of place. Virtues of forgiveness and reconciliation were so loudly and roundly applauded that emotions of vengeance, hatred, and bitterness were rendered unacceptable, an ugly intrusion on a peaceful, healing process.

What were the responses to the TRC's narrative on reconciliation in the townships of South Africa? How did local actors respond to the transnational human rights discourse when it was introduced to their communities via the TRC? My twelve months' research focused on the Vaal Triangle to the south of Johannesburg, an industrialized and urban region of approximately 2 million people. It is an area with a long and intense history of political violence, from the Sharpeville massacre in 1960 to the necklacing of black councilors in 1984 to the undeclared war between the ANC and the IFP in the 1990s that temporarily derailed the peace talks between Nelson Mandela and F. W. De Klerk. Politically motivated massacres continued into late 1993, just months before the nonracial elections. My analysis of this research identifies no single definable relationship between human rights and "society"; instead, the language of rights has had uneven and varied social effects. Religious values and human rights discourse converged on the notion of reconciliation on the basis of shared value orientations. There was a clear divergence, however, between human rights discourse and popular notions of justice as expressed in a local township court.

Adductive Affinities between Religion and Rights Discourse

The concept of adductive affinities draws its inspiration from Weber's notion of "elective affinities," which pointed to the reciprocal effects of a resonance or coherence between frameworks of values in different social fields. In post-1994 South Africa there has been a discernible correspondence between the state's nation-building discourse on reconciliation and the social doctrine of large sections of the "progressive" Catholic and Protestant churches. This section of the religious community has been a fountainhead of symbolism for the TRC's own conceptualization of reconciliation. It also provided the main societal infrastructure for the TRC.

The collective effervescence of ritualized hearings became the mechanism through which the TRC's idealization of reconciliation was transmitted to participants. The hearings positioned individuals and their private narratives within a public narrative structure which made them aware of themselves as particular types of subjects. The creation of new identities ("victim," "perpetrator") engendered new types of attitudes and dispositions (forgiveness, repentance) which bound the subjects to the TRC's reconciliation project. This process drew upon a context of existing value dispositions or affinities, and new values were forged in the ritual hearings themselves. The important thing here was the ability of the ritual process to create loyalties and identities which had not existed before.

The TRC's organizational structure was intertwined with a number of societal institutions but none like the church sector. The use of the same networks of personnel by the two institutions led to an overlapping of structures and the transmission of national narratives on reconciliation to individual victims. The TRC relied on the churches rather than conflict-resolution NGOs or any new mediating structures, as it saw them as the authentic representatives of the community and civil society.

Because of the overlapping of TRC and religious personnel in the process of statement taking, religious values were conveyed to victims even before the hearings. The majority of statements taken in the Vaal were written down by religious activists in church settings. Statement takers were the first point of contact between the commission and victims. During interviews with statement takers, the TRC's message on reconciliation was woven into their written testimonies as the oral testimony of the victim was rendered as text. This prestructuring of the discourse was a vital part of the shift away from retribution and towards a view of justice as emanating from truth and reparations.

Two of the Vaal's most active statement takers were church stalwarts. One of them, Thabiso Mohasoa of Sebokeng's Zone 7, is an International Pentecostal Church activist. Perhaps strangely for a person writing down oral histories of political violence, he explained that "reconciliation means to forget what happened." When asked how he responded to victims' feelings of revenge during statement writing, Mohasoa described how he steered a victim's perspective in order to, in his words, "uplift reconciliation":

> I had understood those feelings before ... I understood retaliation. People don't know any better. Life in South Africa means fighting one another and retaliating. If he does it to me, I will do it to him and to his grandchild and then I will be satisfied. ... when taking a statement, people would be aggressive, saying "I want these perpetrators to be hanged." But the TRC will be a failure if people send negative ideas to it.

Beyond the overlapping networks of TRC statement takers and church activists, there was an institutional fusion of churches and TRC structures in the Vaal. The TRC relied heavily on a religious infrastructure to carry out important functions such as statement taking, the arranging of hearings, and the reconciliation of conflicts of the past. Religious groups were the only local organizations in the Vaal explicitly working with the TRC towards the goal of reconciliation. Before the HRV hearings in Sebokeng in August 1996, a group of churches led by local Catholic priests led a prayer service in Sebokeng's notoriously violent Zone 7 to encourage victims to testify. Local township clergy helped the TRC to identify victims; their members took the vast bulk of the statements and advised in the selection of cases to come to public hearings.

In addition to direct organizational links, the work of the TRC was indirectly reinforced by the conflict-resolving agendas of local ministers. A key actor in the Vaal was an Irish priest fluent in SeSotho called Father Patrick Noonan. The priest activist had run Nyolohelo Catholic Church in Zone 12 of Sebokeng for 25 years. He had radical political sympathies and was known affectionately by local ANC youth as "Comrade Patrick." Father Noonan was a political firebrand in the 1980s, when the Vaal was made ungovernable by rent and school boycotts, barricades on street corners, and necklacings of alleged "apartheid collaborators." Now his mission is to pursue reconciliation through forgiveness: "The truth commission is like a national confession. There is an injection of morality and ethics and that is good. ... The majority of victims have never gone to counseling, but those that do go mostly through the parishes. That was my program of renewal."

Father Noonan has had a significant impact on the individual members of his congregation. One, Cecilia Ncube, has had to cope with the murder of her husband, David, killed in the Sebokeng Night Vigil Massacre on January 11–12, 1991. David and Cecilia had been attending the night vigil of their nephew Christopher Nangalembe at 11427, Zone 7, Sebokeng. Christopher, a member of the ANC Youth League and a Peace Committee monitor, had been killed by a petty criminal, Victor Khetisi Kheswa, whom he had brought before a court run by the comrades. Cecilia left Christopher's night vigil at 10 P.M. on Friday the 11th and went back to her house across the street. She was awakened at 1 A.M. when members of Kheswa's gang (Kheswa was in hospital with a gunshot wound in the stomach) attacked the gathering of mourners with hand grenades and AK-47s: "I heard shooting and big explosions, like a bomb or hand grenade, and then sirens." Press reports at the time placed the death toll at between 36 and 42 and the number of wounded at least at 100.[15]

Instead of being consumed by a desire for revenge, Mrs. Ncube now embraces the new ethos of reconciliation in the country and credits Father Patrick Noonan for guiding her: "He is the man who gave me the strength to forgive these people. They didn't know what they were doing. That is how I survived. I just forgave and moved on. I was on a local renewal committee, and I had to be strong. From Father Patrick I learned that I couldn't bear a grudge and just had to forgive." She distanced herself from the other relatives of those killed in the Night Vigil Massacre, who combined to form the organization Vaal Victims of Violence under the leadership of a member of an African nationalist political party which opposed the TRC's amnesty provisions in the Constitutional Court. Cecilia commented on the unveiling of the memorial to those killed, "The other victims were still sick. They were aggressive and violent and calling for revenge. I am a teacher and understand better. They are just ordinary people."

In addition to their role in promulgating the values of reconciliation as forgiveness and their symbolic duties, ministers continue to play an important role in mediating ongoing armed conflicts arising from decades of apartheid.[16] Reverend Peter "Gift" Moerane of Sharpeville has urged militarized youth of both the ANC and the IFP to negotiate an end to their cycle of violent revenge killings. He is perhaps the only nonpolitical party leader with any real authority among ANC youth in Sharpeville. Similarly, Father Noonan has used his credibility with armed militants to try to end the cycle of revenge killings begun in the anti-apartheid years.

From the above instances in the Vaal and elsewhere we get a picture of the TRC as having close affinities to religious institutions—sharing personnel and organizational structures, values of forgiveness and reconciliation, and ritual symbolism. This close association between human rights and religious doctrine remains one of the best explanations for the TRC's ability to convert many to its cause of reconciliation. As Chanock (1985: 79–84) has demonstrated, this involvement in legal consciousness on the part of Christian missionaries is nothing new. During the colonial period missionaries sought to shape African attitudes to legal transgression by introducing ideas about individual and humanist rights and

Christian guilt and sin. Nevertheless, local actors also pursued other notions of justice which were less shaped by Christian values, throwing into relief the limitations of religion in resolving political conflicts.

Revenge and Retribution in a Local Court

Juxtaposed to religious affinities to human rights ideas were strong discontinuities which were articulated primarily through local courts. I term these disjunctures "relational discontinuities" to distinguish them from early legal pluralist accounts of customary law and to draw attention to the mutual influences between local, national, and transnational formulations of justice.

Discontinuities in legal consciousness were expressed during and in the aftermath of the HRV hearings held in the Vaal in August 1996. A large section of the week-long hearings held at the Sebokeng teacher training college dealt with the atrocities committed by IFP agents based at KwaMadala hostel at the Iron and Steel Corporation (ISCOR) plant. The most widely known case at the hearing involved the mothers of Christopher Nangalembe and Victor Kheswa, the principals in the events that led to the above-mentioned Night Vigil Massacre and subsequent retaliatory acts. The TRC hearing was the first time that Margaret Nangalembe, mother of Christopher, and Anna Kheswa, the mother of Christopher's killer, Victor Kheswa, had met since their sons' feuding had begun five years earlier. They both gave their differing accounts of events and, at the urging of commissioners, shook hands publicly in an act of seeming reconciliation. Anna Kheswa stated her strong desire to leave the poverty of KwaMadala hostel and return to her old house in Zone 7 of Sebokeng township, across the road from the Nangalembe household. The Nangalembe family expressed no opposition and said that Anna Kheswa need fear no hostility from them. At the time, Tutu and other commissioners extolled this case as the apogee of reconciliation within the TRC process.

Yet the ritual enactment of reconciliation, the shaking of hands between the mothers of militarized youth, has had little purchase in terms of advancing any reconciliation at the local level. No IFP members from KwaMadala have successfully returned to any of the Vaal townships from whence they fled in the 1990–91 period. To the contrary, some IFP members, such as Dennis Moerane of Sharpeville, have been summarily executed by armed ANC Special Defense Units when they have tried to return to their former homes in the townships.[17] This is partly the result of the lack of any dispute resolution mechanisms within the TRC framework to negotiate a lasting local peace and the return of former pariahs to the community. In many townships the TRC represented little more than a symbolic and performative

15. The case against Kheswa and his gang members collapsed after it was found that the confessions were extracted under torture. Kheswa was later found dead on the road to Sasolburg on June 17, 1993, while in police custody. Several members of his gang similarly died in questionable circumstances. Many observers allege that members of his IFP gang were killed off one by one by police when they threatened to expose their links with the latter.
16. Often working closely with human rights NGOs.

17. Moerane was accosted outside the Sharpeville library, tied to a lamppost, and shot dead with an AK-47 by an ANC Special Defense Unit on Christmas Day 1996.

ritual with little organization on the ground to implement its version of reconciliation.

Moreover, there were few initiatives within the TRC to engage with the bodies that actually exercise political authority in the townships—local justice institutions, armed vigilante groups, and local political party branches, which were seen as too compromised by their previous role in the violence. Commissioners I interviewed were hostile to the rough justice of local courts, demonizing them as kangaroo courts antithetical to human rights. This is ironic in that some commissioners linked to the United Democratic Front had actually promoted community courts in the 1980s as prefigurative organizations of revolutionary people's power. In the new centralizing culture of human rights, armed units of the anti-apartheid movement must be either incorporated within policing and military structures or isolated and left to wither away.

In return, there was profound disdain for the TRC among local political actors. The ANC representative to the 1991–92 Peace Committees in Sebokeng, Watch Mothebedi, scorned the Nangalembe-Kheswa reconciliation: "Those two are only individuals. Their reconciliation has no further weight. Ms. Nangalembe cannot forgive on behalf of the community. She cannot allow Ms. Kheswa's return. This must be done by legitimate community institutions, not by the TRC who come in for one week and then say they've sorted everything out." If the TRC's policy on reconciliation was not entirely legitimate and effective in some black townships, then how do former "enemies of the community" negotiate their return? Who absolves them and negotiates on behalf of the community? What does this tell us about the relationship between transnational human rights, state law, and local justice?

In the township of Boipatong, there was the kind of overarching legitimate "community" institution to which Mothebedi referred—a local court—which did seem to have the ability to protect former apartheid councilors and enforce a more lasting peace than in surrounding townships. Boipatong (population about 41,000) is located across the highway from the massive, Dickensian ISCOR works and wedged between several packing and canning factories. This urban social space contains a heterogeneous linguistic mixture, including speakers of SeSotho, Pedi, Shangaan, Zulu, and SeTswana, and a class mixture of wealthy professionals, industrial laborers, domestic workers, and large number of unemployed. It holds a special place in the history of violence in South Africa, as the peace talks between Mandela and De Klerk were broken off in June 1992 after armed IFP members, allegedly with police accompaniment, streamed across from KwaMadala hostel and slaughtered over 40 residents of the squatter settlement of Slovo Park, in Boipatong.[18]

Residents of Boipatong mediate and adjudicate many disputes with little reference to the national legal system

18. There are differences in the numbers reported killed; the Waddington Commission declared 42 dead, whereas the TRC says 46.

or bodies such as the TRC, which was seen by local people I interviewed as weak, ineffectual, and a "sellout." The low level of reparations and the granting of amnesties to perpetrators strengthened the view that human rights ideas violated local understandings of justice. Instead of appealing to human rights commissions to solve problems of social order, local adjudication occurs through a daily *kgotla* (plural *lekgotla*, SeSotho for "meeting" or "court") (see Burman and Sharf 1990, Goodhew 1993, Pavlich 1992, Scheper-Hughes 1995, Sharf and Ngcokoto 1990). This local forum mainly deals with petty crimes and domestic disputes, and its presence has implications for the legacy of political violence. In particular, it has protected black councilors who participated in the apartheid local government structure—the Transvaal Provincial Administration—between 1988 and 1990. In 1984 during the Vaal Uprising three councilors were burnt alive by militant crowds, and Esau Mahlatsi, the mayor of Lekoa Council, was murdered in 1993. Boipatong is now unique among Vaal townships in that apartheid-era councilors can live there free of intimidation.

The neighborhood court has a strong patriarchal character. The permanent members of the court are all male and fall into two groups—those over 45, many of whom were former convicted *tsotsis* or "gangsters", and those between 20 and 30, most of whom were MK combatants. The *kgotla* today is a fusion of two models of township justice—the patrimonial and gerontocratic courts of the 1970s and the "popular" revolutionary courts of the 1980s—and therefore combines two groups that were often violent political adversaries during the height of the liberation struggle in the mid-1980s. The religious dimension is not absent, as the court contains a preponderance of members of the Zionist Christian Church, which has its main bases in rural areas but also appeals to the urban poor. The court hears many family disputes (Tuesdays and Thursdays are "Ladies' Days") and cases of petty theft, assault, inheritance, and unpaid debts. It rarely deals with rape cases and never hears murder cases.

The *kgotla* draws its legitimacy from its claim to be an expression of traditional authority and customary law. Its participants call it "tribal law" and thus assert a discontinuity in relation to the criminal courts and international human rights. Unlike the white magistrate's courts, the *kgotla* avoids sentencing to jail if at all possible. It is said that everyone can speak out fully, anyone can cross-examine the plaintiffs, and sentencing is by consensus. Court members claim that unlike that of the human rights commissions, cross-examination by members of the community always identifies the guilty and achieves justice through punishment rather than reconciliation and amnesty. Thus a discontinuity with national and international legal structures is created by local social actors through notions of "community" and "tribe." This is an image of the township dwellers' own alterity as traditional rural, tribal, premodern peoples. However, few residents have been on an African farm (see Mayer 1971), and most live the thoroughly urbanized existence of an industrial community.

Instead of being vestiges of the traditional African past, the notions of tribe and tribal law are part of a more recent political narrative about "community" and an assertion of autonomous governance vis-à-vis the state (see Seekings 1995).[19] This points to discontinuities between the two legal fora, which are relationally and historically constituted. The pre-1994 legal system was a key institution in authoritarian governance, and opposition to state policing in townships is still shaped by this history. Before 1994, police and magistrate's courts were keen enforcers of an institutionalized bureaucratic framework of racial discrimination. Police were concerned less with controlling common crime than with liquor and pass control raids and suppressing dissident political activity. The judiciary largely upheld apartheid legislation and relegated blacks to an inferior and dependent position within a dual legal system (see Abel 1995).[20]

There are procedural differences between magistrate's and neighborhood courts which bear mentioning: those found guilty by the kgotla are subjected to both restorative justice, which usually takes the form of monetary payments or free labor, and a more punitive justice that frequently involves a public beating with whips, sjamboks, and golf clubs. These beatings can be quite severe, and the punished often require hospital treatment. The convicted usually consent to a public flogging in their own township rather than face being handed over to the van der Bijl Park police for possible beatings, torture, and a jail sentence. The prevalence of revenge in neighborhood courts draws our attention away from transient invocations of reconciliation and demands a greater focus upon "justice" as more important in framing social action.

The place of suffering in the rendering of justice highlights the differences and similarities between community justice, criminal law, and human rights. The TRC called for victims to shun the desire to make the perpetrators suffer. In place of revenge, victims would be recompensed by having their stories integrated into a nation-building narrative and through reparations from the state rather than from the offender. Within the TRC process, only the victims' suffering is brought into the public space. In contrast, public (albeit a different "public") suffering by the offender is at the heart of justice in local courts. As with the lex talionis of the Old Testament, an equivalent and physical exaction of pain witnessed by the victim compensates for prior suffering.

The importance granted to suffering as a form of redress in magistrate's court decisions resonates with local courts' judgements. Sentencing in common law recognizes retribution but seeks to subdue the "collective will" and rationalize inchoate passions of hatred and vengeance.[21] Because of their shared valuing of vengeance, there are a number of connections between local courts and the police. The Boipatong kgotla is officially recognized by the local magistrate and police station, and the court sends certain types of cases it cannot resolve (e.g., murder and rape) to the formal criminal justice system. It assists the police in apprehending suspects and hands over those who will not consent to beatings. This cooperation between systems has increased since the formation of the new South African Police Service, but it is not altogether unprecedented. During the apartheid years, the state at various historical junctures enhanced the integration of a dual system of justice and promoted the setting up of customary courts in rural areas and local courts in the townships.[22]

Yet there are also disjunctures between informal and formal law—the retribution of state law is different from popular justice: it involves not the blood, sweat, and screams of the spectacle of public flogging but a more silent administrative incarceration behind the doors of police stations and prisons. Suffering is still the basis of justice, but it is a slow, hidden suffering which victims cannot witness. In assuming the right to punish, the state deprives the victims of their role in inflicting suffering upon offenders.

These historically produced relationships have taken on new meanings in the post-apartheid period as the neighborhood court in Boipatong has dealt relatively successfully with the political violence of the past. It is no coincidence that two former National Party members and councilors from 1988–90 have remained in their homes in the township, whereas such "apartheid collaborators" have been killed or driven from their homes in all other townships of the Vaal. During interviews, former councilors reported that since 1994 they are no longer verbally or physically assaulted and feel protected by the neighborhood court, which they say is prepared to act punitively against anyone who threatens them. This contrasts strongly with the situation in neighboring townships without local courts such as Sharpeville, where councilors have not returned to their former homes but have been banished to shantytowns or special barbed-wire-enclosed camps constructed by the police. The existence of an overarching justice institution in Boipatong has created an environment less conducive to revenge killings.

19. The "community" became heavily politicized during the years of anti-apartheid struggle and came to represent a cornerstone in the ideology of local ANC cadres opposed to the authoritarian state. Urban communities are not homogeneous, and "community justice" is not a static concept but historically produced. The concept of "community" in the post-apartheid era is subjected to contestation by a variety of actors including new policing forums as well as advocates of local justice.
20. This last point is best illustrated in the case of a man condemned to death for killing a fellow hostel dweller he believed to be a malignant being sent through witchcraft (see Sachs 1996).

21. In his characteristic rebuttal of religious and human rights values, Friedrich Nietzsche (1969:162) in Thus Spoke Zarathustra speaks of how law attempts to dignify itself through the notion of proportional retribution, all the while keeping its spoon in the pot of hatred: "The spirit of revenge: my friends, that, up to now, has been mankind's chief concern: and where there was suffering, there was always supposed to be punishment."
22. The creation of the modern dual legal system is usually traced back to the 1927 Native Administration Act.

The unintended consequences of township justice are worth remarking upon here. Despite the opposition in Boipatong to the TRC, the local court realizes many of the objectives of human rights institutions around conflict mediation. I hesitate to use the word "reconciliation," since no one in Boipatong thought that it accurately described the process of coexistence with former "apartheid collaborators." Yet it is ironic that a neighborhood court which portrays itself as a punitive "tribal" authority and rejects the TRC's humanitarian view of human rights for a more retributive view of justice in the end facilitates the kinds of solutions extolled by the TRC. It does so not through notions of reconciliation and restorative justice derived from Christian ethics and human rights talk but through expressions of traditionalist male authority and the likelihood of physical sanction against any who flout its decisions (see Renteln 1990, Merry 1990).

Conclusions

Until the 1960s, legal anthropology was dominated by a form of legal pluralism that proposed an equivalence and continuum between all types of legal rules and social norms and operated with a static and isolationist view of customary law which too readily assumed the existence of different systems. Over time, it moved from codifying customary rules to advocating a processual approach which portrayed local law as characterized by open and seemingly limitless individual negotiation and choice making. This legal pluralism has for decades been the dominant intellectual paradigm in writings on the Tswana, in what are now South Africa and Botswana. From Schapera (1938) in the early part of the century to Comaroff and Roberts (1981) to more recent writers such as Gulbrandsen (1996), studies of legal practices and discourses among Setswana-speaking peoples have largely accepted the dualistic colonial and apartheid legal system at face value and ignored how state law transformed local adjudicative institutions. This paradigm may have resulted from the actual historical experiences of Setswana-speaking peoples but is in my view more likely to have been the result of an entrenched analytical frame which reproduced assumptions of isolation and autonomy. Certainly the people forcibly categorized as Tswana in the former South African "homeland" of Bophuthatswana, run by the corrupt Lucas Mangope, had intimate knowledge and experience of legal coercion from a violent state.

A different form of legal pluralism emerged in the 1970s from within critical legal studies and the cross-disciplinary law-and-society movement. The emphasis in studies of legal pluralism now became the dialectical relationship between state institutions and local normative orders and the relations of dominance and resistance between them. Marxist legal anthropologists such as Snyder (1981) argued rightly that the processual approach treated dispute processes as too self-contained and thus tended to ignore the wider political context.

Local moralities and norms were in a subordinate but resistant relationship to state law, demanding recognition in their own terms (Merry 1990:181). Studies in this tradition began to look at the politics of judicial processes, drawing from Gramscian notions of hegemony in which law is an ideology that expresses and maintains structures of inequality. Foucauldian readings also took hold, seeing law as a disciplinary apparatus and a site of struggle and contestation between dominant and resistant discourses of power (see Humphreys 1985 and Hunt and Wickham 1994).

This critical version of legal pluralism is adequate in many ways for understanding the uniquely polarized history of apartheid legality. It is particularly well-suited to analyzing the dualistic legal system administered by a white-run political and legal bureaucracy and resisted by the local political actors who carved out a sphere of "popular justice" in the 1980s. Yet, with its narrative of dominance and resistance, it is predisposed to ignore the real connections between local and state law and the ways in which especially elite Africans (in chiefs' courts and "Bantustan" bureaucracies) have participated in and acquiesced in state policies. Relations between formal and informal justice institutions in the initial post-apartheid context are even more volatile and contradictory than before, and they present a socio-legal environment that prior formulations of legal pluralism or centralism cannot fully encompass.

A revised legal pluralism would have to preserve from this one the idea that many states engage in centralizing efforts to resolve their hegemonic crises, but it could not accept that there is always an inherent asymmetry between centralizing and pluralizing processes. Instead of the stark polarity of dominance and resistance which reduces the complexities of a historically produced political-legal context, we must turn our attention to shifting patterns of dominance, resistance, and acquiescence, which occur simultaneously. As we have seen in the Vaal townships, local courts are both connecting up with policing structures and bypassing them in order to exercise a certain degree of autonomy to judge and punish. Religious moralities and institutions, in contrast, encourage a more favorable disposition towards human rights values. The notions of adductive affinities and relational discontinuities take us away from generalizations about law and society and offer more concrete ways of theorizing the uneven reception of human rights ideas in a locale.

In this multivalent context, the degree of plurality of legal fields is often a matter of the strategic perspectives of social actors. The legal system may appear quite pluralistic from the Olympian vantage of the Justice Ministry, which surveys hundreds of unregulated armed units and local courts across the country, each dispensing a different version of "justice" over which it has only tentative control. However, from the perspective of a petty criminal apprehended by Boipatong kgotla members and handed over to the police in van der Bijl Park, the institutions of justice look relatively unified and integrated.

There are multiple connections between state institutions, religious organizations, and local courts, to the extent that we see a splintering of the unified fields of "state" and "society" and an eradication of their firm boundaries. Diverse social fields in African countries are too complex and emergent to be constrained by any explanation which sees "law" and "society" as a priori structural categories to be understood by a single explanatory framework. Instead of two coherent unified systems locked in a structurally determined struggle, we see combinations of actors and collective groups producing norms and creating new historical experiences and experiences of history. The direction of social change in post-apartheid South Africa, what Touraine calls historicity, is the product of the social action of individuals and collective actors (political parties, local courts, religious organizations, etc.) engaged in the reflexive self-production of society.[23]

Just as "civil society" implies too much common purpose among non-state actors with regard to state versions of the idea of human rights, the "state" itself is not unified and coherent in its policies. The diversity in human rights practices within the South African state can be well demonstrated by juxtaposing the activities of different arms of the state in the Vaal in 1995–96. Only months before the TRC began taking statements from victims, arranging its one-week hearing in the Vaal townships, and carrying out public education on human rights in the area, policemen in the Murder and Robbery Unit at the nearby van der Bijl Park police station were routinely torturing criminal suspects using methods honed during years of defending successive National Party regimes (1948–94). Because of successive litigation from human rights lawyers,[24] four Vaal policemen were suspended in late 1995 for torturing 30 prisoners. The presiding judge struck down the prisoners' confessions exacted through torture and recommended an internal police investigation. When I reinterviewed a staff member at the Vaal Legal Aid Centre in 1998 and asked if the situation had improved, he replied, "Yes. Prisoners awaiting trial are no longer being tortured. They are only being assaulted."

The post-apartheid South African regime is in an agonizing process of state reformation; its ANC ministers are unifying, consolidating infrastructure, and desperately trying to transform institutions such as the police, prisons, and magistrate's courts tainted by their involvement in administering apartheid. Such a hegemonic crisis is not unique to South Africa. Jean-François Bayart (1993:249) understood the tentative and emergent hegemonizing projects of postcolonial African states when he wrote, "In order to understand 'governmentality' in Africa we need to understand the concrete procedures by which social actors simultaneously borrow from a range of discursive genres, intermix them and, as a result, are able to invent original cultures of the State."

Human rights is a central discursive genre in the new South Africa, and this article has traced some of the procedures through which state officials combine human rights ideas and practices with religious notions of redemption and forgiveness and how these resonate with local perspectives, are reformulated, or are rejected. The procedures work in different directions simultaneously, both reinforcing and obstructing the introduction of human rights values into a context of semiautonomous legal and moral fields. If revised, legal pluralism remains one useful category which allows us move beyond stark formulations of "state" and "society," to chart the concrete consequences of social action which contest historicity in the area of justice and reconciliation.

---

23. These observations are more generally applicable to narratives on history in Latin America and Eastern Europe. On the latter, see Garton Ash (1997), Moeller (1996), and Rosenberg (1995).

24. Such as Tony Richards and Peter Jordi, then of the Law Clinic at the University of the Witwatersrand.

87a   References Cited

ABEL, RICHARD. 1995. *Politics by other means: Law in the struggle against apartheid, 1980–1994*. London: Routledge.

ANDERSON, BENEDICT. 1991. 2d edition. *Imagined communities: Reflections on the origins and spread of nationalism*. London: Verso.

BAYART, JEAN-FRANÇOIS. 1993. *The state of Africa: The politics of the belly*. New York: Longman.

BETTELHEIM, BRUNO. 1952. *Surviving and other essays*. New York: Vintage Books

CHANOCK, MARTIN. 1985. *Law, custom, and social order: The colonial experience in Malawi and Zambia*. Cambridge: Cambridge University Press.

–(199ia). "*Paradigms, policies, and property: A review of the customary law of land tenure*," in Law in colonial Africa. Edited by K. Mann and R. Roberts. London: James Currey.

COLLIER, JANE. 1975. Legal processes. *Annual Review of Anthropology* 4:12-44.

COMAROFF, JOHN, AND SIMON ROBERTS. 1981. *Rules and processes: The cultural logic of dispute in an African context*. Chicago: University of Chicago Press.

DEMBOUR, MARIE-BÉNÉDICTE. 1990. Le pluralisme juridique: Une démarche parmi d'autres, et non plus innocente. *Revue Interdisciplinaire d'Etudes Juridiques* 24:43–59.

ENSALACO, MARK. 1994. Truth commissions for Chile and El Salvador: A report and assessment. *Human Rights Quarterly* 16:656–75.

GOODHEW, DAVID. 1993. The people's police force: Communal policing initiatives in the western areas of Johannesburg, circa 1930–1962. *Journal of Southern African Studies* 19: 447–70.

GULBRANDSEN, ØRNULF. 1996. "Living their lives in courts: The counter-hegemonic force of the Tswana kgotla in a colonial context," *in Inside and outside the law: Anthropological studies in authority and ambiguity*. Edited by O. Harris. London: Routledge.

HAYNER, PRISCILLA B. 1994. Fifteen truth commissions–1974 to 1994: A comparative study. *Human Rights Quarterly* 16: 597–655.

HUMPHREYS, SALLY. 1985. Law as discourse. *History and Anthropology*, no.I pp. 241–64.

HUNT, ALAN, AND GARY WICKHAM. 1994. *Foucault and law*. London: Pluto Press.

HUYSE, LUC. 1995. Justice after transition: On the choices successor elites make in dealing with the past. *Law and Social Enquiry*, no. I, pp. 51–78.

JACOBY, SUSAN. (1983). Wild justice: *The evolution of revenge*. New York: Harper and Row.

KLUG, HEINZ. 1995. *Defining the property rights of others: Political power, indigenous tenure, and the construction of customary law*. Center for Applied Legal Studies, University of the Witwatersrand, Working Paper 23.

KROG, ANTJIE. 1998. *Country of my skull*. Johannesburg: Random House.

LODGE, TOM, AND BILL NASSON. 1992. *All, here and now: Black politics in South Africa in the 1980s*. London: Hurst.

MALINOWSKI, BRONISLAW. 1926. *Crime and custom in savage society*. London: Kegan Paul.

MANN, KRISTIN, AND RICHARD ROBERTS. Editors. 1991. *Law in colonial Africa*. London: James Currey.

MERRY, SALLY ENGLE. 1988. Legal pluralism. *Law and Society Review* 22:869–901.

–1990. *Getting justice and getting even: Legal consciousness among working-class Americans*. Chicago: University of Chicago Press.

MINOW, MARTHA. 1998. *Between vengeance and forgiveness: Facing history after genocide and mass violence*. Boston: Beacon Press.

MOORE, SALLY FALK. 1978. *Law as process: An anthropological approach*. London: Routledge.

PAVLICH, GEORGE. 1992. People's courts, postmodern difference, and socialist justice in South Africa. *Social Justice* 19.

87b

RENTELN, ALISON. 1990. *International human rights: Universalism versus relativism.* London: Sage.

ROBERTS, SIMON. 1991 "Tswana government and law in the time of Seepapitso, 1910–1916," in *Law in colonial Africa.* Edited by K. Mann and R. Roberts. London: James Currey.

SANTNER, ERIC. 1992. "History beyond the pleasure principle," in Probing the limits of representation: Nazism and the Final Solution. Edited by Saul Friedlander. Cambridge: Harvard University Press.

SANTOS, BOAVENTURA DE SOUSA. 1995. *Toward a new common sense: Law, science, and politics in the paradigmatic transition.* New York: Routledge.

SARKIN, JEREMY. 1998. The development of a human rights culture in South Africa. *Human Rights Quarterly* 20:628–65.

SCHAPERA, ISAAC. 1938. *A handbook of Tswana law and custom.* London: Oxford University Press.

SEEKINGS, JEREMY. 1995. Social ordering and control in South Africa's black townships: An historical overview of extra-state initiatives from the 1940s to the 1990s. Paper presented at the meetings of the South African Sociological Association, Rhodes University, July 2–5.

SHARF, W. AND BABA NGCOKOTO. 1990."Images of punishment in the people's courts of Cape Town 1985–7" in *Political violence and the struggle in South Africa.* Edited by C. Mangananyi and A. Du Toit. London: Macmillan.

SNYDER, FRANCIS. 1981. Colonialism and legal form: The creation of "customary law" in Senegal. *Journal of Legal Pluralism* 19:49–90.

STRATHERN, MARILYN. 1985. Discovering "social control." *Journal of Law and Society* 12:111–34.

SUAREZ-OROZCO, M. 1991. The heritage of enduring a "dirty war": Psychosocial aspects of terror in Argentina, 1976–1988. *Journal of Psychohistory* 18:469–505

TAMANAHA, BRIAN. 1993. The folly of the "social scientific" concept of legal pluralism. Journal of Law and Society 20: 192–217.

TEUBNER, G. EDITOR. 1997. Global law without a state. Aldershot, U.K.: Dartmouth

TOURAINE, ALAIN. 1971. The post-industrial society, tomorrow's social history: Class, conflict, and culture in programmed society. Translated by Leonard Fox Mayhew. New York: Random House.

–(1995). *Critique of modernity.* Oxford: Blackwell.TRUTH AND RECONCILIATION COMMISSION OF SOUTH AFRICA. 1998. Final report. Cape Town: Juta.

VINCENT, JOAN. 1990. Anthropology and politics: Visions, traditions, and trends. Tucson: University of Arizona Press.

WILSON, RICHARD A. 1996. The *sizwe* will not go away: The Truth and Reconciliation Commission, human rights, and nation-building in South Africa. *African Studies* 55(2):1–20.

–(1997a). *Human rights, culture, and context: Anthropological approaches.* London and Chicago: Pluto Press.

–(1997b). *The people's conscience? Civil groups, peace, and justice in the South African and Guatemalan transitions.* London: Catholic Institute of International Relations.

Part III
Human Rights Discourse
and Social Movements

[10]

International Law and Social Movements: Challenges of Theorizing Resistance

BALAKRISHNAN RAJAGOPAL[*]

This Article offers an analysis of the key theoretical challenges that arise from the impact of local and transnational social movement action—as witnessed in Seattle in 1999—on international law and institutions. In spite of a vast scholarly literature in the social sciences on social movements and their relationship to the state and other actors, international lawyers have not engaged this literature so far. Given the increasing importance of non-state and individual action in international affairs, this Article suggests that it is now timely to engage with this literature. This Article presents the outlines of a larger project to rethink international law through social movements rather than through states or individuals, as realists and liberals do. At the heart of the analysis in this article is the question of how international lawyers can understand the mass resistance around the world to

* Ford International Assistant Professor of Law and Development and Director, Program on Human Rights and Justice, Massachusetts Institute of Technology. SJD (Harvard Law School, 2000); LLM (The American University, 1992); BL (University of Madras, 1990). I wish to thank Obiora Okafor and Anthony Anghie for conversations and comments. I also wish to thank Nathaniel Berman, Richard Falk, James Gathii, David Kennedy and Martti Koskenniemi for conversations and debates about various issues during the past two years. A version of this article was presented at the University of Toronto Law Faculty Legal Theory Colloquium in March 2002, and I thank Kerry Rittich for her enormous enthusiasm and support. Some ideas from this article have also been presented at the Conference of the Law and Society Association and the Research Committee on the Sociology of Law, Budapest, Hungary, July 4, 2001; the Conference on The "Third" World and the International Order: Law, Politics and Globalization, Osgoode Hall Law School, York University, Oct. 12–13, 2001; and at the Opening Plenary, Latcrit Conference on "Coalitional Theory and Praxis: Social Justice Movements and Latcrit Community," University of Oregon Law School, May 2, 2002. The usual caveats apply. This article presents some key themes from my forthcoming book to be published by Cambridge University Press, INTERNATIONAL LAW FROM BELOW: DEVELOPMENT, SOCIAL MOVEMENTS AND THIRD WORLD RESISTANCE (forthcoming 2003).

398   COLUMBIA JOURNAL OF TRANSNATIONAL LAW   [41:397

global legal structures. The article argues that international lawyers need a theory of resistance, not simply one of governance, to ensure that the voices of the ordinary people, who are increasingly marginalized by the current global order, are properly heard. After outlining some of the key theoretical barriers in international law that prevent a real engagement with social movements, the Article explores some possible foundations for a cultural politics of international law that would enable international legal scholarship to pay proper regard to the empirical reality of international relations and to remain committed to the best cosmopolitan ideals of the discipline.

"A focus on social movements with restructuring agendas itself incorporates a political judgment on how drastic global reform can best be achieved at this stage of history."[1]

---

1.   Richard Falk, *The Global Promise of Social Movements: Explorations at the Edge*

I. INTRODUCTION

The much-maligned "anti-globalization" protests in Seattle, Genoa, and Washington, D.C., as well as the World Social Summit meeting in Porto Allegre, Brazil, have ignited an interest in understanding mass action on a global scale. Concerted social movement action has driven several recent international legal developments (including the Ottawa Convention on Anti-Personnel Landmines,[2] the establishment of the World Bank Complaints Panel,[3] the establishment of the World Commission on Dams,[4] the Doha Declaration regarding the World Trade Organization's Agreement on Trade-Related Aspects of Intellectual Property Rights ("TRIPS") and Public Health,[5] an advisory opinion of the International Court of Justice regarding the threat or use of nuclear weapons)[6] and the emergence of new soft law standards for corporate social responsibility.[7] In most, if not all, of these actions, well-organized social movements in the Third World have formed alliances with those in the West and have transformed the political space[8] of

---

of Time, 12 ALTERNATIVES 173, 173 (1987).

2. Convention on the Prohibition of the Use, Stockpiling, Production and Transfer of Anti-Personnel Mines and on Their Destruction, signed Sept. 18, 1997, 36 I.L.M. 1507, (entered into force Mar. 1, 1999) [hereinafter Ottawa Convention]. *See also* THE BANNING OF ANTI-PERSONNEL LANDMINES: THE LEGAL CONTRIBUTION OF THE INTERNATIONAL COMMITTEE OF THE RED CROSS (Louis Maresca & Stuart Maslen eds., 2000).

3. On the World Bank Complaints Panel, see http://wbln0018.worldbank.org/ipn/ipn web.nsf. *See* Daniel Bradlow, *International Organizations and Private Complaints: The Case of the World Bank Inspection Panel*, 34 VA. J. INT'L L. 553 (1994).

4. On the World Commission on Dams, see http://www.dams.org/default.php. See also the symposium issue *in* Kader Asmal, *Introduction: World Commission on Dams Report, Dams and Development*, 16 AM. U. INT'L L. REV. 1411 (2001).

5. *See Doha Declaration on the TRIPS Agreement and Public Health*, WT/MIN(01)/Dec/2 Para. 4 (Nov. 14, 2001). This Declaration was partly the result of grassroots pressure to reinterpret the TRIPS Agreement so as to allow the sale of generic HIV/AIDS drugs.

6. *See* Legality of the Threat or Use of Nuclear Weapons, 1996 I.C.J. 95 (note, in particular, Justice Weeramantry's dissent). This advisory opinion was the result of a global movement against nuclear weapons. For a perceptive analysis of the role played by global civil society in making this case possible, see RICHARD FALK, *The Nuclear Weapons Advisory Opinion and the New Jurisprudence of Global Civil Society*, *in* LAW IN AN EMERGING GLOBAL VILLAGE 165–88 (1998).

7. *See Business and Human Rights*, *in* HUMAN RIGHTS WATCH WORLD REPORT (2001); HUMAN RIGHTS—IS IT ANY OF YOUR BUSINESS? (2000) *available at* http://www.iblf.org/csr/csrwebassist.nsf/content/f1d2a3a4c5.html#1. On soft law norms, see COMMITMENT AND COMPLIANCE: THE ROLE OF NON-BINDING NORMS IN THE INTERNATIONAL LEGAL SYSTEM (Dinah Shelton ed., 2000).

8. For the purposes of this article, "political space" refers to the sanctioned—but contested—boundaries within which normative evolution and compliance occur.

rulemaking and implementation in international law. Indeed, global norms are increasingly being produced and shaped through an interaction between States, international institutions, and rebellious networks of peasants, farmers, women, and environmentalists, while legal enforcement is increasingly influenced by the everyday resistance of ordinary people.   Despite these developments, international law does not yet have a theory of resistance. This article proposes that international law requires a theory of resistance to remain relevant, both to the empirical reality of international relations, and to the cosmopolitan values, such as human dignity, equality, and peace, that have traditionally attracted the Third World states to international law. This theory of resistance must take Third World social movements seriously. While taking social movements seriously has never been an easy task for international lawyers, in the aftermath of the attacks on September 11, 2001 and the subsequent war on "terror," they have a greater responsibility to pay close attention to social movements and to ensure that legitimate protests are not also labeled as "terrorism."[9] Nevertheless, international law can no longer pretend that mass resistance from the Third World does not fundamentally shape its domain. Indeed, the central focus of the inquiry here must be: how does one write this resistance into international law?

The articulation of a theory of resistance in international law will both compel a fundamental rethinking of the very meaning of the term "Third World" as a collection of States in international law[10] and raise profound theoretical challenges to the international legal order as it presently stands. In the following four Parts, this article presents the outlines of an undertaking to consider international law through social movements, rather than through States or individuals.[11] In Part II, the author presents some of the causes for the inability or unwillingness of international lawyers to seriously consider social movements and review some recent literature that suggests ways to overcome this tendency.   In Part III, the author suggests some preliminary ways to think about a theory of politics for an

---

9. The Italian Prime Minister is reputed to have remarked, in the aftermath of the September 11th attacks, that the protestors against the World Economic Forum in Genoa were also terrorists.

10. For a detailed argument to this effect, see Balakrishnan Rajagopal, *Locating the Third World in Cultural Geography*, THIRD WORLD LEGAL STUD. 1 (1998–99).

11. The broader project is forthcoming, as noted above, as a book by Cambridge University Press in 2003. For a preview of some of the themes and issues contained in the broader project, see Balakrishnan Rajagopal, *From Resistance to Renewal: The Third World, Social Movements and the Expansion of International Institutions*, 41 HARV. INT'L L.J. 529 (2000).

international law that takes into serious consideration the resistance of Third World social movements in contrast to the traditional international law approach to politics. To do so, this article introduces a series of conceptual tools from literature on social movements and links those tools to international legal debates. It further suggests that analyzing international law through the lens of social movements is much more rewarding than analyzing it exclusively from the perspectives of either states (as realists/positivists do) or individuals (as liberals/naturalists do). International law needs to de-center itself from the unitary conception of the political sphere on which it is based, which takes the state or the individual as the principal political actor. In Part IV, the author attempts to articulate some bases for a theory of resistance in international law by drawing on the work of Michel Foucault, Antonio Gramsci, Frantz Fanon, and Partha Chatterjee. Part V is a brief conclusion.

II. INTERNATIONAL LAW AND SOCIAL MOVEMENTS: SEEING PAST EACH OTHER

Despite the fact that international relations is no stranger to mass action—epochal twentieth century developments, after all, were catalyzed through mass action (e.g., nationalism, anti-colonialism, Marxism, identity-based mobilizations, and pro-democracy movements)—international lawyers traditionally have neither attempted to interpret mass actions nor engage the rich literature on social movements.[12] International and domestic lawyers are traditionally interested in governance, not resistance. As a result of professional training, intellectual orientation, political and class alignment, and tradition, lawyers focus on various kinds of governmental and private institutions. With this focus, they tend to ask different sets of questions about social change and the role of law in it. For instance, in domestic law, lawyers examine the "contribution" of courts to the civil rights movement in the United States by studying landmark cases such as *Brown v. Board of Education*.[13] Such "technical" or "legal" discussions filter out the contributions of the masses from historical transformations and highlight the roles played by judges and lawyers. In this clinical reduction of facts, the case itself becomes the historical event, so that

---

12. For a discussion, see *infra* Part III and note 40 for literature.
13. Brown v. Bd. of Educ., 347 U.S. 483 (1954).

legal history is reduced to a cataloguing of factually abstracted episodes that bear little relation to each other.

This traditional tendency in Western domestic law to ignore the contribution of the masses is a result of many factors that are too complex to examine here, but two that are discussed below are relevant to international law; they are problems of source and method.[14] With regard to the problem of source, lawyers tend to have a juro-centric approach that focuses on the texts emerging from public institutions such as legislatures, courts such as the International Court of Justice, the United Nations, and the World Trade Organization's Dispute Settlement Authority. In this approach, there is no space for "texts of resistance"[15]—i.e., either informal or explicitly illegal interpretive acts by individuals and groups that are contrary to institutional interpretations of the law. Thus, for lawyers, the source of normative legitimacy and authority is consistently the statist institutions. For example, environmental lawyers are more concerned with the regulatory behavior of the state than with the rise of environmental consciousness or the mass action that may have led to the regulatory behavior of the state. This has the result of ignoring the social origins of legal rules and institutions and, therefore, the role of laypeople in legal analysis.

Regarding the problem of method, much of legal analysis is focused entirely on the cogency and the internal logical structure of the language of the law. As such, the prescriptive stance of legal analysis focuses on figuring out the gaps, conflicts and ambiguities in the language of the law, even if to reveal the existence of ideology.[16] While this focus is enormously valuable for many purposes, merely revealing the structural flaws in legal reasoning does nothing to ground it in particular social and political contexts and makes the law look surprisingly static.[17] Furthermore, although a revelation of the internal incoherence of law may undermine the authority of law, it does not offer an indication of how it should be reformed.

---

14. *See* Symposium, *Passing Through the Door: Social Movement Literature and Legal Scholarship*, 150 U. PA. L. REV. 1, 54–55 (2001).

15. This term is borrowed from Robert M. Cover, *The Supreme Court, 1982 Term: Foreward: Nomos and Narrative*, 97 HARV. L. REV. 4, 45–50 (1983).

16. This is a classic stance adopted by critical legal studies scholars. *See, e.g.*, DUNCAN KENNEDY, A CRITIQUE OF ADJUDICATION: FIN DE SIÈCLE 113–214 (1997). Even here, the focus is not on the massive regulatory apparatus of the state, which is the source of so much "law" in the Third World, but on judge-made law. As the title of this book indicates, it is adjudication, not regulation, that is critiqued.

17. For a recent acknowledgement from a leading critical scholar, see MARTTI KOSKENNIEMI, THE GENTLE CIVILIZER OF NATIONS: THE RISE AND FALL OF INTERNATIONAL LAW 1870–1960 2 (2002).

Incorporating the social dimensions of law into legal analysis—e.g., viewing the history of the sex discrimination doctrine in U.S. constitutional law as one that arose from a larger women's suffrage movement rather than from the Fourteenth Amendment[18]—has vast consequences for legal reasoning, broader social reform, and the role that law plays in reform. In international law, such incorporation leads to a mode of legal analysis that places much more significance on the consequences of particular legal rules and doctrines for those who do not have a voice or power in the legal system[19] and that, importantly, does not shy away from acknowledging the need to reinterpret international law in order to account for their interests.

The tendency in Western domestic law to ignore the contribution of the masses has been criticized by at least two camps in recent years. One camp within the United States, a group of critical race theorists, feminists, and gay-lesbian theorists, has criticized this decontextualized, technocratic-rational model of law and legal history on the ground that it ignores both the role that law plays in everyday life and empowerment and the role played by ordinary people as agents of legal transformation.[20] For them, the liberal legal model[21] that has remained dominant in the United States so far is fatally flawed due to these blind spots, among others, and needs to be fundamentally reconceptualized. Although some of their writings

---

18. Reva Siegal, *She the People: The Nineteenth Amendment, Sex Equality, Federalism, and the Family*, 115 HARV. L. REV. 947 (2002).

19. The jurisprudence of Justice C.G. Weeramantry stands out as a shining example. See, in particular, his dissent in Legality of the Threat or Use of Nuclear Weapons, 1996 I.C.J. 95.

20. For examples of critical race scholarship, see CRITICAL RACE THEORY: THE KEY WRITINGS THAT FORMED THE MOVEMENT (Kimberlé Crenshaw et al. eds., 1995); PATRICIA WILLIAMS, THE ALCHEMY OF RACE AND RIGHTS (1991); Kimberlé Williams Crenshaw, *Race, Reform and Retrenchment: Transformation and Legitimation in Anti-Discrimination Law*, 101 HARV. L. REV. 1331 (1988). Examples of feminist legal scholarship include CATHERINE A. MACKINNON, TOWARD A FEMINIST THEORY OF THE STATE (1989); MARTHA MINOW, MAKING ALL THE DIFFERENCE: INCLUSION, EXCLUSION AND AMERICAN LAW (1990); Katherine Bartlett, *Feminist Legal Methods*, 103 HARV. L. REV. 829 (1990); Ann Scales, *The Emergence of a Feminist Jurisprudence: An Essay*, 95 YALE L.J. 1373 (1986); Robin West, *Jurisprudence and Gender*, 55 U. CHI. L. REV. 1 (1988). For recent gay-lesbian legal scholarship, see WILLIAM ESKRIDGE JR., GAYLAW: CHALLENGING THE APARTHEID OF THE CLOSET (1999); Janet Halley, *Gay Rights and Identity Imitation: Issues in the Ethics of Representation*, in THE POLITICS OF LAW: A PROGRESSIVE CRITIQUE 115 (David Kairys ed., 1998); Kendall Thomas, *Beyond the Privacy Principle*, 92 COLUM. L. REV. 1431 (1992).

21. In the domestic legal context, liberal legalism is said to consist of a set of premises that are supposed to underlie a specific mode of analyzing legal (and human) relations. These include the notion of the atomistic individual, the distinction between public and private spheres, and law as a neutral and impartial mechanism for resolving disputes between atomistic individuals. For a classic critique of liberalism, see ROBERTO UNGER, KNOWLEDGE AND POLITICS (1975).

allude to social movements, they do not explicitly engage social movement literature.[22] They draw inspiration, inter alia, from the legal theoretical work of Robert Cover, which posits the notion of "interpretive communities"[23] that create law and give it meaning through their personal experiences.

The other camp, a small number of socio-legal theorists and comparativists from the United States and Europe, along with several constitutional scholars from non-Western countries, has engaged in important critiques of liberal theories of rights, justice, and democracy, sometimes by engaging social movements literature. These critiques include the works of: Joel Handler on civil rights, welfare, and other movements in the United States;[24] Austin Sarat on identity and rights and cause lawyering;[25] Jüergen Habermas on social movements, democracy, and rights;[26] Alan Hunt and Neil Stammers on human rights;[27] Sousa Santos on legal theory and human rights;[28] Upendra Baxi on democracy, rights, and justice;[29] and more recently, Diane Otto on human rights and postcolonial theory[30] and Julie Mertus on transnational civil society.[31] These critiques have pointed

---

22. Although critical scholarship has not directly engaged it so far, some recent developments indicate an increasing interest in social movement literature. The Latcrit conference for the year 2002 has taken social movements as its main theme and the University of Pennsylvania Law Review recently held a symposium on "Social Movements and Law Reform." *See* Symposium, *Social Movements and Law Reform: Passing Through the Door: Social Movement Literature and Legal Scholarship*, 150 U. PA. L. REV. 1 (2001).

23. Cover, *supra* note 15, at 40.

24. JOEL HANDLER, SOCIAL MOVEMENTS AND THE LEGAL SYSTEM: A THEORY OF LAW REFORM AND SOCIAL CHANGE (1978).

25. IDENTITIES, POLITICS AND RIGHTS (Austin Sarat & Thomas Kearns eds., 1995); CAUSE LAWYERING (Austin Sarat & Stuart Scheingold eds., 1998).

26. JÜERGEN HABERMAS, BETWEEN FACTS AND NORMS: CONTRIBUTIONS TO A DISCOURSE THEORY OF LAW AND DEMOCRACY (1996); Jüergen Habermas, *New Social Movements*, 49 TELOS 33–37 (1981).

27. Alan Hunt, *Rights and Social Movements: Counter-Hegemonic Strategies*, 17 J.L. & SOC'Y 309, 309–28 (1990); Neil Stammers, *A Critique of Social Approaches to Human Rights*, 17 HUM. RTS. Q. 488 (1995).

28. BOAVENTURA DE SOUSA SANTOS, TOWARD A NEW COMMON SENSE: LAW, SCIENCE AND POLITICS IN THE PARADIGMATIC TRANSITION (1995).

29. THE RIGHTS OF SUBORDINATED PEOPLES (Oliver Mendelsohn & Upendra Baxi eds., 1994); Upendra Baxi, *Taking Suffering Seriously: Social Action Litigation Before the Supreme Court of India, in* JUDGES AND JUDICIAL POWER: ESSAYS IN HONOUR OF JUSTICE V. R. KRISHNA IYER (Rajeev Dhavan et al. eds., 1985); Upendra Baxi, *Voices of Suffering and the Future of Human Rights*, 8 TRANSNAT'L L. & CONTEMP. PROBS. 125 (1998).

30. Diane Otto, *Rethinking the "Universality" of Human Rights Law*, 29 COLUM. HUM. RTS. L. REV. 1 (1997); Diane Otto, *Subalternity and International Law: The Problems of Global Community and the Incommensurability of Difference*, 5 SOC. & LEGAL STUD. 337 (1996).

31. Julie Mertus, *From Legal Transplants to Transformative Justice: Human Rights*

out the elitist bias of extant rights theories and conceptions of democracy and have attempted to formulate general conceptions of law that would accommodate the role of subaltern communities and individuals.

A central aspect of the two camps of literature discussed above has been a scrutiny of the role that law plays in regulating power in everyday life and, in turn, the impact of everyday practices on the law itself.[32] This study of the dynamic between the institutional and extra-institutional aspects of social life and of the importance of extra-institutional mobilization for the success or failure of institutions, has injected new elements into an understanding of law. Indeed, one of the main distinguishing characteristics of social movements literature has been this emphasis on the interconnectedness, at both the national and global levels, between everyday forms of power struggles and institutional politics.[33] Stated differently, a social movement perspective emphasizes the importance of extra-institutional forms of mobilization for the "success" or "failure" of institutional forms.[34] In this sense, these extra-institutional forms of mobilization constitute important arenas of resistance that remain beyond the cognitive boundaries of international law's sole, approved discourse of resistance—human rights.

Few of these perspectives have yet permeated international law despite recent scholarship in international relations that seriously considers social movements.[35] International law remains trapped in a

---

and the Promise of Transnational Civil Society, 14 AM. U. INT'L L. REV. 1335 (1999).

32. This is the understanding of power that Michel Foucault has advanced—i.e., power is not confined to the institutional, political arenas, but "circulates" through all spheres of life as a relational phenomenon. *See* MICHEL FOUCAULT, POWER/KNOWLEDGE: SELECTED INTERVIEWS AND OTHER WRITINGS, 1972–1977 (1980).

33. *See, e.g.*, Falk, *supra* note 1.

34. This is what Rajni Kothari calls "non-party political process," and Claus Offe calls "noninstitutional politics." Rajni Kothari, *Masses, Classes and the State, in* NEW SOCIAL MOVEMENTS IN THE SOUTH: EMPOWERING THE PEOPLE 59 (Ponna Wignaraja ed., 1993); Claus Offe, *New Social Movements: Challenging the Boundaries of Institutional Politics*, 52 SOC. RES. 817 (1985).

35. *See, e.g.*, ROGER BURBACH ET AL., GLOBALIZATION AND ITS DISCONTENTS: THE RISE OF POSTMODERN SOCIALISMS (1997); ROBERT O'BRIEN ET AL., CONTESTING GLOBAL GOVERNANCE: MULTILATERAL ECONOMIC INSTITUTIONS AND GLOBAL SOCIAL MOVEMENTS (2000); KATHRYN SIKKINK AND MARGARET KECK, ACTIVISTS BEYOND BORDERS: ADVOCACY NETWORKS IN INTERNATIONAL POLITICS (1998); TRANSNATIONAL SOCIAL MOVEMENTS AND GLOBAL POLITICS: SOLIDARITY BEYOND THE STATE (Jackie Smith et al. eds., 1997); Paul Ghils, *International Civil Society: International Non-Governmental Organizations in the International System*, 44 INT'L SOC. SCI. J. 417 (1992); Ronnie D. Lipschutz, *Reconstructing World Politics: The Emergence of Global Civil Society*, 21 MILLENIUM 389 (1992); Martin Shaw, *Global Society and Global Responsibility: The Theoretical, Historical, and Political*

version of politics that is narrowly focused on institutional practice and an understanding of the "social" that accepts the unity of the agent as a given. This has resulted in an artificially narrow outlook in international law. Some leading scholars, aware of this, have attempted to construct a broader approach to international law, mainly by identifying non-state actors as "international" actors[36] and by arguing for a right to personal identity that would permit international law to accommodate a plurality of social agents (on the basis of class, gender, race, ethnicity, etc.).[37] Despite this attempt, much of what occurs in extra-institutional spaces in the Third World remains invisible to international law. Indeed, the limitations of liberal categories such as rights, employed to represent social movements, are part of the reason that such blind spots continue to exist. While this argument cannot be pursued here, it is important to recognize that it is difficult to acknowledge the role of mass action in international law because of its institutionalist bias, jurocentrism, and elitism. Given that most Third World social movements consist of the urban poor, peasants, workers in the informal sector, illiterate women, and indigenous peoples whose resources are being destroyed, the legal categories—such as human rights—that are being used to represent "voices" of suffering[38] tend to have elitist blind spots.

Limits of "International Society," 21 MILLENIUM 421 (1992); Kathryn Sikkink, *Human Rights, Principled Issue-Networks and Sovereignty in Latin America,* 47 INT'L ORG. 411 (1993); Paul Wapner, *Environmental Activism and Global Civil Society,* 41 DISSENT 389 (1994); Peter J. Spiro, *New Global Communities: Nongovernmental Organizations in International Decision-Making Institutions,* 18 WASH. Q. 45 (1995).

36. This has a rich pedigree in international law. The first wave of scholarship argued for the recognition of international institutions and multinational corporations as legal actors. *See* WOLFGANG FRIEDMANN, THE CHANGING STRUCTURE OF INTERNATIONAL LAW (1964); WILFRED JENKS, THE COMMON LAW OF MANKIND (1958); PHILIP JESSUP, TRANSNATIONAL LAW (1956); Percy Corbett, *What is the League of Nations, in* BRITISH YEAR BOOK OF INT'L L. 119–48 (1924). A second wave argued for the recognition of individuals, peoples, and liberation movements as legal actors. *See* HERSCH LAUTERPACHT, INTERNATIONAL LAW AND HUMAN RIGHTS (1950); CHRISTOPHER QUAYE, LIBERATION STRUGGLES IN INTERNATIONAL LAW (1991); Louis Sohn, *The New International Law: Protection of the Rights of Individuals Rather Than States,* 32 AM. U. L. REV. 1 (1982). A third wave has now been arguing for recognition of NGOs as international legal actors. *See* Steve Charnovitz, *Two Centuries of Participation: NGOs and International Governance,* 18 MICH. J. INT'L L. 183 (1997); Spiro, *supra* note 35. Richard Falk has been calling for a post-Westphalian world order based on the emergence of a "globalization from below." *See* RICHARD FALK, LAW IN AN EMERGING GLOBAL VILLAGE: A POST-WESTPHALIAN PERSPECTIVE (1998).

37. Thomas Franck, *Clan and Super Clan: Loyalty, Identity and Community in Law and Practice,* 90 AM. J. INT'L L. 359 (1996).

38. *See* Baxi, *Voices of Suffering and the Future of Human Rights, supra* note 29.

III.   RETHINKING THE POLITICAL IN INTERNATIONAL LAW: BEYOND
        LIBERALISM AND MARXISM

This Part will first provide a contextual introduction to the theoretical challenges that arise when we adopt a social movement perspective toward international law. The current interest in social movements must be traced to the historical context in which forms of popular mobilizations began to transform the Third World. During the 1950s and 1960s, the principal forms of popular mobilizations in the Third World were organized around the "nation," aimed mainly at national liberation from colonial rule, and around "class," aimed at a structural transformation of the colonial/comprador economic and social orders within Third World countries.[39] Such mass radicalism lay behind the elite Third World radicalism one witnessed at the United Nations, calling for a New International Economic Order ("NIEO"). This mass radicalism was accompanied and followed by large public mobilizations in Western countries, such as: movements involving civil rights, black nationalism, women's rights, and gay and lesbian rights in the United States; the Green movement in West Germany; and the 1968 student protests in France.[40] In the early 1970s, however, after the engineered "fall" of Allende in Chile, the splintering of the Third World coalition, the containment of nationalist and class movements by the two Super Powers, and the genuine grassroots disillusionment with the violence of the nation-building project in many Third World countries, new forms of popular mobilization began to emerge, based on novel forms of domination and exploitation (such as migrant labor, urban squatters, and women). These mobilizations began to transform the political, economic, and social landscape of many Third World countries. Yet, they could not be analyzed within the Marxist paradigm, which had provided the tools for interpreting radical social change in the Third World for several decades. Literature on social movements emerged largely as a response to these new forms of mobilizations, even as it sought to explicate the exhaustion of leftist ideology. This explains

---

39. *See generally* FRANTZ FANON, THE WRETCHED OF THE EARTH (1963); FRANK FUREDI, COLONIAL WARS AND THE POLITICS OF THIRD WORLD NATIONALISM (1994).

40. The literature on these movements is vast. For a sample, see DOUG MCADAM ET AL., DYNAMICS OF CONTENTION (2001); ALBERTO MELUCCI, NOMADS OF THE PRESENT: SOCIAL MOVEMENTS AND INDIVIDUAL NEEDS IN CONTEMPORARY SOCIETY (1989); FRANCES FOX PIVEN & RICHARD CLOWARD, POOR PEOPLES' MOVEMENTS: WHY THEY SUCCEED, HOW THEY FAIL (1977); EDWARD SHORTER & CHARLES TILLY, STRIKES IN FRANCE, 1830-1968 (1974); SIDNEY TARROW, POWER IN MOVEMENT: SOCIAL MOVEMENTS AND CONTENTIOUS POLITICS (1998); CHARLES TILLY, THE FORMATION OF NATIONAL STATES IN WESTERN EUROPE (1975).

the attempt to distinguish the new forms of popular mobilizations as "new social movements" (based on identity politics), as opposed to presumably "old" social movements (based on national liberation or class).[41] By the end of the 1990s, identity-based movements ran out of steam and became subject to severe questioning from post-Marxists, among others.[42] This followed the discovery that the "move to markets" in development policy in the early 1990s conveniently coincided with the move away from class to identity. The whole spectrum of literature that discusses the above political and social developments is what this article refers to broadly as social movements literature. This literature is complex, varied, and dispersed across several disciplines including sociology, comparative politics, anthropology, and critical development studies.[43]

Social movements literature contains a multitude of views about what constitutes a social movement and what distinguishes a "new" from an "old" movement. To take one example, Mario Diani identifies the following general elements in a social movement: (1) they involve networks of informal interactions between a plurality of actors; (2) they are engaged in political or cultural conflicts; and (3) they organize on the basis of shared beliefs and collective identities.[44] This definition raises several important issues.

First is the issue of what causes one movement to mobilize more successfully than another—that is, what kinds of networks of interaction are necessary to convert popular discontent or sporadic disaffection into a viable movement. A general answer is that "social

---

41. For a good example of this analysis, see Jüergen Habermas, *New Social Movements*, 49 TELOS 33 (1981).

42. It is important to recognize that, in the social sciences, the debate about the newness of the "new" social movements is now sterile and ignored. *See, e.g.*, David Plotke, *What's So New About New Social Movements?*, 20 SOC. REV. 81, 81–102 (1990).

43. For recent works on social movements, see CULTURES OF POLITICS/POLITICS OF CULTURES: RE-VISIONING LATIN AMERICAN SOCIAL MOVEMENTS (Sonia E. Alvarez et al. eds., 1998) [hereinafter CULTURES OF POLITICS/POLITICS OF CULTURES]; KLAUS EDER, THE NEW POLITICS OF CLASS: SOCIAL MOVEMENTS AND CULTURAL DYNAMICS IN ADVANCED SOCIETY (1993); RAMACHANDRA GUHA, THE UNQUIET WOODS: ECOLOGICAL CHANGE AND PEASANT RESISTANCE IN THE HIMALAYAS (1989); NEW SOCIAL MOVEMENTS AND THE STATE IN LATIN AMERICA (David Slater ed., 1985); NEW SOCIAL MOVEMENTS IN THE SOUTH (Ponna Wignaraja ed., 1993); ANTHONY OBERSCHALL, SOCIAL MOVEMENTS: IDEOLOGIES, INTERESTS AND IDENTITIES (1993); GAIL OMVEDT, REINVENTING REVOLUTION: NEW SOCIAL MOVEMENTS AND THE SOCIALIST TRADITION IN INDIA (1993); SIDNEY G. TARROW, POWER IN MOVEMENT: SOCIAL MOVEMENTS, COLLECTIVE ACTION AND POLITICS (1994); THE CHALLENGE OF LOCAL FEMINISMS (Amrita Basu ed., 1995); THE MAKING OF SOCIAL MOVEMENTS IN LATIN AMERICA: IDENTITY, STRATEGY AND DEMOCRACY (Arturo Escobar et al. eds., 1992) [hereinafter THE MAKING OF SOCIAL MOVEMENTS IN LATIN AMERICA]; ALAIN TOURAINE, RETURN OF THE ACTOR: SOCIAL THEORY IN POST INDUSTRIAL SOCIETY (1988).

44. Mario Diani, *The Concept of Social Movement*, 40 SOC. REV. 1 (1992).

movement organizations," such as non-governmental organizations ("NGOs"), provide the glue for the coordination of actors with multiple motives to join the movement.[45] This does not mean, however, that NGOs lead social movements[46] nor that they, themselves, constitute social movements.[47] Amnesty International, for example, is not a social movement, but may form a part of specific social movements, such as the movement against capital punishment, in particular locations. This basic insight is often lost in international law and international relations scholarship that confuses social movements with NGOs[48] or conflates NGOs with civil society.[49] One major reason for this confusion is, as noted in Part II, the institutionalist bias in legal scholarship, which compels notice of mass action only when it is institutionalized either by emergence as a state or by registration as an NGO. While a lack of institutionalization is an Achilles' heel of social movements, legal scholarship misses much of social reality when it focuses only on institutions.

The second issue raised by Diani's definition of a social movement involves the plurality of actors in social movements including organizations, groups of individuals, and individuals, all of whom may have different motivations for joining the movements. The "anti-globalization" movement—recently witnessed in Seattle in 1999 and in Washington, D.C. and Genoa in 2000—is an example of this plurality. Members of the movement include an eclectic mix of Western labor activists worried about the loss of jobs, unions that push for protectionism, environmental activists concerned about the ecological damage of global business practices, human rights activists who worry about the unaccountability of corporations and international organizations, governments who exploit these fears to promote geopolitical interests, Third World social movements for whom the struggle against globalization is a struggle to live, and a number of other hangers-on who may lack an immediate stake but who still desire to be a part of the activity. Exploring and understanding these different motivations is crucial to a proper appreciation of how international legal norms and processes work in practice.

---

45. TARROW, *supra* note 43, at 15.

46. As Tarrow asserts, a "bimodal relationship between leaders and followers . . . is absent from movements." *Id.*

47. Diani, *supra* note 44, at 13–14. *See* William Fisher, *Doing Good? The Politics and Antipolitics of NGOs Practices*, 26 ANN. REV. ANTHROPOLOGY 439, 436–64 (1997).

48. *See, e.g.*, Spiro, *supra* note 35.

49. *See, e.g.*, Charnovitz, *supra* note 36.

A third issue noted by Diani is that different scholars understand the notion of conflict in different ways.[50] Some view the notion of conflict as primarily interpersonal and cultural,[51] while others view it as one directed toward economic and political change.[52] In the context of the Third World, most social movements emerge through a conflict with capitalist development. As Barry Adam points out:

> To ignore the dynamics of capitalist development, the role of the labour markets in reorganizing spatial and familial relations, and the interaction of new and traditional categories of people with dis/employment patterns is to ignore the structural prerequisites which have made the new social movements not only possible, but predictable.[53]

The literature on social movements also notes that how a conflict plays out (e.g., the strategies used, the means deployed and shunned, and, simply, what gets counted as "political") will depend upon each society's own historical methods of protest—what Tarrow refers to as "contention by convention."[54] This calls for a very contextual understanding of resistance, unlike the totalizing category of rights, which presumes that resistance is expressed only in the secular, rational, and bureaucratic arenas of the modern state, particularly through the judiciary. Thus, Parisians build barricades[55] and Indians stage dharnas and satyagrahas. "Political culture," as a concept, is critical for understanding what gets counted as "political" when conflicts arise in particular societies. International law and law in general, however, reduce complex conflicts in non-Western societies to the "rationalist, universalist and individualist" political culture of the West.[56]

The final element of Diani's definition of a social movement

---

50. Diani, *supra* note 44, at 10.

51. ALBERTO MELUCCI, NOMADS OF THE PRESENT: SOCIAL MOVEMENTS AND INDIVIDUAL NEEDS IN CONTEMPORARY SOCIETY (1989).

52. Sidney Tarrow theorizes that movements respond to political opportunity and advance their causes through direct confrontation with formal political spheres. *See* TARROW, *supra* note 43, at 18. Post-Marxists emphasize how movements emerge through their ongoing struggles with the state and capital. *See* Barry Adam, *Post-Marxism and the New Social Movements*, 30 CAN. REV. SOC. & ANTHROPOLOGY 316 (1993).

53. Adam, *supra* note 52, at 322.

54. TARROW, *supra* note 43, at 18.

55. *Id.* at 19.

56. CHANTAL MOUFFE, THE RETURN OF THE POLITICAL 2 (1993).

is that it is organized on the basis of shared beliefs and collective identities. This raises the fourth, and final, issue of how such identities are initially formed. Some suggest that "consensus mobilization" is an on-going part of a movement's formation,[57] while others acknowledge that irreconcilable differences lead to a "process of realignment and negotiation between actors."[58] It appears that both of these processes occur in many social movements, often simultaneously. As gaps between different actors widen and consensus eludes them, realignment of identities begins to occur. This process is wholly different from the "right to identity" approach adopted by international law, which looks at identity as merely an individual choice.

A. Beyond Liberalism

For a number of reasons, the new forms of mobilization in the Third World cannot be analyzed using liberal categories such as rights. First, liberal theory assumes a sharp distinction between public and private, privileging only that which belongs to the public sphere for legal protection.[59] As the feminist slogan "personal is political" vividly showed, this assumption simply fails to take into account the relations of power in the domestic or private arenas. The distinction between public and private was based on a sharply delimited arena of the "political," which feminists, among others, have shown to be inadequate.[60]

Second, liberal theory assumes all legitimate power to be united in a "sovereign will" and all political activity to be conducted through institutional arenas such as legislatures and through institutions such as political parties.[61] Third World mass movements

---

57. TARROW, *supra* note 43, at 22–23.

58. Diani, *supra* note 44, at 9 (citing D.C. Snow et al., *Frame Alignment Processes, Micromobilization, and Movement Participation*, 51 AM. SOC. REV. 464 (1986)).

59. *See* Frances Olsen, *Constitutional Law: Feminist Critiques of the Public/Private Distinction*, 10 CONST. COMMENT. 319 (1993). For an analysis in international law, see Karen Engle, *After the Collapse of the Public/Private Distinction: Strategizing Women's Rights*, *in* RECONCEIVING REALITY: WOMEN AND INTERNATIONAL LAW 143 (Dorinda G. Dallmeyer ed., 1993).

60. *See* J. Oloka-Onyango & Sylvia Tamale, *"The Personal is Political" or Why Women's Rights are Indeed Human Rights: An African Perspective on International Feminism*, 17 HUM. RTS. Q. 691 (1995); Celina Romany, *Women as Aliens: A Feminist Critique of the Public/Private Distinction in International Human Rights Law*, 6 HARV. HUM. RTS. J. 87 (1993); Olsen, *supra* note 59.

61. Thus, even while describing his "law of peoples," John Rawls imposes the requirement of a constitutional democratic government through which liberal people act as he

experienced this assumption as too restrictive because it excluded other arenas of doing politics and promoted a corrupt version of statism. European social theorists, particularly Jüergen Habermas, Alain Touraine, Claus Offe, and Alberto Melucci, criticized this liberal tendency to unify the political space.[62] Habermas, in particular, theorized about new social movements, drawing on the experience of German Green movements, and postulated the idea of a "public sphere" where opinion formation takes place prior to will formation in the sanctioned political arenas.[63] This "public sphere" has been a useful tool for conceptualizing social movements.

Third, liberal theory assumes the unity of the social actor (as a consumer, producer, citizen, etc.) and creates formal arenas where the interests of such social actors would be represented.[64] The praxis of social movements in the Third World shows that the heterogeneity and plurality of the social actor is an essential feature of mass mobilization, which the representational model is unable to accommodate without doing violence to its heterogeneous character.[65]

Fourth, liberal theory assumes a harmonious view toward economic growth, as it assumes that the post-World War II welfare state would shoulder the responsibility of humanizing it. This assumption is based on the Weberian understanding that the contradictions created by the institutions of civil society—property, market, the family, etc.—would be "neutrally" resolved by the State.[66] Instead of achieving this result, however, the State simply colonized civil society and, indeed, all life spaces.[67] This was particularly true in Latin America and Asia, which followed State-led industrialization as part of an import-substitution strategy in the decades following World War II. Thus, social movements in the Third World have

---

tries to balance the law of peoples with the law of states. *See* JOHN RAWLS, THE LAW OF PEOPLES 23–24 (1999).

62. *See* sources cited *supra* notes 40 and 43.

63. *See* JÜERGEN HABERMAS, BETWEEN FACTS AND NORMS: CONTRIBUTIONS TO A DISCOURSE THEORY OF LAW AND DEMOCRACY (1996). Admittedly, Habermas' theory is entirely domestically-focused and does not examine international politics. Nevertheless, his theory has been influential in thinking about civil society in democratic transitions, and it offers a model for contemplating global civil society.

64. For a critique, see Chantol Mouffe, *Democracy, Power and the "Political,"* in SEYLA BENHABIB, DEMOCRACY AND DIFFERENCE: CONTESTING THE BOUNDARIES OF THE POLITICAL 245–56 (1996).

65. See CULTURES OF POLITICS/POLITICS OF CULTURES, *supra* note 43, at 10–14.

66. In Weberian terms, this meant the bureaucracy and the law. *See* FROM MAX WEBER: ESSAYS IN SOCIOLOGY (H.H. Gerth & C.W. Mills eds., 1946).

67. For an analysis, see Ashis Nandy, *State, in* DEVELOPMENT DICTIONARY: A GUIDE TO KNOWLEDGE AS POWER (Wolfgang Sachs ed., 1992).

arisen partly as an attempt to liberate these life spaces from the State and partly to politicize the very institutions of civil society so that it is no longer dependent upon increasing regulation and control.

B. Beyond Marxism

What is the role of Marxist theory in the new forms of Third World mobilization? After all, Marxism provided theoretical tools for analyzing social conflicts in the Third World for almost half a century. The short answer is that social movements in the Third World emerged substantially as a response to the failure of Marxism as a discourse of liberation. This was due to many factors. First, Marxism assumes the identity of social agents (peasant, labor, etc.) through fixed social structures that privileges some categories over others (for example, the proletariat as the vanguard).[68] This means, for example, that a struggle that lacks a "real" class basis—e.g., "bourgeois feminism" or "kulak farmers"—cannot be comprehended. Thus, Marxism became marginal to the most important social struggles in the Third World that were organized around, for example, environmental degradation, the oppression of women, and dispossession of labor and assets from farmers.

Second, Marxism is wedded to an evolutionary view of society and, for example, tends to interpret all social struggles in terms of a move from feudalism to capitalism.[69] Besides being rigid and essentialistic, this historical determinism misses the real nature of many Third World social movements, which combine struggles over material aspects (economic struggles) with struggles over symbolic meanings (cultural struggles).[70] In addition, the evolutionary view borders on ethnocentrism as it automatically assumes the superiority of specific forms of Western modernity over non-Western tradition. This was rejected by several social movements in the Third World, such as the Zapatistas, that organized around a particularly strong

---

68. *See* Karl Marx & Friedrich Engels, *Manifesto of the Communist Party*, *in* THE MARX-ENGELS READER 469–500 (Robert C. Tucker ed., 1978).

69. *See e.g.*, Karl Marx, *On Imperialism in India*, *in* THE MARX-ENGELS READER, *supra* note 68, at 653–64. For a critique, see Balakrishnan Rajagopal, *Locating the Third World in Cultural Geography*, THIRD WORLD LEGAL STUD. 1, 17–18 (1998–99).

70. For a good discussion of the theoretical issues in the context of the Latin American feminist movement, see Norma Stoltz Chinchilla, *Marxism, Feminism and the Struggle for Democracy in Latin America*, *in* THE MAKING OF SOCIAL MOVEMENTS IN LATIN AMERICA, *supra* note 43, at 37–51.

cultural identity.[71]

Third, Marxism shares with liberal theory the understanding of a unified political space and, thus, the State as the main agent of social and economic change.[72] Consequently, the purpose of mass mobilization, as theorized, is the capture of state power. This understanding was reinforced by the statism of Third World development models in the post-World War II period, such as import-substitution and export-promotion. Social movements, on the other hand, reject the State as the main agent of socio-political transformation and do not seek state power as an end in itself. Instead, they seek to obtain their own political space in which they can set the pace and direction of economic change.[73]

Fourth, with globalization, Marxism began to lose touch with new forms of economic arrangements and new forms of struggles that accompanied them, not only in advanced industrial societies, but also in the Third World. These new economies, demonstrated most clearly by the emergence of foreign direct investment, trade, and capital markets, began to reveal that the sphere of capital accumulation and its processes were wider than those of commodity production and exchange. It was wider in at least two ways: (1) capital accumulation increasingly took place on a global scale, whereas commodity production had been theorized within the boundaries of the nation-state; and (2) capital accumulation began to include substantial amounts of labor (domestic labor and informal immigrant labor in low-wage apparel industries) and wealth (natural resources) that were not included in commodity production and exchange. In short, there was a global economy in the making. Marxism was simply unable to supply the theoretical tools to comprehend and respond to it. The social movements that emerged in the Third World surfaced largely as a response to the new, harsh forms of global economy.[74] Indigenous peoples' movements, fishworkers' movements, farmers' movements, and "anti-globalization" protests are a result of the failure of Marxism

---

71. *See* George Yudice, *The Globalization of Culture and the New Civil Society, in* CULTURES OF POLITICS/POLITICS OF CULTURES, *supra* note 43, at 367–68.

72. This was most clearly manifested in the way Marxism differentiated itself from anarchism. *See* Friedrich Engels, *Versus the Anarchists, in* THE MARX-ENGELS READER *supra* note 68, at 728–29. For a critique, see PARTHA CHATTERJEE, THE NATION AND ITS FRAGMENTS (1993).

73. *See* Gustavo Esteva, *Regenerating Peoples' Space,* 12 ALTERNATIVES 125 (1987).

74. *See generally* Samir Amin, *Social Movements at the Periphery, in* NEW SOCIAL MOVEMENTS IN THE SOUTH, *supra* note 43, at 76–100; David Slater, *Rethinking the Spatialities of Social Movements: Questions of (B)orders, Culture and Politics in Global Times, in* CULTURES OF POLITICS/POLITICS OF CULTURES, *supra* note 43, at 380–404.

as a coherent leftist doctrine. To follow Gail Omvedt,[75] what is needed is a historical materialism of all groups adversely affected by the new global economy.

C. Toward a "Cultural Politics"

Social movements arise as a challenge to liberalism, Marxism and, by extension, to extant theories of international law. These theories extend from the utopian (liberal/Western/naturalist) to the apologist (Marxist/Third World/positivist/Realist).[76] The utopians imagine a world without sovereignty (but not necessarily without the state) in which the individual is the primary political actor. Alternatively, the apologists take the political community of the nation-state as the primary political actor and seek to imagine an international legal order that is simultaneously created and constrained by its sovereignty.

Social movements differ from both the utopian and apologist approaches of conceptualizing an international order. Social movements seek to preserve the autonomy implied in the positivist vision, but to abandon the nation-state as the collectivity that would guarantee such autonomy. They also share the naturalists' deep suspicion of the leviathan, but allow a multiplicity of arenas, including the community (rather than the individual), as political actors. Instead of accepting the unified political space propounded by these extant theories, social movements seek to redefine the very boundaries of what is properly "political."

Indeed, most social movements enact a unique form of politics that the author would label "cultural politics." This label is not meant to privilege those movements that are more clearly cultural as "authentic." In the past, this focus on culture resulted in a false dichotomy between "new" and "old" social movements. The former focused on identity and new forms of politics (involving, e.g., human rights, sexual orientation, environment, etc.), whereas the latter movements focused on the struggle for resources to cope with the contradictions of a capitalist economy (such as urban squatters', peasants', and fishworkers' movements). Rather, for all of these movements, identity is strongly associated with survival strategies.

---

75. OMVEDT, *supra* note 43, at xvi.

76. The apology versus utopia contrast is borrowed from Martti Koskenniemi's path-breaking book, FROM APOLOGY TO UTOPIA: THE STRUCTURE OF INTERNATIONAL LEGAL ARGUMENT (1989).

This gives rise to a much richer, contextual, and relational form of politics. As the introduction to an important, recent collection of essays noted:

> We interpret cultural politics as the process enacted when sets of social actors shaped by, and embodying, different cultural meanings and practices come into conflict with each other .... Culture is political because meanings are constitutive of processes that, implicitly or explicitly, seek to redefine social power. That is, when movements deploy alternative conceptions of women, nature, race, economy, democracy, or citizenship that unsettle dominant cultural meanings, they enact a cultural politics.[77]

The above definition of cultural politics makes it clear that politics is much more than a set of actions taken in formal political arenas (such as legislatures). Rather, it is a decentralized phenomenon that encompasses power struggles enacted in private, social, economic, and cultural arenas, in addition to the formal arenas. By challenging and redefining what counts as political and who defines what is political, social movements foster alternative conceptions of the political itself.

To illustrate more clearly what the rich, relational definition of the "political" in cultural politics means for international law, an outline of its elements is as follows:

> Politics goes beyond what we do in formal arenas, and therefore beyond formal voting rights and representation. Human rights law and mainstream political science, however, continue to focus on what happens in the formal institutions to the exclusion of non-institutional mobilizations. For example, a leading democracy theorist states that political institutionalization is "the single most important and urgent factor in the consolidation of democracy."[78]

This narrow outlook governs several areas of international law including peacekeeping and peacebuilding, international economic law, good governance, and humanitarian interventions to save "failed states."

---

77. CULTURES OF POLITICS/POLITICS OF CULTURES, *supra* note 43, at 7.

78. *See* CAPITALISM, SOCIALISM, AND DEMOCRACY REVISITED (Larry Diamond & Marc F. Plattner eds., 1993).

Struggles over meanings and values in the domain of culture are also political. The personal is finally political. This reverses a bias against culture that international law has historically exhibited.

Political struggles are relational; they are not individual. This abandons the "billiard ball" model of politics that has governed liberal rights theory and realist international legal theory. These theories assume that individuals and States are rational self-maximizing actors and therefore focus on their "right to choose" alternative political paths. A social movements approach, by contrast, focuses on the actual way political choices are shaped in collective settings, thereby allowing analyses to either "scale up" from the level of individuals, or to "scale down" from the level of states.

Conflict is at the heart of politics. This element, borrowed from Marxism, reverses the liberal theory's presumption in favor of harmony between social classes (and resultant covering-up of underlying conflicts). These conflicts, which arise at both the material and symbolic levels, are not among nation-states, but among classes. Such a focus on conflict can then aid in infusing a notion of social justice into the analysis of legal rules and institutions in areas such as international economic law.

By positing a cultural politics, social movements effectively foster alternative modernities. As Fernando Calderon puts it, some movements focus on the question of how to be both modern and different.[79] By mobilizing meanings that cannot be defined within standard paradigms of Western modernity, such movements challenge the authority of international law to speak on what is modern and traditional.

Finally, identities do not result merely from individual choice, but from relational activities among a group of people who unite to achieve a common purpose in the form of a movement. In this sense, the "rights" to identity may be inherently relational.[80] This notion is entirely foreign to both the utopian and apologist approaches to international law described above.[81]

---

79. Fernando Calderon, *quoted in* CULTURES OF POLITICS/POLITICS OF CULTURES, *supra* note 43, at 9.

80. Recent rights and property scholarship in North America has moved to articulate a social relations approach. *See, e.g.,* JOSEPH WILLIAM SINGER, ENTITLEMENT: THE PARADOXES OF PROPERTY (2000); Jennifer Nedelsky, *Reconceiving Rights as Relationship*, 1 REV. CONS. STUD. 1 (1993); Joseph Singer, *The Reliance Interest in Property*, 40 STAN. L. REV. 611 (1988); Joseph Singer & Jack Beerman, *The Social Origins of Property*, 6 CAN. J.L. & JUR. 217 (1993).

81. *See supra* note 76 and accompanying text.

It may appear then that the praxes of social movements centrally challenge the very foundations of international law, and provide a more realistic and promising means of imagining a post-Westphalian order, as Richard Falk has labeled it.[82] Instead of defending the "universal" categories of sovereignty and rights, social movements offer a "pluriversal" defense of local communities. In doing so, they reveal the limitations of both a Kantian liberal world order, based primarily on individual autonomy and rights, and also a realist world order based primarily on State sovereignty.

IV.   RESISTANCE AS AN ANALYTICAL CATEGORY IN
       INTERNATIONAL LAW

Traditional international law is unconcerned with mass action unless it is directed at the creation of states in the form of movements that assert the right to self-determination. Even in such cases, international law usually leaves the murky terrain of mass action and "returns" only to welcome the victor as a legitimate representative of State sovereignty.[83] This doctrinal position enabled European and American colonial empires to defeat the legal claims of Third World, anti-colonial, and nationalist movements for independence under international law. Regardless of how much "resistance" such groups posed—for example, during the Mau Mau rebellion in British Kenya—traditional international law has no vocabulary for understanding and accommodating it. This enabled the colonial authorities to treat anti-colonial resistance as criminal acts and to deal with it through law enforcement measures, especially through the doctrine of emergency. Indeed, traditional international law is notorious for the ease with which it has sanctioned violence against non-Western peoples. As Professor Anthony Anghie has emphasized so eloquently about nineteenth-century positivism:

> The violence of positivist language in relation to non-European peoples is hard to overlook. Positivists

---

82. RICHARD FALK, LAW IN AN EMERGING GLOBAL VILLAGE: A POST-WESTPHALIAN PERSPECTIVE (1998).

83. *See* LEAGUE OF NATIONS O.J. Spec. Supp. 3, at 6 (1920) (stating that when a state undergoes a transformation of dissolution, its legal status is uncertain). For a trenchant critique of this case and the self-determination doctrine, see Nathaniel Berman, *Sovereignty in Abeyance: Self-Determination and International Law*, 7 WIS. INT'L L.J. 51 (1988). *See also* Anthony Carroll & B. Rajagopal, *The Case for the Independent Statehood of Somaliland*, 8 AM. U. J. INT'L L. & POL'Y 653, 666–74 (1992).

developed an elaborate vocabulary for denigrating these peoples, presenting them as suitable objects for conquest, and legitimizing the most extreme violence against them, all in the furtherance of the civilizing mission—the discharge of the white man's burden.[84]

The hope that formal political independence for the colonized territories would quickly lead to the creation of a new international law was dashed as the efforts by the newly independent countries to create a NIEO in the 1970s grounded to a halt.[85] During the last couple of decades, it has become increasingly difficult to place much hope in the capacity of Third World states to act as effective guarantors of the democratic aspirations of the masses in the Third World. State sovereignty has been parceled both upwards (to international institutions such as the World Trade Organization and Bretton Woods institutions) and downwards (to market actors and NGOs). The idea of development, with its catching-up rationale that provided the motivation for nation-building in the post-World War II period, has come to be seen as an ideological enterprise with profoundly dangerous implications for the most vulnerable and voiceless in society.[86] In addition, the Third World State has come to colonize all life spaces in civil society and has effectively championed the interests of the global elite that control the world economy. The democratic deficit experienced by global governance processes has been exacerbated due to the democratic deficit of Third World States that act as the agents of the "globalitarian" class.[87] The reformist sensibility in international law during the post-World War II period, which revolved around a commitment to individual human rights and an expanded concept of international development including the law of "welfare," also failed to reverse the rot in the system. Though the

---

84. Antony Anghie, *Finding the Peripheries: Sovereignty and Colonialism in Nineteenth Century International Law*, 40 HARV. INT'L L.J. 1, 7 (1999).

85. This effort by newly independent countries took the form of a number of U.N. General Assembly resolutions and declarations, which legal status was contested by Western international lawyers. *See Charter of Economic Rights and Duties of States*, G.A. Res. 3281, U.N. GAOR, 29th Sess., Supp. No. 30, at 50, U.N. Doc. A/9030 (1974); *Declaration on the Establishment of a New International Economic Order*, G.A. Res. 3201, U.N. GAOR, 6th Special Sess., Supp. No. 1, at 3, U.N. Doc. A/9559 (1974). On the NIEO, see MOHAMMED BEDJAOUI, TOWARDS A NEW INTERNATIONAL ECONOMIC ORDER (1977).

86. For an analysis, see Balakrishnan Rajagopal, *International Law and the Development Encounter: Violence and Resistance at the Margins*, 93 A.S.I.L. PROC. 16 (1999).

87. *See generally* DAVID HELD, DEMOCRACY AND THE GLOBAL ORDER: FROM THE MODERN STATE TO COSMOPOLITAN GOVERNANCE (1995).

causes of this are too complex to examine here,[88] it may be noted that the idea of human rights has proven to be too Western, disciplinary, and anti-political. At the same time, the idea of development has proven to be associated with the containment of mass resistance (especially anti-communist peasant) and a destructive modernity (destructive as in having a devastating impact on natural resources and livelihoods). The post-World War II "settlement" of the colonial question through the grant of political sovereignty did not end mass movements in the Third World. Instead, this resistance took myriad other forms, through social movement action, that have not been sufficiently understood by international lawyers, partly due to the disciplinary limitations discussed above. It is now becoming obvious that Third World social movements represent the cutting edge of resistance in the Third World to antidemocratic and destructive developments. It is important for international lawyers to seek to develop a theory of resistance that would enable them to, at least partially, respond to the political challenge to assure a just and stable world order.

In what ways may a theory of resistance be articulated in international law? We may begin with the elements of the new notion of cultural politics, outlined in Part III above. If politics goes beyond what we do in representative arenas and encompasses civil society, if struggles over symbolic values and meanings matter as much as those over resources, if political struggles and identities are inherently relational, if conflict is central to politics, and if alternative modernities may be fostered by alternative conceptions of the political, then a theory of resistance must begin by questioning many elements of the existing theories of international law and relations. It must cease treating the state and the ideology of development with irrational reverence. It must develop a more flexible and dynamic conception of the dialectic between institutions and extra-institutional mass action. It must pay diligent and honest attention to the social origin of the rules of international law. It must rethink the relationship between international law-making and domestic enforcement. It must pay much closer attention to the actual workings of norms and institutions by studying the everyday forms of power struggles in which they are implicated. It must be reinvigorated by a new, Third World identity that allows new and more useful coalitions of states and social movements to be built, for

---

88. For a detailed examination of the encounter between post-World War II international lawyers' new sensibility to reconstruct international law and the emergence of a new discourse of development to foster growth and reduce poverty in the Third World, see Rajagopal, *supra* note 86.

example on issues such as agricultural subsidies or health and trade issues.

A.   Inspirations for Formulating a Theory of Resistance

A theory of resistance in international law must pay particular attention to the rearticulation of four issues: (1) against what? (the nature of the exercise of power in current international society, including the exercise of power by the modern state); (2) toward what end? (the nature of human liberation that is sought, including the relationship between resistance and the psychology of deprivation); (3) using what strategies? (the relationship between reformist and radical resistance); and (4) what should be the role of the postcolonial state in resistance? (the state as a plural, fragmented, and contested terrain). While this project has not yet truly begun, the writings of some prominent theorists such as Michel Foucault, Frantz Fanon, Antonio Gramsci, and Partha Chatterjee may offer some potential inspirations for building such a theory of resistance and addressing each of the above four issues.

1.   Michel Foucault

The first such source of inspiration is the notion of governmentality or governmental rationality, expounded by Michel Foucault in a series of lectures in the late 1970s.[89] This notion aids in a better understanding of the nature of particular exercises of power upon which a theory of resistance must focus. As defined by Foucault, governmentality means:

> The ensemble formed by the institutions, procedures, analyses and reflections, the calculations and tactics that allow the exercise of this very specific albeit complex form of power, which has as its target population, as its principal form of knowledge political economy, and as its essential technical means apparatuses of security.
>
> The tendency which, over a long period and throughout the West, has steadily led toward the pre-eminence over all other forms (sovereignty, discipline,

---

89. *See* THE FOUCAULT EFFECT: STUDIES IN GOVERNMENTALITY (Graham Burchell et al. eds., 1991).

etc.) of this type of power which may be termed government, resulting, on the one hand, in the formation of a whole series of specific governmental apparatuses, and on the other, in the development of a whole complex of *savoirs*.

The process, or rather the result of the process, through which the state of justice of the Middle Ages, transformed into the administrative state during the fifteenth and sixteenth centuries, gradually becomes "governmentalized."[90]

The nature of the exercise of power in the Third World makes it clear that it is a mistake to regard the power emerging from the State as the principal power. Rather, most effective power has shifted to apparatuses of government that are both above and below the state, as well as to both domestic and transnational private actors. As such, there needs to be a theory of power in the Third World that is broader than that which emerges from state institutions. Also, the form of the exercise of power in the Third World has a particularly bureaucratic aspect to it, consisting of techniques designed to observe, monitor, shape, and control the behavior of individuals situated within the state. This focus on the population is particularly intense with regard to the indigent, who constitute the primary object of the exercise of governmental rationality. This is not new, of course. As a mid-nineteenth-century French author wrote, "assisting the poor is a means of government, a potent way of containing the most difficult section of the population and improving all other sections."[91] Poverty alleviation is currently perhaps the most important motivation behind the operation of international institutions and significant areas of international law.[92] At a time of more intense social mobilization in the Third World, this focus on poverty alleviation raises troubling questions regarding the ideological nature of international law and institutions.

Foucault's definition is useful for developing a theory of resistance that departs from the treatment of the state as an obsession.

---

90. *Id.* at 102–03.

91. *Id.* at 151 (quoting Firmin Marbeau, *Du paupérisme en France et des moyens d'y rémédier au principles d'économic charitable*, Paris, 1847).

92. *See, e.g.*, WORLD DEVELOPMENT REPORT 2001/2002: ATTACKING POVERTY (2000) *available at* http://www.worldbank.org/poverty/wdrpoverty/report/. Even the IMF has reframed its mission with the umbrella of poverty alleviation, renaming, for instance, the Enhanced Structural Adjustment Facility (ESAF) as the Poverty Reduction and Growth Facility (PRGF). *See* IMF website *at* www.imf.org.

Traditional state theory in the Third World, influenced by Marxism, holds that the modern activities of government must be deduced from the properties and propensities of the state.[93] Foucault reverses that presumption and suggests that the nature of state institutions is a function of changes in the practice of government. This reversal has the salutary effect of moving the focus of political theory away from an excessive attention on institutions and toward practices.[94]

Finally, Foucault's definition allows for a focus on both the micropolitics of power relations and their strategic reversibility. The former permits a theory of resistance to take into account how individuals and groups experience power relations, thereby enabling international law to accommodate the feminist slogan, "personal is political" without theoretical discomfort.[95] The latter, strategic reversibility of power relations, essentially shows the contestability of seemingly entrenched power structures by demonstrating how governmental practices themselves can be turned into a focus of resistance in what Foucault calls the "history of dissenting 'counter-conducts.'"[96] This focus on micropolitics and strategic reversibility offers a richer basis for articulating a theory of resistance that focuses on social movements.

2.   Frantz Fanon

A second issue in the articulation of a theory of resistance is toward what end the resistance must aim. In two of his well-known essays, *Concerning Violence*, and *The Pitfalls of National Consciousness*,[97] Fanon lays out the psychological aspects of colonialism as well as those of anti-colonial resistance. Three themes, discussed below, arising from his work are relevant to the articulation of a theory of resistance that engages Third World social movement action.

The first theme is that a complete view of human liberation cannot be confined to the nationalist paradigm. As Amilcar Cabral

---

93. *See* THE FOUCAULT EFFECT: STUDIES IN GOVERNMENTALITY, *supra* note 89, at 4.

94. *Id.*

95. *See* Fernando Teson, *Feminism and International Law: A Reply*, 33 VA. J. INT'L L. 647 (1993) (discussing an example of discomfort with feminist approaches to international law).

96. THE FOUCALT EFFECT: STUDIES IN GOVERNMENTALITY, *supra* note 89, at 5.

97. FRANTZ FANON, THE WRETCHED OF THE EARTH 35–106, 148–205 (Constance Farrington trans., 1963).

stated, "national liberation is an act of culture."[98] This basic lesson is amply illustrated by the emergence of thousands of social movements of farmers, peasants, urban poor, indigenous peoples, women, and workers, who have felt excluded by the nation-building project during the postcolonial period. The idea that nationalism is a sufficient response to colonialism has proven to be inadequate. As Fanon says, "[h]istory teaches us that the battle against colonialism does not run straight away along the lines of nationalism."[99] Instead, he advocates a range of measures that can be adopted to avoid the dangers of nationalist consciousness, including the danger of that singular postcolonial institution, the political party, the ideological underpinnings of which rest on the Western assumption that the masses are incapable of governing themselves.[100] These views have profound importance for articulating the ends of mass resistance in already-independent nation states as they move away from the ends, such as secession, that are traditionally postulated for mass movements in international law. Indeed, the practice of several social movements, such as the Zapatistas in Mexico and the National Alliance for Tribal Self Rule ("NATSR") in India, has moved away from nationalist framings of their demands.[101] Nevertheless, these movements often see their strategies as contributing to a vision of human liberation that is as profound as anti-colonial nationalism. As Pradip Prabhu, one of the conveners of the NATSR, remarked about the passage of a law in India in 1996 that extended village self-rule to tribal areas, "it is the first serious nail in the coffin of colonialism."[102]

The second theme that emerges from the work of Fanon relates to resistance and economic power. A traditional understanding of mass action holds that, to be viable, mass action must rest on economic strength. This economic theory of violence is derived from Marxist theory, which holds that economic substructure determines all social outcomes. As Engels states:

> To put it briefly, the triumph of violence depends upon the production of armaments, and this in its turn depends on production in general, and thus . . . on

---

98. Amilcar Cabral, *National Liberation and Culture, in* RETURN TO THE SOURCE: SELECTED SPEECHES (1974).

99. FANON, *supra* note 97, at 148.

100. *Id.* at 187–88.

101. *See* George Yudice, *The Globalization of Culture and the New Civil Society, in* CULTURES OF POLITICS/POLITICS OF CULTURES, *supra* note 43, at 353–79 (analyzing Zapatista culture).

102. Personal communication, Fall 1997.

economic strength, on the economy of the State and in
the last resort on the material means which that
violence commands.[103]

This logic often drives the accumulation of economic power
by nation-states and forms the core of the catching-up rationale in the
development paradigm. It also underlies the traditional Third World
lawyer's response to colonialism as a peculiar economic exploitation
(as opposed to racial or religious domination) that could, they
believed, be reversed through doctrines such as Permanent
Sovereignty Over Natural Resources.[104]   As suggested above,
however, mass action in the Third World is often a combination of
struggles over material resources and symbolic meanings.   It is
simultaneously cultural and economic.   Fanon recognizes the
importance of this aspect. On the one hand, he bluntly states that,
"[i]n the colonies, the economic substructure is also the
superstructure. The cause is the consequence; you are rich because
you are white, you are white because you are rich."[105]   In the
postcolonial context, the intersection between economic dominance
and caste, racial, ethnic, or religious dominance is a fact of life. It is
also a fact of life in international relations. On the other hand, Fanon
notes that even economic and military dominance has not historically
assured colonial countries of victories over the colonized peoples,
partly due to tactics such as guerilla warfare.[106] Fanon's theory avoids
the underestimation of mass resistance in a non-hegemonic context, a
context in which most social movements operate.

Finally, the third theme that is relevant to a theory of
resistance is Fanon's understanding that the new forms of capitalism
in the Third World have transformed the political space for
governance and resistance. Although he was writing well before the
advent of the new global economy, Fanon notes that, as the colony is
transformed from a sphere of exploitation to a market for goods, blind
domination of the natives based on slavery is replaced by a desire to
protect the market, including the "legitimate interests," of the colonial
business elite.[107] In his view, this transformation creates a "detached

---

103. *Cited in* FANON, *supra* note 97, at 64.

104. G.A. Res. 1803, U.N. GAOR, 17th Sess., Supp. No. 17 at 15, U.N. Doc. A/5217
(1962). *See also* PERMANENT SOVEREIGNTY OVER NATURAL RESOURCES IN INTERNATIONAL
LAW (Kamal Hossain & Subrata Roy Chowdhury eds., 1984).

105. FANON, *supra* note 97, at 40.

106. *Id.* at 64–65.

107. *Id.* at 65.

complicity" between capitalism and anti-colonial resistance.[108] In addition, the creation of a work force in the colony leads to a politics of reformism wherein strikes and boycotts take the place of anti-colonial rebellion.[109] This analysis contributes significantly to an understanding of how global capitalism works and how resistance to it is structured. Global capitalism works to create and protect markets and, increasingly the "rights," of the consumers. Its presence in Third World societies results in workers and others who directly benefit from it and whose politics are aimed at reformism. This analysis reveals how the spread of free markets is so often equated with the spread of freedom in general. For articulating a theory of resistance under conditions of globalization, there must be an acute understanding of how globalization structures opportunities for resistance. Fanon's work offers some clues with regard to how to proceed.

3.   Antonio Gramsci

A third inspiration for a theory of resistance in international law is the well-known work of Antonio Gramsci in *The Prison Notebooks*.[110] Though Eurocentric[111] like his contemporaries, Gramsci postulates three ideas that are of enormous value for articulating a theory of resistance that focuses on the practice of social movements.

The first is his notion of "hegemony," which, as defined by Gramsci, means:

> The spontaneous consent given by the great masses of the population to the general direction imposed on social life by the dominant fundamental group; this consent is "historically" caused by the prestige (and consequent confidence) which the dominant group enjoys because of its position and function in the world of production;
>
> [t]he apparatus of state coercive power which "legally"

---

108. *Id.*

109. *Id.* at 66.

110. ANTONIO GRAMSCI, SELECTIONS FROM THE PRISON NOTEBOOKS OF ANTONIO GRAMSCI (Quintin Hoare & Geoffrey Nowell Smith eds. and trans., 1971).

111. *Id.* at 416 (noting the "[h]egemony of Western Culture over the whole World Culture" and certifying that European culture is the only "historically and concretely universal culture").

enforces discipline on those groups who do not "consent" either actively or passively. This apparatus is, however, constituted for the whole of society in anticipation of moments of crisis of command and direction when spontaneous consent has failed.[112]

Hegemony to Gramsci, then, is an active process involving the production, reproduction, and mobilization of popular consent, which can be constructed by any "dominant group" that takes hold of and uses it. This meaning is different from the more common understanding of "hegemony" as domination through force, and corresponds realistically to the global process of governance that rests, not only on brute military force, but also on the confluence between force and moral ideas. Thus, it is the case that the interests of great powers are sought to be justified by the language of "humanitarian intervention," and that containment of mass resistance is justified through "poverty alleviation." As such, the "consent" given by the international society of states to the general direction imposed on world affairs is a function of the domination of the force and ideas of the West.

For several centuries, the West's hegemony was unshakeable. After decolonization and the rise in the economic power of Asia, as well as the emergence of multiple voices of dissent from within Western societies, however, opportunities have existed for some decades for creative political and legal strategies for the Third World. Social movements, including both those directed at corporate accountability for environmental and human rights abuses and single-issue movements, such as those for banning anti-personnel landmines, have attempted to manufacture the consent of the population for alternative paths of sustainable development, peace, or democracy. While these movements continue to lack the state's coercive apparatus for enforcing discipline on those who do not consent, it is arguable that this part of Gramsci's definition does not apply and has never applied to international affairs because international relations has always lacked an enforcement mechanism. It is plausible that in international law and relations, the conditions under which "spontaneous consent" may be manufactured are as, if not more, important than the existence of forceful enforcement mechanisms. One can understand this idea in the disciplinary sensibility that states obey most rules of international law most of the time, even in the absence of enforcement[113] or in the recognition of the increasingly

---

112. *Id.* at 12.
113. *See* LOUIS HENKIN, HOW NATIONS BEHAVE (1979). Admittedly, the reason given

important role that transnational advocacy networks play in international politics.[114]

The second idea articulated by Gramsci relates to the definition of "passive revolution" and the distinction between "war of position" and "war of movement/maneuver." This theme is critical for understanding the relationship between civil society and the state broadly, and for theorizing about the tactical efforts of social movements to influence global law and policy. He defines passive revolution in two ways: (1) as a revolution without mass participation; and (2) as a "molecular" social transformation that occurs beneath the surface of society where the progressive class cannot advance openly.[115] The latter definition, for which he cites Gandhi's non-violent movement against British rule as an example,[116] helps to introduce into political theory the everyday forms of resistance to economic and political hegemony. Although he is critical of passive revolution as a political program, he uses the term broadly enough to indicate that when a frontal attack may be impossible, a passive revolution may occur despite the surface stability of particular regimes or even the global order. Class and other forms of struggle may continue, even if only at an interpersonal level.[117] This perspective is important for expanding the analysis of international law and politics to include extensive descriptions of the micro-politics of change. Without engaging social movement literature and the tools of anthropological analysis that it provides, international law and relations cannot hope to accomplish this type of analysis.

It is important to note the distinction between "war of position" and "war of movement/maneuver" in Gramscian thought. Gramsci uses the term "war of position" to mean a muted form of political struggle that is only possible during periods of relatively stable equilibrium between fundamental classes.[118] In particular, he emphasizes that this struggle takes the form of triumph over civil

---

for this does not rest on a Gramscian framework, but on an understanding of legal process. Nevertheless, this perspective recognizes the value of maintaining Western "hegemony" through the application of a legal process that produces consent. *See also* Harold Koh, *Why Do Nations Obey International Law?*, 106 YALE L.J. 2599 (1997).

114. *See* SIKKINK & KECK, *supra* note 35.

115. GRAMSCI, *supra* note 110, at 46. (Note that Gramsci is critical of passive revolution.).

116. *Id.* at 107.

117. *Id.* at 47. Partha Chatterjee suggests that passive revolution is, in fact, the general framework of capitalist transformation in societies where bourgeois hegemony has not been accomplished in the classical way. *See* CHATTERJEE, *supra* note 72, at 212.

118. CHATTERJEE, *supra* note 72, at 206.

society before engaging the state. As he puts it, "a social group can, and indeed must, already exercise 'leadership' before winning governmental power (this indeed is one of the principal conditions for winning of such power)."[119] A "war of movement/maneuver," on the other hand, is a frontal attack that aims to seize the institutions of hegemony. Boycotts are a form of a war of position, strikes a form of a war of movement.[120] The same struggle may constitute both a war of position and war of movement. Thus, he notes that Gandhi's passive resistance is a war of position which, at certain times, became a war of movement and, at other times, underground warfare.[121] Social movement action is mostly a passive revolution, which can, at times, be a war of position (as when transnational movements press demands for boycotts of brands or insist on eco-labeling) or a war of movement (as when ethical investors divest stocks of companies that are deemed by social movement actors to be unfriendly to environmental or human rights concerns). A political theory of international law that ignores the role of passive revolution or war of position is in danger of becoming irrelevant or, worse, being blind to the role of non-state groups that do not qualify as NGOs.

The third and final idea that is important to a theory of resistance is that of the relationship between the masses and intellectuals. Several social movements that arose during the 1990s have revealed the existence of a symbiotic relationship between mass action, on the one hand, and movement intellectuals, on the other, who act as mediators between the movements and the global cosmopolitan class. Some intellectuals have assumed leadership positions themselves in various social movements. Examples include Gustavo Esteva (Zapatistas), Pradip Prabhu (NATSR), Vandana Shiva (ecological feminism) and Arundhati Roy (Narmada Bachao Andolan in India). However, there are few, if any, international lawyers who are associated with social movements. This regrettable fact causes even progressive international lawyers to seem rather clubby and elitist with no real connection to the most important mass struggles of our time. This is especially the case in the Third World, where international lawyers have an ethical responsibility to the masses, but remain committed to highly formalistic and statist analyses of the international order. This leads them to take positions on international legal issues that reflect state positions and ignore social reality. An example is the ready acceptance by Third World

---

119. *Id.* at 57.

120. *Id.* at 229.

121. *Id.*

international lawyers in the 1970s of the developing countries' position that environmental concerns were those of the rich and that poverty was the greatest polluter. This position entirely overlooked the existence of environmental movements in their own societies.[122] It also overlooked the exclusive focus of Western international lawyers on NGOs as the only legitimate non-governmental actors.[123]

Gramsci's analysis assists in formulating a theory about the proper relationship between international lawyers (as intellectuals) and social movements. He explains that the supremacy of the social group manifests itself in two ways—as "domination" and as "intellectual and moral leadership."[124] It is imperative that a struggle capture at least some intellectual and moral leadership and this opens a role for intellectuals. Agreeing with Lenin that the division of labor between intellectuals and the working class is false,[125] Gramsci suggests that the working class is capable of developing from within itself "organic intellectuals" with a dual role—that of production and organization of work and that of a "directive political" role.[126] This approach has the salutary effect of drawing attention to the class character and other ruling characteristics of international lawyers while recognizing the connection between their role in "producing" legal knowledge and the dominant group of which they are a part. It is imperative that a theory of resistance in international law pay close attention to these aspects of elite/non-elite and law/social interaction to remain effective and credible.

4.   Partha Chatterjee

Of primary importance to the articulation of a theory of resistance in international law is the role of the state. The sanctioned language of resistance in international law, i.e., human rights, is generally thought to be an anti-state discourse, though this is increasingly recognized as an inaccurate description.[127] Given that

---

122.   *See, e.g.*, R.P. Anand, *Development and Environment: The Case of the Developing Countries*, 24 INDIAN J. INT'L L. 1 (1980). Several environmental movements such as Chipko had already been taking place in India since the early 1970s. *See* GUHA, *supra* note 43.

123.   *See, e.g.*, Charnovitz, *supra* note 36.

124.   GRAMSCI, *supra* note 110, at 57.

125.   *Id.* at 3–4.

126.   *Id.* at 4.

127.   This is due to the increasing salience of economic, social, and cultural rights that require an active role for the State, as well as the recognition that effective protection of human rights and the rule of law sometimes requires state-building. On the first, see UNDP, *Human Development Report: Human Rights and Human Development* (2000). On the

many social movements arose as a result of the pathologies of the developmental state, as suggested above,[128] what is and what should be the relationship between resistance and the state? Should the state be a target or an ally? It is impossible to answer this question in the abstract as it depends upon the particular relationship between states and social movements on particular issues. Nevertheless, Partha Chatterjee's work[129] on the nature of the postcolonial state provides some clues on how social movements relate to Third World states.

The first theme that Partha Chatterjee develops is the centrality of the ideology of development for the very self-definition of the postcolonial state.[130] This resulted directly from an economic critique of colonial rule that attacked the legitimacy of such rule because it resulted in the exploitation of the colonized nation.[131] As Chatterjee discusses this critique, the state represents the only legitimate form of the exercise of power because it is a necessary condition for the development of the nation. The legitimacy of the state, then, does not come merely from elections; rather it derives from its rational character to direct a program of economic development for the nation.[132] As a result, the challenge posed by social movements to the developmental ideology of the state, whether it be through environmental or human rights critiques of its developmental activities, is seen as anti-national.[133] What is instead required is a theory of resistance that questions the developmental ideology of the state and seeks to build alternative sources of legitimacy for the state.

A second theme relates to the assumed neutrality of the state in the development process. The postcolonial goal was to establish a Hegelian rational state that would engage in the planning for and implementation of development. This soon proved to be difficult as the state itself proved to be a contested terrain where the power relations that it sought to reorder through development planning were

---

second, see Gregory Fox, *Strengthening the State*, 7 IND. J. GLOB. LEGAL STUD. 35–77 (1999).

128. See the initial discussion *supra* Part III.

129. *See* CHATTERJEE, *supra* note 72.

130. *Id.* at 202–05.

131. *Id.* at 202.

132. *Id.*

133. For example, the critics of the Narmada dam project in India have been dubbed by its Home Minister as foreign elements. *See* Balakrishnan Rajagopal, *Opinion, The Supreme Court & Human Rights*, THE HINDU (Dec. 6, 2000), *available at* http://www.hindu.com/2000/12/06/stories/05062524.htm.

already shaping the very identity of the state[134] and that of civil society. This means that the objects and subjects of planning merge into each other and that politics is never just an external constraint on the state in the development process.[135]   Rather, politics deeply penetrates the state even as the state constitutes itself as the chief agent of development.   This insight has deep implications for international law since it, also, assumes a neutral state that undertakes to execute legal obligations in a technical and rational manner with respect to the objects of intervention that are located in politics. A theory of resistance in international law must allow for the interpenetration of state and society, of domestic and international, and of law and politics.   In fact, social movement practice demonstrates that this has already been happening. For example, the leaders of social movements and the state agencies in Latin America in areas such as environment and women's rights continually switch jobs and blur the lines between the state and the objects of its intervention. Often, social movements and the states have complex, interpenetrative relationships, as exemplified by the Servicio Nacional de la Mujer (SERNAM) in Chile,[136] which is the National Women's Bureau (a government agency), or the Venezuelan ecology movement that began with a state Organic Law on the Environment in 1976.[137] This complexity indicates that a theory of resistance in international law must treat the state as a plural and fragmented terrain of contestation rather than as a monolith.

V.   CONCLUSION

The call for a theory of resistance that addresses the need to understand social movement action should not be misunderstood as a call for a rejection of international legal order. Rather, international law and institutions provide important arenas for social movement action, as they expand the political space available for transformative politics.   For international lawyers, engaging social movement literature and developing the sensibility of concerned activists, who

---

134. CHATTERJEE, *supra* note 72, at 207–08.

135.   *Id.* at 208.

136.   *See* Veronica Schild, *New Subjects of Rights? Women's Movements and the Construction of Citizenship in the "New Democracies,"* in CULTURES OF POLITICS/POLITICS OF CULTURES, *supra* note 43, at 91–117.

137.   Maria Pilar Garcia, *The Venezuelan Ecology Movement: Symbolic Effectiveness, Social Practices and Political Strategies, in* THE MAKING OF SOCIAL MOVEMENTS IN LATIN AMERICA, *supra* note 43, at 151.

are motivated by the best cosmopolitan ideals of the discipline, awaits. Mass action is a social reality in contemporary society, and international lawyers cannot remain ignorant of it. A new Third World approach to international law will need to engage social movements to transcend the impasse in which it finds itself. This new international law has the potential to contribute to a new understanding of not only the doctrines and ideas of international law, but also the very ethical purpose of the discipline.

This article has traced some of the theoretical challenges faced by international lawyers as they seek to understand their encounter with social movements. It has also suggested some preliminary considerations for articulating a theory of cultural politics that could ground a theory of resistance in international law. During most of its existence, international law has remained too Western, elitist, male-centered, and imperial, and an encounter with social movements offers an opportunity for it to fundamentally transform.

[11]

Cause Lawyering in Transnational Perspective: National Conflict and Human Rights in Israel/Palestine

Lisa Hajjar

There is an interest among scholars working on cause lawyering to "globalize" the subject by studying professional and political networks that span national boundaries. The globalizing scope of human rights provides a particularly relevant perspective, complementing the more narrowly attenuated focus on the roles and activities of cause lawyers. The subjects of this article are Israeli and Palestinian cause lawyers who have worked in the Israeli military court system in the Occupied Territories. This study adopts a transnational perspective both because the context itself (Israel/Palestine) is composed of relations that span national boundaries (statal and ethnonational) and because it befits a consideration of the international networks of human rights. Following an introductory discussion of transnationalism and a brief background on Israel/Palestine and the military courts, I turn to three aspects of cause lawyering: the political motivations inspiring lawyers to engage in such work; a comparative assessment of the legal and extralegal strategies pursued by lawyers; and the influence of human rights on the politics of lawyering in this context.

I. Thinking Transnationally

Around the world, lawyers often play important roles in formulating and advancing social or political causes. "Cause lawyering" refers to the legal and extralegal engagements of politically motivated lawyers, whether the cause is comprehensive transformation, such as independence or democratization, or a more limited aspect of public policy, such as expanded rights or

Earlier versions of this article were presented at the 1996 Law and Society Association annual meeting (Glasgow, Scotland) and the Working Group for the Comparative Study of the Legal Professions (Peyresq, France). For these opportunities, I would like to thank Austin Sarat, Stuart Scheingold, and William Felstiner. Ronen Shamir and George Bisharat have provided extremely useful counsel and information over the past few years, including comments on earlier drafts of this article. I am very grateful to the three anonymous reviewers and to Joe Stork and Bashar Tarabieh for insightful criticism and suggestions. Field research was supported by grants from the American Association of University Women, the Joint Committee on the Near and Middle East of the American Council of Learned Societies and the Social Science Research Council, the Institute for Intercultural Studies, and The American University, Washington, DC. Address correspondence to Lisa Hajjar, Department of Sociology and Anthropology, Swarthmore College, 500 College Ave., Swarthmore, PA 19081 (e-mail: lhajjar1@swarthmore.edu).

guaranteed protections of some kind. In contrast to "conventional" or "client lawyering," which is tailored to accommodate prevailing arrangements of power, cause lawyering involves the application of professional skills and services to transform some aspect of the status quo.[1]

The very notion of "cause" implies agency, motivation, social identifications, political relations, and goals. The other side of the coin is the ways in which sociopolitical dynamics affect cause lawyering as opportunities for intervention expand or contract, political alliances shift, and causes become redefined by circumstance or deliberation. The study of cause lawyering, then, involves analysis of the contours of resistance through the medium of law within a given field of hegemonic relations.

Much of the work done on cause lawyering thus far has focused on national contexts wherein lawyers' causes relate to the politics or policies of their own state or to issues affecting their own society. Even when the subjects are lawyers working in support of causes which have an internationalist agenda, cause lawyering often is organized and operationalized within national boundaries.[2] However, there is an interest among scholars working on cause lawyering to incorporate a more "global" perspective. The objective is to study professional and political networks that span national boundaries in order to gain an understanding of the factors and forces that drive and/or inhibit cause lawyering in "local" contexts.

Although cause lawyering manifests itself in widely varied ways around the world in terms of the causes and practices of lawyers, the quest for change provides a kind of organizing principle at the heart of the concept. Globalizing the study of cause lawyering would not (necessarily) alter the subject (lawyers and their activities); rather, it would involve an opening up of the boundaries—often national—that frame the analysis.

Human rights, as both a normative discourse and a form of international politics, provides a global perspective particularly relevant to the study of cause lawyering. It offers a way of imagining the world or, more specifically, a way of imagining a world changed for the better. Many examples of cause lawyering are tantamount to human rights work of some kind, and human rights "works" in large part through the efforts and activities of lawyers. As Stanley Cohen (1995:5) notes, "Lawyers are the dominant profession to claim ownership of the human rights problem and have succeeded in establishing a virtual monopoly of knowl-

---

[1] While much of the focus on cause lawyering thus far has been directed toward those who are engaged in "progressive" causes (e.g., anti-apartheid, anti-death penalty, labor, environment, immigrants' rights), as a concept cause lawyering can certainly include lawyers working on behalf of conservative or reactionary causes.

[2] Sarat and Scheingold (1997) have edited a volume on cause lawyering which includes a number of case studies from around the world.

edge (how the subject is framed) and power (what strategies of intervention are used)." Yet there is a distinction between cause lawyering and human rights: the latter is *already globalized;* the genealogy of human rights is rooted in the globalization of modernist conceptions and powers of law, notably the ideologico-political significance of the rule of law.[3] Human rights *standards* are "supranational," thus transcending and penetrating the boundaries of state sovereignty. Nevertheless, the state remains the premiere (albeit not exclusive) object and subject of human rights. This tension in human rights between the national and the international is instructive for efforts to globalize the study of cause lawyering.

Human rights is both a promising and a problematic form of international politics. On the one hand, its overarching goal is to establish universal norms of government extending to all societies. This goal is promoted and advanced by a growing international human rights movement, in which lawyers play an important part. On the other hand, human rights goals often are marginalized in local contexts by the politics of sovereignty (i.e., through abuses perpetrated or made possible by the domestic authority of states over the populations they govern),[4] and in the international order by a lack of effective means or suprastate institutions capable of enforcing human rights standards as embodied in international laws and conventions (Henkin 1990).

The human rights dilemma is the need to accommodate while also challenging other forms of authority, notably state governments. A human rights perspective is simultaneously local and global because it enables and elicits international scrutiny of local conditions. Human rights work, like most cause lawyering, is targeted to national polities; there is not, except in the most abstract terms, an "international society." But whereas cause lawyering invokes a given local order through a focus on the roles and activities of lawyers, human rights invokes the international order through a focus on supranational standards (setting, monitoring, and enforcing). In this way the two are conceptually and politically complimentary. According to Richard Falk (1985:34), "[T]he protection of human rights is dependent on the interplay of normative standards and social forces committed to their implementation."

Cause lawyering on behalf of some human rights–type goal is one kind of social force to which Falk is referring. One question that this article seeks to explore is "the interplay": how cause law-

---

   [3] The globalization of human rights is often described in terms of "generations" of rights. The first generation refers to civil and political rights, to which the rule of law is central. While it can hardly be said that there is an international consensus on human rights, this does not detract from the point that human rights has force and meaning at a global level.

   [4] This is not to imply that abuses are limited to states and other institutions in the public sphere, but this is where most of the attention has been focused.

yers make use of the discourse and politics of human rights in a localized setting. The specific subject is cause lawyering by Israelis and Palestinians in the Israeli military court system in the occupied West Bank and Gaza.[5] The time frame under consideration extends through early 1994 when the Israeli occupation was unmediated by the transition to Palestinian "self-government" in parts of the territories.[6]

This case study approach allows for an assessment of the interrelations between local and global factors and forces as they affect a particular group of lawyers and their activities. At the risk of being contradictory, however, the scope of analysis of this study is best described not as global but rather as "transnational."

> The growing significance of a transnational perspective reflects the increasing interdependence of international life combined with the persisting weakness of global institutions. The transnational focus is an ordering halfway house responding to global needs, yet accepting the territoriality of power and authority. Transnational order as a logic is intermediate between the horizontal language of statism and hegemony, and the vertical language of supranationalism. (Falk 1985:49)

The ordering logic of transnationalism has three discernable dimensions relevant to the subject of cause lawyering in the Israeli military court system. One is the spatially abstract regulatory language of human rights, which circulates through the international order by producing and incorporating transnational networks. Monitoring and reporting on violations and other problems by organizations like Amnesty International and Human Rights Watch depends on information provided by local sources, including lawyers. This information is then relayed through the publication of reports, which criticize existing practices or policies and recommend changes. Optimally, from the perspective of human rights organizations and activists, those reports then become a reference point for all kinds of political concerns and activities, from foreign aid to military sales to United Nations resolutions. Human rights informs cause lawyering in the Israeli military courts through the use of human rights language by local lawyers and the development of contacts between them and human rights organizations for purposes of trying to

---

[5] This research on cause lawyering is part of a larger study of the Israeli military court system (Hajjar 1995), based on fieldwork done in Israel and the territories in 1991–93. The research methods include extensive participant observation in all the military courts and over 100 interviews with people representing the various categories of participants, including some 45 lawyers. I spent days or even weeks with a number of lawyers. In addition to providing information about their own roles and activities, lawyers were an important source of information about the history and workings of the system and contacts among the other categories (judges, prosecutors, and defendants).

[6] I returned to Israel/Palestine in June 1997 to examine the effects of the peace process on the military court system. See Hajjar 1997a.

elicit international support to challenge the status quo of occupation.[7]

The other two dimensions of transnationalism that apply to this study are spatially grounded in the history and politics of Israel and the Occupied Territories (Israel/Palestine). They involve trans-statal and trans-ethnonational relations (see Connor 1994; Verdery 1994). The Israeli-Palestinian conflict has been a constitutive aspect of these relations.[8] A second issue which this article addresses is the localized dimensions of transnationalism as they affect cause lawyering. The objective is to illuminate the processes and effects of government-in-conflict in relations among population groups in Israel/Palestine, and people's relations to the Israeli state.[9] At the most basic level, transnationalism manifests itself locally through the significance of differences between Jews and Palestinian Arabs, and the politico-legal distinctions between citizens of the Israeli state and residents of the Israeli-occupied territories.

Section II provides background information on the political and legal context of Israel/Palestine and a brief overview of the military court system. The remainder of the article focuses on the subject of cause lawyering in the military courts. Sections III and IV concentrate on the local dimensions and dynamics of transnationalism as they inform lawyers' motivations (sec. III) and lawyers' legal and extralegal strategies (sec. IV). Section V extends the transnational perspective to the international level by considering the varying influences of human rights on cause lawyering in this context.

II. Israel/Palestine as a Case Study of Transnationalism

A. Background

In 1967 when Israel occupied the West Bank and Gaza, the territorial boundaries of Palestine during the British Mandate were reestablished by the spatialization of control through a single power, now the Israeli state (Kimmerling 1989). But this geographic contiguity manifested itself in an explicitly transnational form. Israeli rule was jurisdictionally divided among several political formations with varying legal statuses: sovereign territory (Israel proper, i.e., inside the borders of the 1949 armistice com-

---

[7] A full consideration of the transnational nature of the work of international human rights organizations is beyond the scope of this study. See S. Cohen 1995.

[8] This claim could be extended far beyond Israel/Palestine, as various governments in the Middle East have used the conflict to set national agendas, prioritize the use of resources, and develop various kinds of foreign relations (political, economic and military).

[9] The term "government" is used throughout in the Foucauldian sense of process rather than, or in addition to, institutional formation. See Gordon 1991; Hunt 1993; Mitchell 1990, 1991.

monly referred to as the Green Line), military administration
(Palestinian population centers in the territories),[10] and those
parts of the Occupied Territories that have been legalistically
transformed into de facto annexations (East Jerusalem, Jewish
settlements, military holdings, and confiscated lands).[11]

Thus, political authority in Israel/Palestine provides one example of trans-statal relations, both because of the heterogeneity
of ruling structures and because military occupation is, by definition, an "international" matter. Locally, *government* (the administration and control of land and people) is a prerogative vested in
the Israeli state, which was empowered through the fact of conquest to extend its rule to the territories. The transnationaliza-
tion of Israeli government was instituted through the various
political and legal processes of jurisdictional mapping and administration. But this localized politico-legal arrangement is mediated by the overlapping authority of the international community, which bears—and at times assumes—a degree of
accountability for the governance and fate of occupied Palestinians and the lands seized in war (see Playfair 1992).

The trans-ethnonational dimension is comparably complex.
Ideologically and politically, the population in Israel/Palestine is
comprised of "two people," specifically two ethnonations, Jewish
and Palestinian Arab. This distinction was institutionalized and
politicized over the last century, a product of the sweeping rise of
modernist nationalism. The Israeli-Palestinian conflict is, at root,
a contest of national claims to the historic homeland, an area
that conforms to the contemporary boundaries of Israel/Pales-
tine.

In terms of the character of its sovereignty, Israel is an
ethnonational state because it is a Jewish state, but its citizenry
includes people not of the Jewish "nation." The term "Israeli,"
which refers to citizenship status, includes Jews (conflating religion and nationality), Arabs (Muslim and Christian Palestinians)
and Druze (Palestinians defined communally by their religion;
they were categorized as Arabs until 1961 when the state accorded them the status of a distinct nation).[12] In ethnonational
terms, "Palestinian" includes both Arab citizens of Israel and
noncitizen residents of the territories.[13] The sociopolitical order

---

[10] Since 1994 the Israeli military has been withdrawing forces from Palestinian population centers, but the larger political implications of such moves on the ground do not
alter the fact that as long as the military retains its authority in the territories, they remain
occupied.

[11] For sources detailing the history and implications of these jurisdictional distinctions in the territories occupied in 1967, see Benvenisti 1990; Lustick 1997; Shehadeh
1993.

[12] There are two additional categories of identity among Israeli citizens: Beduin are
Muslim Arab pastoralists and Circassians are non-Arab Muslims.

[13] The term "Palestinian" also encompasses the millions living in diaspora beyond
the boundaries of Israel/Palestine.

in Israel/Palestine is structured hierarchically by the political disparities of Jewish statehood (i.e., Israel) and Palestinian statelessness.[14]

The combined significance of these trans-statal and transethnonational factors poses a number of distinct challenges for sociolegal analysis on Israel/Palestine. First, the relationship between law and society is complicated by the fact that the parameters of analysis do not correspond to the boundaries of a sovereign state. There is no single legal order applicable throughout this area nor any common legal status or shared set of rights available to all people. Second, there is a serious question as to the semiautonomy of the law when it comes to matters relating to Palestinians because of the ways in which Israeli national security is given precedence over legal rationality within the legal codes and systems (see Briskman 1988; Lahav 1988; Shamir 1990, 1991; Zamir 1989). Third, the absence of a single "polity" corresponds to the absence of any kind of unifying legal ideology. There is no shared perspective on rights, justice, security, and so on.

Cause lawyering in the military court system has been a manifestation of the contested legitimacy of Israeli authority in the West Bank and Gaza. Most of the lawyers who have chosen to work in these courts have done so for political reasons which are rooted in their critique of Israeli government in the territories. However, cause lawyering in this context is a diversified enterprise. Some lawyers, primarily Jewish Israeli liberals, are critical of the *form* of Israeli rule, particularly to the extent that it involves the violation of rule of law standards. Other lawyers, including Jewish Israeli leftists, Arab Israelis, and Palestinian residents of the territories, take the occupation itself as the basis for their criticisms.

The situation in apartheid South Africa provides a salient contrast. There, cause lawyering exhibited a coherence of cause which included not only organized resistance to the racialized politico-legal order, but also a transcendent vision of a democratic future (Abel 1995; Ellmann 1992). Among lawyers working in the Israeli military courts, there is no such shared vision about the desired course of political change or common aspirations about the future of Israel/Palestine. Analytically and politically, the contrast illustrates the difference between lawyers working for a cause of national proportion or significance, and those working in a transnational context.

---

[14] Even though a Palestinian Authority (PA) was established in 1994, its powers are subsidiary to the Israeli state and limited to municipal government over Palestinian population centers (see Usher 1995). This development does not substantively transform the hierarchical order wherein the Israeli state retains an overarching hegemony even over areas of Palestinian "self-government." Whether such a change, in the form of an independent sovereign Palestinian state, will be an outcome of the peace process remains to be seen.

In South Africa, the politics of sovereignty provided an organizing framework for resistance because the state was not only a target for change but a goal. Cause lawyering strategies were coordinated with a larger political movement to reform existing governing structures and to remake the sociopolitical order into an inclusive democracy. In a transnational context, resistance can involve reformist strategies to alter existing governing practices, and counterhegemonic forms aiming to reconfigure government entirely. In Israel/Palestine, both are in evidence. There are movements oriented to the goal of a two-state solution, and others adamantly opposed to such an option. There are movements to democratize the Israeli state by transforming its ethnonational character and others that seek to expand the provision of civil liberties under the existing order. Consequently, when it comes to cause lawyering in Israel/Palestine, the relationship between politics and law reflects a political terrain where consensus on anything is hard to find.

B. The Military Court System

The military court system is a rather unique institution in that it is one of the few contexts where Israeli citizens and Palestinian residents of the territories have had regular and sustained contact. The system was established in 1967. Its authority and jurisdiction extends from the Israeli military government in the territories, which is part of the Israel Defense Forces (IDF) (Shamgar 1982a). However, the IDF's authority in the territories derives from the duties inhering in an occupant, as set out in international humanitarian laws (i.e., laws of war).[15]

The courts are manned by soldiers. Judges and prosecutors, virtually all of whom are Jewish Israelis, include both career soldiers and reservists.[16] Translators, most of whom are Druze Israelis, are essential to the functioning of the system, given the language barriers between Hebrew-only and Arabic-only speakers.

---

[15] The official Israeli position on the state's rights and duties in the territories differs radically and explicitly from international legal opinion. Briefly, the Israeli position devolves on the argument that the West Bank and Gaza are not technically "occupied" because they were not the sovereign territory of the states ruling them at the time of the war (Jordan and Egypt, respectively). Rather, the argument holds, their status was sui generis, making them "administered" rather than occupied territory. Consequently, the laws of war pertaining to occupation, notably the Fourth Geneva Convention, do not apply to Israeli rule on a de jure basis, although the government does claim to abide by the "humanitarian" provisions of the Convention on a de facto basis (never specifying which provisions it regards as humanitarian; the International Committee of the Red Cross, guardian of the Geneva Conventions, regards them as humanitarian in their entirety). For details on this issue, see Hajjar 1997b.

[16] All military court judges and prosecutors are lawyers. As of 1988, Israeli judges sitting on domestic benches have been excluded from doing reserve duty in the military courts, a decision taken by the military leadership to avoid any appearance of a "conflict of interest."

The defense lawyers who work in the military courts include Jewish and Arab Israeli citizens as well as Palestinian residents of the territories. In addition to these politico-legal status distinctions, lawyers' legal skills and education vary, in part along lines of identity: most Israeli citizens were educated in Israeli faculties of law, while most Palestinians from the territories were educated somewhere in the Arab world (primarily Egypt and Lebanon).[17] These differences are so significant as to make it impossible to regard military court lawyers as a cohesive group. However, they do constitute a category because they perform a common role: they all represent Palestinian clients.

The military courts have been used to prosecute Palestinians charged with security violations, which encompass activities ranging from violent actions to tax evasion to political expression.[18] Israeli government of Palestinians in the territories can be regarded as a rule/rights continuum characterized by a shifting give-and-take as determined by considerations of Israeli security and other national interests. Indeed, the Israeli state has deployed law to establish a relationship between security and virtually all aspects of Palestinian life. Over the decades since 1967, hundreds of thousands of Palestinians have passed through the military court system.[19]

Despite the Israeli state's rhetorical claims to abide by rule of law standards, the military court system is rife with problems which seriously compromise the availability of due process protections.[20] The problems include the prevalent use of torture and ill treatment to extract confessions from suspects, prolonged periods of incommunicado detention, the difficulties lawyers face in meeting clients and obtaining information about cases, the use of third-party confessions that are extremely difficult to challenge, the use of "secret evidence" that is unavailable to de-

---

[17] Israeli-trained lawyers have a certain advantage because the military legal system roughly resembles other Israeli legal systems, at least to the extent that all are modeled on the Anglo-American systems. In the Arab world, where most Palestinian lawyers are educated, the Continental legal system provides the general model. This is compounded by the problem that they have little preexisting understanding of Israeli laws of procedure and evidence when they begin working in the military courts.

[18] The laws enforced through the military court system include several thousand original Israeli military orders (see Rabah & Fairweather 1993; Shehadeh & Kuttab 1980; Shehadeh 1988) and the British Defense (Emergency) Regulations, 1945, the latter a holdover from the British Mandate in Palestine (see Moffett 1989; Hajjar 1994).

[19] Between 1988 and 1993 alone there were 83,321 cases. Of this total, only 2,731 defendants were acquitted (Human Rights Watch/Middle East 1994:2). There is also an extensive apparatus for detaining and imprisoning Palestinians extralegally, referred to as "administrative detention."

[20] Virtually everyone, including Israeli judges and prosecutors, discusses the system in terms of its problems, although the nature and cause of the various problems that people choose to highlight vary.

fendants or their lawyers, and the strong trend of judicial preference for prosecution witnesses, particularly soldiers.[21]

The cumulative effects of these problems serve to place onerous burdens on defense lawyers, both as legal practitioners and
as representatives of Palestinian clients. Within the adversarial
legal process, lawyers are *legally* positioned on the "side" of Palestinian residents of the territories and "against" the Israeli military
administration. It is a taken-for-granted feature of the system that
prosecutors enjoy a vast disproportion of advantages over defense lawyers, given that the purpose of the system is to sustain
order and rule in a conflict situation (see Straschnov 1994; Yahav
1993).[22] Consequently, lawyers have few legal options to achieve
the standard mark of "victory": acquittal through trial. Rather,
for the most part they are forced to scramble for some lesser victory through plea bargaining: shorter sentences, the dropping of
charges, exclusion of some flagrantly flawed evidence, and so on.

The pressure to plea bargain also comes from clients. For
one thing, Palestinians generally have refused to regard the military legal system itself as a site of struggle. For another, dealing is
widely recognized as the best means of getting a shorter sentence, thereby enabling people to be back on the streets where, it
is popularly regarded, the "real" struggle takes place. Clients' insistence on dealing, however, does not derive from a single vision. Some are motivated simply by pragmatic considerations to
minimize the consequences of their arrest, while others offer a
politicized rationalization that dealing appropriately reflects
their disregard for Israeli "justice." Consequently, given the structural and interpersonal pressures on lawyers to plea bargain, it
should be no surprise that some 90–95% of military court cases
end in a deal.[23]

Dealing is an individualizing process where the contents of a
single case (evidence, history of past convictions, etc.) largely determine defense-prosecution negotiations over the outcome. The
practice of plea bargaining, which constitutes the vast majority of
lawyers' legal work in this system, undermines lawyers' abilities to

[21] For studies criticizing aspects of the military court system, see Amnesty Interna-
tional 1991; Cohen & Golan 1991, 1992; Dillman & Bakri 1992; Ginbar 1993; Ginbar &
Stein 1994; Golan 1989; Gordon & Mazali 1993; Human Rights Watch/Middle East 1994;
Lawyers' Committee for Human Rights 1992, 1993; Public Committee against Torture in
Israel 1990; Thornhill 1992.

[22] Many judges and prosecutors I interviewed readily acknowledged these advantages, and the fact that they tend to come at the expense of defendants' due process
rights. They rationalized this on the grounds that such measures are necessary in the fight
against terrorism.

[23] Of the cases that do not end in a plea bargain, most are dropped by the prosecution. The instances of a defense victory through trial constitute a miniscule proportion of
the total outcomes. Among lawyers I interviewed, the few who have on occasion taken
cases to trial can count their victories in the low digits—if they are that lucky. For example, one lawyer from Gaza, who claimed to have the best record in the Strip (a claim
supported by a number of other Gazan lawyers), said that in 11 years of practicing, he
won 11 cases.

use the legal process itself for political ends (e.g., presenting arguments challenging the state's authority in general or some aspect thereof). But the legal process narrowly defined neither encompasses nor explains how many defense lawyers perceive their work. While most lawyers do not believe that political change would or could come from *within* the legal system—in large part because the prevalence of dealing—they do see their roles and activities in political terms. Most ascribe their motivation for working in the military courts to the desire to *be politicized* legal practitioners.

The military court system has always functioned as an institutional intersection in the conflict. During the period of the Palestinian uprising against the occupation, which began in December 1987 and lasted through the early 1990s, Israeli-Palestinian relations reached new levels of violence and repression. Tens of thousands of Palestinians were drawn into confrontations of various kinds with the Israeli military, many for the first time. Israeli measures to contain and stop the resistance included a vastly expanded use of the military courts.

The uprising had a transformative effect on cause lawyering. In addition to the chaos caused by the flood of cases, countless people with no previous experience or preexisting knowledge of the legal system were being arrested, interrogated, and charged. Many lawyers with long-time experience made sharp negative comparisons between their "uprising clients" and the types of people they had represented in the past, who were more politically seasoned, aware of the legal costs of resistance, and willing to pay the price for their activism. Whereas prior to the uprising, defendants were often organized along the factional lines of the Palestine Liberation Organization (PLO) and certain lawyers regularly represented people from one faction or another, when the uprising started, these lines became blurred (see Hiltermann 1991; Nassar & Heacock 1991). And by the end of the 1980s, Islamist activists affiliated with Hamas and Islamic Jihad (which are not part of the PLO) were being arrested in increasing numbers. Since Islamist militancy gained prominence only during the uprising, there were virtually no prestanding arrangements for legal representation. Lawyers stepped in to meet the demand, but secular/sectarian political differences added a new potential for tensions in lawyer-client relations. Nevertheless, for all intents and purposes Islamists shared at least the short-term political goal of secular activists: ending the occupation.

The legal terrain was also affected by the uprising. The escalating demand for legal services drew some 200 additional Palestinian lawyers into military court work, many for the first time. While plea bargaining remained the strategy of choice and necessity, the variations in skills, experience, and political views were sources of tension among lawyers and between lawyers and other categories of participants.

But the uprising also had some positive effects on cause lawyering. One significant consequence was a heightened interest in the international community stimulated by media and human rights reports about conditions in the territories, including the military court system. This attention fueled and fortified a "human rights consciousness" among lawyers and enabled a whole new level of political and legal criticism of the court system that some lawyers had been striving to generate for years. In retrospect, this criticism can be seen as part of the political pressures that led to a transformation in the status quo of occupation, as manifested in the start of Israeli-Palestinian negotiations in November 1991.

III. On Being Politicized: The Importance of Identity

In the early years of the occupation, only a small number of lawyers worked in the military courts. In Gaza, four Palestinian lawyers (out of a total of ten) were willing to take military court cases from the outset. The West Bank had a larger population of lawyers, but none worked in the military courts—or any Israeli-run courts—in the early years because the entire profession was on strike to protest the occupation (see Bisharat 1989).

Felicia Langer, the first Israeli cause lawyer, began taking military court cases in 1968.[24] Langer, who is Jewish, was motivated by two interrelated goals: one was to provide legal assistance to Palestinians suffering injustices at the hands of the Israeli military and security personnel, and the other was to break down the "conspiracy of silence" within Jewish Israeli society about the nature of military rule in the territories. She believed that the former was made possible and perpetuated by the latter.

Langer played a groundbreaking role in struggling to raise public awareness about the problems in the military courts, using her first-hand experience to publicize information about Israeli abuses, including the use of torture (see Langer 1975, 1979, 1988). To enhance her legitimacy as a critic among Jewish Israelis, she drew lines around the kinds of cases she was willing to take: she refused to represent people charged with violent crimes. While she did succeed in gaining public visibility, it did not have transformative effects on Israeli public opinion. It did, however, earn her condemnation by Israeli officials as a "terrorist sympathizer" (see Shefi 1982:322–23). But her activities and visibility paved the way for a new generation of Israeli cause lawyers,

---

[24] Prior to Langer's entry into the military court system, Israeli lawyers who defended Palestinians were not cause lawyers. They included military lawyers assigned to the task and some private lawyers who saw the military courts as a new market for their services.

Jews and Arabs, who decided to take up military court work. They were joined by a growing number of Palestinian lawyers.[25]

By the 1980s, the number of lawyers working in the military courts either full or part time had climbed to nearly 200. They included about two dozen Jewish Israelis, four dozen Arab Israelis, and about 120 Palestinians from the West Bank and Gaza.[26] As mentioned above, the uprising drew additional Palestinian lawyers into military court work, but their tenure was brief, and many dropped out as the number of cases declined by the early 1990s.

The reasons Israeli lawyers cite for having chosen to work in the military courts vary. Jewish liberals have been inspired primarily by a concern that the military authorities were failing to abide by rule of law principles, thereby infringing on Palestinians' rights. While they would describe themselves as loyal citizens of Israel, they were critical of the state's tactics to maintain the occupation. Their motivation, then, was to inspire—and if necessary to pressure—the authorities to adhere to the relevant standards of legality for a military occupation. One liberal lawyer describing his work in this regard said that he is an enigma for judges and prosecutors. On the one hand, having served in an elite unit of the IDF he is literally "one of them." On the other hand, he makes a regular practice of reporting on events in the military courts in order to provoke a critical reaction among Jewish Israelis, the one constituency with a capacity to exert pressure on the state to change those policies and practices that contradict the exercise of legitimate authority. He said,

> There is only so much I, or any lawyer, can do in the courts. But when I see a problem, something really outrageous, I run to the media. I have good connections with journalists and they believe what I say because they know me. When I give them a story about something outrageous, like a kid being sent to jail with some long sentence just for throwing stones, or if someone comes to court with bruises from a beating, I want people to know about it. I don't want people to say they didn't know. . . . This is my real service.

Such views, if not necessarily such media tactics, are shared by other liberal Jewish Israeli military court lawyers, who are concerned about the negative effects the occupation is having on

---

[25] The increasing number of Palestinian lawyers working in the military courts was due to both a growth in the profession and the decision among some West Bank lawyers to break the strike.

[26] Because of the politico-legal distinctions among lawyers, no single organization represents them all. Israeli citizens belong to the Israel Bar Association, but this organization has largely resisted involving itself in the professional concerns of its members who defend Palestinians in the military courts. In 1976, Gazan lawyers organized themselves into the Gaza Bar Association, and in 1980, West Bank lawyers formed the Arab Lawyers' Committee. The organizational disunity also makes it difficult to determine the exact number of lawyers working in the courts at any period. The figures cited in the text are estimates provided by knowledgeable informants.

their own society and on Israeli legal culture. When liberals cross the Green Line to defend Palestinians against the state, it serves to disrupt the complacency about what goes on "over there." They are struggling to alter a strong popular view within Jewish Israeli society that it is legitimate to accord legal standards secondary status to national security,[27] which is held to be at constant risk from the dangers posed by the Palestinian collectivity in the territories (see Arian, Talmud, & Hermann 1988). Jewish Israeli liberals are motivated by a desire to intervene in the balance between security concerns and legal principles. According to one who occasionally takes military court cases:

> There is no formula to assess national security, and every Arab in the territories is not *necessarily* a security threat. Because of the procedural problems [referring to the use of "secret evidence"] lawyers have no way of knowing whether the judges and prosecutors are acting fairly in any case. . . . We have to be concerned that people get what they can from the court.

In contrast, Jewish leftists and Arab Israelis have seen their work as an opportunity to support the Palestinian nationalist struggle for independence and to develop solidarity relations with Palestinians in the territories. They share in the view that the occupation is in and of itself a violation of Palestinian rights, not simply a context within which human rights violations occur. However, the Jewish-Arab distinction has implications for their own perspectives on cause and for the way they are regarded by others.

Leftist Jewish lawyers tend to describe themselves as non-Zionists or even anti-Zionists who do not identify with the political establishment.[28] Yet, as Jews they are privileged within the sociopolitical hierarchy in comparison to all categories of non-Jews. Because they politically support the Palestinian struggle against the occupation, their activities as cause lawyers are considered suspect by many Jewish Israelis and the more outspoken among them are regarded as traitors to their own "side." As one lawyer described his decision to take up military court work:

> When I was young, I was ideologically sympathetic to the left, but I wasn't politically active. Then I started working for [a leftist lawyer] and that opened my eyes. I saw the conditions in the territories and I saw what kind of suffering the Palestinians face. . . . I understand the political motivations of Palestinians. It is my job to help them weather down the damage. . . . Being a Jewish Israeli makes it easier for me than for Palestinian law-

---

[27] Within official and politically mainstream Israeli discourse, the prioritizing of security over legality is often justified on the "necessity" argument. For an example, see Landau et al. 1987; for a critique, see Kremnitzer 1989.

[28] Within the Israeli political spectrum, these lawyers would actually be regarded as "ultra-leftists," since the term "leftist" is used to refer to people associated with Zionist left parties like Meretz (a coalition of Ratz, Mapam, and Shinui) and political movements like Peace Now and Yesh Gvul.

yers. Palestinian lawyers have a very hard time and many of them take too much shit. I am not going to take shit from some soldier, and they know it.

For leftist Jewish lawyers, being politicized legal practitioners means defending people engaged in a struggle against a status quo of continuing oppression and disenfranchisement. As one well-known leftist lawyer described her cause: "I have done no favors and deserve no thanks. I am simply trying to make the place where I live [i.e., Israel/Palestine] free of occupation, oppression, exploitation and racism."

Arab Israeli lawyers compare themselves politically to like-minded leftist Jewish Israelis. But Arabs have a more ambiguous relationship with both Jewish Israeli society and their fellow Palestinians who live under occupation. Within the Israeli polity, Arabs are marginalized by definition as non-Jews. For those Arab Israelis who choose to practice across the Green Line, cause lawyering has been integrally linked to issues of identity. The question is not only what is the cause but also who are they—in relation to "their" state (Israel) and "their" people (Palestinians). One Arab Israeli lawyer expressed the contradiction: "I am a soldier in my people's army and I use the cards I have been dealt." His cards include Israeli citizenship.[29]

An Arab Israeli lawyer from Nazareth, who had been working in the military courts since 1973, described his motivation in comparative terms:

> Felicia [Langer] works for other people. I work for my people. Felicia is an Israeli [i.e., Jewish]. She does this work because she is a communist, and she has done great work. . . . But when I defend a Palestinian, I am in a sense defending myself, because the Palestinian struggle is my struggle.

Many Arab Israeli lawyers relate their cause directly to their ethnonational ties to Palestinians in the territories—they are "one people" in the "two people" ideologico-political dichotomy of Israel/Palestine. Indeed, some expressly say that they relish such work as a chance to engage in nationalist activities against the state, which has been less than kind and fair to their own community (see Kretzmer 1990; Lustick 1980; Shamir 1996; Zureik 1979). Others relate their cause more directly to leftist politics than national identity. Said one,

> The most committed lawyers are the leftists, whether we are Jews or Arabs. When [Israelis or Palestinians] criticize us, the first thing they point to is the fact that we are communists. But if we weren't communists, we wouldn't be here. We would be working somewhere else.

Arab Israelis see their status as citizens and their legal education in Israeli universities as very important points of distinction

---

[29] The military metaphor is ironic, because Arabs (with the exception of Druze) are not conscripted into the IDF.

between themselves and Palestinians from the territories, particularly as it bears upon their legal practice. Several describe themselves as having been "Israelized," which manifests itself as aggressiveness in dealing with opponents in the legal domain. One lawyer, who moved from the Galilee to East Jerusalem to work full time in the military courts, said that solidarity motivated him, but the fighting spirit is what has made him the most in-demand lawyer working in the military courts.

> I am a strong man. I respect myself as a lawyer and people respect me. Knowing the language is number one, then knowing the laws and precedents, and finally being able to have good relations with judges and prosecutors. Because I work well, I have a special relationship with the courts, and clients come to me for that reason. I can get things done. I always advise other lawyers [i.e., Palestinians from the territories] to respect themselves and behave with dignity so that the enemy will respect them. When you show weakness, you become weaker because people take advantage.

Arab Israelis' decision to cross the Green Line does not bear the same implications as a similar career decision by either liberal Jewish lawyers, who are motivated by a desire to effect change within their own society, or leftist Jewish lawyers, whose solidarity with Palestinians is tempered by the significance of the Jewish/non-Jewish distinction. Because of the rampant and pervasive discrimination against Arab Israelis inside the Green Line, any question of finding cause in loyalty to the state is unthinkable. Rather, for them the politics of cause is a matter of finding a space to be political: specifically, to act on their critique of the state and to support people with whom they have a national identification.

The example of Arab Israeli cause lawyers illustrates several important developments in the broader context. First, their decision to take military court cases has challenged the significance of the Green Line. Arab lawyers put ethnonational solidarity with Palestinians across the line into practice. One lawyer from Umm al-Fahum describes these relations as complementary:

> Military court work is routine, since most of what we do is plea bargain. I like complicated cases with lots of evidence because this is where I can make a contribution since I have the skills to really work the system. But for simple cases, it is actually better for people to use lawyers from [the territories] who live right there and can visit people in prison and keep in touch with the families. For me, just getting to Gaza presents lots of problems. [Israeli] lawyers can't visit as often as the clients or their families would like, and can't follow cases as closely since they aren't in the military courts every day. That's why I only agree to take the hard cases.

A second and contrasting development is the limits of such solidarity; hardly any younger Arab Israeli lawyers have taken up practice in the territories, preferring to pursue careers within the domestic Israeli legal system. Older practitioners explain this generational gap as a consequence of the scanty legal accomplishments and material rewards that military court lawyers can claim. According to one, "They look at us and think we wasted our lives. We are poor even though we work hard . . . and the jails are still full of Palestinians."

A third development relates to political changes resulting from the Israeli-Palestinian negotiations, which began in 1991. The peace process has had a fracturing effect on the Palestinian "people" in Israel/Palestine, who are divided between citizens and residents of the territories. Among Arab Israeli lawyers, this has manifested itself as a trend to downsize or even end their practice in the territories. Many felt they had "paid their dues" to the Palestinian cause and could walk away with dignity. In the words of one lawyer who decided to quit military court work and take up practice in a northern Israeli city, "Israelis do 3 years of national service [i.e., conscription in the military]. I did 11."

Like the people they defend, Palestinian lawyers from the territories live under occupation and as such occupy a tenuous position *as lawyers* (see Bisharat 1995). The most common answer to the question of why they work in the military courts is that these lawyers want to involve themselves in the Palestinian national struggle for self-determination. Thus, their motivation is solidarity deriving from a common identity with the collective client: the Palestinian population in the territories. Some believe that their work is an integral part of the struggle, while others take a somewhat more detached view of the relationship between politics and legal practice. Of course, this distinction is limited by the fact that many lawyers have been arrested themselves. According to one West Bank lawyer:

> I would visit clients in prison about four days every week. When I was arrested, it wasn't in the night like other people. I was "invited" to meet with [a security services officer]. That's how they arrested me. First they questioned me in Fara'a [an Israeli prison near Nablus] about being a leader of [a Palestinian faction] and passing information from my clients in prison to people on the outside. Then they sent me to the desert [Ansar III, the prison camp in the Negev]. Even though it was totally disgusting, being there was a good experience for me. Now I could really understand how things work from the other side.

Palestinian lawyers frequently describe their motivation in terms of "national duty" and "honor." One young lawyer who started practicing during the uprising said,

> I always ask myself if working in the military courts is what I should be doing, if I am doing anybody any good. I feel sorry for the people. Being arrested or having a family member arrested and going through the whole process is very difficult for

everyone. Visiting the prisons is depressing. The detainees
stink, they are cold and scared and tired. But you are not talking about strangers. These are my people. I know I am helping
them, even if all I am doing is bringing clothes and some news
from their families. . . . People go to lawyers because they need
them. Lawyers are part of the big picture of the struggle.

Although Palestinians have the occupation in common, there
are some important distinctions among Gaza, the West Bank and
East Jerusalem deriving from the differing political histories, socioeconomic conditions and Israeli governing policies in these
three areas. In relative terms, the situation in Gaza has always
been more desperate economically and highly charged politically. When the uprising began, Gaza lawyers went on strike for
11 months to protest the military's repressive policies toward the
population at large and what they claimed were unworkable conditions in the military courts. The strike ended as a result of public pressure to provide legal services for the thousands of people
who were being arrested. However, Gaza lawyers collectively decided not to charge fees for "security cases." This decision was a
demonstration of corporate solidarity with other sectors of the
population for whom the uprising was creating an economic crisis. Thus, working actually cost lawyers money, as they had to sub-
sidize their own activities on behalf of their clients. One Gaza
lawyer commented on this issue:

> The economic situation is a big dilemma. People are so poor,
> and there is a relation between the lawyers and the families, a
> social relationship, which makes it very hard to separate per-
> sonal friendships from professional relations. . . . I lose perspec-
> tive on the separation between myself and my clients and their
> families. . . . Because lawyers are the ones who pass between the
> families and the prisoners, we become like members of the
> family. I know more about my clients' lives and their problems
> than I know about my cousins.

In addition to the financial hardships, working in the military
courts in Gaza is more dangerous, relatively speaking, than in the
West Bank. In one telling example, an Arab Israeli lawyer was
beaten by a soldier for protesting the expulsion of the wife of his
client, who had waved at her husband in the dock. Afterwards,
according to other lawyers on the scene, when the soldier
learned that the lawyer was an Israeli citizen and not a Gaza resi-
dent, he reportedly said that he had hit him "because he thought
that he was a Gazan lawyer and therefore it didn't matter" (Lawyers' Committee for Human Rights 1992:16). Raji Sourani, a
Gaza lawyer who received the Jimmy Carter Human Rights Award
in 1991,[30] said this of the situation: "Being a lawyer in Gaza is the

---

[30] Sourani shared the award with Avigdor Feldman, an Israeli lawyer who handles
many cases of Palestinians before the Israeli High Court of Justice.

worst. Lawyers and detainees are almost equally assaulted and abused by soldiers in the prisons and courts."

While many of the hardships and problems facing Gazans are also faced by West Bankers, the West Bank is relatively more affluent, and most lawyers can count themselves among the middle class. Unlike in Gaza, during the uprising West Bankers retained the right to charge for their work, notwithstanding that thousands of cases were handled on a pro bono basis. In addition to fees which lawyers could collect directly from clients, there were several legal aid programs which provided lawyers' fees;[31] there were no comparable programs in Gaza, illustrating the more well-developed structure of nongovernmental organizations in the West Bank. In addition, many West Bank lawyers were able to receive payment "from Jordan," which meant that Palestinian factions with offices in Amman would dispense funds to cover legal fees of faction members; again, Gaza lawyers had no such options, illustrating the differing histories and relations between the two regions and the Palestinian leadership outside. So while work in the military courts was not particularly lucrative, West Bank lawyers never suffered the absence of income that Gaza lawyers faced. And for those who shifted over to the military courts during the uprising, it was their means of preserving a certain standard of living.

As is probably the case in other parts of the world, even cause lawyers are not immune from criticism about their financial motivations. Money was a very common theme among West Bankers when discussing themselves and their colleagues. One lawyer from Bethlehem, who said that she can barely afford to run an office, complained: "Lawyers are considered thieves by many people, and some of them deserve this reputation because they profit from other people's suffering. But for others, we are not even compensated for the work we do."

The legal environment in the West Bank is more complicated and diversified than that which obtains in Gaza for two main reasons: first, most Israeli lawyers practicing in the territories do so in the West Bank, and second, the differing legal status between East Jerusalemites and other West Bank Palestinians provides them with different personal rights and, thus, professional options.

While many Palestinian and Israeli lawyers have strong informal relations, there are also significant tensions rooted in the ways in which identity is politicized. For example, the West Bank lawyers' organization, the Arab Lawyers Committee, does not accept Israeli citizens as members. This not only reflects but exacerbates the politicization of difference within the profession. The

---

[31] Legal aid was provided on behalf of people with the status of refugees through UNRWA and for nonrefugees through the Quakers' East Jerusalem office.

ALC has expected Israeli lawyers to abide by strikes and other collective decisions, which many do, but has resisted expanding the role that nonmembers could play in setting or influencing those policies.

Identity differences find expression in the ways West Bank and Israeli lawyers view one another. There is a tendency among some Palestinian lawyers to regard Israeli citizens (both Jews and Arabs) as "usurpers." According to a prominent West Bank lawyer, "Palestinian lawyers are different from Israeli lawyers because we are Palestinians first and lawyers second. Many Israeli lawyers see their work as *work*, not as politics. Israelis never handle files for free." For their part, Israeli lawyers often reciprocate the criticism by looking down on Palestinian lawyers as less skilled. Responding to a question about why the ALC has never taken up the offer made by some Arab and Jewish Israeli lawyers to provide seminars in Israeli laws and procedures, one leader of the ALC said,

> Israeli lawyers who emphasize how important knowing the system is are just promoting themselves. We [in the ALC] considered the idea of seminars, but learning Israeli law isn't important because the military courts don't apply the laws. And we don't need any help learning procedures because none exist. Whenever we try to raise issues of procedure or law, judges say, "This isn't Israel."

Lawyers from East Jerusalem have a politico-legal status as "noncitizen residents" of Israel, which distinguishes them from other West Bankers. During periods when the Israeli authorities "close" or "seal" the territories, West Bankers cannot enter Jerusalem because it is regarded by the state as a sovereign part of Israel. Since the roads connecting the northern and southern parts of the West Bank run through Jerusalem, the region is effectively divided into two impassable halves. This has the effect of barring West Bankers residing in one part from access to the other. East Jerusalemites are not affected by such mobility restrictions. Consequently, they have the option during periods of closure to pick up many cases that West Bankers can't handle due to their inability to travel to courts or prisons located in other areas. As the number of arrests began to wane by the early 1990s, competition among lawyers for cases generated resentment on the part of some West Bankers. A lawyer from Bethlehem complained:

> Because of the closure I have had to delay all my files for Ramallah and the north. Jerusalem lawyers are starting to get a monopoly on new cases. Now when people come into my office, the first thing they ask me is if I can do prison visits, which I can't because I can't cross the Green Line. This is enough for many to decide not to hire me. I think we should all go on strike. This would solve at least part of the problem.

The political and professional issues associated with identity differences among the various subcategories of lawyers practicing in the military courts are reflected in the discrepant views on cause. With the exception of liberal Jewish Israelis, all others tend to see their cause as an expression of solidarity with the Palestinian population. But the politics of solidarity provokes debates over who has a greater "right" to act on behalf of the Palestinian people in the legal system. Clearly, the exigencies of sociopolitical identifications in the broader context of Israel/Palestine are important to the interactional dynamics within the court system. Lawyers' motivations, experiences, and relations with others reveal the contradictions of a localized transnationalism.

IV. Strategies of Resistance

How do cause lawyers' practices constitute forms of resistance to the status quo, and to what effects? Resistance is undertaken to challenge the nature of Israeli rule by propounding adherence to rule of law principles or to displace Israeli rule in the territories entirely by working for the goal of Palestinian self-determination. Cause lawyering strategies can be divided into three general categories: legal maneuvers, extralegal solidarity work, and publicizing problems to local and/or international audiences. This section focuses on the first two, and the following section addresses the third.

All lawyers engage in both legal and extralegal activities, but the significance they attach to each varies. Israeli citizens tend to put a greater emphasis on legal options, while Palestinian residents of the territories tend to foreground the extralegal dimensions of their work because of their greater social proximity and shared status with the collective client. One afternoon in 1993, two Gazans and a leftist Jewish Israeli debated this issue. Their discussion started with them concurring on the problems they face. But it soon took a turn as the Israeli lawyer started arguing that Palestinian lawyers actually do a disservice to their clients—and, by implication, to the cause of resistance—by not exploiting even the limited legal options available to them. She was frustrated in particular by the fact that they rarely challenge the authorities when they are denied access to clients being held incommunicado.

One of the Gazan lawyers chided her for not giving adequate consideration to the fact that, *as Palestinians*, they are vulnerable to the Israeli authorities and therefore can't capitalize on the technicalities of their professional rights. She countered that most lawyers don't exercise their rights because they haven't bothered to find out what their options are. She went on to argue that many participate in their own victimization (and that of

International Law and Society

their clients) through ignorance or inertia. How, the Gazan asked, can lawyers know their options or act differently under the prevailing circumstances? Most lawyers live in poverty, employed by people who are even poorer than they are. Furthermore, they suffer the same political conditions as the rest of the population. He added:

> You talk about our rights as if Israel actually respected our rights, as if they were there for the asking. The basic rights we deserve are part of international law [the Fourth Geneva Convention], and what is the Israeli position on that? Forget it! We have lived without any rights since 1967. No lawyer is going to change that.

The structural inequalities in Israel/Palestine place Palestinian lawyers at greater disadvantage within the legal system. Under these circumstances, it is hardly surprising that many Palestinian lawyers see their role primarily as interlocutors between the people and the state, trying to minimize the negative repercussions of the occupation with the limited professional options at their disposal. Being lawyers provides them with the opportunity to have contact with people who have been arrested, and with their families. Thus, beyond the legal work of handling of cases, they function effectively like social workers by offering emotional and other extralegal forms of support. But such activities do constitute forms of resistance: within Palestinian nationalist discourse, *sumud* (steadfastness) is recognized as a part of the struggle against the occupation. Acts of solidarity can be undertaken as conscious efforts to erase the boundaries between the profession and the community it serves.

For Israeli citizens, who generally have fewer social contacts with Palestinian society at large, their sense of cause is often more focused on the legal terrain. One leftist Jewish lawyer with a long tenure in the courts said that she has had some differences with clients over her strategies:

> My first priority is always people in interrogation. I will do everything I can to help someone while he is in interrogation, even sacrificing my work on other files. With the [uprising], so many people were in interrogation, I didn't have time to do prison visits. It hurt me that [my clients] who are very *political* couldn't understand *my* politics. . . . I don't mind losing clients, or even feeling unappreciated. But it bothers me that people put their own interests [i.e., being visited in prison] before the bigger problems. . . . We all have our role to play, and they should understand mine.

Within the legal process itself, plea bargaining dominates, leading lawyers to refer to the military courts as a "*suq* [marketplace] of deals" and to describe themselves as "deal merchants." Lawyers are well aware that a collective refusal to plea bargain could have been a politically effective strategy, if for no other reason than that it would create an enormous backlog for the authorities. But for a variety of reasons, lawyers have never been able to mount and sustain such a strategy. For one thing, the consequences for individual clients would be devastating. The structural advantages favoring the prosecution so seriously compromise the possibility of a defense victory at trial that the outcomes would inevitably be longer sentences for all involved. Lawyers' past experiences with trials strongly mitigate against the appeal of such a strategy, and those who have on occasion taken cases to trial say they regretted the decision in retrospect. One Gaza lawyer described an experience of taking what he believed was a sure-win case to trial:

> I brought 11 defense witnesses to testify against one soldier. The judge said that [despite the overwhelming number of witnesses], he couldn't let their testimony override the "dignity" of the word of a soldier because this would diminish the legitimacy of the IDF [in the territories]. So even though there was no confession, and so many witnesses saying that they had arrested the wrong person, my client went to prison.

Another factor working against the option of taking cases to trial relates to a sheer lack of time and adequate remuneration to make it worth lawyers' while. Although the uprising merely worsened the situation, many lawyers who practice regularly in the military courts have been too consistently overwhelmed with work to give the necessary attention to any one file. Furthermore, because release on bail is rarely granted, and given the delays which are endemic to the system, pretrial detention could be longer than the sentence, especially for people charged with minor crimes.

The prevalence of plea bargaining epitomizes the contradictory relationship between the politics of struggle and the legal process: plea bargaining systematically fragments political resistance through the individualization of cases. According to one Gaza lawyer, "By always plea bargaining, we just help the Israelis put Palestinians in jail faster." There is an obvious disjuncture between dealing, which involves concession, and the charged discourse of resistance beyond the court system. Throughout the years of occupation, the Palestinian political leadership demonstrated little interest and almost no involvement in the workings of the system or the legal activities of lawyers, aside from statements of solidarity and support for political prisoners.

This lack of political direction has left legal strategies to the discretion of lawyers. Their problems in organizing themselves, either formally through one group or informally on an ad hoc basis, have meant that this discretion has largely been a matter between individual lawyers and their clients. For those lawyers who would have liked to politicize legal practice by taking a collective stand to refuse to deal—something that many Israeli and

Palestinian lawyers have said they desire—such a strategy would only have been possible if undertaken by all or at least most lawyers working in the military courts. As long as any lawyer plea bargains and thus gets lower sentences for his or her clients, there is pressure on all lawyers to do the same or risk losing clients.

Within the legal process itself, lawyers have engaged in resistance activities on an individual basis. Examples of these strategies include trying to challenge confessions by calling for *zuta* (voir dire), just threatening to take a case to trial which sometimes motivates overworked prosecutors to lower the sentence or drop some charges, or even the troubling tactic of "dealing against files" by giving the prosecutor something on one case in order to get a break on another. A common strategy has been to delay, either to put pressure on prosecutors who were under orders to finish files quickly or to wait for a judge or prosecutor who might be more amenable to lowering the sentence or dropping some charges.

Even the most common practices, what lawyers describe as "begging for mercy," can be regarded as a form of resistance if the goal is understood as getting the shortest possible sentence for the client. One Arab Israeli lawyer described his strategy to tell judges and prosecutors what they want to hear in order to inspire them to lower the sentence:

> Sometimes I tell them that the occupation is really good for Palestinians, because this is what they believe. Sometimes I tell that my client is a poor fool who was taken advantage of by some troublemaker who made him throw stones or burn tires. They like this too, because they want to believe that the [uprising] is not really popular. . . . Good lawyers are the ones who can make their clients seem "innocent," not of the charges—because there is a confession—but innocent in a bigger sense, like being forced into activism.

Ultimately, individual lawyers' strategies hinge on a combination of skills and commitment, legal options related somewhat to issues of identity, and the nature of lawyers' relations with others. But despite the differences, their common role defending Palestinians has provided a basis for certain shared criticisms of the operations of the system and the way Israeli rule in the territories is maintained.

V. Cause Lawyering as Resistance Politics: Between Hegemony and Human Rights

Defense lawyers are the only category of participants whose involvement in the military courts is voluntary.[32] For most, their decision is based on a conscious desire to traffic in the highly charged fray of occupation politics. Those lawyers who are most politically *effective* are the ones who have been able to use the information they gain through their work to bring outside attention to the operations of the system and conditions in the territories. In this regard, human rights has been important both as a conceptual framework that enables lawyers to articulate their criticisms,[33] and as a transnational array of institutions that have provided clearinghouses for this information.[34]

The human rights business, including cause lawyering for human rights–type goals, is an elite enterprise (S. Cohen 1995:12). It requires the cultural capital to utilize and disseminate information. This is certainly true in the context of the Israeli military courts, because the lawyers who have been most successful in translating their individualized work into part of a larger social force have been (1) those with the political and intellectual savvy to cultivate connections with the local media and local human rights organizations (Israeli and/or Palestinian) and (2) a smaller number who have the language skills (particularly English) and political stature to serve as contacts to the international media and international human rights organizations. In these ways, cause lawyering involves not simply working in support of a cause but helping to establish what that cause is, at least to the extent that law and politics intersect. This intersection has been increasingly relevant over the last decade as resistance to the occupation has involved a marshaling of resources to appeal to the international community for substantive interventions.

The human rights dilemma comes to bear in this enterprise of framing and publicizing problems as means of evoking interventionary measures. States, in this case Israel, are the recognized arbiters of the rights of populations under their rule. While states are bound in principle to respect the internationally institutionalized standards of government (as embodied in the various human rights instruments), in practice the international order has little capacity to enforce those standards. Consequently,

---

[32] Defendants are there because they have been arrested, and judges, prosecutors, and translators are assigned to their roles as military duty.

[33] It is the very fact that Israel/Palestine is a transnational context that human rights rather than civil rights provides the normative reference.

[34] One effect of the uprising within Israel was the establishment of a number of new local human rights organizations with mandates to monitor and protest conditions in the territories. New Palestinian organizations in the territories were also established, joining the efforts of already existing institutions.

challenging states' violations of human rights demands ad hoc strategies to effect changes. Cause lawyering for human rights constitutes one such set of strategies. Yet there are significant differences in military court lawyers' views of cause, which have informed the kinds of connections they developed and the types of interventions they have sought to elicit.

Within Jewish Israeli society, the uprising confirmed mainstream and rightist popular views of Palestinians as inherently violent and threatening enemies. For liberal Jewish Israeli lawyers concerned about the rule of law, the implications were challenging. Their work with Palestinian clients gave them access to knowledge about the abuses being perpetrated by agents of the state. The contradictions between loyalty and legalism reached new heights. "A full acknowledgement of the truth about what your own government is doing, together with an active engagement with the implications of this knowledge, would threaten deeply cherished beliefs" (S. Cohen 1995:43).

Liberals have tried to mediate between the demands of rule and the principles of rights for people who are subjects of the Israeli state. Unlike the other subcategories of lawyers, Jewish Israeli liberals are inclined to identify with the state's discourse on security, which is a pillar of the Israeli hegemonic normative formation. But they have sought to generate a human rights consciousness by criticizing contraventions of legality and abuses of power. Liberals use human rights discourse, specifically legal norms and values, as a means to inspire social awareness and responsibility, disseminating their knowledge about problems and violations to the Jewish Israeli public. Their transformative project is to legitimize Palestinian rights within Israeli state practices. In the words of one liberal lawyer, "There are problems in Israel as there are in Northern Ireland when security is an issue. Terrorists can't expect our support, but the courts have an obligation to try them fairly. . . . Everyone has a right to certain legal rights."

The other subcategories of lawyers are less accommodating—if at all—of Israeli security concerns. Leftist Jewish and Arab Israelis are critical of the discourse of Israeli security, and Palestinians from the territories are outside of it entirely. For these three subcategories, the primary issue is not adherence to the rule of law (although the short-term relevance of this is not dismissed), but the human rights principle of self-determination, to which Israeli rule is seen as the (main) obstacle. The connections they cultivate and the strategies they deploy are aimed at ending the occupation, not simply modifying the way in which the state's authority is exercised on the ground. Being politicized legal practitioners means defending people engaged in a struggle against a status quo which, in their view, amounts to a colonial situation.

Their opposition to Israeli government of the territories is a form of anticolonial politics.

The international record on anticolonialism is mixed. There are important sources of potential support, such as the General Assembly of the United Nations, which has exhibited an enduring commitment to the cause of Palestinian self-determination. But in the arenas that actually count, international politics tends to exhibit a strong obstructivist trend against struggles of stateless people and in support of already-existing states. The problems facing Palestinians in the territories are rooted in the contradictions between local Israeli hegemony and the international ideal of self-determination. The state-centered international order provides an inspiration for seeking the creation of a Palestinian state. More immediately, the international community is a potential source of support to which Palestinians and their Israeli supporters appeal to counter the travails of life under occupation.

Although leftist Jewish and Arab Israeli and Palestinian cause lawyers have had little success directly linking their legal practices in the military courts to the larger goals of ending the occupation, they have succeeded in drawing international attention to circumstances in the territories. As one Arab Israeli described the consequences of ongoing efforts to make the criticisms public:

> We have to use our position as lawyers by publicizing how inhumane the occupation is and the injustices of the [court] system. This inside view can be used to deal with a number of factors relating to the occupation. First, [lawyers] have a right to go to the prisons, to see the actual effects of interrogation, what the authorities do to prisoners and their families. A lawyer must be courageous to write about what is going on without exaggerating or being afraid of the consequences. On this count, Felicia [Langer] has done one of the greatest steps to let the world know what was going on. . . . But it took the efforts of many lawyers to bring international attention to what is going on. A few years ago, no organization dared to challenge or criticize Israel, one reason being that there just weren't enough facts to counter the pro-Israel propaganda. But by exposing the facts about the occupation, now organizations and people not only can criticize Israel but must do so because the evidence is growing. Even the US State Department criticizes Israel for its policies in the [occupied territories]. This is an achievement for Palestinians.

The consequences of such efforts have been indirect in regard to the larger political goals of Palestinian self-determination and may seem inconsequential in comparison to cause lawyering in other contexts. But if we appreciate the fact that circumstances on the ground are affected by transnational flows of information and the political reactions they can generate, we can see that the implications of such activities are not unimportant. The Israeli government certainly felt the pressure from the escalating criticisms lawyers helped to generate, and reacted by trying to challenge the legitimacy of the lawyers themselves as well as the veracity of their information and analysis (see H. Cohen 1981:xii). In one official Israeli response to an Amnesty International report on the military courts, the author wrote:

> The Report is, for the most part, based on unverified accusations of unnamed, often politically motivated, sources. In particular, the Report's author relied on allegations of "defense lawyers", many of whom have a vested interest in undermining the Israeli authorities. The Report contains no criticism of the defense lawyers' attempts to obstruct justice, nor does it attempt to cross-check their claims by objective means. It should have been explained that these defense lawyers often function not as "officers of the court", but rather as political actors willing to sacrifice the interests of justice and of their clients for political ends. (Gaulan 1992:2)

International concern about the occupation and the ongoing problem of Palestinian statelessness was increased dramatically by the uprising, thus providing an outlet for the criticisms being articulated by cause lawyers. The uprising resonated with the international community because the right to self-determination is widely regarded as one of the most important rights since it provides the basis for other kinds of rights and protections, at least in principle. To the degree that self-determination is contingent on the establishment of a sovereign state, we can see that the problems facing Palestinians—in the territories and beyond—are inextricably intertwined with international politics in a world of states. To be stateless is to be vulnerable in an international order that provides no institutionalized refuge, solace, or recourse. To be under military occupation, however, provides a clear and contestable obstacle to self-determination.

The problems associated with government-in-conflict in Israel/Palestine, while shaped by the historico-political specificities of this context, are not unique. Rather, they illustrate the inherent contradiction between supranational human rights ideals and the local politics of hegemony. Until the uprising, international human rights activities on behalf of Palestinians in the territories were limited, for the most part, to criticisms of the policies and practices of the Israeli military administration. With the uprising, it became increasingly apparent that the status quo of occupation must end. This critical awareness created a discursive space for projecting counterhegemonic views within the conceptual framework and language of international human rights.

Cause lawyers, many of whom had been dealing with these problems for years, were well positioned to focus attention in particular ways to raise the level of human rights consciousness locally as conditions on the ground reached crisis proportions.

They were also able to connect with human rights investigators and foreign journalists who were coming in droves to monitor and expose abuses. Such monitoring efforts served as conduits for information about Palestinian suffering and their aspirations for independence. These efforts were enhanced by the fact that by the late 1980s the international human rights movement had reached a stage of development (institutionally and discursively) where the implementation of human rights standards could be advanced, or at least advocated, with much greater force and influence than had been the case even a decade earlier. Thus, the more effective cause lawyers working in the military courts played an important role in producing knowledge about *how* the occupation was problematic, and the most effective ones marketed that knowledge to the international community.

In conclusion, cause lawyering in the Israeli military courts provides an example of the interrelations between the local and the international in one specific context. What we can deduce from this is that the state-centered international order sustains and reinforces certain fundamental contradictions between sovereignty and security on the one hand, and human rights protections and guarantees on the other. To the extent that cause lawyering in general assumes the possibility of "justice" and a principle of rights, globalizing the study of cause lawyering invites attention to the various ways in which international human rights inspire and empower lawyers to be politicized legal professionals and to reform or transform local orders.

References

Abel, Richard L. (1995) *Politics by Other Means: Law in the Struggle against Apartheid, 1980–1994.* New York: Routledge.

Amnesty International (1991) *Israel and the Occupied Territories: The Military Justice System in the Occupied Territories: Detention, Interrogation, and Trial Procedures.* New York: Amnesty International USA.

Arian, Asher, Ilan Talmud, & Tamar Hermann (1988) *National Security and Public Opinion in Israel.* Tel Aviv & Boulder, CO: Jaffee Center for Strategic Studies & Westview Press.

Benvenisti, Eyal (1990) *Legal Dualism: The Absorption of the Occupied Territories into Israel.* Boulder, CO: Westview Press.

Bisharat, George Emile (1989) *Palestinian Lawyers and Israeli Rule: Law and Disorder in the West Bank.* Austin: Univ. of Texas Press.

——— (1995) "Courting Justice? Legitimation in Lawyering under Israeli Occupation," 20 *Law & Social Inquiry* 349–405.

Briskman, Dana (1988) "National Security versus Human Rights: An Analysis of the Approach of the Israeli Supreme Court to the Conflict between National Security and Civil Liberties." M.A. thesis, Harvard University Law School.

Cohen, Haim (1981) "Foreword," in *The Rule of Law in the Areas Administered by Israel.* Tel Aviv: Israel National Section of the International Commission of Jurists.

Cohen, Stanley (1995) *Denial and Acknowledgement: The Impact of Information about Human Rights Violations.* Jerusalem: Center for Human Rights, Hebrew Univ.

Cohen, Stanley, & Daphna Golan (1991) *The Interrogation of Palestinians during the Intifada: Ill-Treatment, "Moderate Physical Pressure" or Torture?* Jerusalem: B'Tselem, Israeli Information Center for Human Rights in the Occupied Territories.

—— (1992) *The Interrogation of Palestinians during the Intifada: Follow-up to March 1991 B'Tselem Report.* Jerusalem: B'Tselem, Israeli Information Center for Human Rights in the Occupied Territories.

Connor, Walker (1994) *Ethnonationalism: The Quest for Understanding.* Princeton, NJ: Princeton Univ. Press.

Dillman, Jeffrey D., & Musa A. Bakri (1992) *Israel's Use of Electric Shock Torture in the Interrogation of Palestinian Detainees.* Jerusalem: Palestine Human Rights Information Center.

Ellmann, Stephen (1992) *In a Time of Trouble: Law and Liberty in South Africa's State of Emergency.* New York: Oxford Univ. Press, Clarendon Press.

Falk, Richard A. (1985) *Human Rights and State Sovereignty.* New York: Holmes & Meier Publishers.

Gaulan, Tamar (1992) Letter from the Ministry of Justice dated April 8, 1992, published as introduction to *Response of the IDF Military Advocate General's Unit to the Amnesty International Report on the Military Justice System in the Administered Areas.* Tel Aviv: Office of the Military Advocate General.

Ginbar, Yuval (1993) *The "New Procedure" in GSS Interrogation: The Case of 'Abd a-Nasser 'Ubeid,* trans. R. Mandel. Jerusalem: B'Tselem, Israeli Information Center for Human Rights in the Occupied Territories.

Ginbar, Yuval, & Yael Stein (1994) *Torture during Interrogations: Testimony of Palestinian Detainees, Testimony of Interrogators.* Jerusalem: B'Tselem, Israeli Information Center for Human Rights in the Occupied Territories.

Golan, Daphna (1989) *The Military Judicial System in the West Bank.* Jerusalem: B'Tselem, Israeli Information Center for Human Rights in the Occupied Territories.

Gordon, Colin (1991) "Governmental Rationality: An Introduction," in G. Burchell, C. Gordon, & P. Miller, eds., *The Foucault Effect: Studies in Governmentality.* Chicago: Univ. of Chicago Press.

Gordon, Neve, & Rela Mazali (1993) *"The Slaughter House": Sketch of the General Security Service Interrogation Center at Gaza Central Prison.* Tel Aviv: Association of Israeli-Palestinian Physicians for Human Rights.

Hajjar, Lisa (1994) "Zionist Politics and the Law: The Meaning of the Green Line," 2 *Arab Studies J.* 44–51.

—— (1995) "Authority, Resistance and the Law: A Study of the Israeli Military Court System in the Occupied Territories." Ph.D. diss., Dept. of Sociology, American Univ.

—— (1997a) *Changes in Human Rights Activism in Israel/Palestine since Oslo.* Center for Policy Analysis on Palestine Occasional Paper No. 8 Washington: Center for Policy Analysis on Palestine.

—— (1997b) "Two People, One State: War, Peace, Sovereignty and Law in Israel/Palestine." Unpublished, Swarthmore College.

Henkin, Louis (1990) *The Age of Rights.* New York: Columbia Univ. Press.

Hiltermann, Joost R. (1991) *Behind the Intifada: Labor and Women's Movements in the Occupied Territories.* Princeton, NJ: Princeton Univ. Press.

Human Rights Watch/Middle East (1994) *Israel—Torture and Ill-Treatment: Israel's Interrogation of Palestinians from the Occupied Territories.* New York: Human Rights Watch.

Hunt, Alan (1993) *Explorations in Law and Society: Toward a Constitutive Theory of Law.* New York: Routledge.

Kimmerling, Baruch (1989) "Boundaries and Frontiers of the Israeli Control System: Analytic Conclusions," in B. Kimmerling, ed., *The Israeli State and Society: Boundaries and Frontiers.* Albany: State Univ. of New York Press.

Kremnitzer, Mordechai (1989) "The Landau Commission Report—Was the Security Service Subordinated to the Law, or the Law to the 'Needs' of the Security Service?" 23 *Israel Law Rev.* 216–79.

Kretzmer, David (1990) *The Legal Status of the Arabs in Israel.* Boulder, CO: Westview Press.

Lahav, Pnina (1988) "A Barrel without Hoops: The Impact of Counterterrorism on Israel's Legal Culture," 10 *Cardozo Law Rev.* 529–60.

Langer, Felicia (1975) *With My Own Eyes: Israel and the Occupied Territories, 1967–1973.* London: Ithaca Press.

——— (1979) *These Are My Brothers: Israel and the Occupied Territories*, Pt. II. London: Ithaca Press.

——— (1988) *An Age of Stone.* New York: Quartet.

Landau, Moshe, et al. (1987) *Commission of Inquiry into the Methods of Investigation of the General Security Service Regarding Hostile Terrorist Activity.* Jerusalem: Government Press Office.

Lawyers' Committee for Human Rights (1992) *Lawyers and the Military Justice System of the Israeli-Occupied Territories.* New York: The Committee.

——— (1993) *A Continuing Cause for Concern: The Military Justice System of the Israeli-Occupied Territories.* New York: The Committee.

Lustick, Ian S. (1980) *Arabs in the Jewish State: Israel's Control of a National Minority.* Austin: Univ. of Texas Press.

——— (1997) "Has Israel Annexed East Jerusalem?" 5 (12) *Middle East Policy* 34–39.

Mitchell, Timothy (1990) "Everyday Metaphors of Power," 19 *Theory & Society* 545–77.

——— (1991) "The Limits of the State: Beyond Statist Approaches and Their Critics," 85 *American Political Science Rev.* 77–97.

Moffett, Martha Roadstrum (1989) *Perpetual Emergency: A Legal Analysis of Israel's Use of the British Defense (Emergency) Regulations, 1945, in the Occupied Territories.* Ramallah, West Bank: Al-Haq/Law in the Service of Man.

Nassar, Jamal R., & Roger Heacock, eds. (1991) *Intifada: Palestine at the Crossroads.* New York: Birzeit Univ. & Praeger Publishers.

Playfair, Emma, ed. (1992) *International Law and the Administration of Occupied Territories: Two Decades of the Israeli Occupation of the West Bank and Gaza Strip.* New York: Oxford Univ. Press, Clarendon Press.

Public Committee against Torture in Israel (1990) *Moderate Physical Pressure: Interrogation Methods in Israel.* Jerusalem: The Committee.

Rabah, Jamil, & Natasha Fairweather (1993) *Israeli Military Orders in the Occupied Palestinian West Bank, 1967–1992.* Jerusalem: Jerusalem Media and Communication Centre.

Sarat, Austin, & Stuart A. Scheingold, eds. (1997) *Cause Lawyering: Political Commitments and Professional Responsibilities.* New York: Oxford Univ. Press.

Shamgar, Meir (1982a) "Legal Concepts and Problems of the Israeli Military Government—The Initial Stage," in Shamgar, ed., 1982b.

———, ed. (1982b) *Military Government in the Territories Administered by Israel 1967-1980: The Legal Aspects.* Jerusalem: Harry Sacher Institute for Legislative Research & Comparative Law, Hebrew University, Faculty of Law.

Shamir, Ronen (1990) "'Landmark Cases' and the Reproduction of Legitimacy: The Case of Israel's High Court of Justice," 24 *Law & Society Rev.* 781–805.

——— (1991) "Legal Discourse, Media Discourse, and Speech Rights: The Shift from Content to Identity—the Case of Israel," 19 *International J. of the Sociology of Law* 45–65.

——— (1996) "Suspended in Space: Bedouins under the Law of Israel," 30 *Law & Society Rev.* 231–57.

Shefi, Dov (1982) "The Reports of the UN Special Committees on Israeli Prac-
    tices in the Territories: A Survey and Evaluation," in Shamgar 1982b.
Shehadeh, Raja (1988) *Occupier's Law: Israel and the West Bank*. Washington, DC:
    Institute for Palestine Studies.
———— (1993) *The Law of the Land: Settlements and Land Issues under Israeli Mili-
    tary Occupation*. Jerusalem: Palestinian Academic Society for the Study of
    International Affairs.
Shehadeh, Raja, & Jonathan Kuttab (1980) *The West Bank and the Rule of Law: A
    Study*. Geneva: International Commission of Jurists.
Straschnov, Amnon (1994) *Justice under Fire: The Legal System during the Intifada*.
    Tel Aviv: Yediot Aharanot [Hebrew].
Thornhill, Teresa (1992) *Making Women Talk: The Interrogation of Palestinian Wo-
    men Security Detainees by the Israeli General Security Services*. London: Lawyers
    for Palestinian Human Rights.
Usher, Graham (1995) *Palestine in Crisis: The Struggle for Peace and Political Inde-
    pendence after Oslo*. London: Pluto Press, in association with the Transna-
    tional Institute and the Middle East Research & Information Project.
Verdery, Katherine (1994) "Beyond the Nation in Eastern Europe," *Social Text*,
    No. 38 (Spring), 1–19.
Yahav, David, ed. (1993) *Israel, the "Intifada" and the Rule of Law*. Tel Aviv: Israeli
    Ministry of Defense Publications.
Zamir, Itzhak (1989) "Human Rights and National Security," 23 *Israel Law Rev.*
    375–406.
Zureik, Elia (1979) *The Palestinians in Israel: A Study in Internal Colonialism*. Bos-
    ton: Routledge & Kegan Paul.

[12]

The Female Inheritance Movement in Hong Kong

Theorizing the Local/Global Interface[1]

by Sally Engle Merry and Rachel E. Stern

Human rights concepts dominate discussions about social justice at the global level, but how much local communities have adopted this language and what it means to them are far less clear. As individuals and local social movements take on human rights ideas, they transform the shape and meaning of rights to accommodate local understandings. At the same time, they retain aspects of the global framework as signs of a global modernity that they wish to share. How and when individuals in various social locations come to see themselves in terms of human rights is a complicated but critically important question for anthropologists of globalization as well as for human rights activists. Using the female inheritance movement in Hong Kong in the early 1990s as a case study, this article argues that the localization of global human rights ideas depends on a complicated set of activist groups with different ideological orientations along with translators who bridge the gaps. As it explores the local appropriation of global cultural products, it reveals the instabilities of global and local and the importance of tracing the processes of translation and collaboration that make communication across this continuum possible.

SALLY ENGLE MERRY is Marion Butler McLean Professor in the History of Ideas and Professor of Anthropology at Wellesley College (Pendleton East, Rm. 334, 106 Central St., Wellesley, MA 02481, U.S.A. [smerry@wellesley.edu]). She is also codirector of the Peace and Justice Studies Program. She was born December 1, 1944, and received her B.A. from Wellesley College in 1966, her M.A. from Yale University in 1968, and her Ph.D. from Brandeis University in 1978. Her *Colonizing Hawai'i: The Cultural Power of Law* (Princeton: Princeton University Press, 2000) received the 2001 J. Willard Hurst Prize from the Law and Society Association. Her other publications include *Law and Empire in the Pacific: Hawai'i and Fiji* (coedited with Donald Brenneis, Santa Fe: School of American Research Press, 2004), *Getting Jus-*

1. We are grateful to Wellesley College for support for several months of research by Rachel Stern. Research was also supported by a Mellon New Directions Fellowship and a grant from the National Science Foundation, Cultural Anthropology and Law and Social Sciences Programs, BCS-0094441, to Sally Merry. We received helpful comments from James Hayes, Kevin O'Brien, Harriet Samuels, and Alan Smart and from audiences at the University of Pennsylvania, New York University, and Columbia University Law School. We appreciate the willingness of the participants in the movement to talk to us about it and are grateful for their insights.

tice and Getting Even (Chicago: University of Chicago Press, 1990), and *Urban Danger* (Philadelphia: Temple University Press, 1981). She is currently completing a book on international human rights and localization processes.

RACHEL E. STERN is a Ph.D. student in the Political Science Department at the University of California, Berkeley, and a National Science Foundation Graduate Fellow. Her previous publications include articles in *Asian Survey* and the *China Environment Series*. Her current research deals with environmental activism in China.

The present paper was submitted 28 X 03 and accepted 4 VIII 04.

In the spring of 1994, everyone in Hong Kong was talking about female inheritance. Women in the New Territories were subject to Chinese customary law and, under British colonialism, still unable to inherit land. That year, a group of rural indigenous women joined forces with Hong Kong women's groups to demand legal change. In the plaza in front of the Legislative Council building, amid shining office buildings, the indigenous women, dressed in the oversized hats of farm women, sang folk laments with new lyrics about injustice and inequality. Demonstrators from women's groups made speeches about gender equality and, at times, tore paper chains from their necks to symbolize liberation from Chinese customary law (Chan 1995:4). Across the plaza, a conservative group representing rural elite interests, the Heung Yee Kuk, gathered in large numbers to protest female inheritance on the grounds that it would undermine tradition. One banner held the plaintive message "Why are you killing our culture?" (p. 30).

The starting point for this research was the odd juxtaposition of rural women wearing farm hats and the transnational rhetoric of rights and gender equality that they employed to lobby for legal change. The majority of these women had never been in the central business district before. How did they become part of a movement that framed their grievances as a violation of their human rights when they needed directions even to find downtown? How did they recognize the potential of legislative change to solve their particular problems? In other words, how were human rights made local? To what extent were they indigenized, that is, translated into local terms that made sense to rural village women?

On a small scale, the 1993–94 female inheritance movement is a case study of globalization. There is a widespread assumption that the global circulation of ideas is increasing cultural homogeneity, but, as Appadurai (1996:7) suggests, global ideas circulated through the mass media also spark resistance, selectivity, and agency, creating vernacular forms of globalization.[2] Scholars emphasize the global circulation of ideas and images but rarely examine how transnational ideas and discourses become localized. The female inheritance movement offers an opportunity to examine a vernacular form of globalization and to think about how global ideas are reinterpreted in terms of local categories of meaning.

2. Some studies show that global ideas build on local referents to establish their meaning and value, as in transnational fashions and music (see, e.g., Feld 2001).

International Law and Society

388 | CURRENT ANTHROPOLOGY *Volume 46, Number 3, June 2005*

This process of localization is a high-stakes question in the universalism-versus-relativism debate. Although the idea of human rights creates universal standards (Donnelly 2003), proponents of Asian values, most famously Lee Kuan Yew of Singapore, argue that it is based on Western individualism and does not readily apply to more collectivist Asian societies (see Bauer and Bell 1999:3–23). Although support for Asian values has diminished, it is common for members of non-European societies to argue that the idea of human rights is an alien, Western concept which does not fit into their cultural framework. By focusing on how human rights are interpreted in local cultural terms and gain legitimacy within local communities, localization offers one way to bridge the divide between universalism and relativism. Anthropological research on human rights, for example, focuses on processes of appropriating rights and critiques the notion of an opposition between universalism and relativism (Wilson 1996, Cowan, Dembour, and Wilson 2001). Abdullahi An-Na'im also argues that "human rights are much more credible . . . if they are perceived to be legitimate within the various cultural traditions of the world" (1992a:3, see also An-Na'im 1992b, 2002). He advocates a cross-cultural approach in which rights are "conceived and articulated within the widest possible range of cultural traditions" as a way of increasing their credibility, legitimacy, and efficacy (1992a:2).

From another angle, there is a growing body of research on transnational social movements that blends social movement theory with transnational network analysis. This work asks how transnational movements and actors promote normative and political change at the global level (Keck and Sikkink 1998, Khagram, Ricker, and Sikkink 2002, Risse, Ropp, and Sikkink 1999). There is much discussion of norm creation because the political impact of transnational nongovernmental organizations (NGOs) often depends on the use of information, persuasion, and moral pressure (Khagram, Ricker, and Sikkink 2002:11). Framing, defined as "action-oriented sets of beliefs and meanings that inspire and legitimate the activities and campaigns of a social movement organization," is also an important ingredient in movement success as well as a way to push the creation of new norms (Snow and Benford 2000:614; see also Tarrow 1998). Work on framing, transnational networks, and norm creation generally explores interaction between domestic NGOs, transnational NGOs, movements, and states. Case studies often look at how coalitions both take advantage of existing international norms and institutions and create new ones. For example, Alison Brysk (2000) shows that Latin American indigenous people turned to international institutions only after efforts to frame their grievances in terms of rights had failed at home.

This scholarship on transnational movements, however, pays little attention to how local actors come to see their everyday grievances as violations of human rights or negotiate between their existing cultural frameworks and rights concepts. For those sympathetic to An-Na'im's argument, there is little detailed exploration of

what a dialogic approach to human rights means in practice. How do places like Hong Kong manage to employ rights language in a way that taps the power of universalism while responding to local conditions? Using an anthropological perspective, we examine the female inheritance movement in its historical, social, economic, and political context as an example of meaning-making at the grass roots in a rights-based movement. We develop a framework for thinking about process—charting how and why human rights ideas moved from their global sites of creation to local social movements. Two ideas are important here: *layers* and *translators*.

We see the female inheritance movement as a coalition of distinct layers. We call the different camps "layers" rather than "groups" as a way of conceptualizing their relationship to rights language and their relative distance from transnational ideas. Following the pioneering work of Stuart Scheingold (1974) and other socio-legal scholars (e.g., McCann 1994, Engel and Munger 2002), we see rights as a resource, albeit a limited one. The layers of the female inheritance movement formed a rough hierarchy in terms of the degree to which they tapped into this resource. For example, one layer emphasized the rights dimension of female inheritance while another framed the issue in terms of patriarchy and feudal thinking. The indigenous women themselves, whose stories formed the narrative core of the movement, generally saw themselves as the victims of unfeeling and rapacious male relatives, although they also came to see themselves as subject to gender discrimination. The movement was an amalgamation of the ways in which these different layers perceived the issue, incorporating both particularistic understandings of grievances and the more generalized framework of human rights.

Despite significant ideological differences, these layers were able to communicate through the services of people whom we term "translators." Translators were able to switch between different ways of framing the problem, facilitating collaboration between people in various layers who did not necessarily say the same thing or think about the issue in the same way. Translators, for example, helped the indigenous women recast their stories as violations of a right to protection from gender discrimination, something guaranteed by the Hong Kong government. These intermediaries provided critical bridges between a human rights discourse connected to modernity and universalism and more particular and individualized ways of thinking about injuries.

This discussion of layers and translators shows that the human rights framework can play an important role even when rights talk only trickles down to protagonists through the mediation of translators. For a focus on human rights to be an effective political strategy, the idea of rights need not be adopted by participants at all levels of the movement and need not be culturally legitimate throughout the society. However, timing is critical. The Chinese crackdown at Tiananmen Square in 1989 and the anticipated handover to China in 1997 worried Hong Kong leaders and citizens concerned about protection for individual rights (Petersen 1996; Chan 1995:27). At this historical juncture, human rights were an important source of what Kevin O'Brien terms "rightful resistance" (1996). By citing the gulf between international norms and the situation in Hong Kong, the women and their allies gained both legitimacy and public support.

Our research on the movement relies on ethnographic studies done at the time of the movement and subsequent field research in 2002–3, including interviews with many of the protagonists. These interviews took place nearly ten years after the movement. While they provided insight into how people saw the issue, we have relied heavily on secondary sources to reconstruct a timeline of events. Eliza Chan's (1995) master's thesis in anthropology at the Chinese University of Hong Kong was particularly valuable because Chan spent significant time with the indigenous women during the movement and placed emphasis on how they perceived events at the time. It was Chan's insightful analysis of the difference between the way indigenous women saw the movement and the way it was understood by others that started us on a further exploration of the female inheritance movement as a way of understanding the process of localizing human rights.

The Female Inheritance Movement

The central actors in the female inheritance movement are people labeled "indigenous," a term used in Hong Kong to describe the descendants of the population living in the New Territories at the time of the British colonial takeover in 1899. In anthropology, the term "indigenous" is usually used to refer to relatively homogeneous groups that were the initial inhabitants of a territory and have now been incorporated into larger national states. They often occupy a subordinate status within the state. In contrast, the New Territories is an ethnically diverse region that has experienced continuous immigration and settlement of various ethnic groups, largely Cantonese, Hakka, and Punti, over a long period of time (see Watson 1985). Groups typically claim indigenous identity on the basis of prior residence, custom, and community and use these claims as the basis for entitlements to land and resources. Thus, indigeneity is a political claim as well as a cultural status. In the Hong Kong context, "indigenous" was a label first imposed by the British and locally adopted to differentiate those with pre-1899 roots from more recent urban arrivals.

The catalyst for the movement was an indigenous woman, Lai-sheung Cheng, who became a key leader by tracking down other aggrieved women in the New Territories and contacting Hong Kong women's groups to push their claims. When Ms. Cheng's father died without a will (a common occurrence in the New Territories),[3]

3. Wills are considered bad luck in traditional Chinese culture because of their association with death. For this reason, wills detailing the division of property are rare. However, men occasionally leave "voice from the grave" wills that exhort family members to behave well or give a widow permission to remarry (Selby 1991:72–73; see also Wong 2000:173).

her two brothers inherited his house in Yuen Long. In May 1991 the brothers decided to sell the house to a developer. Ms. Cheng was still living on the second floor of the house, and she refused to leave unless she was given a share of the proceeds from the sale, citing a Qing-Dynasty custom allowing unmarried women to reside indefinitely in the family's home after a father's death (*South China Morning Post*, August 23, 1993, and Cheng interview, 2003). For the next two years she was harassed by the buyer of the house to force her to leave. The buyer routinely broke into the house, once smearing excrement and urine around the interior and on another occasion releasing mice (*Sunday Telegraph*, October 24, 1993, and Cheng interview, 2003). The harassment was so intense that Ms. Cheng said she had to call the police nearly every night.

Fed up, Ms. Cheng decided to make her story public. Her first step was to write a letter to Chris Patten, then governor of Hong Kong, saying, "I was persecuted because of the law" (Cheng interview, 2003). Not content with alerting Governor Patten, she wrote a letter to the Chinese newspaper *Oriental Daily* explaining her situation. The *Oriental Daily* did not publish the letter, but someone at the paper put Ms. Cheng in touch with Linda Wong, a social worker at the Hong Kong Federation of Women's Centres who was known to the staff because her organization was lobbying hard for a women's commission (Wong interview, 2003). Ms. Cheng told Linda Wong that she knew several other indigenous women in a similar situation, including Ying Tang, a patient at Ms. Cheng's Chinese-medicine clinic. She also said that several women had contacted her after they saw her name and story in a Chinese newspaper, the *Wah Kui Daily*. Ms. Wong asked Ms. Cheng to contact these women and bring them to a meeting, which she did in late 1993 (Wong interview, 2003). After this first meeting, the women began to publicize their stories. They met informally with various government officials, including members of the Hong Kong Legislative Council Anna Wu and Christine Loh, to explore their legal options. Their first formal step was a meeting at the Complaints Division of the Office of Members of the Legislative Council (Wong interview, 2003).

Framing the Issue

As the indigenous women were organizing, prohibition of female inheritance in the New Territories was gaining prominence as a political issue. On the most basic level, the conflict over female inheritance stemmed from Hong Kong's dual legal system regarding land. While Hong Kong Island and Kowloon, the two other regions of Hong Kong, are governed by laws and a legal system imported from Britain, the New Territories fall under the 1910 New Territories Ordinance, which recognizes Chinese customary law. Although the original legislation makes it sound as if courts had the option of using Chinese customary law to resolve land cases ("the courts have the power to enforce Chinese custom or customary right"), the *Tang v Tang* decision (1970) established that application of Chinese custom to New Territories land cases was mandatory (Selby 1991:48; see also Loh 1997). As a result, there were two laws governing inheritance in Hong Kong in 1994: one in urban Hong Kong and another in the rural New Territories.

Discrimination against New Territories women had been on the radar screen of women's groups for a long time. When the Association for the Advancement of Feminism (AAF) was founded in 1984, abolishing discriminatory laws in the New Territories was mentioned in its position paper (Tong 1999:64). In addition, five women's groups asked the government to set up a working group to look into New Territories discrimination in July 1990 (Howarth et al. 1991:17). The issue of female inheritance took on increased importance after a 1991 shadow report by the Hong Kong Council of Women prepared in conjunction with Hong Kong's report to the Human Rights Committee in Geneva on compliance with the International Covenant on Civil and Political Rights (ICCPR).

NGO reports on UN treaties tend to vanish into the ether of documents surrounding UN work. However, this particular submission came at a high point of interest in human rights in Hong Kong. Hong Kong's Bill of Rights had been passed in July 1991,[4] and in the wake of the events in Tiananmen Square Hong Kong was newly concerned with civil liberties and discrimination (Petersen 1996; see also Petersen and Samuels 2002: 47–48). Although the Heung Yee Kuk, a political organization representing rural villages, had lobbied to exempt "traditional rights" of male villagers from the Bill of Rights, it had failed to win an exemption (Petersen 1996:353–55).[5] As a result, the Hong Kong Council of Women's report was able to claim that this was a form of gender discrimination that contravened the newly passed Bill of Rights (Howarth et al. 1991:16).

The shadow report was important because it framed the female inheritance issue in human rights terms. The four authors, all Western women with strong academic backgrounds, argued that male-only inheritance violated both the Convention on the Elimination of Discrimination Against Women (CEDAW) and the ICCPR (Ho-

warth et al. 1991:12).[6] They further explained that Hong Kong's legislation governing succession—the Intestates' Estate Ordinance and the Probate and Administration Ordinance—did not apply to New Territories women (p. 14). The report included a well-reasoned argument as to why male-only inheritance was not protected by either the Joint Declaration or the Basic Law, the two documents outlining the terms of the handover (pp. 16–17). These legal arguments provided the critical intellectual framework for activists and legislators to push for equal inheritance. They also helped clear up confusion about the complicated dual legal system. The government could no longer claim, as the attorney general did in 1986, that they were "not aware of any provisions of [Hong Kong] law which discriminate against women" (quoted in Lui 1997: chap. 3, 5). The report called male-only inheritance a "feudal" result of a patriarchal Confucian social order and noted that it persisted in Hong Kong long after its abolition in China, Taiwan, and Singapore because the New Territories Ordinance had "led to a rigidification of customary law" (pp. 13, 15, 17).

The most important contribution of the report, however, was its discovery that the jurisdiction of the New Territories Ordinance was based on territory, not on indigenous identity, and therefore its prohibition of female inheritance applied to all residents of the New Territories. In 1994, 42% of the population of Hong Kong lived in the New Territories (Tong 1999:53). Most of the people lived in public housing estates or private flats that were not exempted from the New Territories Ordinance. As a result, women were ineligible to inherit property throughout most of the New Territories (Petersen 1996: 341; Jones interview, 2003).[7] Amazingly, practically no one had realized this. The news of this discovery broke in the Chinese newspaper *Ming Pao* on September 6, 1993, and immediately created a crisis for the government (Wong 2000:299; see also Fischler 2000:215).[8] The 340,000 owners of apartments and houses in urban parts of the New Territories suddenly discovered that Chinese customary law applied to them (Home Affairs Branch 1993). Clearly, the New Territories Ordinance would have to be amended to allow female urban residents to inherit property when the owner died intestate, following the laws in place in urban Hong Kong.

On November 19, 1993, the government introduced the New Territories Land (Exemption) Bill. The bill ex-

---

4. There were calls for a Bill of Rights prior to 1989, but the proposal was not endorsed by the government until after Tiananmen (Petersen 1996:350). In a tricky bit of legislation drafting, Hong Kong's Bill of Rights was modeled on the ICCPR to make it harder to repeal after the handover. China had already agreed in the Joint Declaration (the document outlining the terms of the handover) that the ICCPR would remain in force.

5. The Heung Yee Kuk, founded in 1926, has acted as a leader in protecting the interests of indigenous villagers, particularly with reference to land, and is the highest tier of the representative organization of the villagers (Chan 2003:67, 87). Kuk members consist of the chair and vice chair of each of 27 rural committees made up of representatives elected by their villages (Asian Television Network, February 27, 2001). These conservative clan leaders have in the past opposed development, but since the late 1950s they have stopped doing so and sought to increase compensation for land from the government (Chan 2003:71).

6. The Hong Kong Council of Women was formed in 1947. Because of an explosion in the number of local women's groups during the 1980s, membership in the early 1990s was limited to a small number of expatriate women.

7. The Hong Kong Council of Women also discovered that women had once been permitted to administer New Territories property after the death of a husband, father, or son, but 1971 changes to the laws governing inheritance had eliminated this possibility (Carol Jones, personal communication, October 14, 2003).

8. By the time the news broke, the Hong Kong Council of Women had already informed the government of the problem. In June 1993 the government started automatically exempting all new grants of lands (with the exception of land grants to indigenous villagers) from the New Territories Ordinance (*South China Morning Post*, March 11, 1994).

empted urban land, land generally inhabited by Hong Kong residents who had moved into the New Territories, from the New Territories Ordinance. This change was not contested by the rural political leaders or the government. It was only when a legislator proposed extending the right to inherit family land to rural indigenous women that a wave of protest erupted. Giving rural women the right to inherit family land was a dramatic departure from a practice dating back at least a hundred years. The first step in making this momentous change came with the creation of the Anti-Discrimination Female Indigenous Residents Committee.

The Anti-Discrimination Female Indigenous Residents Committee

On October 3, 1993, the indigenous women lodged their complaint with the Complaints Division of the Legislative Council. Less than a week later, the Legislative Council passed a nonbinding motion calling for female inheritance in the New Territories (*South China Morning Post*, October 14, 1993). Despite two hours of fierce debate, the motion passed easily, with 36 in favor and only 4 opposed. The Anti-Discrimination Female Indigenous Residents Committee was founded about the time of this debate (Wong 2000:299; Chan 1995:47). In addition to the indigenous women, it included Linda Wong, a representative of the AAF, a Radio Television Hong Kong reporter, an anthropology graduate student, and a labor organizer.[9] With the help of these outsiders, the indigenous women began to tell their stories to a wider audience. Most important, they learned to tell these stories in a way that was politically effective.

In the beginning, the women saw their situations as personal wrongs perpetrated by particular relatives and stressed that they had been denied affection by their natal and marital relatives (Chan 1995:72). According to Linda Wong, the women were not thinking about changing the law until the first demonstration outside the Legislative Council. Rather, they were hoping that Legislative Council members would address their individual cases (interview, 2003).[10] Chan (1995) argues that most of the women saw their claims in terms of kinship obligations, not equal rights. Most of the women did not criticize the patrilineal kinship system itself but blamed particular relatives who had reneged on their kinship obligations to provide them financial and emotional support in lieu of their fathers' land. One woman interviewed by Chan was most angry that her relatives had failed to keep in touch with her, forgetting that she was her fathers' "root and sprout" and "flesh and blood." If

she had inherited, she said, she would have allowed her relatives to live in her father's house as long as they maintained close ties with her (pp. 88–89).

When the women did make inheritance claims, they justified them on the basis of their filial ties to their father and sought to assert their membership in the lineage (Chan 1995:39). In telling their stories, several of the women emphasized the role they had played in their fathers' funerals to underscore their close ties to their fathers (pp. 82–85). Because they had been filial, affectionate daughters, they argued, they were entitled to inherit.[11] By using kinship ties to justify inheritance, they reinforced the patrilineal family system even as they asserted their rights (p. 97). Tellingly, only one of the women in the Anti-Discrimination Female Indigenous Residents Committee had a brother. The rest of the women were all "last-of-line" daughters (*juefangnu*) and, as a result, their fathers' land had been inherited by distant male relatives.[12] In Chan's interviews, most of the women said they would have been willing to give up their inheritance rights if they had had brothers (Chan 1995:72). Regardless, many villagers criticized them for behaving unreasonably in demanding a share of their natal family's property (p. 39). As the women began lobbying for a change in the law, they came under pressure for being "ungrateful" and for being "collaborators" with the Westernized "outsiders" (p. 126).

Through the Anti-Discrimination Female Indigenous Residents Committee, the indigenous women learned how to translate their kinship grievances into the language of rights and equality. This translation was critical because, in order to be politically persuasive, the women needed to phrase their needs in a language acceptable to those hearing their claims (Chan 1995:56). The Legislative Council and the media were interested not in family disputes over property but in stories that spoke to wider themes of gender equality and human rights. The women had to "learn" to put on an "elitist and rational pose," to present themselves as victims with a "detached" attitude, in language devoid of personal grievances and emotions (p. 100).

Although the Hong Kong Federation of Women's Centres claimed that the "women took all the initiatives by themselves while the Centre just concentrated on providing resources support," the process was more complicated (Hong Kong Federation of Women's Centres 1994):20; see also Lui 1997: chap. 4, 20). Chan describes how outsiders on the Residents Committee played an important role in framing the indigenous women's stories and, more generally, facilitating the transition to a more generalized, rights-based perspective (1995:119). The social workers drilled the women, teaching them

9. The exact number of members of the Residents Committee is unclear. Chan (1995:39) cites six active members, although one is a news reporter without a grievance. Wong and Chan (interview, 2003) list seven core members. Most likely, there was some flux over time.
10. This is a matter of dispute. In a 2003 interview Ms. Cheng claimed that the women knew that the law had to be changed from the start.

11. In some cases, affection and kinship were valid criteria for female inheritance. Chan (1997:155–59) discusses a case from the 1970s in which a village council ruled that a daughter could become trustee of her father's land because she was the person closest to her father.
12. All Chinese terms are in Mandarin. For a more extended discussion of what it means to be a "last-of-line" daughter, see Chan (1995:40, 60–63).

392 | CURRENT ANTHROPOLOGY *Volume 46, Number 3, June 2005*

not to use slang and how to present themselves to the public (p. 120). They learned to ask for a broad change to an unfair law rather than mediation and a more equal division of property. On several occasions the outsiders in the group groomed the women in dealing with the media, particularly in how to respond to reporters. The emphasis, beyond avoiding slang and speaking with sufficient detachment, was on keeping the women's stories short and quotable. They wanted the women to reiterate a standard claim rather than telling their personal stories so that the movement did not appear to be motivated only by personal interest (p. 117). The women practiced responding to questions such as "There are some women in the New Territories who say that they do not need the rights of inheritance. Why do you still insist on it?" and "What experience of yours in the New Territories aroused you to speak out so boldly?" pp. 117–19; see also Chan interview, 2003, and Cheng interview, 2003). In one session, the social worker imitated the tone of the reporters in asking this question and taped the response given by one of the women. She then played the tape for the group to illustrate the power of placing an individual story in a wider context. For one woman, the principle of gender equality and human rights enabled her to claim inheritance even though her natal kin claimed that she was only an adopted, not a biological daughter (pp. 119–20). Under the human rights framework, she had rights regardless of her adopted status.

In addition, the Residents Committee helped the women branch out into different modes of expression, creating dramas and songs to illustrate the injustice of male-only inheritance. A labor organizer in the group became the "stage director" for the drama. As one interviewee put it, "She put together elements to strike those cameras," such as suggesting that the women dress in traditional clothes (Chan interview, 2003; see also Cheng interview, 2003). As part of this dramatization, the women needed to present a united front regardless of differences in age, ethnicity, and education. They had to negotiate a common identity as indigenous women, an identity forged through a series of small decisions within the group. When the women rewrote a traditional song to include new lyrics about injustice, for example, they had to find a song that everyone knew. In the end, they chose a Hakka mountain song (*shan ge*) even though the majority of the indigenous women were not Hakka (Cheng interview, 2003).

In creating the dramas, the organizers were responding to the stereotypes that they knew the media wanted to see. The media had long seen the New Territories as a bastion of outdated tradition. In a documentary on New Territories life entitled *An Indigenous Village: A Case for Concern*, aired on Radio Television Hong Kong June 20 1986, the narrator closed with the thought that "traditional modes of thinking vastly out of step with the modern world are still deep-rooted in the hearts of indigenous villagers in the New Territories." During the female inheritance movement, the Kuk was portrayed as traditional, rural, and male while the female inheritance coalition was urban, modern, and female (Chan

1995:50). For the most part, the indigenous women were seen as victims of "tradition" and lineage hegemony (p. 100). One TV series broadcast during the movement depicted the lineage system as a "living fossil" of Chinese tradition (p. 107). Other reporters posed the women in front of ancestral halls staring into the distance, using the elegant Chinese calligraphy as a foil for the women's apparent helplessness (p. 103). The press encouraged the women to wear the loose-fitting black suits and large-brimmed hats traditionally associated with rural women, a departure from their normal attire (p. 53).

Indigenous women who failed to generalize their particular grievances into stories of rights violations were silenced (Chan 1995:131–32). In the middle of one Legislative Council debate, for example, an indigenous woman, the oldest participant in the movement, suddenly interrupted the chairperson and started shouting in Hakka about how badly her relatives had treated her. The chairperson cut the woman off, saying, "Your story is not related to our discussion." A representative of the Kuk then told her that her story was just a family dispute and should be filed with the Kuk (pp. 131–32). Portraying the women's stories as individual disputes without broader significance was an important way of discrediting the indigenous women (p. 5). During the debate over the passage of the land exemption bill, one legislator dismissed the indigenous women by saying, "As regards the case of Ms. Cheng Lai-Sheung . . . her family members have already clarified publicly that it was only a matter of dispute on fighting for legacy" (Hong Kong Hansard 1994:4553).

In contrast, the women's stories were very effective when filtered through the lens developed in the Anti-Discrimination Female Indigenous Residents Committee and presented as examples of gender inequality. Social movement scholars have noted the degree to which individual testimonials can help legitimate a cause and, by extension, rally support behind it (Keck and Sikkink 1998:19–20). In the female inheritance movement, the women's stories played a critical role in giving a human face to the problem and discrediting the Kuk's claim that it was the sole voice of indigenous villagers. During the October 1993 motion debate, several of the legislative councillors mentioned having met the indigenous women and having been moved by the women's stories. These women's stories also refuted Kuk claims that no one complained about male-only inheritance (Hong Kong Hansard 1993:249, 253, 256).

It would be easy to believe that the indigenous women lost control of their stories and were exploited for political change, as has occurred elsewhere (Keck and Sikkink 1998:20). The reality, however, is more nuanced. While the outsiders on the Residents Committee helped the women present themselves to the outside world, the women themselves played an active role in shaping the strategy. The idea of writing new lyrics for indigenous songs, for example, came from the women (Chan 1995: 108; see also Cheng interview, 2003). The idea was a public relations coup: the image of indigenous women singing traditional songs became an icon of the movement. The women also had a voice in the wider women's movement through the chairperson of the Residents Committee, Ms. Cheng, who attended meetings of a coalition of women's groups. Perhaps most important, the women spoke for themselves. While the outside members of the Residents Committee coached the women, they also felt strongly that the women should have their own voice (Chan 1995:117; see also Wong interview, 2003).

As the indigenous women learned to tell their stories differently, they moved from framing their problems as kinship violations to presenting them as a product of discrimination and gender inequality. This shift in consciousness seems to have been an additive process. Although the women developed a new perception of the problem as gender discrimination, they retained their old sense of individual wrongs perpetrated by male relatives. Consciousness is slippery and unquantifiable, and it is difficult to know how completely the indigenous women assimilated the gender-equality framework. One woman told her story using terms such as "gender discrimination" and "injustice," for example, terms that she had not known before joining the Residents Committee (Chan 1995:146). The Hakka mountain song that the women developed also refers to injustice. The first two lines of the song show an awareness that the indigenous women stand together as an oppressed group with common concerns: "Female indigenous women are the most unfortunate people / This world is unfair to them" (p. 98). The second two lines go farther, asking the Legislative Council to address the problem and, by implication, change the law: "The Hong Kong society is unjust / I hope that the Legislative Councillors will uphold justice" (p. 98).

Yet the Hakka song does not mention rights, and there is little evidence that the indigenous women developed a sustained critique of their problems based on human rights. Despite one woman's statement that "now and after [the handover in] 1997, I will continue to bravely stand up and fight for the rights of indigenous women," the indigenous women dropped out of the women's movement after the land exemption ordinance was passed (Hong Kong Women Christian Council 1995:126; see also interviews). No doubt they were tired of fighting, but this may also be a sign that their concerns were rooted in their particular problems with uncooperative male relatives rather than a larger struggle for gender equality. The women's frustration with demonstrations that did not focus exclusively on them is another sign that the rights perspective never entirely replaced the kinship-violation frame. Moreover, Chan reports that some of the women were upset when their stories were subsumed by the larger themes of gender equality or antidiscrimination (1995:116, 146).

Passage of the Bill

After the initial debate and the formation of the Anti-Discrimination Female Indigenous Residents Commit-

tee, events began unfolding rapidly. Inside the Legislative Council, Christine Loh took up the female inheritance cause for the rural indigenous women. Loh, educated in both Hong Kong and England, says that the issue appealed to her because she thought it was "very odd" that indigenous women had "less rights" than everyone else in Hong Kong (interview, 2003). On January 31, 1994, she submitted an amendment to extend the land exemption ordinance to include rural land. If passed, it would have allowed female indigenous women to inherit family property, although not the ancestral trust lands held by lineages.

For a few months after Loh submitted her amendment, things were quiet. The Heung Yee Kuk, relying on old-style colonial politics, ignored the issue because it assumed that the amendment would never receive government support. But on March 10 the government announced that it would not oppose Loh's amendment. This was a turning point, particularly because it had initially seemed that extending female inheritance to indigenous women would be an uphill battle. While the outcome seems inevitable in retrospect, the colonial government had long courted the support of the Kuk to ensure that rural development was not met with serious resistance, and many thought the government would continue to back it on the inheritance issue. In fact, it is not clear why the colonial government had a change of heart. Some Kuk members felt that the government had sold them out because it no longer required Kuk support to develop the New Territories (*South China Morning Post*, March 27, 1993). The Kuk's pro-Beijing stance and opposition to Governor Patten's political reforms may also have played a role (*South China Morning Post*, March 27, 1993).

In response to the change in the government's position, the Kuk organized a rally on March 22 attended by over 1,200 supporters (*South China Morning Post*, March 23, 1993). At 3:50 p.m., 20 incensed indigenous villagers broke through security barriers during a protest outside the Legislative Council building. They attacked people demonstrating for equal inheritance rights, ripped up banners, threw water bottles, and shouted curses (*South China Morning Post*, March 23, 1994; see also Tse interview, 2003). Lee Wing-tat, a legislative councillor caught in the fray, fell to the ground after a punch to the back. After March 22, both sides realized the strength of the opposition and the scale of the fight ahead of them. At that point, 12 women's groups formed the Coalition for Equal Inheritance Rights to fight for rural women's inheritance rights in the New Territories (Tong 1999: 55–56).[13] Three days later, the Kuk formed the Head-

13. The Coalition included the following groups: Anti-Discrimination Female Residents Committee, Hong Kong Federation of Women's Centres, Association for the Advancement of Feminism, Hong Kong Women Christian Council, Women's Rights Concern Group of the Chan Hing Social Service Centre, Hong Kong Women Workers Association, AWARE, Hong Kong Council of Women, Business and Professional Women, the Hong Kong Federation of Women, and two other community groups (Tong 1999:64–65; see also Wong 2000:62).

394 | CURRENT ANTHROPOLOGY *Volume 46, Number 3, June 2005*

quarters for the Protection for the Village and Defense of the Clan (p. 58). For the next three months, these two groups worked hard to gain support, holding frequent demonstrations and facing off dozens of times.

In both the March 22 rally and subsequent demonstrations, the Kuk positioned itself as the defender of tradition and culture.[14] Traditionally, women left their home village and became part of their husbands' lineages. Allowing female inheritance, the Kuk argued, would lead to a disintegration of clan identity because land would eventually be owned by nonlineage members (Chan 1998:45). To buttress its claim, it appealed to the authority of the ancestors. Male-only inheritance is "in accordance with the wishes of [the] ancestors" and, as a result, "any outsider tampering with these customs shall not be tolerated" (Heung Yee Kuk Proclamation, quoted in Chan 1998:45). In order for this claim to be seen as legitimate, the male-dominated Kuk realized that it would need the support of indigenous women. It found women who agreed with Angela Li York-lan: "[We] do not think we are discriminated against. We love our traditions. We have the right not to accept any change" (*South China Morning Post*, April 4, 1994). At one demonstration, the Kuk vice chairman, Daniel Lam, said, "We have shown the community that villagers are able to demonstrate endurance, calm and reason in the fight against the destruction of our customs" (*Hong Kong Standard*, April 12, 1994).

As defenders of tradition, the Kuk placed emphasis on being Chinese. One song often sung at demonstrations was "The Brave Chinese," renamed "The Brave New Territories People" (Chan 1998:47). Being Chinese meant renewing attention to the anticolonial strands of indigenous history. In April 1994, 1,000 villagers gathered to commemorate an 1899 uprising against the British at Tai Po (p. 45; see also *South China Morning Post*, April 18, 1994). Ironically, it was the first time the uprising had ever been publicly commemorated (p. 46). Kuk demonstrations lent themselves to dramatic media coverage. The inheritance issue remained in the public eye from October 1993 (the motion debate) through June 1994 (the passage of the bill) because Kuk members did things such as beheading a doll representing Governor Patten (*South China Morning Post*, April 18, 1994). On another occasion, angry villagers threatened to rape Loh if she dared set foot in the New Territories (*South China Morning Post*, March 26, 1994). When it came to media attention, Loh said, "One couldn't have better opponents than the Heung Yee Kuk" (interview, 2003).

Although there were times when the outcome of Loh's amendment was unclear, the issue was pretty much settled by May 1994. The public overwhelmingly supported female inheritance rights, by a margin of 77% in favor to 9% opposed (*South China Morning Post*, May 9,

1994).[15] There was little sympathy for the Heung Yee Kuk both because people generally believed in gender equality and because they were resentful of what they saw as the special privileges granted to indigenous villagers. Recognizing the extent of public support for extending female inheritance rights from urban women in the New Territories to indigenous women, the government incorporated Loh's amendment into its own bill, along with suggestions from several other legislative councillors (Tsang and Wan 1994:13). On May 24, 1994, the Bills Committee of the Legislative Council accepted the government's amended bill and voted down Heung Yee Kuk Chairman Lau Wong-fat's suggestion of a referendum in the New Territories to settle the issue (Tsang and Wan 1994:12). By the time of the actual vote on June 22, the result was a foregone conclusion. The New Territories Land (Exemption) Ordinance passed easily, with 36 votes in favor, 2 against, and 3 abstentions (Hong Kong Hansard 1994:4656).

Creating Custom: The History Behind the Debate

The female inheritance movement is full of deep ironies about the meanings of tradition and modernity. Most basically, it was a struggle over land rights and political power in which powerful male leaders claimed to be defending culture, tradition, and the lineage while poor indigenous women and their elite urban allies claimed to speak for gender equality and universal human rights. Yet this dichotomy between tradition and modernity was a constructed truth, created both by the protagonists and by the historical legacy of colonialism.

COLONIAL ROOTS

Hong Kong's dual legal system was the result of the unusual circumstances under which the British gained control of the New Territories. In contrast to Hong Kong Island and Kowloon, which were ceded to Britain in perpetuity, the terms of the 1899 Convention of Peking specified that the New Territories would be leased to Britain for 99 years. This was the lease that expired on July 1, 1997, when Hong Kong (including Hong Kong Island and Kowloon) was handed back to China. The limited scope of Britain's right to rule was one reason to preserve local custom as much as possible (Petersen 1996:339; Jones 1995:167–70). After gaining control of the New Territories, the British issued a number of proclamations assuring New Territories villagers that the New Territories would be "governed . . . according to the laws, customs and usages of the Chinese by the elders of villages, subject to the control of the British magistrate" (quoted in Chan 1999:234). The 1899 Blake Proclamation, often cited as the grounds for deference to Chinese custom, further reassured villagers that "your

---

14. This appeal to tradition is an old argument. Defenders of the practice of keeping concubines argued that it was "an institution . . . sanctioned by immemorial Chinese law and customs; it has been preserved by the Colony's Charter; it has received the highest judicial recognition" (quoted in Lee 2000:232).

15. This was a survey of all of Hong Kong.

usages and good customs will not in any way be interfered with" (Lockhart 1900:appendix no. 9). Before World War II, villagers were governed by local elders according to Chinese custom and law with a British district officer to resolve disputes.

This strategy was dictated by economics and a desire to avoid conflict. Remembering the expensive and bloody 1857 Sepoy Rebellion in India, British colonial administrators decided that adherence to Chinese customary law in the New Territories was the best way to ensure local support for colonialism at minimal cost (Chiu and Hung 2000:226; see also Jones 1995:168). Because the British never believed that the New Territories would be particularly profitable (Chun 2000:48), they saw the New Territories villagers in terms of culture and kinship, not as potential laborers. In contrast to Hong Kong Island, which saw rapid change, the New Territories villages were treated as bearers of tradition, isolated and expected not to change. For many colonial administrators, preserving village life became a romantic goal (Jones 1995:180). Until urbanization and industrialization hit the New Territories in the 1970s and 1980s, the area was seen as "a virtual laboratory for the study of rural Chinese society" (Watson 1983:486).

The New Territories were dominated by powerful patrilineages, corporate groups that traced membership through male descent. While multilineage villages did exist, most males in a community could trace their family back to a common ancestor. The members of the patrilineage had common land, held celebrations to worship common ancestors, and cooperated for political purposes (Watson 1983:486). In contrast to the situation in the rest of Hong Kong, it was permissible in the New Territories to make gifts of land to ancestral trusts in perpetuity. In 1948 about one-third of the land was held in such ancestral trusts, with sale permitted only by all beneficiaries (Strickland Report 1953:62). The female inheritance dispute focused not on lands held in ancestral trusts but on family lands.

Despite a common belief that patrilineages were unified corporate groups, there was considerable inequality in the villages and within lineages. Watson's (1985) careful ethnographic study from the 1970s reveals that smallholder tenants were heavily dependent on their wealthy agnates.[16] These two classes were quite distinct, with different forms of marriage, levels of education, kinds of houses, and social lives for wives and daughters. Although it was important for the lineage to present itself as a unified corporation to the outside world and to its members, it existed in a highly stratified society. More-

over, during the last quarter of the twentieth century, inheritance patterns slowly started changing. Local lawyers sometimes found ways around the ban on women's inheritance of family land, particularly if the village head was supportive. In the absence of a male heir, widows or daughters occasionally inherited land or acquired the cash after the properties were sold (Chan 1997:169). Sometimes a woman could keep land if she did not remarry. Her position was, in essence, "trustee for life" (Selby 1991:73).

DEFINING CUSTOM

Since Chinese custom was not codified, it was typically interpreted by British magistrates serving in the New Territories and the courts (see, e.g., Coates 1956, Wesley-Smith 1994). For colonial administrators, preserving local customs meant identifying them, a problematic process. Despite references to homogeneous "Chinese customs," there was variation in customs among lineages, villages, and districts (Wesley-Smith 1994:218; Strickland Report 1953:13). No doubt overwhelmed by this diversity, the British began an effort to record Chinese customs in 1899. The result was a particularly idealized version of Chinese custom because their informants were mostly village elders and scholars, men—they were all men—with an interest in preserving the status quo (Chan 1999:236). District officers developed a "bible" of points of custom, which they passed on to others. Coupled with testimony from expert witnesses alive in 1899, these notes were used by British district officers to resolve land disputes according to traditional Chinese law until they were lost in the 1941–44 Japanese occupation (Wesley-Smith 1994:206).

This was an ironic situation. Despite their confessed ignorance, British district officers functioned as upholders of Chinese tradition.[17] Perhaps as a result of uncertainty, district officers tended to be conservative, with the result that adherence to Chinese law and custom was reinforced and solidified (Wesley-Smith 1994:206, 222–23). The additional irony was that other Chinese societies, such as Taiwan and Mainland China, reformed Chinese law and custom to allow equal inheritance. By refusing to allow this kind of change, the British froze New Territories life in a mythic, imagined past. This model of colonial administration worked in the prewar era because the New Territories were still largely rural. In 1931 the population of the New Territories was 98,000. Most residents were still farmers, and district officers could hear most disputes (Watson 1983:484). Most important, the New Territories were isolated enough from urban Hong Kong to maintain a different

16. In a New Territories region that Watson studied, a small merchant and landowning elite headed lineages made up of tenant farmers (1985:54). The landlord-merchants controlled crucial resources such as land, ancestral estates, markets, pawnshops, boats for cargo, and factories. They employed fellow lineage members as well as outsiders in their many enterprises (p. 81). James Hayes notes that "Watson mainly worked with the oldest, biggest lineages and class divisions were less marked in the majority of New Territories lineages, many of which were quite small" (personal communication, October 2003).

17. On the bench there was a minority view that custom should be allowed to change with the times. In a 1956 decision (*Wong Ying-kuen v Wong Yi-shi and Ors*) J. Briggs held that "the correct law to apply is the Qing law and custom as it existed in 1842 with such modifications in custom and in the interpretation in the law as have taken place in Hong Kong since that period" (quoted in Selby 1991:50).

396 | CURRENT ANTHROPOLOGY *Volume 46, Number 3, June 2005*

legal system and set of rights. This isolation ended in the postwar era.

POSTWAR CHANGES: THE END OF VILLAGE LIFE

The end of World War II brought a wave of migrants from China. Residents who had fled Hong Kong during the Japanese occupation returned, accompanied by refugees from the Chinese civil war. Between 1945 and 1950 the population of Hong Kong jumped from 600,000 to between 2 and 2.5 million, an increase of roughly 400% (Bray 2001:16; see also Chun 2000:111). This jump in population created an intense need for new public housing. After a 1953 fire in the Shek Kip Mei squatter community, the Hong Kong government decided to build public housing on a massive scale. Urban Hong Kong was already overcrowded, so the new public housing estates had to be built in the New Territories. The government built seven New Towns in the New Territories, each of which included industry, public housing, community services, and infrastructure (Scott 1982:660).

This development was tremendously disruptive to rural life. In the most direct measure of disruption, about 50 villages were physically moved to make room for the New Towns and another 25 villages were moved in order to create reservoirs to meet the water needs of the expanding urban population (Hayes 2001:72). Not surprisingly, the old district officer system could not keep up with population growth and the new burdens of New Town administration. Starting in 1961, land dispute cases were resolved by the courts; the district officers were no longer "father mother officials" (*fu mu guan*) but pure administrators.

Most important, development changed the economy of the New Territories by creating new sources of wealth. Land for the New Towns was largely purchased from New Territories villagers, either with cash or through a land swap (Nissim 1998:102). Between 1984 and 1997, the period just before reunification with China, there was a rapid increase in wealth based in part on the skyrocketing value of real estate (Smart and Lee 2003:167; see also Chan 2001:272). In 1993 one legislative councilor said, "When I was small, people were still talking about 'country people' with 'feet covered with cow dung' and 'illiterate.' But today we see that the members of the Heung Yee Kuk are all tycoons in smart suits and traveling in Rolls Royces" (Hong Kong Hansard 1993:240). The development value of land was part of a larger move away from an agricultural economy. Cheap rice imports from Thailand flooded Hong Kong in the 1950s. Rice farming, the traditional occupation in the New Territories, was suddenly unprofitable (Watson 1983:483). Some farmers switched to vegetables, but many others decided to emigrate. Suddenly, villages were transformed from physical communities based on a shared physical space to transnational communities based on shared traditions and birthplace (Chan 2001:280).[18] As the rural

18. In a study of two villages, Watson (1985:150) found that one-third of the households had one or more members living abroad.

wealthy became absentee landlords, a group of new entrepreneurs, distinct from the old elite of wealthy landlord-merchants, emerged. The new entrepreneurs were supported and nurtured by colonial officials because they were more willing to cooperate with Hong Kong officials in their development plans than the old elite (Watson 1985:147–48). In addition, they tended to be less concerned with lineage unity (p. 148).

It was against this backdrop of urbanization, industrialization, and dislocation that the rural women stepped forward to protest their inability to inherit land.

Layers and Translators: Theorizing the Movement

The story of how indigenous women came to demand a change in inheritance shows how international human rights can be used to address local grievances. Yet this is not a simple story of elite outsiders introducing or imposing rights language. Rather, rights language, mediated through translators, was adopted, modified, supplemented, and ignored by the various participants. Here, we introduce four layers as a way of thinking about the degree to which actors were tied to international rights language. These four layers—expatriates, the Legislative Council, women's groups, and indigenous women—differed significantly from each other in ideology, level of education, extent of international travel, degree of international rights consciousness, and language.

EXPATRIATES

Expatriates played a critical role in bringing the female inheritance issue to prominence and framing it in rights terms. Although it is difficult to remember in hindsight, there was no reason male-only inheritance had to be addressed through legislative change. In 1993, five indigenous women had applied for legal aid to sue for equal inheritance. They were denied legal aid, but their efforts show that the inheritance issue could have been settled on a case-by-case basis by the courts instead of by legislative change (*South China Morning Post*, October 23, 1993). Inheritance was resolved through legislation because, in the course of preparing its ICCPR report, the Hong Kong Council of Women discovered that female inheritance was illegal throughout the New Territories, not just in the villages (Jones interview, 2003).

After securing the necessity of changes to the New Territories Ordinance, expatriates lobbied for female inheritance as a question of international law. The Hong Kong Council of Women's report clearly stated that male-only inheritance "should have been declared *unlawful* long ago, as [it is] contrary to Article 26 of the ICCPR" and is "in conflict with the principle of equality between sexes contained in the internationally accepted Declaration of Elimination of Discrimination Against Women" (Howarth et al. 1991:16, 12). These expatriates were primarily academics and lawyers, several of whom dealt with international law professionally. They were mostly from the United States, Britain, or Australia and spoke English fluently, if not as a first language. On a local-global continuum they were undeniably global, and they saw denying women inheritance rights as a violation of women's right to protection from gender discrimination.

THE LEGISLATIVE COUNCIL

The Legislative Council, Hong Kong's national elite, saw female inheritance primarily as a choice between tradition and modernity. In the final debate over the land exemption ordinance, opponents of the bill claimed that it would "attack the age-old fine tradition of the clan system" and "disturb the peace in the countryside" (Hong Kong Hansard 1994:4579).[19] Others sympathetic to the Kuk complained about the pace of change.[20] In the words of one legislator, "This is an attempt to change the social customs of the indigenous population. Such thinking will gradually be overtaken by newer concepts. In view of this, should we take the hasty move of enforcing the changes through the legislative process?" (p. 4544). Not even Kuk supporters, however, dared question the tenet of gender equality (Lee 2000:248). Chairman Lau Wong-fat maintained that the indigenous women "are not actually treated unequally. In fact, they are equal in other respects. Many of them may even often bully their husbands" (Hong Kong Hansard 1994:4559).

On the other side of the debate, supporters of the bill argued that Hong Kong could not be an international city as long as it had laws that discriminated against women. As one legislator put it, "Hong Kong is a prosperous and progressive metropolis. The fact that the indigenous women of the New Territories are still openly discriminated against is a disgrace for the people of Hong Kong" (Hong Kong Hansard 1994:4565). Others made an explicit connection between the Kuk's rowdy behavior and support for the land exemption ordinance: "When the 20th century is coming to a close, that someone should so shamelessly and overtly threaten to rape is indeed a shame on this modern international city of Hong Kong. Today members of this Council must use their vote to remove such a stigma on Hong Kong" (p. 4542).

Christine Loh, originally attracted to the issue because she saw it in rights terms, continued to talk about equality and human rights: "The idea of human rights is that we have to protect every individual's basic right. Not to mention that there are 200 indigenous women complaining, even if there were only two of them, we as legislators still have the responsibility of ensuring their equal right

before the law" (quoted in Lee 2000:250). Some legislators also referred to international rights, echoing the rhetoric used by the expatriate layer. Legislative Councillor Anna Wu, herself a lawyer, was one of the first to pick up the connection between female inheritance and international law. In a December 1993 letter to members of the Bills Committee, she wrote: "The 1976 extension of the ICCPR to Hong Kong and the 1991 enactment of the Bill of Rights Ordinance should have cast serious doubt on the continuing validity of the system established by the NTO (New Territories Ordinance)" (1994: 1).

For legislators, there were two appealing aspects of international law. First, international law could be used to shame the government into action. In question-and-answer sessions with government representatives, Legislative Council members occasionally inquired about international covenants as a way of holding the government responsible to the ideals expressed in UN documents (Hong Kong Hansard 1993:156–57, 159–60). The other appealing aspect of international law was its perceived connection to modernity. In the debate over the passage of the land exemption ordinance, Legislative Councillor Fung called it "both out of date and inappropriate to deprive women of their land rights," particularly because the Bill of Rights, the ICCPR, and CEDAW all stated that all citizens should be equal before the law (Hong Kong Hansard 1994:4547).

Most supporters of the bill were not much concerned about the abolition of custom, perhaps because neither they nor their constituencies would be affected by the change in law. "Outdated customs are a burden," declared one legislator (Hong Kong Hansard 1993:139; see also 1994:4542). However, Anna Wu was concerned that the ordinance would inadvertently abolish a positive tradition: women's rights under Chinese customary law to maintenance from the estate (see also Loh 1997:6). Although these customary rights were never enforced by the courts, male relatives were traditionally responsible for the ongoing maintenance of widows and unmarried daughters. Ms. Cheng's original complaint, for example, was that her brothers had violated Chinese custom by refusing to allow her to stay in her father's house. In a March 1993 letter to the members of the Bills Committee, Wu expressed her concern that the bill would be "placing in jeopardy the welfare" of women "dependent on the residual customary obligations of the landowner" (1993:2). While not widely shared, her apprehension showed sensitivity to the strengths of the old system. It suggests that her vision of the problem bridged the perspectives of the expatriate, national, and local groups.

WOMEN'S GROUPS

In 1989, 20 women's groups formed a coalition to lobby for a women's commission and the extension of CEDAW to Hong Kong (Wong 2000:60–61). Until the Coalition for Equal Inheritance Rights was founded in March 1994, the women's groups shared information and coordinated action on female inheritance through regular meetings

---

19. This debate took place in both English and Cantonese, the two official languages of Hong Kong.
20. The Hong Kong Federation of Women, a conservative women's group founded in 1993, also favored a more gradual approach: "We aim at progress without upsetting stability" (Hong Kong Federation of Women 1994). Peggy Lam, a founding member of the federation as well as a legislative councillor, argued that haste to pass the amended land exemption ordinance had caused anxiety and conflict that could have been avoided (Hong Kong Hansard 1994:4548–49).

of this coalition. In contrast to the Legislative Council or the expatriates, the coalition functioned entirely in Cantonese. Like the wider women's movement, it consisted primarily of middle-class, educated women, including students and social workers (see Tong n.d.:648).

The women's groups conceptualized the female inheritance issue mainly in terms of gender equality. T-shirts and banners from the movement often carried the logo " ♀ = ♂ ." In keeping with this theme, one women's group issued a statement that "based on the principle of equality, land inheritance right is the right of every indigenous inhabitant. If women inhabitants are not entitled to it because of their gender, it is blatant discrimination, something we cannot accept" (quoted in Lee 2000:250). The women's groups treated gender equality as a self-evident tenet and, for the most part, saw no need to justify it in terms of law. When they did talk about the law, women's groups borrowed their arguments and even their language from the ICCPR report. One AAF publication directly quoted the report, saying that male-only inheritance rights "should have been declared *unlawful* long ago" (Association for the Advancement of Feminism 1993:14). Like the legislative councillors, the women's groups made an explicit connection between gender equality and modernity. Male-only inheritance was "archaic and out of step with society's development." The Hong Women Christian Council went so far as to say, "Gender equality is a shared goal of the modern world" (quoted in Wong 2000:192). Along with the legislative councillors, the women's groups focused on changing the law, not on providing solutions for individual women.

However, there were some important differences in perspective between the women's groups and the legislative councillors. The women's groups saw male-only inheritance as a product of patriarchy, a strand of thought that never emerged in the Legislative Council.[21] One group accused the Heung Yee Kuk of "patriarchal hegemony" (Wong 2000:192). Another suggested that the majority of indigenous women were not aware of their oppression because of "patriarchal socialization. . . . A harmony that conceals injustice is not one to be applauded" (quoted in Lee 2000:250–51). This critique of patriarchy was closely mixed with antifeudalism, a term associated with postrevolutionary thought in China. The term "feudalism" functioned as a kind of shorthand to connote backward customs in need of change. During the rally outside the Legislative Council in connection with the October motion debate, demonstrators shouted "Down with feudal traditions!" (*Hong Kong Standard*, October 14, 1993). Antifeudalism was the theme of the May 4, 1994, demonstration outside the Legislative Council in honor of China's May 4th movement (Cheung 1994:7). By "feudal traditions" the women's groups generally meant gender inequality, usually stemming from patriarchy. Male-only succession was said to reinforce "the feudalistic idea that

women are inferior to men" (Association for the Advancement of Feminism 1993:7). One women's group wrote that "depending on fathers, husbands and children is exactly what the 'three subordinations' teaches in feudal society" and is in opposition "to the principle of independence for women" (quoted in Lee 2000:250).

In striving toward modernity and renouncing "backward" customs, women's groups and legislative councillors were drawing on themes familiar from twentieth-century Chinese history. Both May 4th reformers and Cultural Revolution zealots fought against custom and feudalism in the name of progress. Nevertheless, many of the concepts used by the women's groups—gender equality, human rights, and patriarchy—were appropriated from Western thought. Gender inequality based on the critique of patriarchy is a standard feminist message, as familiar to the women's groups and legislative councillors as to the U.S. National Organization of Women as to Hong Kong's AAF. The women's groups' techniques of activism—demonstrations, T-shirts, and banners—are also familiar from Western feminism, as is the ♀ = ♂ logo. While the broader themes were appropriated from abroad, local symbols were used to express international ideas. Singing their modified Hakka songs, the women wore traditional hats colloquially known as "Hakka hats"—an ironic choice of symbols given that Hakkas are a denigrated group in the New Territories. Even the slogans about feudalism were a way to put gender equality in a regional historical context.

The overarching appropriation of Western feminist concepts and activist techniques is interesting because many of Hong Kong's women's groups were founded specifically to indigenize Western feminism. AAF, for example, was founded "to bring together people who speak our language and share a similar background" and "work within our own culture" (AAF founder quoted in Choi 1995:95).[22] Still, even if ideas and tactics were borrowed from abroad, the women's groups were indigenized in the sense that the leaders were Hong Kong women and discussions were conducted primarily in Cantonese. In discussing the role of the Hong Kong Women Christian Council, one of the founding members emphasized the importance of local leadership: "[We are] a local Christian women's group, not the expatriates. If they join us, then they may play a supporter's role . . . but we have a local basis" (quoted in Choi 1995:97).

INDIGENOUS WOMEN

The indigenous women's were the only lower-class voices in the female inheritance movement. While 200 indigenous women signed petitions supporting the movement, only 6 had high-profile roles (Chan 1995:17). Of these 5 were relatively poor, 4 had very limited education, 3 were Hakka, and 1 spoke only Hakka (pp.

---

21. Some later criticized the female inheritance movement because it failed to offer a fundamental challenge to patriarchy (Lui 1997: chap. 4, 22).

22. Fanny Cheung, the founder of the Hong Kong Federation of Women's Centres, says that it takes a "community approach" that differs from Western feminism; in addition to mobilizing community resources, it seeks to avoid confrontation and militancy (Lee 2000:253).

42–46).[23] One spoke fluent English and had been educated at a local university, traveled widely, and worked as a reporter (pp. 46, 95); while the other women hoped to recover their parents' property and assert their identities as lineage members, this woman participated in the movement to support gender equality and human rights (pp. 40, 42, 46). Comparing these six women with the Kuk elite, it is clear that there was a class-struggle aspect to the movement. One of the indigenous women remarked, "Before, when all the villagers were poor, we helped each other out. Now we are enemies" (pp. 30–32). However, the movement focused on gender, not class. One of the few references to class came from Ms. Cheng: "Before we had nothing while the male villagers had everything. There was a wide gap between rich and poor, and women were inferior at that time" (interview, Asia Television News, February 27, 2001). In her mind, class and gender were intertwined. Women were inferior not just because they were women but because they were poor.

The indigenous women slowly shifted from seeing their stories as individual kinship violations to broader examples of discrimination. The theme of rights and gender equality was prominent in documents collectively written by the Residents Committee. In an article published in the Hong Kong Federation of Women's Centres annual report, the committee called the denial of female inheritance "a century-long discriminatory barrier to the indigenous women's basic rights" (Hong Kong Federation of Women's Centres 1994:88). A submission to the Legislative Council talked about the "inherent right" to succession and mentioned "the protection to women that has been laid down in the United Nations Universal Declaration of Human Rights" (Anti-Discrimination Female Indigenous Residents Committee 1994). Because the majority of the indigenous women were illiterate, it is probable that such articles and statements were guided, if not written, by Linda Wong or the other outsiders on the Residents Committee.

On an individual level, Ms. Cheng was both the person most comfortable talking about female inheritance in terms of equality and rights and the person most comfortable talking to the press. In one interview she said, "What I am fighting for is sexual equality" (*Sunday Telegraph*, October 24, 1993). At another point she said that if the government refused to change the law it "would be violating the Bill of Rights" (*Hong Kong Standard*, October 14, 1993). In contrast, another indigenous woman's critique of the New Territories Ordinance was limited to the fact that "the legislation does not take care of situations where families do not have any sons, which is my case" (*South China Morning Post*, February 25, 1993). Because she spoke rights language, Ms. Cheng could bring the women's concerns to a wider public.

23. According to interviews with Wong and Chan in 2003, of the seven indigenous women who formed the core of the Residents Committee, four were illiterate. None were educated beyond secondary school.

TRANSLATORS

There were relatively few points of contact between the four layers. After their initial work framing the issue, the expatriates attended rallies but rarely went to coalition meetings. The fact that coalition meetings were held in Cantonese was an important barrier. The women's groups informed Christine Loh about upcoming demonstrations, but there was little dialogue with Loh or her office. And the indigenous women had little contact with any of the other layers except to attend formal Legislative Council hearings and rallies. Nevertheless, these four layers formed a coalition that made the female inheritance movement possible. Each layer was aware that it had to work with the others for the movement to succeed. For example, when the head of the Kuk, Lau Wong-fat, claimed that respect for the traditions of indigenous people helped promote harmony in society, a supporter of the movement in the Legislative Council retorted that they had received complaints from female indigenous residents that they were "oppressed by the sexist traditions" (*South China Morning Post*, October 14, 1993). The legislator was able to call on indigenous women's voices to refute the Kuk's call for respecting tradition.

A few translators connected the layers. Translators can move between layers because they conceptualize the issue in more than one way and can translate one set of principles and terms into another. They created a movement in which rights language and indigenous women's stories could come together to create political change. Although the women did acquire some consciousness of rights through participation in the Residents Committee, rights language was mainly promoted by others. Through translators, the indigenous women joined their stories to a larger movement concerned with human rights and discrimination.

Our research uncovered at least three people who acted as translators: Lai-sheung Cheng, Linda Wong, and Anna Wu. Ms. Cheng, in essence, created the Residents Committee by finding other women with similar stories who were ready to step forward. Through her participation in coalition meetings and her contacts with the media, she brought the women's concerns to a wider audience. She was able to generalize individual kinship grievances and lobby for a change in the law. By having a voice in the coalition's strategy, she was also able to shape how the women's stories were used in the movement.

Although she did not have a formal leadership title, Linda Wong was a critical link between the indigenous women and the broader world. The women were able to tell their stories in the Legislative Council because Linda Wong created the opportunity and showed them how to do it. With the help of other outsiders, she helped frame the women's stories in terms of equality and rights so that they were politically viable. In contrast to the indigenous women, who rarely traveled outside of the New Territories, Wong had experience in activism and had a good idea what the media and the public would find appealing. The carefully orchestrated dramas and songs

400 | CURRENT ANTHROPOLOGY *Volume 46, Number 3, June 2005*

had, in the words of one participant, a "symbolic meeting" that "became an icon for the whole movement" (Chan interview, 2003). Wong also literally translated the Cantonese and Hakka used by the indigenous women into English. Using English ensured that the women's stories reached a wider audience and were taken seriously by elites. In a sense, both Linda Wong and Laisheung Cheng translated "up"; they took stories anchored in a local kinship idiom and talked about them in global rights language.

In the Legislative Council, Anna Wu was a translator of quite a different kind. With help from other legislative councillors, Wu brought international law, a concern mainly expressed by the expatriate layer, into the Legislative Council debate. However, it is clear from her attempt to codify indigenous women's customary rights that she also understood and appreciated the kinship system.[24] By bringing the kinship system into a dialogue about rights, she helped to localize the debate. This localization could have gone farther if other legislative councillors had been sensitive to the kinship dimension. The issue died quietly because the discussion was dominated by the tradition-versus-rights debate.

LOCAL AS A MATTER OF DEGREE?

Taking about the female inheritance movement in terms of layers is implicitly a discussion about what it means to be local and global. As an international import, rights talk is, by definition, global. More global layers tended to see female inheritance as an international human rights issue, more local layers as a kinship violation. However, the terms "global" and "local" are not particularly useful. They are often a stand-in for social class. To say that the indigenous women are local while the expatriates are global is to say that the expatriates are educated, mobile, and rich while the indigenous women are illiterate, fixed, and poor. In an international city like Hong Kong, it is not even clear that there is any "local." Global influences are so pervasive that "local" is a matter of degree.

"Local" is a particularly slippery word because no one in the female inheritance movement is a truly local actor. The indigenous women seem local, for example, but one of the core members of the Residents Committee lived in Holland; she had found out about the inheritance debate during a visit home (Wong and Chan interview, 2003). The Heung Yee Kuk is actually a transnational group because so many villagers have emigrated but retain their New Territories identity. They help pay for celebrations, and many come back to reconnect with their villages during yearly rituals (Chan 2001:276). They feel strongly about preserving the past, and, as a result, indigenous tradition is largely financed, protected, and

promulgated by people who no longer live in Hong Kong. Overseas villagers were encouraged to participate in demonstrations against the female inheritance movement, and the Headquarters for the Protection for the Village and Defense of the Clan even established a U.K. branch (Tong 1999:58).

As a transnational actor, the Kuk was attuned to the persuasiveness of human rights language. In the late 1960s it had closely watched Britain's behavior in Gibraltar and learned that indigenous people were entitled to certain rights (Chan 1998:41). In a 1994 proclamation, the Kuk appealed to international norms to protect local tradition: "The indigenous inhabitants of any country in the world all have their legitimate traditions and customs well protected by law. . . . Therefore the existing provisions in the legislation to safeguard the traditional customs of New Territories indigenous inhabitants are . . . a primary obligation of the Hong Kong government" (quoted in Chan 1998:42). It was a stretch, but during the October 1993 motion debate one legislative councillor argued that female inheritance would violate the human rights of ancestors. "There should not be a double standard in human rights," he said. "As we have to respect the human rights of our contemporaries, we have also to respect the human rights of our ancient ancestors" (Hong Kong Hansard 1993:268).

"Global" and "local" become particularly meaningless in the context of international politics. Against the backdrop of the 1997 handover and the larger question of Sino-British relations, every issue in Hong Kong had a global dimension. The Kuk lobbied hard for China's support as a way of putting pressure on individual legislators to vote down the land exemption ordinance.[25] Although China's top leaders did not comment on the inheritance question, China was initially supportive of the Kuk. Both the Xinhua news agency, China's de facto embassy in Hong Kong, and the Hong Kong and Macau Affairs office released statements in March 1994 warning the Hong Kong government that the amended ordinance violated the Basic Law (Lui 1997:chap. 4, 13; Wong 2000:187). Following up on this, Kuk representatives met China's ambassador in England on April 5 (Tsang and Wan 1994: 10) and found the ambassador supportive. China's support noticeably waned, however, as the vote on the ordinance drew closer. The internal workings of the Chinese Communist Party (CCP) are opaque, but it must have decided that international bad press about lack of support for gender equality was not worth the support of the Kuk.[26]

---

24. In an early meeting with the indigenous women, Wu suggested that the women might be able to sue male relatives for failing to live up to their responsibilities. Compared with other legislative councillors, Wu left the indigenous women with a sense that her view of the issue was closest to theirs (Wong interview, 2003).

25. The tactic of appealing to China continued even after the ordinance was passed. In 1997, the Kuk lobbied the Preparatory Committee, the body reviewing Hong Kong's laws in preparation for the handover, to repeal female inheritance in the rural New Territories. When the Preparatory Committee let the land exemption ordinance stand, the Kuk appealed to the National People's Congress. Ultimately, this tactic also failed.

26. At the time, China was under substantial international pressure because of its human rights record. In contrast, China had a relatively good record on gender equality, and this must have been something that the CCP wanted to preserve (Petersen interview, 2003).

Moreover, the "local" problem of female inheritance was created by the world's ultimate global system—colonialism. The root of the problem was, of course, the preservation of Chinese customary land law under the British, but this was not the root cause of the Kuk's opposition to the land exemption ordinance. Customs were slowly changing in the New Territories, and it was becoming more and more common for women to inherit money, if not land (Chan 1997:169). The Kuk was not horrified by the idea of female inheritance per se; it wanted to protect the profits guaranteed under another colonial policy, the 1972 small-house policy. The small-house policy allowed any male villager who could trace his lineage back to 1898 to obtain a 700-square-foot piece of land, free of land premium, to build a house for himself within the borders of the village (Chan 2003:72).[27] All New Territories men, even those overseas, are eligible for this once-in-lifetime land grant. The original aim of the policy was to replace temporary housing and allow for natural growth in the New Territories, but a glut of small houses has led to rapid development (Hopkinson and Lei 2003:2). Although the small-house policy was originally considered a privilege that would be abolished if abused, it has come to be seen as a right (Hopkinson and Lei 2003:4, 31), and because of rising land values it is a very valuable one. Although the Kuk cites clan continuity as the primary justification for the policy, houses are often sold or rented to outsiders for a profit (Chan 1999:238–40). During the female inheritance movement it was an open secret that the Kuk was concerned that female inheritance would lead to the repeal of other indigenous rights, particularly the small-house policy (see Chan 2003). The village elder Bruce Kan even said publicly, "The next thing the government would do is cancel our rights on applying for land" (*South China Morning Post*, March 27, 1993).

But the zeitgeist was simply against the Kuk. The years 1989–97 were the high tide of human rights consciousness in Hong Kong (Petersen interview, 2003). The 1991 passage of the Bill of Rights, based on the ICCPR, encouraged everyone, including women, to think in terms of human rights (Petersen and Samuels 2002:24). Greater awareness of human rights coincided with Patten's democratic reforms, particularly the 1992 reform package and the 1991 introduction of direct elections to the Legislative Council. Democratization led to increased attention to local problems.[28] As Christine Loh said, "It was the golden age of democracy in Hong Kong, and I was honored to be the salad tosser" (Loh interview, 2003).

Conclusion

The female inheritance movement illustrates the localization of global ideas. Gender equality, feminism, and human rights are ideas borrowed from another cultural context, spread through the UN system of treaties and major world conferences which draw government and nongovernmental activists together from all parts of the globe. This language was clearly critical to this movement at all levels, although to varying degrees. Much has been written about the importance of technology, particularly the Internet, as a force behind the globalization of ideas, but the female inheritance movement underscores the importance of people. Much of the rights discourse was introduced by expatriates. It was subsequently picked up by Hong Kong residents who had either spent time abroad, like Christine Loh and Anna Wu, or been exposed to this kind of language by others. As people flow across borders in search of jobs or education, they carry ideas with them. Cultural translators reinterpret these ideas in ways that make sense in more particular and local terms.

Success is important to the spread of traveling theories such as that of human rights. During the campaign, the indigenous women expected that the new law would allow them to inherit their fathers' property, although some also filed lawsuits (Chan 1995:48). However, the land exemption ordinance was not retroactive, so the original claimants whose fathers had already died did not benefit. They had to file lawsuits under Chinese customary law and could only sue for compensation for male relatives' failure to fulfill their kinship obligations (pp. 18, 50, 134). Lack of success probably contributed to these women's disappearance from rights-based movements. Yet some of the indigenous women in the movement continued to talk about their misfortunes in terms of gender discrimination, injustice, and the land exemption ordinance. They still articulated their grievances in rights terms, even if they did not regain their property or become recognized as daughters in the lineage system (p. 146). In contrast, the passage of the law gave the women's groups, some legislators, and the expatriates a dramatic victory. And it is these groups rather than the indigenous women who sustained a long-term commitment to a rights framework.

The female inheritance movement shows that the power of rights discourse lies in its flexibility and contingency. As the recent literature on rights suggests, the broad umbrella of rights language can allow people with very different conceptions of the issue to work together (see Milner 1986, McCann 1994, Gilliom 2001, Goldberg-Hiller 2002, Goldberg-Hiller and Milner 2003). Through a system of layers and translators, women at the grass roots used rights language in a far more contingent and limited way than elites. Moreover, the rights frame was layered over the kinship frame, producing a kind of double consciousness. The female inheritance movement shows that rights mobilization does not require a deep and abiding commitment. Rather, it can be

---

27. In 1995 the UN Committee on Economic and Social Rights complained that the small-house policy discriminated against women (Hopkinson and Lei 2003:23). Although the policy has been under review since 1996, extending it to include women is not seen as an option because there is simply not enough land.

28. A great deal of attention has been given to the connection between democratization and increased support for women's rights (see Fischler 2000; Lui 1997; Tong 1999, n.d.).

402 | CURRENT ANTHROPOLOGY *Volume 46, Number 3, June 2005*

adopted in a more transitory and tentative way contingent on success. Although framing rights in local terms may increase their legitimacy and effectiveness, this analysis shows that not all participants in a movement need to be deeply committed to this framework.

The female inheritance movement also shows that rights language is appropriated because it is politically useful, not because it is imposed. In 1994 Hong Kong, rights had political currency precisely because they were associated with the international world and modernity. Both citizens and the government were concerned about losing Hong Kong's liberal traditions after the 1997 handover. Allegiance to gender equality and human rights was a sign, both to the people in Hong Kong and to the outside world, that things in Hong Kong were not going to change—that Hong Kong deserved a place in the "civilized" community of nations.

Comments

MONIQUE DEVEAUX
Department of Political Science, Williams College, Williamstown, MA 01267, U.S.A. (monique.deveaux@ williams.edu). 19 x 4

Merry and Stern are right to reject as oversimple the assumption that rights discourse is culturally exogenous to indigenous societies and the dichotomies that sustain it: tradition versus modernity, local versus global, relativism versus universalism. Their exploration of how rights talk was "indigenized," translated, and appropriated by the female inheritance movement in Hong Kong's New Territories in the early 1990s is an excellent illustration of the fungible, flexible character of rights. As such, it helps to debunk dogmatic and surely false claims to the effect that where rights are invoked by, say, indigenous peoples, it is only because this normative framework has been imposed.

Having said that, it is remarkable how much of the evidence Merry and Stern assemble to show how indigenous women came to use human rights language to articulate and defend their demands actually *reinforces* this view of rights as external artifice. The strategic and ultimately temporary character of their appropriation of rights is readily acknowledged. Coached by urban gender-equality activists, those active in the women's inheritance movement learned to protest unjust customary laws in the language of rights and equality; those who did not, we learn, were silenced or ignored. While this attests to the political purchase of rights—the unfair inheritance rules were, after all, overturned—it also reveals the unsurprising conclusion that rights remained external to the self-understandings of many people, including rural, indigenous women in the New Territories. That they needed to learn to translate their demands is a function of the national and transnational political institutions and frameworks that bear directly on the legal

status of discriminatory inheritance laws and does not necessarily attest to the inherent appropriateness of rights discourse to their particular struggle.

Clearly it is not Merry and Stern's aim to *evaluate* the use of rights in this case in normative terms; their interest is to investigate in practical and analytical terms the "local appropriation of global cultural products," namely, human rights. But surely it is worth asking about the fit of rights language and about the power relations—both local and global—that made the adoption of rights language the only viable political option. Merry and Stern note that "there is little evidence that the indigenous women developed a sustained critique of their problems based on human rights"; one cannot help but wonder whether this language was not, despite their conclusion to the contrary, an imposition on the way rural women think about their lives and entitlements. The requirement that they frame their concerns in the language of rights is perfectly understandable from the standpoint of political strategy, but this does not mean that we should not ask hard questions about the troubling power relationships (e.g., between urban political elites and rural indigenous women, between indigenous justice narratives and transnational political frameworks) that make it necessary.

Why ask these questions at all? Rights discourse is the preeminent language for demanding justice in our time, but rights have occupied a fraught place in struggles by indigenous peoples, including indigenous women's quests for sexual justice. As Merry and Stern argue, however, rights discourse can be taken up even by those who are ambivalent about their content; "rights mobilization does not require a deep and abiding commitment." Certainly aboriginal peoples, including women, have appealed widely to rights in the context of national social, legal, and political frameworks, as well as to human rights, in asserting collective aboriginal entitlements and demanding recognition and protections from states (Barsh 1995, Bell 1992). From land claims to indigenous group rights, both the jargon and the legal reality of rights are difficult to avoid.

At the same time, however, rights discourse has been denounced by some indigenous scholars and activists alike as reflecting colonial, European conceptions of the individual and of individuals' relation to the broader community (Alfred 1999, Turpel and Monture 1990, Tully 2000). Indeed, in the case of indigenous women's movements, the ideal of gender equality has been criticized as "inappropriate conceptually and culturally" and as "not an important political or social concept" for aboriginal communities, in the words of one First Nations woman scholar (Turpel 1993:179). Aboriginal ideals of community harmony, healing, and gender complementarity are frequently cited as alternatives to European concepts of justice and equality, while oral history, storytelling, and life narratives are readily defended by indigenous peoples as legitimate discursive strategies in political life (Lake 2003), ones that can even supplant legal rights talk. While Merry and Stern—no doubt wisely—do not seek to enter the fray of this particular debate, it is nevertheless the missing normative context of their argument. Indigenous women, as the female inheritance movement example shows, can readily couch their justice struggles in the framework of rights, and their political success may depend upon it; but do they want to, and should they have to?

MASAMICHI S. INOUE
Japan Studies Program/Department of Modern and Classical Languages, Literatures and Cultures, University of Kentucky, 1055 Patterson Office Tower, Lexington, KY 40506-0027, U.S.A. (msinoue@uky.edu). 31 X 04

Merry and Stern's engaged and nuanced analysis of the female inheritance movement in Hong Kong helps us pose critical questions concerning contemporary social movements, local identity, and globalization in a new theoretical perspective. As an anthropologist working on a similar set of questions in Okinawa (e.g., Inoue 2004), I find their concepts of "layers" and "translators" particularly interesting, informative, and thought-provoking. By placing these ideas in critical conversation with Talal Asad's notion of the concept of cultural translation, the significance—in spite of certain problems—of their article will come into even sharper focus.

Asad (1986) explored anthropological (i.e., cultural) translation as "a process of power" (p. 148) and noted that "because the languages of Third World societies—including, of course, the societies that social anthropologists have traditionally studied—are 'weaker' in relation to Western languages (and today, especially to English), they are more likely to submit to forcible transformation in the translation process than the other way around" (pp. 157-58). Merry and Stern's article both refutes and reinforces Asad's observation.

It refutes or at least complicates the notion that the languages of Third World societies are being subjected to "forcible transformation in the translation process" in three interrelated ways. First, Merry and Stern demonstrate that the female inheritance movement actively modified, redefined, and appropriated international rights language instead of being simply translated by that language. Second, they show that the language mobilized by this movement was not monolithic but differentiated—sometimes fragmented—into multiple layers whose potencies were not equal. In other words, layers significantly differing from each other in social class, ideological orientation, education, and so forth, were not all "weak" in relation to Western languages/English in the same way. Third, Merry and Stern themselves function as excellent "translators." They move across different layers of the women's struggle and different moments of Hong Kong history to present a comprehensive and complex picture of the female inheritance movement to the international audience of CURRENT ANTHROPOLOGY and, in so doing, contribute to empowering a specific Third World language.

Yet Merry and Stern inadvertently reinforce what Asad calls "the inequality of languages" (1986:156) in the very act of complicating it, because the direction of their translation seems to be primarily from the lower layers (the indigenous women) to the upper ones (supranational expatriates, elite national legislators, and local middle-class activists, students, and social workers) and not the other way around. Put differently, in the midst of exploring the female inheritance movement in terms of global metropolitan rights language, there is a general inattention to the particular forms that cultural meanings and social identities of these indigenous women took in the process and aftermath of the movement. For example, why did indigenous women drop out of the movement after the land exemption ordinance was passed? What did the indigenous women feel and think when the elite women disciplined them to take the local out of their stories? What did the oldest participant (an indigenous woman) in the movement experience, in her own words, when she was suddenly interrupted by the chairperson of a Legislative Council session? The indigenous women's frustration with the rights language is briefly mentioned and surmised, but the nature, thrust, and intensity of this "frustration" is not fully explored in spite of the indigenous women's status as the protagonists of this social drama. In sum, while we see clearly the ways in which stories grounded in a local kinship idiom came to be framed "up" within international rights language through the efforts of various participants in the movement, we are not entirely clear about the ways in which rights language was anchored, interpreted, and framed "down" in kinship and other specific local idioms by the lower layer of the movement.

Merry and Stern's work implies that anthropologists are an integral part of "layers" of various political and social struggles in the world. It also reinforces Asad's idea that anthropologists can potentially function as cultural "translators" who make a difference by fully exploring the experiences of local subjects and, perhaps, also by writing and speaking in Third World languages as well as in English. It has not yet fully delivered what it has promised. I wonder what Merry and Stern think about such potentialities and about the responsibilities of anthropologists in this age of globalization.

SIUMI MARIA TAM
Department of Anthropology, Chinese University of Hong Kong, Hong Kong (b307763@mailserv.cuhk.edu. hk). 31 X 04

The way in which localization and globalization interact has been an important issue for anthropologists, and Merry and Stern's analysis of the female inheritance rights movement in Hong Kong offers a very good case study. Proposing a framework of "layers" and "translators" for understanding the players and action that constituted the movement, they have demonstrated effectively how the indigenous women gradually adopted the international language of rights because it was found to be more efficacious than the language of mistreatment by male kin.

404 | CURRENT ANTHROPOLOGY *Volume 46, Number 3, June 2005*

They have also illustrated how changes in the social environment in Hong Kong—the increase in urbanites living in the New Territories (making inheritance an issue that went beyond the indigenous population), the Hong Kong government's eagerness to uphold the image of a Westernized metropolis, and a post-1989 Beijing taking care to avoid accusations of gender discrimination, of being "uncivilized" and "feudal"—contributed to a political ecology that favored the passage of the ordinance amendment. This timeliness of the movement—with memories of the 1989 Tiananmen incident fresh and the 1997 handover impending—made human rights language a most appropriate strategy for participants.

While I appreciate the delineation of the four "layers" of the movement, namely, the expatriates, the Legislative Council, the women's groups, and the indigenous women themselves, I find it difficult to agree that these were hierarchically related in terms of their closeness to rights language as a resource. In addition, while the four were no doubt major players in the movement, Merry and Stern might also have noted the roles of other important players without which the rights language could not have been utilized so effectively. The media, men, and the Heung Yee Kuk itself were in a very real sense as much the bridge between the local and the global as the four groups discussed. This points to the need for further contextualization of the movement to appreciate the complexity of the process. In this connection, my questions are as follows:

1. What was the role of men, particularly the profeminists, the kinsmen of the protagonists, and the new residents of the New Territories whose daughters' inheritance rights were affected—complicated by their degrees of affinity with a "global" idea of gender equality and a "Chinese" concept of male superiority?

2. How did the local media contribute to the movement at different stages? The local Chinese press was the first to publicize the issue, and as the movement went on it became quite clear that the media were on the side of "progress" and "rights" as universal values and generally portrayed village men in a negative light.

3. Why is the Heung Yee Kuk, itself a transnational organization, as Merry and Stern argue, and employing rights language (such as ancestors', family, and kinship rights) and at one point portraying itself as a victim, not one of the "layers" and "translators" (albeit on the other side of the interests being fought over)?

4. In some important ways the researchers depart from local understandings of the role of certain key "translators" such as Christine Loh, who was almost the personal face of the Legislative Council's sympathy to the movement. The AAF (and very often the legislators as well) respected village traditions (however defined) and put the blame on (male) village heads for either not clarifying the nature of the amendment to villagers or misleading them. Thus, like Anna Wu, these other players understood the potential advantage of a male-centered kinship system for the welfare of the women, as well as the strategic importance of not demonizing all men and the patriarchal village structure. The role of "traditional"

Chinese culture and the way in which individuals were seen to be related to it deserve more in-depth discussion.

These questions might have been more readily answered if the researchers had had the benefit of participant observation at the time of the movement. The series of happenings in 1993–94 could have been interpreted as a triumph of women's rights, but this has not generalized into gender equality. As a number of feminists in Hong Kong have argued, this is because in most of the local "women's rights" movements women's rights have been interpreted as women's welfare, leaving the patriarchal system unchallenged.

KWONG-LEUNG TANG
Department of Social Work, Chinese University of Hong Kong, Shatin, Hong Kong (kitang@swk.cuhk. edu.hk). 1 XI 04

Much has been written about the development of the human rights canon through the United Nations. Yet, human rights treaties adopted in an international forum face obstacles to their implementation in local contexts. The promotion of women's human rights is a case in point. While advocates believe that women's oppression and discrimination can be overcome by international law, it remains doubtful whether the overarching human rights framework can be effectively used to champion the cause of disadvantaged women in national/local contexts. Many analysts continue to question whether international formulations of rights are useful for women. Acknowledging that transnational rights ideas cannot be scrutinized apart from the local movements, current research has shifted towards studying the intersection between local movements and global processes. Theorizing of such an interface is critically important and ought to be empirically grounded.

In light of these considerations, Merry and Stern offer an eloquent and perceptive theorizing of local translation of global rights. Essentially, they examine how gender equality and human rights could be used to deal with discrimination against women by traditional cultures. Using the female inheritance movement in Hong Kong as a case study, they suggest that the localization of women's human rights hinges on activist groups ("layers") and "translators" who bring about collaboration between layers. Among the numerous obstacles encountered, the important gap between women's experiences and the indeterminacy of statements of human rights (Cook 1994) remains to be bridged. The translators play a pivotal role here. "Cultural translators" interpret global ideas in the form that is intelligible to local people. They help indigenous women to reframe their stories as violations of a right to protection from gender discrimination.

Overall, the characterization of the layers is apt, but one particular layer may be undergoing transformation over time. Four layers, distinguished by "their relationships to rights language and their relative distance from transnational ideas," are identified: expatriates, legislative councillors, women's groups, and indigenous women. Yet, the layer of legislative councillors is not a homogeneous entity. In fact, the Legislative Council has been noted for constant tugs-of-war among members, particularly between those who hold ultra-conservative ideas and those who embrace global rights ideas.

The researchers allude to the importance of timing. It is true that it worked in favor of the women's groups, since the female inheritance movement took place in the "age of democracy" right after the Tiananmen Square crackdown of 1989. However, the role of the state and its relationships with key actors merit closer scrutiny. The colonial state, ready to give up its control in 1997, was still in a powerful position to determine the outcome of the movement. The arrival in 1992 of Chris Patten, the last governor and an astute professional politician championing democratic rights for the people, made a real difference.

Another direction involves the study of inhibiting factors in the politics of protest: actors that resist global ideas and limit human rights discourses to protect their interests. As the researchers contend, the weakening of the previously strong alliance between the Heung Yee Kuk (ultimately outmaneuvered by the women's movement) and the colonial elites mattered. But the paper offers only a glimpse of the Kuk's ideologies, interests, and strategies and misses the subtle changes in its relationship with the state as it became more and more pro-Beijing in outlook. Unsurprisingly, the Kuk is now viewed by many as a strong voice opposing international law and local policy on women's rights should these undermine its economic interests. It is a much more powerful group, as the post-colonial state has been its strong ally since the transition. One wonders whether the success of the female inheritance movement could be "replicated" under these changed conditions.

While Merry and Stern see human rights as a resource for local movements, there are complex dimensions to the interface between global ideas and local processes. In particular, their analysis of the local/global interface would have been more illuminating had the impacts of local processes on global rights discourse been analyzed. Nevertheless, they rightly observe that the potency of rights discourses is contingent and flexible. Paradoxically, its very strength is its weakness. Strategically, while global human rights discourse offers a focus for women's groups, local movements have not been enduring. A deep and sustainable commitment to women's human rights may be lacking among the activists and indigenous women. Despite the success of the female inheritance movement, similar actions to promote women's human rights remain few and far between. In fact, key developments in women's human rights go unheeded. Concerns regarding continued discrimination against women have recently resulted in the UN's adoption (in 1999) of the Optional Protocol, giving women the right to complain to the UN about violations of the Convention and providing for a remedy for victims (Tang 2004). While women's groups in other countries have actively pursued its ratification, the Optional Protocol is glossed over by the post-colonial state, the newly established Women's Commission, and, to the surprise of many, some of the women's groups that were involved in the female inheritance movement.

KEEBET VON BENDA-BECKMANN
Max-Planck-Institut für Ethnologische Forschung,
Projektgruppe Rechtspluralismus, Advokatenweg 36,
06114 Halle/S., Germany (kbenda@eth.mpg.de).
18 X 04

Merry and Stern's study of the female inheritance movement in Hong Kong is an important empirically grounded contribution to the debate on globalization and human rights. Rather than looking at local interpretations of human rights themselves, often labeled vernacularized or hybrid, the authors look into the processes through which this "local appropriation" takes place. It involves chains of groups of actors operating at different levels and with distinct ideological orientations through which the human rights ideas are communicated. The main theoretical problem they address is how it is possible for these groups, with their distinct ideological orientations, to cooperate and to gain political influence. They show that it requires "translators," people who are able to translate a problem from one vernacular to another. This mechanism of translation between "layers" is crucial to the success of the movement. They argue convincingly that it is not necessary that human rights language be regarded as legitimate by all members of a society or even adopted by all the layers of the movement to be effective. They explain how the debate about female inheritance is caught up in a wider range of political issues, among them the privileges in housing policies of the indigenous population of the New Territories.

The paper discusses two fundamental problems entailed in the translating process: the problem of alienation and the tension between individual and structural approaches. Some of the participants in the lowest layer of the movement see their stories and worries disappear in the translation process, to be replaced by formulations to which they cannot relate. There is a class issue here, as the layers are hierarchically ordered and those in the top layer set the agenda and determine the idiom in which stories are to be told. Similar processes of alienation and dispossession have been known since the 1970s from research in the sociology and anthropology of law in Europe and the U.S.A.: the disputing parties often no longer recognize their dispute once it has been reformulated by lawyers to make it acceptable to the courts.

Secondly, research in the 1970s on legal clinics and social advocates' practices in a country like the Netherlands showed the deep contradictions between protagonists of structural change and clients wanting to resolve individual problems. The female inheritance movement in Hong Kong shows similar internal contradictions among the layers within the movement. Here, too, participants in the lowest layer, seeking redress for their individual grievances without challenging the inheritance rules as such, withdraw from a movement that has

406 | CURRENT ANTHROPOLOGY *Volume 46, Number 3, June 2005*

no interest in individual problems but aims at structural change, the main interest of the upper layers.

The lowest layer of the movement has some intriguing characteristics. Most participants are not purely local actors. Merry and Stern attribute this to the fact that Hong Kong is an international city whose citizens generally have connections beyond its borders, though the extent of globalized connections differs. This may be the case, but one wonders whether involvement in the movement might be skewed towards women with such connections. This is all the more likely if one considers another feature that Merry and Stern mention but do not discuss in great detail. Almost all members of the lowest layer of the movement are women without male siblings. In fact, several mentioned that they would have no objection to their brothers' inheriting everything; they just think that in the absence of brothers women should be allowed to inherit and should not be made dependent on the whims of cousins or uncles. Women suffering under patriarchal brothers apparently do not dare to speak up in public. The participants in the movement, then, are atypical. Interestingly, they are atypical for Hong Kong but not for China, where the one-child policy must have left many women without brothers. But then, China has long made female inheritance the legal norm, though it is not clear to what extent this has replaced customary law in practice. Paradoxically, Hong Kong remains in this respect in isolation, despite its many connections with the outside world.

The paper does not allow us to judge whether the participants involved in the movement are indeed atypical. If they are, the question is how the results of the movement relate to women who do have brothers and who have few contacts beyond the borders of Hong Kong. Do the creative translation techniques of songs and plays reach these women, and how do they respond? While the paper discusses the conditions for political success at the top, it is less specific about the bottom. This calls for further research.

Reply

SALLY ENGLE MERRY AND RACHEL STERN
Wellesley, Mass., U.S.A. 10 XII 04

It is a pleasure to hear readers' thoughts and to begin a dialogue about both the details of the female inheritance movement and its wider meaning. As many of the readers point out, there are limitations on research conducted ten years after an event took place. They express a desire for more information about how the indigenous women themselves saw the use of rights language. Did they feel that rights language was imposed from above? How, if at all, was rights language "framed down," or anchored in claims about kinship? And how did indigenous women outside the movement respond to rights language? Was rights language a temporary strategic choice,

or did it change the way participants—or the wider Hong Kong public—thought about gender? These are interesting and important questions that are difficult to answer without the benefit of watching the events of 1993–94 unfold firsthand. Although we interviewed many of the key participants later, we would love to have observed the nuances of indigenous women's balancing of two sets of justice ideologies, one based on rights and one based on kinship obligations.

But it is also the case that we were particularly interested in the use of the idea of rights as a political strategy and in how rights language is introduced and interacts with alternative understandings of a problem. While we speculate on the effect of rights language on consciousness, it is a separate project to consider how rights are *understood* locally and how that understanding changes through activism. As in McCann's research on the pay equity movement (1994), Gilliom's study of welfare recipients (2001), and McAdam's treatment of the civil rights movement (1989), answers to these questions require sustained contact with movement participants to document how activism transforms understandings. We are now both exploring rights consciousness in other contexts, as are other researchers.

Deveaux begins with the issue that animated this project in the first place: is using a human-rights frame for the political struggle of indigenous women a "good thing"? The question has several dimensions. Does this individualistic way of framing a grievance do violence to the women's own understanding of their situation? It is imposed or voluntarily adopted? Is it politically effective? Deveaux is right to pose these questions, and we are aware that our article answers only some of them. This is largely because we recognize that answers depend heavily on what standards one adopts for a "good thing." Instead, we focused on the complicated linkages between indigenous women and a global human-rights discourse. We wanted to unpack the idea of imposition in order to see the indigenous women themselves as strategic actors, regardless of whether they maintained a long-term normative commitment to a rights framework.

Inoue calls translation a "process of power" and suggests that our analysis reinforces the "inequality of languages" by focusing on translation in only one direction. Instead, she asks for more attention to the consciousness of the indigenous women and the way in which their perspectives were incorporated into rights language. This is a valuable point and one that warrants further research. Piecing together the information we did gather, it appears that the inequality in translation, while significant, was not absolute and that the indigenous women, to various degrees, were engaged in reinterpretation and translation. Yet even as we look at multiple processes of translation, it is important to recognize that translators differ in terms of power and capacity to translate. And when power comes into play, languages are not necessarily treated equally.

Von Benda-Beckmann also points to the power dynamics of translation when she observes that the indigenous women, at the bottom of the class hierarchy, watched their stories disappear in the translation process. She shows important parallels with the legal process, in which conflicts are transformed by lawyers and courts. Her further point about the tension between helping individuals and promoting structural change—present in both the female inheritance movement and activist legal clinics in the Netherlands—is well taken.

Thus, Deveaux, Inoue, and Von Benda-Beckmann are all concerned with translation as a form of power. Inoue sees the female inheritance case study, at least as we have written it, as reinforcing a zero-sum view of power which pits indigenous understandings against rights language with the idea that some discourses are more valid and powerful than others. In a similar vein, Deveaux and Von Benda-Beckmann push us to ask hard questions about how indigenous women's voices may have been steamrollered. These commentators point out that language can be exclusive and discourse hegemonic. It is problematic that rights language was the only legitimate way to talk about inheritance in the public sphere and that the indigenous women's complementary understandings of their grievances were, of necessity, private. As Deveaux points out, questions about the inadequacy of rights language and frustration over its limitations have already emerged in the area of indigenous rights, as they have in the sphere of women's rights. Further research on the translation process could explore what is lost when this kind of language is used.

Yet this is not a simple story of coercion in which rights language is imposed from above. The indigenous women had choice and agency. There was a lot of pressure from neighbors and friends for them to drop their claims, and they could easily have dropped out of the movement. The fact that they did not indicates that, at a minimum, they understood the efficacy of rights language. For the indigenous women and, in fact, for the broader inheritance movement, the idea of rights was a tool for overturning a deeply entrenched status quo. As Martha Minow puts it, rights are the "possessions of the dispossessed," the refuge of the powerless (quoted in McCann 1993:773).

We think that the female inheritance case study moves us toward a more additive view of power in which rights language and indigenous understandings coexist and, by coexisting, become more than the sum of their parts. In the female inheritance movement, rights language was significantly strengthened by the addition of the indigenous women's individual stories. While the indigenous women would not have won the right to inheritance without framing their claims in terms of rights, the wider women's movement would not have been able to amend the New Territories Ordinance without recourse to the women's individual stories. Power moves in both directions here. Rights language craves specificity just as specific stories benefit from a wider frame.

Another strand of commentary either requests more detail about other players in the movement or suggests slightly different ways of aligning them. Tam, Tang, and Von Benda-Beckmann would like to know more about men, the media, other indigenous women in the New

Territories, and the Heung Yee Kuk. They are particularly interested in how these other actors either used rights language or responded to it.

While we are also quite interested in other actors, our four layers are a deconstruction of the female inheritance movement, not an exhaustive list of everyone involved in the debate. We inevitably simplified in order to develop a schematic description and analyze the translation processes. In addition, we were specifically interested in the coalition of people who came together to pursue female inheritance and the different ways in which international rights language was used within this coalition to advocate change. Our hope is that scholars will fill in gaps and add nuance, as Tang and Tam do in their comments. Tang offers a particularly interesting postscript, noting that even the women's groups have not sustained their focus on women's human rights.

Inoue calls on us to speculate about the "responsibilities of anthropologists in this age of globalization." In contrast to the image of isolated academics holed up in an ivory tower, our research shows that academics can have great influence. Expatriate academics in Hong Kong played a major role in introducing rights language to the discussion over female inheritance, especially rights language anchored in international law. And, as Inoue points out, we also played a role as translators by bringing these different frames to an international audience. We raised the profile of rights language by simply showing up and asking questions about it.

With influence comes responsibility. Anthropologists have engaged in considerable debates over the power of the author to shape stories and represent other people's lives. We agree that academics need to be self-reflective and aware of the impact of their research. We, of course, brought the female inheritance movement a wider academic audience and put our own spin on it. Because our work implicitly addresses the normative question that Deveaux poses—is this a "good thing"?—it may be ducking responsibility not to have addressed that question directly. We preferred, however, to offer our translation and allow readers to draw their own conclusions according to their own values.

References Cited

ALFRED, TAIAIAKE. 1999. *Peace, power, and righteousness: An indigenous manifesto.* Oxford: Oxford University Press. [MD]

AN-NA'IM, ABDULLAHI. 1992a. "Introduction," in *Human rights in cross-cultural perspective: A quest for consensus.* Edited by Abdullahi Ahmed An-Na'im. Philadelphia: University of Pennsylvania Press.

———. 1992b. "Toward a cross-cultural approach to defining international standards of human rights: The meaning of cruel, inhuman, or degrading treatment or punishment," in *Human rights in cross-cultural perspective: A quest for consensus.* Edited by Ahmed An-Na'im. Philadelphia: University of Pennsylvania Press.

408 | CURRENT ANTHROPOLOGY Volume 46, Number 3, June 2005

———. Editor. 2002. Cultural transformation and human rights in Africa. London: Zed Books.

ANTI-DISCRIMINATION FEMALE INDIGENOUS RESIDENTS COMMITTEE. 1994. Submission on the green paper on opportunities for women and men. MS.

APPADURAI, ARJUN. 1996. Modernity at large: Cultural dimensions of globalization. Minneapolis: University of Minnesota Press.

ASAD, TALAL. 1986. "The concept of cultural translation in British social anthropology," in Writing culture. Edited by James Clifford and George E. Marcus, pp. 141–64. Berkeley: University of California Press. [MSI]

ASSOCIATION FOR THE ADVANCEMENT OF FEMINISM. 1993. New Territories women denied right to inherit. Women's News Digest 29:13–14.

BARSH, RUSSEL LAWRENCE. 1995. Indigenous peoples and the idea of individual human rights. Native Studies Review 10 (2):35–54. [MD]

BAUER, JOANNE R., AND DANIEL A. BELL. Editors. 1999. The East Asian challenge for human rights. London and New York: Cambridge University Press.

BELL, DIANE. 1992. "Considering gender: Are human rights for women, too? An Australian case," in Human rights in cross-cultural perspective. Edited by Abdullahi Ahmed An-Na'im. Philadelphia: University of Pennsylvania Press. [MD]

BRAY, DENIS. 2001. "Recollections of a cadet officer Class II," in Hong Kong, British Crown Colony, revisited. Edited by Elizabeth Sinn. Hong Kong: Centre of Asian Studies, University of Hong Kong.

BRYSK, ALISON. 2000. From tribal village to global village: Indian rights and international relations in Latin America. Stanford: Stanford University Press.

CHAN, JOANNE CHONG-LAI. 1995. Negotiating daughterhood: A case study of the female inheritance movement in the New Territories, Hong Kong, M.A. thesis, Chinese University, Hong Kong.

CHAN, SELINA CHING. 1997. "Negotiating tradition: Customary succession in the New Territories of Hong Kong," in Hong Kong: The anthropology of a metropolis. Edited by Grant Evans and Maria Tani. Honolulu: University of Hawai'i Press.

———. 1998. Politicizing tradition: The identity of indigenous inhabitants of Hong Kong. Ethnology 37:39–54.

———. 1999. Colonial policy in a borrowed place and time: Invented tradition in the New Territories of Hong Kong. European Planning Studies 7:231–42.

———. 2001. Selling the ancestor's land: A Hong Kong lineage adapts. Modern China 27:262–84.

———. 2003. Memory making, identity building: The dynamics of economics and politics in the New Territories of Hong Kong. China Information 17:66–91.

CHEUNG, CHOI WAN. 1994. New Territories indigenous women reclaimed inheritance rights. Women's News Digest 32–33:6–7.

CHIU, STEPHEN, W. K., AND HO-FUNG HUNG. 2000. "Rural stability under colonialism: A new look at an old issue," in Social development and political change in Hong Kong. Edited by Siu-kai Lau. Hong Kong: Chinese University Press.

CHOI PO-KING. 1995. Identities and diversities: Hong Kong women's movement in 1980s and 1990s. Hong Kong Cultural Studies Bulletin 4:95–103.

CHUN, ALLEN. 2000. Unstructuring Chinese society: The fictions of colonial practice and the changing realities of "land" in the New Territories of Hong Kong. New York: Harwood Academic Publishers.

COATES, AUSTIN. 1969. Myself a Mandarin. New York: John Day. New York: Harwood Academic Publishers.

COOK, R. Editor. 1994. Human rights of women. Philadelphia: University of Pennsylvania Press. [KLT]

COWAN, JANE, MARIE-BENEDICT DEMBOUR, AND RICHARD WILSON. Editors. 2001. Culture and rights. Cambridge: Cambridge University Press.

DONNELLY, JACK. 2003. Universal human rights in theory and practice. Ithaca: Cornell University Press.

ENGEL, DAVID M., AND FRANK W. MUNGER. 2002. Rights of inclusion: Law and identity in the life stories of Americans with disabilities. Chicago: University of Chicago Press.

FELD, STEPHEN. 2001. "A sweet lullaby for world music," in Globalization. Edited by Arjun Appadurai. Durham: Duke University Press.

FISCHLER, LISA COLLYNN. 2000. Women at the margin: Challenging boundaries of the political in Hong Kong. Ph.D. diss., University of Wisconsin at Madison, Madison, Wis.

GILLIOM, JOHN. 2001. Overseers of the poor: Surveillance, resistance, and the limits of privacy. Chicago: University of Chicago Press.

GOLDBERG-HILLER, JONATHAN. 2002. The limits to union: Same-sex marriage and the politics of civil rights. Ann Arbor: University of Michigan Press.

GOLDBERG-HILLER, JONATHAN, AND NEAL MILNER. 2003. Rights as excess: Understanding the politics of special rights. Law and Social Inquiry 28(3).

HAYES, JAMES W. 2001. "Colonial administration in British Hong Kong and Chinese customary law," in Hong Kong, British Crown Colony, revisited. Edited by Elizabeth Sinn. Hong Kong: Centre of Asian Studies, University of Hong Kong.

HOME AFFAIRS BRANCH. 1993. Legislative Council brief: New Territories Land (Exemption) Bill. CNTA/L/CON/26/21/ Pt. II.

HONG KONG FEDERATION OF WOMEN. 1994. Statement on conflict arising from New Territories women's right of succession. MS.

HONG KONG FEDERATION OF WOMEN'S CENTRES. 1994. Annual report: 1993–1994. Hong Kong.

HONG KONG HANSARD. 1993. Proceedings of the Legislative Council. http://www.legco.gov.hk/yr93–94/englihs/lc_sitg/hansard/h931013.pdf.

———. 1994. Proceedings of the Legislative Council. http://www.legco.gov.hk/yr93–94/englihs/lc_sitg/hansard/h940622.pdf.

HONG KONG WOMEN CHRISTIAN COUNCIL. Editor. 1995. Uncertain times: Hong Kong women facing 1997. Hong Kong.

HOPKINSON, LISA, AND MANDY LAO MAN LEI. 2003. Rethinking the small house policy. Hong Kong: Civic Exchange.

HOWARTH, CARLA, CAROL JONES, CAROLE PETERSEN, AND HARRIET SAMUELS. 1991. Report by the Hong Kong Council of Women on the Third Periodic Report by Hong Kong under Article 40 of the International Covenant on Civil and Political Rights. Hong Kong: Hong Kong Council of Women.

INOUE, MASAMICHI S. 2004. "We are Okinawans but of a different kind": New/old social movements and the U.S. military in Okinawa. CURRENT ANTHROPOLOGY 45:85–104. [MSI]

JONES, CAROL. 1995. "New Territories inheritance law. Colonization and the elites," in Women in Hong Kong. Edited by Benjamin K. P. Leung and Veronica Pearson. Hong Kong: Oxford University Press.

KECK, MARGARET E., AND KATHRYN SIKKINK. 1998. Activists beyond borders: Advocacy networks in international politics. Ithaca: Cornell University Press.

KHAGRAM, SANJEEV, JAMES V. RIKER, AND KATHRYN SIKKINK. Editors. 2002. Restructuring world politics: Transnational social movements, networks, and norms. Minneapolis: University of Minnesota Press.

LAKE, MARILYN. 2003. "Woman, black, indigenous: Recognition struggles in dialogue," in Recognition struggles and social movements: Contested identities, agency, and power. Edited by Barbara Hobson. Cambridge: Cambridge University Press. [MD]

LEE, CHING KWAN. 2000. "Public disclosures and collective identities: Emergence of women as a collective actor in the women's movement in Hong Kong," in The dynamics of social *movements in Hong Kong.* Edited by Stephen Wing Kai Chiu and Tai Lok Lui. Hong Kong: Hong Kong University Press.

LOCKHART, J. H. STEWART. 1900. *Report on the New Territory at Hong Kong.* London: Darling & Son.

LOH, CHRISTINE. 1997. *Inheritance rights of indigenous women of the New Territories.* http://www.christineloh.bizland.com/cloh/vz_mainframe.htm.

LUI, YUK-LIN. 1997. The emergence and development of the feminist movement in Hong Kong from the mid-1980s to the mid-1990s. M.A. thesis, Chinese University, Hong Kong.

MCADAM, DOUG. 1989. The biographical consequences of activism. *American Sociological Review* 54:744–60.

MCCANN, MICHAEL W. 1993. Reform litigation on trial. *Law and Social Inquiry* 17.

———. 1994. *Rights at work: Pay equity reform and the politics of legal mobilization.* Chicago: University of Chicago Press.

MILNER, NEAL. 1986. The dilemmas of legal mobilization: Ideologies and strategies of mental patient liberation. *Law and Policy* 8:105–29.

NISSIM, ROGER. 1988. *Land administration and practice in Hong Kong.* Hong Kong: University of Hong Kong Press.

O'BRIEN, KEVIN. 1996. Rightful resistance. *World Politics* 49(1):31–55.

PETERSEN, CAROLE. 1996. Equality as a human right: The development of anti-discrimination law in Hong Kong. *Columbia Journal of Transnational Law* 34:335–87.

PETERSEN, CAROLE, AND HARRIET SAMUELS. 2002. The International Convention on the Elimination of All Forms of Discrimination Against Women: A comparison of its implementation and the role of non-governmental organizations in the United Kingdom and Hong Kong. *Hastings International and Comparative Law Review* 26:1–51.

RISSE, THOMAS, STEPHEN ROPP, AND KATHRYN SIKKINK. Editors. 1999. *The power of human rights: International norms and domestic change.* Cambridge: Cambridge University Press.

SCHEINGOLD, STUART. 1974. *The politics of rights.* New Haven: Yale University Press.

SCOTT, IAN. 1982. Administering the New Towns of Hong Kong. *Asian Survey* 22:659–75.

SELBY, STEPHEN. 1991. Everything you wanted to know about Chinese customary law (but were afraid to ask). *Hong Kong Law Journal* 21:45–77.

SMART, ALAN, AND JAMES LEE. 2003. Financialization and the role of real estate in Hong Kong's regime of accumulation. *Economic Geography* 79(1):153–71.

SNOW, DAVID, AND ROBERT BENFORD. 2000. Framing processes and social movements: An overview and assessment. *American Review of Sociology* 26:611–39.

STRICKLAND REPORT: REPORT OF A COMMITTEE APPOINTED BY THE GOVERNOR IN OCTOBER, 1948. 1953. *Chinese law and custom in Hong Kong.* Hong Kong: Government Printer.

TANG, K. L. 2004. Internationalizing women's struggle against discrimination: The UN Women's Convention and the Optional Protocol. *British Journal of Social Work* 34:1175–90. [KLT]

TARROW, SIDNEY. 1998. 2d edition. *Power in movement: Social movements and contentious politics.* Cambridge: Cambridge University Press.

TONG, IRENE. 1999. "Re-inheriting women in decolonizing Hong Kong," in *Democratization and women's movements.* Edited by Jill M. Bystydzienski and Joti Sekhon. Bloomington: Indiana University Press.

———. n.d. The women's movement in Hong Kong's transition. MS, Department of Politics and Public Administration, University of Hong Kong.

TSANG GAR YIN AND CHI KIE WAN. 1994. Campaign for equal inheritance rights. *Women's News Digest* 32–33:8–13.

TULLY, JAMES. 2000. "The struggles of indigenous peoples for and of freedom," in *Political theory and the rights of indigenous peoples.* Edited by Duncan Ivison et al. Cambridge: Cambridge University Press. [MD]

TURPEL, MARY ELLEN. 1993. Patriarchy and paternalism: The legacy of the Canadian state for First Nations women. *Canadian Journal of Women and the Law* 6:174–92. [MD]

TURPEL, M. E., AND P. A. MONTURE. 1990. Ode to Elijah: Reflections of two First Nations women on the rekindling of spirit at the wake for the Meech Lake Accord. *Queen's Law Journal* 15:345–59. [MD]

WATSON, JAMES L. 1983. Rural society: Hong Kong's New Territories. *China Quarterly* 95:480–90.

WATSON, RUBIE S. 1985. *Inequality among brothers: Class and kinship in South China.* Cambridge: Cambridge University Press.

WESLEY-SMITH, PETER. 1994. *The sources of Hong Kong law.* Hong Kong: Hong Kong University Press.

WILSON, RICHARD A. 1996. "Introduction: Human rights, culture, and context," in *Human rights, culture, and context: Anthropological perspectives.* Edited by Richard A. Wilson. London: Pluto Press.

WONG, PIK WAN. 2000. Negotiating gender: The women's movement for legal reform in colonial Hong Kong. Ph.D. diss., University of California, Los Angeles, Los Angeles, Calif.

WU, ANNA. 1993. Letter to the members of the Bills Committee considering the New Territories Land (Exemption) Bill. MS.

Name Index